About the Authors

Leonard M. (Len) Jessup is Vice President for University Development at Washington State University and President of the WSU Foundation, roles he has held since May 2005. He leads a transformation of the development operation at WSU in order to achieve significantly higher levels of fundraising and to prepare the University for its next comprehensive campaign. Prior to this post, he served as Dean of the College of Business and Economics at WSU since June 2002 and as the Philip L. Kays Distinguished Professor in Management Information Systems (MIS). As Dean, he led a complete, two-year reengineering of the business program, which resulted in the successful AACSB reaccreditation of the College in spring 2004. The College has now embarked on a new strategic plan with a vision to be among the best and most innovative programs in the country. In that role he also helped to lead a University-wide Entrepreneurship and Innovation Initiative, driven by the College of Business and Economics and its top-ranked entrepreneurship program. He also helped to focus the College on innovative approaches to teaching and learning and has guided the development of innovative new facilities such as the Boeing Wireless Classroom of the Future, the Carson Center for Placement and Professional Development, and the James C. Nelson Gallery of Excellence, a computer-based, interactive display of excellence throughout the business program.

Dr. Jessup received his B.A. in Information and Communication Studies in 1983 and his M.B.A. in 1985 from California State University, Chico, where he was voted Outstanding M.B.A. Student. He received his Ph.D. in Organizational Behavior and Management Information Systems from the University of Arizona in 1989. He is a member of the Association for Information Systems and Alpha Iota Delta, was Associate Editor for the *Management Information Systems Quarterly*; is a past member of the Editorial Board for Small Group Research, and was Conference Co-Chair for the International Conference on Information Systems, hosted by WSU and held in Seattle in 2003.

Jessup has taught in various areas of management and MIS and has published, presented, and consulted on electronic commerce, computer-supported collaborative work, technology-supported teaching and learning, emerging information technologies, entrepreneurship, leadership, and related topics. He has earned numerous awards for teaching excellence and innovation. Jessup came to WSU from Indiana University in June 2000 as Coordinator of the MIS program in the College. While managing the MIS program he helped to implement a Web-based, online version of the undergraduate MIS program and an "MIS Fellows" program that enabled top undergraduate MIS students to work side-by-side with MIS faculty on cutting-edge research projects.

Joseph S. (Joe) Valacich is the George and Carolyn Hubman Distinguished Professor in MIS and the inaugural Marian E. Smith Presidential Endowed Chair at Washington State University. He was previously an Associate Professor with tenure (early) at Indiana University, Bloomington, and was named the Sanjay Subhedar Faculty Fellow. He has had visiting faculty appointments at the University of Arizona, City University of Hong Kong, Buskerud College (Norway), The Norwegian University of Life Sciences, Riga Technical University (Latvia), and the Helsinki School of Economics and Business. He received his Ph.D. degree from the University of Arizona (MIS), and his M.B.A. and B.S. (computer science) degrees from the University of Montana. His teaching interests include systems analysis and design, collaborative computing, project management, and management of information systems. Professor Valacich served on the national task forces to design *IS '97* and *2002: The Model Curriculum and Guidelines for Undergraduate Degree Programs in Information Systems* as well as *MSIS 2000* and *2006: The Master of Science in Information Systems Model Curriculum.* He also served on the Executive Committee, funded by the National Science Foundation, to define the *IS Program Accreditation Standards* and on the Board of Directors for CSAB (formally, the Computing Sciences Accreditation Board), rep-

resenting the Association for Information Systems (AIS). He was the general conference co-chair for the 2003 International Conference on Information Systems (ICIS) in Seattle and was the vice-chair of ICIS 1999 in Charlotte, NC.

Dr. Valacich has conducted numerous corporate training and executive development programs for organizations, including: AT&T, Boeing, Dow Chemical, EDS, Exxon, FedEx, General Motors, Microsoft, and Xerox. He previously served on the editorial boards of *MIS Quarterly* (two terms) and *Information Systems Research*, and is currently serving on the boards at *Decision Science* and *Small Group Research*. His primary research interests include technology-mediated collaboration, human-computer interaction, mobile and emerging technologies, e-business, and distance education. He is a prolific researcher, with publications in numerous prestigious journals, including: *MIS Quarterly, Information Systems Research, Management Science, Academy of Management Journal, Communications of the ACM, Decision Science, Communications of the AIS, Journal of AIS, Organizational Behavior and Human Decision Processes, Journal of Applied Psychology, Journal of Management Information System*, and many others. He is a co-author of the best-selling *Modern Systems Analysis and Design,* 5th Edition, as well as *Essentials of Systems Analysis and Design, 3rd* Edition, *Object-Oriented Systems Analysis and Design,* 2nd Edition, and *Information Systems Project Management;* all are published by Prentice Hall.

Brief Contents

Contents

**Chapter 10   Managing Information Systems Ethics
and Crime   406**

Preface

Approach

One of the greatest challenges that we face in teaching information systems courses is how to keep pace in the class with what is happening out in the real world. Hardware, software, telecommunications, and networking equipment—all of it—continues to become faster, cheaper, and better, with business organizations continuing to adopt and adapt these new technologies rapidly. Whereas a decade ago large businesses would spend two or three percent of their revenues on information technology, today, spending on information technology for many large businesses can range from five to ten percent of their revenue. Most important, organizations are now relying on that technology as a fundamental part of their business strategy and their competitiveness.

As a result of this pervasiveness and the fast pace of technology change and use in organizations, teaching people about information systems has never been more valuable or challenging.

Given the dynamic nature of information systems, and given that it is difficult to find introductory information systems textbooks that are both up-to-date and student-friendly, we wrote *Information Systems Today*, Third Edition, with three primary goals in mind. First, we wanted readers not only to learn about information systems, but to clearly understand the importance of information systems for companies and people operating in the digital world. Second, we did not simply want to spoon-feed students with technical terms and the history of information systems. Instead, we want students to understand exactly what innovative organizations are doing with contemporary information systems and, more important, where things are headed. Third, we wanted to empower students with the essential knowledge they need to be successful in the use and understanding of information technology in their careers.

To this end, we wrote *Information Systems Today*, Third Edition, so that it is contemporary, fun to read, and useful, focusing on what business students need to know about information systems.

Audience

Information Systems Today, Third Edition, is primarily for the undergraduate introductory information systems course required of all business students. The introductory information systems course typically has a diverse audience of students majoring in many different areas, such as accounting, economics, finance, marketing, general management, human resource management, production and operations, international business, entrepreneurship, and information systems. Given the range of students taking this type of course, we have written this book so that it is a valuable guide to all business students and provides them with the essential information they need to know. Students majoring in areas outside of business may also attend the introductory information systems course. Therefore, this book has been written to appeal to a diverse audience.

Information Systems Today, Third Edition, can also be used for the introductory course offered at the graduate level—for example, in the first year of an MBA program.

What's New to the Third Edition

Our primary goal for *Information Systems Today*, Third Edition, was to emphasize the importance of information systems to all business students as the role of information technology and systems continues to expand within organizations and society. Most notably, we extensively examine how information systems are fueling globalization—making the world smaller and more competitive—in virtually every industry and at an ever-increasing pace. Given this clear focus, we are better able to identify those topics most critical to students and future business professionals. Consequently, we have made substantial revisions to the basic content of the chapters and pedagogical elements, as well as included several new elements that we believe achieve this goal. A sample of the new or expanded chapter topics include:

- A new chapter examining the evolution of globalization and its impacts for individuals, organizations, and society that draws heavily on Thomas Friedman's best seller *The World Is Flat*.
- A new chapter examining the design and management of information systems infrastructures.
- Expanded coverage on the complexities related to assessing information systems investment decisions, building on key concepts from Clayton Christensen's *The Innovator's Dilemma*.
- Expanded coverage on information systems security, control, auditing, and disaster recovery planning.
- Expanded and updated coverage on legislative and legal issues including the USA PATRIOT and Sarbanes-Oxley Acts.
- Expanded and updated coverage of how the Internet is transforming commerce and society through the lens of Chris Anderson's *The Long Tails* and other contemporary views of the digital world.
- New and expanded coverage of cyberwar and cyberterrorism, particularly focusing on how the "business processes" of global terrorism are being transformed in the digital world.
- New and expanded coverage of a broad range of information systems in order to explore how these systems improve business intelligence and decision making as well as enable stronger partnerships with suppliers and customers.
- Updated and expanded technology briefings, five in all, that cover the underpinnings of how core information systems technology works.

In addition to the changes within the main chapter content, we have also added two new features to each chapter—"Change Agents" and "Industry Analyses." Change Agents briefly present the major players in the information systems industry, and how their companies or technologies have helped shape the world as we see it today. The Industry Analyses highlight how different industries have fundamentally changed with the advent of the Internet and the prevalence of information systems in today's digital world.

Beyond the chapter content and features, we have also made substantial changes and refinements to the end of each chapter. First, we carefully revised the end-of-chapter problems and exercises to reflect content change and new material. Second, we have introduced all new end-of-chapter cases about real, contemporary organizations to illustrate the issues businesses face when operating in the digital world. Third, the real-world business case called "e-Enabling the Air Transport Industry" has been updated to outline Boeing's strategy for infusing information systems into the air transport industry to help airlines better manage fleets and operations in this highly turbulent industry. Each installment of the case mirrors the primary content of its chapter to better emphasize its relevancy within the context of a real organization. All these elements are discussed more thoroughly next.

Our goal has always been to provide only the information that is relevant to all business students, nothing more and nothing less. We believe that we have again achieved this goal with *Information Systems Today*, Third Edition. We hope you agree.

Key Features

As authors, teachers, developers, and managers of information systems, we understand that in order for students to best learn about information systems with this book, they must be motivated to learn. To this end we have included a number of unique features to help students quickly and easily assess the true value of information systems and their impact on everyday life. We show how today's professionals are using information systems to help modern organizations become more efficient and competitive. Our focus is on the application of technology to real-world, contemporary situations. Next, we describe each of the features that contribute to that focus.

A Multitiered Approach

Each chapter utilizes cases in a variety of ways to emphasize and highlight how contemporary organizations are utilizing information systems to gain competitive advantage, streamline organizational processes, or improve customer satisfaction.

Opening Case—Managing in the Digital World   All chapters begin with an opening case describing a real-world company, technology, and/or issue to spark students' interest in the chapter topic. We have chosen engaging cases that relate to students' interests and concerns by highlighting why information systems have become central for managing in the digital world. Each opening case includes a series of associated questions the students will be able to answer after reading the chapter contents. The organizations and products highlighted in these cases include:

- Apple Computer's rise, fall, and reemergence as a global technology giant.
- MGM Grand's use of information systems to transform the gaming industry.
- How TiVo has changed the television industry, laying the foundation for video on demand and other services.
- Google's meteoric rise and the challenges associated with maintaining its success.
- eBay's ongoing struggles with counterfeit products and fraudulent Web sites.
- How widely available tools such as Netstumbler are making your information and networks more vulnerable to hackers.
- Amazon.com's use of customer data to improve security, product offerings, and ability to gain and sustain competitive advantage over rivals.
- How MLB.com (Major League Baseball) took control of its data to improve branding, create new revenue sources, and strengthen relationships with customers.
- How Sony, Nintendo, Electronic Arts, and Microsoft are designing the future of online gaming systems.
- How technologies such as BitTorrent are staying one step ahead of illegal file sharing legislation.

Brief Case   Each chapter also includes a brief case that is taken directly from the news and discusses contemporary companies and technologies. These are embedded right in the text of the chapter and highlight concepts from the surrounding chapter material. Discussion questions are provided to seed critical thinking assignments or class discussions. Some of the organizations, trends, and products highlighted in these cases include:

Brief Case ⊙

- How MTV Europe is deploying mobile video services to expand the reach and range of its market.
- How candy and chewing gum giant Wrigley is developing transnational information systems to achieve global efficiencies.
- How domainers—those who buy and sell lucrative domain names on the Internet—have grown into a multibillion-dollar industry.
- How Toyota is using information systems to consolidate and manage its growing global empire.
- How instant messaging is being used both productively and unproductively in organizations.
- How organizations are using various technologies to track and monitor employees.
- How London's Ministry of Sound has evolved from a dance club to a global force in the entertainment industry.
- How McDonald's is outsourcing drive-through order placement.
- How Microsoft *aids* hackers by releasing security update patches.
- How hacking has evolved into a global business, often holding companies and their data hostage for a big ransom.

End-of-Chapter Case   To test and reinforce chapter content, we present a current real-world case at the end of each chapter. Sources for these cases include *InformationWeek*, *BusinessWeek*, *CIO* Magazine, and various Web sites. Like the Brief Cases within the chapter, these are taken from the news and are contemporary. However, these are longer and more substantive than the Brief Cases. They too are followed by discussion questions that help the student apply and master the chapter. In addition, popular cases from *Information Systems Today*, Second Edition can be found at the Companion Website www.prenhall.com/jessup. The organizations and products highlighted in these cases include:

- How social networking sites like MySpace and Facebook have become big business on the Internet.
- How picture exchange site Flickr aids in the globalization movement.
- How NetFlix is transforming the movie and gaming industries.
- How the Sundance Film Festival is utilizing digital technology and the Internet to transform both the creation and distribution of entertainment content.
- How IBM has developed one of the world's top intranet sites to improve employee productivity.
- How and why cybercriminals target eBay, PayPal, and other popular Web sites and resources.
- How retail giant Home Depot is utilizing information systems to maximize the value of in-store product placements.
- How FedEx and Microsoft are using the Internet to provide superior customer service and increase customer loyalty.
- How the advent of open source software systems, such as the Linux operating system, Apache Web server, and Firefox Web browser, are transforming the software industry.
- How national defense and security is vulnerable to a plethora of local and global security threats.

E-enabling the Air Transport Industry   This real-world business case is used throughout the book and follows each chapter in order to enable students to apply lessons from each chapter in the business world. The Boeing Company took a vision for using high-speed Internet connectivity within commercial airplanes and developed this concept into a range of services that will indeed permanently transform the airline industry. Discussion questions are included with this running case after each chapter in order to promote critical thinking and class participation.

Common Chapter Features

Throughout every chapter, a variety of short pedagogical elements are presented to highlight key information systems issues and concepts in a variety of contexts. These elements help to show students the broader organizational and societal implications of various topics.

Industry Analysis

Every industry is being transformed by the Internet and the increasing use of information systems by individuals and organizations. To give you a feel for just how pervasive and profound these changes are, each chapter presents an analysis of a specific industry to highlight the new rules for operating in the digital world. Given that no industry or profession is immune from these changes, each Industry Analysis highlights the importance of understanding information systems for *every* business student, not only for information systems majors. Discussion questions help students better understand the rapidly changing opportunities and risks of operating in the digital world. Chapter 1 examines how the digital world is transforming the opportunities for virtually all business professions. Subsequent chapters examine how globalization and the digital world has eliminated or has forever transformed various industries, including the photo, radio, travel, banking, automobile manufacturing, programming, television, law enforcement, and even the comics industry. Clearly, we are in a time of tremendous change, and understanding this evolution will better equip students to not only survive but thrive in the digital world.

Key Enablers

We worked hard to ensure that this book is contemporary. We cover literally hundreds of different emerging technologies throughout the book. This feature focuses on the underlying innovations that enable the development of new, emerging technologies that are likely to impact organizations or society. Topics include:

- Nanotubes
- Spintronics
- Cognitive radio
- Pulsed arrested spark discharge
- Organic light emitting diodes
- Brainwave interfaces
- Liquid lenses
- Voice print
- Fabbing
- Photonic crystal fibers

When Things Go Wrong

Textbooks don't usually describe what not to do, but this can be very helpful to students. This feature enables students to learn about a real-world situation in which information systems did not work or were not built or used well. Topics include:

- Blackberry's copyright infringement that nearly shut down its network for millions of customers.
- Sony's "rootkit" spyware used to track customer's listening behavior and prevent illegal copying.
- Errors and deliberate misrepresentations of information at Wikipedia for ego, political gains, and profits.
- Loss of customer data at ChoicePoint, leading to a spike in identity theft victims.
- Challenges associated with the discarding the growing mountain of electronic waste, such as obsolete computers, cell phones and other gadgets.
- How illegal file sharing by employees creates huge liabilities for companies.
- Unusual cyberthreats, such as accidentally (or purposely) digging up largely unprotected fiber optic networks.
- Misusing customer relationship management (CRM) data to profile and take advantage of customers.
- Software failure at the Tokyo Stock Exchange costing hundreds of millions of dollars.
- How spam and spyware are creating traffic jams on the information superhighway.

Net Stats

The Internet is now a significant part of every organization as well as our personal lives. Net Stats provide interesting, important trends and forecasts related to Internet usage within a variety of contexts. These insights help students better understand the Internet's role in fueling globalization and transforming the digital world. Topics include:

- Global Internet usage
- File sharing
- Broadband access
- Blogging
- RFID tags
- Search engines
- E-business growth

- Spyware
- Infrastructure investment
- Bundled services

Ethical Dilemma

Ethical business practices are now a predominant part of contemporary management education and practice. This feature examines contemporary dilemmas related to the chapter content and highlights the implications of these dilemmas for managers, organizations, and society. Topics include:

- Differences in online rights throughout the world
- Ownership of company data
- Employee monitoring
- Cookies to "enhance" your Web surfing
- Vendor/client relationships
- Using CRM systems to target or discriminate
- System designs that eliminate jobs
- Ethical hacking
- Underground gaming industry to sell virtual goods for "real" money
- RFID privacy

Change Agent

A variety of key players have shaped the current landscape by inventing, selling, or promoting products and services that just a few years ago, few people would have imagined, and today, many people can't live without. While there are countless people who have contributed to today's digital world, this feature presents some of the more prominent players that have significantly advanced technologies or lead important companies. These people include:

- Steve Jobs of Apple
- Niklas Zennström of Skype
- Michael Dell of Dell
- Sergey Brin and Larry Page of Google
- Meg Whitman of eBay
- Anne Mulcahy of Xerox
- Jeff Bezos of Amazon.com
- Larry Ellison of Oracle
- Bill Gates of Microsoft
- Judy McGrath of MTV

End-of-Chapter Material

Our end-of-chapter material is designed to accommodate various teaching and learning styles. It promotes learning beyond the book and the classroom. Elements include the following:

- Key Terms—Highlight key concepts within the chapter.
- Review Questions—Test students' understanding of basic content.
- Self-Study Questions—Enable students to assess whether they are ready for a test.
- Matching Questions—Check quickly to see if students understand basic terms.
- Problems and Exercises—Push students deeper into the material and encourage them to synthesize and apply it.
- Application Exercises—Challenge students to solve two real-world management problems using spreadsheet and database applications from a running case centered on a university travel agency. Student data files referenced within the exercises are available on the Companion Website: www.prenhall.com/jessup.
- Team Work Exercise—Enable students to work in teams to solve a problem and/or address an issue related to the chapter material.
- We have extensively updated these elements to reflect new chapter content and the natural evolution of the material.

Pedagogy

In addition to the features described above, we provide a list of learning objectives to lay the foundation for each chapter. At the end of the chapter, the Key Points Review repeats these learning objectives and describes how each objective was achieved. A list of references is located at the end of the text, organized by chapter.

Organization

The content and organization of this book are based on our own teaching, as well as on feedback from reviewers and colleagues throughout the field. Each chapter builds on the others to reinforce key concepts and allow for a seamless learning experience. Essentially, the book has been structured to answer three fundamental questions:

1. What are contemporary information systems, and how are they being used in innovative ways?
2. Why are information systems so important and interesting?
3. How best can we build, acquire, manage, and safeguard information systems?

The ordering and content of our chapters was also significantly influenced by a recent article, "What Every Business Student Needs to Know About Information Systems."[1] This article was written by 40 prominent information systems scholars to define the information systems core body of knowledge for all business students. By design, the content of *Information Systems Today*, Third Edition, carefully follows the guidance of this article. We are, therefore, very confident that our book provides a solid and widely agreed upon foundation for any introductory information systems course.

The chapters are organized as follows:

- **Chapter 1: "Managing in the Digital World"**—This chapter helps the student understand what information systems are and how they have become a vital part of modern organizations. We walk the student through the technology, people, and organizational components of an information system, and we lay out types of jobs and career opportunities in information systems and in related fields. We use a number of cases and examples, such as that of Apple Computers, to show the student the types of systems being used and to point out common "best practices" in systems use and management.
- **Chapter 2: "Fueling Globalization through Information Systems"**—In this new chapter, which draws heavily on Thomas Freidman's bestseller *The World is Flat*, we provide a discussion of how globalization evolved, and what opportunities globalization presents for organizations. Using examples, such as the MGM Grand, we highlight the factors organizations have to consider when operating in the digital world. We also present different business and information systems strategies for companies operating in the digital world.
- **Chapter 3: "Valuing Information Systems Investments"**—Here, we discuss how companies, such as TiVo, can use information systems for automation, organizational learning, and strategic advantage. Further, we describe how to formulate and present the business case for an information system. Given the rapid advancement of new technologies, we also explain why and how companies are continually looking for innovative ways to use information systems for competitive advantage.

---

[1] Ives, B., Valacich, J., Watson, R., Zmud, R. (2002). "What Every Business Student Needs to Know about Information Systems." *Communications of the Association for Information Systems*, 9(30). Other contributing scholars to this article include: Maryam Alavi, Richard Baskerville, Jack J Baroudi, Cynthia Beath, Thomas Clark, Eric K. Clemons, Gordon B. Davis, Fred Davis, Alan R. Dennis, Omar A. El Sawy, Jane Fedorowicz, Robert D. Galliers, Joey George, Michael Ginzberg, Paul Gray, Rudy Hirschheim, Sirkka Jarvenpaa, Len Jessup, Chris F. Kemerer, John L. King, Benn Konsynski, Ken Kraemer, Jerry N. Luftman, Salvatore T. March, M. Lynne Markus, Richard O. Mason, F. Warren McFarlan, Ephraim R. McLean, Lorne Olfman, Margrethe H. Olson, John Rockart, V. Sambamurthy, Peter Todd, Michael Vitale, Ron Weber, and Andrew B. Whinston.

- **Chapter 4: "Managing the Information Systems Infrastructure"**—In this chapter, we provide an overview of the essential information systems infrastructure components and describe why they are necessary for satisfying an organization's informational needs. With the ever-increasing complexity of maintaining a solid information systems infrastructure, it becomes increasingly important for organizations, such as Google, to design a reliable, robust, and secure infrastructure. We discuss recent trends to support an information systems infrastructure, and describe how organizations can ensure a reliable and secure infrastructure, and plan for potential disasters.

- **Chapter 5: "Enabling Commerce Using the Internet"**—Perhaps nothing has changed the landscape of business more than the use of the Internet for electronic commerce. In this extensively updated chapter, we describe how a number of firms, such as eBay, use the Internet to conduct commerce in cyberspace. Further, we explain how organizations build intranets to support internal processes and build extranets to interact with other firms. We then describe the stages of business-to-consumer electronic commerce and discuss emerging trends in consumer-to-consumer e-commerce and mobile commerce. Finally, we explain different forms of e-government, and show how governmental regulations can become a threat to e-commerce.

- **Chapter 6: "Securing Information Systems"**—With the pervasive use of information systems, new dangers have arisen for organizations, and information security has become a paramount issue within the context of global information management. In this chapter, we expanded the topic of securing information systems to a full chapter by examining the primary threats to information systems security and how systems are compromised. Using examples of organizations, such as PayPal, we show how companies can implement both technological and human-based safeguards to better manage information systems.

- **Chapter 7: "Enhancing Business Intelligence Using Information Systems"**—Given how many different types of information systems organizations use, in this chapter we use examples from Amazon.com and other firms to describe the various types of systems. In this extensively updated chapter, we provide ways to categorize the systems so that the student can better make sense of them all. Further, we discuss a variety of systems that span different organizational levels, such as decision support systems, intelligent systems, data mining and visualization systems, office automation systems, collaboration technologies, knowledge management systems, geographic information systems, and functional area information systems.

- **Chapter 8: "Building Organizational Partnerships Using Enterprise Information Systems"**—In this extensively updated chapter, we focus on enterprise systems, which are a popular type of information system used to integrate information and span organizations' boundaries to better connect a firm with customers, suppliers, and other partners. We show the student how MLB.com, the Web site for Major League Baseball, and other firms use enterprise resource planning, customer relationship management, and supply chain management to compete in the digital world.

- **Chapter 9: "Developing Information Systems"**—How are all these systems built? In this chapter, we examine how Sony, Electronic Arts, and other firms build and acquire new information systems. We walk the student through the traditional systems development approach, as well as more contemporary approaches, such as prototyping, rapid application development, and object-oriented analysis and design.

- **Chapter 10: "Managing Information Systems Ethics and Crime"**—In this chapter, we describe the ethical dilemmas associated with information systems, as well as common forms of computer crime. We examine the ethical concerns Napster and other firms deal with in the information age, and how computer ethics influences the use of information systems. We also define computer crime and list several types of computer crime. Lastly, given its growing relevance to managing and living in the digital world, we significantly updated and expanded our discussion of cyberwar and cyberterrorism.

In addition to these 10 chapters, we include five Technology Briefings focusing on basic concepts regarding hardware, software, databases, networking, and the Internet. Specifically, these briefings are:

- **Technology Briefing 1: Information Systems Hardware**—This briefing provides an overview of computer hardware components and various classes and configurations of computers that are implemented in modern organizations.
- **Technology Briefing 2: Information Systems Software**—This briefing provides an overview of what software is and how it is created.
- **Technology Briefing 3: Database Management**—This briefing provides an overview of how database and database management systems (DBMS) work, examining how DBMS are used, designed, and implemented.
- **Technology Briefing 4: Networking**—This briefing examines central components and concepts core to understanding networking fundamentals.
- **Technology Briefing 5: The Internet and the World Wide Web**—This briefing introduces students to a high-level view of the Internet and Web by examining concepts such as the purpose of a URL, how web browsers talk to web servers, or how traffic is maintained and routed.

Although our market research found that many students have a solid understanding of these technological building blocks, this material is provided as a reference or to be used as a central part of the course. By delivering this material as a Technology Briefing, we provide instructors the greatest flexibility in how and when they can apply it.

Supplement Support

Instructor's Resource Center Online and on CD-ROM

The convenient Instructor's Resource Center is available both online and on CD-ROM. The online center is accessible from *www.prenhall.com/jessup* by choosing the "Instructor Resources" link from the catalog page. Both the online center and CD-ROM include all the supplements: *Instructor's Manual, Test Item File, TestGen, TestGen conversions in WebCT and BlackBoard-ready files, PowerPoint presentations*, and *Image Library (text art)*. The Instructor's Manual includes answers to all review and discussion questions, exercises, and case questions. The Test Item File (Test Bank) includes multiple-choice, true-false, and essay questions for each chapter. The Test Bank is delivered in MS Word, as well as in the form of TestGen. The PowerPoint presentations highlight text learning objectives and key topics. Finally, the Image Library is a collection of the figures and tables from the text for instructor use in PowerPoint slides and class lectures.

Companion Website: www.prenhall.com/jessup

This text is supported by a dynamic Companion Website that features:

1. Interactive Study Guide that includes multiple-choice, true-false, and essay questions for each chapter. Each question includes a hint for students' reference. Students receive automatic feedback upon submitting each quiz.
2. Student Data files for use with the end-of-chapter Application Software Exercises.
3. Glossary.

Online Courses

WebCT, www.prenhall.com/webct, Gold Level Customer Support available exclusively to adopters of Prentice Hall courses, is provided upon adoption and provides you with priority assistance, training discounts, and dedicated technical support.

BlackBoard, www.prenhall.com/blackboard, Prentice Hall's abundant online content, combined with BlackBoard's popular tools and interface, result in robust Web-based courses that are easy to implement, manage, and use—taking your courses to new heights in student interaction and learning.

Reviewers

We wish to thank the following faculty who participated in reviews for this and previous editions:

Lawrence L. Andrew, Western Illinois University

Karin A. Bast, University of Wisconsin–La Crosse

Brian Carpani, Southwestern College

Amita Chin, Virginia Commonwealth University

David Firth, University of Montana

Frederick Fisher, Florida State University

James Frost, Idaho State University

Frederick Gallegos, California State Polytechnic University–Pomona

Dale Gust, Central Michigan University

Traci Hess, Washington State University

Bruce Hunt, California State University–Fullerton

Carol Jensen, Southwestern College

Bhushan Kappor, California State University–Fullerton

Elizabeth Kemm, Central Michigan University

Beth Kiggins, University of Indianapolis

Chang E. Koh, University of North Texas

Brian R. Kovar, Kansas State University

Kapil Ladha, Drexel University

Linda K. Lau, Longwood University

Cameron Lawrence, University of Montana

Martha Leva, Penn State University–Abington

Weiqi Li, University of Michigan–Flint

Dana L. McCann, Central Michigan University

Richard McCarthy, Quinnipiac University

Patricia McQuaid, California State Polytechnic University

Timothy Peterson, University of Minnesota–Duluth

Eugene Rathswohl, University of San Diego

Rene F. Reitsma, Oregon State University

Kenneth Rowe, Purdue University

G. Shankaranarayanan, Boston University

James Sneeringer, St. Edward's University

Cheri Speier, Michigan State University

Bill Turnquist, Central Washington University

Craig K. Tyran, Western Washington University

William Wagner, Villanova University

Minhua Wang, State University of New York–Canton

John Wells, Washington State University

Nilmini Wickramasinghe, Cleveland State University

Acknowledgments

Although only our two names will be listed as the authors for this book (in alphabetical order), this was truly a team effort that went well beyond the two of us. Prentice Hall has been an outstanding publishing company to work with. They are innovative, have high standards, and are as competitive as we are.

Among the many amazingly helpful people at Prentice Hall, there are a handful of people we wish to thank specifically. First, Ana Jankowski, our assistant editor, helped to whip us and this book into shape and get it finished on time. Additionally, Suzanne Grappi, our production editor, helped in getting approval for photos, figures, Web sites, and other graphics as well as coordinating refinements as the book moved through stages of production. Finally, our executive editor, Bob Horan, guided the book and us from its inception, and he dared us to dream of and to write the best introductory information systems textbook ever.

In addition to our colleagues at Prentice Hall, a number of other people have helped us by conducting background research or creating early drafts of elements and chapter material. They are Traci Hess, Clay Looney, John Mathew, Darren Nicholson, Jennifer Nicholson, Saonee Sarker, Anna Sidorova, John Wells, and Carol Wysocki. In particular, three individuals were particularly instrumental in making the third edition the best ever. First, Karen Judson did an outstanding job editing and refining all our new cases and chapter elements. Likewise, Ryan Wright provided many innovative ideas for chapter updates, end-of-chapter problems, and chapter elements as well as leading the effort to streamline and update the Technology Briefings. Last, and most significantly, Christoph Schneider not only was instrumental in developing and updating the e-Enabled end-of-chapter running case, but also drafting key parts of the new globalization and infrastructure chapters. Additionally, without the support of our Boeing colleagues, Scott Carson, president and CEO of commercial airplanes, and Robert Dietterle, chief technology officer of Connexion by Boeing, the development of the end-of-chapter running case would not have been possible. Thanks, team! We could not have done it without you.

Most important, we thank our families for their patience and assistance in helping us to complete this book. Len's daughter Jamie and his son David were a constant inspiration, as were Joe's wife Jackie, his daughter Jordan, and his son James. This one is for you all.

Information Systems Today

chapter *1*

Managing in the Digital World

p r e v i e w >   Today, organizations from Apple Computer to Zales Jewelers use computer-based information systems to better manage their organizations in the digital world. These organizations use information systems to provide high-quality goods and services as well as to gain or sustain competitive advantage over rivals. Our objective for Chapter 1 is to help you understand what information systems are, how they have evolved to become a vital part of modern organizations, and why this understanding is necessary for you to become an effective manager in the digital world. After reading this chapter, you will be able to do the following:

1. Explain what an information system is, contrasting its data, technology, people, and organizational components.

2. Describe types of jobs and career opportunities in information systems and in related fields.

3. Describe the dual nature of information systems in the success and failure of modern organizations.

The next section provides a brief overview of the book. Then, we explain what information systems are and how they have evolved. We conclude by illustrating how information systems can be utilized to improve organizational performance.

Managing in the Digital World: Apple Computer

FIGURE 1.1

Apple has been an innovation leader in the computer and consumer electronics industries.

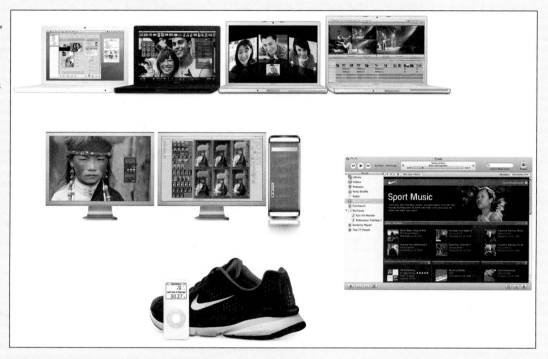

It happened on April Fool's Day 1976, but history has shown it was no joke. On that date, Stephen "Woz" Wozniak and Steven Paul Jobs officially formed the Apple Computer Company. The two friends had been fascinated with computers since their days as students at Homestead High School in Cupertino, California. Wozniak graduated first, in 1967, because he is five years older than Jobs, but their shared interest in anything digital kept bringing the two together, both before Jobs graduated from high school and after he graduated in 1972.

The two Steves both dropped out of college to work on building computers—first in Jobs' bedroom, then in his garage when the bedroom got too crowded. (Wozniak later returned to school at the University of California in Berkeley and graduated with a degree in engineering in 1986.) At first they were interested just in building circuit boards but decided to build entire computers and sell them to home users. The Apple I debuted shortly after the company was formed and sold for $666.66.

Before the Apple I came the Altair 8800—the first home computer. Buyers had to assemble the machine themselves, there was no interface, and switches had to be tripped manually and in proper sequence for the machine to function at all. The machine was a fun tool for geeks but not practical for the average computer user.

However, the introduction of the Apple I computer paved the way for profound changes in the way everyday people would use computers. Shortly after the introduction of the Apple I, Wozniak and Jobs developed the Apple II, which included a keyboard, a floppy disk drive, and color graphics. Because of its jazzy appearance and ease of use (which can't be compared with today's personal computers), consumers liked the Apple II, and the Apple Company eventually sold 50,000 units. It continued to be Apple's dominant product until 1993. To date, the Apple II's 17-year life span is a record within the computer industry.

Wozniak and Jobs' working relationship was key to Apple's success. Wozniak, the engineer, was concerned primarily with a computer's function, while Jobs focused on ease of use and design. Thanks to the two-Steves team, the Apple II was an attractive and functional addition to a family's living room. Apple continues to offer products that are a blend of engineering and aesthetics, and many consumers are devoted to the products. The history of Apple Computers, however, includes a series of high highs and low lows. For example, the Lisa, introduced in 1983, was a commercial disaster, and the Apple III, introduced shortly after the Apple II, was discontinued after only a year on the market when it failed to entice consumers. In 1984, Apple once again had a hit when it introduced the popular

Macintosh 128K, featuring the AppleMouse II (the first computer mouse introduced to the mass market) and the first true graphical user interface. When Apple introduced the Macintosh Portable (an early laptop), it had only limited success, but it was redesigned and renamed the PowerBook and proved a marketplace success. Other near failures for Apple included the Apple Newton (an early PDA) and the G3 enterprise server computer.

Jobs left Apple in 1985 amid employee complaints that he was an erratic and tempestuous manager; Wozniak left Apple for good in 1986. Jobs was so disgruntled when he left Apple that he sold all but one share of his stock in the company. Jobs then started another computer company, NeXT Computer, which designed and marketed a technologically advanced computer that did not sell well because of its high price. Apple's leadership foundered for a while, but the company purchased NeXT for $402 million in 1996, and Jobs again took over the helm. Jobs brought Apple back to profitability by revamping its product line. The iMac, a PowerBook featuring a 14-inch display and Mac OS X—a new operating system—was the most successful unit in the 1998 product line.

Jobs has remained Apple's chief executive officer (CEO), seeing the company through yet another product success with the introduction of the iPod, a hard drive–based MP3 music player, which debuted in November 2001 (4 GB, $250) and went mainstream in 2003. The simple user interface and small size were the major factors that made the iPod one of the most sought after digital music players.

Also attractive to consumers is the fact that the iPod is offered with several customizable features, such as connectability to a car stereo system or to external speakers, a camera, and choices of outer skin color. Apple soon improved on the original iPod design, offering the iPod mini, iPod color, iPod shuffle, iPod nano, and so on. Although competitors have released their own digital music players, none have achieved Apple's market share.

To add to the iPod's success, Apple created an online music store called iTunes, where users could download digital music for 99 cents per track. The combination of product (the iPod) and service (online iTunes store) resulted in massive profits for Apple. Although initially the music from the online store could only be downloaded using an Apple computer, later the downloads could be made from any machine (though they still can only be played on iPods). Recently, iTunes has expanded into the video market, providing videos—mostly reruns of television shows—for video-capable iPods.

In 2005, environmentalists criticized Apple Computers for its lack of an e-waste recycling policy. Jobs was at first defiant, dismissing such complaints as trivial, but shortly after Apple's annual meeting in April 2005, he announced that Apple would take back iPods for free. In 2006, he further expanded Apple's recycling programs to any customer who buys a new Mac. This program includes shipping and "environmentally friendly disposal" of customers' old systems.

After reading this chapter, you will be able to answer the following:

1. Given the pace at which technology is converging (e.g., phones, music players, cameras, and so on), what do you think is next for Apple?

2. Apple has had many "near death" experiences throughout its history; is Apple now here to stay?

3. Jobs has been the catalyst for many of Apple's successes (and failures); can Apple survive without Jobs?

Sources:

iTunes Video Boosts TV Ratings: Downloads of *The Office* and *LOST* Are on the Rise, and so Are Their Ratings, http://money.cnn.com/2006/01/17/technology/browser0117/index.htm

Apple's iTunes Raises Privacy Concerns, http://news.zdnet.com/2100-1009_22-6026542.html

http://www.mcelhearn.com/article.php?story=200601111150127268

http://apple2history.org/history/ah01.html

http://apple2history.org/history/appy/ahc.html

http://www.apple-history.com/

http://packmug.ncsu.edu/woz/history.html

What You Will Find in this Book

Figure 1.2 provides an overview of this book. The chapters provide a comprehensive presentation of the information systems body of knowledge, including the following:

- *Chapter 1—Managing in the Digital World.* Here we provide an overview of what information systems are and how they are being used in modern organizations.
- *Chapter 2—Fueling Globalization through Information Systems.* Here we provide an overview of how the pervasive use of information systems is fueling globalization and rapid change in the world.
- *Chapter 3—Valuing Information Systems Investments.* Here we examine how information systems can be utilized to improve organizational performance as well as provide a return on investment.
- *Chapter 4—Managing the Information Systems Infrastructure.* Here we provide an overview of the various components of a comprehensive infrastructure and how organizations are managing this infrastructure to best utilize their information systems investments.
- *Chapter 5—Enabling Commerce Using the Internet.* Here we focus on how organizations are utilizing the Internet to create and sustain business opportunities competitive advantage.
- *Chapter 6—Securing Information Systems.* Here we examine how organizations can best secure their information systems.
- *Chapter 7—Enhancing Business Intelligence Using Information Systems.* Here we describe various kinds of information systems that firms use to improve business processes and decision making.
- *Chapter 8—Building Organizational Partnerships Using Enterprise Information Systems.* Here we examine how information systems can be used to help integrate the entire organization and help connect the firm to customers, suppliers, and partners.
- *Chapter 9—Developing Information Systems.* Here we describe how information systems and services are developed and/or acquired.
- *Chapter 10—Managing Information Systems Ethics and Crime.* Here we discuss key legal and ethical issues for successfully managing information systems.

In addition to these chapters, we also provide five short technology-focused overviews that will provide a better understanding of how these various components function and can be configured to create the power of modern information systems. These briefings include the following:

- *Technology Briefing 1—Information Systems Hardware.* Here we provide a brief overview of a modern computer, its components, and various computer categories and types.

Introduction	Chapter 1 Managing in the Digital World	
Information Systems Body of Knowledge	Chapter 2 Fueling Globalization through Information Systems	Chapter 3 Valuing Information Systems Investments
	Chapter 4 Managing the Information Systems Infrastructure	
	Chapter 5 Enabling Commerce Using the Internet	Chapter 6 Securing Information Systems
	Chapter 7 Enhancing Business Intelligence Using Information Systems	
	Chapter 8 Building Organizational Partnerships Using Enterprise Information Systems	Chapter 9 Developing Information Systems
	Chapter 10 Managing Information Systems Ethics and Crime	
Technology Foundations	Technology Briefing 1 Information Systems Hardware	Technology Briefing 2 Information Systems Software
	Technology Briefing 3 Database Management	
	Technology Briefing 4 Networking	Technology Briefing 5 The Internet and World Wide Web

FIGURE 1.2

The overview of this book, representing key information for managing computer-based information systems in organizations.

- *Technology Briefing 2—Information Systems Software.* Here we provide a brief overview of computer software, including types, evolution, and how software is created.
- *Technology Briefing 3—Database Management.* Here we provide a brief overview of database management systems and how they are designed.
- *Technology Briefing 4—Networking.* Here we provide a brief overview of computer networking concepts, technologies, and applications.
- *Technology Briefing 5—The Internet and World Wide Web.* Here we provide an overview of the Internet, its evolution, and its future.

Our primary objective when designing this book was to focus on the big picture, trying not to bog you down with unnecessary technological jargon. Nevertheless, to effectively manage in the digital world, you need a comprehensive understanding of what information systems are, the necessary vocabulary to understand and explain these technologies, what factors are shaping the digital world, the categories and types of information systems, and how organizations are deploying these systems to create value and competitive advantage. We hope that you agree after reading the book that we have achieved this objective.

Information Systems Today

In 1959, Peter Drucker predicted this rise in the importance of information and of information technology, and at that point, over four decades ago, he coined the term **knowledge worker**. Knowledge workers are typically professionals who are relatively well educated and who create, modify, and/or synthesize knowledge as a fundamental part of their jobs.

Drucker's predictions about knowledge workers were very accurate. As he predicted, they are generally paid better than their prior agricultural and industrial counterparts; they rely on and are empowered by formal education, yet they often also possess valuable real-world skills; they are continually learning how to do their jobs better; they have much better career opportunities and far more bargaining power than workers ever had before; they make up about a quarter of the workforce in the United States and in other developed nations; and their numbers are rising quickly.

Drucker also predicted that, with the growth in the number of knowledge workers and with their rise in importance and leadership, a **knowledge society** would emerge. He reasoned that, given the importance of education and learning to knowledge workers and the firms that need them, education would become the cornerstone of the knowledge society. Possessing knowledge, he argued, would be as important as possessing land, labor, or capital (if not more so) (see Figure 1.3). Indeed, research shows that people equipped to prosper in the knowledge society, such as those with a college education, earn far more on average than people without a college education and that gap is increasing. In fact, information from the U.S. Census Bureau (2005 data) reinforces the value of a college education: workers 18 and over with a bachelor's degree earn an average of $51,206 a year, while those with a high school diploma earn $27,915. Workers with an advanced degree make an average of $74,602, and those without a high school diploma average $18,734. Additionally, getting a college degree will qualify you for many jobs that would not be available to you otherwise and will distinguish you from other job candidates. Finally, a college degree is often a requirement to qualify for career advancement and promotion opportunities once you do get that job.

People generally agree that Drucker was accurate about knowledge workers and the evolution of society. While people have settled on Drucker's term "knowledge worker," there are many alternatives to the term "knowledge society." For example, Manuel Castell has written that we now live in a network society. *Wired* magazine has published that we now live in a **new economy** and described it as follows:

So what is the new economy? When we talk about the new economy, we're talking about a world in which people work with their brains instead of their hands. A world in which communications technology creates global competition—not just for

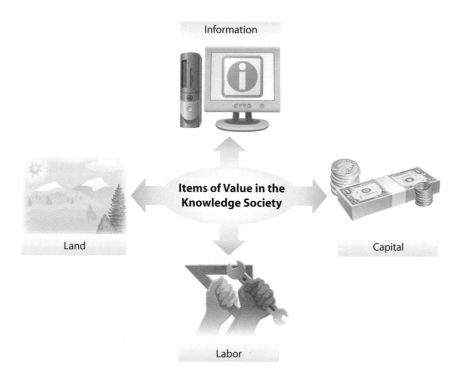

FIGURE 1.3

In the knowledge society, information has become as important as—and many feel *more important than*—land, labor, and capital resources.

running shoes and laptop computers, but also for bank loans and other services that can't be packed into a crate and shipped. A world in which innovation is more important than mass production. A world in which investment buys new concepts or the means to create them, rather than new machines. A world in which rapid change is a constant. A world at least as different from what came before it as the industrial age was from its agricultural predecessor. A world so different its emergence can only be described as a revolution. (Excerpt from *Wired* magazine's "Encyclopedia of the New Economy," http://hotwired.wired.com/special/ene/)

Others have referred to this phenomenon as the knowledge economy, the digital society, the network era, the Internet era, and other names. We simply refer to this as the *digital world.* All these ideas have in common the premise that information and related technologies and systems have become very important to us and that knowledge workers are vital.

Some have argued, however, that there is a downside to being a knowledge worker and to living in the digital world. For example, Kit Sims-Taylor has argued that knowledge workers will be the first to be replaced by automation with information technology. Jeremy Rifkin has argued that our overreliance on information technology has caused us to think and act hastily and to lose our perspective. Others have argued that in the new economy there is a *digital divide,* where those with access to information technology have great advantages over those without access to information technology.

To be sure, there is a downside to overreliance on knowledge workers and information technology, but one thing is for certain: knowledge workers and information technologies are now critical to the success of modern organizations, economies, and societies. What are some of the characteristics of the digital world? This is examined next.

Characteristics of the Digital World

Computers are the core component of information systems. Over the past decade, the advent of powerful, relatively inexpensive, easy-to-use computers has had a major impact on business. To see this impact, look around your school or place of work. At your school, you may register for classes online, use e-mail to communicate with fellow students and your instructors, and complete or submit assignments on networked personal computers. At work, you may use a personal computer for e-mail and other tasks. Your paychecks are probably generated by computer and automatically deposited in your checking account via high-speed networks. Chances are that each year you see more information technology than you did the year before, and this technology is a more fundamental and important part of your learning and work than ever before.

When you stop and think about it, it is easy to see why information technology is important. Increasing global competitiveness has forced companies to find ways to be better and to do things less expensively. The answer for many firms continues to be to use information systems to do things better, faster, and cheaper. Using global telecommunications networks, companies can more easily integrate their operations to access new markets for their products and services as well as access a large pool of talented labor in countries with lower wages.

This integration of economies throughout the world, enabled by technological progress, is called *globalization* (see Chapter 2). You can see the effects of globalization in many ways, such as the greater international movement of commodities, money, information, and labor, as well as the development of technologies, standards, and processes to facilitate this movement (see Figure 1.4). Specifically, a more global and competitive world includes visible economic, cultural, and technological changes, including the following:

- *Economic Changes.* Increases in international trade, in the development of global financial systems and currency, and in the outsourcing of labor.
- *Cultural Changes.* Increases in the availability of multiculturalism through television and movies; the frequency of international travel, tourism, and immigration; the availability of ethnic foods and restaurants; and the frequency of worldwide fads and phenomena such as Pokemon, Sudoku, Idol television, and MySpace.
- *Technological Changes.* The development of low-cost computing platforms and communication technologies; the availability of low-cost communication systems such as e-mail, Skype, and instant messaging; the ubiquitous nature of low-cost global telecommunications infrastructure like the Internet; and the enforcement of global patent and copyright laws to spur further innovation.

Through the convergence of economies and culture, fueled by a robust global technology infrastructure, the world has forever changed. Given its central role in this ongoing global revolution, information systems are defined next.

FIGURE 1.4

Globalization can be seen in visible economic, cultural, and technological changes.

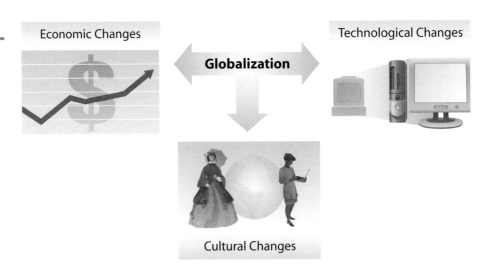

Ethical Dilemma

Online Rights Not Always Universal

American Internet users have been fortunate in that online content is not censored, and U.S.-based bloggers, journalists, and e-mailers are generally not subject to government intrusion or harassment. As the world becomes flatter, however, and the Internet becomes available to users in diverse countries, the question of who owns and/or controls Web-published data becomes an issue.

To use one country as an example, China has often been in the news for alleged violations of human rights. Since American companies have provided software and hardware for China's Internet infrastructure, the question arises, When China restricts online rights for its citizens, should U.S. companies providing services be cooperative? Consider the following:

- Cisco built the entire Chinese Internet infrastructure and allegedly agreed to supply equipment that allows the Chinese government to monitor Internet users.
- Chinese Internet users use Microsoft's blog tool, MSN Spaces. Microsoft censors the Chinese version of its software, using a blacklist supplied by Beijing. Among words that will be automatically rejected by the Chinese system are "democracy" and "capitalism."
- In order to do business in China, in 2004 Google agreed to censor out "subversive" articles from Google News China or from their search results.

Reporters Without Borders and other critics have called such censorship agreements unethical. Cisco, Microsoft, and Google have replied that they are simply following local laws. Opponents argue, however, that online product and service providers based outside of China should not assist the Chinese government in its campaign against Internet users' online rights.

A case in point: A Chinese journalist in Beijing recently posted content that, although probably factually correct, was deemed inappropriate by the Chinese government. The government then requested that Microsoft shut down the blog, and Microsoft complied. The Chinese government monitors all online activity, shutting down "dissident" Web sites and deleting "subversive" postings. Since Chinese bloggers often write under pseudonyms, the Chinese government has recently asked Internet access provider firms to reveal the identities of bloggers who post "inappropriate" content. As a result, several Chinese bloggers have been arrested and sentenced to lengthy jail terms after their identities were revealed.

For human rights activists, the major issue is that American companies such as Microsoft and Google that profess to value free speech are acting unethically when they cooperate with governments that curtail Internet users' rights to freedom of expression. The fact that Article 19 of the Universal Declaration of Human Rights supports freedom of expression lends legitimacy to this argument.

Another question that arises in such situations is, "Who owns Web-posted data"? Since the data is often not physically present in the local country supplying Internet access, do the local authorities have the right to censor the data? (Local authorities would probably argue that the impact of the content posted online is felt locally.) Do local authorities have a right to regulate online content when Internet access is hosted by companies located outside a country?

Most important, is the online environment independent of the digital world we live in, or is it subject to all the rules and regulations of countries the Internet passes through? Should the Internet adapt its own laws that all hosting companies must follow?

These are questions that will need to be answered in the twenty-first century as the world gets smaller and the Internet becomes an integral service in all countries.

Sources: Julien Pain, "Perspective: A Cyber Blind Spot on Human Rights," *CNet News.com* (December 1, 2005), http://news.com.com/A+cyber+blind+spot+on+human+rights/2010-1028_3-5977410.html

David Barboza and Tom Zellar Jr., "Microsoft's Shutdown of Chinese Blog Is Condemned," *International Herald Tribune* (January 8, 2006), http://www.iht.com/articles/2006/01/06/technology/web.0107msft.php

Information Systems Defined

Information systems (IS) are combinations of **hardware**, **software**, and **telecommunications networks** that people build and use to collect, create, and distribute useful data, typically in organizational settings. Hardware refers to physical computer equipment, such as the computer monitor, central processing unit, or keyboard. Software refers to a program or set of programs that tell the computer to perform certain tasks. Telecommunications networks refer to a group of two or more computer systems linked together with communications equipment. Although we discuss the design, implementation, use, and implications of hardware, software, and telecommunications throughout the chapters, the specifics on hardware, software, and telecommunications are discussed in detail in the Technology Briefings. In Figure 1.5, we show the relationships among these IS components.

People in organizations use information systems to process sales transactions, manage loan applications, or help financial analysts decide where, when, and how to invest. Product managers also use them to help decide where, when, and how to market their products and related services, and production managers use them to help decide when and how to manufacture products. Information systems also enable us to get cash from ATMs, communicate by live video with people in other parts of the world, and buy concert or airplane tickets. (Note that the term "information systems" is also used to describe the field comprising people who develop, use, manage, and study information systems in organizations.)

It is important to note that people use various terms to describe the field of information systems, such as management information systems, data processing management, systems management, business computer systems, computer information systems, and simply "systems." Since the term "information systems" is most common, we will stick with this term and its acronym, IS. Next, we more thoroughly examine each of the key components of the information systems definition.

Data: The Root and Purpose of Information Systems

Earlier, we defined IS as combinations of hardware, software, and telecommunications networks that people build and use to collect, create, and distribute useful data, typically in organizational settings. We will begin by talking about data, the most basic element of any information system.

FIGURE 1.5

An information system is a combination of five key elements: people, hardware, software, data, and telecommunications networks.

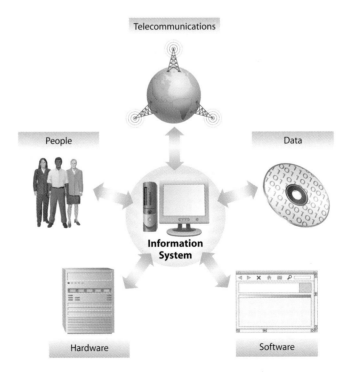

Data. Before you can understand how information systems work, it is important to distinguish between data and information, terms that are often erroneously used interchangeably. **Data** is raw material—recorded, unformatted information, such as words and numbers. Data has no meaning in and of itself. For example, if I asked you what 465889727 meant or stood for, you could not tell me (see Figure 1.6). However, if I presented the same data as 465-88-9727 and told you it was located in a certain database, in John Doe's file, in a field labeled "SSN," you might rightly surmise that the number was actually the Social Security number of someone named John Doe.

Information. Data formatted with dashes or labels is more useful than unformatted data. It is transformed into **information**, which can be defined as a representation of reality. In the previous example, 465-88-9727 was used to represent and identify an individual person, John Doe (see Figure 1.6). Contextual cues, such as a label, are needed to turn data into information that is familiar to the reader. Think about your experience with ATMs. A list of all the transactions at a bank's ATMs over the course of a month would be fairly useless data. However, a table that divided ATM users into two categories, bank customers and non–bank customers, and compared the two groups' use of the machine—their purpose for using the ATMs and the times and days on which they use them—would be incredibly useful information. A bank manager could use this information to create marketing mailings to attract new customers. Without information systems, it would be difficult to make data useful by turning it into information.

Knowledge. In addition to data and information, knowledge and wisdom are also important. **Knowledge** is needed to understand relationships between different pieces of information. For example, you must have knowledge to be aware that only one Social Security number can uniquely identify each individual (see Figure 1.6). Knowledge is a body of governing procedures, such as guidelines or rules, that are used to organize or manipulate data to make it suitable for a given task.

Wisdom. Finally, **wisdom** is accumulated knowledge. Wisdom goes beyond knowledge in that it represents broader, more generalized rules and schemas for understanding a specific domain or domains. Wisdom allows you to understand how to apply concepts from one domain to new situations or problems. Understanding that a unique individual identifier, such as a Social Security number, can be applied in certain programming situations to single out an individual record in a database is the result of accumulated knowledge (see Figure 1.6). Wisdom can be gained through a combination of academic study and personal experience.

Understanding the distinctions between data, information, knowledge, and wisdom is important because all are used in the study, development, and use of information systems.

Data	Information	Knowledge	Wisdom
465889727	465-88-9727	465-88-9727 → John Doe	465-88-9727 → John Doe ⟶ School Records, Employment Records, Medical Records
Unformatted Data	Formatted Data	Data Relationships	Data Relationships for Multiple Domains
Meaning: ???	Meaning: A SSN	Meaning: SSN → Unique Person	Meaning: SSN → Unique Person → Any information about the Person

FIGURE 1.6

Data, information, knowledge, and wisdom.

Information Technology: The Components of Information Systems

When we use the term "information system," we are talking about **computer-based information systems**. Computer-based information systems are a type of technology. Here we briefly distinguish between technology, information technology (IT), and information systems.

Technology versus Information Technology. **Technology** is any mechanical and/or electrical means to supplement, extend, or replace human, manual operations or devices. Sample technologies include the heating and cooling system for a building, the braking system for an automobile, and a laser used for surgery. In Figure 1.7, we show the relationship between technologies and computer-based information systems. Throughout this book, when we speak of technology, we are typically referring to IT unless noted.

The term **information technology (IT)** refers to machine technology that is controlled by or uses information. One type of information technology is a programmable robot on the shop floor of a manufacturing firm that receives component specifications and operational instructions from a computer-based database.

We could argue that any technology makes use of information in some fundamental way, as does each of the three examples of basic technology listed earlier (heating system, braking system, and a laser). However, information technologies, such as programmable manufacturing robots, use more information and in a more sophisticated way. It may appear that we are splitting hairs by distinguishing among technologies and information technologies. While the distinction is subtle, it is important. Information technologies use machine technologies as building blocks and then combine them with computing and networking technologies. A technology such as a mechanical drill press is useful, but it is more useful when combined with a computer database that instructs that drill press when and how to act.

Information Technology versus Information Systems. Information technologies and information systems are also similar but also different. Remember that we defined an information system as a combination of hardware, software, and telecommunications networks that people build and use to collect, create, and distribute data. The goal of an information system is to provide useful data to people. An example of an information system is the use of specialized software on a computer-controlled, mechanical machine used to produce compact discs (CDs), combined with other shop-floor equipment that allows a person to monitor and control the production of each CD from a separate, possibly remote, computer.

FIGURE 1.7

Computer-based information systems are a subset of information technologies and of technologies in general.

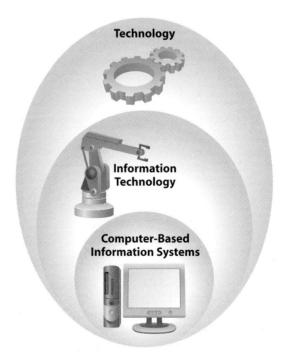

Key Enabler

Spintronics

You can't get far into electronics until seeing the term "semiconductor." Semiconductors are materials such as silicon and germanium that don't conduct electricity as well as copper and don't insulate as well as rubber. Computer chips—both CPU and memory—are typically composed of semiconductors. Semiconductors have made it possible to miniaturize transistors while at the same time increasing speed and energy efficiency.

Conventionally, electrons within semiconductors are in a binary state, where a 0 or a 1 is represented by the electron's charge of plus or minus. This semiconductor technology has been a mainstay in the computer and telecommunications industries for over 50 years. Now, a new technology offers several improvements that can not only speed up the data transmission process but can do so using materials other than semiconductors. This technology is known as spintronics.

Spintronics uses the spin of the electrons rather than the charge to represent binary states. Electrons either can "spin up" or "spin down" to represent 0s and 1s. The theory of spintronics is based on the concept that every particle demonstrates spin; though actual spinning does not take place, the term more easily explains the idea. This recent breakthrough in nanotechnology offers the opportunity to control the "spin" property of particles, making it an attractive alternative for information storage.

The underlying enabler is the quality of electrons' "spin" properties to hold their states for a much longer period of time. This allows the production of electronic devices that will not lose their fast-access memory as soon as the electric current is interrupted. Furthermore, more information can be stored in the same space, thus giving rise to a new generation of storage devices.

Perhaps spintronics' largest potential lies in embedded memory in devices such as home appliances, televisions, and automobiles; the technology also shows a potential for use in magnetic tunnel junction materials (for computer memory), magnetic sensors, and spintronic couplers (to transmit data between electronic systems).

Mass-storage devices that use spintronic technology are now a reality. In 2002, IBM used spintronics to compress massive amounts of data into a small area, at approximately 1 trillion bits per square inch (1.5 Gbit/mm^2). This roughly equals 1 terabyte on a single-sided 3.5-inch-diameter disc (for comparison, the U.S. Library of Congress claims to have more than 40 terabytes of data, so the entire library's content would fit on 40 disks). Future applications may include a quantum microchip and spin-based transistors, further improving the performance of microprocessors.

Source: Wikipedia.org: http://en.wikipedia.org/wiki/Spintronics

Other examples of information systems include a series of integrated electronic spreadsheets used for a budget, an order-fulfillment system for managing customers' purchases, and a set of linked pages on the Web. You may be asking, "Does my PC at work or school count as part of the company's or university's overall information system?" Our answer is yes. Information systems include personal, group, organizational, interorganizational, and even global computing systems.

People: The Builders and Managers of Information Systems

The information systems field includes a vast collection of people who develop, maintain, manage, and study information systems. The career opportunities for a person with IS training continue to be strong, and they are expected to continue to improve over the next 10 years. For example, in 2006, the U.S. Bureau of Labor Statistics is predicting that employment for computer and information systems managers will grow faster than the average for all occupations through 2014. This boost in employment will occur in nearly every industry, not just computer hardware and software companies, as more and more

TABLE 1.1 Best Jobs for the Next Decade

Rank	Career	Job Growth (10-year forecast)	Average Pay (salary and bonus)
1	Software engineer	46.07%	$80,427
2	College professor	31.39%	$81,491
3	Financial adviser	25.92%	$122,462
4	Human resources manager	23.47%	$73,731
5	Physician assistant	49.65%	$75,117
6	Market research analyst	20.19%	$82,317
7	**Computer/IT analyst**	**36.10%**	**$83,427**
8	Real estate appraiser	22.78%	$66,216
9	Pharmacist	24.57%	$91,998
10	Psychologist	19.14%	$66,359

Source: http://money.cnn.com/magazines/moneymag/bestjobs/.

organizations more heavily rely on IS professionals. Likewise, *Money* magazine (http://money.cnn.com/magazines/moneymag/bestjobs/) ranked "Computer/IT Analyst" as one of its top 10 best jobs for the next decade (see Table 1.1); also, fastcompany.com (http://www.fastcompany.com/articles/2006/01/top-jobs-main.html) rated "Computer and Information Systems Managers" as its fifth-best job over the coming decade.

In addition to an ample supply of jobs, earnings for information systems professionals will remain strong. According to the U.S. Bureau of Labor Statistics, median annual earnings of these managers in May 2005 were $102,360. The middle 50 percent earned between $74,700 and $126,120. Also, according to professional staffing firm Robert Half International, average starting salaries in 2005 for high-level information technology managers ranged from $80,250 to $112,250. According to a 2005 survey by the National Association of Colleges and Employers, starting salary offers for those with a master of business administration degree, a technical undergraduate degree, and one year or less of experience averaged $52,300; for those with a master's degree in management information systems/business data processing, the starting salary averaged $56,909. Finally, computer and information systems managers, especially those at higher levels, often receive more employment-related benefits—such as expense accounts, stock option plans, and bonuses—than do nonmanagerial workers in their organizations.

Even with lower-level technical jobs such as systems programmers being *outsourced* (i.e., performed by lower-paid workers in countries other than the country in which the host company resides—discussed later in this chapter), there continues to be a strong need for people with information systems knowledge, skills, and abilities—in particular, people with advanced information systems capabilities, as we will describe here.

Careers in IS The field of IS includes those people in organizations who design and build systems, those who use these systems, and those responsible for managing these systems. In Table 1.2, we list careers in IS and the salaries you might earn in those positions. The people who help develop and manage systems in organizations include systems analysts, systems programmers, systems operators, network administrators, database administrators, systems designers, systems managers, and chief information officers.

Another significant part of the IS field is the group of people who work in IS consulting firms, such as IBM, EDS, and Accenture. Experts in these consulting firms advise organizations on how to build and manage their systems and sometimes actually build and run those systems. Companies such as IBM that have traditionally been hardware/software companies are now doing a lot of systems consulting and related work. Similarly, companies such as Accenture that specialize in systems consulting are very successful—hiring more people, opening new offices, taking on new business, and generating lots of revenue.

TABLE 1.2 **Careers and Salaries in the Information Systems Field (National Average)**

IS Activities	Typical Careers	Salary Ranges in Percentiles (25%–75%)
Develop	Systems analyst	$50,000–$85,000
	Systems programmer	$50,000–$80,000
	Systems consultant	$80,000–$120,000
Maintain	Information systems auditor	$45,000–$75,000
	Database administrator	$75,000–$100,000
	Webmaster	$55,000–$80,000
Manage	IS manager	$60,000–$90,000
	IS director	$85,000–$120,000
	Chief information officer (CIO)	$150,000–$250,000
Study	University professor	$70,000–$180,000
	Government scientist	$60,000–$200,000

Sources: www.salary.com; cnnmoney.com.

University professors are another group of people in IS. These professors conduct research on the development, use, and management of information systems. Nonacademic researchers who conduct research for agencies such as the Department of Defense or for large corporations such as IBM, Xerox, Hewlett-Packard, and AT&T face almost unlimited opportunities. These professionals generally conduct more applied research and development than academic researchers. For example, a researcher for a major computer manufacturer might be developing a new computer product or examining ways to extend the life of a current product by integrating leading-edge components with the older architecture.

The Advent of the Chief Information Officer A number of important indications show that organizations are trying hard to manage information systems better. But perhaps nothing better demonstrates the growing importance of information systems in organizations than the advent of the **chief information officer (CIO)** and related positions in contemporary organizations.

EVOLUTION OF THE CIO. In the early 1980s, the CIO position became popular as the new title given to executive-level individuals who were responsible for the information systems component within their organizations. The CIO was charged with integrating new technologies into the organization's business strategy. Traditionally, the responsibility for integrating technology and strategy had not officially rested with any one manager. Responsibility for managing the day-to-day information systems function had previously rested with a midlevel operations manager or, in some cases, with a vice president of information systems. Ultimate responsibility for these activities would now rest with a high-level executive, the CIO. People began to realize that the information systems department was not simply a cost center—a necessary evil that simply consumed resources. They realized that information systems could be of tremendous strategic value to the organization. As a result, this new IS executive would work much like other executives, sitting at the strategy table, working right alongside the chief executive officer, chief financial officer, chief operating officer, and other chief executives and key people in the organization. When strategic decisions were to be made, technology would play a major role, and the CIO needed to participate in the strategic decision-making process.

Not surprisingly, many organizations jumped on the CIO bandwagon and either hired or named a CIO. As a result, many people thought that the CIO boom was a fad that would soon end, as do many other popular management trends. In fact, in early 1990, *BusinessWeek* printed a story titled "CIO Is Starting to Stand for 'Career Is Over': Once Deemed Indispensable, the Chief Information Officer Has Become an Endangered Species" (Rothfeder and Driscoll, 1990). In this story and in the cartoon in

FIGURE 1.8

BusinessWeek cartoon showing the dangers of being a CIO.

© Dave Cutler.

Figure 1.8, the authors reported statistics showing that in 1989 the CIO dismissal rate had doubled to 13 percent, which was noticeably higher than the 9 percent for all top executives. They explained that the primary reasons for CIO dismissals included tightening budgets for technology and management's overblown expectations of CIO functions. Apparently, many organizations had been caught up in the rush to have a CIO without thinking enough about why they needed a CIO in the first place. The authors countered, however, that given the growing trend toward using information systems to achieve competitive advantage, the CIO could become relevant and important again. How right they were.

THE CIO TODAY. Today, most large organizations have a CIO or an equivalent position. It is also now common for midsized and smaller organizations to have a CIO-like position within their organizations, although they may give this person a title, such as director of information systems. In 2006, *Information Week* named Rob Carter of FedEx its CIO of the year. FedEx has some of the most sophisticated information systems in the world, delivering more than 6 million packages a day (see Figure 1.9). A recent information systems project that Carter believes provides FedEx with a competitive advantage is called Insight—an enhancement over existing package tracking systems that tells customers all packages being sent to them that day, *even if the customer doesn't know about the package.* In some markets, businesses, such as a company that does nationwide bone marrow sample testing for transplants, need to know in advance what is arriving each day. Given that these highly perishable samples are viable for only 24 hours, adequate personnel and lab resources must be on standby as the samples arrive. Prior to Insight, the company would often have idle resources or be understaffed. Today, managers can use Insight to optimize their laboratory and human resources to match the flow of samples. Insight is a system that provides competitive advantage over rivals such as United Parcel Service (UPS), but such advantages are often short lived; it is often easy to copy innovations or even surpass them. Being a business innovation leader is an ongoing process for most CIOs. We will talk much more about gaining, and sustaining, competitive advantage using information systems in Chapter 3.

IS MANAGERIAL PERSONNEL. In large organizations, there typically are many other different management positions in addition to the CIO position within the IS function. In Table 1.3, we describe several such positions. This list is not exhaustive; rather, it is

FIGURE 1.9

FedEx is a pioneer in using information systems and technologies for competitive advantage.

intended to provide a sampling of IS management positions. Furthermore, many firms will use the same job title, but each is likely to define it in a different way, or companies will have different titles for the same basic function. As you can see from Table 1.3, the range of career opportunities for IS managers is very broad.

What Makes IS Personnel So Valuable? In addition to the growing importance of people in the IS field, there have been changes in the nature of this type of work. No longer are IS departments in organizations filled only with nerdy men with pocket protectors (Figure 1.10). Many more women are in IS positions now. Also, it is now more common for an IS professional to be a polished, professional systems analyst who can talk fluently about both business and technology. IS personnel are now well-trained, highly skilled, valuable professionals who garner high wages and prestige and who play a pivotal role in helping firms be successful.

Past   Present

FIGURE 1.10

Information systems personnel are no longer nerds.

TABLE 1.3 Some IS Management Job Titles and Brief Job Descriptions

Job Title	Job Description
CIO	Highest-ranking IS manager. Responsible for strategic planning and IS use throughout the firm
IS director	Responsible for managing all systems throughout the firm and the day-to-day operations of the entire IS unit
Division or account executive	Responsible for managing the day-to-day operations of all aspects of IS within one particular division, plant, functional business area, or product unit
Information center manager	Responsible for managing IS services, such as help desks, hotlines, training, consulting, and so on
Development manager	Responsible for coordinating and managing all new systems projects
Project manager	Responsible for managing a particular new systems project
Maintenance manager	Responsible for coordinating and managing all systems maintenance projects
Systems manager	Responsible for managing a particular existing system
IS planning manager	Responsible for developing an enterprise-wide hardware, software, and networking architecture and for planning for systems growth and change
Operations manager	Responsible for supervising the day-to-day operations of the data and/or computer center
Programming manager	Responsible for coordinating all applications programming efforts
Systems programming manager	Responsible for coordinating support for maintenance of all systems software (e.g., operating systems, utilities, programming languages, and so on)
Manager of emerging technologies	Responsible for forecasting technology trends and for evaluating and experimenting with new technologies
Telecommunications manager	Responsible for coordinating and managing the entire voice and data network
Network manager	Responsible for managing one piece of the enterprise-wide network
Database administrator	Responsible for managing database and database management software use
Audit or computer security manager	Responsible for managing ethical and legal use of information systems within the firm
Quality assurance manager	Responsible for developing and monitoring standards and procedures to ensure that systems within the firm are accurate and of good quality
Webmaster	Responsible for managing the firm's Web site

Many studies have been aimed at helping us understand what knowledge and skills are necessary for a person in the IS area to be successful (see, e.g., Todd, McKeen, and Gallupe, 1995). Interestingly, these studies also point out just what it is about IS personnel that makes them so valuable to their organizations. In a nutshell, good IS personnel possess valuable, integrated knowledge and skills in three areas—technical, business, and systems— as outlined in Table 1.4.

TECHNICAL COMFPETENCY. The technical competency area includes knowledge and skills in hardware, software, networking, and security. In a sense, this is the "nuts and bolts" of IS. This is not to say that the IS professional must be a high-level technical expert in these areas. On the contrary, the IS professional must know just enough about these areas to understand how they work and how they can and should be applied. Typically, the IS professional manages or directs those who have deeper, more detailed technical knowledge.

The technical area of competency is, perhaps, the most difficult to maintain because the popularity of individual technologies is so fleeting. However, according to industry analysts, many programming jobs or support jobs will have been outsourced to third-party providers in the U.S. or abroad by 2010, so there is a shift in the hot skills the market will demand (Collett, 2006). While there is the need for a diverse set of technical skills such as network design or data warehousing, other, easier-to-codify jobs will be automated or outsourced (see Table 1.5). In fact, many of the hot skills listed in Table 1.5 are focused on the business domain, which will be discussed next.

TABLE 1.4 IS Professional Core Competencies

Domain	Description
Technical Knowledge and Skills	
Hardware	Hardware platforms, peripherals
Software	Operating systems, application software, drivers
Networking	Network operating systems, cabling and network interface cards, LANs, WANs, wireless, Internet, security
Business Knowledge and Skills	
Business integration, industry	Business processes, functional areas of business and their integration, industry
Managing people and projects	Planning, organizing, leading, controlling, managing people and projects
Social	Interpersonal, group dynamics, political
Communication	Verbal, written, and technological communication and presentation
Systems Knowledge and Skills	
Systems integration	Connectivity, compatibility, integrating subsystems and systems
Development methodologies	Steps in systems analysis and design, systems development life cycle, alternative development methodologies
Critical thinking	Challenging one's and others' assumptions and ideas
Problem solving	Information gathering and synthesis, problem identification, solution formulation, comparison, and choice

BUSINESS COMPETENCY. The business competency area is one that sets the IS professional apart from others who have only technical knowledge and skills, and in an era of increased outsourcing it may well save a person's job. For example, even though low-level technology jobs may be outsourced, MSNBC.com recently reported (http://www.msnbc.msn.com/id/5077435/) that information systems management is one of 10 professions that is not likely to be outsourced. As a result, it is absolutely vital for IS professionals to understand the technical areas AND the nature of the business as well. IS professionals must also be able to understand and manage people and projects, not just the technology. These business skills propel IS professionals into project management and, ultimately, high-paying middle- and upper-level management positions.

SYSTEMS COMPETENCY. Systems competency is another area that sets the IS professional apart from others with only technical knowledge and skills. Those who understand how to build and integrate systems and how to solve problems will ultimately manage large, complex systems projects as well as manage those in the firm who have only technical knowledge and skills.

Perhaps now you can see why IS professionals are so valuable to their organizations. These individuals have a solid, integrated foundation in technical, business, and systems knowledge and skills. Perhaps most important, they also have the social skills to understand how to work well with and motivate others. It is these core competencies that continue to make IS professionals valuable employees.

Given how important technology is, what does this mean for your career? Technology is being used to radically change how business is conducted—from the way products and services are produced, distributed, and accounted for to the ways they are marketed and sold. Whether you are majoring in information systems, finance, accounting, operations

TABLE 1.5 Hot Skills for 2010 and Beyond

Domain	Hot	Cold
Business Domain	• Enterprise architecture • Project leadership • Business process modeling • Project planning, budgeting, and scheduling • Third-party provider management	
Technology Infrastructure and Services	• Systems analysis • Systems design • Network design • Systems auditing	• Programming • Routine coding • Systems testing • Support and help desk • Operations – server hosting, telecommunications, operating systems
Security	• IT security planning and management	• Continuity and recovery
Storage	• Storage administration	
Application Development	• Customer-facing application development	• Legacy skills
Internet	• Customer-facing Web application systems • Artificial intelligence • Data mining • Data warehousing	
Business Intelligence	• Business intelligence • Data warehousing • Data mining	

Source: Adapted from Collett, 2006.

management, human resource management, business law, or marketing, knowledge of technology is critical to a successful career in business.

Organizations: The Context of Information Systems

We have talked about data versus information, the technology side of IS, and the people side of IS. The last part of our IS definition is the term "organization." People use information systems to help their organization to be more productive and profitable, to help their firm gain competitive advantage, to help their firm reach more customers, or to improve service to their customers. This holds true for all types of organizations—professional, social, religious, educational, and governmental. In fact, not too long ago, the U.S. Internal Revenue Service launched its own site on the Web for the reasons just described (see Figure 1.12). The IRS Web site was so popular that approximately 220,000 users visited it during the first 24 hours, and more than a million visited it in its first week—even before the Web address for the site was officially announced. Today, popular Web sites like MySpace.com and Yahoo.com receive millions of visitors every day.

Types of Information Systems Throughout this book, we will explore various types of information systems commonly used in organizations. It makes sense, however, for us to describe briefly here the various types of systems used so that you will better understand what we mean by the term "information system" as we use it throughout the rest of the book. Table 1.6 provides a list of the major types of information systems used in organizations.

Topping the list in the table are some of the more traditional, major categories that are used to describe information systems. These include *transaction processing systems,*

Change Agents

Steve Jobs, Cofounder and CEO, Apple Computer

Steve Jobs, cofounder and CEO of Apple Computer, named the company after the apple orchards in California where he worked as a young man. Jobs is also the chairman and CEO of Pixar Animation Studios, the film production company responsible for such animated movie hits as *Toy Story 1, Toy Story 2, Monsters, Inc., The Incredibles,* and *Cars.*

Jobs was born on 24 February 1955 in San Francisco, California. He graduated from Homestead High School in Cupertino, California, in 1972 and enrolled in Reed College in Portland, Oregon, but dropped out after one semester. After leaving college, Jobs worked as a technician at Atari, saved his wages, and made a personal pilgrimage to India. When Jobs returned to work at Atari, where Steve Wozniak was also employed, the "two Steves" worked together on a circuit board design project.

Jobs and Wozniak discovered they worked well together and finally started their own company—Apple Computer—in 1976. At Apple, Wozniak focused on function, while Jobs looked at design and ease of use. Jobs believed computers should be designed not solely as computation tools but also as attractive objects in a house.

While Apple Computer enjoyed much success, such as Apple II, the Mac, and the iPod, it also suffered much-publicized failures such as the Lisa, Apple III, Newton, and G3. Jobs, personally, also experienced downfalls, such as leaving Apple in 1985 (when John Sculley was CEO) to start his own company, NeXT, which did not succeed in the marketplace.

When Jobs returned to Apple in 1996, he found a failing company. He was appointed as an interim CEO (and later confirmed as the CEO) and turned Apple around by cutting some projects and initiating others. Two new products, the iMac and the iPod, were to endear new generations to the Apple brand.

The media have often quoted Jobs, who seems willing to speak on any topic:

- On his rival, Bill Gates: "I wish him the best, I really do. I just think he and Microsoft are a bit narrow. He'd be a broader guy if he had dropped acid once or gone off to an ashram when he was younger."
- On his goals: "I want to put a ding in the universe."
- On his love life: "My girlfriend always laughs during sex, no matter what she's reading."
- On pleasing customers: "You can't just ask people what they want and then try to give that to them. By the time you get it built, they'll want something new."

Steven Paul Jobs, CEO of Apple Computer, lives with his wife and three children in Silicon Valley, California, where apple orchards once grew.

Sources:http://www.brainyquote.com/quotes/authors/s/steve_jobs.html

http://www.apple.com/pr/bios/jobs.html

http://en.wikipedia.org/wiki/Steve_Jobs

FIGURE 1.11

Steve Jobs, cofounder and CEO, Apple Computer.

FIGURE 1.12

Web site of the U.S. Department of the Treasury, Internal Revenue Service, http://www.irs.gov/.

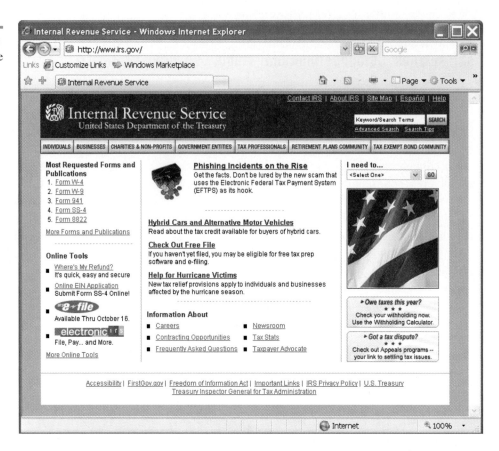

management information systems, executive information systems, decision support systems, intelligent systems, data mining and visualization systems, knowledge management systems, geographic information systems, and *functional area information systems.* Five to 10 years ago, it would have been typical to see systems that fell cleanly into one of these categories. Today, with **internetworking**—connecting host computers and their networks together to form even larger networks like the Internet—and **systems integration**—connecting separate information systems and data to improve business processes and decision making—it is difficult to say that any given information system fits into only one of these categories (e.g., that a system is a management information system only and nothing else). Modern-day information systems tend to span several of these categories of information systems, helping not only to collect data from throughout the firm and from customers but also to integrate all that diverse data and present it to busy decision makers, along with tools to manipulate and analyze those data. *Customer relationship management, supply chain management,* and *enterprise resource planning* systems are good examples of these types of systems that encompass many features and types of data and cannot easily be categorized.

Office automation systems and *collaboration systems* are typically bought "off the shelf" and enable people to (1) perform their own work and (2) work with others. A handful of software packages dominate this sector of the software industry and are commonly found on personal computers in people's homes and offices. Microsoft Office and OpenOffice are examples of popular office automation systems that provide word processing, spreadsheet, and other personal productivity tools. Microsoft's Exchange/Outlook and Lotus Notes are good examples of very popular collaboration systems that provide people with e-mail, automated calendaring, and online, threaded discussions.

Systems for electronic commerce, such as corporate Web sites, are also very popular and important. These systems are typically Internet-based and enable (1) consumers to find information about and to purchase goods and services from each other and from business firms and (2) business firms to electronically exchange products, services, and information.

TABLE 1.6 Types of Information Systems Used in Organizations

Type of System	Purpose	Sample Application
Transaction processing system	Process day-to-day business event data at the operational level of the organization	Grocery store checkout cash register with connection to network
Management information system	Produce detailed information to help manage a firm or a part of the firm	Inventory management and planning system
Executive information system	Provide very high-level, aggregate information to support executive-level decision making	News retrieval and stock update information system
Decision support system	Provide analysis tools and access to databases in order to support quantitative decision making	Product demand forecasting system
Intelligent system	Emulate or enhance human capabilities	Automated system for analyzing bank loan applications
Data mining and visualization system	Methods and systems for analyzing data warehouses to better understand various aspects of a business	Market analysis
Office automation system (a.k.a. personal productivity software)	Support a wide range of predefined day-to-day work activities of individuals and small groups	Word processor
Collaboration system	Enable people to communicate, collaborate, and coordinate with each other	Electronic mail system with automated, shared calendar
Knowledge management system	Collection of technology-based tools to enable the generation, storage, sharing, and management of knowledge assets	Groupware
Geographical information system (GIS)	Create, store, analyze, and manage spatial data	Site selection for new shopping mall
Functional area information system	Support the activities within a specific functional area of the firm	System for planning for personnel training and work assignments
Customer relationship management (CRM) system	Support interaction between the firm and its customers	Sales force automation
Enterprise resource planning (ERP) system	Support and integrate all facets of the business, including planning, manufacturing, sales, marketing, and so on	Financial, operations, and human resource management
Supply chain management (SCM) system	Support the coordination of suppliers, product or service production, and distribution	Procurement planning
Electronic commerce system	Enable customers to buy goods and services from a firm's Web site	Amazon.com

Given the pervasive use of the Internet to support electronic commerce, we devote a great deal of time to this topic in subsequent chapters. In Technology Briefing 5, we talk about the nuts and bolts of how the Internet works, and in Chapter 5, we talk about how people are using the Internet to conduct electronic commerce.

While many modern-day information systems span several of these IS categories, it is still useful to understand these categories. Doing so enables you to better understand the myriad approaches, goals, features, and functions of modern information systems.

We have talked about each of the parts of our definition of IS, and we have talked about different types of information systems. In the next section, we focus on how information systems can be managed within organizations.

Organizing the Information Systems Function The current emphasis on the use of technology within businesses is not a fad. Indeed, all indicators point to the increased use of technology and to organizations' continued awareness of the importance of technology,

FIGURE 1.13

Evolution of the information systems function.

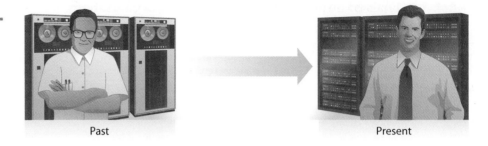

Past   Present

both as a tool for productivity and as a vehicle for achieving competitive advantage and organizational change. Just as information systems have evolved over the past several years, so too has the IS function. Next, we briefly review the evolution of the IS function within organizations (see Figure 1.13).

EARLY HISTORY: POOR SERVICE AND WORSE ATTITUDES. Early IS departments typically had huge project backlogs, and IS personnel would often deliver systems that were over budget, were completed much too late, were difficult to use, and did not always work well. In addition, many of these old-school IS personnel believed they owned and controlled the computing resources, that they knew better than users did, and that they should tell users what they could and could not do with the computing resources. Needless to say, this was not a recipe for success and good relationships. Indeed, relations between IS personnel and users within a firm were often sour and were sometimes bitter.

THE RISE AND FALL OF END-USER DEVELOPMENT. In the early years of information systems within organizations, users were often forced to put up with the poor service and the poor attitude. Then technology started to become significantly better—faster, easier to build and use, and cheaper—with the advent of the personal computer (PC) and standard software packages (see Figure 1.14). As a result, end users began to develop their own

FIGURE 1.14

The advent of the IBM PC and early applications packages led to end-user development.

BASIC programming language

Dbase database application

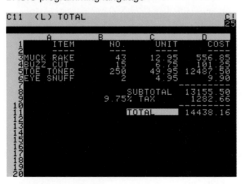

Visicalc Spreadsheet

IBM PC

Source: http://upload.wikimedia.org/wikipedia/en/6/62/BASIC_3.0.png; http://upload.wikimedia.org/wikipedia/en/7/73/Dbaseshot.png; http://upload.wikimedia.org/wikipedia/commons/7/7a/Visicalc.png; http://upload.wikimedia.org/wikipedia/commons/6/69/IBM_PC_5150.jpg.

computing applications using PC-based spreadsheet packages (e.g., Visicalc), database management systems (e.g., dBase), and programming languages (e.g., BASIC). Disgruntled users simply said, "If the IS staff cannot or will not do this for us, then we will build our own systems." In many cases, they did just that, and they did it well, much to the dismay of some of the IS managers. Although end-user development clearly has strengths and still exists in some organizations, it also has serious weaknesses (see Chapter 9); thus, today, most organizations leave the systems development to the professionals.

THE MODERN INFORMATION SYSTEMS ORGANIZATION. Business managers soon became more savvy about technology and the possibilities and opportunities that it offered, and they reasoned that the possibilities and opportunities were too great to let the IS function simply wither away as end-user development took over. In addition, smart, concerned IS personnel realized that they needed an attitude adjustment. Some people believe that the changes in the nature of technology forced people to cooperate more. For example, the shift from large "mainframe" computers to a "client-server" model (i.e., relatively powerful personal computers spread throughout the organization that share data, applications, or peripherals that are hosted by more powerful server computers—see Technology Briefing 1 and Technology Briefing 4) may have forced people within the IS function to improve their operations and their relationships with people in other units of the firm. The client-server model required a new kind of relationship between IS and other people throughout the firm (Stevens, 1994). As a result of these forces, in modern IS units that do a good job, the atmosphere, attitude, and culture are very different and much more sensitive and responsive than they used to be.

In these more responsive IS units, the personnel have taken on more of a consulting relationship with their users. The IS personnel believe that, fundamentally, they are there to help the users solve problems and be more productive. Indeed, in many cases, the IS personnel do not even refer to the users as "users." They are "clients" or "customers," or, even better, they are "colleagues" within the organization. This new attitude is a major change from the old days, when IS personnel did not want to be bothered by users and thought that the techies knew better than users. It is unfortunate that this old-school mentality still exists in some organizations.

The new IS culture is much like that found in successful service organizations. Think of how customers are treated in service organizations, such as Citigroup's Smith Barney or Ernst & Young, or in product-based organizations where service is also important, such as McDonald's or Nordstrom. Great service to the customer is absolutely critical, and employees do everything they can to please customers. They often live by the credo that "the customer is always right."

The same holds for IS units that have taken on this new **service mentality**. The IS personnel do everything they can to ensure that they are satisfying their systems customers within the firm. They reach out to customers and proactively seek their input and needs rather than waiting for customers to come in with systems complaints. They modify the systems at a moment's notice just to meet customer needs quickly and effectively. They celebrate the customer's new systems ideas rather than putting up roadblocks and giving reasons that the new ideas cannot or will not work. They fundamentally believe that the customers own the technology and the information and that the technology and information are there for the customers, not for the systems personnel. They create help desks, hotlines, information centers, and training centers to support customers. These service-oriented IS units structure the IS function so that it can better serve the customer.

The implications of this new service mentality for the IS function are staggering. It is simply amazing how unproductive a company can be when the IS personnel and other people within the firm are at odds with one another. On the other hand, it is even more amazing how productive and enjoyable work can be when people in the IS function work hand in hand with people throughout the organization. Technology is, potentially, the great lever, but it works best when people work together, not against each other, to use it.

The Spread of Technology in Organizations Another phenomenon that shows how integral and vital information systems and their proper management have become to organizations is the extent to which the technology is firmly integrated and entrenched within the various business units (such as accounting, sales, and marketing).

In many organizations today, you will find that the builders and managers of a particular information system or subsystem spend most of their time out in the business unit, along with the users of that particular system. Many times, these systems personnel are permanently placed—with an office, desk, phone, and personal computer—in the business unit along with the users.

In addition, it is not uncommon for systems personnel to have formal education, training, and work experience in information systems as well as in the functional area that the system supports, such as finance. It is becoming increasingly difficult to separate the technology from the business or the systems staff from the other people in the organization. For this reason, how information systems are managed is important to you, no matter what career option you pursue.

As information systems are used more broadly throughout organizations, IS personnel often have dual-reporting relationships—reporting to both the central IS group and the business function they serve. Therefore, at least some need for centralized IS planning, deployment, and management continues—particularly with respect to achieving economies of scale in systems acquisition and development and in optimizing systems integration, enterprise networking, and the like. Even in organizations that are decentralizing technology and related decisions, a need for technology and related decisions to be coordinated well across the firm still persists. This coordination is likely to continue to happen through some form of a centralized (or, at least, centrally coordinated) IS staff. Organizations are likely to continue to want to reap the benefits of IS decentralization (flexibility, adaptability, and systems responsiveness), but it is equally likely that they will not want to—and will not be able to—forgo the benefits of IS centralization (coordination, economies of scale, compatibility, and connectivity).

Given the trend toward pushing people from the IS staff out into the various business units of the firm and given the need for people within each of the functional areas of the business to have technology skills, there is clearly a need for people who know the technology side *and* the business side of the business well. We suspect that the need for people to play these boundary-spanning roles will continue.

Downsizing and Outsourcing Many organizations that are **downsizing**, or rightsizing as some call it, are looking toward the IS function and technology as the lever for simultaneously shrinking the organization by reducing personnel headcount and making the organization more productive (i.e., doing more with less). In short, they are using technology to streamline business functions and, in some cases, to slash costs and replace people. Although this approach may not be fair for the people who lose their jobs, many firms are forced to do this to remain competitive and, in some cases, to continue to exist. Such uses of information systems have interesting implications for the size and structure of organizations and for the size and structure of the IS function.

Similarly, **outsourcing** is on the rise for all aspects of business. In outsourcing, many of the more routine jobs are "outsourced": these jobs and/or tasks are being conducted by people in another firm, in another part of the country, or on another continent at less cost. Some of these outsourced jobs are within the information systems function. For example, many computer programming tasks are now being completed by firms in India and China. *CIO* magazine reported that although the United States leads the world when it comes to the number and quality of IS-related workers, outsourcing to low-wage countries has become a large and key component of managing most IS organizations. Today, 73 percent of Fortune 2000 companies utilize global outsourcing, with worldwide spending reaching $50 billion in 2007 (*CIO,* 2006), up from $16 billion in 2004. What implications does that have for people considering careers in business or, in particular, in information systems?

Career Prospects and Opportunities Although technology at some levels continues to become easier to use, there is still and is likely to continue to be an acute need for people within the organization to have the responsibility of planning for, designing, developing, maintaining, and managing technologies. Much of this will happen within the business units and will be done by those with primarily business duties and tasks as opposed to systems duties and tasks. However, we are a long way from the day when technology is so easy to deploy that a need no longer exists for people with deep information systems knowledge and skills. In fact, many people believe that this day may never come. Although increasing numbers of people will incorporate systems responsibilities within their nonsystems jobs, there will continue to be a need for people with primarily systems responsibilities. In short, IS staffs and departments will likely continue to exist and play an important role in the foreseeable future.

While many organizations are downsizing and while some are shrinking their IS staffs and/or sending the more routine jobs abroad, overall hiring within IS is back again and is expected to grow. Given that information systems continue to be a critical tool for business success, it is not likely that IS departments will go away or even shrink significantly. Indeed, all projections are for long-term growth of IS in both scale and scope. Also, as is the case in any area of business, those people who are continually learning, continuing to grow, and continuing to find new ways to add value and who have advanced and/or unique skills will always be sought after, whether in information systems or in any area of the firm.

Net Stats

Worldwide Internet Usage

In 2006, about 20 percent of the world's active Internet users were located in the United States. This is down from about half, just two years ago. Overall, it was estimated that there were just over 1 billion active Internet users worldwide, with over 380 million users in Asia, 294 million in Europe, and 227 million in North America (and about 200 million active users in the United States alone) (see Table 1.7). The Internet is mostly heavily used in North America, with nearly 70 percent of the total population; Africa has the lowest penetration, with less than 3 percent. The United States has the most users, followed by China with 123 million. As the world continues to embrace the Internet, it is inevitable that the U.S. proportion will continue to get smaller. What do you think these statistics will look like in 10 years? In 20 years?

TABLE 1.7 World Internet Usage and Population Statistics

World Regions	Population (2006 estimates)	Population (% of world)	Internet Usage, Latest Data	% Population (penetration)	Usage (% of world)	Usage Growth (2000–2005)
Africa	915,210,928	14.1%	23,649,000	2.6%	2.3%	423.9%
Asia	3,667,774,066	56.4%	380,400,713	10.4%	36.5%	232.8%
Europe	807,289,020	12.4%	294,101,844	36.4%	28.2%	179.8%
Middle East	190,084,161	2.9%	18,203,500	9.6%	1.7%	454.2%
North America	331,473,276	5.1%	227,470,713	68.6%	21.8%	110.4%
Latin America/ Caribbean	553,908,632	8.5%	79,962,809	14.7%	7.8%	350.5%
Oceania/ Australia	33,956,977	0.5%	17,872,707	52.6%	1.7%	134.6%
World Total	6,499,697,060	100.0%	1,043,104,886	16.0%	100.0%	189.0%

Note: Internet usage and world population statistics were updated for June 30, 2006. ©Copyright 2006, Miniwatts Marketing Group. All rights reserved.
Source: http://www.internetworldstats.com/stats.htm.

The future opportunities in the IS field are likely to be found in a variety of areas, which is good news for everyone. The diversity in the technology area can embrace us all. It really does not matter much which area of IS you choose to pursue—there will likely be a promising future there for you. Even if your career interests are outside IS, being a well-informed and capable user of information technologies will greatly enhance your career prospects.

The Dual Nature of Information Systems

Given how important and expensive information systems have become, information technology is like a sword—you can use it effectively as a competitive weapon, but, as the old saying goes, those who live by the sword sometimes die by the sword. The two following cases illustrate this dual nature of information systems.

Case in Point: An Information System Gone Awry: ERP Implementation at the U.S. Navy

What happens when an information system is implemented poorly? According to the U.S. Government Accountability Office (GAO), the U.S. Navy has "wasted" $1 billion on four failed enterprise resource planning (ERP) pilot projects, spanning 1998–2005, with software giant SAP (Songini, 2005).

In 2006, the Navy was in the middle of an even larger project to consolidate the pilot projects in an effort to create a massive ERP system scheduled for completion by 2011. The GAO warns that the current project is also in jeopardy unless the Navy is able to universally adopt and follow pre-established best practices, rather than needing to extensively customize the massive software system.

Both the Navy and SAP disagree that any of the pilots were failures, even if all the systems will be or have already been scrapped. Both feel that the pilots demonstrated that off-the-shelf ERP software could work in the Navy's massive and complex environment. Nevertheless, the GAO still feels that the project is a big risk and that it is unlikely the ERP will provide the "all-inclusive, end-to-end corporate solution for the Navy." Although nearly $2 billion have been spent (or committed) on the project that began in 1998, it is still too early to tell whether this information system will help the Navy streamline its operations.

Case in Point: An Information System That Works: FedEx

Just as there are examples of information systems gone wrong, there are many examples of information systems gone right. For example, take the innovative use of information systems on the FedEx Web site (earlier we mentioned their "Insight" project).

FedEx, now a $32 billion family of companies, is the world's largest express transportation company and delivers millions of packages and millions of pounds of freight to 220 countries and territories each business day. FedEx uses extensive, interconnected information systems to coordinate more than 260,000 employees, hundreds of aircraft, and tens of thousands of ground vehicles worldwide.

To improve its services and sustain a competitive advantage, FedEx offers extensive services on the Internet. FedEx.com has more than 15 million unique visitors per month and over 3 million tracking requests per day. FedEx.com has become the information hub for a business where managing information *is the business.* In addition to shipment tracking, customers use the site for finding out about delivery options and costs, use tools to prepare their own packages, verify them online, and print bar-coded shipping documents. These and other information systems have positioned FedEx as the global leader in express transportation.

Information Systems for Competitive Advantage

The U.S. Navy's ERP system and FedEx Web site are typical of those used in large, complex organizations. These systems are so large in scale and scope that they are difficult to build. It is important to handle the development of such systems the right way the first time

ChoicePoint Inc.

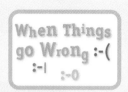

Identity theft is *the* crime of the twenty-first century, claiming 8.9 million victims in the first seven months of 2006. Individuals can practice a few preventative measures—don't give out Social Security numbers, financial account numbers, and so on—but are unable to control a credit-checking organization's storage and dissemination of personal data.

Whenever you're applying for a job, getting insurance, or renting an apartment, chances are that someone is conducting a background check on you to see whether you are trustworthy. Personal information clearinghouses, such as ChoicePoint, based in Georgia, typically provide personal information, for a fee, to the U.S. government and others conducting background checks. ChoicePoint maintains about 19 billion pieces of information on virtually every adult American, including names, addresses, telephone numbers, Social Security numbers, prior insurance claims, bank accounts, credit card accounts, criminal records, bankruptcy filings, and so on—in short, an identity thief's dream.

Although one would hope that personal information clearinghouses take great care to check whether someone is authorized to obtain consumer records, unfortunately this is not always the case. In an unprecedented incident in 2005, a ring of California identity thieves posing as legitimate businesses bought more than 100,000 electronic records from ChoicePoint. The identity thieves placed the requests for information from Kinko's stores, and before internal investigators noticed the scheme, records of more than 163,000 people were delivered online to more than 50 fraudulent accounts. The incident had no serious implications for many of the individuals whose data was disseminated, but more than 750 became victims of identity theft.

In addition to earning a bad reputation for ChoicePoint, the data dissemination to unauthorized recipients had further adverse consequences for ChoicePoint. In 2006, the Federal Trade Commission (FTC) fined ChoicePoint $10 million for the security breach, the largest fine ever imposed by the FTC. In addition, ChoicePoint was ordered to pay $5 million to compensate consumers who were affected by the incident. Although the fines might be small compared to ChoicePoint's annual profit of over $140 million, the FTC also ordered ChoicePoint to implement new security procedures and submit to audits by an independent security professional every two years for the next 20 years.

Most worrisome for consumers is the fact that ChoicePoint is only one personal information clearinghouse among many, and strict federal regulation is probably the only way consumers can hope to gain more control over the information maintained by such clearinghouses.

Sources: Caron Carlson, "ChoicePoint's Data Breach Fine Sets Record," *eWeek* (January 26, 2006), http://www.eweek.com/article2/0,1895,1915768,00.asp
Robert O'Harrow Jr., "ID Data Conned from Firm," *Washington Post* (February 17, 2005), http://www.washingtonpost.com/wp-dyn/articles /A30897-2005Feb16.html
http://www.forbes.com/feeds/ap/2006/01/26/ap2479440.html

around. These examples also show that as we rely more and more on information systems, the capabilities of these systems is paramount to business success.

Not only were these systems large and complicated, but they were—and continue to be—critical to the success of the firms that built them. The choices made in developing the new systems at both the Navy and FedEx were **strategic** in their intent. These systems were not developed solely because managers in these organizations wanted to do things faster or because they wanted to have the latest, greatest technology. These organizations developed these systems strategically to help gain or sustain some **competitive advantage** (Porter, 1985; Porter and Millar, 1985) over their rivals. Let us not let this notion slip by us—while the use of technology can enable efficiency and while information systems must provide a return on investment, technology use can also be strategic and can be a powerful enabler of competitive advantage.

Although we described information systems' uses at two relatively large organizations, firms of all types and sizes can use information systems to gain or sustain a competitive advantage over their rivals. Whether it is a small mom-and-pop boutique or a large government agency, every organization can find a way to use information technology to beat its rivals. In Chapter 3, we will talk more about this opportunity to use information systems strategically.

Brief Case ⊙

MTV Europe

What's the most international television network in the world? No doubt it's MTV (see Figure 1.15). MTV Networks, with 120 channels and 1.2 billion viewers via 94 TV channels and 62 Web sites, has become a force in international television. Owned by Viacom, MTV is now working to break into a new medium: mobile television screens. Not surprisingly, MTV Europe (MTV-E), the largest TV network in Europe, will be the testing ground for this new technology.

MTV-E has been chosen to test this new medium because of the widespread use of 3G cell phones in Europe. (The United States has been relatively slow at adopting this newer technology and offers services only in major metropolitan areas.) 3G stands for "third-generation protocol." This protocol allows for greater speeds to be transmitted to the mobile phone (roughly three times faster than a dial-up modem).

MTV-E has sought partnerships with the major European cell carriers, including Vodaphone, Orange, and T-Mobile. With these partnerships, the distribution reach via cell phones is almost as high as MTV-E's traditional television channels. Partnerships are a vital aspect of MTV-E's distribution strategy; without these joint ventures, it would be virtually impossible to use Europe's cell phone network to deliver content.

Another issue the executives of MTV-E had to consider was the content. Most companies in the area of mobile distribution (such as Verizon V-Cast, which also offers content created by MSNBC or VH-1) simply port TV shows over to the mobile screen, thereby offering looped segments of shows. Although Verizon has enjoyed some success with the V-Cast service, they lack the geographical reach that Europe's cell phone infrastructure enjoys.

Intending to offer the best and most relevant content possible, MTV-E decided to use a different strategy for content creation. MTV-E hopes that by creating exclusive content for the cell phone service, they will create a new way of watching programs on a cell phone. This media will include everything from short TV segments to live video feeds. The key is "snack-size content," which consumers can watch while commuting on a subway train, waiting for a friend, or killing some time between classes. While MTV's traditional strategy has been to design content for short attention spans,

FIGURE 1.15

MTV is one of the most international TV networks in the world.

their new mobile content has to be designed for even shorter attention spans.

MTV-E has found that one genre that works particularly well for this purpose is comedy. Parents are even utilizing the mobile video services to entertain their kids when they are stuck waiting somewhere, as in a doctor's office. To also appeal to current MTV viewers, MTV-E has decided to tightly integrate its content with that offered by MTV. For example, while the MTV music awards, one of the highest-rated shows for the company, are broadcast via traditional television channels, live backstage streams are broadcast to MTV-E's mobile customers.

This new on-demand content also provides MTV-E with important information regarding customers' needs and wants, data that can be used for direct marketing, and thus adding to the network's revenues.

Questions

1. Describe from both technology and customer perspectives why MTV-E is a good test bed for on-demand mobile services.
2. Define several types of potential customers for mobile, on-demand video and list what types of video content each would be interested in; rank each potential customer as to their likelihood of adoption.

Sources: http://www.businessweek.com/technology/content/jan2006/tc20060131_294681.htm
http://www.brandrepublic.com/bulletins/br/article/537580/media-analysis-local-custom/

Why Information Systems Matter

On May 1, 2003, Nicholas Carr published an article titled "IT Doesn't Matter" in *Harvard Business Review* that created quite a stir. He argued that as IT becomes more pervasive it will become more standardized and ubiquitous, more of a commodity that is absolutely necessary for every company. He reasoned then that companies should focus IT strictly on cost reduction and risk mitigation and that investing in IT for differentiation or for competitive advantage is futile. Many experts in academia, in the popular press, and within technology companies not only disagreed with that argument but also felt that, if taken literally, such a line of thinking could hurt companies' competitiveness.

Given the debate that this article caused, on May 1, 2004, *CIO* magazine's editor in chief, Abbie Lundberg, published an interview with Carr on the subject, along with an invited counterpoint essay titled "The Engine That Drives Success: The Best Companies Have the Best Business Models Because They Have the Best IT Strategies" by noted technology and business strategy author Don Tapscott. Tapscott argued that companies with bad business models tend to fail regardless of whether they use information technology or not. On the other hand, companies that have good business models and use information technology successfully to carry out those business models tend to be very successful. He described many examples, across a variety of industries, where firms dominate their respective markets; have superior customer relationships, business designs, and differentiated offerings; and are well known for their superior use of IT in supporting a unique business strategy. His examples included Amazon.com, Best Buy, Citigroup, PepsiCo, Herman Miller, Cisco, Progressive Casualty Insurance, Marriott, FedEx, GE, Southwest Airlines, and Starbucks.

We tend to side with Tapscott on this one. We believe that information systems are a necessary part of doing business, that they can be used to create efficiencies, and that they can also be used as an enabler of competitive advantage. We do agree with Carr, however, that the competitive advantage from the use of information systems can be fleeting, as competitors can eventually do the same thing. Also, given how expensive information systems projects have become and given how cost conscious and competitive businesses now are, nearly every information system project today must show a clear return on investment. Again, we'll talk more about the role of information systems in competitive advantage and return on investment in Chapter 3 and throughout the book.

Industry Analysis

Business Career Outlook

In Chapter 2, we carefully examine how information systems are fueling globalization and tremendous changes throughout the world. Today, organizations are increasingly moving away from focusing exclusively on local markets. For example, Price Waterhouse LLP is focusing on forming overseas partnerships to increase its client base and better serve the regions located away from their U.S. home. This means that it is not only more likely that you will need to travel overseas in your career or even take an overseas assignment but also extremely likely that you will have to work with customers, suppliers, or colleagues from other parts of the world. Given this globalization trend, there is a shortage of business professionals with the necessary "global skills" for operating in the digital world. Three strategies for improving your opportunities include the following:

1. *Gain International Experience.* The first strategy is very straightforward. Simply put, by gaining international experiences, you will more likely possess the necessary cultural sensitivity to empathize with other cultures and, more important, will greatly enhance a global organization.

2. *Learn More Than One Language.* A second strategy is to learn more than your native language. Language problems within global organizations are often hidden

beneath the surface. Many people are embarrassed to admit when they don't completely understand a foreign colleague. Unfortunately, the miscommunication of important information can have disastrous effects on the business.

3. ***Sensitize Yourself to Global Cultural and Political Issues.*** A third strategy focuses on developing greater sensitivity to the various cultural and political differences within the world. Such sensitivity and awareness can be developed through coursework, seminars, and international travel. Understanding current events and the political climate of international colleagues will enhance communication, cohesiveness, and job performance.

In addition to these strategies, prior to making an international visit or taking an international assignment, there are many things you can do to improve your effectiveness as well as enhance your chances of having fun, including the following:

1. Read books, newspapers, magazines, and Web sites about the country.
2. Talk to people who already know the country and its culture.
3. Avoid literal translations of work materials, brochures, memos, and other important documents.
4. Watch locally produced television as well as monitor the local news through international news stations and Web sites.
5. After arriving in the new country, take time to tour local parks, monuments, museums, entertainment locations, and other cultural venues.
6. Share meals and breaks with local workers and discuss more than just work-related issues such as current local events and issues.
7. Learn several words and phrases in the local languages.

Regardless of what business profession you choose, globalization is a reality within the digital world. In addition to globalization, the proliferation of information systems is having specific ramifications for all business careers. This is discussed next.

For Accounting and Finance: In today's digital world, accounting and finance professionals rely heavily on information systems. Information systems are used to support various resource planning and control processes as well as to provide managers with up-to-date information. Accounting and finance professionals use a variety of information systems, networks, and databases to effectively perform their functions. In addition to changing the ways internal processes are managed and performed, information systems have also changed the ways organizations exchange financial information with suppliers, distributors, and customers. If you choose a career in accounting or finance, it is very likely that you will be working with various types of information systems every day.

For Operations Management: Information systems have also greatly changed the operations management profession. In the past, orders for supplies had to be placed over the phone, production processes had to be optimized using tedious calculations, and forecasts were sometimes only educated guesses. Today, enterprise resource planning and supply chain management systems have eliminated much of the "busywork" associated with making production forecasts and placing orders. Additionally, with the use of corporate extranets, companies are connecting to their suppliers' and distributors' networks, helping to reduce costs in procurement and distribution processes. If you choose operations management as your profession, the use of information systems will likely be a big part of your workday.

For Human Resources Management: The human resources management profession has experienced widespread use of information systems for recruiting employees via Internet job sites, distributing information through corporate intranets, or analyzing employee data stored in databases. In addition to using information systems within your daily work activities, you will also have to deal with other issues related to information systems use and misuse within your organization. For example, what are the best methods for motivating employees to use a system they do not want to use? What policies should you use regarding monitoring employee productivity or Internet misuse? If you choose human resource management as a profession, information systems have become an invaluable addition to the recruitment and management of personnel.

For Marketing: Information systems have changed the way organizations promote and sell their products. For example, business-to-consumer electronic commerce, enabled by the Internet, allows companies to directly interact with their customers without the need for intermediaries; likewise, customer relationship management systems facilitate the targeting of narrow market segments with highly personalized promotional campaigns. Marketing professionals must therefore be proficient in the use of various types of information systems in order to attract and retain loyal customers.

For Information Systems: Information systems have become a ubiquitous part of organizational life, where systems are used by all organizational levels and functions. Because of this, there is a growing need for professionals to develop and support these systems. To most effectively utilize the investment in information systems, professionals must be proficient in both business—management, marketing, finance, and accounting—and technology. In other words, information systems professionals must understand the business rationale for implementing a particular system as well as how organizations can use various systems to obtain a competitive advantage. Being able to bridge the business needs of the organization to information systems-based solutions will provide you with a competitive advantage on the job market.

Source: R. Treitel, "Global Success" (October 9, 2000), http://www.ganthead.com/articles/articlesPrint.cfm?ID=12706

Key Points Review

1. *Explain what an information system is, contrasting its data, technology, people, and organizational components.* Information systems are combinations of hardware, software, and telecommunications networks that people build and use to collect, create, and distribute useful data, typically in organizational settings. When data are organized in a way that is useful to people, these data are defined as information. The term "information systems" is also used to represent the field in which people develop, use, manage, and study computer-based information systems in organizations. The field of IS is huge, diverse, and growing and encompasses many different people, purposes, systems, and technologies. The technology part of information systems is the hardware, software, and telecommunications networks. The people who build, manage, use, and study information systems make up the people component. They include systems analysts, systems programmers, information systems professors, and many others. Finally, information systems typically reside and are used within organizations, so they are said to have an organizational component. Together, these three aspects form an information system.

2. *Describe types of jobs and career opportunities in information systems and in related fields.* The people who help develop and manage systems in organizations include systems analysts, systems programmers, systems operators, network administrators, database administrators, systems designers, systems managers, and chief information officers. All of these types of people are in heavy demand; as a result, salaries are high and continue to rise. The field of IS has changed such that IS personnel are now thought of as valuable business professionals rather than as "nerds" or "techies." The need for technology-related knowledge and skills has spread to other careers as well in fields such as finance, accounting, operations management, human resource management, business law, and marketing.

3. *Describe the dual nature of information systems in the success and failure of modern organizations.* If information systems are conceived, designed, used, and managed effectively and strategically, then together with a sound business model they can enable organizations to be more effective, to be more productive, to expand their reach, and to gain or sustain competitive advantage over rivals. If information systems are not conceived, designed, used, or managed well, they can have negative effects on organizations, such as loss of money, loss of time, loss of customers' goodwill, and, ultimately, loss of customers. Modern organizations that embrace and manage information systems effectively and strategically and combine that with sound business models tend to be the organizations that are successful and competitive.

Key Terms

chief information officer
   (CIO)   15
competitive advantage   29
computer-based information
   systems   12
data   11
downsizing   26
hardware   10

information   11
information systems (IS)   10
information technology (IT)   12
internetworking   22
knowledge   11
knowledge society   6
knowledge worker   6
new economy   6

outsourcing   26
service mentality   25
software   10
strategic   29
systems integration   22
technology   12
telecommunications networks   10
wisdom   11

Review Questions

1. Define the term "knowledge worker." Who coined the term?
2. Describe and contrast the economic, cultural, and technological changes occurring in the digital world.
3. Define the term "information systems" (IS) and explain its data, technology, people, and organizational components.
4. Define and contrast data, information, knowledge, and wisdom.
5. Define and contrast technology, information technology, and information system.
6. Describe three or four types of jobs and career opportunities in information systems and in related fields.
7. What is a CIO, and why has the CIO grown in importance?
8. List and define three technical knowledge and/or skills core competencies.
9. List and define four business knowledge and/or skills core competencies.
10. List and define four of the systems knowledge and/or skills core competencies.
11. List and define five types of information systems used in organizations.
12. Describe the evolution of the information systems function within organizations.

Self-Study Questions

Visit the Interactive Study Guide on the text Web site for additional Self-Study Questions: **www.prenhall.com/jessup**.

1. Information systems today are _____.
   A. slower than in the past
   B. continuing to evolve with improvements to the hardware and software
   C. utilized by only a few select individuals
   D. stable and should not change
2. Information systems are used in which of the following organizations?
   A. professional
   B. educational
   C. governmental
   D. all of the above
3. Whereas data are raw unformatted pieces or lists of words or numbers, information is _____.
   A. data that has been organized in a form that is useful
   B. accumulated knowledge
   C. what you put in your computer
   D. what your computer prints out for you
4. Computer-based information systems were described in this chapter as _____.

A. any complicated technology that requires expert use
B. a combination of hardware, software, and telecommunications networks that people build and use to collect, create, and distribute data
C. any technology (mechanical or electronic) used to supplement, extend, or replace human, manual labor
D. any technology used to leverage human capital

5. In the 1980s, which of the following became a popular new title given to executives who were responsible for the information systems function?
   A. CFO
   B. CIO
   C. CEO
   D. CMA
6. Other terms that can be used to represent the knowledge society include _____.
   A. the new economy
   B. the network society
   C. the digital world
   D. all of the above

7. Which of the following IS job titles is used for a person whose primary responsibility is directly doing maintenance on an information system?
A. IS director
B. maintenance manager
C. systems analyst
D. chief information officer

8. Which of the following is not classified as business knowledge and skills?
A. management
B. communication
C. systems integration
D. social

9. Which of the following was not discussed as a common type, or category, of information system used in organizations?

A. transaction processing
B. decision support
C. enterprise resource planning
D. Web graphics

10. Which of the following is not an example of an information system?
A. an accounting system in a business
B. a concession stand
C. a combination of different software packages in a company
D. a database of customers

Answers are on page 37.

Problems and Exercises

1. Match the following terms with the appropriate definitions:
  i. Wisdom
  ii. New economy
  iii. Information
  iv. Knowledge society
  v. Outsourcing
  vi. Systems integration
  vii. Downsizing
  viii. Chief information officer
  ix. Information systems
  x. Service mentality
    a. A society with a high proportion of knowledge workers who play an important leadership role
    b. An executive-level individual who has overall responsibilities for the information systems component within the organization and is concerned primarily with the effective integration of technology and business strategy
    c. Accumulated knowledge that represents broader, more generalized rules and schemas for understanding a specific domain or domains
    d. The moving of routine jobs and/or tasks to people in another firm, in another part of the country, or in another country at less cost
    e. Data that have been formatted in a way that is useful
    f. When companies slash costs, streamline operations, and/or let employees go
    g. Connecting separate information systems and data to improve business processes and decision making
    h. An economy in which information technology plays a significant role and that enables producers of both the tangible (computers, shoes, etc.) and intangible (services, ideas, etc.) products to compete efficiently in global markets

    i. The mind-set that your goal is to enable others to be successful and that the "customer is always right"
    j. Combinations of hardware, software, and telecommunications networks that people build and use to collect, create, and distribute useful data, typically in organizational settings

2. Using the Web, research how FedEx has invested and updated its information systems and information technologies. List some of the most significant items and argue whether these investments have been good or bad. Discuss how you feel these investments affected FedEx's competitors.

3. Peter Drucker has defined the knowledge worker and knowledge society. What are his definitions? Do you agree with them? What examples can you give to support or disprove these concepts?

4. List three major IS professional core competencies or general areas from the textbook. Do you agree or disagree that all three are needed to become a professional? Why? What competencies do you currently possess, and what do you need to improve on or acquire? What is your strategy to acquire new skills? Where and when will you acquire them?

5. Of the several information systems listed in the chapter, how many do you have experience with? What systems would you like to work with? What types of systems do you encounter at the university you are attending? The Web is also a good source for additional information.

6. Consider an organization that you are familiar with, perhaps one that you have worked for or have done business with in the past. Describe the types of information systems that organization uses and tell whether they are useful or up to date. List specific examples for updating or installing information systems that improve productivity or efficiency.

7. Identify someone who works within the field of information systems as an information systems instructor, professor, or practitioner (e.g., as a systems analyst or systems manager). Find out why this individual got into this field and what this person likes and dislikes about working within the field of IS. What advice can this person offer to someone entering the field?

8. Based on your previous work and/or professional experiences, describe your relationships with the personnel in the IS department. Was the IS department easy to work with? Why or why not? Were projects and requests completed on time and correctly? What was the organizational structure of this IS department? How do your answers compare with those of other classmates?

9. As a small group, conduct a search on the Web for job placement services. Pick at least four of these services and find as many IS job titles as you can. You may want to try monster.com or careerbuilder.com. How many did you find? Were any of them different from those presented in this chapter? Could you determine the responsibilities of these positions based on the information given to you?

10. What type of IT/IS investment should Starbucks Coffee have, and how would it be used in the corporate office and the individual stores? What would it need to track inventory and sales? Search the Web or visit a Starbucks Coffee store in your city to determine whether you can see what technology is available in your local store.

11. The IS support group within the School of Business at Indiana University changed its name from "Business Computing Facility" to "Technology Services." Along with the change in name came an appropriate change in services and offerings to their clientele. Research the evolution of the information systems support function within your university or within a company. Make sure you track names changes, reporting structures, service orientation, and so on.

12. Contrast, using specific examples in your own life, technology, information technology, and computer-based information systems.

13. Do information systems matter to modern organizations? Why or why not?

Application Exercises

Note: The existing data files referenced in these exercises are available on the Student Companion Web site: **www.prenhall. com/jessup**.

Spreadsheet Application: Ticket Sales at Campus Travel

The local travel center, Campus Travel, has been losing sales. The presence of online ticketing Web sites such as travelocity.com and expedia.com has lured many students away. However, given the complexity of making international travel arrangements, Campus Travel could have a thriving and profitable business if they concentrate their efforts in this area. You have been asked by the director of sales and marketing to help with analyzing prior sales data in order to design better marketing strategies. Looking at these data, you realize that it is nearly impossible to perform a detailed analysis of ticket sales given that it is not summarized or organized in a useful way to inform business decision making. The spreadsheet TicketSales.csv contains the ticket sales data for spring 2006. Your director has asked you for the following information regarding ticket sales. Modify the TicketSales.csv spreadsheet to provide the following information for your director:

1. The total number of tickets sold for each month.
   a. Select the data from the "tickets sold" column.
   b. Then select the autosum function.
2. The largest amount of tickets sold by a certain salesperson to any one location:
   a. Select the appropriate cell.

b. Use the "MAX" function to calculate each salesperson's highest ticket total in one transaction.

3. The least amount of tickets sold by a certain salesperson to any one location:
   a. Select the appropriate cells.
   b. Use the "MIN" function to calculate the "least tickets sold."
4. The average number of tickets sold:
   a. Select the cells.
   b. Use the "AVERAGE" function to calculate the "average number of tickets sold" using the same data you had selected in the previous steps.

Database Application: Tracking Frequent Flier Miles at the Campus Travel Agency

The director of sales and marketing of the travel agency would like to increase the efficiency of handling those who have frequent flier accounts. Often, frequent fliers have regular travel routes or want to change their preferred seating area or meal category. In the previous years, the data has been manually entered in a three-ring binder. In order to handle the frequent flyers' requests more efficiently, your director has asked you to build an Access database containing the following information:

- Customer name (first and last name)
- Customer address
- Customer phone number
- Frequent flier number

- Frequent flier airline
- Meal category
- Preferred seating area

To do this, you will need to do the following:

1. Create an empty database named "frequent flier."
2. Import the data contained in the file FrequentFliers.txt using the function "Get external Data >> Import. . .".

Hint: use tab delimiters when importing the data; note that the first row contains field names.

After importing the data, create a report displaying the names and addresses of all frequent fliers by doing the following:

1. Select "Create report by using Wizard."
2. Select the field first name, last name, addresses into the report.
3. Save the report as "frequent fliers."

Team Work Exercise: How to Find Out What Is Current in IS

Visit a Web site of an information systems-related content provider, such as *InformationWeek, Computerworld, CIO* magazine, or *NewsFactor,* and scan the current headlines. You can find these online resources at www.informationweek. com, www.computerworld.com, www.cio.com, and www. newsfactor.com. After having scanned the headlines, get together with your team and discuss your findings. What is the focus of the different sites? What are the hot technologies and related issues? Which seem to be most important to business managers? Prepare a brief presentation for your classmates.

Answers to the Self-Study Questions

1. B, p. 6 **2.** D. p. 20 **3.** A, p. 10 **4.** B, p. 12 **5.** B, p. 15 **6.** D, p. 6 **7.** B, p. 15
8. C, p. 19 **9.** D, p. 23 **10.** B, p. 10

---

case

Click Clique: Facebook.com

Facebook.com calls itself "a social utility that helps people better understand the world around them . . . through social networks allowing people to share information online the same way they do in the real world." That it does. Reportedly, 85 percent of all U.S. college students—over 12 million—have registered with Facebook.

Founded by a group of Harvard University students and launched in February 2004, Facebook was set to provide everything a college student needs to know about other students. Users list their interests ("soccer," "buying shoes"), friends, classes, and any other "tasteful" information about themselves. Anyone can form a subgroup within Facebook, such as "Cancer Corner" for smokers, "Collars Up!" for members who like to wear their shirts with the collars turned up, and the self-described "Republican Princesses." Members post detailed profiles of themselves and admit to logging on to browse Facebook four or five times a day.

While Facebook can help people get acquainted, it can also be used as a "weapon," according to some users. "It's communication lean" and a little fake, says an undergraduate sociology major at George Washington University. But even so, she logs on to the site whenever she has some spare time.

Initially, Facebook provided students with a secluded online directory that could be accessed only by people having an e-mail address ending in ".edu" (an ending that is usually reserved for educational institutions). This constraint was the major difference between Facebook and other online friendship and dating Web sites. Students registered on Facebook apparently felt safe in divulging personal information, probably because the network is closed to campus outsiders. In some instances, however, sororities and fraternities ask students not to list their Greek affiliations on Facebook to prevent potential pledges from researching which students are members of which sororities and fraternities. This restriction protects sorority and fraternity members from being constantly approached, both online and in person, and also reduces animosity and competition between students vying for certain sororities and fraternities.

Over time, Facebook realized that the restriction to just students alienated a large number of people. What was founded as a social networking site just for Harvard students was opened up to college students throughout the U.S., to high school students, and, in 2006, to anyone who wanted to join. To give its members the feeling of protection, the privacy controls were expanded, allowing people to prevent being included in search results and being contacted by people outside their networks. Further, Facebook's college and work networks require authenticated email addresses to join.

Due to such restrictions, Facebook is also a good place for announcements—or not. For example, one student advertised a party in an off-campus apartment complex.

As expected, fellow students who were on Facebook learned about the time and location of the party, but, unfortunately (for the host), a pair of roommates living next door to the party site also read about the party on Facebook. The pair of roommates dreaded the impending commotion and advised the police to be on alert that night. The party started mildly at 8:00 P.M. but got rowdy by 9:00 P.M. The police cars that were parked just outside the apartment complex stopped the party promptly at 10:00 P.M. to comply with the city's noise ordinance. The moral is, don't advertise an event on Facebook unless you want a crowd to show up. To summarize, Facebook provides a popular networking service for college students and other people alike. Anyone belonging to the Facebook community can access other members' profiles and browse their interests and friends. The "wall" is

another popular feature. Anyone can post messages to a member's wall, and members can delete posted messages. Other Facebook features include adding photo albums, listing coming activities, and "poking," a ritual equivalent to a handshake. Facebook also provides rating scales for music, books, movies, television series, and other interests and activities.

Facebook is not the first Web site to deliver social networking activities. Other social networking sites include Friendster, MySpace, Tribe Networks, LinkedIn, NamesDataBase, and Google's Orkut, all of which have features similar to Facebook. Social networking sites use a variety of techniques to increase user base. Some allow direct registration from their Web sites; others do not. Those that do not allow direct registration follow the "viral marketing" premise, by which only

those who receive an invitation from a registered friend may be allowed to join the network. This process not only reinforces the networking philosophy but also makes sure that an entire circle of friends is registered on one site.

Venture capitalists have expressed an interest in funding online social networking because of the advertising prospects. When friends recommend a product or service to friends, an ad has more impact. Therefore, when marketers use online social networks, sales can increase exponentially.

Because often the only source of revenue is advertisements placed on every page, many online social networks have not yet paid off financially for founders, but the concept has definitely proven popular with users and will continue to attract those who simply enjoy being part of a cybercommunity.

Questions

1. Do you use a social networking site like Facebook.com? If so, why? If not, why not?
2. Besides advertising, how else could a social networking site generate revenue?
3. What are the pros and cons of using a social networking site?

Sources: Ryan Naraine, "Social Networks in Search of Business Models," *Business* (February 13, 2004), http://www.internetnews.com/bus-news/article.php/3312491

Zoe Barton, "Facebook's Greek Drama," *C/Net News.com* (October 17, 2005), http://news.com/Facebooks+Greek+drama/2100-1046_3-5895963.html

Michael Arrington, "85% of College Students Use Facebook," *TechCrunch* (February 4, 2004), http://www.techcrunch.com/2005/09/07/85-of-college-students-use-facebook/

Libby Copeland, "Click Clique—Facebook's Online College Community," *Washington Post.com,* December 28, 2004, http://www.washingtonpost.com/wp-dyn/articles/A30002-2004Dec27.html

case ②

e-Enabling the Air Transport Industry: Managing in the Digital World

Over the past several years, there has been a tremendous downturn in worldwide travel, and this downturn has greatly impacted the air transport industry. Several factors have led to this downturn, including the dot-com bust, the economic recession, the terrorist attacks of 2001, the SARS crisis in the Far East, and the ongoing war on terror. The poor economy affected many companies worldwide, resulting in layoffs and other cost-cutting measures, such as reduced travel. A significant amount of the revenue generated within the air transport industry is through the frequent business travelers. Thus, during this downturn, a large part of the lucrative business travel segment

has collapsed, and several major international airlines, such as United Airlines and USAir, were driven to the verge of bankruptcy; it was only through drastic cost-cutting measures and improved efficiencies that they were able to survive.

Information systems have played a major role in helping airlines reduce costs and improve efficiencies through streamlined crew, aircraft, and maintenance scheduling. While airlines all over the world continue to demand more from their sophisticated information systems, so too have the airlines' most valued customers, namely, the business travelers. Over the past few years, most hotels that cater to business travelers have installed high-speed Internet access, to the point

that it has now become a commodity. Likewise, most major airports provide wired kiosks and wireless access throughout the terminals so that busy travelers can access the Internet as they wait for a flight. However, one place where business travelers have been largely out of touch with their colleagues and customers while on the road has been when they were on a flight. Sometimes, a few hours of not being available online can be quite relaxing. At other times, however, it may be very beneficial to be online for processing e-mail messages, placing customer orders, or chatting with family and friends. Until recently, the only way for an airline traveler to communicate with the outside world was through a very expensive and very slow onboard telephone.

To address this need, the Boeing Company, headquartered in Chicago, began offering solutions to help airlines meet their own and their customers' need for real-time information. To better support the airlines, Boeing is developing the "e-Enabled airplane," which integrates various airline operational processes using a variety of information systems and communication technologies (collectively, these systems and technologies are marketed by Boeing as the "e-Enabled Advantage"). The e-Enabled airplane allows airlines to streamline operations and to better serve their various customer segments by providing sophisticated systems and real-time information to support various aspects of the airline's operations, including crew scheduling and aircraft maintenance. Further, part of the project was to provide in-flight broadband Internet access to support airline customers. The communication infrastructure to enable these capabilities was initially provided by a new Boeing company called Connexion by Boeing, a mobile information services provider bringing high-speed Internet and data services to in-flight aircraft and maritime operators for the benefit of passengers, crew, and operations. To provide connectivity, Connexion leased capacity on geostationary satellites, which enabled transmission speeds of 5 mbps downstream and up to 1 mbps upstream, virtually anywhere in the world. In other words, passengers could connect to the Internet at speeds comparable to broadband connections at their homes or offices.

After the development of the system and periods of extensive testing, Connexion received an operating license from the Federal Aviation Administration for in-flight broadband services in late 2001. Since then, the service has been available for corporate and government aircraft and was installed in early 2003 on

select Lufthansa and British Airways flights between Europe and the United States. Although many airlines had initially indicated interest in this system, the crisis in the air transport industry (discussed previously) led many airlines to back off from their plans to deploy the system. Lufthansa became the first airline to install the service, putting it on several of its Airbus jets for use on transatlantic routes. Given the success of Lufthansa, many other airlines quickly followed to become Connexion customers, including Scandinavian Airlines, ANA, China Airlines, and Singapore Airlines.

In addition to offering in-flight Internet services to their customers, airlines could use Connexion's systems for internal processes, such as crew members' access to the airline's reservation system or real-time transfer of maintenance requests to the destination airport. Furthermore, Connexion's systems could be used to receive satellite TV or the latest weather data so that the pilots could choose alternative routes, if necessary. Mitigating potential delays caused by adverse weather conditions can be a major factor leading to increased customer satisfaction.

Thus, this broadband connectivity was an important component of Boeing's vision of the e-Enabled airplane. Unfortunately, things did not turn out the way they were supposed to, and fewer airlines than expected adopted Connexion's service. This, paired with ongoing terrorist threats, led Boeing to pull the plug on the Connexion project in mid-2006. Additionally, since alternatives for providing the necessary connectivity for the e-Enabled project existed (albeit offering lower bandwidth), Boeing was nevertheless able to continue with its e-Enabled vision.

Using the integrated services provided by the e-Enabled airplane, the airplane's central maintenance computer or the airplane crew can now automatically trans-

Passengers using Connexion in-flight Internet Services

mit alerts about potential service events to the airline's service center. When they receive the transmission, maintenance staff can remotely research and diagnose a problem in order to reduce the time needed to solve the problem once the aircraft has landed. As soon as the problem has been diagnosed and a service plan has been established, the necessary parts can be automatically ordered and delivered to the gate so that the maintenance crew can begin working on the problem as soon as the airplane arrives.

Similarly, automatic alerts about thunderstorms looming behind the horizon can be generated and instantaneously transmitted to the airline's operations center as well as to the flight crew. Sophisticated software systems can then calculate the possibility of the weather conditions' impacting the flight schedule and suggest alternatives to mitigate potential delays.

In most industries, organizations constantly have to evolve to stay in business. For example, just a few years ago, no coffee shop needed to provide wireless Internet access; today, however, it has become a necessity for keeping and attracting new customers. Airline industry experts also predict that the same will happen for airlines. And, since history is often the best predictor of the future, it is likely that all airlines will one day be e-Enabled.

Questions

1. Briefly outline how airlines can use e-Enabled services to stay ahead of their competition.
2. Do you think connectivity will be indispensable for travelers in the near future? Why or why not? Under which conditions could a promising system like broadband access for customers become a success or failure?
3. Which factors help or impede Boeing's e-Enabled vision in times when their major customers face massive financial difficulties?

Sources: http://www.connexionbyboeing.com.

"France Telecom Mobile Satellite Communications to Become First Sales Associate for Connexion by Boeing Maritime Service" (April 5, 2006), retrieved July 28, 2006, from http://www.boeing.com/connexion/news/2006/q2/060405a_nr.html

chapter 2

Fueling Globalization through Information Systems

p r e v i e w > In today's world, the effects of globalization can be seen everywhere. Whether you buy products or services, almost everything (except for maybe a haircut at your local barbershop) can be produced somewhere else in the world. For example, retailer Wal-Mart buys much of the products it sells from China—it is said that if Wal-Mart were a country, it would be China's eighth-largest trading partner (Jingjing, 2004). Similarly, all kinds of services are now being outsourced to foreign countries, no matter whether the service is software development, the transcription of documents, or the design of components for large commercial aircraft. In this chapter, you will learn how globalization evolved and how information systems fuel this trend towards an ever-shrinking world. After reading this chapter, you will be able to answer the following:

1. Define globalization, describe how it evolved over time, and describe the key drivers of globalization.

2. Describe the emerging opportunities for companies operating in the digital world.

3. Explain the factors companies have to consider when operating in the digital world.

4. Describe international business and information systems strategies used by companies operating in the digital world.

The next section examines the evolution of globalization, followed by a discussion of challenges facing companies operating in a global digital world. Then different international business strategies and associated international information systems strategies are examined. Other aspects of the relationship between globalization and information systems, such as the *digital divide* (see Chapter 10—Managing Information Systems Ethics and Crime), will be examined throughout the remainder of the book. Finally, our discussion of globalization is intentionally limited to how information systems are fueling globalization; for more comprehensive discussions, see Friedman's *The World Is Flat* (2005) or Viotti and Kauppi's *International Relations and World Politics* (2006).

Managing in the Digital World: Casino Gaming

Las Vegas, Nevada, continues to draw 38 million visitors a year—who spend $36 billion annually, $6 billion on gaming alone—because people love playing the slot machines, matching wits with other gamblers at the poker and black-jack tables, playing roulette, and otherwise placing bets on games of chance. The concept is called gaming, and experts say it's probably ingrained in the human psyche.

As you might suspect, given the popularity of gaming, the industry has been at the forefront of technological innovation. Take, for example, the MGM Grand casino and hotel in Las Vegas. The Grand's enterprise resource planning (ERP) system encompasses booking, ticket sales, housekeeping, employee hiring and firing, dining, security, and other activities for all of the following:

- 5,034 guest rooms, including 751 suites
- 2,000-seat theater with live performances nightly
- 16,800-seat Grand Garden Arena featuring megaconcerts and special events
- Five bars and two world-renowned nightclubs
- 740-seat theater featuring headline entertainers
- 14 large restaurants and many smaller concessions
- 380,000-square-foot, state-of-the-art conference facilities
- Shopping mall with high-end shops
- Championship 18-hole golf course
- More than 170,000 square feet of gaming facilities

Technology allows the MGM Grand to manage all this with ease through its ERP system, where integration is the name of the game. Take gamer (player) information services, for example. A valued high-stakes player can enjoy complimentary meals, MGM Grand–financed shopping sprees, or free tickets to a boxing match—all of which are tracked by the player's room key. Room-key tracking of valued players lets the hotel/casino offer services and products tailored to those players. Thanks to MGM's technological resources, customers can be tracked at any of the company's facilities, including MGM Grand Las Vegas, Bellagio, The Mirage, Treasure Island, New York-New York, and MGM Grand Detroit.

Gaming-management software vendors include such well-known companies as Konami, the Japanese software development company known for the popular games Frogger and Dance Dance Revolution. The 30-year-old company maintains a division devoted strictly to manufacturing and selling gaming machines and gaming management systems internationally.

Radio frequency identification (RFID), a technology used for years in employee ID badges, the cattle industry,

FIGURE 2.1

Online gaming is a global business.

toll roads, merchandise monitoring, and passports, is also set to become a prominent player in the gaming industry. For instance, in the past, card players presented their cards to a pit boss who manually recorded the amount players bet and how long they gambled. Now, casinos can use RFID technology to accomplish the same task. Through equipment integrated into a casino's ERP system, RFID monitors at gambling tables can access in real time information such as how much the player is holding in chips and the amount bet per hour.

The next big innovation after coinless slot machines (that use charge cards instead of cash) in the casino industry is mobile gaming. Las Vegas casinos such as the Venetian have started field trials with converted PDAs that enable guests to play a variety of games from almost anywhere in the hotel. As Nevada state law only allows gambling in public spaces, such devices cannot be used in hotel rooms or parking garages. Other than that, people can use mobile devices to gamble while waiting in the ticket line for a nightly show, while waiting for the next course at dinner, or while being in a meeting at the hotel's convention center.

While brick-and-mortar gaming palaces will always be popular with the betting public, online gambling is one of the fastest-growing segments of electronic commerce (see Figure 2.1). Despite the fact that online gambling is mostly illegal in the United States, American gamblers wager an estimated $6 billion annually. Since the estimated 2,300 online gambling sites are based overseas, U.S. anti–online-gambling laws have been difficult if not impossible to enforce. In May 2006, in an attempt to crack down on cyberspace gambling, the U.S.

House of Representatives passed a bill that would prohibit online games such as poker, blackjack, and roulette. The bill sought to update the 1961 Federal Wire Wager Act by outlawing the electronic transmission of funds to pay gambling fees and debts. The American Gaming Association (AGA), the gambling industry's largest lobbyist, once opposed online gambling but is against current attempts at legislation outlawing online gambling, and in 2006 the AGA recommended a study of the feasibility of legalizing it.

Undoubtedly, businesses that make up the gambling industry will continue to take advantage of technological innovation to manage their organizations. And online gambling, which is totally dependent on technology, will either thrive as in the past or will dwindle in the United States as laws are passed prohibiting it.

Questions

1. How do you feel about online gaming, should it be open and legalized? Why or why not?
2. How could global Internet gambling be regulated or controlled so that consumers were protected from fraudulent sites?
3. How does Internet gambling lead to increased globalization?

Sources:

Erica Werne, "Crackdown on Internet Gambling Advances in Congress," *Digital CAD*, May 25, 2006, http://www.digitalcad.com/articles/viewarticle.jsp?id=44332

http://news.com.com/Chips+for+cheaters/2009-7355_3-5568411.html?tag=st.bp.story

http://news.com.com/Vegas+casino+bets+on+RFID/2100-7355_3-5568288.html

http://news.zdnet.com/2100-1009_22-5568288.html

http://www.suntimes.com/output/gaming/wkp-news-bet231.html

http://www.mgmgrand.com/pages/pressroom_hotel_view.asp?HotelPressID=39

Key Enabler

Detecting Intermittent Electrical Faults

Picture this: Your car sputters when you step on the gas to drive up steep hills. You take it to the repair shop and explain the problem, but mechanics can find nothing wrong, and when they drive the car, it doesn't sputter going up hills. You're frustrated but have no choice but to pay your bill and hope it doesn't happen again.

Now, picture this: A light comes on in an airplane cockpit during a flight, indicating that an emergency door is not properly sealed. When the plane lands, mechanics check the light and the door and find nothing wrong. The incident repeats several times, but mechanics fail to find a problem. Finally, an emergency exit door comes off during flight, and the plane crashes, killing all passengers and crew members.

In both scenarios, the problem was "intermittent electrical faults"—inconvenient in the first instance, fatal in the second.

The good news is that Sandia National Laboratories, a national security company that works closely with the U.S. government, has produced a technique called pulsed arrested spark discharge (PASD), which makes hard-to-find intermittent electrical faults easier to locate and repair.

The Boeing Company, manufacturer of commercial airplanes, is among the first to use PASD technology. For instance, in July 2006, Boeing mechanics using PASD found a potentially dangerous short circuit hiding in the miles of electrical wiring in a Boeing 747 tested in New Mexico. As used in airplane maintenance, the technology works like this: Technicians plug the PASD device (about the size of a suitcase) into bundles of wires simultaneously. The device then checks for small insulation breaks that could cause intermittent faults. The device sends a nanosecond burst of high-voltage electricity through wiring bundles, making any potential short circuit appear before it would normally do so. Because the voltage is higher than that normally used in airplanes, the electrical pulse jumps from the smallest wiring insulation fault (which to ordinary instrumentation seems undamaged) either to the bulkhead or to another nearby damaged wire. The spark generated by the PASD device—like static electricity leaping from hand to doorknob—in effect lights up the invisibly damaged spot like car headlights at night light up a deer's eyes. The nanosecond burst is then measured to see the amount of time it takes to return to its source. Thus, the test tells technicians the exact location of the problem. The high-voltage burst does no damage because it lasts for such a short time.

In addition to the commercial airline industry, the military is interested in using PASD technology to test wiring in submarines and tanks, where wiring is difficult to access. Undoubtedly, other industries, such as auto repair, will find the technology useful as well.

Since wiring ages, tiny breaks can occur and present huge problems. PASD technology can help ensure that vital connections, as in aircraft, do not lead to irreparable damage.

Sources: Anonymous, "Preemptive Spark Helps Find Intermittent Electrical Short Circuits in Airplanes," *Science Daily* (June 21, 2006), http://www.sciencedaily.com/releases/2006/06/060621084401.htm

---

in many former communist countries could enjoy greater freedoms. For many companies, this meant a tremendous increase in potential customers as well as access to a huge, talented labor pool in the former Eastern bloc countries.

Around the same time, Microsoft released the first version of the Windows operating system, which over time became the world standard in PC operating systems, enabling people from all over the world to use a common computing platform.

FLATTENER #2: 8/9/95—THE RELEASE OF THE NETSCAPE WEB BROWSER. The second big flattener was the Internet browser—the "killer app" that enabled everyone who had a computer and a modem to view Web pages. While the first Web site went live in 1991, viewing and navigating early Web sites was very cumbersome, and the Internet, in its

TABLE 2.2 Ten Forces That Flattened the World

Flattener	Event or Trend	Description
1	November 9, 1989	The fall of the Berlin Wall and the fall of communism, opening up of new markets for talent and products
2	August 9, 1995	Netscape went public; the company introduced the first mainstream Web browser
3	Work flow software	Standards and de facto standards enabling computers to "talk to each other" and facilitate collaboration
4	Supply chaining	Horizontal collaboration between suppliers, retailers, and customers
5	Open sourcing	Online communities building software and continuously improve it using peer review
6	Outsourcing	Companies having certain business functions (such as telephone support) conducted by other companies, often in a different country
7	Offshoring	Companies setting up entire plants in different countries to reduce costs
8	In-sourcing	Logistics companies (such as UPS) offering complete supply chain solutions to other businesses
9	In-forming	Everyone with Internet access having incredible amounts of information and entertainment at their fingertips
10	The steroids	Technologies amplifying the other flatteners by making things digital, mobile, virtual, and personal

FIGURE 2.3

Flattener #1: Tearing Down the Berlin Wall.

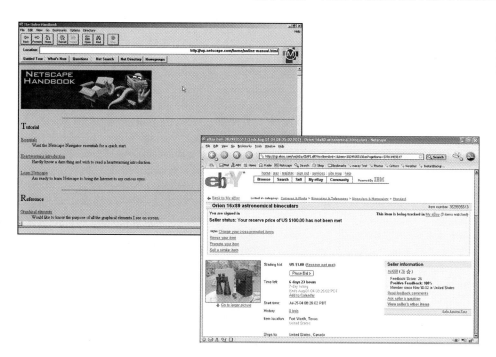

FIGURE 2.4

Flattener #2: Netscape
Browser—Then and Today.

infancy, was not used by the general public (see Technology Briefing 5—The Internet and the World Wide Web). On August 9, 1995, Netscape, the company that released the first mainstream browser only a year before (see Figure 2.4), went public. Later in 1995, Netscape even integrated an e-mail component into its browser, allowing people not only to view Web pages but also to communicate using the Internet. Thus, the Netscape browser can be regarded as a cornerstone in giving individuals easy access to the Internet. In addition to opening up the possibilities of the Internet for the general public, Netscape helped set a standard for the transport and display of data that other companies and individuals could build on, making the Internet even easier to use and more powerful than ever. Although many companies had

Net Stats

Online Searching

The Google search engine has become so popular with Internet users that the word "Google" is often used as a verb.[1] (I "Googled" the restaurant to see its reviews.) Yahoo! and Microsoft's MSN are also well-known search engines. Table 2.3 compares the percentage Internet surfers used each search engine in 2004 and 2005.

TABLE 2.3 Top Three U.S. Search Share Rankings by Percentage Points, December 2004 and 2005

Search Engine	December 2004 Search Share (%)	December 2005 Search Share (%)	Change (percentage points)
Google	43.1	48.8	5.7
Yahoo!	21.7	21.4	–0.3
MSN	14.0	10.9	–3.1

Source: Nielsen//NetRatings, February 2006.

[1]Although "googled" is synonymous with searching, Google.com is becoming concerned that its use as a verb is a copyright infringement. See http://www.nzherald.co.nz/ category/story.cfm?c_id=55&objectid=10396133.

some internal computer networks, it was the widespread adoption of the Internet that enabled companies to interconnect in new ways. Widespread adoption of the Internet also allowed organizations to benefit from the political and societal changes during that time.

In the final years of Globalization 2.0, the Internet really took off, and many young entrepreneurs envisioned a variety of new business models based on the possibilities the Internet offered. At the same time, companies supplying the network infrastructure saw the need to provide more and faster connections, leading to a tremendous *overinvestment* in telecommunications infrastructure, such as fiber-optic cable, which is used to transmit very large amounts of data at the speed of light (see Technology Briefing 4—Networking). Only a few years later, many of the new ventures (most of which operated at a loss in order to gain initial market share) proved not to be viable, often because of inexperienced management and uncontrolled spending. With the bursting of the dot-com bubble, stock prices plummeted, causing many people to lose much of their retirement money that had been invested in the stock market. However, the burst of the dot-com bubble also helped make the transition from Globalization 2.0 to Globalization 3.0.

In the aftermath of the burst of the dot-com bubble, many Internet companies went into bankruptcy, creating less demand for and oversupply of the telecommunications infrastructure that had been installed just a few years before. This, in turn, caused infrastructure providers to fail, and much of the infrastructure had to be sold for a fraction of the cost. While the short-term consequences were devastating for many companies and individual investors, the most notable long-term consequence was falling telecommunications costs, enabling the collaboration of individuals and small groups we see today.

FLATTENER #3: WORK FLOW SOFTWARE. The third flattener Friedman mentions is what he broadly calls **work flow software** (see Figure 2.5), a variety of software applications that allow people worldwide to communicate. While the Netscape browser

FIGURE 2.5

Flattener #3: Work flow software.

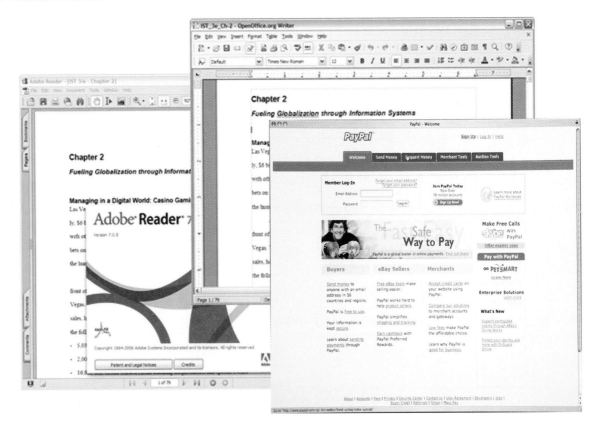

enabled people to access the Internet, other standards allowed different people and different companies all over the world to communicate seamlessly. For example, eXtensible Markup Language (XML; see Chapter 8—Building Organizational Partnerships using Enterprise Information Systems) enabled computer programs to "talk" to other programs so that, for example, a computer in an automobile manufacturing plant could automatically order a new shipment of windshield wipers from a supplier once the inventory reached a certain level. This and a variety of other transactions could be handled without human intervention, thanks to standards allowing different computers from different computer manufacturers, running different operating systems, to communicate. Today, XML is even used for saving document formatting information in open source applications such as OpenOffice (see Technology Briefing 2—Information Systems Software).

In addition to XML, various other de facto standards emerged, easing the ability for individuals and companies from all over the world to communicate and engage in commerce. Worldwide use of productivity software such as Microsoft Word or Adobe Acrobat enabled information sharing, while standard online payment systems such as PayPal provided a common global currency to fuel commerce (see Chapter 5—Enabling Commerce Using the Internet). Providing individuals anywhere in the world with the ability to communicate, share documents, or transfer money, regardless of the underlying computing platform or local currency, is fueling global collaboration of companies, small groups, and individuals.

FLATTENER #4: SUPPLY CHAINING. The fourth flattener is *supply chaining,* the tight integration of retailers, their suppliers, and their customers. One of the best-known examples is the supply chain of the giant retailer Wal-Mart (see Figure 2.6). Wal-Mart leverages the other flatteners to create a seamless supply chain (see Chapter 8) to get the goods from the manufacturers to the customers. Not only does Wal-Mart receive the information about their stores' sales, they also transmit this vital data to the manufacturers so that they can anticipate when the next shipment is needed, how their products sell, and what products may need improvement to increase sales. Wal-Mart has recently introduced *RFID (radio frequency identification)* tags into their supply chain, allowing them to track where the goods are in the supply chain as well as when their products are sold and to whom.

FIGURE 2.6

Flattener #4: Supply chaining at Wal-Mart is fueling globalization.

FIGURE 2.7

Flattener #5: Open sourcing.

FLATTENER #5: OPEN SOURCING. Demonstrated by software products such as the Linux operating system, the Firefox Web browser, or the OpenOffice office suite, the open-source community has made different software, as well as the software's source code, freely available to everyone (see Figure 2.7). As discussed in Technology Briefing 2, software developers, geeks, and other techies all over the world use the communication and collaboration capabilities offered by the Internet to create new pieces of software. The software created is in a constant state of evolution, as people critique each other's work, improve the software, fix flaws, and so on. The enormous success of the Firefox Web browser or of the Web server software Apache has even forced established software companies to launch new and improved versions of their own, proprietary software. The power of open sourcing is further demonstrated by the fact that in September 2006, 61 percent of all Web sites were hosted on Apache Web servers (Netcraft, 2006).

Another example of open sourcing is the successful online encyclopedia *Wikipedia,* the content of which can be created and updated by anyone with an Internet connection. As there is a huge community reviewing all latest edits, flaws in the entries are usually quickly detected and fixed. Open sourcing thus has made content, information, and software available to anyone with an Internet connection, enabling new and easier forms of collaboration between individuals, small groups, and companies.

The term **wiki** refers to Web sites allowing users to add, remove, or edit content, and is now often used synonymously with open-source dictionaries. Many organizations are now developing their own wiki sites to provide a place where users can share their knowledge. One example of this is eBay (www.ebaywiki.com), which utilizes this open source system to allow users to create, edit, and police the contents of eBay's gigantic wiki.

FLATTENER #6: OUTSOURCING. One country that has benefited tremendously from the flatteners mentioned before is India. While the American economy paid for the huge

FIGURE 2.8

Flattener #6: Outsourcing

overinvestment in telecommunications infrastructure during the dot-com bubble, India profited from the sudden drop in telecommunications cost after the dot-com bubble burst. During the dot-com era, many American companies turned to India for talented employees, as the supply of American engineers was all but dried up and companies had to look overseas for qualified employees (see Figure 2.8). After the stock market crashed, companies had to watch their expenditures much more closely than before and again turned to India. This time, they decided to hire Indian engineers not only because of the availability but primarily because outsourcing work to India was much more cost effective than performing those functions at home. We introduced outsourcing in Chapter 1— Managing in the Digital World and examine this important topic later in this and subsequent chapters.

FLATTENER #7: OFFSHORING. While outsourcing means having certain organizational functions (such as back-office functions) performed by other companies and potentially in other countries, **offshoring** adds a whole new dimension. When China officially joined the World Trade Organization in 2001, it agreed to follow certain accepted standards of trade and fair business practices. Before, the slow opening of the Chinese market was seen as an opportunity to *sell products* to the huge Chinese markets; afterward, companies saw the opportunity to *produce goods* in China (see Figure 2.9). Now, instead of just outsourcing certain activities, companies set up entire factories in countries such as China in order to mass-produce goods at a fraction of the price it would cost to produce these goods in the United States or even in Mexico.

FLATTENER #8: IN-SOURCING. The eighth major flattener is **in-sourcing**, which refers to the delegation of a company's core operations to a subcontractor that specializes in that operation. For example, United Parcel Service (UPS) is becoming a leading sourcing provider. In addition to providing their traditional service offerings of delivering packages to worldwide destinations, UPS started offering complete supply chain solutions to companies (see Figure 2.10). Traditionally, online retailers such as Nike.com would handle all online customer orders themselves. However, through an in-sourcing arrangement, UPS manages Nike's warehouse and handles product packing and shipping as well as payment collection from customers so that Nike can concentrate on its core competencies, such as the design of new athletic shoes. Similarly, near their sort station in Lexington, Kentucky, UPS employees manage distribution facilities for a vast array of companies, even packaging bulk consumer electronics into retail packages or repairing Toshiba laptop

FIGURE 2.9

Flattener #7: Offshoring.

FIGURE 2.10

Flattener #8: In-sourcing at UPS.

computers. In some instances, it is not the manufacturer's repair team coming to a customer to perform on-site repair or maintenance but rather a team of certified UPS technicians. In these examples, UPS acts as a department within the organizations; UPS employees come into an organization, analyze the organization's processes, and take over entire functions. Thus, such in-sourcing agreements require great amounts of trust, and for the outside observer, it is often hard to see that a different company (such as UPS) is performing the actual work. Given the scope of the in-sourcing arrangements and the nature of the tasks (i.e., complete supply chain solutions), such activities could usually not be performed from offshore locations.

FLATTENER #9: IN-FORMING. For the individual, **in-forming** is what outsourcing, in-sourcing, or supply chaining is for companies. With the Web and powerful search engines such as Google, Yahoo!, or MSN, every person who has access to the Internet can now build his or her "own personal supply chain ... of information, knowledge, and entertainment" (Friedman, 2005, p. 153). Using the possibilities of the Internet, an incredible number of people all over the world now have access to all kinds of information; this access to information has enabled people to get a more complete picture of what's happening in the world, and people have to depend less on propaganda and censored media (see Figure 2.11). Now, people have an incredible amount of information at their fingertips, and in the near future, people will be able to access almost any book without even having to go to a physical library.

FLATTENER #10: THE STEROIDS. The last group of flatteners, which Friedman calls "the steroids," are technologies that make different forms of collaboration "digital, mobile, virtual, and personal" (p. 161). This group of technologies amplifies all the flatteners discussed previously (see Figure 2.12). By digitizing content—from books, to music,

FIGURE 2.11

Flattener #9: In-forming.

FIGURE 2.12

Flattener #10: The steroids.

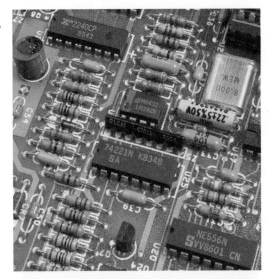

photographs, or virtually any business document—people can collaborate easier than ever before, benefiting from lightning-fast transmission of information. Similarly, the collaboration becomes virtual in that people using these technologies never have to think about the underlying standards or technologies enabling the collaboration; greater mobility enables collaboration from a wide variety of locations without being tied to one's office or desk. Finally, certain flatteners, such as in-forming, are available to everyone with an Internet connection, making the new forms of collaboration very personal.

What are some examples of these "steroids"? The tremendous increase in computing power and storage capacity is one of these steroids, enabling people to collaborate, manipulate pictures, or even record songs using their computers. Further, people can collaborate worldwide using technologies such as Skype, which allows free PC-to-PC video and voice calls to anywhere in the world. A final example is the growth in mobile infrastructures, to the point where people can access the vast resources enabled by the other nine flatteners no matter where they are—be it on a train, in a coffee shop, or even aboard an aircraft.

Although any one of these flatteners may be powerful, it's their *convergence* that makes Globalization 3.0 possible. Friedman refers to this as a "triple convergence," where three complementary events ushered in Globalization 3.0. First, as with many things, the flatteners are complementary, but it is their combination that leads to effects greater than

Change Agents

Niklas Zennström, Cofounder and Chief Executive Officer of Skype

Niklas Zennström, born in 1966, a Swedish citizen with degrees in business and computer science from Uppsala University in Sweden, cofounded Skype, a free Internet communication service, with Janus Friis. Although other VoIP

FIGURE 2.13

Niklas Zennström, cofounder and chief executive officer of Skype.

(Voice-over Internet Protocol) services exist, Skype is unique in that it is free, and the telecommunications service now boasts over 28 million subscribers. Skype users can make online calls for free and for a small charge can also call anyone with a landline. "The idea of charging for calls belongs to the last century," Zennström has remarked. "Skype software gives people new power to affordably stay in touch with their friends and family by taking advantage of their technology and connectivity investments."

Zennström began his career at Tele2, a small European telecommunications service, where he acquired valuable knowledge about the telecommunication industry. Also before Skype, Zennström and Janus Friis created KaZaA, peer-to-peer file downloading software that became the most downloaded software on the Internet, now totaling approximately 380 million downloads. KaZaA was later sold to Sharman Networks. Zennström also created get2net, a European ISP, and Altnet, a company that was the first to provide secure P2P services.

Zennström sold Skype to eBay in October 2005 and remains the company's chief executive officer. In 2006, Time magazine called Zennström and Friis "Telephone Revolutionaries" and named them to be among the 100 most influential people who are transforming the world.

Sources: http://www.businessweek.com/magazine/content/05_22/b3935421.htm

http://en.wikipedia.org/wiki/Niklas_Zennstr%C3%B6m

http://www.time.com/time/magazine/article/0,9171,1187489,00.html

---

the sum of their parts. Second, many people wonder why, even though some of these flatteners have been around for a while, their impacts have yet to be significantly felt. Friedman argues that, as with any major breakthrough, there is often a time lag until one sees the impact in a measurable way. In other words, just because a change is not initially viewed as groundbreaking does not mean that significant changes are not taking place. Finally, because of the global scale of the flatteners, enabling more people than ever to participate in new forms of collaboration who are at various stages of participation in the global village, we are only at the *beginning* of Globalization 3.0—the deep and pervasive impacts of this phase are in its infancy.

The Rise of Outsourcing   As discussed previously, one phenomenon that has seen a huge increase due to the decrease in telecommunication costs is the *outsourcing* of services. Traditionally, functions such as the manufacturing of goods were outsourced to other countries, based primarily on the cost of labor. For example, while many *manufactured* goods are imported from China, many U.S. companies also have their goods produced in so-called **maquiladoras**—assembly plants located on the Mexican side of the U.S.–Mexican border—to take advantage of lower wages and less stringent regulations. Then, in the years leading to Globalization 3.0, companies started to outsource *services* to other countries, starting with the development of computer software and the staffing of customer support and marketing call centers. Today, a wide variety of services—ranging from telephone support to tax returns—are outsourced to different countries, be it Ireland, China, or India. Even highly specialized services such as reading X-rays by skilled radiologists are outsourced by U.S. hospitals to doctors around the globe, often while doctors in the United States are sleeping. However, companies operating in the digital world have to carefully choose where to outsource, looking at factors such as English proficiency, salaries, or geopolitical risk. While countries such as India remain popular for outsourcers, other formerly popular countries (such as Singapore, Canada, or Ireland) are declining due to rising salaries. With these shifts, outsourcers are constantly looking at nascent and emerging countries such as Bulgaria, Egypt, Ghana, or Vietnam, each of which has some particular benefits to offer (see Table 2.4). Obviously, outsourcers have to weigh the potential benefits (e.g., cost savings) and drawbacks (e.g., higher geopolitical risk) of outsourcing to a particular country.

TABLE 2.4 Outsourcing Destinations by Country

Country	Ranking	English Proficiency	Entry-level Programmer Salary (US$ 1,000)	Relative Geopolitical Risk
Asia				
India	Leading	Very good	5-10	Moderate
China	Challenging	Poor	5-10	Moderate
Malaysia	Challenging	Fair	10-15	Moderate
Philippines	Challenging	Very good	5-10	High
Vietnam	Nascent	Fair	<5	Moderate
Thailand	Nascent	Poor	5-10	Moderate
Singapore	Declining	Fair	15-20	Low
Europe				
Czech Republic	Challenging	Good	10-15	Moderate
Poland	Challenging	Good	10-15	Moderate
Hungary	Challenging	Poor	10-15	Moderate
Russia	Challenging	Poor	10-15	Moderate
Romania	Emerging	Good	5-10	Moderate
Bulgaria	Emerging	Fair	5-10	Moderate
Ukraine	Emerging	Poor	5-10	Moderate
Ireland	Declining	Excellent	>20	Low
Middle East				
Egypt	Emerging	Very good	<5	High
Israel	Declining	Very good	15-20	Moderate
Africa				
South Africa	Challenging	Very good	10-15	Moderate
Ghana	Nascent	Very good	5-10	High
The Americas				
Mexico	Challenging	Poor	10-15	Moderate
Costa Rica	Emerging	Very good	10-15	Moderate
Brazil	Emerging	Poor	5-10	High
Argentina	Nascent	Fair	5-10	Moderate
Canada	Declining	Excellent	>20	Low

Source: Adapted from "Global Outsourcing Guide, CIO Magazine, July 15, 2006.

TABLE 2.5 Examples of Global Outsourcing

Industry	Examples
Airlines	British Airways outsources customer relations and passenger revenue accounting to India.
	Delta outsources reservation functions to India.
Airplane design	Parts of Airbus and Boeing airplanes are designed and engineered in Moscow, Russia.
Consulting	McKinsey outsources global research division to India.
	Ernst & Young moves part of tax preparation to India.
Insurance	British firm Prudential PLC moves call center operations to India.
Investment banking	Lehman Brothers outsources IT services to India.
Retail banking	Worldwide banking group HSBC moves back-office operations to India.
Credit card operations	American Express moves a variety of services to India.
Government	The Greater London Authority outsourced the development of a road toll system to India.
Telecommunications	T-mobile outsources part of its content development and portal configuration to India.

Source: Adapted from EBS (2006).

Today, the outsourcing market exceeds $500 billion annually and is predicted to rapidly increase over the next decade. Additionally, nearly 90 percent of all large organizations were expected to use some form of global IT outsourcing in 2006. Companies are choosing to outsource business activities for a variety of reasons, including the following (King, 2003):

- To reduce or control costs
- To free up internal resources
- To gain access to world-class capabilities
- To increase revenue potential of the organization
- To reduce time to market
- To increase process efficiencies
- To outsource noncore activities
- To compensate for a lack of specific capabilities or skills

Fueled by Globalization 2.0 and 3.0, outsourcing is now a fact of life, and no matter which industry you're in, you will likely feel the effects of outsourcing (see Table 2.5). With Globalization 3.0, individuals will have to ask themselves how they can seize the global opportunities and how they will be able to compete with individuals from all over the world who might be able to do their job at the same quality but at a lower cost. The next sections will outline some opportunities made possible by increasing globalization.

Opportunities of Operating in the Digital World

Clearly, globalization has opened up many opportunities, brought about by falling transportation and telecommunication costs. Today, shipping a bottle of wine from Australia to Europe merely costs a few cents, and using the Internet, people can make PC-to-PC phone calls around the globe for free. To a large extent, fueled by television and other forms of media, the increasing globalization has moved cultures closer together—to the point where people now talk about a "global village." Customers in all corners of the world can receive television programming from other countries or watch movies produced in Hollywood,

Munich, or Mumbai, helping to create a shared understanding about forms of behavior or interaction, desirable goods or services, or even forms of government. Over the past decades, the world has seen a democratization of many nations, enabling millions of people to enjoy freedoms they had never experienced before. All of this makes operating in the digital world much easier than ever before.

Opportunities of Reaching New Markets

After the fall of communism, new markets opened up for countless companies. The fall of the Berlin Wall and the following reunification of Germany, for example, increased the size of the German market from 64 million to 80 million people. Similarly, the fall of communism in other Eastern Bloc countries such as Poland, Romania, and the former Soviet Union enabled the sales of products to literally millions of new customers (see Figure 2.14).

Opportunities of a Global Workforce

With the decrease in communication costs, companies can now draw on a large pool of skilled professionals from all over the globe. Some companies outsource to different regions exactly because the availability of skilled labor is high. Many countries, such as Russia, China, and India, offer high-quality education, leading to an ample supply of well-trained people at low cost. While enrollment in the sciences or engineering is dropping in the United States, other countries are producing engineering graduates at an unprecedented pace (Mallaby, 2006). In 2005, for example, 200,000 young engineers graduated from Indian universities, while the United States produced only about a third as many; likewise, Europe produced only about half the number of India (see Figure 2.15).

FIGURE 2.14

Former Eastern Bloc countries.

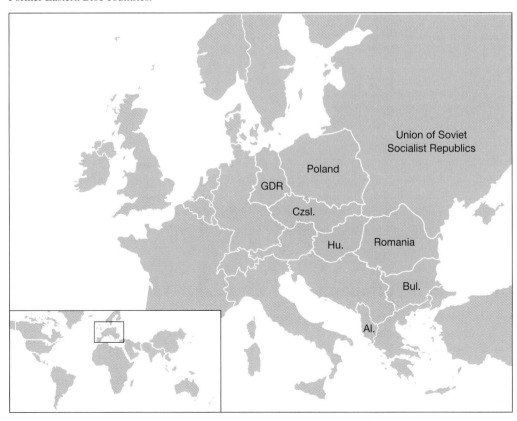

Source: http://upload.wikimedia.org/wikipedia/en/7/71/Eastern_bloc.png.

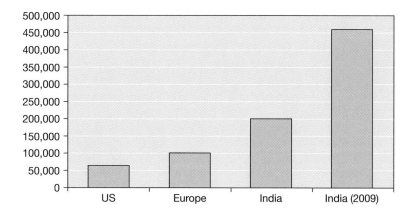

FIGURE 2.15

Engineering graduates in the United States, Europe, and India.

Source: Mallaby, 2006
http://www.washingtonpost.com/
wp-dyn/content/article/2006/01/02/
AR2006010200566.html.

While the number of engineering students in the West is plummeting, enrollments in Asia and India in particular are rapidly expanding (e.g., India reported having over 450,000 students enrolled in engineering programs in 2005). Some countries are actively building entire industries around certain competencies, such as software development or tax preparation in India and call centers in Ireland. For companies operating in the digital world, this can be a huge opportunity, as they can "shop" for qualified, low-cost labor all over the world. On the other hand, the consulting company McKinsey believes that out of the 2.5 million Indian university graduates, only 10 to 25 percent (depending on the field of study) are considered employable by multinational companies, mainly because of differences in the quality of the education and the differences in language skills (Farrell, Kaka, and Stürze, 2005).

The factors discussed in this section translate into a number of direct opportunities for companies, including greater and larger markets to sell products and larger pools of qualified labor. Nevertheless, while globalization has brought tremendous opportunities to companies, they also face a number of daunting challenges when operating in the global marketplace. Next, we highlight some of these challenges.

Challenges of Operating in the Digital World

Traditionally, companies acquired resources and produced and sold goods or services all within the same country. Such domestic businesses did not have to deal with any challenges posed by globalization but also could not leverage the host of opportunities. The challenges faced can be broadly classified into governmental, geoeconomic, and cultural challenges. See Table 2.6 for a summary of the challenges of operating in the digital world.

Governmental Challenges

Many challenges faced by companies are of governmental nature. These challenges are associated with factors such as the overall political system, regulations (including data sharing), or even Internet access. In the following sections, we will highlight some of these challenges faced when operating in the digital world.

Political System Challenges First and foremost, companies operating in the digital world have to consider the overall political climate of their host country. One factor to consider here is whether the host country is a market economy or whether it is a planned economy. When operating in a country that is less free than the home country, a company might face tight restrictions regarding what can be produced or sold, how much can be produced or sold, or to whom the products can be sold.

Further, although companies now have access to more countries than ever before, political stability is one issue to consider when operating outside one's home country. In many countries, the political systems are less stable than in the United States or in Western

TABLE 2.6 **Challenges of Operating in the Digital World**

Broad Challenges	Specific Challenges	Examples
Governmental	Political system	Market versus planned economy; political instability
	Regulatory	Taxes and tariffs; import and export regulations
	Data sharing	EU Data Protection Directive
	Internet access and individual freedom	Internet censorship in various countries
Geoeconomic	Time zone differences	Videoconferences across different time zones
	Infrastructure related reliability	Differences in network infrastructures throughout the world
	Differences in welfare	Migration and political instability caused by welfare differences between rich and poor countries
	Demographic	Aging population in the United States and Western Europe; younger workforce in other countries
	Expertise	Availability of labor force and salary differences
Cultural	Working with different cultures	Differences in power distance, uncertainty avoidance, individualism/collectivism, masculinity/femininity, concept of time, and life focus
	Challenges of offering products or services in different cultures	Naming and advertising for products; intellectual property

Europe, and companies have to consider whether to invest huge sums into specific countries, as foreign companies operating in politically unstable countries risk losing their assets due to confiscation, military coups, upheavals, or civil wars.

Regulatory Challenges As most countries have their own sovereign governments, taxes, laws, and regulations differ from country to country, and companies have to follow the rules of their host countries. For example, many countries impose a variety of different taxes and **tariffs** in order to regulate the flow of goods and services into and out of the country. Such taxes and tariffs exist for almost all categories of products, from bananas to computer hardware, and differ widely depending on the product category. The nature and amount of such taxes and tariffs has to be considered when deciding whether to import or export goods and services, manufacture in a foreign country, and so on.

Other regulations concerning the flow of goods and services are embargoes and export regulations. **Embargoes** are typically limiting (or prohibiting) trade with one particular country. For example, the U.S. embargo of Cuba is intended to isolate the Cuban government economically; thus, it prohibits the export of goods into Cuba, the import of Cuban goods (such as rum or cigars) into the United States, and most forms of travel to Cuba. Other embargoes are targeted at countries accused of sponsoring terrorist activities; these countries include Syria, Iran, and North Korea, among others. Thus, embargoes limit many forms of trade with a specific country.

In contrast, **export regulations** are directed at limiting the export of certain goods to other countries. While the export of goods such as missile technology from the United States to almost any country is severely restricted, other products may be exported to some, but not other countries. The U.S. Department of Commerce maintains lists to cross-check which types of products cannot be exported to which countries. For some products, such regulations can be quite complicated. For example, while the desktop version of the computer program PGP (Pretty Good Privacy, a data encryption technology; see Chapter 6—Securing Information Systems) can be exported to almost any country (with the exception of embargoed countries), PGP's software development kit can be sold only to users (including government users) in European Union (EU) member countries and close trading partners, to nongovernment users only in all other countries, and not at all to users in embargoed countries. As you can see, companies dealing with certain product categories have to be well aware of the laws and regulations governing the sale of their products.

Often, companies have to produce in certain countries in order to win sales contracts. For example, Boeing produces some airplane parts in China for two important reasons. First, there are significant cost savings associated with manufacturing in China. Second and more important, the Chinese government requires the manufacturing of at least some aircraft components in China in exchange for large aircraft orders (Holmes, 2006). Similarly, the United States has various **quotas** permitting foreign businesses to export only a certain number of products to the country; therefore, to overcome such quotas, many foreign car manufacturers (such as BMW, Toyota, or Mercedes-Benz) started producing automobiles in the United States.

Data-Sharing Challenges One area that has recently come to concern is the regulation of **transborder data flows**. Spurred by the decrease in telecommunications costs, companies started to outsource many business functions to other countries; for example, companies today outsource integral functions such as accounting or human resources to India, where the same quality of service can be provided at a fraction of the cost of performing the same functions in the United States or the EU. However, to outsource such functions, much (sometimes sensitive) data has to be transferred to different countries, which is where the problems start. Recently, the EU passed a directive that prohibits the transfer of data to countries with less stringent data protection laws. Thus, while it is now easier to transfer data between countries within the EU, it is much harder to transfer data from an EU member country to a nonmember country. While this poses challenges to companies from EU member countries (e.g., a German insurance company outsourcing its call center to India), this also introduces difficulties for international companies operating in the EU; for example, can a U.S.-based company transfer certain data from a European subsidiary back to the home office? In most cases no. As such, these limitations significantly restrict a company's ability to utilize common business processes (e.g., in the financial or health care sector), making it much more difficult and expensive to operate globally. However, currently, only a few countries have data protection laws as stringent as those of the EU, and a U.S. company outsourcing certain services to India, for example, does not face such challenges.

Internet Access and Individual Freedom When operating in a global digital world, companies will also have to consider Internet access issues. While people in some countries probably have access to almost all places on the Internet, people in others face many limitations in terms of the content they will be able to see or the applications they will be able to use. For example, in Germany and France, sites displaying fascist symbols and racist propaganda are banned by law; however, their citizens still have the possibility to visit prohibited content on sites hosted outside those countries. In other countries, such content is completely blocked, and people have no way to access banned content. Likewise, China restricts the use of Voice over Internet Protocol technology (a technology enabling phone calls over the Internet; see Technology Briefing 4) in order to be able to monitor phone conversations. Thus, Chinese Internet users are not able to use such technologies.

The French organization "Reporters without Borders" (www.rsf.fr) maintains a list of countries listed as "enemies of the Internet." Countries ranging from Belarus to Vietnam block all types of content that the governments deem inappropriate, with topics including primarily politics, religion, and sex. While many countries regulate the Internet by maintaining blacklists of sites and providing Internet access only through state-owned Internet service providers, some countries (such as Cuba or North Korea) block Internet access altogether, allowing only a handful of people with special permission to access the Internet. Operating in such countries brings about all sorts of issues regarding mainly how to comply with such regulations and whether a company should comply with such rules on ethical grounds. For example, U.S. Internet search portals MSN and Yahoo! recently faced an ethical dilemma when they were requested to reveal the identity of Chinese citizens posting dissident messages on Web logs hosted on those sites. Clearly, the Internet poses great challenges not only for companies operating globally but also for countries that are imposing control or limiting the freedom of their citizens.

Geoeconomic Challenges

These are just a few factors companies have to consider when operating in the digital world. Other factors to consider are of **geoeconomic** nature, that is, the combination of economic and political factors that influence a region. Especially in the times before Globalization 3.0, the necessity to travel in order to conduct business in a foreign country was a big factor, considering the time needed to reach overseas destinations, the lost productivity due to time differences, and so on. For highly paid executives, a two-day trip to London can cost large sums of money, for airplane tickets, overnight stays, travel days, and lost productivity due to jet lag and other factors. The Internet in general and Globalization 3.0 in particular have reduced much of the need for business travel by enabling low-cost and high-quality videoconferencing. One such example is the partnership between computer company Hewlett-Packard and Dreamworks SKG (the makers of animated movies such as *Shrek*), who built a collaboration studio intended to simulate face-to-face meetings across the globe. Although only one such room costs about $400,000 and the monthly service fees can be as high as $18,000, the reduced need for business travel can still easily translate into significant savings in costs and time for companies conducting business globally.

Time Zone Challenges   One factor that videoconferencing cannot resolve is the time difference between different countries. On the one hand, companies can use the time difference for their advantage; on the other hand, the time difference may actually hinder collaboration. For example, Symantec, a maker of antivirus software, has set up laboratories around the globe such that different teams can work on fighting viruses around the clock. When a team in California quits for the night, a team in Tokyo (where it's morning) can take over; when the team in Tokyo has finished their day's work, they hand off the project to a team in Europe, which then hands it back to the team in the United States (an approach called "following the sun"). However, the time differences can also cause friction, especially if real-time meetings (such as videoconferences) are needed. A good example is that of a U.S. telecommunications giant with subsidiaries in different European countries. Traditionally, the company's employees in Los Angeles prefer to hold weekly business meetings on a particular day of the week right after lunch. For employees of the European subsidiaries who have to "join" the conferences (via either phone or videoconferencing), this means coming in to work late in the evening once a week, as 1:00 P.M. in Los Angeles is 10:00 P.M. in Frankfurt (see Figure 2.16).

Infrastructure-Related Challenges   Another challenge facing companies operating in the digital world is differences in infrastructure, both in terms of the classic infrastructure (such as roads, electricity, and sewage systems) and in terms of connectivity. While in most Western countries the telecommunications infrastructures are fast and reliable, in many other countries connectivity is not always a given. A network outage somewhere in Africa can effectively bring the communications infrastructure of an entire country to a screeching halt. Having backup plans for such incidents is imperative when operating in different regions providing different level of services. We will discuss infrastructure-related issues in more detail in Chapter 4—Managing the Information Systems Infrastructure.

Challenges Related to Economic Welfare   Although the fall of communism and the other factors enabling Globalization 3.0 have helped to open up new markets and globalization has contributed to unprecedented growth in global per-capita gross domestic

FIGURE 2.16

International time zones.

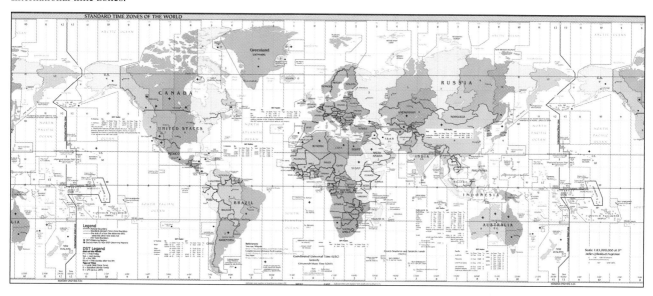

product (GDP), this growth has not been evenly distributed throughout the world. According to organizations such as the International Monetary Fund, the gap between rich and poor countries has widened, as the per-capita GDP has increased sixfold in the richest 25 percent of all nations, whereas it only has increased threefold in the poorest 25 percent. For many companies, the poorest countries thus do not constitute viable markets, and the expansion in potential customer base is only hypothetical. Further, this inequality can have other (and potentially more serious) consequences, such as political instability or increased migration toward the richer countries.

For many established companies, there is also new competition coming from poorer countries. For example, companies like the Brazilian aircraft manufacturer Embraer, the Chinese appliances manufacturer Haier, or the Indian tractor and auto manufacturer Mahindra have gained extensive experience in operating in markets characterized by tough competition and low profit margins. Now, these emerging giants have started entering the European and American markets, and established companies do not only face their competition in emerging markets, but also in their traditional home markets, as the emerging giants can offer products at prices much below those established companies can offer (Engardio, Arndt, and Smith, 2006).

Demographic Challenges

Companies operating in the digital world will also have to consider different demographic trends occurring worldwide. Specifically, the populations of the United States, many European countries, and Japan are increasingly getting older. At the same time, the population of other countries is getting younger and younger. While this may be an opportunity for companies to try to replace their aging workforce with new talent, it can also pose a challenge, as much of this younger workforce is lacking the necessary work experience.

Many low-wage countries have an abundance of people; in addition, the populations of such countries are growing at much higher rates than those of most Western nations (see Figure 2.17). As these countries are very poor, it is unlikely that the population growth will directly translate into a larger qualified labor pool or a larger market for products and services.

Expertise Related Challenges The nature of the workforce can also pose significant challenges for companies operating in the digital world. Different countries have different concentrations of skilled workers and differing costs for those workers (see Table 2.7).

FIGURE 2.17

World population, 1950–2050 (in billions).

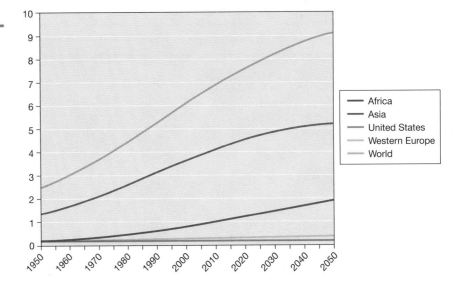

For example, most industrial nations have made significant investments in building a large base of skilled information systems personnel. However, these workers will typically also be much more costly to employ than those from less developed countries. The types of skills prevalent in different countries may also vary. Depending on the region, the lack of skilled labor can be a real problem for companies operating in other countries, as companies might not always be able to hire people with the right set of skills.

Cultural Challenges

The third broad class of challenges can be classified as cultural challenges. Although people speak of the emerging "global village," its existence is often very superficial, and companies operating in the digital world still have to consider a variety of cultural differences, some of which can pose quite complex challenges.

How National Cultures Differ Hofstede (2001) defines **culture** as the "collective programming of the mind that distinguishes the members of one group or category of people from another" (p. 9). Culture is manifested in how individuals view a variety of

TABLE 2.7 Salary Differences Have Helped to Make Global Outsourcing Popular

2006 Average Salary for Experienced IT Managers in Various Countries		
Rank	Country	Pay (US$)
1	Switzerland	161,900
2	Germany	126,700
3	Denmark	116,000
4	Japan	112,300
5	Belgium	109,600
6	Ireland	108,800
7	UK	105,700
8	Hong Kong	97,600
9	Italy	93,900
10	Spain	93,200
14	**United States**	**89,100**
34	India	26,500

Source: Adapted from: www.finfacts.com.

Ethical Dilemma

Underground Gaming Economy

In the United States in 2006, real estate appreciated at a colossal rate, pricing many middle-income families out of buying a house; gasoline prices rose to a phenomenal $3.00 per gallon and up; and health care costs again spiraled out of sight. It's the real world, and those of us who live and work in it develop skills to cope.

Things in Project Entropia, a virtual world with a real cash economy, aren't much better. Colonists on Calypso must still fight off dangerous enemies, the Ped is still worth only 10 cents against the U.S. dollar, and the price of ore-rich property is rising.

Project Entropia is one of many massive multiplayer online role-playing games (MMORPGs). Other online role-playing games include but are not limited to Sony's Everquest, George Lucas's Star Wars Galaxies, Second Life, and Ultima Online. Players pay monthly subscription fees and assume virtual identities called avatars. Estimates are that more than 100 million people play worldwide, and the gaming companies report that subscriptions total over $3.6 billion a year.

In most MMORPGs, gamers slay enemies, build houses and businesses, choose professions, pick up mystical attributes, and fill their virtual bank accounts with gold and cash. Each player's avatar "lives" in the game's virtual community. A recent trend, however, is for players who do not play just for fun to play to collect virtual tools, gold, or cash and then sell the booty for real cash. The dollar amounts involved are usually relatively small, say, $70 for 10 million gold sets in Ultima Online, but there have been notable exceptions. In November 2005, for example, Jon Jacobs, a film producer from Miami, Florida, paid $100,000 for a virtual resort in Project Entropia. "I have invested in a business that offers numerous opportunities for generating revenue," Jacobs said. He pointed out that the digital resort includes 1,000 hotel rooms that could be sold for $100 each, a stadium for hosting hunting or combat competitions, and a nightclub.

The practice of buying and selling assets from MMORPGs has become so prevalent that the virtual moguls have a name: "farmers." The popular auction site eBay daily lists thousands of items taken from MMORPGs under its Internet Games category. Items for sale range from characters that have advanced to higher levels of a game to weapons, gold, and other items captured in a game.

Farming has become especially popular in China, where companies employ rows of gamers who play for up to 12 hours at a time, collecting virtual assets and ascending to the highest levels of a game—all of which the companies will sell.

Critics of this new virtual economy say that it penalizes gamers who play strictly for fun but allows those with cash to spend to advance through levels of a game they have not mastered. Others say there is nothing wrong with players buying advantages that let them play at higher levels without putting in large amounts of time.

Some game companies have banned farmers from the playing field. For example, Blizzard Entertainment, the makers of World of Warcraft, a game that boasts more than 5.5 million subscribers, has permanently banned over 1,000 users following its investigation into the selling of virtual goods. Similarly, *PC Gamer,* America's largest gaming magazine, stopped taking advertisements from companies that trade in virtual goods and characters from MMORPGs, and in early 2007, eBay banned the sale of virtual goods, such as currency or avatars.

The companies cite ethical reasons for penalizing farmers, but they also realize that farmers can eventually impact revenues, as gamers who don't buy and sell attributes refuse to play with those who do.

Sources: Jay Wrolstad, "Virtual Resort Sells for $100,000," *Newsfactor Magazine Online* (November 11, 2005), http://www.newsfactor.com/story.xhtml?story_id=39369

Elizabeth Millard, "Inside the Underground Economy of Computer Gaming," *Newsfactor Magazine Online* (January 4, 2006), http://www.newsfactor.com/story.xhtml?story_id=40592&page=2

About Entropia Universe, http://www.entropiauniverse.com/en/rich/5035.html

cultural dimensions, such as power distance, uncertainty avoidance, individualism/collectivism, masculinity/femininity, concept of time, and life focus (see Table 2.8). In essence, each nation has its own culture, which can often have important implications for companies operating in the digital world. One area where such challenges often surface is the interaction between a company's headquarters and a subsidiary in a different culture.

POWER DISTANCE. **Power distance** refers to how different societies handle the issue of human inequality and sheds light on the inherent power structure within organizations and teams. Some cultures are higher in power distance, preferring strong authority or autocracy, while other cultures are lower in power distance, fostering more collaborative teamwork and less hierarchical structures. Consequently, differences in power distance can pose serious challenges.

UNCERTAINTY AVOIDANCE. The degree of **uncertainty avoidance** helps in understanding the risk-taking nature of a culture. From an outsourcing perspective, this might result in workers from some cultures being more cautious; this can be particularly troublesome when some workers, because of high levels of uncertainty avoidance, are not eager to adopt new technologies or techniques.

INDIVIDUALISM/COLLECTIVISM. A related dimension, **individualism/collectivism**, reflects the extent to which a society values the position of an individual versus the position of a group. In societies that are collectivist, peer pressure often plays an important role in shaping group interaction and decision making. Mixing both individually and collectively oriented individuals in an outsourcing project can often cause excessive conflict if not carefully managed.

MASCULINITY/FEMININITY. Additionally, **masculinity/femininity** refers to the degree to which a society is characterized by masculine qualities, such as assertiveness, or by feminine characteristics, such as nurturance, which can have important implications in terms of user preferences for technology, how user requirements are collected, or how teams assign roles and collaborate.

CONCEPT OF TIME. The **concept of time** can also differ across cultures, with some cultures having a relatively longer-term orientation, reflecting an appreciation for future

TABLE 2.8 Critical Cultural Dimensions for Various Countries

Critical Cultural Dimensions	Countries				
	Group 1: United States, Canada, Australia	Group 2: Germany, Austria, Switzerland	Group 3: Mexico Venezuela, Peru	Group 4: Japan	Group 5: India, Hong Kong, Singapore
Power distance	Moderately low	Moderately low	Moderately high	Moderately high	High
Individualism/ collectivism	High individualistic	Moderately individualistic	Moderate to highly collectivistic	Moderately collectivistic	Moderate to highly collectivistic
Masculinity/ femininity	Moderately masculine	Moderately masculine	Moderately to highly masculine	High masculinity	Masculine
Uncertainty avoidance	Moderately weak	Moderately strong	Moderately weak	Strong	Moderately weak
Concept of time	Long term	Long term	Short term	Long term	Short term
Life focus	Quantity	Quantity	Quality	More quality than quantity	Changing from quality to quantity

Source: Verma (1997); adapted from Owens and McLaurin (1993).

rewards, perseverance, and long-term planning. On the other hand, cultures with shorter-term orientation focus on the past and the current situation.

LIFE FOCUS. A last cultural dimension, **life focus**, contrasts the extent to which a culture focuses on the *quantity* versus the *quality* of life. A quantity-of-life orientation reflects a more competitive culture that values achievements and the acquisition of material goods. A quality-of-life orientation values relationships, interdependence, and concern for others. Life focus differences can influence group development, task and role assignments, and cause difficulties in the interaction between a company's headquarters and a subsidiary in a different culture.

Other Cultural Barriers In addition to the cultural barriers mentioned by Hofstede, there are many other barriers that can pose a challenge to companies operating in the digital world, including the following:

- *Language.* Communication language and norms
- *Work Culture.* Work skills, habits, and attitudes toward work
- *Aesthetics.* Art, music, and culture
- *Education.* Attitudes toward education and literacy
- *Religion, Beliefs, and Attitudes.* Spiritual institutions and values
- *Social Organizations.* Family and social cohesiveness

Each of these cultural elements can greatly influence interaction between employees in different countries, as outlined in Table 2.9. For example, the lack of a common language can often lead to disastrous results when communicating technical information, such as user requirements or design specifications. Likewise, differences in work culture can influence the employee's interaction. For instance, Europeans typically approach a project by focusing on its beginning and incrementally moving forward until the project is concluded. Americans, on the other hand, typically look at the end first and work backward to the start (Heichler, 2000). In sum, differences in language, work culture, and other cultural elements can have serious implications for managing in the digital world.

Other Challenges of Offering Products or Services in Different Cultures Companies selling their products in foreign markets also have to consider different local cultures when deciding what to sell and how to market their products. For example,

TABLE 2.9 How Various Cultural Elements Can Affect Communication, Interaction, and Performance

Cultural Element	How It Can Impact Globalization Success
Language	Communication problems can influence efficiency, understanding, and performance.
Work culture	Different skills, work habits, and attitudes can influence performance and manpower constraints.
Aesthetics	Art, music, and dance reflect nonwork interests that can be used to enrich team communication and cohesiveness.
Education	Education level limits skill levels, technological sophistication, and infrastructure.
Religion, beliefs, and attitudes	Basic values and beliefs can influence attitudes toward work, promptness, punctuality, mutual trust, respect, and cooperation.
Social organization	Social norms of a society can influence formal and informal communication, including negotiations and job assignments.
Political life	Differing political systems can influence the delivery of supplies and equipment, human rights, legal system, and overall stability.

Source: Adapted from Verma (1997).

FIGURE 2.18

Illegally copied intellectual property is openly bought and sold in many countries.

different countries have different standards concerning what type of advertising is socially acceptable. Also, different cultures have different standards of dealing with intellectual property, such as computer software, digital music, or movies. While in most Western nations intellectual property is considered very important and is even protected by law, in other nations copying someone else's work is not seen as problematic. In fact, some cultures even regard it as flattery to copy the work of others. Thus, intellectual property infringements are common in many countries, reaching from counterfeiting Nivea Creme to mass-producing illegal copies of DVDs or computer software (see Figure 2.18). Finally, different norms and standards can cause problems for companies. For example, Wal-Mart did not consider that the standard sizes of pillowcases differed between the United States and Germany, and as a result, Wal-Mart's German stores ended up sitting on huge piles of U.S.-sized pillowcases. These and other problems eventually caused the retail giant to withdraw from the highly competitive German retail market.

Going Global: International Business Strategies in the Digital World

Before the era of globalization, most companies were solely operating in the domestic arena, conducting their activities exclusively in one country, starting from the acquisition of raw materials to the selling of final products. Although such businesses are likely to benefit from the flatteners that also spurred Globalization 3.0, **domestic companies** do not have to deal with many of the challenges brought about by globalization.

In today's digital world, the number of domestic companies is continually shrinking, with most domestic companies being relatively small (often local) businesses, such as local service providers, restaurants, farms, or retailers (e.g., independent grocery stores). Most of today's large companies, no matter if they are in car manufacturing (such as GM, Toyota, or DaimlerChrysler), insurance (Allianz or Munich Re), or consumer goods (Nestlé or Procter and Gamble), have some **international business strategy** for competing in different global markets.

e-Waste

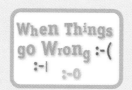

Americans bought an estimated $125 billion worth of electronics in 2005—computers, monitors, cell phones, PDAs, DVD players, microwave ovens, and so on. Electronic products contain a mix of components that contain material, such as lead, mercury, cadmium, or PVCs, which are highly toxic when incinerated or buried in a landfill. For example, a conventional computer monitor contains 4 to 8 pounds of lead, and newer LCD screens contain mercury.

Since local landfills won't take hazardous waste, what happens to electronic gadgets when consumers no longer need or want them? (Landfills don't want them, but some consumers bury them in ordinary household garbage.) Some owners hand them down to someone else or pack them away in the back of a closet or garage. Others donate the items—whether they still function or not—to a charitable organization. But maybe the donations aren't so welcome.

In 2004 alone, Goodwill Industries International Inc. was flooded with more than 23 million pounds of electronic goods, most of which were unusable. Since recycling electronics costs money, Goodwill spokesperson Christine Nyirjesy Bragale told a reporter in January 2006, "Electronic waste is becoming a costly problem for us."

Three U.S. states—California, Maine, and Maryland—have followed examples from Europe and Japan in handling electronic waste disposal in that they impose a mandatory recycling fee either on consumers or manufacturers, they require manufacturers to take back the equipment for recycling, or they place responsibility on local governments for providing recycling centers. Although federal law in the United States prevents businesses from improperly disposing of e-waste, this law does not extend to households.

Unfortunately, although the export of hazardous waste to developing countries was banned in 1992, between 50 and 80 percent of America's e-waste continues to be shipped to Third World countries, where environmental standards are less strict. So much e-waste has been deported that, in 2002, China banned its import.

To reduce the environmental impact and to facilitate recycling efforts, as of mid-2006, the EU has banned toxic ingredients, such as lead, mercury, cadmium, and so on, from electronics, appliances, lighting equipment, medical equipment, and other consumer products. Prior to the EU mandate, a sparse few companies were concerned with the production of "green" hardware. Now, however, since Europe represents about 30 percent of the world market for electronic equipment, manufacturers are rushing to comply with the EU directive.

The need for stricter regulations concerning e-waste disposal has been recognized in the United States, and in January 2006, Congress had appointed a working group to determine a course of action. Legislation could take a while, however, but in the meantime more states may decide to formulate their own legislation. Clearly, disposing properly of e-waste is a problem that needs a solution if the environment is to be protected.

Sources: http://www.intel.com/technology/mooreslaw/ index.htm

http://www.strategiy.com/inews.asp?id=20051130063030

Sherry Watkins, "E-Waste Epidemic," *Government Technology* (January 2, 2006), http://www.govtech.net/magazine/channel_story. php/97724

http://www.canada.com/topics/technology/story.html?id=e8def77a-3a8f-420b-ad29-a9e08d03fca0&k=4739&p=3

Anonymous, "Is America Exporting a Huge Environmental Problem?," *ABC News* (January 6, 2006), http://www.abcnews.go.com/2020/ Technology/story?id=1479506

http://www.wired.com/news/technology/0,57151-1.html?tw=wn_story_page_next1

http://www.cnn.com/2006/TECH/ptech/01/18/recycling.computers.ap/index.html

http://www.mercurynews.com/mld/mercurynews/news/local/states/california/peninsula/13697994.htm

http://europa.eu.int/scadplus/leg/en/lvb/l21210.htm

Such companies pursue either a multidomestic, global, or transnational strategy, depending on the degree of supply chain integration and necessary local customer responsiveness (Prahalad and Doz, 1987; Hitt, Ireland, and Hoskisson, 2005). On the one hand, businesses can benefit from global integration by utilizing economies of scale; on the other hand, a company's local subunits may benefit strongly from being able to quickly respond to changing conditions in local markets. Different

FIGURE 2.19

International business strategies.

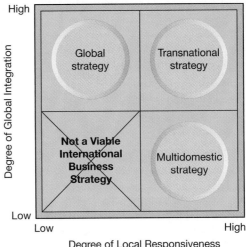

international business strategies are suited better for different situations (see Figure 2.19 and Table 2.10). In the following sections, we describe each of these various business strategies.

Multidomestic Business Strategy

The **multidomestic business strategy** is particularly suited for operations in markets differing widely. The multidomestic business strategy uses a loose federation of associated business units, each of which is rather independent in their strategic decisions. In other words, the degree of integration is very low, and the individual subunits can respond quickly to their respective market demands (Ghoshal, 1987). Multidomestic companies can thus be extremely flexible and responsive to the needs and demands of local markets, and any opportunities arising in local markets can be quickly seized. An example of a multidomestic company is the international arm of General Motors, the national subsidiaries of which produce cars that are customized to the specific local markets (e.g., Opel in Germany and Vauxhall in Great Britain). However, working in a decentralized fashion, much of the knowledge generated is retained at the local subsidiaries, and knowledge transfer between the individual subsidiaries is often limited, leading to inefficiencies and mistakes that potentially can be repeated across subsidiaries (Bartlett and Ghoshal, 1998). In sum, for companies following a multidomestic business strategy, very little data and control information flows between the home and subsidiary locations (see Figure 2.20).

TABLE 2.10 When to Use International Business Strategies

Strategy	Description	Strengths	Weaknesses	When to Use
Multidomestic	Federation of associated business units; decentralized	Ability to quickly react to local conditions	Differing product offerings limit economies of scale, and limited interunit communication limits knowledge sharing	Very heterogeneous markets
Global	Centralized organization with standardized offerings across markets	Standardized product offerings allow achieving economies of scale	Inability to react to local market conditions	Homogeneous markets
Transnational	Some aspects centralized, others decentralized; integrated network	Can achieve benefits of multidomestic and global strategies	Difficult to manage; very complex	Integrated global markets

FIGURE 2.20

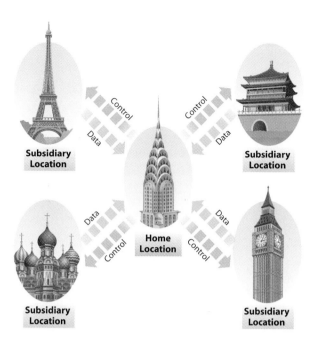

Multidomestic business strategy.

Global Business Strategy

The **global business strategy**, in contrast, works much more in a centralized fashion. Companies are using this strategy primarily to achieve economies of scale by producing identical products in large quantities for a variety of different markets. As the decisions are made at the headquarters, the organization can be characterized as a centralized hub (Bartlett and Goshal, 1998). A good example of a global strategy is Coca-Cola; while there are some products made for local tastes, the core product (Coke) is the same in all markets, and only aspects such as product advertising differ. The headquarters gives the overall strategic direction and thus has tight control of the entire company as well as the knowledge that is generated within the company. However, the need to achieve economies of scale prohibits implementation of local strategies, and thus a global company cannot react to local challenges and opportunities as quickly as multidomestic companies. Here, extensive data flows from the subsidiaries to the home location, and the home location exerts strong control on the subsidiaries (see Figure 2.21).

Transnational Business Strategy

An emerging strategy is the **transnational business strategy**. Having realized the benefits and drawbacks of multidomestic and global business strategies, companies using a transnational business strategy selectively decide which aspects of the organization should be under central control and which should be decentralized. This business strategy allows companies to leverage the flexibility offered by a decentralized organization (to be more responsive to local conditions) while at the same time reaping economies of scale enjoyed by centralization. An example of a transnational company is Unilever, which decides when to centralize and when to decentralize, depending on the products and the local markets. However, this business strategy is also the most difficult, as the company has to strike a balance between centralization and decentralization. In contrast to global organizations, where most of the resources are centralized in the companies' home countries, different resources in a transnational company can be centralized in different countries, depending on where the company can achieve the greatest returns or cost savings. Further, different decentralized resources are interdependent; this is in contrast to the other organizational forms, where there is usually one direction of the flow of resources. In a transnational company, for example, semiconductors for computer chips might be

FIGURE 2.21

Global business strategy.

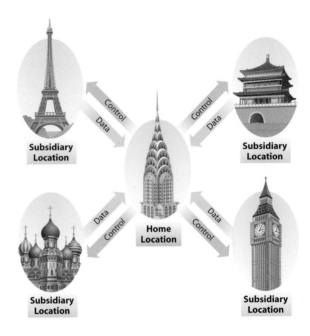

produced in a state-of-the-art factory in Dresden, Germany; shipped to a Southeast Asian country to be assembled into a final product; and then shipped back to Western Europe to be sold to an individual customer. Bartlett and Ghoshal (1998) characterize transnational companies as integrated networks, requiring a great deal of effort in terms of managing the different interdependencies, tasks, and communication among the different units. In sum, both data and control can flow in any direction, depending on the specific business process (see Figure 2.22).

Different types of information systems can best support these different organizational forms. While we will discuss global implications throughout the book, in the next section we will provide a high-level overview of information systems supporting companies operating in the digital world.

FIGURE 2.22

Transnational business strategy.

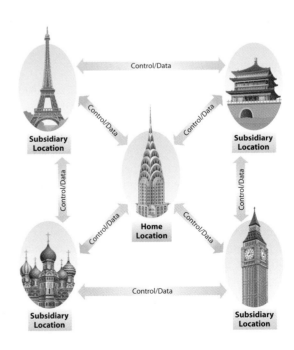

Brief Case ✪

Transnational Development

As information systems gain complexity, they often cost more for companies to maintain, especially in such areas as employee training, supply chain simplification, accounting practices, customer service, tracking customer trends and preferences, and information systems maintenance. As IS costs increase, those services become well suited to outsourcing. And since a company's bottom line is always a vital concern, if outside sources can provide IT services at less cost than providing them in-house, the decision to outsource is often a no-brainer.

Take, for example, the Wrigley Company, the world's largest manufacturer of chewing gum, including such brands as Juicy Fruit, Big Red, Doublemint, and Wrigley's Spearmint. Wrigley sells nearly half of all gum sold in the United States, and consumers in 150 countries buy Wrigley's brands.

Marketing research is considered the top priority in the Wrigley Company, including such activities as consumer preference studies, marketing trends tracking, and advertis-

ing campaign and new product testing. The company's Marketing Research Department plans and coordinates activities with European branches located in Germany, the United Kingdom, the Czech Republic, and Russia.

Wrigley's Marketing Research Department needed a single corporate marketing research database, and in 2002 the Russian Marketing Research branch initiated the development of a marketing research work flow automation system. The system was implemented first in the Moscow branch and, after a year of successful use, was also installed in the Marketing Research branches in Germany, the United Kingdom, and the Czech Republic. In the future, Wrigley plans to install the automated system in all branches globally.

Questions

1. What can companies like Wrigley learn in one market and apply in another?
2. Is Wrigley's transnational IS development approach optimal, or should a more centralized approach be used?

Sources: http://www.aplana.com/pcbase/customerinfo.asp?id=16

Operating in the Digital World Using Information Systems

Organizations use a variety of information systems strategies to manage international operations most effectively. For example, Nestlé, one of the world's largest food producers, with over 500 factories and operations in more than 70 countries, is also considered to be one of the world's most globalized companies. Firms such as Nestlé that are operating in multiple nations can pursue three distinct types of information systems strategies: (1) multinational, (2) global, and (3) transnational information systems strategies (Ramarapu and Lado, 1995) (see Table 2.11). We describe each in this section.

TABLE 2.11 Global Information Systems Strategies

IS/Business Strategy	Systems	Communications	Data Resources
Multinational	Decentralized systems	Direct communication between home office and subsidiaries	Local databases
Global	Centralized systems	Multiple networks between home office and subsidiaries	Data sharing between central home office and subsidiaries
Transnational	Distributed/shared systems; Internet-enabled applications	Enterprise-wide linkages	Common global data resources

Source: Adapted from Ramarapu and Lado (1995).

Multinational Information Systems Strategy

Multidomestic companies often pursue a **multinational information systems strategy** to support their international operations. In order to support the loose confederacy of various different local subsidiaries and the decentralized nature of the decision making, each organizational subsidiary has its own decentralized systems. Although the systems within the different business units may be integrated, there is no centralized IS structure. The communications take place primarily between the different subsidiaries and the home office; thus, there is no focus on the communication between the different subsidiaries (this is why there is only limited knowledge transfer among the subsidiaries). As the different subsidiaries are very independent, they retain the decentralized local data processing centers that are responsive to local needs and regulations and at the same time use information technology to integrate them loosely into the framework of the parent organization.

Global Information Systems Strategy

In contrast, the tightly controlled global business strategy greatly benefits from the integration achieved by a **global information systems strategy**. To achieve this, standards are introduced to enable a centralized infrastructure. As the home office coordinates most of the strategic decisions of the local subsidiaries, multiple networks between the home office and the subsidiaries are needed for both communication and data sharing. In contrast to the multinational IS strategy, data does not stay at the local subsidiaries, which reduces the potential for duplication, but at the same time introduces issues related to transborder data flows (primarily in EU countries).

Transnational Information Systems Strategy

In order to create an integrated network between the home office and the multiple local subsidiaries, transnational businesses usually pursue a **transnational information systems strategy**. In such strategy, there is much communication among the different subunits as well as between the home office and the subunits, and many systems are distributed and/or shared; in this way, a subsidiary can access the systems and resources of other subsidiaries. Similarly, key data is shared throughout the company to enable a seamless integration of processes. Much of the communication, data, and application sharing is enabled by intranet, extranet, and Web-based applications (see Chapter 5).

Industry Analysis

The Automobile Industry

Could Ford Motor Company end up as the last of Detroit's "big three" car companies to be based in the United States? This question buzzed around the automobile industry in July 2006 after billionaire Kirk Kerkorian, General Motors' (GM's) largest individual shareholder, proposed that GM merge with Japan's Nissan Motor Company and France's Renault.

Auto industry experts have claimed for years that globalization—the flattening of the world—would result in a widespread consolidation of automakers.

What is happening within the auto industry is indicative of globalization in general. A "flattened" world implies that the world is becoming more homogeneous. As the process continues, distinctions between national markets are fading and for some products may disappear entirely.

For instance, for decades manufacturers within the automobile industry have worked toward developing a "world car"—a basic car that with a few modifications can be sold all over the world. In the 1990s, three attempts were made to produce and market a world car: Honda's Accord, Ford's Mondeo/Contour, and GM's Cadillac Catera/Opel Omega. None of the models sold as well as hoped in North America, Europe, and Asia for several reasons:

- Consumers in different areas of the world have different tastes in automobiles. For example, small cab size has long been accepted in Europe, but American consumers prefer larger cabs.
- Europeans prefer steel construction over plastic, as in door panels, which are largely used in car manufacturing in the United States.
- Differences in infrastructure among countries lead to varying preferences in cars. Asians, for example, prefer smaller-sized cars that can maneuver well through narrow, crowded streets, while Americans are fond of SUVs and pickups.
- The price of gasoline varies throughout the world. Europeans think first of fuel economy when buying a car, while Americans base decisions more on a car's performance and appearance.
- Variations in regulations governing cars, such as emission standards, also vary with countries and affect car buyers' choices.

The development of a "world car" may yet be accomplished but probably not until cultural and economic conditions undergo even more globalization.

In the meantime, the automobile industry continues to move beyond geographic boundaries. Auto companies traditionally based in the United States are moving plants overseas, and foreign manufacturers are moving production facilities to the United States. Toyota, a Japanese auto company, has production plants in Alabama and West Virginia. Ford Motor Company is based in the United States but operates satellite companies in Asia and Europe. China recently bought a Brazilian auto engine manufacturing plant and transported it to China.

Another significant change in the auto industry involves sales channels. Traditionally, U.S. automakers maintain localized franchises that handle auto sales in a specific region. Now there are Internet franchises that have also created worldwide sales centers that did not previously exist.

The global marketplace has changed the automobile industry profoundly, but it has also created new opportunities. In a 2006 press interview, author David Magee of Tennessee, who has written books on the automobile industry, said of the possible GM–Renault–Nissan merger, "I couldn't have been less surprised. This is the twenty-first century."

Questions

1. How is Globalization 3.0 fueling change in the auto industry?
2. Examine how cultural differences make it difficult to create a world car.

Sources: Chuck Chandler, "Globalization: The Automobile Industry's Quest for a 'World Car' Strategy" (May 22, 2000), http://globaledge.msu.edu/NewsAndViews/views/papers/0018.pdf

Garry Emmons, "American Auto's Troubled Road," *Working Knowledge* (May 10, 2006), http://hbswk.hbs.edu/ item.jhtml?id=5290&t=innovation

Sarah A. Webster, "Future of Autos Is Global," *Detroit Free Press* (July 2, 2006), http://www.freep.com/apps/pbcs.dll/article?AID=/20060702/BUSINESS01/607020577/1014/BUSINESS

Key Points Review

1. *Define globalization, describe how it evolved over time, and describe the key drivers of globalization.* Globalization is the integration of economies throughout the world, fueled by technological progress and innovation. Over the past centuries, globalization has come a long way; starting with Columbus's discovery of America, Globalization 1.0 was fueled by power. Then, in 1800, Globalization 2.0 started, fueled mainly by a fall in transportation and telecommunications costs. Globalization 3.0, starting in 2000, was enabled by the convergence of a number of "flatteners," namely, the fall of the Berlin Wall, Netscape going public, work flow software, supply chaining, open sourcing, outsourcing, offshoring, in-sourcing, in-forming, and "the steroids." This has led to a rise in outsourcing and has helped to shape the world as we know it today.

2. *Describe the emerging opportunities for companies operating in the digital world.* Companies

operating in the digital world see a number of opportunities, many of which are enabled by Globalization 3.0. For companies, the primary opportunities are the access to new markets for their products and services as well as the access to a talented labor pool in countries with lower wages.

3. *Explain the factors companies have to consider when operating in the digital world.* In addition to the opportunities, operating in the digital world also poses a number of challenges to companies. The first broad set of challenges is of governmental nature and includes challenges related to the political system (such as market vs. planned economy or political instability), regulatory challenges, data-sharing challenges, and challenges related to Internet access and individual freedom. The next class of challenges is of geoeconomic nature. Such challenges arise due to differences in world time zones, communication reliability, and workforce quality. Further, differences in economic welfare potentially lead to challenges, both for companies and for countries. The final set of challenges relate to national cultural differences, including differences in power distance, uncertainty avoidance, individualism/collectivism, masculinity/femininity, concept of time, and life focus as well as differences in language, education, and religion. Finally, companies face various challenges when offering products or services in many countries, depending on what is considered a socially acceptable product or advertisement.

4. *Describe international business and information system strategies used by companies operating in the digital world.* Companies operating in the digital world can use three different business strategies. As it can quickly respond to changing local conditions, the multidomestic business strategy is best suited for heterogeneous markets and includes having a decentralized federation of loosely associated business units in different countries. The global business strategy includes having a centralized organization to offer standardized products in different markets. This helps to achieve economies of scale and is best suited for homogeneous markets. The transnational business strategy is very well suited for operating in the digital world, as it combines the benefits of the multidomestic and the global business strategies by enabling economies of scale while being responsive to local market conditions. In a transnational business strategy, some aspects of the company are centralized, while others are decentralized. When operating in the digital world, multidomestic companies often pursue a multinational information systems strategy. A multinational IS strategy is characterized by decentralized systems and very limited data sharing. In contrast, global organizations pursuing a global business strategy often utilize a global IS strategy, with very centralized systems, and much data flows from the subsidiaries to the headquarters. Finally, transnational companies use a transnational IS strategy, which depends on distributed systems, increased communication between the headquarters and the subsidiaries as well as between the subsidiaries, and common access to critical data. Transnational information systems are primarily enabled by intranets, extranets, and the Internet.

Key Terms

concept of time   66

culture   64

domestic company   68

embargoes   60

export regulations   60

geoeconomic   62

global business strategy   71

global information systems strategy   75

globalization   43

Globalization 1.0   43

Globalization 2.0   44

Globalization 3.0   44

individualism/collectivism   66

in-forming   53

in-sourcing   51

international business strategy   68

life focus   67

maquiladoras   56

masculinity/femininity   66

multidomestic business strategy   70

multinational information systems strategy   75

offshoring   51

power distance   66

quotas   61

tariffs   60

transborder data flows   61

transnational business strategy   71

transnational information systems strategy   75

uncertainty avoidance   66

wiki   50

work flow software   48

Review Questions

1. List the 10 factors that led to Globalization 3.0.
2. How did the fall of the Berlin Wall flatten the world according to Friedman?
3. Describe work flow software. How did this technology drive the flattening of the world?
4. What is the process of setting up entire factories in China in order to produce goods at a fraction of the cost? How does this drive the flattening of the world?
5. Describe in-sourcing and provide examples of how organizations use in-sourcing.
6. List and describe several reasons why companies are choosing to outsource business activities.
7. List and contrast several challenges of operating in the digital world.
8. Explain the concept of geoeconomic challenges and how organizations can overcome these challenges.
9. What is meant by transborder data flows, and why is this a concern?
10. Define culture and describe how it affects globalization.
11. List and describe several ways in which cultures differ.
12. Describe the multidomestic business strategy and how it affects the flow of control information.
13. Describe and contrast the multidomestic, global, and transnational information systems strategies.

Self-Study Questions

Visit the Interactive Study Guide on the text Web site for additional Self-Study Questions: **www.prenhall.com/Jessup**.

1. What stage of globalization started with expansion of trade to India, where the horse and wind and in later stages steam were the primary drivers?
   A. Globalization 0.5
   B. Globalization 1.0
   C. Globalization 2.0
   D. Globalization 3.0
2. The release of the Netscape Web browser had the following effects on the flattening of the world *except*:
   A. setting the standard for Web browsing
   B. providing easy access to the Internet
   C. providing integrated e-mail
   D. launching the World Wide Web
3. Which of the following is *not* considered a world flattener by Friedman?
   A. open sourcing
   B. supply chaining
   C. in-forming
   D. customer service software
4. Which of the following is *not* consisted open-source software:
   A. Microsoft Office
   B. Apache
   C. Firefox
   D. Linux
5. The assembly plants on the Mexican side of the U.S.–Mexican border that mass-produce goods for the U.S. market are called _____.
   A. Mexicanizations
   B. maquiladoras
   C. Mexcaias
   D. gringoias

6. Embargoes are considered which part of the following challenges operating in the digital world?
   A. regulatory
   B. data sharing
   C. political system
   D. governmental changes
7. One of the geoeconomic challenges that videoconferencing *cannot* resolve is _____.
   A. time zone challenges
   B. infrastructure challenges
   C. data-sharing challenges
   D. cultural challenges
8. Which of the cultural dimensions is described as "the extent to which a culture focuses on quantity versus quality of life"?
   A. concept of time
   B. uncertainty avoidance
   C. life focus
   D. work culture
9. _____ reflects the extent to which a society values the position of an individual versus the position of a group.
   A. masculinity/femininity
   B. uncertainty avoidance
   C. individualism/collectivism
   D. life focus
10. What emerging strategy do companies use when deciding which aspect should be under central control and which should be decentralized?
    A. global business strategy
    B. transnational business strategy
    C. multidomestic business strategy
    D. operational business strategy

Answers are on page 79.

Problems and Exercises

1. Match the following terms to the appropriate definitions:
   i. transnational business strategy
   ii. multidomestic business strategy
   iii. in-forming
   iv. Globalization 3.0
   v. quotas
   vi. Maquiladoras
   vii. geoeconomic
   viii. uncertainty avoidance
   ix. culture
   x. embargoes
      a. Collective programming of the mind that distinguishes the members of one group or category of people from another
      b. Assembly plants located on the Mexican side of the U.S.-Mexican border; utilized mainly to take advantage of lower wages and less stringent regulations
      c. Began with individuals and small groups from virtually every nation to shrink the world from "size small to size tiny"
      d. An international business strategy employed to be flexible and responsive to needs and demands of heterogenous local markets
      e. The combination of economic and political factors that influence a region
      f. Using the Internet to access information to enable people to get a more complete picture of what is happening in the world
      g. Are typically limiting (or prohibiting) trade with one particular country
      h. The cultural characteristic that helps in understanding the risk-taking nature of a culture
      i. The act of foreign governments to limit certain product's imports
      j. Allows companies to leverage the flexibility offered by a decentralized organization while at the same time reaping economies of scale enjoyed by centralization

2. Visit the Go4Customers Web site (www. go4customer .com). What does this company do? Where are they located? Who are Go4Customers customers? Give an example of how a U.S. company would use go4customer.

3. Visit Wal-Mart China (www.wal-martchina/english/). Compare and contrast your local Wal-Mart with Wal-Mart China. Are the items sold in China the same as your local Wal-Mart? How does Wal-Mart China differ from your Wal-Mart? Explain your answer.

4. Interview an IS professional and document their views on outsourcing. Specifically, find out if his or her company is using outsourcing; if so, what do they outsource and why? If not, why not? If they utilize outsourcing, have them critique its quality, cost, and so on.

5. What search engine do you use? Compare and contrast your search engine preference with one of the other big search engines available (Google.com, msn.com, yahoo.com). How would these search engines be used to create your "own personal supply chain"?

6. What digital news media do you use to get your news? According to this textbook's definitions, are you in-forming? If you are in-forming, describe how. What other ways could you in-form?

7. What are some examples of key technologies that utilize "steroids"? Using the technology definition provided by this textbook, how do you use technological steroids in your everyday life?

8. Should the U.S. government allow companies to use outsourcing if qualified U.S. citizens are willing and able to do a job? Should the government regulate the amount that can be outsourced by any company? Why or why not?

9. Work flow software allows an organization to move documents and/or tasks through a work process. Using your own experiences and observations, either professionally or personally, describe how the work flow software worked.

10. As outlined in the chapter, UPS provides in-sourcing services for many businesses. Visit www.ups.com and identify some examples of UPS providing in-sourcing services and include a listing of some of UPS's in-sourcing customers.

11. Interview an IS professional regarding some possible uses for open-source software. Is open-source software being used in the IS professional's organization? If so, document what software they use and how it is working; if not, document why they are not using open source software.

12. List 10 reasons why you would (or would not) be a good global manager.

13. Global outsourcing appears to be here to stay. Use the Web to identify a company who is providing low-cost labor from some less developed part of the world. Provide a short report that explains who they are, where they are located, who their customers are, what services and capabilities they provide, how long they have been in business, and any other interesting information you can find in your research.

14. Examine Table 2.8 and rate yourself for each of the critical cultural dimensions. Do your ratings match those of your country in every instance? If so, why do you think this occurred? If not, why?

15. Download and use the open source Firefox Web browser (www.mozilla.com/firefox/) and compare and rank its features against those of Microsoft Internet Explorer or Netscape Navigator. Which do you prefer and why?

Application Exercises

The existing data files referenced in these exercises are available on the Student Companion Web site: **www.prenhall.com/Jessup**.

 Spreadsheet Application: Building a Business Case for Online Ticketing

On graduation, you were hired by Campus Travel to assist in creating an infrastructure to sell travel services over the Internet. One aspect of this online system is a module to handle travel-related requests so that the customers can see whether a particular product of service is available. In order to do this, you will have to be able to manipulate data to allow for management to see what is really going on. To do so, your manager has asked for the following:

1. Sort the data by date, then by sales.
   a. Open the file sortdata.csv.
   b. Highlight all data.
   c. Select sort from the "Data" menu.
   d. Sort by "Date Sold," then by "Salesperson." Print out a copy of each for your instructor.

2. Count the number of Tickets sold in the provided table.
   a. In cell H3, enter the countif formula to count the number of tickets each salesperson has sold. Hint: Use "=countif(b2:b36,g3)."
   b. Copy cell h3 down to the other salespeople.
   c. Sum the total number of tickets sold in the appropriate field.

 Database Application: Locating Campus Travel Agencies

Campus Travel is now trying to market toward specific customers in their frequent flier database. This includes targeting customers from certain airlines that reside in certain areas. You have been asked to import the frequent flier database and then to filter records accordingly. To do so, you must complete the following:

1. Open the file frequentflier.mdb.
2. Use "filter by selection" to filter records from customers in Pullman.
3. Filter customers by "Delta Airlines."

Team Work Exercise: Becoming a Global Leader

Many universities believe, rightfully so, that they have a duty to help internationalize students through a variety of events, courses, and experiences in order to help prepare students for managing in the digital world. Work in teams of four or five students and compile a list of all the different things you feel your school is doing to help students develop into better global leaders.

Answers to the Self-Study Questions

1. B, p. 43   2. D, p. 45   3. D, p. 46   4. A, p. 50   5. B, p. 56   6. A, p. 60   7. A, p. 62
8. C, p. 67   9. C, p. 66   10. B, p. 71

case ❶

Global Picture Sharing with Flickr

Has there been a wedding, birth, confirmation, graduation, one-hundredth birthday celebration, or other commemorative event in your family lately? Would you like to see the photos your sister, Uncle Walt, and Grandma Mary took at the event? Invite everyone who attended to post their photos on Flickr.com—one of the easiest and most popular means of sharing photos online.

Flickr.com was developed by Ludicorp, a Vancouver, Canada–based company founded in 2002 and launched online in 2004. Yahoo! purchased Flickr in 2005. In just over a year after Flickr's launch, the site had over 350,000 members, who had collectively uploaded 31 million images.

Flickr didn't invent online photo sharing, but the tools members can use to navigate the photos on the site are unique. "Tags" let photo owners and viewers label photos to prescribe a category that makes them easier to find. For example, popular tags include summer, winter, cute, Europe, dog, cat, and so on. Flickr takes the tag concept further with clustering, a better way to explore photos through tags. Key in "summer beach vacations," for instance, and you can view a page of clustered photos with just those tags. Clustering has resulted in such far-out photo categories as confusing street signs, dogs' noses, Halloween costumes, margaritas, and mannequins.

Flickr sees photo sharing and the use of tags as a social process users call "folksonomy." That is, since viewers can add comments to photos, there is level of involvement similar to a social gathering. For a person who is browsing through a set of photos, the notes on the photos tell little stories, as if that person were sitting

by the photographer, who is explaining the photo.

Flickr photo viewers can also rate a photo according to "interestingness." Each calendar day, a few highly valued "interestingness" photos are posted to a common page for viewer exploration.

Flickr also allows for basic photo manipulation such as rotation, ordering prints, sending to a group of people, adding to a blog, deleting, and so on. Photos can be open for everyone everywhere to view, or viewing can be restricted to one's friends and family.

User space on Flickr is unlimited; however, there is a restriction based on the bandwidth used per month. (For only a few dollars per month, there are no bandwidth restrictions.)

Since Flickr's basic photo-sharing service is free, revenue for the company is based on Yahoo!-placed ads on Flickr

Web pages. Photographers who post images on the Flickr site, however, are free to sell their photos. The legal aspects of copyright are handled by a license called the "creative commons." This license has many different levels and copyright protection but is primarily for not-for-profit use of a user's photographs. Flickr offers a simple interface that allows photographers to choose a license for protecting copyright.

For programming enthusiasts, Flickr has released all application program interfaces (APIs) for public use. For example, programmers have used the APIs to develop uploading applications for the Mac, Windows, camera phones, and other devices.

The worldwide popularity of Flickr is another way in which information systems are fueling a flatter world.

Questions

1. Why do you think Flickr has been so popular throughout the world?
2. What lessons could a Web site for a local business learn from Flickr?
3. How do Web sites like Flickr act to increase globalization?

Sources: Brad Stone, "Photos for the Masses," *MSNBC-Newsweek* (March 18, 2004), http://www.msnbc.msn.com/id/7160855/site/newsweek/

Anonymous, "The New New Things," *Flickr Blog* (August 1, 2005), http://blog.flickr.com/ flickrblog/2005/08/the_new_new_thi.html

Daniel Terdiman, "New Flickr Tools Rein in Photo Chaos" (August 2, 2005), http://news.com.com/Shedding+light+on+Flickr/2100-1025_3-5997943.html

http://news.com.com/Tagging+gives+Web+a+human+meaning/2009-1025_3-5944502.html

case

e-Enabling the Air Transport Industry: Globalization of the Airline Industry

In its early years, airlines were primarily carriers of airmail, and their primary customers were governments, and it was only after World War II that passenger airlines really took off. As many pioneering airlines were state owned, the air transport industry grew to be heavily regulated, for example, in terms of the route network, pricing structures, or other operational requirements. Most of these regulations stayed in place until the late 1970s, when the U.S. government, as well as other countries, started deregulating the air transport industry, shifting airline ownership patterns from government funded to primarily privately owned.

This opened up the market for a large number of new entrants, especially for carriers in the low-cost niche.

Suddenly, both new entrants and established airlines faced a new competitive environment and had to reduce operating costs in order to survive. However, it was not only established airlines such as Pan Am or TWA that struggled for survival; a large number of new entrants to the air transport industry also had to file for bankruptcy shortly after beginning service. Contributing to this is the highly cyclical nature of the air transport industry; historically, four or five poor years were followed by five or six good years

for the industry, and many new entrants could not survive periods of stagnation or decline. The most recent downturn following the terrorist attacks of September 11, 2001, has imposed extreme hardships for many airlines. As a result, many airlines went out of business or were consolidated within stronger competition; likewise, aircraft manufacturers such as Boeing and Airbus faced a slump in new aircraft orders. In fact, many new aircraft scheduled to be delivered in the months after 9/11 were flown directly to aircraft "boneyards" in the southwestern United States to be stored indefinitely, never having transported a single passenger.

However, while the U.S. air transport industry has seen a massive downturn, nations such as India and China have seen tremendous economic growth, making air travel accessible to vast amounts of people. For example, in the past few years, India has seen a number of low-cost carriers such as Kingfisher Airlines enter the domestic market, making air travel more affordable. As a result, the Indian air transport industry has seen unprecedented growth rates, with an increase in air travel of more than 20 percent in the 2005–2006 fiscal year. For aircraft manufacturers, this translates into formidable economic opportunities; recently, Boeing adjusted its 20-year market forecast for new commercial airplanes in India to $35 billion, up from $25 billion. Similarly, Boeing predicts an annual growth rate of almost 9 percent for the Chinese market, a growth rate that cannot be achieved in most Western markets because of the maturity of the air transport industry (the growth rate of the U.S. market is only about 3.5 percent). While the Chinese market is currently only one-sixth the size of the U.S. market, Boeing estimates that the Chinese domestic market will reach half the size of the U.S. market within the next 20 years.

Given the rise of these markets, it is no surprise that large international airline manufacturers such as Boeing or Airbus are competing fiercely for new aircraft orders. In markets such as India or China, these manufacturers have largely been successful; in other markets, the products offered may not meet local needs. For example, many Russian domestic carriers rely on a fleet of legacy Russian aircraft that can cope with infrastructure issues such as snow-covered gravel runways in remote destinations or lacking ground infrastructure for handling luggage or passengers (see Figure 2.22). On the other hand, even late-model aircraft built by the traditional Russian manufacturers Ilyushin or Tupolev have not been received too well by the market (especially outside the former Soviet Union), despite being cheaper than their Western counterparts, partly because of factors such as excessive noise levels. In an attempt to remain an aviation superpower, Russia recently decided to merge the country's six largest aircraft manufacturers into a single, state-controlled holding named United Aircraft Corporation. For Boeing and Airbus, who already employ several hundred Russian engineers in their design offices in Moscow, this is good news. First, the newly formed holding has announced its intent to specialize in a smaller, regional jet, thus reducing the competition in the market for long-range passenger jets; the Russian airline Aeroflot now has to choose between Boeing and Airbus as their supplier (e.g., a recent Aeroflot order was estimated at $3 billion for 22 to 23 aircraft). Second, both Boeing and Airbus hope to draw on the large talent pool (especially in the areas of aeronautical engineering and design) that may leave the former Russian aircraft manufacturers after the creation of the state controlled holding.

Although the opening of new markets may seem promising for airline

Airlines serving remote destinations are facing different infrastructure issues.

start-ups and aircraft manufacturers alike, there are still hurdles to overcome. For example, even though China and India's combined population is about 2.4 billion people, the number of people actually able to afford air travel remains very small. Further, for many low-cost carriers, it is impossible to directly copy the business models of successful North American or European no-frills airlines such as Southwest Airlines, Ryanair, or EasyJet. For example, low-cost carriers in the United States or Europe can reduce operating costs tremendously by bypassing the traditional distribution infrastructure; in fact, tickets for many of such airlines are not even available in traditional travel agencies, and travelers have to turn to the airlines' Web sites in order to purchase a ticket. In India or China, however, such cost cutting would mean excluding large segments of potential customers from ever purchasing a ticket because of the low levels of Internet penetration and widespread concerns regarding the security of online transactions.

Questions

1. List the different ways aircraft manufacturers can benefit from globalization. How can information systems help to reap the benefits from globalization?
2. Several emerging countries have seen tremendous growth in air travel. Do you think this growth is sustainable? Why or why not?
3. Most aircraft manufacturers produce the same product for markets across the globe. Should such companies adopt a different international business strategy? What type of international business strategy would you recommend for airplane manufacturers?

Sources: http://www.boeing.com/commercial/cmo/regions.html

A. E. Kramer, "Russian Aircraft Industry Seeks Revival through Merger," *New York Times,* February 22, 2006, C-1

Times of India, "Global Players Vie for Indian Sky" (July 19, 2006), http://timesofindia.indiatimes.com/articleshow/1778998.cms

chapter 3

Valuing Information Systems Investments

preview > This chapter will examine how organizations evaluate information systems investments and how these investments can be used strategically, enabling firms to gain or sustain competitive advantage over their rivals. As described in Chapter 1—Managing in the Digital World, a firm has competitive advantage over rival firms when it can do something better, faster, more economically, or uniquely. We will show why it is vital but sometimes difficult for people to determine the value of an information systems investment. Presenting the "case" for an information system is necessary for making good investment decisions; these decisions are particularly difficult given the pace of technological innovations. After reading this chapter, you will be able to do the following:

1. Discuss how organizations can use information systems for automation, organizational learning, and strategic advantage.

2. Describe how to formulate and present the business case for an information system.

3. Explain why and how companies are continually looking for innovative ways to use information systems for competitive advantage.

In this chapter, we begin by examining how organizations can gain the greatest value from their information systems investments. We then describe what it means to make the business case and examine several factors that must be identified and considered when building a successful business case. Finally, we talk about the continual need to find innovative ways to succeed with and through information systems.

Managing in the Digital World: TiVo

"You've got a life. TiVo gets it." With that catchy motto, in 1999 TiVo Incorporated introduced a service that gave users unprecedented control over television viewing. Hate to miss that football game for your sister's wedding? TiVo will record it for you, and you can watch it at your convenience. Are there certain shows you always have to miss because you work late hours? TiVo solves the problem again. On the TiVo Web site, the service describes itself: "Your TiVo® box, powered by the amazing TiVo® service, automatically finds and digitally records all of your favorite shows, every time they're on. Every episode of your favorite series. Every Coppola movie. Every home improvement program. Even Dora cartoons! Whatever you choose. All while you're out living life. Plus, only TiVo lets you watch your favorite shows any time, anywhere."

Mike Ramsay and Jim Barton developed their TiVo business plan in 1997. The first TiVo "boxes" shipped to customers in 1999. A 2006 subscriber to TiVo's service got the box, ranging from the basic model for free that records up to 80 hours of TV, through models that could record two shows at once priced at $30 and $130, up to the $180 model that included a 40-hour TiVo box, DVD player, and DVD burner. Monthly subscription fees ranged from $16.95 to $19.95 and a three-year prepay option was also available. The subscription service allows users to select shows to record without knowing scheduled times.

TiVo is basically a simple computer with a hard drive recorder that incorporates the following capabilities:

- Automatically record your favorite shows whenever they are on; works with cable, satellite dish, or antenna
- A search engine to find and automatically record the shows that match your interests (by title, actor, director, category, and even key word)
- Easy home networking features that enable online services like Podcasts, Yahoo! Weather and Traffic, and local movie listings and tickets from Fandango
- Easy-to-use to-go features that let you transfer shows to your laptop or portable device or easily burn them to DVD
- Scheduling last-minute shows from the Web

TiVo makes TV watching an interactive experience in that you can pause the action if the phone rings, answer the phone, and then either return to the show exactly where you left off or fast-forward to the story where it is when you return. You can also do instant replay without missing a moment of the action.

The internal architecture of a TiVo box consists of a microprocessor, a video encoder/decoder chip, and an internal hard drive. The hard drive's capacity initially was

FIGURE 3.1

TiVo allows consumers to watch television programming on their time schedule.

13 to 60 GB, which has steadily increased over the years to 250 GB. The new TiVo models have the capability to record high-definition TV, record from two channels simultaneously, burn DVDs of the content of the internal hard drive, and connect to Ethernet and wireless networks. Licensed manufacturers produce all the hardware, and TiVo provides the software that runs the hardware. The software is a Linux-based operating system and has frequent updates.

The variety of selections available to users include the following:

- You can select a genre of movies, such as comedy, mystery, or romance, and request that your TiVo record them.
- You can select only those shows for recording that have your favorite actor.
- You can select specific types of shows that have your favorite actor.
- You can drill down selections to include one person or item, such as recipes for asparagus.
- In addition, if you connect the TiVo box to your home computer network, you can play music from your computer on your TiVo system.

- You can view photos stored on your computer using TiVo. They are displayed on the TV screen, so everyone does not have to crowd around the computer to see photos.

TiVo has recently launched on online service called TiVo Central, which allows users to schedule the recording of any program by accessing the Internet from any location, regardless of the location of the TiVo box.

As with any successful new technology, other companies have imitated TiVo. Several cable TV companies offer digital video recorders (DVRs) to customers that can record programs for later viewing. To date, however, the competition does not offer the wide variety of services TiVo offers.

Rivalry affected TiVo's customer base, however, forcing the company to change its marketing plan accordingly. For example, TiVo no longer charges for the cost of the basic TiVo box with remote control—the price is included in the monthly subscription fee. TiVo has also joined with Comcast Cable Company to provide service to their customers. And in March 2006, TiVo struck a deal with Verizon Wireless that allowed Verizon cell phone users to program their TiVo recorders from their cell phones. In another venture called TiVoToGo, TiVo is providing software to users that will let them move recorded programming from the TiVo recorder to laptop computers. Furthermore, in the future TiVo may add an advertisement display feature since marketers have complained that TiVo users can fast-forward to skip ads. (This feature will undoubtedly raise the ire of some TiVo customers.)

TiVo announced a new service in March 2006 called KidZone, where parents could look for shows appropriate for their children and then separate that content from recorded adult shows.

Clearly, TiVo will continue innovating and changing its services to meet customer needs and preferences.

After reading this chapter, you will be able to answer the following:

1. What would your "business case" be to convince your family or roommates to purchase TiVo?
2. In what way was TiVo a disruptive innovation?
3. How would you forecast the future of TiVo in regard to the advent of on-demand video where any type of video content is available at any time on any device?

Sources:

http://en.wikipedia.org/wiki/TiVo

Margarite Reardon, "TV Looks to Verizon Phones for TV Recording," *CNet News* (March 7, 2006), http://news.com.com/TiVo+looks+to+Verizon+phones+for+TV+recording/2100-1039_3-6046759.html

http://news.com.com/Love+in+the+time+of+TiVo/2100-1041_3-6039433.html

http://www.tivo.com

Valuing Information Systems

In Chapter 1, we introduced the notion that information systems can have strategic value to an organization. Here, we describe three ways to use an information system: for automating, for organizational learning, and for achieving strategy (see Figure 3.2). These three activities are not necessarily mutually exclusive, but we believe that each is progressively more useful to the firm and thus adds more value to the business. In the final category, information systems are used to support a firm's strategy and to enable a firm to gain or sustain competitive advantage over rivals.

Information Systems for Automating: Doing Things Faster

Someone with an **automating** perspective thinks of technology as a way to help complete a task within an organization faster, more cheaply, and perhaps with greater accuracy and/or consistency. Let us look at a typical example. A person with an automating mentality would take a loan application screening process and automate it by inputting the loan applications into a computer database so that those involved in decision making for the loans could process the applications faster, more easily, and with fewer errors. Such a system might also enable customers to complete the loan application online. A transition from a manual to an automated loan application process might enable the organization to deploy employees more efficiently, leading to even more cost savings.

To illustrate the benefits of automating with an information system, in Table 3.1 we compare three different loan application processes. In the first example, everything is done by hand. In the second example, a technology-supported process, potential customers fill out applications by hand, and then an employee inputs them into a computer system. The third example is a completely automated process in which potential customers input loan applications directly online via the Web, and then the system automatically receives these applications into a database and processes them.

The real-time savings with the fully automated system come into play with the applications for loans under $250,000, which typically comprise the bulk of applications received. Conversely, one common thread across all three scenarios is that it takes the executive committee over two full weeks to make decisions on applications for loans over $250,000. Automation can do only so much.

Although many significant gains from computing in organizations have come from automating previously manual processes, computing solely for automation is a bit short-sighted. In the next section, we will explain how technology can be used more effectively.

Information Systems for Organizational Learning: Doing Things Better

We can also use information systems to learn and improve. Shoshana Zuboff (1988) described this as **informating**. Zuboff explained that a technology informates when it provides information about its operation and the underlying work process that it supports. The system helps us not only to automate a business process but also to learn to improve the day-to-day activities within that process.

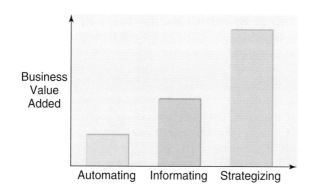

FIGURE 3.2

The business value added from automating, learning, and supporting strategy with IS.

TABLE 3.1 Activities Involved Under Three Different Loan Application Processes and The Average Time for Each Activity

Primary Activities of Loan Processing	Manual Loan Process (Time)	Technology-Supported Process (Time)	Fully Automated Process (Time)
1. Complete and submit loan application	Customer takes the application home, completes it, returns it (1.5 days)	Customer takes the application home, completes it, returns it (1.5 days)	Customer fills out application from home via the Web (1 hour)
2. Check application for errors	Employee does this in batches (2.5 days)	Employee does this in batches (2.5 days)	Computer does this as it is being completed (3.5 seconds)
3. Input data from application into information system	Applications kept in paper form, although there is handling time involved (1 hour)	Employee does this in batches (2.5 days)	Done as part of the online application process (no extra time needed)
4. Assess loan applications under $250,000 to determine whether to fund them	Employee does this completely by hand (15 days)	Employee does this with the help of the computer (1 hour)	Computer does this automatically (1 second)
5. Committee decides on any loan over $250,000	(15 days)	(15 days)	(15 days)
6. Applicant notified	Employee generates letters manually in batches (1 week)	Employee generates letters with the help of the computer (1 day)	System notifies applicant via e-mail (3.5 seconds)
Total Time:	Anywhere from **25 to 40 days**, depending on size of loan	Anywhere from **5 to 20 days**, depending on size of loan	Anywhere from **1 hour to 15 days**, depending on size of loan

Note that many online loan application services can now give you instant "tentative" approval pending verification of data you report in your online application. Also, only some of the activities within the manual and technology-supported processes can occur in parallel.

The learning mentality builds on the automating mentality because it recognizes that information systems can be used as a vehicle for **organizational learning**—the ability of an organization to learn from past behavior and information, improving as a result—and change as well as for automation. In a 1993 *Harvard Business Review* article, David Garvin described a **learning organization** as one that is "skilled at creating, acquiring, and transferring knowledge, and at modifying its behavior to reflect new knowledge and insights."

To illustrate a learning mentality, let us think again about our loan processing example. Figure 3.3 shows how a computer-based loan processing system tracks types of loan applications by date, month, and season. The manager easily sees the trends and can plan for the timely ordering of blank application forms and the staffing and training of personnel in the loan department. The manager can also more efficiently manage the funds used to fulfill loans.

A learning approach allows people to track and learn about the types of applications filed by certain types of people at certain times of the year (e.g., more auto loan applications in the fall, mostly from men in their twenties and thirties), the patterns of the loan decisions made, or the subsequent performance of those loans. This new system creates data about the underlying business process that can be used to better monitor, control, and change that process. In other words, you learn from this information system about loan applications and approvals; as a result, you can do a better job at evaluating loan applications.

A combined automating and learning approach, in the long run, is more effective than an automating approach alone. If the underlying business process supported by technology is inherently flawed, a learning use of the technology might help you detect the problems with the process and change it. For instance, in our loan processing example, a learning use of technology may help us uncover a pattern among the accepted loans that enables us to distinguish between low- and high-performing loans over their lives and subsequently to change the criteria for loan acceptance.

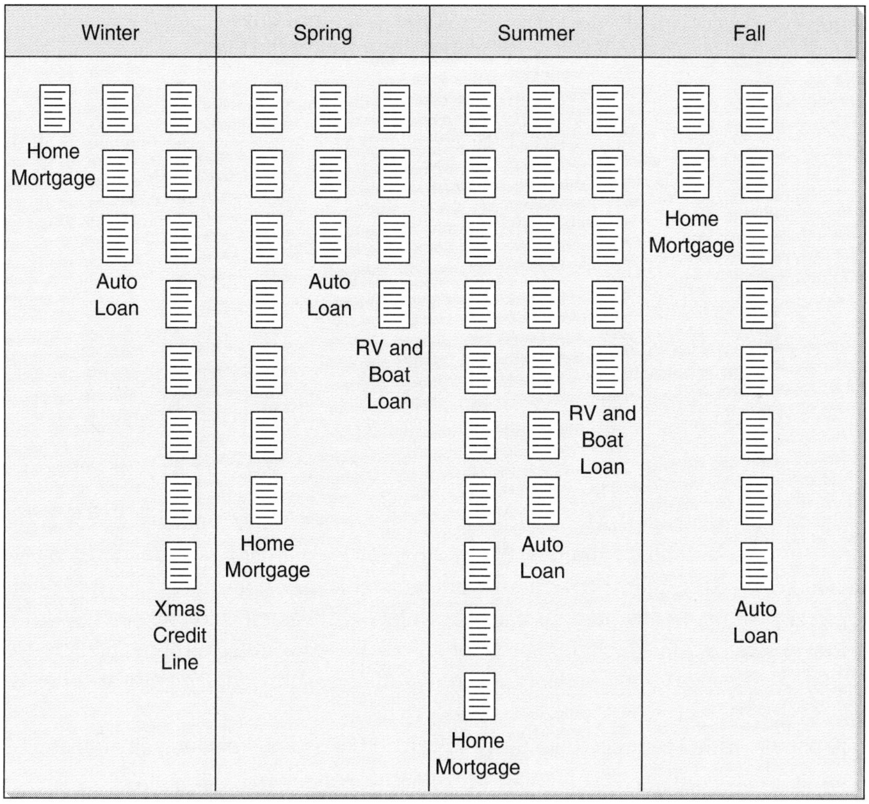

Winter	Spring	Summer	Fall

FIGURE 3.3

A computer-based loan processing system tells the bank manager which types of loans are highest during each season.

If, however, the underlying business process is bad and you are using technology only for automating (i.e., you would not uncover the data that would tell you this process is bad), you are more likely to continue with a flawed or less-than-optimal business process. In fact, such an automating use of technology may mask the process problems.

With a bad underlying set of loan acceptance criteria (e.g., rules that would allow you to approve a loan for someone who had a high level of debt as long as they had not been late on any payments recently), a person might manually review four applications in a day and, because of the problematic criteria used, inadvertently accept on average two "bad" applications per week. If you automated the same faulty process, with no learning aspects built in, the system might help a person review 12 applications per day, with six "bad" applications accepted per week on average. The technology would serve only to magnify the existing business problems. Without learning, it is more difficult to uncover bad business processes underlying the information system.

Information Systems for Supporting Strategy: Doing Things Smarter

Using information systems to automate or improve processes has advantages, as described previously. In most cases, however, the best way to use an information system is to support the organization's strategy in a way that enables the firm to gain or sustain competitive advantage over rivals. To understand why, think about **organizational strategy**—a firm's plan to accomplish its mission and goals as well as to gain or sustain competitive advantage over rivals—and how it relates to information systems. When senior managers conduct **strategic planning**, they form a vision of where the organization needs to head, convert that vision into measurable objectives and performance targets, and craft a strategy to achieve the desired results. In Figure 3.4, we show some common organizational strategies. An organization might decide to pursue a **low-cost leadership strategy**, as do Wal-Mart and Dell, by which it offers the best prices in its industry on its goods and/or services. Alternatively, an organization might decide to pursue a **differentiation strategy**, as do

FIGURE 3.4

Five general types of
organizational strategy: broad
differentiation, focused
differentiation, focused low-cost,
overall low-cost leadership, and
best-cost provider.

Source: Courtesy A. A. Thompson
and A. J. Strickland III, *Strategic
Management: Concepts and Cases,*
8th ed. (Homewood, Ill.: Richard D.
Irwin, 1995).

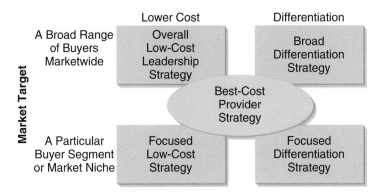

Porsche, Nordstrom, and IBM, by which it tries to provide better products or services than its competitors. A company might aim that differentiation broadly at many different types of consumers, or it might focus on a particular segment of consumers, as Apple did for many years with its focus on high-quality computers for home and educational markets. Still other organizations might pursue a middle-of-the-road strategy, following a **best-cost provider strategy**, offering products or services of reasonably good quality at competitive prices, as does Target.

A person with a strategic mentality toward information systems goes beyond mere automating and learning and instead tries to find ways to use information systems to achieve the organization's chosen strategy. This individual wants the benefits of automating and learning but also looks for some strategic, competitive advantage from the system. In fact, in today's business environment, if a proposed information system isn't going to clearly deliver some strategic value (i.e., help to improve the business so that it can compete better) while also helping people to work smarter and saving money in the process, then it isn't likely to be funded.

Sources of Competitive Advantage

How do business firms typically get competitive advantage? An organization has competitive advantage whenever it has an edge over rivals in attracting customers and defending against competitive forces (Porter, 1985, 2001). In order to be successful, a business must

Ethical Dilemma ▶

Protect Company Profits or Employees?

Consider the following scenario. Dave, a human resources manager at ACME, Inc., has been asked for his input concerning a new payroll processing system the company's information systems department is designing. Dave knows that user input is important to successful information systems development, and he hopes to be helpful to the IS development staff.

As he evaluates the new payroll processing system, Dave can see that it will save the company much money and will reduce errors, but it will also eliminate many jobs—jobs that his friends and colleagues need to support their families. Which decision would be most ethical for Dave: (1) to recommend installation and implementation of the new payroll processing system or (2) to find as much fault as he can with the new system so that workers he knows and likes can keep their jobs?

have a clear vision, one that focuses investments in resources such as information systems and technologies to help achieve competitive advantage. Some sources of competitive advantage include the following:

- Having the best-made product on the market
- Delivering superior customer service
- Achieving lower costs than rivals
- Having a proprietary manufacturing technology
- Having shorter lead times in developing and testing new products
- Having a well-known brand name and reputation
- Giving customers more value for their money

Companies can gain or sustain each of these sources of competitive advantage by effectively using information systems. Returning to our loan example, a person with a strategic view of information systems would choose a computer-based loan application process because it can help achieve the organization's strategic plan to process loan applications faster and better than rivals and to improve the selection criteria for loans. This process and the supporting information system add value to the organization and match the organization's strategy. It is, therefore, essential to the long-term survival of the organization. If, on the other hand, managers determine that the organization's strategy is to grow and generate new products and services, the computer-based loan application process and underlying system might not be an efficient, effective use of resources, even though the system could provide automating and learning benefits.

Information Systems and Value Chain Analysis

Managers use value chain analysis to identify opportunities to use information systems for competitive advantage (Porter, 1985, 2001; Shank and Govindarajan, 1993). Think of an organization as a big input/output process. At one end, supplies are purchased and brought into the organization (see Figure 3.5). The organization integrates those supplies to create products and services that it markets, sells, and then distributes to customers. The organization provides customer service after the sale of these products and services. Throughout this process, opportunities arise for employees to add value to the organization by acquiring supplies in a more effective manner, improving products, and selling more products. This set of activities that add value throughout the organization is known as the **value chain** within an organization.

Value chain analysis is the process of analyzing an organization's activities to determine where value is added to products and/or services and what costs are incurred for doing so. Because IS can automate many activities along the value chain, value chain analysis has become a popular tool for applying IS for competitive advantage. In value chain analysis, you first draw the value chain for your organization by fleshing out each of the activities, functions, and processes where value is or should be added. Next, you determine the costs—and the factors that drive costs or cause them to fluctuate—within each of the

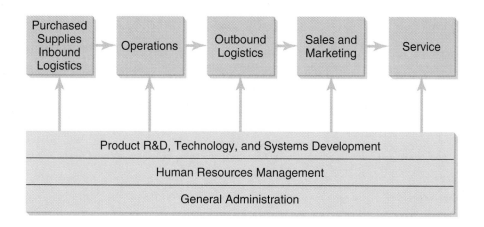

FIGURE 3.5

A sample generic organizational value chain.

areas in your value chain diagram. You then benchmark (compare) your value chain and associated costs with those of your competitors. You can then make changes and improvements in your value chain to either gain or sustain competitive advantage.

The Role of Information Systems in Value Chain Analysis

The use of information systems has become one of the primary ways that organizations improve their value chains. In Figure 3.6 we show a sample value chain and some ways that use of information systems can improve productivity within it. For example, many organizations use the Internet to connect businesses with one another electronically so that they can exchange orders, invoices, and receipts online in real time. Using the Internet has become a popular method for improving the front end of the organizational value chain. In fact, many firms now use the Internet for such business-to-business interactions; these systems are called *extranets* (described in greater detail in Chapter 5—Enabling Commerce Using the Internet).

The Technology/Strategy Fit

You might be asking, if any information system helps do things faster and better and helps save money, who cares whether it matches the company's strategy? Good question. If money grew on trees, you probably would build and use just about every information system you could imagine. Organizations could build many different valuable systems, but they are constrained by time and money to build only those that add the most value: those that help automate and learn as well as have strategic value. In most cases, you do not want systems that do not match the strategy, even if they offer automating and learning benefits. Further, while spending on information systems is rising again, most companies are willing to spend money on projects only when they can see clear, significant value.

Given this focus on the value that the system will add, you probably do not want a system that helps differentiate your products based on high quality when the organizational strategy is to be the overall industry low-cost leader. In other words, if a firm were pursuing a strategy for low-cost leadership, investments to help drive costs down would be valued over those that didn't.

We should also caution that merely choosing and implementing an emerging information system is not sufficient to gain or sustain competitive advantage. In any significant information systems implementation, there must be commensurate, significant organizational change. This typically comes in the form of *business process management (BPM)* and other similar methods of improving the functioning of the organization as opposed to merely dropping in an information system with no attempts at changing and improving the organization. We will talk more in Chapter 8—Building Organizational Partnerships Using Enterprise Information Systems—about the role of BPM for transforming organizational business processes.

FIGURE 3.6

Sample value chain and corresponding sample uses of information systems to add value.

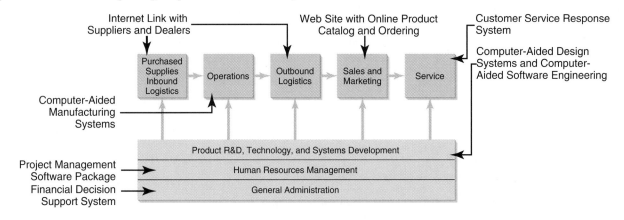

Making the Business Case for an Information System

Given that money does not grow on trees, people in organizations are constantly trying to justify spending money on anything, especially information systems. Before people are willing to spend money to build a new information system or spend more money on an existing system, they want to be convinced that this will be a good investment. Will the system provide automating, learning, and/or strategic benefits? The phrase that is used to describe the process of identifying, quantifying, and presenting the value provided by an information system is **making the business case**.

Business Case Objectives

What does making the business case for an information system mean? Think for a moment about what defense lawyers do in court trials. They carefully build a strong, integrated set of arguments and evidence to prove that their clients are innocent: they build and present their case to those who will pass judgment on their clients. In much the same way, people in business often have to build a strong, integrated set of arguments and evidence to prove that an information system is adding value to the organization or its constituents. This is, in business lingo, "making the business case" for a system.

As a business professional, you will be called on to make the business case for systems and other capital investments. As a finance, accounting, marketing, or management professional, you are likely to be involved in this process and will therefore need to know how to effectively make the business case for a system and to understand the relevant organizational issues involved. It will be in the organization's best interest—and in your own—to ferret out systems that are not adding value. In these cases, you will need to either improve the systems or replace them.

Sony's Secret

In November 2005, Mark Russinovich was testing computer security software he had cowritten when he discovered something new and uninvited hiding deep inside his PC. Russinovich is an experienced programmer who has written a book about the Windows operating system, and even he could not immediately identify the interloper. Russinovich finally traced the foreign object to code left behind when he purchased and played a Van Zant album from Amazon.com.

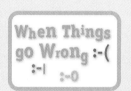

The album was produced by Sony BMG Music Entertainment and had been advertised as "copyright protected" when Russinovich bought it. He later found that the "protection" consisted of code called a "rootkit," a cloaking mechanism that was installed on his hard drive without his permission. Each time the CD was played, the program behind the rootkit notified Sony BMG.

Russinovich posted his discovery on his blog, immediately igniting a discussion about Sony BMG's methods. Copyright protection was one thing, the debaters said, but Sony BMG had gone too far.

The rootkit itself was not harmful to computers, experts explained, but it could serve as a hidden portal for viruses and Trojan horses. Shortly after the Sony rootkit news was publicized, virus makers did, indeed, exploit the rootkit access to spread infection via a Trojan horse. Thereafter, Sony announced it would quit distributing CDs that contained the rootkit, and the company has since issued uninstall instructions to customers.

Sony BMG argued that it sought only to protect the copyright of songs it produced. The British company that authored the software Sony used said it had tested the program and had not found it a problem. CD customers, however, begged to differ. It was sneaky, they countered, and not only took away control of their own computers but also left them vulnerable to malicious intruders.

Which side of the debate could you argue?

Sources: Ingrid Marson, "Sony Rootkit Victims in Every State, Researcher Says," *CNet News* (January 17, 2006), http://news.com.com/Sony+rootkit+victims+in+every+U.S.+state%2C+researcher+says/2100-1029_3-6027857.html?part=rss&tag=6027857&subj=news
http://news.com.com/FAQ+Sonys+rootkit+CDs/2100-1029_3-5946760.html?tag=nl

Making the business case is as important for proposed systems as it is for existing systems. For a proposed system, the case will be used to determine whether the new system is a "go" or a "no go." For an existing system, the case determines whether the company will continue to fund the system. Whether a new system or an existing one is being considered, your goal is to make sure that the system adds value, that it helps the firm to achieve its strategy and competitive advantage over its rivals, and that money is being spent wisely.

The Productivity Paradox

Unfortunately, while it is easy to quantify the costs associated with developing an information system, it is often difficult to quantify tangible productivity gains from its use. Over the past several years, the press has given a lot of attention to the impact of information systems investments on worker productivity. In many cases, IS expenditures, salaries, and the number of people on the IS staff have all been rising, but results from these investments have been disappointing. For instance, worldwide spending on IS approached $2.6 trillion in 2006, up 0.8 percent from 2005. American and Canadian companies are spending, on average, 2 percent of company revenues on IS investments, up from 1.7 percent in 2005. As a result, justifying the costs for IS investments has been a hot topic among senior managers at many firms. In particular, "white-collar" productivity, especially in the service sector, has not increased at the rate one might expect, given the trillions of dollars spent.

Why has it been difficult to show that these vast expenditures on information systems have led to productivity gains? Have information systems somehow failed us, promising increases in performance and productivity and then failing to deliver on that promise? Determining the answer is not easy. Information systems may have increased productivity, but other forces may have simultaneously worked to reduce it, the end results being difficult to identify. Factors such as government regulation, more complex tax codes and stricter financial reporting requirements (such as the Sarbanes-Oxley Act; see Chapter 4—Managing the Information Systems Infrastructure), and more complex products can all have major impacts on a firm's productivity.

It is also true that information systems built with the best intentions may have had unintended consequences—employees spending excessive amounts of time surfing the Web to check sports scores on the ESPN Web site, volumes of electronic junk mail being sent by Internet marketing companies or from personal friends, and company PCs being used to download and play software games (see Figure 3.7). In these situations, information systems can result in less efficient and less effective communication among employees and less productive uses of employee time than before the IS was implemented. Does this kind of employee behavior affect productivity figures? You bet it does. Still, in general, sound IS investments should increase organizational productivity. If this is so, why have organizations not been able to show larger productivity gains? A number of reasons have been given for the apparent **productivity paradox** of IS investments (Figure 3.8). This is examined next.

FIGURE 3.7

Unintended consequences can limit the productivity gains from information systems investments.

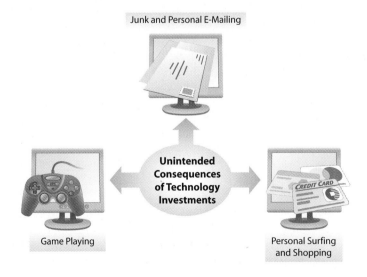

FIGURE 3.8

Factors leading to the information systems productivity paradox.

Measurement Problems In many cases, the benefits of information systems are difficult to pinpoint because firms may be measuring the wrong things. Often, the biggest increases in productivity result from increased **system effectiveness** (i.e., the extent to which a system enables people and/or the firm to accomplish goals or tasks well). Unfortunately, many business metrics focus on **system efficiency** (i.e., the extent to which a system enables people and/or the firm to do things faster, at lower cost, or with relatively little time and effort). Although information systems may have real benefits, those benefits may not be detected. Effectiveness improvements are sometimes difficult to measure. Also, expected benefits from IS are not always defined in advance, so they are never seen: in order to see something, you usually have to know what to look for. Measurement problems are not limited to traditional office information systems, either. All types of systems have potential measurement problems.

A good example of measurement problems associated with IS investment is the use of automatic teller machines (ATMs). How much have ATMs contributed to banking productivity? Traditional statistics might look at the number of transactions or output as some multiple of the labor input needed to produce that output (e.g., a transaction). However, such statistics do not work well for the ATM example. The number of checks written may actually decrease with ATMs, making productivity statistics appear lower. On the other hand, can you imagine a bank staying competitive without offering ATM services? The value added for the customer in terms of improved delivery of services almost dictates that banks offer a wide range of ATM services in today's competitive market. Deploying these information systems has become a **strategic necessity**—something an organization must do in order to survive.

Time Lags A second explanation for why productivity is difficult to demonstrate for IS investments is that a significant time lag may occur from when a company makes the investment until that investment is translated into improvement in the bottom line. Brynjolfsson (1993) reports that lags of two to three years are typical before strong organizational impacts of IS investments are felt.

The explanation for lags is fairly simple. At one level, it takes time for people to become proficient at using new technologies. Remember the first time you ever used a computer? It probably seemed difficult and cryptic to use. It may have taken you more time to figure out how to use the computer than it would have to complete a task manually.

Nonetheless, the computer probably became easier to use as you became more proficient with it. If you multiply this learning curve over everyone in an organization who may be using a given technology, you can see that until a firm has some experience in using a technology, the benefits associated with using it may be deferred. Everyone must become proficient with that technology in order to gain the benefits from its use.

It may also take some time before the tangible benefits of a new information system can be felt. Let us return to our ATM example. It may take years from the first implementation of this new system before the benefits may be felt. The system must first be implemented, which could take years in a large, widely distributed financial institution. Then the system must be fine-tuned to operate optimally and must be tied into all of the necessary subsystems. Employees and customers must be trained in how to use the system properly, and it may take years before they become truly proficient and comfortable with using it.

When the system is working well and people are using it efficiently, productivity gains may be measured. It takes time for the system to produce any labor savings within the organization and for customers' satisfaction levels to rise. Given that the ATMs have become a strategic necessity, perhaps one of their benefits is that they enable banks to gain—or simply keep—customers. It can take years for a financial institution to feel the effects of its deployment of ATM machines.

If time lags are the reason IS investments do not show up in productivity figures, then eventually IS managers should be able to report some very good news about organizational return on IS investment. Still, for managers faced with the day-to-day pressures of coming up with a demonstrable impact on firm performance, the explanation of time lags may not be very helpful or comforting.

Redistribution   A third possible explanation for why IS productivity figures are not easy to find is that IS may be beneficial for individual firms but not for a particular industry or the economy as a whole. Particularly in competitive situations, IS may be used to redistribute the pieces of the pie rather than making the whole pie bigger. In other words, strategic information systems may help one firm to increase its market share; however, this may come at the expense of another firm, which loses its market share as consumers transfer to the first firm. The result for the industry or economy as a whole is a wash—that is, the same number of products is being sold and the same number of dollars is being spent across all the firms. The only difference is that now one firm is getting a larger share of the business, while another firm is getting a smaller share.

While such an explanation may be feasible for some markets and industries, it does not fully explain why productivity figures would be stagnant at the level of one individual firm. Shouldn't each organization be more productive than before? Part of the problem is that our expectations of performance are somewhat biased. We tend to take for granted that technology fundamentally enables people to do things that would otherwise be nearly impossible. In effect, we continue to "raise the bar" with our expectations of what people can accomplish when supported by technology. For example, you might wonder whether the electronic spreadsheet on the PC on your desk is really helping you do your job better. To best answer this, you should think back to what it was like to create a spreadsheet by hand. It was a much slower process, was far more likely to produce errors, and left people significantly less time to work on other, more important tasks.

Mismanagement   A fourth explanation is that the IS has not been implemented and managed well. Some believe that people often simply build bad systems, implement them poorly, and rely on technology fixes when the organization has problems that require a joint technology/process solution. Rather than increasing outputs or profits, IS investments might merely be a temporary bandage and may serve to mask or even increase organizational slack and inefficiency. Also, as we mentioned in Chapter 1, an information system can be only as effective as the business model that it serves. Bad business models can't be overcome by good information systems. Similarly, the rapid decrease in processing time enabled by IS can result in unanticipated bottlenecks. For example, if automation has increased the potential output of a system but part of that system relies on human input, then the system can operate only as fast as the human can feed input into or through that system.

Eli Goldratt very aptly showed how this happens in his best-selling book *The Goal*, in which he uses the format of a novel to show how people can think logically and consistently about organizational problems in order to determine true cause-and-effect relationships between their actions and the results. In the novel, the characters do this so well that they save their manufacturing plant and make it successful. Spending money on IS does not help increase the firm's productivity until all of the bottlenecks are addressed. From a management standpoint, this means that managers must be sure that they evaluate the entire process being automated, making changes to old processes as necessary, in order to truly benefit from IS investment. If managers simply overlay new technology on old processes, sometimes known as "paving the cow path," then they will likely be disappointed in the meager productivity gains reaped from their investment.

Change Agents

Michael Dell, Founder and Chairman, Dell, Inc.

Michael Dell, founder and chairman of the board of Dell, Inc., the world's largest computer manufacturing company, was reportedly told by one of his high school teachers at Memorial High School in Houston, Texas, that he would "probably never go anywhere in life."

Dell did not do especially well scholastically in high school, but he apparently had a sense for where the PC market was headed. While a premed

FIGURE 3.9

Michael Dell, founder and chairman, Dell, Inc.

student at the University of Texas in Austin, Dell started a computer company called PCs Limited. (He assembled the computers he sold in his dorm room.) The company did well enough that at 19 Dell dropped out of school, borrowed $1,000 from his grandparents, and ran his company full time.

Currently a billionaire, *Forbes* magazine ranked Dell the twelfth richest man in the world in 2006 and the ninth richest in the United States. He based his successful business on selling low-cost computer systems directly to consumers through telephone sales and the dell.com Web site.

In the early 1990s, Dell was the youngest chief executive officer to head a Fortune 500 company. He authored a book titled *Direct from Dell: Strategies That Revolutionized an Industry* and serves on the Foundation Board of the World Economic Forum and the executive committee of the International Business Council and is a member of the U.S. Business Council. Dell also serves on the U.S. President's Council of Advisers on Science and Technology and the governing board of the Indian School of Business in Hyderabad, India. The Michael and Susan Dell Foundation strives to improve the lives of children around the world.

Dell lives with his wife Susan and four children in Austin, Texas, in the fifteenth-largest home in the world, valued at $18.7 million.

Sources: http://en.wikipedia.org/wiki/Michael_Dell
http://www1.us.dell.com/content/topics/global.aspx/corp/
biographies/en/msd_index?c=us&l=en&s=corp

If it is so difficult to quantify the benefits of information systems for individual firms and for entire industries, why do managers continue to invest in information systems? The answer is that competitive pressures force managers to invest in information systems whether they like it or not. You might ask, then, so why waste time making the business case for a system? Why not just build them? The answer: money doesn't grow on trees. These are typically expensive projects for companies, and a strong case must be made for investing in them.

Making a Successful Business Case

People make a variety of arguments in their business cases for information systems. When managers make the business case for an information system, they typically base their arguments on faith, fear, and/or facts (Wheeler, 2002a). (Wheeler also adds a fourth "F," that being for "fiction," and notes that, unfortunately, managers sometimes base their arguments on pure fiction, which is not only bad for their careers but also not at all healthy for their firms.) Table 3.2 shows examples of these three types of arguments.

Do not assume that you must base your business case on facts only. It is entirely appropriate to base the business case on faith, fear, or facts (see Figure 3.10). Indeed, the strongest and most comprehensive business case will include a little of each type of argument. In the following sections, we talk about each of these types of arguments for the business case.

Business Case Arguments Based on Faith In some situations, arguments based on faith (or fear) can be the most compelling and can drive the decision to invest in an information system despite the lack of any hard data on system costs or even in the face of some data that say that the dollar costs for the system will be high. Arguments based on faith often hold that an information system must be implemented in order to achieve the organization's strategy effectively and to gain or sustain a competitive advantage over rivals, despite the dollar costs associated with that system. Given the power of modern information systems, their rapid evolution, and their pervasiveness in business today, information systems have become a common tool for enabling business strategy. Consequently, the business cases for systems are frequently grounded in strategic arguments.

For example, a firm has set as its strategy that it will be the dominant, global force in its industry. As a result, this firm must adopt a global telecommunications network and a variety of collaboration technologies, such as e-mail, desktop videoconferencing, and groupware tools, in order to enable employees from different parts of the globe to work together effectively and efficiently. Similarly, a firm that has set as its strategy that it will have a broad scope—producing products and services across a wide range of consumer

TABLE 3.2 Three Types of Arguments Commonly Made in The Business Case for an Information System

Type of Argument	Description	Example
Faith	Arguments based on beliefs about organizational strategy, competitive advantage, industry forces, customer perceptions, market share, and so on.	"I know I don't have good data to back this up, but I'm convinced that having this customer relationship management system will enable us to serve our customers significantly better than do our competitors and, as a result, we'll beat the competition. . . . You just have to take it on faith."
Fear	Arguments based on the notion that if the system is not implemented, the firm will lose out to the competition or, worse, go out of business.	"If we don't implement this enterprise resource planning system we'll get killed by our competitors because they're all implementing these kinds of systems. . . . We either do this or we die."
Fact	Arguments based on data, quantitative analysis, and/or indisputable factors.	"This analysis shows that implementing the inventory control system will help us reduce errors by 50%, reduce operating costs by 15% a year, increase production by 5% a year, and will pay for itself within 18 months."

FIGURE 3.10

A successful business case will
be based on faith, fear, and facts.

needs—must adopt some form of an enterprise resource planning system to coordinate
business activities across its diverse product lines. For example, Procter & Gamble produces dozens of household products that are consumed under various brand names
throughout the world—Noxzema, Folgers coffee, Tide laundry detergent, Cover Girl cos-
metics, Crest toothpaste, and Pringles potato chips, to name a few. Integration across various product lines and divisions is a key goal for IS investments. Such integration allows
Procter & Gamble to streamline inventory, thus improving efficiency.

In short, successful business case arguments based on faith should clearly describe the
firm's mission and objectives, the strategy for achieving them, and the types of information
systems that are needed in order to enact the strategy. A word of caution is warranted here.
In today's business environment, cases based solely on strategic arguments, with no hard
numbers demonstrating the value of the information system under consideration, are not
likely to be funded.

Business Case Arguments Based on Fear There are several different factors to take
into account when making a business case in which you will provide arguments based on
fear. These include a number of factors involving competition and other elements of the
industry in which the firm operates, which are shown in Figure 3.11 (Harris and Katz,
1991). For example, a mature and stable industry, such as the automotive industry, may
need IS simply to maintain the current pace of operations. While having the newest IS

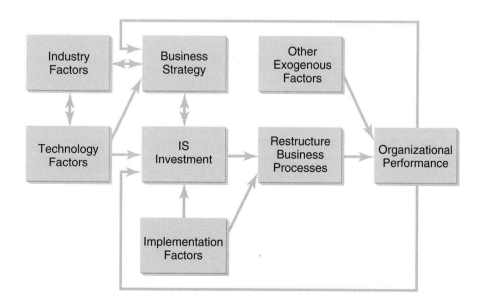

FIGURE 3.11

Factors in IS investment
decisions.

available may be nice, it may not be needed to stay in business. However, a company in a newer, more volatile industry, such as the cellular phone industry, may find it more important to be on the leading edge of technology in order to compete effectively in the marketplace. Likewise, some industries are more highly regulated than others. In these cases, companies can use IS to control processes and ensure compliance with appropriate regulations. The argument for the business case here would be something like, "If we do not implement this information system, we run the risk of being sued or, worse, being thrown in jail" (see Chapter 4 and the discussion related to IS controls).

Probably the most important industry factor that can affect IS investment is the nature of competition or rivalry in the industry. For example, when competition in an industry is high and use of information systems is rampant, as it is in the personal computer industry, strategic necessity more than anything else forces firms to adopt information systems. Given how tight profit margins are in the PC industry, Dell and other manufacturers must use inventory control systems, Web-based purchasing and customer service, and a host of other systems that help them to be more effective and efficient. If they do not adopt these information systems, they will likely go out of business. One framework often used to analyze the competition within an industry is Porter's notion of the five primary competitive forces (Porter, 1979): (1) the rivalry among competing sellers in your industry, (2) the threat of potential new entrants into your industry, (3) the bargaining power that customers have within your industry, (4) the bargaining power that suppliers have within your industry, and (5) the potential for substitute products from other industries (see Figure 3.12). Table 3.3 provides examples of how IS can have an impact on the various competitive forces in an industry.

Porter's five-forces model of competition can help you determine which specific technologies will be more or less useful, depending on the nature of your industry. You can then use these as the bases for your arguments as to whether to invest in new or existing information systems. This kind of industry-based business case might not enable you to attach specific monetary benefits to particular information systems, but it can show you and others that specific uses of particular systems are necessary to compete in your markets. Business case arguments formulated this way sound something like, "If we do not implement this information system, our competitors are going to beat us on price, we will lose market share, and we will go out of business."

Business Case Arguments Based on Fact Many people, including most chief financial officers, want to see the business case for an information system be based on some convincing, quantitative analysis that proves beyond a shadow of doubt that the benefits of the system will outweigh the costs. The most common way to prove this is to provide a

FIGURE 3.12

Porter's five-forces model.

Source: M. Porter, "How Competitive Forces Shape Strategy," *Harvard Business Review,* March/April 1979.

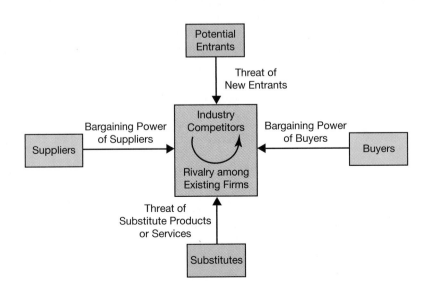

TABLE 3.3 IS Impact on Competitive Forces

Competitive Force	Implication for Firm	Potential Use of IS to Combat Competitive Force
Traditional rivals within your industry	Competition in price, product distribution, and service	Implement enterprise resource planning system to reduce costs and be able to act and react more quickly
		Implement Web site to offer better service to customers
Threat of new entrants into your market	Increased capacity in the industry	Better Web site to reach customers and differentiate product
	Reduced prices	
	Decreased market share	Inventory control system to lower costs and better manage excess capacity
Customers' bargaining power	Reduced prices	Implement customer relationship management system to serve customers better
	Need for increased quality	
	Demand for more services	Implement computer-aided design and/or computer-aided manufacturing system to improve product quality
Suppliers' bargaining power	Increased costs	Use Internet to establish closer electronic ties with suppliers and to create relationships with new suppliers located far away
	Reduced quality	
Threat of substitute products from other industries	Potential returns on products	Use decision support system and customer purchase database to better assess trends and customer needs
	Decreased market share	
	Losing customers for life	Use computer-aided design systems to redesign products

Source: Adapted from Applegate, Austin, and McFarlan. *Corporate Information Strategy and Management*, 7th ed. (Columbus, Ohio: McGraw-Hill/Irwin, 2007).

detailed cost-benefit analysis of the information system. Although this step is critical, the manager must remember that there are inherent difficulties in and limits to cost-benefit analyses for information systems. To illustrate how a cost-benefit analysis could be used to build a fact-based business case, let us consider the development of a Web-based order entry system for a relatively small firm.

IDENTIFYING COSTS. One goal of a cost-benefit analysis is to accurately determine the **total cost of ownership (TCO)** for the IS investment. TCO is focused on understanding not only the total cost of *acquisition* but also all costs associated with ongoing *use and maintenance* of a system. Consequently, costs can usually be divided into two categories, **nonrecurring costs** and **recurring costs**. Nonrecurring costs are one-time costs that are not expected to continue after the system is implemented. These include costs for things such as the Web server, telecommunications equipment, Web server software, HTML editors, Java, Flash, and other tools. These *one-time costs* also include the costs of attracting and training a Webmaster, renovating some office space to serve as the location of the Web server, and paying analysts and programmers to develop the system.

Recurring costs are ongoing costs that occur throughout the life cycle of systems development, implementation, and maintenance. Recurring costs include the salary and benefits of the Webmaster and any other personnel assigned to maintain the system, upgrades and maintenance for the system components, monthly fees paid to a local Internet service provider, and the continuing costs for the space in which the Webmaster works or the *collocation facility* where the server resides. Personnel costs are usually the largest recurring costs, and the Web-based system is no exception in this regard. These recurring expenses can go well beyond the Webmaster to include expenses for help desk personnel, maintenance programmers, IS management, and data entry personnel.

The sample costs described thus far have been fairly **tangible costs**, which are easy to quantify. Some **intangible costs** ought to be accounted for as well, even though they will not fit neatly into the quantitative analysis. These might include the costs of reducing traditional sales, losing some customers that are not "Web ready," or losing customers if the Web application is poorly designed or not on par with competitors' sites. You can choose either to quantify these in some way (i.e., determine the cost of losing a customer) or simply to reserve these as important costs to consider outside of—but along with—the quantitative cost-benefit analysis.

IDENTIFYING BENEFITS. Next, you determine both **tangible benefits** and **intangible benefits**. Some tangible benefits are relatively easy to determine. For example, you can estimate that the increased customer reach of the new Web-based system will result in at least a modest increase in sales. Based on evidence from similar projects, you might estimate, say, a 5 percent increase in sales the first year, a 10 percent increase the second year, and a 15 percent increase the third year. In addition, you might also include as tangible benefits the reduction of order entry errors because orders will now be tracked electronically and shipped automatically. You could calculate the money previously lost on faulty and lost orders, along with the salaries and wages of personnel assigned to find and fix these orders, and then consider the reduction of these costs as a quantifiable benefit of the new system. Cost avoidance is a legitimate, quantifiable benefit of an information system. Similarly, the new system may enable the company to use fewer order entry clerks or redeploy these personnel to other, more important functions within the company. You could consider these cost reductions as benefits of the new system.

A Web-based system has intangible benefits as well. Some intangible benefits of this new system might include faster turnaround on fulfilling orders and resulting improvements in customer service. These are real benefits, but they might be hard to quantify with confidence. Perhaps an even more intangible benefit would be the overall improved perception of the firm. Customers might consider it more progressive and customer service oriented than its rivals; in addition to attracting new customers, this might increase the value of the firm's stock if it were a publicly traded firm. Another intangible benefit might be simply that it was a strategic necessity to offer customers Web-based ordering to keep pace with rivals. While these intangibles are difficult to quantify, they must be considered along with the more quantitative analysis of benefits. In fact, the intangible benefits of this Web-based system might be so important that they could carry the day despite an inconclusive or even negative cost-benefit analysis.

PERFORMING COST-BENEFIT ANALYSES. An example of a simplified **cost-benefit analysis** that contrasts the total expected tangible costs versus the tangible benefits is presented in Figure 3.13. Notice the fairly large investment up front, with another significant outlay in the fifth year for a system upgrade. You could now use the net costs/benefits for each year as the basis of your conclusion about this system. Alternatively, you could perform a **break-even analysis**—a type of cost-benefit analysis to identify at what point (if ever) tangible benefits equal tangible costs (note that breakeven occurs early in the second year of the system's life in this example)—or a more formal **net-present-value analysis** of the relevant cash flow streams associated with the system at the organization's **discount rate** (i.e., the rate of return used by an organization to compute the present value of future cash flows). In any event, this cost-benefit analysis helps you make the business case for this proposed Web-based order fulfillment system. It clearly shows that the investment for this system is relatively small, and the company can fairly quickly recapture the investment. In addition, there appear to be intangible strategic benefits to deploying this system. This analysis—and the accompanying arguments and evidence—goes a long way toward convincing senior managers in the firm that this new system makes sense.

COMPARING COMPETING INVESTMENTS. One method for deciding among different information systems investments or when considering alternative designs for a given system is illustrated in Figure 3.14. For example, suppose that for a given system being considered, there are three alternative designs that could be pursued—A, B, or C. Let's also suppose that early planning meetings identified three key system requirements and four key constraints that could be used to help make a decision on which alternative to pursue. In the left column of Figure 3.14, three system requirements and four constraints are listed. Because not all

		2006	2007	2008	2009	2010
Costs						
Nonrecurring						
Hardware		$ 20,000				
Software		$ 7,500				
Networking		$ 4,500				
Infrastructure		$ 7,500				
Personnel		$100,000				
Recurring						
Hardware			$ 500	$ 1,000	$ 2,500	$ 15,000
Software			$ 500	$ 500	$ 1,000	$ 2,500
Networking			$ 250	$ 250	$ 500	$ 1,000
Service fees			$ 250	$ 250	$ 250	$ 500
Infrastructure				$ 250	$ 500	$ 1,500
Personnel			$ 60,000	$ 62,500	$ 70,000	$ 90,000
Total costs		$139,500	$ 61,500	$ 64,750	$ 74,750	$110,500
Benefits						
Increased sales		$ 20,000	$ 50,000	$ 80,000	$115,000	$175,000
Error reduction		$ 15,000	$ 15,000	$ 15,000	$ 15,000	$ 15,000
Cost reduction		$100,000	$100,000	$100,000	$100,000	$100,000
Total benefits		$135,000	$165,000	$195,000	$230,000	$290,000
Net costs/benefit		$ (4,500)	$103,500	$130,250	$155,250	$179,500

FIGURE 3.13

Worksheet showing a simplified cost-benefit analysis for the Web-based order fulfillment system.

Criteria	Weight	Alternative A		Alternative B		Alternative C	
		Rating	Score	Rating	Score	Rating	Score
Requirements							
Real-time data entry	18	5	90	5	90	5	90
Automatic reorder	18	1	18	5	90	5	90
Real-time data query	14	1	14	5	70	5	70
	50		122		250		250
Constraints							
Developer costs	15	4	60	5	75	3	45
Hardware costs	15	4	60	4	60	3	45
Operating costs	15	5	75	1	15	5	75
Ease of training	5	5	25	3	15	3	15
	50		220		165		180
Total	100		342		415		430

FIGURE 3.14

Alternative projects and system design decisions can be assisted using weighted multicriteria analysis.

requirements and constraints are of equal importance, they are weighted on the basis of their relative importance. In other words, you do not have to weight requirements and constraints equally; it is certainly possible to make requirements more or less important than constraints. Weights are arrived at in discussions among the analysis team, users, and sometimes managers. Weights tend to be fairly subjective and, for that reason, should be determined through a process of open discussion to reveal underlying assumptions, followed by an attempt to reach consensus among stakeholders. Notice that the total of the weights for both the requirements and constraints is 100 (percent).

Next, each requirement and constraint is rated on a scale of 1 to 5. A rating of 1 indicates that the alternative does not meet the requirement very well or that the alternative violates the constraint. A rating of 5 indicates that the alternative meets or exceeds the requirement or clearly abides by the constraint. Ratings are even more subjective than weights and should also be determined through open discussion among users, analysts, and managers. For each requirement and constraint, a score is calculated by multiplying the rating for each requirement and each constraint by its weight. The final step is to add up the weighted scores for each alternative. Notice that we have included three sets of totals: for requirements, for constraints, and overall totals. If you look at the totals for requirements, alternative B or C is the best choice because each meets or exceeds all requirements. However, if you look only at constraints, alternative A is the best choice because it does not violate any constraints. When we combine the totals for requirements and constraints, we see that the best choice is alternative C. Whether alternative C is actually chosen for development, however, is another issue. The decision makers may choose alternative A, knowing that it does not meet two key requirements, because it has the lowest cost. In short, what may appear to be the best choice for a systems development project may not always be the one that ends up being developed. By conducting a thorough analysis, organizations can greatly improve their decision-making performance.

Presenting the Business Case

Up to this point, we have discussed the key issues to consider as you prepare to make the business case for a system. We have also shown you some tools for determining the value that a system adds to an organization. Now you are actually ready to make the

Net Stats

Valuing IT Investments: File Sharing

In 2005, the Pew Internet and American Life Project interviewed 1,421 Internet users, via telephone, about their music and video downloading practices. The study found that approximately 27 percent of Internet users (36 million people) download music or video files. About half have done so outside of peer-to-peer networks or paid online services. Approximately 28 percent (10 million people) say they obtain music and video files through e-mail and instant messages. Another 19 percent (7 million people) say they obtain music and video files from someone else's MP3 player. The study did not differentiate between illegal and legal means of obtaining music and video files online. Table 3.4 summarizes where people currently download music. Additionally, a majority of current music and video downloaders felt that the U.S. government could do little or nothing about music file sharing (see Table 3.5).

Sources: Rob McGann, "File Sharers Go beyond P2P," *Clickz* (March 23, 2005), http://www.clickz.com/stats/sectors/ governmentarticle.php/3492356
Electronic Freedom Foundation Press Release, "Trademark Owners Can't Control Your Desktop" (June 29, 2005), http://www.eff.org/news/archives/2005_06.php#003748

TABLE 3.4 Sources for Current Music Downloaders

Do you CURRENTLY download music or video files from any of the following places? Have you EVER downloaded music or video files from this source?

	Yes, currently do	No, but have in the past	No, and never have	Don't Know/ Refused
An Online music service like iTunes or BuyMusic.com	27%	8%	64%	1%
Email or instant messages you receive	20	8	72	0
Other music-related websites, such as online music magazines or musicians' homepages	17	6	78	0
A peer-to-peer network like KaZaA or Morpheus	16	17	65	1
Someone's iPod or other MP3 player	15	4	80	0
Other movie-related websites, such as online movie magazine or review sites	7	2	90	1
Music or movie blogs	4	3	91	2
An online movie download service like Movielink	2	4	94	*

Source: Pew Internet & American Life Project Tracking Survey, January 2005.

TABLE 3.5 Can the U.S. Government Reduce Music File Sharing?

Responses from each demographic group	U.S. gov't can reduce	Little or nothing gov't can do about it	Don't Know/ Refused
General Public	38%	42%	20%
Internet Users	39	48	13
Home and Work Broadband Users	32	57	11
Young Adults 18–29	36	55	9
Current Music and Video Downloaders	39	54	7
iPod/MP3 Owners	40	52	8

Source: Pew Internet & American Life Project Tracking Survey, January 2005.

case—to present your arguments and evidence to the decision makers in the firm. This task is much like that of a lawyer presenting a persuasive written and oral argument to win a judgment in her client's favor. Making a business case for IS really is not much different. You are simply trying to clearly articulate the value of the investment to your organization.

Know the Audience Depending on the firm, a number of people from various areas of the firm might be involved in the decision-making process for a new IS investment. People from different areas of the firm typically hold very different perspectives about what investments should be made and how those investments should be managed (see Table 3.6). Consequently, presenting the business case for a new IS investment can be quite challenging. Ultimately, a number of factors come into play in making investment

TABLE 3.6 Characteristics of Different Stakeholders Involved in Making Information Systems Investment Decisions

Stakeholder	Perspective	Focus/Project Characteristics
Management	Representatives or managers from each of the functional areas within the firm	Greater strategic focus; largest project sizes; longest project durations
Steering committee	Representatives from various interest groups within the organization (they may have their own agendas at stake when making investment decisions)	Cross-functional focus; greater organizational change; formal cost-benefit analysis; larger and riskier projects
User department	Representatives of the intended users of the system	Narrow, nonstrategic focus; faster development
IS executive	Has overall responsibility for managing IS development, implementation, and maintenance of selected systems	Integration with existing systems focus; fewer development delays; less concern with cost-benefit analysis

Source: Adapted from McKeen, Guimaraes, and Wetherbe (1994).

decisions, and numerous outcomes can occur (see Figure 3.16). Understanding the audience and the issues important to them is a first step in making an effective presentation. Various ways to improve the development of a business case are examined next.

Convert Benefits to Monetary Terms When making the case for an information systems investment, it is desirable to translate all potential benefits into monetary terms. For example, if a new system saves department managers an hour per day, try to quantify that savings in terms of dollars. Figure 3.16 shows how you might convert time savings into dollar figures. While merely explaining this benefit as "saving managers time" makes it sound useful, managers may not consider it a significant enough inducement to warrant spending a significant amount of money. Justifying a $50,000 system because it will "save time" may not be persuasive enough. However, an annual savings of $90,000 is more likely to capture the attention of decision makers and is more likely to result in project approval. Senior managers can easily rationalize a $50,000 expense for a $90,000 savings and can easily see why they should approve such a request. They can also more easily rationalize their decision later on if something goes wrong with the system.

FIGURE 3.15

Investment selection decisions must consider numerous factors and can have numerous outcomes.

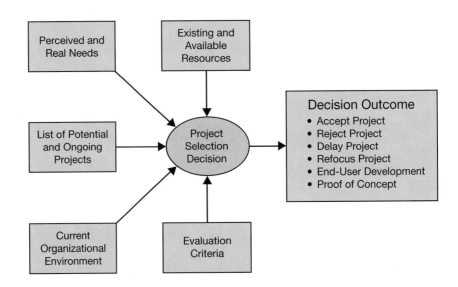

FIGURE 3.16

Converting time savings into dollar figures.

Benefit:

New system saves at least one hour per day for 12 midlevel managers.

Quantified as:

Manager's salary (per hour)	$30.00
Number of managers affected	12
Daily savings (one hour saved × 12 managers)	$360.00
Weekly savings (daily savings × 5)	$1,800.00
Annual savings (weekly savings × 50)	$90,000.00

Devise Proxy Variables   The situation presented in Figure 3.16 is fairly straightforward. Anyone can see that a $50,000 investment is a good idea because the return on that investment is $90,000 the first year. Unfortunately, not all cases are this clear-cut. In cases in which it is not as easy to quantify the impact of an investment, you can come up with **proxy variables** to help clarify what the impact on the firm will be. Proxy variables can be used to measure changes in terms of their perceived value to the organization. For example, if mundane administrative tasks are seen as a low value (perhaps a 1 on a 5-point scale) while direct contact with customers is seen as a high value (a 5), you can use these perceptions to indicate how new systems will add value to the organization. In this example, you can show that a new system will allow personnel to have more contact with customers while at the same time reducing the administrative workload. Senior managers can quickly see that individual workload is being shifted from low-value to high-value activities.

Alternatively, you can create a customer contact scale from 1 to 5, with 1 representing very low customer contact and 5 representing very high customer contact. You can argue that currently your firm rates a 2 on the customer contact scale and that with the new information system your firm will rate a significantly higher number on the scale.

You can communicate these differences using percentages, increases or decreases, and so on—whatever best conveys the idea that the new system is creating changes in work, in performance, and in the way people think about their work. This gives decision makers some relatively solid data on which to base their decision.

Measure What Is Important to Management   One of the most important things you can do to show the benefits of a system is one of the simplest: measure what senior managers think is important. You may think this is trivial advice, but you would be surprised how often people calculate impressive-looking statistics in terms of downtime, reliability, and so on, only to find that senior managers disregard or only briefly skim over those figures. You should concentrate on the issues senior business managers care about. The "hot button" issues with senior managers should be easy to discover, and they are not always financial reports. Hot issues with senior managers could include cycle time (how long it takes to process an order), customer feedback, and employee morale. By focusing on what senior business managers believe to be important, you can make the business case for systems in a way that is more meaningful for those managers, which makes selling systems to decision makers much easier. Managers are more likely to buy in to the importance of systems if they can see the impact on areas that are important to them.

Assessing Value for the Information Systems Infrastructure

Howard Rubin, executive vice president of Meta Group, argued that we should take a more holistic view when assessing IS value (*CIO,* June 2004), particularly in areas such as IS infrastructure, where assessing tangible value may be difficult (see Chapter 4). IS infrastructure includes an organization's facilities, hardware, software, personnel, and so on. While these things are important and expensive to acquire and maintain, they are often difficult to place a value on. Rubin suggested four categories for assessing investments in regard to their value to the overall infrastructure.

Economic Value First, economic value is the contribution an investment makes toward improving the infrastructure's ability to enhance the profitability of the business. Rubin recommended that we use important business metrics in order to gauge the economic value of a given investment. An airline, for example, might use a metric such as revenue per passenger per mile per year to determine effectiveness. To assess an investment, the airline could then calculate the IS infrastructure cost per passenger mile and observe how investments in the infrastructure over time has an impact on profitability.

Architectural Value Second, architectural value is derived from an investment's ability to extend the infrastructure's capabilities to meet business needs today and in the future. To measure architectural value, "before and after" assessments of infrastructure characteristics such as interoperability, portability, scalability, recoverability, and compatibility can be taken. Rubin recommended that for each area of the business, infrastructure characteristics be rated on a scale of 1 to 10 as to how well various investments influence the infrastructure's ability to meet those needs.

Operational Value Third, operational value is derived from assessing an investment's impact on enabling the infrastructure to better meet business processing requirements. To assess this, Rubin recommended that we measure the impact of not investing in a particular project. For example, what would be the cost of not investing in a new customer relationship management system in terms of lost staff productivity, lost business revenue, or even lost customer base?

Regulatory and Compliance Value Fourth, regulatory and compliance value is derived from assessing the extent to which an investment helps to meet requirements for control, security, and integrity as required by a governing body or a key customer. For example, what is the impact of, say, noncompliance with government reporting requirements necessitated by the Sarbanes-Oxley Act of 2002?

Rubin also argues that, where possible, all evaluation measures should be compared with external benchmarks. In any event, these provide a useful framework for more broadly evaluating a particular investment.

Changing Mind-Sets about Information Systems

Perhaps the most significant change in the information systems field has been in mind-sets about technology rather than in technology itself. The old way for managers to think about information systems was that information systems are a necessary service, a necessary evil, and a necessary, distasteful expense that is to be minimized. Managers cannot afford to think this way anymore. Successful managers now think of information systems as a competitive asset to be nurtured and invested in. This does not mean that managers should not require a sound business case for every information systems investment. Nor does this mean that managers should not also need to have facts as part of a business case for a system. It does mean, however, that managers must stop thinking about systems as an expense and start thinking about systems as an asset to invest in wisely. Managers have to become strategic about information systems and think of them as an enabler of opportunities.

Valuing Innovations

To differentiate itself, an organization often must deploy new, state-of-the-art technologies to do things even better, faster, and more cheaply than rivals that are using older technologies. Although firms can choose to continually upgrade older systems rather than investing in new systems, these improvements can at best give only a short-lived competitive edge. To gain and sustain significant competitive advantage, firms must often deploy the latest technologies or redeploy and reinvest in existing technologies in clever, new ways.

Brief Case ⊙

For Sale by Owner: Your Company's Name.com

They don't sell houses or land, but they do deal in Internet real estate, and most turn a handsome profit. "They" are called domainers, and the real estate they buy and sell consists of domain names. Although they keep a low profile and usually don't flaunt their success, domainers participate in a virtual land grab worth $9 billion in 2006 and projected to soar to $23 billion by 2009.

As you know, every Web site on the Internet has a domain name, also called a uniform resource locator (URL) or Web address. Domain names may or may not identify the business or person who owns the Web site. For example, msn.com, yahoo.com, and google.com are domain names that do, in fact, identify the Web site owner by name. Domain names such as pty.com and xa2z7.com, however, do not.

Domainers trade on the fact that many businesses, organizations, and celebrities want domain names for their Web sites that clearly identify the site's owner and are, therefore, easy for Internet surfers to find. A domainer might buy the domain name "fordmotorcompany.com," for instance, and then try to sell it to the Ford Motor Company; that is exactly how the domain-buying business operated in the 1990s. Buy a name, hold it, and wait for a buyer who wanted it to make an offer. But when pay-per-click advertising was developed, the game changed. Currently, domainers can profit most by renting advertising space on the domain names they hold to marketers. Here is how the domainer makes his or her profit from renting ad space:

1. Buy and hold a general domain name, such as "candy.com" or "cellphones.com." (The financial wisdom in buying such domain names became apparent to domainers when they realized that many Internet surfers conduct searches simply by entering a search word or term followed by .com in the URL address box of their browsers.) Alternatively, domainers buy domain names that represent common misspellings of popular domains (such as amazo.com), hoping to benefit from Web surfers' typos.

2. Direct Web traffic to a middleman, called an aggregator, who designs a Web site and then taps into Yahoo!, Google, or Microsoft's advertising networks and lists the best-paying clients. When a searcher enters the domain name, such as "cellphone.com," the "cellphone.com" Web page comes up, with a list of cell phone Web site URLs.

3. Each time a searcher clicks on one of the URLs listed on the domain name's page, the search engine owner (Yahoo!, Google, or Microsoft) or advertiser pays the domainer a fee.

Renting domain names is a secondary market for domainers that can bring in hundreds of dollars per day. The key to this market is not necessarily search engine traffic—rather, it is type-in traffic or user-directed navigation because millions of Internet users type what they are looking for directly in the address bar of their browser, such as "candy.com." (Candy.com was recently sold for over $100,000 and makes a profit of $1,000 a week for its owner.)

Figures are not available for this type of URL type-in traffic since the larger search engines, such as Yahoo! and Google, do not disclose how much of their revenue comes from domain name rental. Experts report, however, that as much as 15 percent of Google's and Yahoo's revenue may come from per-click advertising.

Domainers could face a loss of revenue if, as has been suggested, Google, Yahoo!, and Microsoft cut out the domainer in the middle and serve Internet browser type-in traffic directly. But until that happens, domainers are raking in the cash.

Questions

1. How do you feel about domainers? Is it an ethical business?
2. Discuss the pros and cons of having Google, Yahoo!, MSN, and others "cut out" domainers as middle men in the Web search process.

Source: Paul Sloan, "Masters of Their Domains," *CNN Money.com* (December 1, 2005), http://money.cnn.com/magazines/business2/business2_archive/2005/12/01/8364591/index.htm

But with the plethora of new information technologies and systems available, how can you possibly choose winners? Indeed, how can you even keep track of all the new breakthroughs, new products, new versions, and new ways of using technologies? For example, in Figure 3.17 we present a small subset of some new information technologies and systems, ranging from some that are here now and currently being used to some that are easily a decade away from being a reality. Which one is important for you? Which one will make or break your business? Does this list even include the one that you need to be concerned about?

FIGURE 3.17

Some enabling technologies on the horizon.

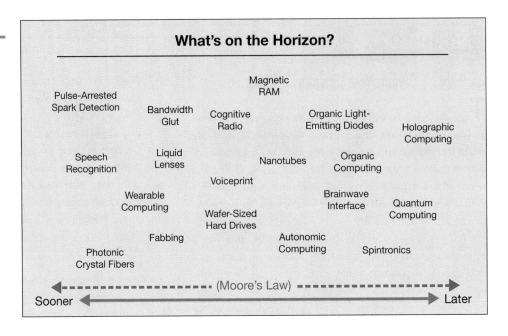

The Need for Constant IS Innovation

Sir John Maddox, a physicist and the editor of the influential scientific journal *Nature* for 22 years, was quoted in *Scientific American* in 1999 as saying, "The most important discoveries of the next 50 years are likely to be ones of which we cannot now even conceive." Think about that for a moment. Most of the important discoveries of the next 50 years are likely to be things that, at present, we have no clue about. To illustrate that point, think back to just a short decade ago about what the state of the Internet was. Then, the Internet was not on the radar screens of many business organizations. Those that had Web sites were mostly providing an electronic brochure to customers and weren't exploiting the technology to streamline business processes as is the norm today. Look now at how the Internet has transformed modern business; how could something so transformational not have been easier for businesses to imagine or predict a decade earlier? Well, it is difficult to see these things coming. Next, we examine how you can improve your ability to spot and exploit new innovations.

Successful Innovation Is Difficult

As we hinted at previously, there are limits to using emerging information systems to gain or sustain a competitive advantage. Information systems are often bought from or built by someone else. They are often either purchased from a vendor or developed by a consultant or outsourcing partner. In these situations, the information systems are usually not proprietary technologies owned by the organization. For example, although a soft-drink company can patent the formula of a cola or a pharmaceutical company can patent a new drug, an organization typically cannot patent its use of an information system, particularly if someone else developed it. The data in the system may be proprietary, but the information system typically is not. One classic counterexample, however, is Amazon.com's patented "one-click" ordering process that has been successfully defended in the courts.

Innovation Is Often Fleeting Given the pace of change in the digital world, advantages gained by innovations often have a limited life span. For example, even in situations where an organization has developed an innovative information system in-house, they usually do so with hardware, software, and networking components others can purchase. In short, rivals can copy emerging information systems, so this form of competitive advantage can be short lived. Indeed, if use of the new system causes one organization to gain a significant advantage over others, smart rivals are quick to duplicate or improve on that use of the system.

Innovation Is Often Risky Developing innovative information systems always entails a risk. The classic example from consumer electronics is the choice of a VCR in the early days of that technology and the competing Betamax and VHS designs (see Figure 3.18). Most experts agreed that the Betamax had superior recording and playback quality, but VHS ultimately won the battle in the marketplace. People who made the "smart" choice at the time probably would have chosen a VCR with the Betamax design. Ultimately, however, that turned out to be an unfortunate choice. Other examples in the field of consumer electronics abound today. For example, when buying a stereo today, should you invest in traditional compact disc technology (such as the read-only CD-ROM), recordable compact discs, digital audiotape, an MP3 device, or some other technology? Many people have been stuck with huge collections of vinyl records, cassette tapes, or (gulp!) eight-track tapes. It is easy to make poor choices in consumer electronics or to make choices that are good at the time but soon turn out to be poor choices.

Innovation Choices Are Often Difficult Choosing among innovative information systems–related investments is just as difficult as choosing consumer electronics. In fact, for organizations, choosing among the plethora of available innovative technologies is far more difficult, given the size and often mission-critical nature of the investment. Choosing a suboptimal home stereo, although disappointing, is usually not devastating.

Choosing new technologies in the information systems area is like trying to hit one of several equally attractive fast-moving targets. You can find examples of the difficulty of forecasting emerging technologies in the experiences that many organizations have had in forecasting the growth, use, and importance of the Internet. The 1994 Technology Forecast prepared by the major consulting firm Price Waterhouse (now PriceWaterhouseCoopers) mentioned the word "Internet" on only five pages of the 750-page document. The next year, more than 75 pages addressed the Internet. In the 1997 briefing, the Internet is a pervasive topic throughout. Back in 1994, it would have been difficult, perhaps even foolish, to forecast such pervasive, rapidly growing business use of the Internet today. Table 3.7 illustrates how many people and organizations have had difficulty making technology-related predictions.

Given the pace of research and development in the information systems and components area, staying current has been nearly impossible. Probably one of the most famous metrics of computer evolution has been "Moore's Law." Intel founder Gordon Moore predicted that the number of transistors that could be squeezed onto a silicon chip would double every 18 months, and this prediction has proven itself over the past 40 years (see Technology Briefing 1—Information Systems Hardware). In fact, some computer hardware and software firms roll out new versions of their products every three months. Keeping up with this pace of change can be difficult for any organization.

FIGURE 3.18

Betamax tapes were shaped differently and required different technology inside the VCR than did VHS tapes.

Source: Getty Images, Inc.

TABLE 3.7 Some Predictions About Technology That Were Not Quite Correct

Year	Source	Quote
1876	Western Union, internal memo	"This 'telephone' has too many shortcomings to be seriously considered as a means of communication. The device is inherently of no value to us."
1895	Lord Kelvin, president, British Royal Society	"Radio has no future. Heavier-than-air flying machines are impossible. X-rays will prove to be a hoax."
1899	C.H. Duell, commissioner, U.S. Office of Patents	"Everything that can be invented has been invented."
1927	H.M. Warner, Warner Brothers	"Who the hell wants to hear actors talk?"
1943	Thomas Watson, chairman, IBM	"I think there is a world market for maybe five computers."
1949	Popular Mechanics	"Where a calculator on the ENIAC is equipped with 18,000 vacuum tubes and weighs 30 tons, computers in the future may have only 1,000 vacuum tubes and weigh only 1.5 tons."
1957	Editor, business books, Prentice Hall	"I have traveled the length and breadth of this country and talked with the best people, and I can assure you that data processing is a fad that won't last out the year."
1968	Business Week	"With over 50 foreign cars already on sale here, the Japanese auto industry isn't likely to carve out a big slice of the U.S. market."
1977	Ken Olsen, president, Digital Equipment Corporation	"There is no reason anyone would want a computer in their home."

Organizational Requirements for Innovation

Certain types of competitive environments require that organizations remain at the cutting edge in their use of information systems. For example, consider an organization that operates within an environment with strong competitive forces (Porter, 1979). The organization has competitive pressures coming from existing rival firms or from the threat of entry of new rivals. It is critical for these organizations to do things better, faster, and more cheaply than rivals. These organizations are driven to deploy innovative information systems.

These environmental characteristics alone, however, are not enough to determine whether an organization should deploy a particular information system. Before an organization can deploy any new systems well, its processes, resources, and risk tolerance must be capable of adapting to and sustaining the development and implementation processes.

Process Requirements To deploy innovative information systems well, people in the organization must be willing to do whatever they can to bypass and eliminate internal bureaucracy, set aside political squabbles, and pull together for the common good. Can you imagine, for example, a firm trying to deploy a Web-based order entry system that enables customers to access inventory information directly when people in that firm do not even share such information with each other?

Resource Requirements Organizations deploying innovative information systems must also have the human capital necessary to deploy the new systems. The organization must have enough employees available with the proper systems knowledge, skills, time, and other resources to deploy these systems. Alternatively, the organization must have resources and able systems partners available to outsource the development of such systems if necessary.

Risk Tolerance Requirements The last characteristic of an organization ready for the deployment of innovative information systems is that its members must have the appropriate tolerance of risk and uncertainty as well as the willingness to deploy and use new systems that may not be as proven and pervasive as more traditional technologies. If people within the organization desire low risk in their use of information systems, then gambling on cutting-edge systems will probably not be desirable or tolerable for them.

Predicting the Next New Thing

As you can see, using innovative information systems toward a strategic end will be difficult to identify, implement, and sustain. As Bakos and Treacy (1986) and others have argued, if you are using information systems to gain a competitive advantage in the area of operating efficiencies, it is likely that your rivals can just as easily adopt the same types of information systems and achieve the same gains. For example, you might set up a Web site that enables customers to check on the status of their order without requiring help from a customer service representative, and this might enable you to cut costs. Rivals could, however, easily copy this approach and match your cost reductions. The competitive advantage thus turns into strategic necessity for anyone in this industry.

On the other hand, there are ways to use information systems to gain a competitive advantage in a way that is easier to sustain. For example, Bakos and Treacy argued that if you can use information systems to make your products or services unique or to cause your customers to invest heavily in you so that their switching costs are high, then you are better able to develop competitive advantage that is sustainable over the long haul. For example, you might combine heavy investments in computer-aided design systems with very bright

Key Enabler

Organic Light-Emitting Diodes

When you began to see flat-screen monitors in television shows, you knew that they were "in." Flat screens are now common in both consumer and commercial electronics, including in cell phones, PC monitors, and television screens. Flat screens are typically liquid crystal displays (LCDs) in which pixels are arrayed in front of a light source. Pixels (short for "picture elements") are tiny dots that make up the representation of a picture in a computer's memory. Although LCD technology results in thin screens and uses little power, a new innovation—the organic light-emitting diode (OLED)—allows for substantially thinner screens that use much less power.

A diode is an electronic component that allows an electric current to flow in one direction but restricts its flow in the opposite direction. A light-emitting diode (LED) emits some forms of light when an electric current flows in one direction through it. An OLED is a thin-film, light-emitting diode in which the emissive layer (layer that sends a current out) is an organic compound (made up of carbon and hydrogen molecules).

OLED technology, originally developed by Sanyo and Kodak, offers several advantages over LCD technology:

- Wider viewing angles—The screen can be viewed without distortion up to 160 degrees.
- Brighter and better resolution (clearer and brighter picture).
- Cheaper—OLEDs are up to 20 to 50 percent cheaper to produce than LCDs.
- Less power usage—Low power usage is a major advantage to OLEDs since they use just 2 to 10 volts of electricity.
- Superthin screens—OLEDs can be hundreds of times thinner than paper. This allows for such uses as smart computer monitor wallpaper or smart car paint where the wallpaper or paint can display any color, design, or even video.

Where screens are concerned, thinner, cheaper, and clearer are clearly the watchwords.

Source: Wikipedia.org

engineers in order to perfect your product and make it unique, something relatively difficult to copy. Alternatively, you might use a customer relationship management system to build an extensive database containing the entire history of your interaction with each of your customers and then use that system to provide very high-quality, intimate, rapid, customized service that would convince customers that if they switched to a rival, it would take them years to build up that kind of relationship with the other firm.

The Innovator's Dilemma Deciding which innovations to adopt and pursue has never been easy. In fact, there are many classic examples where so-called industry leaders failed to see the changing opportunities introduced by new innovations (see Table 3.7). In 1962, Everett Rogers theorized that the adoption of innovations usually follows an S-shaped curve (i.e., Diffusion of Innovations, see Figure 3.19). When an innovation is brought to market, initially, only a small group of "innovators" will adopt that innovation. After some time, sales pick up as the innovators are followed by the "early adopters" and the "early majority," and the increase in sales is strongest. Then, sales slowly level off when the "late majority" starts adopting the innovation. Finally, sales stay level as only the "laggards" are left to adopt the innovation.

However, some innovations are more disruptive, turning entire industries upside down. Clayton Christensen's *The **Innovator's Dilemma*** outlines how *disruptive innovations* undermine effective management practices, often leading to the demise of an organization or an industry. **Disruptive innovations** are new technologies, products, or services that eventually surpass the existing dominant technology or product in a market (see Table 3.8). For example, retail giant Sears nearly failed in the early 1990s when they did not recognize the transformational power of the disruptive innovation, discount retailing; today, discounters like Wal-Mart and segment-specific stores like Home Depot dominate retailing.

Within every market, there are customers who have relatively high, moderate, or low performance requirements from the existing product offerings. For example, within the mobile phone industry today, some low-performance customers demand very basic phones and services (e.g., no text messaging, camera, or data services), while high-performance customers use devices and services that rival the capabilities of some personal computers with high-speed Internet connections. Additionally, over time, as disruptive innovations

TABLE 3.8 Examples of Disruptive Innovations and Their Associated Displaced or Marginalized Technology

Disruptive Innovation	Displaced or Marginalized Technology
Digital photography	Silver halide photographic file
Mobile telephony	Wire-line telephony
Handheld digital appliances	Notebook computers
Xbox, PlayStation	Desktop computers
Online stock brokerage	Full-service stock brokerages
Online retailing	Bricks-and-mortar retailing
Free, downloadable greeting cards	Printed greeting cards
Distance education	Classroom education
Unmanned aircraft	Manned aircraft
Nurse practitioners	Medical doctors
Semiconductors	Vacuum tubes
Desktop publishing	Traditional publishing
Automobiles	Horses
Airplanes	Trains
Compact disc	Cassettes and records
MP3 players and music downloading	Compact discs and music stores

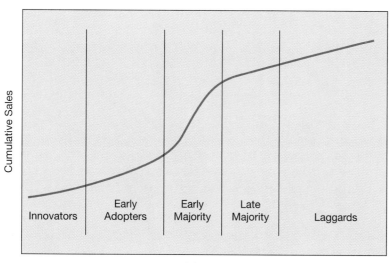

FIGURE 3.19

Diffusion of innovations.

Source: Adapted from Rogers, 1962.

and incremental improvements are introduced into an industry, the capabilities of all products improve; as product capabilities improve at the high-performance end of the market, the number of potential customers gets relatively smaller. At the same time, as the low-end products also improve, they are increasingly able to capture more and more of the mainstream marketplace.

To illustrate this progression, Christensen provides compelling examples within several industries. In particular, the collapse of 1970s midrange (minicomputer) giant Digital Equipment Company (DEC) (and the entire midrange industry for that matter) clearly illustrates the innovator's dilemma. DEC was ultimately surpassed in the marketplace by microprocessor-based computers, with the microprocessor being the disruptive innovation.

In the 1970s, when microcomputers were first introduced, DEC (and their customers) deemed them to be toys and ignored their potential. It is important to note that DEC was a well-run company and was touted as having one of the finest executive teams in the world. Additionally, DEC used leading management techniques, such as conducting extensive market research with their existing customers and industry (i.e., they put "marketing" ahead of technology; for a divergent view, see the discussion of the E-Business Innovation Cycle later in this chapter). When surveyed, none of DECs customers indicated a need for microcomputers, and thus DEC concluded that developing improved capabilities within their *existing* midrange computer product line is where they should focus. At this time, DEC's goal was to serve the needs of "high" and "mid" performance users, which made up the largest part of the total market for computers (see Figure 3.20). The increasing performance of DECs products started meeting the needs of customers who would traditionally purchase mainframe computers, and so DEC could try to "up sell" to mainframe customers of IBM, Burroughs, and Honeywell, where the margins were even greater than in the midrange computer industry.

Initially, there were virtually no competitive product offerings serving the needs of the low-performance users; in other words, current product offerings by established computer manufacturers such as DEC were either too powerful or too expensive (or both) for these low-end customers. In the 1980s, the microcomputer industry was launched by Apple and the (disruptive) microprocessor, developed in the 1970s, was now being turned into a product that had the capabilities and price for users in the low-performance category of the marketplace. DEC was not alone in ignoring the introduction of microcomputers; virtually all established players in the computing industry continued to focus on their existing customers and existing product lines, incrementally improving their products over time. Meanwhile, in just a few years, the microcomputer industry grew and matured, going from toy, to office automation device (e.g., a replacement for the typewriter or adding machine), to a multipurpose business computer for many small and medium-size businesses that

FIGURE 3.20

Innovator's dilemma view of the evolution of the computing industry.

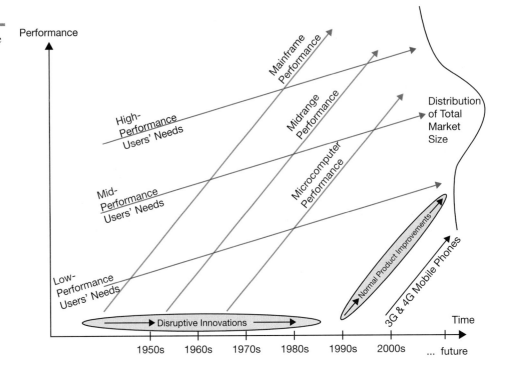

could never before afford a computer. As the low end of the market took shape in the 1980s, DEC continued to focus on their existing customers and business model (e.g., direct selling, personal service, and so on). Rapidly, the capabilities of the disruptive microcomputers improved, meeting the needs of not only the low end but also the midperformance range of the marketplace, which was traditionally served by DEC's midrange computers. Being far more inexpensive than DEC's products, the microcomputers took over the bulk of the market. Sadly, DEC continued to ignore the microcomputer industry until it was too late, and DEC could do nothing but watch the loss of their biggest traditional market segment. By January 26, 1998, what was left of DEC was sold to Compaq Computers; Compaq was later acquired by Hewlett-Packard in 2002.

Today, microprocessor-based computers from Dell, Sony, Apple, and others meet or exceed the needs of much of the *entire* marketplace; additionally, only a handful of high-end computer manufacturers remain. So what is next for this industry? Many believe that the next disruptive innovation will be 3G and 4G mobile phones from companies like Nokia, Motorola, and Samsung (see Technology Briefing 4—Networking). Another example of an industry that has been transformed by disruptive technologies is the photo industry (see the Industry Analysis at the end of the chapter). What DEC experienced, so too have countless other companies in numerous industries. Table 3.9 summarizes the typical progression and effects of a disruptive innovation on an industry.

Organizing to Make Innovation Choices Given the evolution of industries outlined in the innovator's dilemma, how do organizations make decisions on which innovations to embrace and which to ignore? In his follow-up book, *The Innovator's Solution,* Christenson outlines a process, called the *disruptive growth engine,* which all organizations can follow to more effectively respond to disruptive innovations in their industry. This process has the following steps:

1. ***Start Early.*** To gain the greatest opportunities, become a leader in identifying, tracking, and adopting disruptive innovations by making these processes a formal part of the organization (i.e., budgets, personnel, and so on).

TABLE 3.9 Typical Progression and Effects of Disruptive Innovation on an Industry

1. First mover introduces a new technology. It is expensive, focusing on a small number of high-performance, high-margin customers.

2. Over time, the first mover focuses on improving product capabilities to meet the needs of higher-performance customers in order to continue to reap the highest margins.

3. Later entrants, using a disruptive innovation, have an inferior market position, focusing on lower-performance, lower-margin customers.

4. Over time, later entrants focus on incremental product improvements to serve the needs of more lower-performance customers, also focusing on cost efficiencies to offset lack of margins with economies of scale.

5. As the market matures, all products improve, competition increases, and margins diminish; the first mover rarely learns the efficiencies of the later entrants and is entrenched in high-margin business practices; the first mover's market share rapidly erodes as that of the later entrants rapidly grows.

6. Ultimately, the later entrants' products meet or exceed the requirements for the vast majority of the marketplace, they "win" with efficient, low-cost business processes demanded by the majority of the marketplace.

2. *Executive Leadership.* To gain credibility as well as to bridge sustaining and disruptive product development, visible and credible leadership is required.
3. *Build a Team of Expert Innovators.* To most effectively identify and evaluate potential disruptive innovations, build a competent team of expert innovators.
4. *Educate the Organization.* To see opportunities, those closest to customers and competitors (e.g., marketing, customer support, and engineering) need to understand how to identify disruptive innovations.

In addition to formalizing the identification of innovations with the organization, shifts in business processes and the fundamental thinking about disruptive innovations are needed. Next, we examine how to implement the innovation identification process.

Implementing the Innovation Process Executives today who are serious about using information technology in innovative ways have made it a point to have their people be continually on the lookout for new disruptive innovations that will have a significant impact on their business. Wheeler (2002b) has summarized this process nicely as the **E-Business Innovation Cycle** (see Figure 3.21). Like the term "e-commerce," "e-business" refers to the use of information technologies and systems to support the business. Whereas "e-commerce" generally means the use of the Internet and related technologies to support commerce, **e-business** has a broader meaning: the use of nearly any information technologies or systems to support every part of the business. The model essentially holds that the key to success for modern organizations is the extent to which they use information technologies and systems in timely, innovative ways. The vertical dimension of the E-Business Innovation Cycle shows the extent to which an organization derives value from a particular information technology, and the horizontal dimension shows time. Next, we examine the cycle.

CHOOSING ENABLING/EMERGING TECHNOLOGIES. The first bubble left of the graph shows that successful organizations first create jobs, groups, and processes that are all devoted to scanning the environment for new emerging and **enabling technologies** (i.e., information technologies that enable a firm to accomplish a task or goal or to gain or sustain competitive advantage in some way; also called disruptive innovations) that appear to be relevant for the organization. For example, an organization might designate a small group within the Information Systems department as the "Emerging Technologies" unit

FIGURE 3.21

The E-Business Innovation
Cycle.

Source: Wheeler (2002).

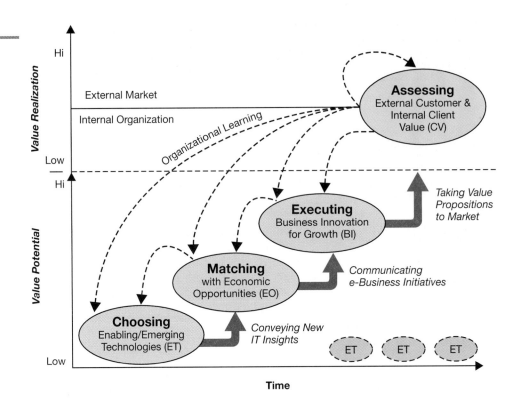

and charge them with looking out for new technologies that will have an impact on the business. As part of their job, this group will pore over current technology magazines, participate in Internet discussion forums on technology topics, go to technology conferences and conventions, and have strong, active relationships with technology researchers at universities and technology companies.

MATCHING TECHNOLOGIES TO OPPORTUNITIES. Next, in the second bubble, the organization matches the most promising new technologies with current **economic opportunities**. For example, the Emerging Technologies group might have identified advances in database management systems (and a dramatic drop in data storage costs) as a key emerging technology that now enables a massive data warehouse to be feasible. In addition, managers within the marketing function of the firm have recognized that competitors have really dropped the ball in terms of customer service and that there is an opportunity to gain customers and market share by serving customers better.

EXECUTING BUSINESS INNOVATION FOR GROWTH. The third bubble represents the process of selecting among myriad opportunities to take advantage of the database and data storage advances and addressing the current opportunity to grab customers and market share. The organization decides to implement an enterprise-wide data warehouse that enables them to have at their fingertips integrated corporate-wide data and an unparalleled capability to understand, react to, and better serve customers.

ASSESSING VALUE. The fourth bubble represents the process of assessing the value of that use of technology, not only to customers but to internal clients (i.e., sales representatives, marketing managers, the chief operating officer, and so on) as well.

The E-Business Innovation Cycle suggests three new ways to think about investments in disruptive innovations:

1. *Put Technology Ahead of Strategy.* This approach says that technology is so important to strategy and to success that you have to begin with technology. Notice that the first bubble involves understanding, identifying, and choosing technologies that are important. The first bubble does not begin with strategy, as a traditional approach to running a business organization would suggest. In fact, many would argue that given how

important technology is today and how fast it changes, if you start with a strategy and then try to retrofit technology into your aging strategy, you are doomed. This approach argues that you begin by understanding technology and develop a strategy from there. This approach is admittedly very uncomfortable for people who think in traditional ways and/or who are not comfortable with technology. We believe, however, that for many modern organizations, thinking about technology in this way is key.

2. ***Put Technology Ahead of Marketing.*** The second way that this approach turns conventional wisdom on its head is that, like strategy, marketing also takes a backseat to the technology. Think about it carefully, and you will see that marketing does not come into play until later in this model. A very traditional marketing-oriented approach would be to go first to your customers and find out from them what their needs are and what you ought to be doing with technology (as did DEC). The trouble with this approach is that, given the rapid evolution of technology, your customers are not likely to know about new technologies and their capabilities. In some sense, they are the last place you ought to be looking for ideas about new technologies and their impact on your business. Indeed, if they know about the new technology, then chances are your competitors already do too, and that technology is not one to rest your competitive advantage on. As Steve Jobs of Apple put it, "You can't just ask people what they want and then try to give that to them. By the time you get it built, they'll want something new."

3. ***Innovation Is Continuous.*** The third way that this approach is interesting—and potentially troubling—is that the process has to be ongoing. As shown along the time dimension along the bottom of the graph, the first bubble repeats over and over again as the Emerging Technologies group is constantly on the lookout for the "next new thing" that will revolutionize the business. The rate of information technology evolution is not likely to slow down, and innovative organizations truly cannot—and do not—ever rest.

Today, dealing with rapid change caused by disruptive innovations is a reality for most industries. If you are a leader in an industry, you must continually learn to embrace and exploit disruptive innovations, potentially *destroying* your existing core business while at the same time building a new business around the disruptive innovation. If you fail to do this, your competition may do it for you.

Industry Analysis

Photo Industry

Have you tried lately to purchase a roll of Kodak 35-mm color film with 12 exposures? It's hard to find because the 12-exposure option is no longer manufactured—24 or 36 exposures are still for sale, but for how long?

Soon new cameras that use film will also be hard to find. For instance, Canon, number one in digital camera sales in the United States in 2006 (Sony was second and Kodak third), announced in June 2006 that the company would no longer develop new film cameras. Canon will concentrate instead on improving its digital cameras and developing new digital models. Other camera/film companies are following Canon's lead:

- Earlier in 2006, Konica Minolta Holdings said it would stop making film cameras, lenses, and even film, then announced it was selling its assets to rival Sony.

- Nikon, a world leader in high-quality camera products, said in January 2006 that it would stop making most models of film cameras to focus solely on digital. Nikon now makes only two film cameras, the F6 for professionals and the FM10 for beginners.

In just over four years (2002–2006), photography moved from film to digital dominance. "The shift from film to digital was way faster than we expected," said Kakushi Kiuchi, an executive in charge of professional photography for Fuji Film at the Photo Imaging Expo in Tokyo in 2006. Digital technology was clearly a disruptive innovation in the photo industry.

Just as PC technology has progressed at a dizzying rate over the past 10 years, so too has digital photography. Film photography has dominated the industry for over 100 years, but once digital cameras came online, the digital photography market exploded.

Apple manufactured the first digital cameras sold to the general public in 1994. One year later, Kodak introduced its first digital camera, the Kodak DC40. The DC40 was extremely successful, and soon several competing camera companies, including Canon, Sony, and Fuji, introduced digital cameras to the consumer market. (Experts predict that Kodak's mainstay— 35-mm movie film products—will inevitably also go completely digital, as digitized movies become the rule, both for theater and for home viewing.)

Polaroid, the first camera company to manufacture a camera that could also instantly develop photos captured on film, has also had to change significantly as digital became the rule. The company has battled back from bankruptcy twice in 1993 and 2004 with a line of nonphotography business products, including commercial ID printing and DVD players. Given consumer demand for digital pictures and increasing options such as high-quality desktop printing, focusing exclusively on instant photos was no longer profitable for Polaroid.

Without the changes in their business models that moved the companies away from film photography and into the digital market, Kodak and Polaroid would probably not have survived.

With Kodak, Polaroid, Canon, and other camera and film companies leading the way, the photography industry now focuses on the digital electronics consumers prefer. The result is that new electronic products, from cell phones to laptops, now have photographic capabilities.

Clearly, as the world continues to flatten, the motto for the photography industry and other industries as well is that digital dominates.

Questions

1. What competitive dynamics are affecting the digital camera marketplace?
2. Contrast the evolution of the digital camera industry with the cellular phone industry. What is similar? What is unique?

Sources: Emi Doi, "As Film Fades, Japan's Camera Industry Changes Focus," *McClatchy Washington Bureau* (June 21, 2006), http://www.realcities.com/mld/krwashington/news/ world/14870142.htm

Danit Lidor, "Perez' Kodak Loses No. 1 U.S. Digital Camera Spot," *Forbes.com* (May 9, 2006), http://www.forbes.com/2006/05/09/kodak-digital-cameras-cx_ gl_0509autofacescan15.html

Anonymous, "Polaroid Dips into DVD Recorder Market," *DVD Recorder World* (May 9, 2006), http://www.dvdrecorderworld.com/news/359

Press Release, "Polaroid Commercial ID Systems Launches Fully Integrated Line of Photo ID Products," *Yahoo! Finance* (April 11, 2006), http://biz.yahoo.com/prnews/060411/ netu019.html?.v=49

Key Points Review

1. *Discuss how information systems can be used for automation, organizational learning, and strategic advantage.* Automating business activities occurs when information systems are used to do a business activity faster or more cheaply. IS can be used to help automate. It can also be used to improve aspects of an operation in order to gain dramatic improvements in the operation as a whole. When this occurs, technology is said to help us learn because it provides information about its operation and the underlying work process that it supports. Using information systems to automate and learn about business processes is a good start. However, information systems can add even more value to an organization if they are conceived, designed, used, and managed with a strategic approach. To apply information systems strategically, you must understand the organization's value chain and be able to identify opportunities in which you can use information systems to make changes or improvements in the value chain to gain or sustain a competitive advantage. This requires a change in mind-set from thinking about information systems as an expense to be minimized to thinking of information systems as an asset to be invested in.

2. *Describe how to formulate and present the business case for a system.* Making the business case is

the process of building and presenting the set of arguments that show that an information system is adding value to the organization and/or its constituents. It is often difficult to quantify the value that an information system provides because of measurement problems, time lags before benefits are realized, industry redistribution, and mismanagement. You must also understand your organization's particular business strategy in order to make an effective business case for systems. In short, technology investments should be closely linked to the organization's business strategy because these investments are becoming one of the major vehicles by which organizations can achieve their strategy. After you gain an understanding of your organization's position in the marketplace, its strategy for investing in systems that add value, and firm-level implementation factors, you can quantify the relative costs and benefits of the system. Considering all of these factors simultaneously will help you formulate an effective business case. In order to make a convincing presentation, you should be specific about the benefits this investment will provide for the organization. To do this, you must convert the benefits into monetary terms, such as the amount of money saved or revenue generated. If you have difficulty identifying specific monetary measures, you should devise some proxy measures to demonstrate the benefits of the system. Finally, make sure that you measure things that are important to the decision makers of the organizations. Choosing the wrong measures can yield a negative decision about a beneficial system.

3. *Explain why and how companies are continually looking for innovative ways to use information systems for competitive advantage.* Organizations are finding innovative ways to use new technologies to help them do things faster, better, and more cost efficiently than rivals. Being at the technological cutting edge has its disadvantages and is typically quite difficult to execute. Given that new technologies are not as stable as traditional ones, relying on innovative information systems and technologies can be problematic. Because constantly upgrading to newer and better systems is expensive, relying on emerging systems can hurt a firm financially. In addition, using innovative information systems for competitive advantage can provide short-lived advantages; competitors can quickly jump on the technological bandwagon and easily mimic the same system. Not every organization should deploy innovative information systems. Those organizations that find themselves in highly competitive environments probably most need to deploy new technologies to stay ahead of rivals. To best deploy these new technologies, organizations must be ready for the business process changes that will ensue, have the resources necessary to deploy new technologies successfully, and be tolerant of the risk and problems involved in being at the cutting edge. Deploying emerging information systems is essentially a risk/return gamble: the risks are relatively high, but the potential rewards are great. Organizations successfully utilizing innovative systems and technologies today have people (and in some cases special units) who scan the environment, looking out for emerging and enabling (and potentially disruptive) technologies that can help their firm. They then narrow down the list to technologies that match with challenges the firm faces or create economic opportunities. Next, they choose a particular technology or a set of technologies and implement them in a way that enables them to gain or sustain competitive advantage. Finally, they assess these technology projects in terms of their value not only to internal people and groups but also to external clients and partners. This process is ongoing, as information technologies and systems continually evolve.

Key Terms

automating 85	informating 85	proxy variables 105
best-cost provider strategy 88	innovator's dilemma 112	recurring costs 99
break-even analysis 100	intangible benefits 100	strategic necessity 93
cost-benefit analysis 100	intangible costs 99	strategic planning 87
differentiation strategy 87	learning organization 86	system effectiveness 93
discount rate 100	low-cost leadership strategy 87	system efficiency 93
disruptive innovations 112	making the business case 91	tangible benefits 100
e-business 115	net-present-value analysis 100	tangible costs 99
E-Business Innovation	nonrecurring costs 99	total cost of ownership
Cycle 115	organizational learning 86	(TCO) 99
economic opportunities 116	organizational strategy 87	value chain 89
enabling technologies 115	productivity paradox 92	value chain analysis 89

Review Questions

1. Compare and contrast automating and learning.
2. Describe the attributes of a learning organization.
3. List five general types of organizational strategy.
4. Describe competitive advantage and list six sources.
5. Describe the productivity paradox.
6. Describe how to make a successful business case, contrasting faith-, fear-, and fact-based arguments.
7. Compare and contrast tangible and intangible benefits and costs.
8. Contrast the perspectives of different stakeholders involved in making information systems investment decisions.
9. Define a proxy variable and give an example.
10. Why is successful application of innovative technologies and systems often difficult?
11. What is the "innovator's dilemma"?
12. Using past examples, explain what is meant by a disruptive innovation.
13. Describe the E-business Innovation Cycle.

Self-Study Questions

Note: Visit the Interactive Study Guide on the text Web site for additional Self-Study Questions: **www.prenhall.com/Jessup**.

1. _____ is using technology as a way to help complete a task within an organization faster and, perhaps, more cheaply.
   A. automating
   B. learning
   C. strategizing
   D. processing
2. What are new technologies, products, or services that eventually surpass the existing dominant technology or product in a market called?
   A. surpassing event
   B. disruptive innovation
   C. innovative technology
   D. technology change
3. Which of the following is an intangible benefit?
   A. negative benefits
   B. qualitative benefits
   C. quantitative costs
   D. positive cash flows
4. Which of the following is *not* improving the value chain?
   A. improving procurement processes
   B. increasing operating costs
   C. minimizing marketing expenditures
   D. selling more products
5. Which of the following is not one of the three types of arguments commonly made in the business case for an information system?
   A. fear
   B. fact
   C. faith
   D. fun

6. A company is said to have _____ when it has gained an edge over its rivals.
   A. monopoly
   B. profitability
   C. competitive advantage
   D. computer advantage
7. Each of the following was described in this chapter as a source of competitive advantage except for _____.
   A. delivering superior customer service
   B. achieving lower cost than rivals
   C. being the subject of a hostile takeover
   D. having shorter lead times in developing and testing new products
8. Making the _____ is the process of building and presenting the set of arguments that show that an information system is adding value to the organization.
   A. organizational chart
   B. organizational case
   C. law case
   D. business case
9. How disruptive innovations undermine effective management practices, often leading to the demise of an organization or an industry, is known as _____.
   A. bad luck
   B. technological obsolescence
   C. life cycle analysis
   D. innovator's dilemma
10. What is a process of choosing, matching, executing, and assessing innovative technologies called?
    A. environmental scanning
    B. E-Business Innovation Cycle
    C. strategic planning
    D. none of the above

Answers are on page 122.

Problems and Exercises

1. Match the following terms with the appropriate definitions:
   i. Value chain analysis
   ii. Tangible costs
   iii. Total cost of ownership (TCO)
   iv. Productivity paradox
   v. Learning organization
   vi. Value chain
   vii. E-Business Innovation Cycle
   viii. Proxy variable
   ix. Disruptive innovation
   x. Innovator's dilemma
      a. How disruptive innovations undermine effective management practices, often leading to the demise of an organization or an industry
      b. Costs that are quantifiable or have physical substance
      c. The process of analyzing an organization's activities to determine where value is added to products and/or services and the costs that are incurred for doing so
      d. New technologies, products, or services that eventually surpass the existing dominant technology or product in a market
      e. A substitute variable (such as customer contact) expressed on a 5-point scale from low to high that is used in place of an information system's intangible benefit, which is difficult to quantify
      f. The cost of owning and operating a system, including the total cost of acquisition, as well as all costs associated with its ongoing use and maintenance
      g. An organization that is able to learn, grow, and manage its knowledge well
      h. The extent to which an organization uses information technologies in innovative ways and derives value from these technologies over time
      i. The observation that productivity increases at a rate that is lower than expected when new technologies are introduced
      j. The set of primary and support activities in an organization where value is added to a product or service

2. After reading this chapter, it should be fairly obvious why an IS professional should be able to make a business case for a given system. Why, however, is it just as important for non-IS professionals? How are they involved in this process? What is their role in making information systems investment decisions?

3. Why is it important to look at industry factors when making a business case? What effect might strong competition have on IS investment and use? What effect might weak competition have on IS investment and use? Why?

4. Argue for or against the following statement: "When making the business case, you should concentrate on the decision makers' 'hot buttons' and gloss over some of the other details."

5. What role does the organizational culture play in IS investments? Is this something that can be easily adjusted when necessary? Why or why not? Who is in control of a firm's organizational culture? Do you have personal experiences with this issue?

6. Why can it be difficult to develop an accurate cost-benefit analysis? What factors may be difficult to quantify? How can this be handled? Is this something that should just be avoided altogether? What are the consequences of that approach?

7. Within a small group of classmates, describe any involvement you have had with making the business case for buying something for yourself or within an organization. To whom were you making the case? Was it a difficult sell? Why? To what extent did you follow the guidelines set forth in this chapter? Were your arguments based on faith, fear, fact, or fiction? How did your business case differ from those of others in your group? Were you successful? Why or why not? Were they successful? Why or why not?

8. Of the five industry forces presented in the chapter (Porter's model), which is the most significant for an organization in terms of making IS investment decisions? Why? Which is the least significant? Why?

9. Discuss the following in a small group of classmates or with a friend. Describe a situation from your own experience in which something was purchased where a cost-benefit analysis showed it to have a negative return when based on tangible factors. Was the purchase decision based on intangible factors? Have these intangible factors proven themselves to be worth the investment? Was it harder to convince others of the purchase because of these intangible factors?

10. Contrast the total cost of acquisition versus the total cost of ownership for the purchase of a new car. Demonstrate how the type of car, year, make, model, and so on change the values of various types of costs and benefits.

11. Identify and describe three different situations where fear, faith, or fact arguments would be most compelling to making an information systems investment decision.

12. Talk to an information systems manager and have him or her describe a system that took some length of time to improve organizational productivity in some significant way. Specifically, find out how long and why it took this much time. Was the time frame longer than expected? Why or why not? Was this a typical situation or a unique one?

13. Contrast the differing perspectives of different stakeholders involved in making information systems investment decisions.

14. Why shouldn't every organization deploy innovative information systems? What are some of the recommended characteristics of an organization that are necessary in order for that organization to successfully deploy innovative technologies?

15. Identify examples not discussed in the chapter of disruptive innovations that successfully displaced or marginalized an industry or technology.

16. Apply the progression and effects of disruptive innovation on an industry (see Table 3.9), describing the evolution of a disruptive technology to a product or industry.

Application Exercises

 Note: The existing data files referenced in these exercises are available on the Student Companion Web site: **www.prenhall.com/ Jessup.**

 Spreadsheet Application: Valuing Information Systems

The cost of maintaining information systems is high for Campus Travel. You have been assigned to evaluate the total cost of owership (TCO) of a few systems that are currently in use by Campus Travel employees. Take a look at the TCO.csv file to obtain the list of systems that are in use and the costs associated with maintaining the software, hardware, and the associated personnel for each type of system. Calculate the following for your operations manager:

1. The costs for server hardware by adding a new column to include Web servers. This includes $4,500 for the main campus and $2,200 for the other campuses.

2. The TCO for the entire IS in Campus Travel (Hint: Sum all the values for all the systems together).

3. The TCO for servers and network components of the IS.

4. Make sure that you format the table, including using the currency format, in a professional manner.

 Database Application: Building a System Usage Database

To understand the assets in Campus Travel, the IS manager has asked you to design a database that would be able to store all the assets. Your manager asks you to do the following:

1. Create a new blank database called asset.mdb.

2. Create a new table called "assets" in the asset database with the following fields:
   a. Item ID (Text field)
   b. Item Name (Text field)
   c. Description (Memo field)
   d. Category (hardware, software, other)
   e. Condition (new, good, fair, poor)
   f. Acquisition Date (Date field)
   g. Purchase Price (Currency field)
   h. Current Value (Currency field)

Team Work Exercise: Pizza, Anyone?

Compare with your classmates your experiences with ordering pizza over the phone for delivery to your home. When you call to order the pizza, do you have to give them your full name, address, and phone number every time you call them, or do they merely ask your phone number and then automatically know who you are and where you live? If it is the latter, then they are using an information system to keep track of you so that they do not continually have to annoy you by asking you for your name, address, and phone number every time you call. How important is this to you? Is this giving the pizza company a competitive advantage? Is it as important to you as the price of the pizza or how fast it is delivered? Are there conditions under which superior use of information systems can compensate for inferior products (think about products other than pizza, too)?

Answers to the Self-Study Questions

1. A, p. 85   2. B, p. 112   3. B, p. 100   4. B, p. 89   5. D, p. 96
6. C, p. 88   7. C, p. 89   8. D, p. 91   9. D, p. 112   10. B, p. 115

case ①

Netflix

Remember the old brick-and-mortar movie rental services? You drove to the physical location, scanned shelves for your movie of choice (too frequently, it wasn't in), paid the clerk, and left. The flick was due back in 24 hours (usually three to five days max), or you were billed a hefty late fee. In some cases, forgetful customers answered the door to find a police officer asking why they hadn't returned a rental movie.

Movie rental stores still exist, of course—Blockbuster may come to mind first—but now there are alternatives. Pay-per-view is an option for cable and satellite dish TV subscribers, but choices are limited to the services' picks and are available only after movies have been offered as rental DVDs and videos for 30 days. Since customers are not always satisfied with limits inherent in these options—late fees, unavailability of newer films, short turnaround times, and so on—it had to follow that someone would come up with the idea to offer a click-based online movie rental service.

Enter Netflix in 2002, the first and now the largest online movie rental service. As of 2007, Netflix offered 6 million subscribers 70,000 movie choices. The term "subscriber" is the key to Netflix's unique idea. Movie aficionados subscribe to the Netflix service by paying a monthly fee based on the number of movies they want to rent each month. For $4.99 per month (the lowest-priced plan), customers can rent two movies per month. Fees continue upward as the number of movie rentals per month increase, with the top fee set at $23.99 per month—four DVDs out at a time and unlimited rentals per month. For all plans, postage is paid each way, the U.S. Postal Service handles mailed DVDs both ways, and there are no late fees. When one movie is returned, a second is mailed from a list of preferences the customer sets.

Soon after Netflix's inception in 2002, Blockbuster, the nation's largest movie rental chain, and Wal-Mart, the largest business in the United States, began to offer in-store subscription services similar to Netflix's model. By 2006, however, Wal-Mart had dropped its movie rental subscription service, and Blockbuster's subscription service was losing money.

Netflix's extraordinary and, therefore, popular service has outpaced competitive movie rental services, including pay-per-view because it personalizes a customer's movie rental experience to a degree not possible before. This personalized service asks the customer to rate up to 40 movies. From this information, software called Cinematch creates a profile of each customer and a "queue" of recommended movies. If, for example, a customer liked "Troy," he or she may also like "Alexander," and that movie will be included in the customer's queue. Netflix's Cinematch system allows customers to tap a wide database of movies, many of which they may not have been aware of at all since it will move to the next movie in a customer's queue if a more recent and popular listing is not immediately available.

Another strategy employed by Netflix is the "friends" feature, which allows subscribers to share and recommend movies to one another. Although not a unique idea to the Internet, this creates online communities of Netflix customers that further drive the business. Netflix is not without critics. It turns out that the service "rewards" customers with the fewest monthly rentals and "punishes" those with the most rentals in terms of popular movie availability and promptness of shipping. This policy is spelled out in the company's Terms of Service, published on the Netflix Web site:

> In determining priority for shipping and inventory allocation, we may utilize many different factors, including without limitation, the number and type of DVDs you rent through our service, the subscription plan you select, as well as other uses of our service by you.

For example, if all other factors are the same, we give priority to those members who receive the fewest DVDs through our service.

According to the Netflix site, when you add a popular movie that is currently unavailable, you are added to the queue. There is an assumption by the customers that the queue is linear, meaning that the first customer to request the movie would be the first customer to get the movie—or first in, first out. In reality, the priority service equation selects customers on the basis of their profitability. With shipping being the major cost for the online movie distributor, customers who cost the most in terms of shipping may not receive popular movies first.

What does this mean for the customers? If you are a customer who uses the service infrequently, then you are highly profitable for Netflix since your shipping costs are low. Therefore, your selections are prioritized. The customers who use the service frequently or what Netflix would deem "overfrequently" are seen as not as profitable and therefore do not receive priority.

In 2004, this policy caused a "frequent" Netflix customer to sue the company in a class action lawsuit titled *Chavez v. Netflix, Inc.* The plaintiff in the case, Frank Chavez, claimed Netflix's claims that a subscriber could rent "unlimited" DVDs each month and receive them in "a day's time" were false. (Chavez had attempted to rent hundreds of DVDs a month but sued when he found he could not.) Although Netflix denied any wrongdoing, they settled the suit in 2005. Chavez received $2,000, and his lawyers got over $2.5 million. Certain Netflix customers who joined the class action suit were upgraded to a higher plan for a short period, and Netflix instituted a limited try-the-plan-for-three-months-free offer.

Although some customers have expressed dissatisfaction, Netflix customer numbers have increased rather than decreased.

Questions

1. Can local video stores survive in the digital world? Contrast their evolution with that of local bookstores. What is similar? What is unique?

2. Forecast the future of Netflix in regard to the advent of on-demand video where any type of video content is available at any time on any device.

3. Discuss whether you believe Netflix's terms of service are fair.

Sources: Anonymous, "Netflix Settlement Details," *Boing, Boing* (November 2, 2005), http://www.boingboing.net/2005/11/02/netflix_lawsuit_sett.html

Netflix Terms of Service and Plans, http://www.netflix.com/MediaCenter?id=1005&hnjr=8 and http://www.netflix.com/StaticPage?id=1004

Jeffrey M. O'Brien, "The Netflix Effect," *Wired* (December 2002), http://www.wired.com/wired/archive/10.12/netflix.html

Timothy J. Mullaney and Robert Hof, "Netflix Starring in Merger Story?," *Business Week Online* (November 10, 2005), http://www.businessweek.com/technology/content/nov2005/tc20051110_143721.htm

Mike Elgan, "How to Hack Netflix," *Information Week* (January 30, 2006), http://www.informationweek.com/news/showArticle.jhtml?articleID =177105341

case ❷

e-Enabling the Air Transport Industry: Valuing Information Systems

In its early years, airlines were primarily carriers of airmail, and their primary customer was the U.S. government. Consequentially, the air transport industry grew to be heavily regulated. The U.S. government has started deregulating the air transport industry in 1978, opening up the market for a large number of new entrants, especially for carriers in the low-cost niche. The global market, however, has remained highly regulated. Typically, routes that airlines can fly between two countries are negotiated in a bilateral fashion. These agreements dictate which routes an airline can fly, where its planes can land, and where it could pick up or drop off passengers—"not exactly an open market," according to Phil Condit, Boeing's former Chairman and chief executive officer. Another factor adding to these complications is that people in one country usually are banned from owning an airline in another country because of the strategic value of the aircraft.

In addition to federal regulations, the International Air Transport Association (IATA) set a number of different standards for many "below the wing" activities. Most notably, IATA created the Passenger and Airport Data Interchange Standards (PADIS) to govern almost all aspects related to passenger air travel. For example, PADIS regulates standards for reservations, electronic ticketing,

check-in, airport/airline communication, and baggage handling, ensuring that passengers can travel on one ticket with different airlines or that they can check their baggage through the final destination regardless of their carriers.

Despite the overall regulatory environment, the deregulation of the air transport industry in the late 1970s has led to the formation of a large number of new airlines, especially in the low-cost segment. Suddenly, both new entrants and established airlines had to reduce operating costs in order to survive in this new competitive environment. Shortly after the deregulation, several established airlines started struggling for survival. Pan Am, founded in 1927, had to file for bankruptcy in 1991, giving in to the pressure of low-cost competitors. Likewise, TWA filed for bankruptcy for three times before being acquired by American Airlines in 2001.

After deregulation, the air transport industry has seen increased competition because of both existing airlines and new entrants; however, most customers do not have an alternative to air travel because of both speed and convenience factors when compared to other means of transportation. Air travel is especially advantageous for business travelers, where other forms of transportation such as automobile or rail cannot be considered a

comparable alternative. Although every traveler has experienced a drastic decrease in convenience due to increased security measures following the September 11, 2001, terrorist attacks in the United States, most travelers still do not have an alternative to air travel. According to Boeing, air travel demand could fluctuate widely in the short term, but forecasts showed a steady growth in demand in the long run. Between 2005 and 2025, the world's fleet of commercial aircraft (regional jets or larger) was forecast to double and total almost 36,000 airplanes. In addition, to the over 17,000 airplanes needed to sustain the growth, about 9,600 new airplanes are needed to replace retired and converted

Additions and Removals of Commercial Aircraft 2005–2025.

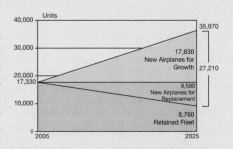

Source: Boeing Market Overview (2006) http://www.boeing.com/nosearch/exec_pres/ CMO.pdf (accessed August 23, 2006)

airplanes, for a total of more than 27,000 new airplanes (see Figure).

An important factor influencing the demand for new aircraft was the airlines' operating structure. While traditionally most airlines have relied on a hub-and-spoke model, more and more airlines are now trying to serve more nonstop markets by offering more direct routes between smaller cities, thus reducing the dependence on hubs. Whereas the traditional hub-and-spoke model was expected to still have some use for intercontinental routes, switching to more nonstop routes was seen as a growing market. For the airlines, this departure from the hub-and-spoke model translated into a need for smaller aircraft in order to be able to offer more direct connections. Especially high-fare customers were seen as sensitive to convenient arrival and departure times, and this would more than offset the additional costs incurred by airlines in order to add these additional flights.

While Boeing expected twin-aisle airplanes to dominate the long-haul,

transoceanic markets, the global regional markets was expected to be served primarily by single-aisle aircraft, which were forecast to make up 75 percent of the world's fleet by 2023. Because of replacements of the current fleets, single-aisle airplanes were expected to dominate future aircraft deliveries. Hot spots for economic growth, like China and Southeast and Southwest Asia, were believed to further contribute to an increased demand for new aircraft.

Boeing's primary customers, the airlines, however, were becoming increasingly fickle. On the one hand, analysts forecast steady growth of passenger volumes. On the other hand, Boeing could not be sure that an airline would be willing to purchase further products and services once a contract had ended. In addition, some of Boeing's customers had filed for bankruptcy protection, creating further uncertainty for Boeing.

While several "legacy" carriers struggled in the years after September 11, 2001, a large number of low-cost

carriers entered the market. With a completely different operating structure, these carriers could be profitable despite overall losses of the airline industries. In addition to eliminating traditional sales channels, these airlines would reduce costs by decreasing turnaround time at the gate or using only one aircraft model. For Boeing, helping their customers reduce their operating costs could be an important way to aid their survival and, ultimately, a reduced number of lost customers due to factors such as bankruptcy.

For Boeing's executives, e-Enabling was regarded as the "silver bullet" to deal with the situation. The products and services of the e-Enabled Advantage program could help the airlines increase their efficiencies, which would ultimately help them survive. In addition to that, the products and services would help to differentiate Boeing from Airbus, an important aspect in times when the differences between the different aircraft became more and more blurry.

Questions

1. How does the e-Enabled Advantage program help Boeing obtain a competitive advantage over its rivals?
2. Use Porter's five-forces model to analyze the commercial air transport industry. Compare and contrast this to an analysis of the aircraft manufacturing industry.
3. Create a value chain for the commercial air transport industry and identify several ways that capabilities of the e-Enabled Advantage program can provide benefits.

Sources: http://www.iata.org/whatwedo/standards/padis, retrieved October 1, 2006
http://www.boeing.com/commercial/cmo/pdf/cmo_parisbook.pdf

chapter 4

Managing the Information Systems Infrastructure

preview > As any city depends on a functioning infrastructure, companies operating in a digital world are relying on a comprehensive information systems infrastructure to support their business processes and competitive strategy. With ever-increasing speed, transactions are conducted; likewise, with ever-increasing amounts of data to be captured, analyzed, and stored, companies have to thoroughly plan and manage their infrastructure needs in order to gain the greatest returns on their information systems investments. When planning and managing their information systems architectures, organizations must answer many important and difficult questions. For example, how will we utilize information systems to enable our competitive strategy? What technologies and systems best support our core business processes? Which vendors should we partner with, which technologies do we adopt, and which do we avoid? What hardware, software, or services do we buy, build, or have managed by an outside service provider? How can the organization get the most out of the data captured from internal and external sources? How can the organization best assure that the infrastructure is reliable and secure? Clearly, effectively managing an organization's information systems infrastructure is a complex but necessary activity in today's digital world. After reading this chapter, you will be able to do the following:

1. List the essential information systems infrastructure components and describe why they are necessary for satisfying an organization's informational needs.

2. Describe solutions organizations use to design a reliable, robust, and secure infrastructure.

3. Describe how organizations can ensure a reliable and secure infrastructure, plan for potential disasters, and establish IS controls.

This chapter focuses on helping managers understand the key components of a comprehensive information systems infrastructure and why its careful management is necessary. With an increasing complexity of an organization's information needs and an increasing complexity of the systems needed to satisfy these requirements, the topic of infrastructure management is fundamental for managing in the digital world.

Managing in the Digital World: "I Googled You!"

You're researching a paper for a physics class, and you need information on quarks. Google it (see Figure 4.1). You'd like to locate a high school classmate, but no one in your graduating class knows where she is. Google her. You're watching a movie, and a character says she "googled" a blind date. The term "google" has become so familiar to Internet users that it's often used as a verb. In fact, the term has become so common that Google is becoming concerned that its use as a verb is a copyright infringement, asking dictionaries such as *Merriam-Webster* to change their definition of Google to "to use the Google search engine to obtain information . . . on the World Wide Web."

According to the Google.com Web site, "Google is a play on the word googol, which was coined by Milton Sirotta, nephew of American mathematician Edward Kasner, and was popularized in the book *Mathematics and the Imagination* by Kasner and James Newman. It refers to the number represented by the numeral 1 followed by 100 zeros. Google's use of the term reflects the company's mission to organize the immense, seemingly infinite amount of information available on the web."

According to Google lore, company founders Larry Page and Sergey Brin argued about everything when they first met as Stanford University graduate students in computer science in 1995. Larry was a 24-year-old University of Michigan alumnus on a weekend visit; Sergey, 23, was among a group of students assigned to show him around. Both had strong opinions and divergent viewpoints, but they eventually found common ground in a unique approach to solving one of computing's biggest challenges: retrieving relevant information from a massive set of data.

By January 1996, Page and Brin had begun collaboration on a search engine called BackRub, named for its unique ability to analyze the "back links" pointing to a given Web site. Page, who had always enjoyed tinkering with machinery and had gained some notoriety for building a working printer out of Lego™ bricks, took on the task of creating a new kind of server environment that used low-end PCs instead of big expensive machines. Afflicted by the perennial shortage of cash common to graduate students everywhere, the pair took to haunting the department's loading docks in hopes of tracking down newly arrived computers that they could borrow for their network.

In 1998, Page and Brin were still operating out of a dorm room. They maxed out credit cards buying a terabyte of memory to hold their data and went looking for investors to help them further develop their search engine technology. David Filo, a friend and one of the developers of Yahoo!, told the two their technology was solid and convinced them to start up their own company.

FIGURE 4.1

Google search page.

Page and Brin put out feelers for investors and found Andy Bechtolsheim, a friend of a faculty member, who wrote them a check for $100,000 after one brief meeting. Since the check was made out to "Google Inc.," Page and Brin scrambled to establish a corporation so they could deposit the check. Other investors joined, and Google Inc. began operations in September 1998 in Menlo Park, California—in a friend's garage that included a washer and dryer and a hot tub. The first employee hired was Craig Silverstein, director of technology.

From the start, Google, still in beta in 1998, handled 10,000 search queries a day. The company quickly captured the attention of the press and was extolled in *USA Today, Le Monde,* and *PC Magazine,* which named Google the best search engine of 1998.

Google quickly outgrew its garage location, and by February 1999 the company had moved into an office in Palo Alto, California, and now had eight employees and was handling more than 500,000 search queries a day.

The company continued to expand, removed the "beta" label from the search engine in 1999, and that same year moved into the Googleplex, its current headquarters in Mountain View, California.

In May 2000, Google was already the world's largest search engine answering 18 million queries a day, and was awarded a Webby Award and a People's Voice Award for technical achievement. (By the end of 2000, Google was answering 100 million search queries a day.)

On April 29, 2004, Google filed with the Securities and Exchange Commission for its initial public offering (IPO). In an unprecedented move, the IPO was sold at auction in order to make the shares more widely available. Shares were priced at $85, and Google hoped to raise $3 billion from the initial offering. Expert opinions on the success of the auction were mixed. Some said the stock price was inflated; others said the stock would eventually tank. Experts who warned of doomsday, however, were eventually proved wrong. In December 2006, Google's stock was selling for $466 a share and was expected to go to $548 in the short term.

Google has continued to innovate and move beyond the search engine market. The company offers e-mail, instant messaging, and mobile text messaging services. Other Google services include an automated news site, a Web blogging site, free imaging software, and a site for programmers interested in creating new applications. In mid-2006, Google was poised to challenge PayPal in the Internet account business and to give eBay a run for its money in the online auction business.

Google's e-mail service, like the company itself, is unique. Launched in 2004 as "Gmail," it was initially available to newcomers only on invitation from someone who already had the service. Gmail incorporates e-mail and instant messaging so that users can e-mail in the traditional manner and/or visit in real time.

The highest revenue generator for Google is its AdSense program. This program allows any Web site to publish advertisments on each of its pages. The Web site publisher is paid every time someone clicks on an ad originating from that page. The AdSense program also lets Web site publishers determine how many people look at the site, the cost per click, click-through rates, and so on. The AdSense program can tailor the type of ads that are placed on a Web site—that is, publishers can block ads they don't want to appear, such as competitor ads, ads concerning death or war, and ads for "adult" material.

Another Google service popular with users is froogle, which uses Google search technology to let consumers search for and compare products by product type, price, and so on. Other features include the following:

- The Google News service automatically combines news clippings from various online newspapers and provides them on one page for users' convenience.
- Google scholar helps researchers search through publications.
- Google finance searches for finance-related news and stock information.
- Other specialized search capabilities include video search, image search, mail-order catalog search, book search, blog search, and university search.

In addition, these services can also be accessed through mobile phones using the Google mobile products.

Google has clearly become a significant presence on the Internet and in users' daily lives. Look for new Google products and services at http://labs.google.com/.

After reading this chapter, you will be able to answer the following:

1. To what extent was Google's initial success limited by its infrastructure?

2. If you were asked to identify the ideal location for a new Google facility, where would it be? Explain.

3. How would you rank order the various infrastructure components described in this chapter in their importance to Google's success? Explain your rationale.

Sources:

Anonymous, "Google Milestones," **http://www.google.com/corporate/history.html**

Antone Gonsalves, "Google Testing Possible eBay Competition," *Information Week* (October 25, 2005), **http://www.informationweek.com/story/showArticle.jhtml?articleID=172900366**

Eric J. Sinrod, "Google in a Patent Pickle?," *C/Net News* (January 19, 2006), **http://news.com.com/ Google+in+a+patent+pickle/2010-1071_3-6027546.html**

Thomas Claburn, "Feds Seek Google Search Records in Child Porn Investigation," *Information Week* (January 19, 2006), **http://www.informationweek.com/internet/showArticle.jhtml?articleID=177101999**

The Information Systems Infrastructure

Any area where people live or work needs a supporting **infrastructure**, which entails the interconnection of all basic facilities and services enabling the area to function properly. The infrastructure of a city, for example, includes components such as streets, power, telephone, water, and sewage lines but also schools, retail stores, and law enforcement. Both the area's inhabitants and the businesses depend on that infrastructure; cities with a good infrastructure, for example, are considered more livable than cities with poorer infrastructure and are much more likely to attract businesses and residents (see Figure 4.2). Likewise, valuable employees often choose firms with better facilities, management, and business processes.

For organizations considering where to set up a new manufacturing plant, for example, such decisions are often based on the provision of such infrastructure. Indeed, many municipalities attempt to attract new businesses and industries by setting up new commercial zones with the necessary infrastructure. In some cases, specific infrastructure components are of special importance. One such example is search engine giant Google, which has data centers located all over the world to offer the best performance to its users. Google's newest data center is nearing completion in the small town of The Dalles, Oregon, located on the banks of the

FIGURE 4.2

A city's infrastructure is complex and interconnected.

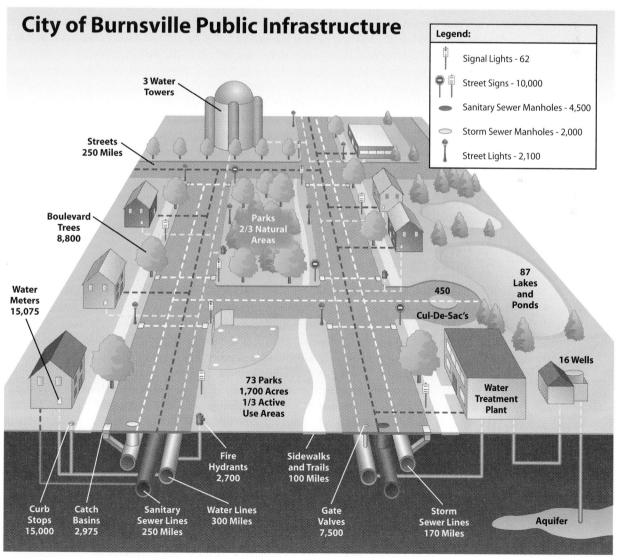

Source: http://www.burnsville.org/ftpfiles/infrabig.jpg.

FIGURE 4.3

Google data center in The
Dalles, Oregon, is nearing
completion.

Columbia River (see Figure 4.3). Why would a company such as Google choose such a rural
location? First, the location offered connectivity, using a state-of-the-art fiber-optic network
to provide high-speed data transfer to the Internet backbone (see Technology Briefing 4—
Networking and Technology Briefing 5—The Internet and World Wide Web). Second—and
maybe more important—the location on the river would give the data center access to water
for its cooling needs and cheap, uninterrupted power from the nearby hydroelectric dam. As
you can see from this example, companies such as Google must consider far more than just
the need for increased data storage space and processing power.

For organizations operating globally, managing a comprehensive, worldwide infrastructure poses additional challenges. This is particularly acute when operating in developing nations. For example, in many parts of the world, organizations cannot count on an
uninterrupted supply of water or electricity. Consequently, many of the large call centers in
India that support customers around the world for companies like Dell Computers or
Citibank have, for example, installed massive power generators to minimize the effects of
frequent power outages or have set up their own satellite links to be independent from the
local, unreliable phone networks.

The Need for an Information Systems Infrastructure

As people and companies rely on basic infrastructures to function, businesses also rely on
an **information systems infrastructure** (consisting of hardware, software, networks, data,
facilities, human resources, and services) to support their decision making, business
processes, and competitive strategy. **Business processes** are the activities that organizations
perform in order to reach their business goals and consist of core processes and supporting
processes. The **core processes** make up the primary activities in the value chain; these are
all the processes that are needed to manufacture goods, sell the products, provide service,
and so on (see Chapter 3—Valuing Information Systems Investments). The **supporting
processes** are all the processes that are needed to perform the value chain's supporting
activities, such as accounting, human resources management, and so on (see Figure 4.4).

Almost all of an organization's business processes depend on the underlying information
systems infrastructure, albeit to different degrees. For example, an organization's management
needs an infrastructure to support a variety of activities, including reliable communication networks to support collaboration between suppliers and customers, accurate and timely data and
knowledge to gain business intelligence, and information systems to aid decision making and
support business processes. In sum, organizations rely on a complex, interrelated information
systems infrastructure to effectively thrive in the ever-increasing, competitive digital world.

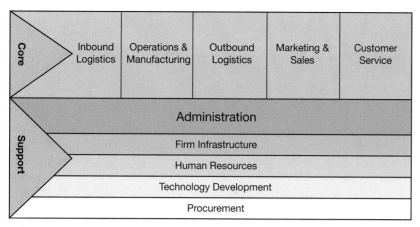

FIGURE 4.4

A generic value chain showing an organization's core and supporting activities.

In order to make better decisions, managers at all levels of the organizations need to analyze information gathered from the different business processes. The processes of gathering the information as well as the information itself are commonly referred to as **business intelligence**. Whereas some of these processes obtain the information from external sources—such as marketing research or competitor analysis—other processes gather business intelligence from internal sources, such as sales figures, customer demographics, or performance indicators. While there are a variety of different systems used for gaining business intelligence (see Chapter 7—Enhancing Business Intelligence Using Information Systems), all gather, process, store, or analyze data in an effort to better manage the organization. In other words, modern organizations rely heavily on their information systems infrastructure; its components include the following (see Figure 4.5):

- Hardware
- Software
- Communications and collaboration
- Data and knowledge
- Facilities

FIGURE 4.5

The information systems infrastructure.

- Human resources
- Services

Next, we briefly discuss each of these components and highlight their role in an organization's information systems infrastructure. To dig deeper into the technical aspects of the various infrastructure components, refer to the Technology Briefings.

Hardware The information systems hardware is an integral part of the IS infrastructure. This hardware consists not only of the computers used in an organization but also of networking hardware (see Technology Briefing 1—Information Systems Hardware and Technology Briefing 4—Networking) (see Figure 4.6). While the computing hardware is integral to an organization's IS infrastructure because it is needed to store and process organizational data, the networking hardware is needed to connect the different systems to allow for collaboration and information sharing.

Companies often face difficult decisions regarding their hardware. Constant innovations within the information technology sector lead to ever-increasing processor speeds and storage capacities but also to rapid obsolescence. Information systems executives therefore face countless complex questions, such as the following:

- Which hardware technologies should be chosen?
- What time interval should equipment be replaced?
- How can the information systems be secured best?
- What performance and storage is needed today? Next year?
- How can reliability be assured?

These and other questions will be addressed throughout this chapter when we discuss how different infrastructure solutions can help to support an organization's competitive strategy, decision making, and business processes.

Software As outlined in Technology Briefing 2—Information Systems Software, various types of software enable companies to utilize their information systems hardware and networks. This software assists organizations in executing their business processes and competitive strategy. Consequently, with increased reliance on information systems for managing the organization, effectively utilizing software resources is becoming increasingly critical and complex. For example, companies have to manage the software installed on each and every computer used, including managing updates, fixing bugs, and managing issues related to software licenses (see Figure 4.7). In addition, companies have to decide whether to upgrade their software or switch to new products and when to do so.

FIGURE 4.6

Hardware is an integral component of an organization's IS infrastructure.

FIGURE 4.7

Installing and maintaining software can be a costly and time-consuming task.

Clearly, managing the software component of an IS infrastructure can be a daunting task. However, there are some developments helping organizations to better manage the software resources, and we will present these later in the chapter.

Communications and Collaboration As you have read in the previous chapters, one of the reasons why information systems in organizations have become so powerful and important is the ability to interconnect, allowing internal and external constituents to communicate and collaborate with each other. The infrastructure supporting this consists of a variety of components, such as the networking hardware and software (see Technology Briefings 4 and 5), that facilitate the interconnection of different computers, enabling collaboration literally around the world.

However, having a number of interconnected computers is necessary but not sufficient for enabling communication and collaboration; companies also need various other hardware and software. For example, e-mail servers, along with communication software such as Microsoft Outlook, are needed to enable a broad range of internal and external communication. Similarly, companies have to decide on whether to utilize tools such as instant messaging and which system to use for such applications (see Figure 4.8). Further, it has become increasingly important for companies to be able to utilize videoconferencing to bridge the distances between a company's offices or between a company and its business partners, saving valuable travel time and enhancing collaboration. However, as there are

FIGURE 4.8

Companies have to decide how to support their communication needs.

vast differences in terms of quality, costs, and functionality of these systems, companies have to assess their communication needs and carefully decide which combination of technologies best support the goals of the organization.

Data and Knowledge Data and knowledge are probably among the most important assets an organization has, as data and knowledge are essential for both gaining business intelligence and executing business processes. Managing this resource thus requires an infrastructure with sufficient capacity, performance, and reliability. For example, companies such as Amazon.com need databases to store customer information, product information, inventory, transactions, and so on. Like Amazon.com, many companies operating in the digital world rely heavily on their databases not only to store information but also to analyze this information to gain business intelligence.

For example, the main data center for United Parcel Service (UPS) handles on average 10 million package tracking requests per day, with peak days approaching 20 million. To support this core business process, UPS has designed a data management architecture that includes an array of Unix-based mainframes running a massive database management system. This data management architecture has a capacity of 471 terabytes of data (approximately 471,000 gigabytes). Additionally, given that data is the lifeblood for UPS, they have replicated this infrastructure in two locations—New Jersey and Georgia—to ensure speed and reliability (see Figure 4.9).

In addition to effectively managing their data resources, organizations must also effectively manage their knowledge. In Chapter 1—Managing in the Digital World, we outlined the rise of the knowledge worker—professionals who are relatively well educated and who create, modify, and/or synthesize knowledge—and the new economy where organizations must effectively utilize their knowledge to gain a competitive advantage. Trends and options for effectively managing data and knowledge are also examined later in the chapter.

Facilities Although not directly needed to support business processes or business intelligence, specialized facilities are needed for the information systems infrastructure. While not every company needs facilities such as Google's data center in The Dalles, managers need to carefully consider where to house the different hardware, software, data centers, and so on. A normal desktop computer might not need much in terms of power, nor does it generate much heat; however, massive clusters of computers or **server farms** (facilities housing a vast number of servers to support the information processing needs of a large organization) have tremendous demands for reliable electricity and air-conditioning. In addition to such technical requirements, there is also the need to protect important equipment from both outside

FIGURE 4.9

UPS's servers handle up to 20 million requests per day.

Ethical Dilemma

Who Owns Company Data?

In years past, beads, land, gold, oil, animal skins, and food were all considered trade currency. Today, information is a prime bargaining chip. And, just like any of these forms of lucre, it can be stolen. For instance, a person might use information belonging to a previous employer to get a better job or to maintain old business contacts after changing jobs. The question is, Is stealing information from a company's database akin to stealing money from the bank?

The answer, of course, is "yes." The act of pilfering data from an employer or previous employer is data theft. From an organization's standpoint, stealing information is not only more harmful than stealing company stationery or a few pencils but even more harmful than stealing sophisticated computer hardware.

Unfortunately, data theft is not rare. A 2004 survey by Ibas, a data forensics firm in the United Kingdom, found that 70 percent of the respondents had stolen key information from an employer.

Seventy-two percent of the people surveyed indicated that they had no ethical problems with taking proposals, presentations, contact databases, or e-mail address books when changing to a new employer. Fifty-eight percent felt that data theft ranked with exaggerating insurance claims. Thirty percent had stolen customer contact information when they left a firm. (Most thefts occurred when employees left to take another job.)

"The surprising thing is the level to which people believe this is acceptable," said Chris Watson of Ibas in an article by BBC News published online in February 2004.

Eighty percent of the employees surveyed justified their actions by using the rationale that "after all, I did the work to build that customer database and create sales leads."

Where do you stand on the issue?

Source: Anonymous, "Workplace Data Theft Runs Rampant," BBC News (February 15, 2004), http://news.bbc.co.uk/1/ hi/technology/3486397.stm

---

intruders and the elements, such as water or fire. The most prominent threats to an organization's IS facilities come from floods, seismic activity, rolling blackouts, hurricanes, and the potential of terrorist activities (see Figure 4.10). How can an organization reliably protect its facilities from such threats? Other issues to consider are the questions of availability; for example, can an organization afford to have its Web site unavailable for a minute, for an hour, or even for a day? Strategies for managing information systems facilities are examined later in the chapter.

Human Resources Another issue faced by companies is the availability of a trained workforce. Although even large facilities do not require large support staff, the staff that is needed should be well trained. This is one of the issues faced by Google's new data center in The Dalles. While the construction of the facility has created a large number of construction jobs, helping the area's unemployment situation, permanent jobs will likely require special skills so that much of the workforce will be "imported" from other regions. For this reason, many companies try to locate facilities in common areas. For example, the automobile industry has historically been centered in Detroit, while many of the technology companies have chosen areas like Austin, Boston, San Jose, and Seattle.

Services A broad range of services is the final infrastructure component. Over the past few years, this component has become increasingly important for many business organizations. Traditionally, an organization would perform all business processes—from acquiring raw materials to selling and servicing the final product—itself, no matter if these processes would be the organization's core competency or not. Today, with increasing pressures from the competition and the organization's shareholders, many processes that are not among a company's core competencies are being delegated to other organizations with considerably higher expertise (see Figure 4.11). For example, business

FIGURE 4.10

Potential threats to IS facilities vary by region include floods, hurricanes, terrorism, power outages, and seismic activity.

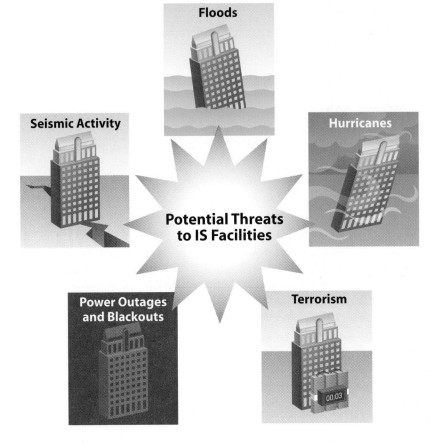

organizations turn over the management of their supply chains to logistics companies such as UPS, or organizations turn over the responsibility for the information systems infrastructure to organizations such as EDS. In fact, many of the solutions used to address organizations' various infrastructure needs are based on services, as you will see in the following sections.

FIGURE 4.11

Traditionally, organizations would execute their entire value chain; today, a variety of other businesses provide services to perform noncore processes.

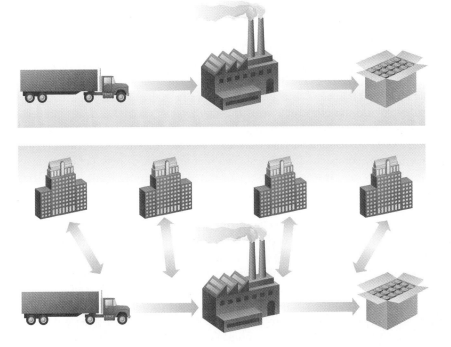

Clearly, there are a variety of infrastructure issues to consider for companies operating in today's digital world. In the next section, we will describe some solutions for designing and managing an organization's information systems infrastructure.

Designing the Information Systems Infrastructure

With organizations' growing needs for a comprehensive information systems infrastructure, a number of solutions have emerged and are continuing to emerge. While some of these solutions are already common business practice, others are just now starting to be adopted. In the following sections, we will present various solutions to information systems infrastructure needs presented in the previous section.

Managing the Hardware Infrastructure

Both businesses and research facilities face an ever-increasing need for computing performance. For example, auto manufacturers, such as the GM German subsidiary Opel or Japanese Toyota, use large supercomputers to simulate automobile crashes as well as evaluate design changes for vibrations and wind noise. Research facilities such as the U.S. Department of Energy's Lawrence Livermore National Laboratory use supercomputers for simulating nuclear explosions, while others simulate earthquakes using supercomputers (see Figure 4.12); such research sites have a tremendously complex hardware infrastructure.

While not every organization faces such large-scale computing problems, the demands for computing resources are often fluctuating, leading to either having too few resources for some problems or having too many idle resources most of the time. To address this problem, many organizations now turn to *on-demand computing* for fluctuating computation needs, *grid computing* for solving large-scale problems, and *autonomic computing* for increasing reliability. In the following sections, we will discuss each of these infrastructure trends.

On-Demand Computing In almost every organization, demand for individual IS resources is highly fluctuating. For example, some high-bandwidth applications, such as videoconferencing, may be needed only during certain times of the day, or some resource-intensive data-mining applications may only be used in irregular intervals. **On-demand computing** is a way to address such fluctuating computing needs; here, the available resources are allocated on the basis of users' needs (usually on a pay-per-use basis). For

FIGURE 4.12

The Earth Simulator supercomputer creates a "virtual twin" of the earth.

Source: http://www.es.jamstec.go.jp/esc/eng/GC/b_photo/esc04.jpg.

FIGURE 4.13

Utility computing allows companies to pay for computing services on an as-needed basis.

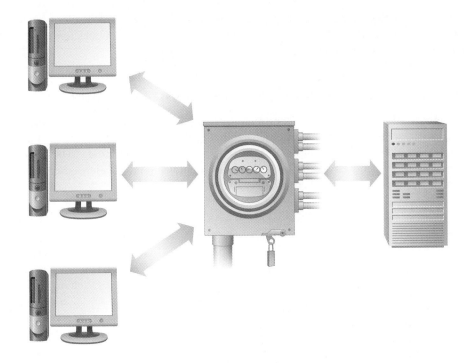

example, more bandwidth will be allocated to a videoconference, while other users who do not need the bandwidth at that time receive less. Similarly, a user running complex data-mining algorithms would receive more processing power than a user merely doing some word processing.

At times, organizations prefer to "rent" resources from an external provider. This form of on-demand computing is referred to as **utility computing**, where the resources in terms of processing, data storage, or networking are rented on an as-needed basis and the organization receives a bill for the services used from the provider at the end of each month (see Figure 4.13). For many companies, utility computing is an effective way for managing fluctuating demand as well as controlling costs; in essence, all tasks associated with managing, maintaining, and upgrading the infrastructure are left to the external provider and are typically bundled into the "utility" bill—if you don't use, you don't pay. Also, as with your utility bill, customers are charged not only on overall usage but also on peak usage (i.e., different rates for different times of the day).

Grid Computing Although today's supercomputers have tremendous computing power, some tasks are even beyond the capacity of a supercomputer. Indeed, some complex simulations can take a year or longer to calculate even on a supercomputer. Sometimes, an organization or a research facility would have the need for a supercomputer but may not be able to afford one because of the extremely high cost. For example, the fastest supercomputers can cost more than $200 million, and this does not represent the "total cost of ownership," which also includes all the other related costs for making the system operational (e.g., personnel, facilities, storage, software, and so on; see Chapter 3). Additionally, the organization may not be able to justify the cost because the supercomputer may be needed only occasionally to solve a few complex problems. In these situations, organizations have had to either rent time on a supercomputer or decided simply not to solve the problem.

However, a relatively recent infrastructure trend for overcoming cost or use limitations is to utilize **grid computing**. Grid computing refers to combining the computing power of a large number of smaller, independent, networked computers (often regular desktop PCs) into a cohesive system in order to solve problems that only supercomputers were previously capable of solving. While supercomputers are very specialized, grid computing allows organizations to solve both very large-scale problems as well as multiple (concurrent) smaller problems. To make grid computing work, large computing tasks are broken into small chunks, each of which can then be completed by the individual computers

FIGURE 4.14

Grid computing uses resources from various different computers located around the world.

(see Figure 4.14). However, as the individual computers are also in regular use, the individual calculations are performed during the computers' idle time so as to maximize the use of existing resources. For example, when writing this book, we used only minimal resources on our computers (i.e., we typically used only a word processor, the Internet, and e-mail); if our computers were part of a grid, the unused resources could be utilized to solve large-scale computing problems. This is especially useful for companies operating on a global scale. In each country, many of the resources are idle during the night hours, often more than 12 hours per day. Because of time zone differences, grid computing helps utilize those resources constructively. One way to put these resources into use would be to join the Berkeley Open Infrastructure for Network Computing (BOINC), which lets individuals "donate" computing time for various research projects, such as searching for extraterrestrial intelligence (SETI@home) or running climate change simulations.

However, as you can imagine, grid computing poses a number of demands in terms of the underlying network infrastructure or the software managing the distribution of the tasks. Further, many grids perform on the speed of the slowest computer, thus slowing down the entire grid. Many companies starting out with a grid computing infrastructure attempt to overcome these problems by using a **dedicated grid**. In a dedicated grid, the individual computers, or nodes, are just there to perform the grid's computing tasks; in other words, the grid consists of a number of homogeneous computers and does not use unutilized resources. A dedicated grid is easier to set up and manage and is for many companies much more cost effective than purchasing a supercomputer. As the grid evolves and new nodes are added, dedicated grids become more heterogeneous over time.

One factor that adds to the popularity of using dedicated grids is the falling cost of computing hardware. Just a few years ago, companies have attempted to utilize idle resources as much as possible and set up heterogeneous computing grids. However, the added complexity of managing heterogeneous grids poses a large cost factor so that today it is often more cost effective to set up a homogeneous, dedicated grid; in this case, the savings in terms of software and management by far offset the added costs for dedicated computing hardware in terms of both acquisition and maintenance.

Edge Computing Another recent trend in IS hardware infrastructure management is **edge computing**. With the decrease in cost for processing and data storage, computing tasks are now often solved at the edge of a company's network. In other words, rather than having massive, centralized computers and databases, multiple smaller servers are located closer to the individual users. This way, resources in terms of network bandwidth and access time are saved. If a computer needs several hours to compute a certain problem, it might be a good choice to send the task over a network to a more powerful computer that might be able to solve that problem faster. However, as the costs for computing power have decreased tremendously over the past years, many problems can now be computed locally within a matter of seconds, so it is not economic to send such problems over a network to a remote computer (Gray, 2004). To save resources, many businesses use edge computing for their online commerce sites. In such cases, customers interact with the servers of an edge-computing service provider (such as Akamai). These servers, in turn, communicate with the business' computers. This form of edge computing helps to reduce wait times for the consumers, as the e-commerce sites are replicated on Akamai's servers, while at the same time reducing the number of requests to the company's own infrastructure. This process not only saves valuable resources such as bandwidth but also offers superior performance that would otherwise be too expensive for organizations to offer. Akamai's services are utilized by organizations such as NBC, Fox Sports, BMW, and Victoria's Secret.

Autonomic Computing One major drawback of these hardware infrastructure trends and the demands for IS infrastructure in general is the increased complexity of such systems. Whereas the primary reason for having this infrastructure is the utilization of the resources, the time and money needed to manage these resources don't add value to the organization; in fact, some people believe that the costs of managing these systems undermine the benefits these systems provide, even if the organization decides to use outside services. To overcome this, academic and industry researchers (e.g., at IBM) have begun working on **autonomic computing** systems, which are self-managing, meaning they need only minimal human intervention to operate (see Figure 4.15). In other words, in a traditional computing environment, system operators often have to fine-tune the computer's configuration in order to most efficiently solve a particular type of complex problem. In an autonomic computing environment, the ultimate goal is to allow the system to do everything else on its own, completely transparent to the user. In order to achieve this, an autonomic computing system must know itself and be self-configuring, self-optimizing, self-healing, and self-protecting.

In order to optimally perform different tasks, an autonomic system must know itself; that is, it must know its configuration, capacity, and current status, but it must also know which resources it can draw on. Second, in order to be able to use different resources based on different needs, the system should be self-configuring so that the user does not have to take care of any configuration issues. Further, as any parts of a system can malfunction, an autonomic system should be self-healing so that any potential problems are detected and the system is reconfigured so as to allow the user to continue performing the tasks, even if parts of the system are not operational. Finally, as almost any computer system can be the target of an attack (see Chapter 6—Securing Information Systems), autonomic computing systems must be aware of any potential dangers and must be able to protect themselves

FIGURE 4.15

Autonomic computing systems have self-awareness and are self-configuring, self-optimizing, self-healing, and self-protecting.

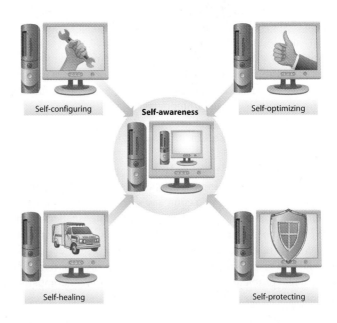

from any malicious attacks (e.g., by automatically quarantining infected parts of a system). Clearly, these are some formidable tasks researchers have to address, but considering the time and money that is currently spent on managing and maintaining IT infrastructures, autonomic computing systems are promising for the future.

Managing the Software Infrastructure

With growing use of information systems to support organizations' business processes and the need for business intelligence, organizations have to rely on a variety of different software. However, continuously upgrading operating systems and applications software (see Technology Briefing 2) can be a huge cost factor for organizations both in terms of labor and in terms of costs for the actual products needed. To reduce such costs, many companies are now turning increasingly to using open-source software, attempting to integrate various software tools, or using application service providers for their software needs. Each of these software infrastructure management approaches is discussed next.

Open-Source Software Open source, seen by Friedman (2005) as one of the 10 flatteners of the world, is a philosophy that promotes developers' and users' access to the source of a product or idea (see Chapter 2—Fueling Globalization Using Information Systems). Particularly in the area of software development, the open-source movement has taken off with the advent of the Internet, and people around the world are contributing their time and expertise to develop or improve software, ranging from operating systems to applications software. As the programs' source code is freely available for use and/or modification, this software is referred to as **open-source software**.

OPEN-SOURCE OPERATING SYSTEMS. One of the most prevalent examples of open-source software is the operating system Linux, which was developed as a hobby by the Finnish university student Linus Torvalds in 1991. Having developed the first version himself, he made the source code of his operating system available to everyone who wanted to use it and improve on it. Because of its unrivaled stability, Linux has become the operating system of choice for Web servers, **embedded systems** (such as TiVo boxes, handheld computers, and network routers; see Figure 4.16), and supercomputers alike (as of 2006, 73 percent of the world's 500 fastest supercomputers ran Linux operating systems; Top 500, 2006).

OPEN-SOURCE APPLICATION SOFTWARE. In addition to the Linux operating system, other open-source software has been gaining increasing popularity because of its stability and low cost. For example, in 2006, 68 percent of all Web sites were powered by the

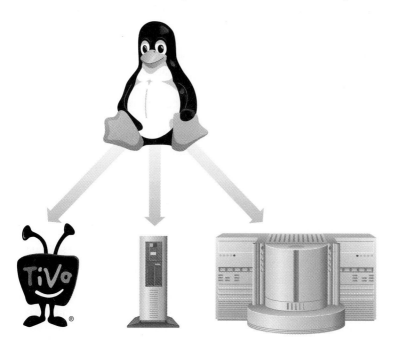

FIGURE 4.16

Linux is the operating system of choice for embedded systems, Web servers, and supercomputers (the penguin "Tux" is the official mascot of Linux).

FIGURE 4.17

The Firefox Web browser.

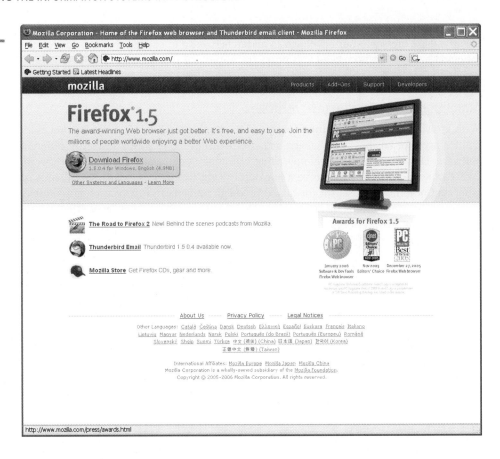

Apache Web server, another open-source project (Netcraft, 2006). Other popular examples of open-source application software include the Firefox Web browser (see Figure 4.17) and the office productivity suite OpenOffice. While there are many upsides to open-source software, vendors of proprietary software are still highlighting "hidden" costs of running open-source software. For example, finding an organization to provide reliable customer support can sometimes be difficult.

Web Services To perform business processes and for business intelligence, it is often essential to draw information from different sources or different applications. However, with the increasing complexity of an organization's software needs, it is often impossible to get all of the various applications to integrate seamlessly. In some cases, software companies (such as Microsoft and IBM) offer a wide range of products, all of which can interoperate quite well. However, business organizations sometimes shy away from being completely dependent on a single vendor for their software needs. One way to increase the independence while still being able to integrate various software applications is the use of **Web services**. Web services are Web-based software systems used to allow the interaction of different programs and databases over a network. Using Web services, companies can integrate information from different applications, running on different platforms. For example, you can use Web services offered by Google to integrate search functionality into your own Web site, or you can use Web services to provide your guests with an interactive map to your house (see Figure 4.18). You can also learn more about Web services in Technology Briefing 2.

One logical extension to using Web services is using a **service-oriented architecture**. The main goal of implementing a service-oriented architecture is the integration of different applications using Web services. In a service-oriented architecture, different repeatable business tasks, or services, are integrated to better perform various business processes. These services are typically vendor independent and can thus be used to integrate data and capabilities of different systems running on different platforms. This capability—and the reusability of different services—allows businesses to quickly react to changes in the business environment.

FIGURE 4.18

An example of a Web service that allows maps to be inserted into Web pages.

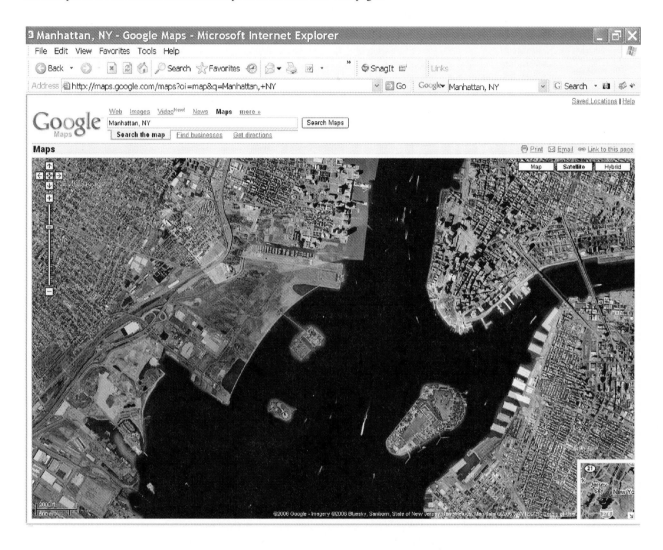

Managing Software Assets   As organizations manage their software infrastructure, there are several issues that must be carefully managed, such as software bugs and licensing. Next, we briefly outline these issues and present some of the tools and strategies organizations are utilizing to better manage these complex tasks.

MANAGING SOFTWARE BUGS.   With the increased complexity of software, it is almost impossible to build applications that are error free, and no matter whether such applications are operating systems, Web sites, or enterprise-wide software, there is the potential of unforeseen problems with the software. Typically, software developers will account for these unforeseen problems by incorporating a **patch management system** into the application. Patch management is typically based on an online system that checks a Web service for available patches. If the software vendor offers a new patch, the application will download and install the patch in order to fix the software bug. An example of a patch management system in wide use is the Windows Update Service. The user's operating system automatically connects to a Microsoft Web service to download critical operating system patches. While some of these patches are intended to fix bugs in the Windows operating system, many patches are built to fix security holes that could be exploited by malicious hackers.

TABLE 4.1 Different Types of Software Licenses

Restrictiveness	Software Type	Rights	Restrictions	Examples
Full rights	Public domain software	Full rights	No restrictions; owner forsakes copyright	Different programs for outdated IBM mainframes
	Nonprotective open source (e.g., Berkeley software development [BSD] license)	Freedom to copy, modify, and redistribute the software; can be incorporated into commercial product	Creator retains copyright	FreeBSD operating system; BSD components in (proprietary) Mac OS X operating system
	Protective open source (e.g., general public license [GPL])	Freedom to copy, modify, and redistribute the software	Modified or redistributed software must be made available under the same license; cannot be incorporated into commercial product	Linux operating system
	Proprietary software	Right to run the software (for licensed users)	Access to source code severely restricted; no rights to copy or modify software	Windows operating system
No rights	Trade secret		Access to source code severely restricted; software is not distributed outside the organization	Google PageRank™ algorithm

MANAGING SOFTWARE LICENSING. Software licensing has been a hot button topic for software companies as they lose billions in piracy and mislicensed customers (see Chapter 10—Managing Information Systems Ethics and Crime). Traditionally, software licensing is defined as the permission and rights that are imposed on applications, and the use of software without a proper license is illegal in most countries.

Most software licenses differ in terms of restrictiveness, ranging from no restrictions at all to completely restricted. Table 4.1 lists different types of software licenses, ordered in terms of restrictiveness. Note that although freeware or shareware is freely available, the copyright owners often retain their rights and do not provide access to the program's source code. For organizations using proprietary software, two types of licenses are of special importance. The first, **shrink-wrap license**, accompanies the software and is used primarily in consumer products. The shrink-wrapped contract has been named as such because the contract is activated when the shrink wrap on the packaging has been removed. The second type of licensing is **enterprise licensing**. Enterprise licensing (also known as **volume licensing**) can vary greatly and is usually negotiated. In addition to rights and permissions, enterprise licenses usually contain limitations of liability and warranty disclaimers that protect the software vendor from being sued if their software does not operate as expected.

As shown in Table 4.1, there are a variety of software licenses. For different business needs, organizations are often depending on a variety of software, each having different licenses, which can cause headaches for many organizations. Not knowing about the software an organization has can have a variety of consequences. For example, companies are not able to negotiate volume licensing options, unused licenses strain the organization's budget, or license violations can lead to fines or public embarrassment. **Software asset management** helps organizations to avoid such negative consequences. Usually, software asset management consists of a set of activities, such as performing a software inventory (either manually or using automated tools), matching the installed software with the licenses, reviewing software-related policies and procedures, and creating a software asset management plan. The results of these processes help organizations to better manage their software infrastructure by being able to consolidate and standardize their software titles, decide to retire unused software, or decide when to upgrade or replace software.

Application Service Providers Undoubtedly, managing the software infrastructure is a complex task, often resulting in large fluctuations in operating costs for organizations. To better control such costs, business organizations increasingly use the services of **application service providers (ASP)**. Analogous to on-demand computing, application service providers offer **on-demand software** for a variety of clients who access the applications on an as-needed basis over the Web. In other words, the software is located on the ASP's servers, and the users interact with the software using Web-enabled interfaces, such as Web browsers; while the software to perform the tasks is provided by the ASP, the organization still performs the task to be completed (such as payroll processing). For organizations, using an ASP offers a variety of benefits, such as a reduced need to maintain or upgrade software, a fixed monthly fee for services (rather than variable IT costs), and the ability to rely on a provider that has gained considerable expertise because of a large number of clients.

One example for a simple, free application service is Google calendar, which allows users to organize their schedules, share calendars, and coordinate meetings with other users. To address different business' needs, there are a variety of application service providers (see Table 4.2 for examples of different ASPs).

Managing the Communication and Collaboration Infrastructure

The organization's communication and collaboration needs are the third major infrastructure component. As with the hardware and software infrastructure, some changes in the organizations' needs have taken place over the past years; for example, e-mail has become the communications medium of choice for many people. However, for some topics, other forms of communication are more suited, so managers turn to the telephone, instant messaging, meetings, or videoconferences. One recent trend to satisfy such diverse communication and collaboration needs is the growing convergence of computing and telecommunications.

Net Stats

Broadband Access Increases

Recent reports show that in 2006, nearly 70 percent of active home Internet users in the United States had access to broadband connections. Web connection speed trends are shown in Figure 4.19.

FIGURE 4.19

Web connection speed trends in U.S. homes.

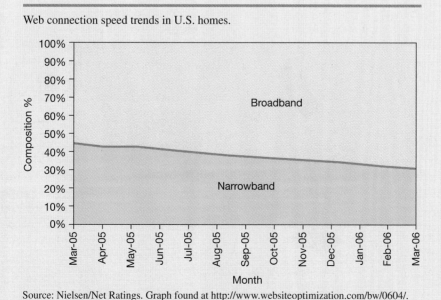

Source: Nielsen/Net Ratings. Graph found at http://www.websiteoptimization.com/bw/0604/.

TABLE 4.2 Examples of Different Types of Application Service Providers (ASPs)

Type	Service Offered	Example
Specialist or functional ASP	Single application	ASP providing payroll processing software for companies to use
Vertical market ASP	Solution package for a specific industry	ASP providing property management systems for hotels
Enterprise ASP	Broad solutions for the needs of different organizations	ASP offering complete enterprise resource planning solutions (see Chapter 7) to different industries
Local ASP	Services for small businesses within a limited geographic area	ASP offering Web site design and maintenance for small-business owners in a community

Convergence of Computing and Telecommunications The computing industry is experiencing an ever-increasing convergence of functionality of various devices. Whereas just a few years ago a cell phone was just a cell phone and a PDA was just a PDA (personal digital assistant; see Technology Briefing 1), such devices are now converging such that the boundaries between devices are becoming increasingly blurred. Today, an increasing number of devices offer a variety of different functionalities—formerly often available only on separate dedicated devices—to address differing needs of knowledge workers and consumers alike (e.g., phones, PDAs, cameras, music players, and so on).

In addition to a convergence of capabilities of devices, there is also increasing convergence within the underlying infrastructures. For example, in the past, the backbone networks for the telephone and Internet were distinct. Today, increasingly, most voice and data traffic shares a common network infrastructure. To facilitate this convergence, also termed **IP convergence**, the use of IP (Internet Protocol; see Technology Briefing 5) for transporting voice, video, fax, and data traffic has allowed enterprises to make use of new forms of communication and collaboration (e.g., instant messaging and online whiteboard collaboration) as well as traditional forms of communication (such as phone and fax) at much lower costs (see Figure 4.20). In the following sections, we will discuss two uses of IP for communication: voice over IP and videoconferencing over IP.

FIGURE 4.20

IP convergence allows various devices to communicate using IP technologies.

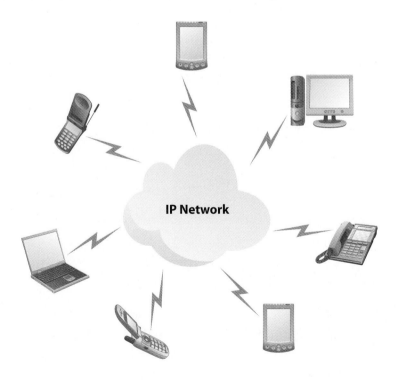

IP Network

VOICE OVER IP. **Voice over IP (VoIP)** (or IP telephony) refers to the use of Internet technologies for placing telephone calls. Whereas just a few years ago the quality of VoIP calls was substandard, recent technological advances now allow the quality of calls to equal or even surpass the quality of traditional calls over (wired) telephone lines. In addition to the quality, VoIP offers a number of other benefits; for example, users can receive calls from almost anywhere they connect to the Internet. In other words, knowledge workers are not bound to their desk to receive VoIP calls; instead, using IP routing, their telephone number "follows" them to wherever they connect to the Internet. Organizations can also benefit from tremendous cost savings, as often there is almost no cost incurred over and above the costs for a broadband Internet connection (VoIP software such as Skype allows home users to make free PC-to-PC calls; see Figure 4.21).

VIDEOCONFERENCING OVER IP. In addition to voice communications, IP can also be used to transmit video data. Traditionally, videoconferences were held via traditional phone lines, which were not made to handle the transfer of data needed for high-quality videoconferencing. Some companies also used dedicated digital lines for videoconferencing; however, this was a very costly option. Similar to VoIP, the Internet also helped to

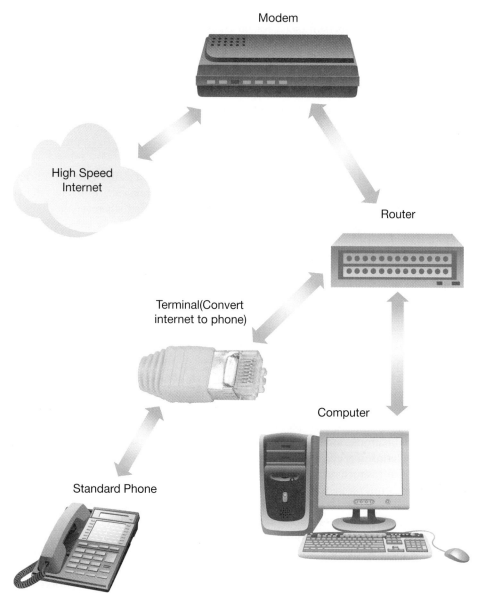

Modem

High Speed
Internet

Router

Terminal(Convert
internet to phone)

Computer

Standard Phone

FIGURE 4.21

VoIP technology enables organizations and individuals to reduce their telecommunications costs.

FIGURE 4.22

The HP HALO meeting room features life-size images.

significantly reduce costs and enhance the versatility of videoconferences by enabling **videoconferencing over IP**.

While for some videoconferences desktop videoconferencing equipment (consisting of a webcam, a microphone, speakers, and software such as Microsoft Office Live Meeting or Skype) may be sufficient, for others higher-end equipment may be needed. Such infrastructure can include specific videoconferencing hardware, or it can even be a $400,000 HP HALO meeting room featuring life-size images allowing people from across the globe to meet as if they were sitting in the same room (see Figure 4.22). In contrast to other applications, with the HALO room, HP provides a videoconferencing service to its customers, offering features such as access to a dedicated network infrastructure or support services for a fixed monthly fee. We will discuss videoconferencing in more detail in Chapter 7.

Increasing Mobility Changes in communication media—such as the growth of e-mail or instant messaging—has led to changes in the way we communicate. In today's digital world, knowledge workers desire being connected, whenever and wherever they are, so that they are able to quickly respond to any communication or use any spare minute to clean up their e-mail in-box. One infrastructure component supporting this need for connectivity is the provision of a wireless infrastructure.

WIRELESS INFRASTRUCTURES. Today's knowledge workers use two primary categories of wireless devices for their communication needs: (1) communication devices (such as cell phones) that use the public telephone infrastructure and (2) wireless devices capable of connecting to an organization's internal network. The convergence of devices and infrastructures allows the sending and receiving of e-mails using a cell phone. Thus, knowledge workers no longer need a laptop computer, nor do they need to be connected to an organization's network to get useful tasks completed. Similarly, using Web-enabled cell phones or PDAs, knowledge workers can access their company's networks and informational resources (see Chapter 5 for a discussion of corporate intranets). However, for many applications, having access to an organization's network can offer many advantages in terms of speed, ease of use, and so on. Thus, organizations are increasingly using wireless infrastructures.

When deciding on installing wireless infrastructures, organizations have to take great care to address issues such as the standards being used as well as the security of the network. For example, wireless networks based on the 802.11 family of standards are the norm today (see Technology Briefing 4). However, with the widespread use, misuse also abounds; as most of today's new laptops are equipped with the necessary hardware to connect to 802.11 networks, people are often trying to find a way to surf the Internet for free while on the road or even try to (illegally) access organization's networks (also called drive-by hacking or "war driving"; see Figure 4.23 and Chapter 6—Securing

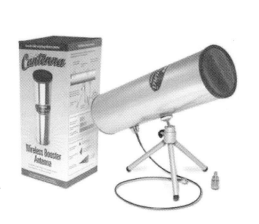

FIGURE 4.23

Accessories for "war driving" are easily obtainable, causing security concerns for organizations.

Source: http://shop.netstumbler.com/ SearchResult.aspx?CategoryID=26.

Key Enabler

Cognitive Radio

Wireless transmission is now the name of the game. Increasingly, cell phones, Wi-Fi, and satellite communication are saturating the airwaves with our personal data. Privacy is one concern, but also of concern is overcrowding of the airwaves. (Try making a cell phone call in Arizona during the peak "snowbird" season, and you will understand the problem.) What happens when calls are dropped? Usually one of three conditions: (1) wireless frequencies are full, (2) wireless towers are too few and far between, or (3) the environment (weather, high mountains, and so on) interferes.

Fortunately, researchers at Virginia Polytechnic Institute and State University in Blacksburg, Virginia, have come up with a plan for increasing the carrying capacity of airwaves. The technology—called "cognitive radio"—was originally designed for use at disaster sites since it gives a wireless signal a certain degree of intelligence. That is, it allows the transmitter to detect whether certain segments of the radio spectrum are in use. The signal can then switch to unused portions of the spectrum.

The radio spectrum in the United States is fixed by the Federal Communications Commission (FCC), with much of the spectrum being allotted for signals that are rarely used. These open areas are used intelligently by the cognitive radio signal to allow maximum carrying capacity.

Cognitive radio's current capabilities include location sensing, detection of other transmission devices, changing frequency, and even adjusting power output of the signal. These capabilities and others provide cognitive radio with the ability to adapt to conditions in real time, thereby maximizing the radio spectrum.

Intel has been a leader in the commercialization of this technology, and the company is now building reconfigurable chips that will analyze the environment and select the optimal protocol and frequency for sending data. The FCC has made special allowances so that these new devices can be tested on a large scale.

Sources: Fette, B. 2004. Cognitive Radio Shows Great Promise. *COTS Journal.* http://www.cotsjournalonline.com/ home/article.php?id=100206

Savage, J. 2006. Cognitive Radio. *Technology Review.* http://www.technologyreview.com/read_article.aspx?ch=specialsections&sc=emergingtech&id=16471

Niknejad, K. 2005. Cognitive radio: a smarter way to use radio frequencies. *Columbia News Service.* http://jscms.jrn.columbia.edu/cns/2005-04-19/niknejad-smartradio

Information Systems). In many cases, having an (unsecured) wireless network is equal to having a live network cable lying in the company's parking lot. Clearly, securing wireless infrastructures still poses challenges for organizations, which have to strike a balance between providing relatively easy access for authorized individuals and limiting access for outsiders.

Managing the Data and Knowledge Infrastructure

To support more effective business processes and gather business intelligence, organizations have to find ways to effectively manage data from different sources as well as manage their internal knowledge. Thus, companies have turned to data-mining and knowledge management tools, which we will discuss in the following sections.

Data Mining **Data mining** is a method companies use to sort and analyze information to better understand their customers, products, markets, or any other phase of their business for which data has been captured. With data-mining tools, you can graphically drill down from summary data to more detailed data, sort or extract data based on certain conditions, and perform a variety of statistical analyses, such as trend analysis, correlation analysis, forecasting, and analysis of variance. The next sections describe how data is being collected when organizations interact with their clients, and how these data are analyzed using data mining techniques.

ONLINE TRANSACTION PROCESSING. Fast customer response is fundamental to having a successful Internet-based business. **Online transaction processing (OLTP)** refers to immediate automated responses to the requests of users. OLTP systems are designed specifically to handle multiple concurrent transactions from customers. Typically, these transactions have a fixed number of inputs, such as order items, payment data, and customer name and address, and a specified output, such as total order price or order tracking number. In other words, the primary use of OLTP systems is gathering new information, transforming that information, and updating information in the system. Common transactions include receiving user information, processing orders, and generating sales receipts. Consequently, OLTP is a big part of interactive electronic commerce applications on the Internet. Since customers can be located virtually anywhere in the world, it is critical that transactions be processed efficiently (see Figure 4.24). The speed with which database management systems can process transactions is, therefore, an important design decision when building Internet systems. In addition to which technology is chosen to process the transactions, how the data is organized is also a major factor in determining system performance. Although the database operations behind most transactions are relatively simple, designers often spend considerable time making adjustments to the database design in order to "tune" processing for optimal system performance. Once an organization has all this data, it must design ways to gain the greatest value from its collection; although each individual OLTP system could be queried individually, the real power for an organization comes from analyzing the aggregation of data from different systems. Online analytical processing is one method being used to analyze these vast amounts of data.

ONLINE ANALYTICAL PROCESSING. **Online analytical processing (OLAP)** refers to the process of quickly conducting complex analysis of data stored in a database, typically using graphical software tools. The chief component of an OLAP system is the **OLAP server**, which understands how data is organized in the database and has special functions for analyzing the data. OLAP tools enable users to analyze different dimensions of data beyond data summary and data aggregations of normal database queries (see Technology Briefing 3—Database Management). For example, OLAP can provide time-series and trend analysis views of data, data drill-downs to deeper levels of consolidation, and the ability to answer "what if" and "why" questions. An OLAP query for Amazon.com might be, "What would be the effect on profits if wholesale book prices increased by 10 percent and transportation costs decreased by 5 percent?" Managers use the complex query capabilities of an OLAP system to answer questions within executive information systems, decision support systems, and enterprise resource planning (ERP) systems (each of these systems is described in later

FIGURE 4.24

Global customers require that online transactions be processed efficiently.

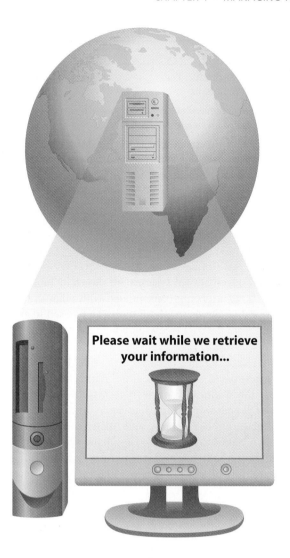

chapters). Given the high volume of transactions within Internet-based systems, analysts must provide extensive OLAP capabilities to managers in order to gain the greatest business value.

MERGING TRANSACTION AND ANALYTICAL PROCESSING. The requirements for designing and supporting transactional and analytical systems are quite different. In a distributed online environment, performing real-time analytical processing diminishes the performance of transaction processing. For example, complex analytical queries from an OLAP system require the locking of data resources for extended periods of execution time, whereas transactional events—data insertions and simple queries from customers—are fast and can often occur simultaneously. Thus, a well-tuned and responsive transaction system may have uneven performance for customers while analytical processing occurs. As a result, many organizations replicate all transactions on a second database server so that analytical processing does not slow customer transaction processing performance. This replication typically occurs in batches during off-peak hours, when site traffic volumes are at a minimum.

The systems that are used to interact with customers and run a business in real time are called **operational systems**. Examples of operational systems are sales order processing and reservation systems. The systems designed to support decision making based on stable point-in-time or historical data are called **informational systems**. The key differences

TABLE 4.3 Comparison of Operational and Informational Systems

Characteristic	Operational System	Informational System
Primary purpose	Run the business on a current basis	Support managerial decision making
Type of data	Current representation of state of the business	Historical or point-in-time (snapshot)
Primary users	Online customers, clerks, salespersons, administrators	Managers, business analysts, customers (checking status, history)
Scope of usage	Narrow and simple updates and queries	Broad and complex queries and analyses
Design goal	Performance	Ease of access and use

between operational and informational systems are shown in Table 4.3. Increasingly, data from informational systems are being consolidated with other organizational data into a comprehensive data warehouse, where OLAP tools can be used to extract the greatest and broadest understanding from the data (see Figure 4.25).

Data Warehousing Large organizations such as Wal-Mart, UPS, and Alaska Airlines have built **data warehouses**, which integrate multiple large databases and other information sources into a single repository. This repository is suitable for direct querying, analysis, or processing. Much like a physical warehouse for products and components, a data warehouse stores and distributes data on computer-based information systems. A data warehouse is a company's virtual storehouse of valuable data from the organization's disparate information systems and external sources. It supports the online analysis of sales, inventory, and other vital business data that have been culled from operational systems. The purpose of a data warehouse is to put key

FIGURE 4.25

Enhancing business intelligence by combining data from different sources.

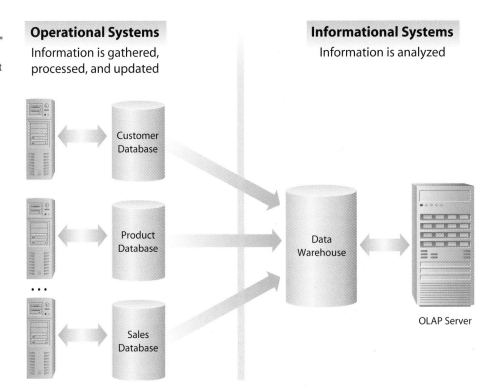

Operational Systems
Information is gathered, processed, and updated

Informational Systems
Information is analyzed

Customer Database

Product Database

Sales Database

Data Warehouse

OLAP Server

TABLE 4.4 Sample Industry Uses of Data Warehousing

Use of Data Warehousing	Representative Companies
Retail	
Analysis of scanner checkout data	Amazon.com
Tracking, analysis, and turning of sales promotions and coupons	Costco
	CVS Corporation
Inventory analysis and redeployment	Home Depot
Price reduction modeling to "move" the product	Office Depot
Negotiating leverage with supplies	Sears
Frequent buyer program management	Target
Profitability analysis	Walgreen
Product selections of granular market segmentation	Wal-Mart
	Williams-Sonoma
Telecommunications	
Analysis of call volume, equipment sales, customer profitability, costs, inventory	AT&T
	Cingular Wireless
Inventory analysis and redeployment	Comcast Cable
Purchasing leverage with suppliers	Hong Kong CSL
Frequent buyer program management	Telefonica SA
Resource and network utilization	T-Mobile
Problem tracking and customer service	Verizon
Banking and Financing	
Relationship banking	Bank of America
Cross-segment marketing	Citigroup
Risk and credit analysis	Goldman Sachs
Merger and acquisition analysis	Merrill Lynch
Customer profiling	Morgan Stanley
Branch performance	UBS AG
Portfolio management	Wells Fargo
Automotive	
Inventory and supply chain management	DaimlerChrysler AG
Resource utilization	Ford
Negotiating leverage with suppliers	General Motors
Warranty tracking and analysis	Honda
Profitability analysis and market segmentation	Toyota

business information into the hands of more decision makers. Table 4.4 lists sample industry uses of data warehouses. Data warehouses can take up hundreds of gigabytes (even terabytes) of data. They usually run on fairly powerful mainframe computers and can cost millions of dollars.

Data warehouses represent more than just big databases. An organization that successfully deploys a data warehouse has committed to pulling together, integrating, and sharing critical corporate data throughout the firm.

Data Marts Rather than storing all enterprise data in one data warehouse, many organizations have created multiple data marts, each containing a subset of the data for a single aspect of a company's business—for example, finance, inventory, or personnel. A **data mart** is a data warehouse that is limited in scope. It contains selected information from the data warehouse such that each separate data mart is customized for the decision support applications of a particular end-user group. For example, an organization may have several data marts, such as a marketing data mart or a finance data mart, that are customized for a particular type of user. Data marts have been popular among small and medium-sized businesses and among departments within larger organizations, all of which were previously prohibited from developing their own data warehouses because of the high costs involved.

Williams-Sonoma, for example, known for its high-class home furnishing stores, is constantly looking to find new ways to increase sales and reach new target markets. Some of the most important data are coming from their catalog mailings, a database that contains 33 million active U.S. households. Using SAS data-mining tools and different models, Williams-Sonoma can segment customers into groups of 30,000 to 50,000 households and can predict the profitability of those segments based on the prior year's sales. These models resulted in the creation of a new catalog for a market segment that had up to then not been served by Williams-Sonoma. Now, for example, Williams-Sonoma markets a variety of new products, such as fringed lamps, chic furniture, and cool accessories, to an identified market segment using its Pottery Barn Teen catalog.

Data marts typically contain tens of gigabytes of data as opposed to the hundreds of gigabytes in data warehouses. Therefore, data marts can be deployed on less powerful hardware. The differences in costs between different types of data marts and data warehouses can be significant. The cost to develop a data mart is typically less than $1 million, while the cost for a data warehouse can exceed $10 million. Clearly, organizations committed to getting the most out of their data must make a large investment in database technology.

While hard data from inside and outside sources are very important to an organization's success, another key ingredient is the employee's knowledge. However, capturing this knowledge and using it for business intelligence processes can be a formidable task. To better capture and use employee's knowledge, companies are turning to knowledge management.

Increasing Business Intelligence with Knowledge Management   There is no universal agreement on what exactly is meant by the term "knowledge management." In general, however, **knowledge management** refers to the processes an organization uses to gain the greatest value from its knowledge assets. In Chapter 1, we contrasted data and information as well as knowledge and wisdom. Recall that data are raw material—recorded, unformatted information, such as words or numbers. Information is data that have been formatted and organized in some way so that the result is useful to people. We need knowledge to understand relationships between different pieces of information; wisdom is accumulated knowledge. Consequently, what constitutes **knowledge assets** are all the underlying skills, routines, practices, principles, formulas, methods, heuristics, and intuitions, whether explicit or tacit. All databases, manuals, reference works, textbooks, diagrams, displays, computer files, proposals, plans, and any other artifacts in which both facts and procedures are recorded and stored are considered knowledge assets (Winter, 2001). From an organizational point of view, properly used knowledge assets enable an organization to improve its efficiency, effectiveness, and, of course, profitability.

Knowledge assets can be distinguished as being either explicit or tacit (Santosus and Surmacz, 2001). **Explicit knowledge assets** reflect knowledge that can be documented, archived, and codified, often with the help of information systems. Explicit knowledge assets reflect much of what is typically stored in a database management system. In contrast, **tacit knowledge assets** reflect the processes and procedures that are located in a person's mind on how to effectively perform a particular task (see Figure 4.26). Identifying key tacit knowledge assets and managing these assets so that they are accurate and available to people throughout the organization remains a significant challenge.

Tacit knowledge assets often reflect an organization's **best practices**—procedures and processes that are widely accepted as being among the most effective and/or efficient. Identifying how to recognize, generate, store, share, and manage this tacit knowledge is the primary objective for deploying a knowledge management system. Consequently, a **knowledge management system** is typically not a single technology but rather a collection of technology-based tools that include communication technologies—such as e-mail, groupware, instant messaging, and the like—as well as information storage and retrieval systems—such as a database management system—to enable the generation, storage, sharing, and management of tacit and explicit knowledge assets (Malhotra, 2005).

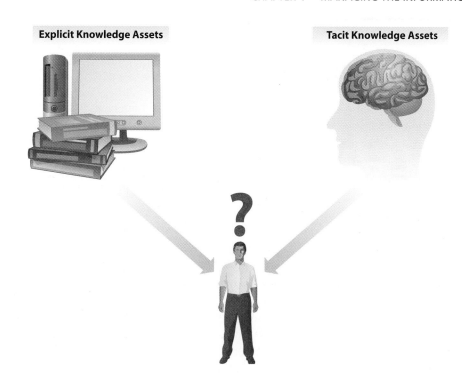

Explicit Knowledge Assets

Tacit Knowledge Assets

FIGURE 4.26

Explicit knowledge assets can easily be documented, archived, and codified, whereas tacit knowledge assets are located in a person's mind.

Managing the Facilities Infrastructure

As described previously, data and knowledge are key assets for most business organizations. Thus, it is vital to ensure that the different IS infrastructure components (such as hardware, software, communication, and data and knowledge) are available when needed and are unaffected by potential outside influences. Given various threats to IS infrastructure components (such as storm, power outages, earthquakes, and so on), organizations have to take great care on where and how to house the infrastructure. In the following sections, we will discuss different aspects of facilities and how they are secured from outside influences.

Ensuring Availability As many potential causes of disasters cannot be avoided (there's no way to stop a hurricane), organizations should attempt to plan for the worst and protect their infrastructure accordingly. For companies operating in the digital world, the information systems infrastructure is often mission critical, so special care has to be taken to secure it. Whereas some applications can tolerate some downtime in case something malfunctions or disaster strikes, other applications (such as UPS's package tracking databases) can't tolerate any downtime—these companies need 24/7/365 reliability.

In order to provide for uninterrupted service, the infrastructure is usually housed in high-availability facilities; such facilities are equipped with different features to assure availability and reliability (see Figure 4.28). The facilities for UPS in Atlanta, Georgia, and Mahwah, New Jersey, are prime examples for such high-availability facilities. To ensure uninterrupted service, the data centers are self-sufficient, and each can operate for up to two days on self-generated power. The power is needed not only for the computers but also for air conditioning, as each facility needs air-conditioning capacity equaling that of or more than 2,000 homes. In case power fails, the cooling is provided using more than 600,000 gallons of chilled water, and the UPS facilities even have backup wells in case the municipal water supply should fail. Other protective measures include raised floors (to protect from floods) and buildings designed to withstand winds of 200 miles per hour. As you can imagine, such facilities are highly complex, and monitoring the operations can be a difficult task, as there are more than 10,000 data points to observe (such as temperature readings, power surges, and so on). To help manage this infrastructure component, these facilities have been designed so that they can be monitored from a single laptop computer.

Many (especially smaller) organizations do not need facilities the size of one of the UPS data centers; instead, they may just need space for a few servers. For such needs,

Change Agents

Larry Page and Sergey Brin, Cofounders of Google (Figure 4.27)

Thanks to Larry Page's and Sergey Brin's creation, everyone who uses the Internet knows that to "google" means to search for information. The coined verb has come into popular use since 1998, when Google, an Internet search engine, first went online. In August 2004, Brin and Page took the company public on NASDAQ and that same year announced first-quarter results as a public company with record revenues of $805.9 million.

Google is unique among search engines in that it indexes more content than most other search engines and finds relevant Web pages in less time. It can also search through a database of almost a million pictures, can personalize searches using a personal profile users create, and produce maps in conjunction with local searches such as "restaurants" in addition to offering free e-mail accounts. Additionally, Google is constantly releasing new applications and fighting for much more turf in the search engine business. Today, Brin and Page are reportedly worth approximately $12.8 billion each. (They recently bought a Boeing 767 for their private use.) Avid environmentalists, the two Google founders drive hybrid cars and encourage their employees to do the same. Brin and Page also came up with several innovative ideas to keep their employees' morale high; among the perks for Google employees are roller-hockey games in the company's parking lot twice a week, on-site workout and massage rooms, or one day per week to spend on their favorite innovations and projects.

In accordance with the company's informal motto "don't be evil," Brin and Page have established Google.org as Google's philanthropic arm (which also includes the Google Foundation). Drawing on Google's resources such as talent or technology, Google.org tries to address some of the world's most pressing problems—including poverty, energy, and the environment—by funding studies to improve water supplies in Western Kenya or programs to increase literacy in India.

Sources: http://en.wikipedia.org/wiki/Lawrence_E._Page

http://en.wikipedia.org/wiki/Sergey_Brin

http://news.bbc.co.uk/2/hi/business/3666241.stm

http://www.google.org/

FIGURE 4.27

Sergey Brin and Larry Page, cofounders of Google.

Source: http://www.google.com/press/images.html.

FIGURE 4.28

High-availability facilities feature sturdy construction, backup generators, air conditioning, access control, intrusion detection systems, and fire suppression systems.

FIGURE 4.29

Collocation facilities allow organizations to rent secure space for their infrastructure.

Source: http://www.sungard.com/corporate/general_pictures.htm.

companies can turn to **collocation facilities**. Organizations can rent space (usually in the form of cabinets or shares of a cabinet; see Figure 4.29) for their servers in such collocation facilities. Organizations managing collocation facilities provide the necessary infrastructure in terms of power, backups, connectivity, and security.

Securing the Facilities Infrastructure An organization's information systems infrastructure always needs to be secured to prevent it from outside intruders. Thus, no matter whether your server is located in a cabinet within your organization or you have rented space in a collocation facility, you should have physical safeguards in place to secure the equipment. Common safeguards include access control, closed-circuit television monitoring (see Chapter 6), and intrusion detection systems. We will discuss these safeguards and other security issues in later chapters.

Managing the Human Resource Infrastructure

With the increased sophistication of the information systems infrastructure, organizations trying to manage their own infrastructure are facing the need for a highly trained workforce. However, access to the necessary human resource infrastructure is not a given in many rural areas. Over time, certain areas have become known for the availability of talented staff in a certain sector, and thus organizations operating in that sector tend to set up shop in such areas. Such areas are often characterized by a high quality of life for the people living there, and it is no surprise that many companies in the information technology sector are headquartered in Silicon Valley, California, or Seattle, Washington. In other areas, organizations can often not depend on an existing human resource infrastructure and have to attract people from other areas. In such cases, organizations have to find ways to both attract and retain employees.

Human resource policies provide another approach for assuring an adequate supply of skilled personnel. For example, many organizations provide educational grants or expense-matching programs to encourage employees to improve their education and skills. Typically, after receiving continuing education benefits, employees must agree to remain with the organization for some specified period of time or be forced to repay the employer. Other human resource policies, such as telecommuting, flextime, and creative benefit packages, can help to attract and retain the best employees.

With increasing globalization, other regions throughout the world are boasting about their existing human resource infrastructure. One such example is the Indian city of Bangalore, where, over a century ago, Maharajas started to lure talented people to the region to build a world-class human resource infrastructure. Although this has certainly helped to attract top Indian companies and multinational corporations alike, many companies have recently started complaining about other infrastructure issues, such as bad roads, power outages, housing conditions, traffic jams, and heavy rains. Clearly, for an area, just having a good human resource infrastructure is not sufficient, as organizations have to

TABLE 4.5 Organizations Use Different Services to Support Their Infrastructure Needs

IS Infrastructure Component	Service	Example
Hardware	Utility computing	Organizations pay for processing or data storage on an as-needed basis
Software	Application service provider (ASP)	Organizations use a payroll system hosted on an ASP's server
Communication and collaboration	Videoconferencing	Organizations install HP HALO rooms and pay a monthly fee for usage and support
Data and knowledge	ASP	Data from applications hosted on an ASP's server is stored by the provider
Facilities	Collocation facility	Companies rent space for their servers in a collocation facility

balance all their infrastructure needs when deciding where to move their headquarters or where to set up a new local subsidiary.

Managing the Services Infrastructure

When operating in today's digital world, organizations have to rely on a complex information systems infrastructure. For many (especially smaller) organizations, maintaining such infrastructure is beyond their means because of the costs for maintaining and upgrading hardware and software, employing in-house experts for support, and so on. Thus, organizations big and small are turning to outside service providers for their infrastructure needs. As you read throughout this chapter, organizations can use different services to support their infrastructure needs. Table 4.5 provides examples for different types of services offered. Next, we will discuss an additional form of services, namely, outsourcing.

Brief Case ◐

Toyota's Savvy Chief Information Officer

Some jingoistic Americans who refuse to buy "foreign" cars have also boycotted Toyota. They might be surprised to learn that, in fact, Toyota operates 14 manufacturing facilities in North America. Toyota employs over 37,000 Americans, and in 2006 the company produced 15 million cars in North America—a 20-year high—investing nearly $16.2 billion in local manufacturing and sales.

As with any large corporation, Toyota's IT investments are also large. Experts report, however, that until 2005, Toyota's IT departments had failed to keep up with increases in production and sales—especially in sales and customer support services.

After closely examining Toyota's IT services in 2003, Barbra Cooper, Toyota's chief information officer, found that these failures were due not to poor software choices, poor implementation, lack of appropriate IT personnel, or lack of expertise but rather to lack of trust in and respect for Toyota's American IT departments. Cooper had been hired in 1996 to oversee IT projects and realized early on that the IT and business departments seldom communicated closely or worked together to solve IS problems. During her retrospective examination of Toyota's IT services, Cooper realized that a major problem was that the IT staff was buried under the weight of six enterprise-wide projects and that staff was spread so thin that they could not adequately address any of the projects. Called the "big six," the projects included a new extranet for dealers, a PeopleSoft ERP implementation, a sales management system, a forecasting system, an advanced warranty system, and a documents management system.

Toyota's head office (business vs. IT) believed all six projects were vital and failed to realize that the IT department could not possibly successfully complete them. Cooper sought to bring the business and IT departments together so that priorities, time lines, and practical delivery dates could be discussed by both sides. Cooper also sought corporate headquarters' help in defining a new IT projects approval process in which the IT department would be involved in all planning phases.

In the beginning, some business managers and other employees did not like the new cooperative planning process, probably because they were reluctant to concede the control they had previously enjoyed over IT projects. They would no longer be able to develop their own IT initiatives and simply deliver their ideas to the IT department for implementation.

The new IT project approval process that Cooper recommended would also result in extensive changes in her IT department. Thus, already-stretched IT employees feared that their responsibilities would increase even more. In the past, Cooper had been protective of her employees' time and of projects undertaken by the IT department, and now she resolved to ensure that IT capabilities be considered before projects were assigned.

As Toyota's IT department met deadlines and delivered high-quality information systems, Cooper and her department gained respect. Toyota's business executives were further impressed when, in 2005, IT services reported a reduction in project costs of 16 percent—translating into several million dollars in savings. As a result, Cooper was given the go-ahead to revamp Toyota's IS model worldwide.

Questions

1. What is more important, leadership or infrastructure?
2. Can you have great information systems infrastructure without a great leader?

Sources: Thomas Wailgum, "The Big Fix," *CIO* (April 15, 2005), http://www.cio.com/archive/041505/toyota.html

http://www.toyota.com/about/operations/manufacturing/index.html

Outsourcing As we have defined in Chapter 1, outsourcing is the turning over of partial or entire responsibility for information systems development and/or management to an outside organization. In a prior section, we talked about application service providers, where an organization uses software services from another organization. In contrast, outsourcers such as Accenture provide services to organizations. Such services can be conducting business processes, such as finance, accounting, or human resources, or the services provided can be the development and maintenance of software or the management of an organization's technology infrastructure. As with other infrastructure solutions such as on-demand computing or on-demand software, outsourcing can help a company focus on its core processes without having to worry about supporting processes. While outsourcing has seen a tremendous increase over past years, outsourcing is typically limited to noncore business functions. However, there are some noncore business functions that organizations tend to keep within their own realm. For example, although more and more companies outsource the management of their information systems infrastructure, only very few outsource information systems security, as it is regarded as being critical for an organization's survival (CSI, 2006).

Ensuring a Reliable and Secure Infrastructure

In the previous sections, you have read about how organizations get most out of their data, how to maximize available resources, and how to use outside providers for the infrastructure needs. While these are all very important issues for an organization to manage, there is one issue that is even more critical for effective infrastructure management. Specifically, what happens when something goes seriously wrong? For organizations such as Amazon.com, a network outage can quickly lead to millions of dollars in terms of lost revenue. Unfortunately, there are many events that can lead to catastrophic system failures, such as natural disasters, criminal activities, or just plain accidents. The most common causes of disaster are power outages, hardware failures, and floods (see Figure 4.30). How can companies managing in a digital world avoid such disasters? In a prior section, you learned how companies proactively try to avoid a disaster by building and maintaining high-availability facilities or by renting space in a collocation facility. In the following

FIGURE 4.30

Power outages, hardware failures, and floods are the most common causes of disaster.

Common causes of disasters

section, you will learn how organizations can attempt to limit the impacts of a disaster or plan for and recover from a disaster should one happen.

Disaster Planning

In some cases, all attempts to provide a reliable and secure information systems infrastructure are in vain, and disasters cannot be avoided. Thus, organizations need to be prepared for when something catastrophic occurs. The most important aspect of preparing for disaster is creating a **disaster recovery plan**, which spells out detailed procedures for recovering from systems-related disasters, such as virus infections and other disasters that might cripple the information systems infrastructure. This way, even under the worst-case scenario, people will be able to replace or reconstruct critical files or data, or they will at least have a plan readily available to begin the recovery process, including a list of service providers. A typical disaster recovery plan includes information that answers the following questions:

- What events are considered a disaster?
- What should be done to prepare the backup site?
- What is the chain of command, and who can declare a disaster?
- What hardware and software is needed to recover from a disaster?
- Which personnel are needed for staffing the backup sites?
- What is the sequence for moving back to the original location after recovery?

Backup Sites   **Backup sites** are critical components in a disaster recovery plan, as they allow businesses to continue functioning in the event a disaster strikes; in other words, backup sites can be thought of as a company's office in a temporary location. Commonly, a distinction is made between cold and hot backup sites. These are discussed next.

COLD BACKUP SITES. A **cold backup site** is nothing more than an empty warehouse with all necessary connections for power and communication but nothing else. In the case of a disaster, a company has to first set up all necessary equipment, ranging from office furniture to Web servers. While this is the least expensive option, it also takes a relatively longer time before a company can resume working after a disaster.

HOT BACKUP SITE. A **hot backup site**, in contrast, is a fully equipped backup facility, having everything from office chairs to a one-to-one replication of the most current data. In the event of a disaster, all that has to be done is to relocate the employees to the backup site to continue working. Obviously, this is a very expensive option, as the backup site has to be kept fully equipped and all the information systems infrastructure duplicated. Further, hot backup sites also have a redundant backup of the data so that the business processes are interrupted as little as possible. To achieve this redundancy, all data are **mirrored** on a separate server (i.e., everything is stored synchronously on two independent systems). This might seem expensive, but for a critical business application involving customers, it may be less expensive to run a redundant backup system in parallel than it would be to disrupt business or lose customers in the event of catastrophic system failure.

CHOOSING A BACKUP SITE LOCATION. Thinking about the location of redundant systems is an important aspect of disaster planning. If a company relies on redundant systems, all of which are located within the same building, a single event can incapacitate both systems. Similarly, events such as a hurricane can damage systems that are located across town from each other. Thus, even if the primary infrastructure is located in-house, when having redundant systems, it pays to have the backup located in a different geographic area to minimize the risk of a disaster happening to both systems.

Designing the Recovery Plan

When planning for disaster, two objectives should be considered by an organization: recovery time and recovery point objectives. **Recovery time objectives** specify the maximum time allowed to recover from a catastrophic event. For example, should the organization be able to resume operations in minutes, hours, or days after the disaster? Having completely redundant systems helps to minimize the recovery time and might be best suited for mission-critical applications, such as e-commerce transaction servers. For other applications, such as data mining, while important, the recovery time can be longer without disrupting primary business processes.

Additionally, **recovery point objectives** specify how current the backup data should be. Imagine that your computer's hard drive crashes while you are working on a term paper. Luckily, you recently backed up your data. Would you prefer the last backup to be a few days old, or would you rather have the last backup include your most recent version of the term paper? Having completely redundant systems that mirror the data helps to minimize (or even avoid) data loss in the event of a catastrophic failure.

The disaster recovery plan is just one part of an overall plan for effectively managing the information systems infrastructure. In Chapter 6, we outline a comprehensive information systems security plan that includes disaster recovery.

Information Systems Controls, Auditing, and the Sarbanes-Oxley Act

As you have seen, there are a variety of components to consider when managing the information systems infrastructure. No matter how organizations choose to manage their infrastructure, **information systems controls** have to be put into place to control costs,

BlackBerry

What would physicians, emergency medical technicians, trial attorneys, government decision makers, military officers, and countless other professionals do without their pagers, cell phones—and BlackBerries?

When Things go Wrong :-(:-| :-0

In 1999, Research in Motion (RIM), based in Waterloo, Ontario, introduced a wireless device it named BlackBerry, after the berry-like buttons on the product. A BlackBerry fits in a user's palm and is operated using a trackwheel and buttons. When first introduced, BlackBerries concentrated on e-mail, but they now support push e-mail (received in real time), mobile telephoning, Internet faxing, text messaging, Web browsing, and other wireless information services. BlackBerries are noted for their reliability, offering connectivity when other telecommunication devices fail.

In the early 2000s, NTP, Incorporated, a Virginia-based patent-holding company, sent notice of their wireless telecommunications patents to several fledgling wireless companies, offering to license their patents to them. None of the companies bought patent licenses from NTP. NTP then sued one of the companies, RIM, claiming patent infringement. RIM claimed in court that a functional wireless e-mail system was already in the public domain before NTP's inventions. The jury, however, found for NTP, and RIM was fined several million dollars. The case continued through several appeals but was finally settled in 2006.

RIM agreed to pay NTP $612.5 million "in full and final settlement of all claims." RIM also announced the use of newly developed technology that would remove all question of whether the BlackBerry used NTP-patented technology. BlackBerry users, who totaled more than 3 million in March 2006, were relieved when the case was settled since many had feared that the beloved devices would be shut down by court order. In fact, the U.S. Department of Defense had testified during the patent infringement lawsuit that loss of the BlackBerry network would be a threat to national security since so many government employees used the device.

Although NTP's patent infringement case was settled, the situation raised several questions. When similar innovations are developed independently but simultaneously, who actually "owns" the invention? If a company pays to license a patent, how long should the company pay royalties on the product using the patent? And, perhaps most important, how secure is intellectual property in a flat world, where technological advances emerge virtually overnight?

Sources: Wikipedia.org/BlackBerry: http://en.wikipedia.org/wiki/BlackBerry

Mark Heinzl and Amol Sharma, "RIM to Pay NTP $612.5 Million to Settle BlackBerry Patent Suit," *Wall Street Journal* (March 4, 2006), http://online.wsj.com/article_email/SB114142276287788965-lMyQjAxMDE2NDAxMzQwMjMyWj.html

gain and protect trust, remain competitive, or comply with internal or external governance (e.g., the Sarbanes-Oxley Act, discussed later in this section). Such controls, which help ensure the reliability of information, can consist of a variety of different measures, such as policies and their physical implementation, access restrictions, or record keeping, to be able to trace actions and transactions and who is responsible for these. IS controls thus need to be applied throughout the entire IS infrastructure. To be most effective, controls should be a combination of three types of controls:

- Preventive controls (to prevent any potentially negative event from occurring, such as by preventing outside intruders from accessing a facility)
- Detective controls (to assess whether anything went wrong, such as unauthorized access attempts)
- Corrective controls (to mitigate the impacts of any problem after it has arisen, such as restoring compromised data)

One way to conceptualize the different forms of controls is by a hierarchy ranging from high-level policies to the implementation at the application level (see Figure 4.31 for the hierarchy of controls; note that the categories are not necessarily mutually exclusive); Table 4.6 gives a brief explanation of the different types of controls and presents examples for each. You have learned about a variety of IS controls in prior sections, and while reading this book, you will continue to come across the different elements of control. In the following sections, we will describe how companies use IS auditing to assess the IS controls in place and whether further IS controls need to be implemented or changed.

Information Systems Auditing Analyzing the IS controls should be an ongoing process for organizations. However, often it can be beneficial for organizations to periodically have an external entity review the controls so as to uncover any potential problems. An **information systems audit**, often performed by external auditors, can help organizations assess the state of their information systems controls to determine necessary changes and to help ensure the information systems' availability, confidentiality, and integrity. The response to the strengths and weaknesses identified in the IS audit is often determined by the potential risks an organization faces. In other words, the IS audit has to assess whether the IS controls in place are sufficient to address the potential risks. Thus, a major component of the IS audit is a **risk assessment**, which aims at determining what

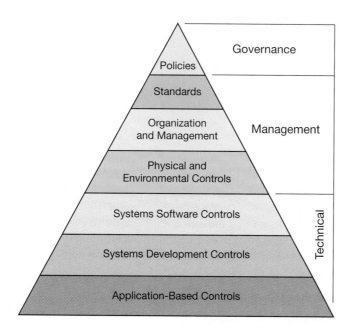

FIGURE 4.31

Hierarchy of IS controls.

Source: http://infotech.aicpa.org/

TABLE 4.6 Different Types of Information Systems Controls

Type of Control	What Is It For?	Examples
Policies	Define aims and objectives of the organization	General policies about: Security and privacy, Rights of access, Data and systems ownership, End-user development, Access to sensitive areas (e.g., high-availability facilities), Disaster planning
Standards	Support the requirements of policies	Standards about: Systems development process Systems software configuration Application controls Data structures Documentation
Organization and management	Define lines of reporting to implement effective control and policy development	Policies about: Security and use Account authorization Backup and recovery Incident reporting
Physical and environmental controls	Protect the organization's IS assets	High-availability facilities Collocation facilities
Systems software controls	Enable applications and users to utilize the systems	Control access to applications Generate activity logs Prevent outside intrusion (e.g., by hackers)
Systems development and acquisition controls	Ensure that systems meet the organization's needs	Document user requirements Use formal processes for systems design, development, testing, and maintenance
Application-based controls	Ensure correct input, processing, storage, and output of data; maintain record of data as it moves through the system	Input controls (such as checking the input into a Web form) Processing controls Output controls (comparing the outputs against intended results) Integrity controls (ensure that data remains correct) Management trail (keep record of transactions to be able to locate sources of potential errors)

type of risks the organization's IS infrastructure faces, the criticality of those risks to the infrastructure, and the level of risks the organization is willing to tolerate. To determine the potential risks, an organization needs to first identify the infrastructure components that are at risk, identify potential vulnerabilities, and map the vulnerabilities to the potential threats. Then the probability of each event's occurring and its potential impact should be estimated. This process will lead to several important questions that must be answered, including the following:

■ What are the costs of restoring the data in case of a threat event?
■ What are potential legal costs in case confidential data are lost?
■ What are the costs to the business if core systems are unavailable for a certain period of time?

Depending on the nature of the risks, the level of risk tolerance, and the severity of the risks identified, an organization can follow various steps. These steps are reducing or eliminating the risk (by implementing stricter IS controls), sharing or transferring the risk (e.g., by outsourcing certain functions to a highly skilled service provider), or just accepting the risk (in case the risk is deemed not critical to an organization's success) (see also Chapter 6).

Once the risk has been assessed, auditors have to evaluate the organization's internal controls. During such audits, the auditor tries to gather evidence regarding the effectiveness of the controls. However, testing all controls under all possible conditions is very inefficient and often infeasible. Thus, auditors frequently rely on **computer-assisted auditing tools (CAAT)**, which is specific software to test applications and data, using test data or simulations. In addition to using specific auditing tools, auditors use audit sampling procedures to assess the controls, enabling the audit to be conducted in the most cost-effective manner. Once the audit has been performed and sufficient evidence has been gathered, reports are issued to the organization. Usually, such reports are followed up with a discussion of the results and potential courses of action.

The Sarbanes Oxley Act Performing an IS audit can help an organization reduce costs or remain competitive by identifying areas where IS controls are lacking and need improvement. Another major factor that has contributed to a high demand for IS auditors is the need to comply with government regulations, most notably the **Sarbanes-Oxley Act** (hereafter S-OX) of 2002. Formed as a reaction to large-scale accounting scandals that led to the downfall of corporations such as WorldCom and Enron, the act primarily addresses the accounting side of organizations. However, given the importance of an IS infrastructure and IS controls for an organization's financial applications, it is of major importance to include IS controls in compliance reviews.

According to S-OX, companies have to demonstrate that there are controls in place to prevent misuse or fraud, controls to detect any potential problems, and effective measures in place to correct any problems; S-OX goes so far that corporate executives face jail time and heavy fines if the appropriate controls are not in place or are ineffective. The information systems architecture plays a key role in S-OX compliance, given that many controls are information-systems based, providing capabilities to detect information exceptions and to provide a management trail for tracing exceptions. However, S-OX itself barely addresses IS controls specifically; rather, it addresses general processes and practices, leaving companies wondering how to comply with the guidelines put forth in the act. Further, it is often cumbersome and time consuming for organizations to identify the relevant systems to be audited for S-OX compliance. Thus, many organizations find it easier to review their entire IS infrastructure, following objectives set forth in guidelines such as the **control objectives for information and related technology (COBIT)**—a set of best practices that help organizations both maximize the benefits from their IS infrastructure and establish appropriate controls.

Another issue faced by organizations because of S-OX is the requirement to preserve evidence to document compliance and for potential lawsuits. Since the inception of S-OX, e-mails and even instant messages have achieved the same status as regular business documents and thus need to be preserved for a period of time, typically up to seven years. Failure to present such documents in case of litigious activity can lead to severe fines being imposed on companies and their executives, and courts usually will not accept the argument that a message could not be located. For example, the investment bank Morgan Stanley faced fines up to $15 million for failing to retain e-mail messages. On the surface, it seems easiest for an organization to simply archive all the e-mail messages sent and received. However, such a "digital landfill" where everything is stored can quickly grow to an unmanageable size, and companies cannot comply with the mandate to present any evidence in a timely manner. Thus, many organizations turn to e-mail management software that archives and categorizes all incoming and outgoing e-mails based on key words. Even using such specialized software, finding e-mails related to a certain topic within the archive can pose a tremendous task: some analysts estimate that a business with 25,000 employees generates over 4 billion e-mail messages over the course of seven years (not counting any increase in e-mail activity), which will be hard to handle for even the most sophisticated programs.

Industry Analysis

Radio

The new satellite and high-definition radio stations have been called "jukeboxes on steroids." Generally, there are no ads and no DJs—just uninterrupted tunes.

Satellite radio, also known as subscription radio, operates via digital signals received from low-orbiting satellites. In the absence of paid advertising, subscribers pay monthly fees for a bundle of music "channels," each one devoted to talk shows or to various types of music, such as country, hip-hop, classical, and so on.

Currently, the prominent players in the satellite radio market are XM Radio and Sirius in North America and WorldSpace in Europe, Asia, and Africa. All of the signals are proprietary—that is, services do not share equipment. Instead, each service owns its own licensed equipment for receiving and relaying signals. The popularity of satellite radio is beginning to affect traditional FM market share, as evidenced by the gravitation of some big names in radio, such as Howard Stern, to satellite stations.

In addition to satellite radio, high-definition (HD) radio has recently become popular with listeners. HD radio is similar to the satellite model in that a digital signal provides CD-quality listening. This technology claims to eliminate the static and hiss associated with the FM analog signal.

The digital medium also offers a promising multicasting feature using current radio equipment. "Multicasting" is the term used for subdividing a radio station's signal into multiple channels. Multicasting means that a station's listeners have a choice of stations that carry talk shows, various genres of music, sports, and so on, much like TV signals are divided into several channels. The potential for current radio stations is limitless since they can now offer several types of high-quality niche programming without having to buy additional equipment.

Clearly, the radio industry is joining other major industries in becoming globalized and digitized to become successful in today's world.

Questions

1. Contrast the infrastructure required to launch a satellite versus traditional radio station.
2. Today there are thousands of AM/FM stations. Forecast their future and provide a strategy for retaining and gaining market share.

Sources: Anonymous, "A New Radio Format, or Just Another Name?," *Audio Graphics* (April 24, 2006), http://www. audiographics.com/agd/042406-3.htm

Anonymous, "Business Briefs" (May 10, 2006), http://ws.gmnews.com/news/2006/0510/Business/013.html

Key Points Review

1. *List the essential information systems infrastructure components and describe why they are necessary for satisfying an organization's informational needs.* Modern organizations heavily rely on information systems infrastructure; its components include hardware, software, communications and collaboration, data and knowledge, facilities, human resources, and services. While the computing hardware is integral to an organization's IS infrastructure, as it is also needed to store and process organizational data, networking hardware is needed to connect the different systems to allow for collaboration and information sharing. Software assists organizations in executing their business processes and competitive strategy. Consequently, with increased reliance on information systems for managing organizations, effectively utilizing software resources is becoming increasingly critical and complex. Communication and collaboration is one of the reasons why information systems have become so powerful and important to modern organizations. The ability to interconnect computers, information systems, and networks ultimately allows the interconnection of both internal and external business processes, facilitating improved communication and collaboration. Data and knowledge are probably among the most important assets an organization has, as data and knowledge are

essential for both gaining business intelligence and executing business processes. Facilities, though not directly needed to support business processes or business intelligence, are necessary for the information systems infrastructure. Human resources are also an important component in information system infrastructure. Although even large facilities do not require large support staff, the staff that is needed should be well trained. Finally, a broad range of services are needed to support the information system infrastructure.

2. *Describe solutions organizations use to design a reliable, robust, and secure infrastructure.* Many organizations now turn to on-demand computing for fluctuating computation needs, utility computing for "renting" of resources, grid computing for solving large-scale problems, edge computing for providing a more decentralized use of resources, and autonomic computing for increasing reliability. To manage the ever-increasing complexity of software needs, organizations turn to open-source software to increase their independence, use Web services to integrate different applications housed on different systems, and use patch management and software asset management systems to keep their systems current. In other cases, organizations want to free themselves from having to address such issues and use on-demand software provided by application service providers. The convergence of computing and telecommunications has helped organizations address their diverse communication needs, such as by enabling voice over IP or videoconferencing over IP. Often, companies implement wireless infrastructures to increase their employees' mobility. To support more effective businesses and to gather business intelligence, organizations have to find ways to manage vast amounts of data, usually using online transaction processing and online analytical processing. Data warehouses and data marts support the integration and analysis of large data sets. Knowledge management systems are a family of tools helping to organize, store, and retrieve a company's tacit and explicit knowledge assets. Finally, organizations have to manage their facilities to ensure security and availability, have to manage the human resource infrastructure to attract and retain qualified personnel, and have to manage the use of different services, often using outsourcing.

3. *Describe how organizations can ensure a reliable and secure infrastructure, plan for potential disasters, and establish IS controls.* In some cases, all attempts to provide a reliable and secure information systems infrastructure are in vain, and disasters cannot be avoided. Thus, organizations need to be prepared when something catastrophic occurs. The most important aspect of preparing for disaster is creating a disaster recovery plan, which spells out detailed procedures for recovering from systems-related disasters, such as virus infections and other disasters that might cripple the information systems infrastructure. This disaster plan should include decisions about where to back up and whether this backup site be hot or cold. A hot backup site completely replicates data and facilities; a cold site is an empty facility with only power and network connectivity. Reliability is also enhanced through the design of a comprehensive disaster recovery plan that outlines recovery goals and tactics. IS controls can help ensure a secure and reliable infrastructure; such controls should be a mix of preventive, detective, and corrective controls. To assess the efficacy of these controls, organizations frequently conduct information systems audits to determine the risks an organization faces and how far the IS controls can limit any potentially negative effects. Further, organizations perform IS audits to comply with government regulations, most notably, the Sarbanes-Oxley Act of 2002. According to S-OX, companies have to demonstrate that there are controls in place to prevent misuse or fraud, controls to detect any potential problems, and effective measures to correct any problems; S-OX goes so far that a business executive could face heavy fines or substantial jail time if appropriate controls are not in place or are ineffective. Performing thorough IS audits on a regular basis can help assess compliance to these regulations.

Key Terms

application service
   provider (ASP) 144
autonomic computing 140
backup sites 161
best practices 156
business intelligence 131
business processes 130

computer-assisted auditing tools
   (CAAT) 165
control objectives for information
   and related technology
   (COBIT) 165
cold backup site 161
collocation facilities 156

core processes 130
data mart 153
data mining 150
data warehouse 151
dedicated grid 139
disaster recovery plan 160
edge computing 139

Review Questions

1. List three reasons why Google chose The Dalles, Oregon, for its newest data center.
2. Describe what business intelligence (BI) is and how organizations use BI to gain a competitive advantage.
3. What is on-demand computing, and how can organizations use this technology to cut costs?
4. Define grid computing and describe its advantages and disadvantages.
5. List the five elements that are essential for autonomic computing.
6. Describe why companies would choose to implement open-source software over fully licensed software.
7. List and describe the two main types of software licenses.
8. Describe what is meant by the term IP convergence.
9. Describe the two main categories of wireless device for communication needs.
10. Compare and contrast data warehouses and data marts.
11. Define outsourcing and how it is used in organizations today.
12. Describe how the Sarbanes-Oxley Act impacts the management of the information systems infrastructure.

Self-Study Questions

Visit the Interactive Study Guide on the text Web site for additional Self-Study Questions: **www.prenhall.com/ Jessup**.

1. _____ processes are the activities organizations perform in order to reach their business goals.
   A. core
   B. support
   C. business
   D. functional

2. In modern organizations, information system infrastructure heavily relies on all of the following except for _____.
   A. hardware
   B. communication
   C. human resources
   D. services
   E. finance

3. _____ is a special form of on-demand computing which is typically used to solve large-scale computing problems.
   A. grid
   B. utility

   C. access
   D. edge

4. Rather than having massive centralized computers and databases, smaller servers are now located closer to individual users. This is called _____ computing.
   A. edge
   B. grid
   C. utility
   D. access

5. Which of the following is *not* an example of open-source software?
   A. Linux
   B. OpenOffice
   C. Apache
   D. Windows Vista

6. This management system allows developers to account for unforeseen problems after the software was shipped to the customer.
   A. account management system
   B. patch management system

C. software bug system

D. software inventory system

7. This system helps organizations avoid the negative impacts of installing unlicensed or private software.

A. software asset management

B. patch management system

C. software bug system

D. software inventory system

8. What method is used to sort and analyze information to better understand an organization's customers, products, market, and so on?

A. OLTP

B. Web services

C. OLAP

D. data mining

9. _____ knowledge assets reflect the process and procedures that are located in a person's mind.

A. tacit

B. explicit

C. implicit

D. real

10. Which is a specific software tool used by auditors to test applications and data or run simulations of business transactions and processes?

A. Sarbanes-Oxley

B. Web services

C. computer-assisted auditing tools (CAAT)

D. risk assessment system

Answers are on page 171.

Problems and Exercises

1. Match the following terms with the appropriate definitions:

i. Utility computing

ii. Web services

iii. Shrink-wrap license

iv. Application service provider

v. Voice over IP

vi. OLTP

vii. Knowledge management

viii. Operational system

ix. Data warehouse

x. OLAP

   a. The integration of large databases into a single repository

   b. The use of the Internet technology for placing telephone calls

   c. A type of license that accompanies software primarily used by consumers

   d. Technology used for immediate automated response to requests of the users

   e. Technology used in transaction and analytical processing to interact with customers and run a business in real time

   f. The process an organization uses to gain the greatest value from its knowledge assets

   g. A form of on-demand computing where resources are rented on an as-needed basis

   h. Web-based software systems that allow the interaction of different programs over a network

   i. Internet technology that provides access to application software via a Web browser

   j. A graphical software tool that provides complex analysis of data

2. Akamai (www.akamai.com) distributes on average 10 to 20 percent of the Web's content on any given day. What function do they provide, and how do they accomplish this?

3. Do you feel that there should be human involvement in the resolution of network, hardware, and software problems? Autonomic computing allows for the computers to self-configure; describe some societal, ethical, and technical problems that might arise from this.

4. Several Fortune 500 companies now use voice over IP (VoIP) for virtually all of their corporate communication. What are the advantages to this technology for business infrastructure? What are some of the consumer VoIP technologies that are currently in place? Which one of these technologies do you see lasting?

5. The HP Halo system allows for videoconferences to mimic face-to-face conferences. Imagine you were in charge of designing a new videoconference system. What are some of the features you would include? Which features do you feel are less important?

6. Based on your experience with online transaction processing systems (in everyday life or in the workplace), which ones seem to work best? What characteristics did you judge the success of these systems by? Would you make any adjustments to the system?

7. Interview an IS employee within an organization at a university or a workplace. What are the important issues for the infrastructure of the organization? Have they had any experiences with data loss due to infrastructure problems? What backup plans do they have in place in case of disaster?

8. Describe how various systems in this chapter might enable organizations to become prepared for a disaster such as a fire or flood. What technologies in particular are of critical importance?

9. Choose an organization with which you are familiar that uses databases. Then brainstorm how this organization could use data mining to gain an understanding of their customers, products, or marketplace. What are some key pieces of information that should be data mined for this organization?

10. Using a search engine, enter the key word "data warehousing." Who are the large vendors in this industry? What type of solutions do they offer to their clients? Do you see any common trends in the data warehousing businesses?

11. Using a Web browser, go to http://www.kmworld. com/. Looking at this site's current stories on knowledge management, find some current trends in knowledge management. Under the "Solutions" link, choose an industry of interest to you. What types of solutions are offered for this industry?

12. Find any Web site that could be considered a "knowledge management" site. What knowledge does the site capture? What are the important attributes included in this site? What suggestions would you have to make the site a better place to find or store knowledge?

13. Interview an IS professional and ask him or her about open-source software. Does he or she see all types of information systems to be candidates for open-source software? Additionally, find out what systems are most likely and least likely to be open source.

14. Browse BOINC's different grid computing projects at http://boinc.berkeley.edu/. Which projects seem most interesting? For which projects would you "donate" your computing resources? If you would not donate any resources, why not?

15. Interview an IS professional about his or her company's use of software asset management processes. How does he or she keep track of the different software installed? If anyone asked you about the software installed on your computer, would you know what you have installed? Would you be able to produce the licenses for each software installed?

Application Exercises

The existing data files referenced in these exercises are available on the Student Companion Web site: **www.prenhall.com/ Jessup.**

Spreadsheet Application: Tracking Frequent Flier Mileage

You have recently landed a part-time job as a business analyst for Campus Travel. In your first meeting, the operations manager learned that you are taking an introductory MIS class. As the manager is not very proficient in using office software tools, he is doing all frequent flier mileage in two separate Excel spreadsheets. One is the customer's contact information, and the second is the miles flown. Being familiar with the possibilities of spreadsheet applications, you suggest setting up one spreadsheet to handle both functions. To complete this, you must do the following:

1. Open the spreadsheet frequentflier2.csv. You will see a tab for customers and a tab labeled "miles flown."

2. Use the vlookup function to enter the miles flown column by looking up the frequent flier number (Hint: If done correctly with absolute references, you should be able enter the vlookup formula in the first cell in the "miles flown" column and copy it down for all the cells).

3. Use conditional formatting to highlight all frequent fliers who have less than 4,000 total miles.

4. Finally, sort the frequent fliers by total miles in descending order and print out the spreadsheet.

Database Application: Building a Knowledge Database

Campus Travel seems to be growing quite rapidly. Now they have franchises in three different states, totaling 16 locations. As the company has grown tremendously over the past few years, it has become increasingly difficult to keep track of the areas of expertise of each travel consultant; often, consultants waste valuable time trying to find out who in the company possesses the knowledge about a particular region. Impressed with your skills, the general manager of Campus Travel has asked you to add, modify, and delete the following records from its employee database:

1. Open employeedata.mdb.

2. Select the "employee" tab.

3. Add the following records:
   a. Eric Tang, Spokane Office, Expert in Southwest, Phone (509)555-2311
   b. Janna Connell, Spokane Office, Expert in Delta, Phone (509)555-1144

4. Delete the following record:
   a. Carl Looney from the Pullman office

5. Modify the following:
   a. Change Frank Herman from the Pullman office to the Spokane office
   b. Switch Ramon Sanchez's home number to (208)549-2544

Team Work Exercise: Your Personal Communication Infrastructure Assessment

Work in a team of four or five students and have each person list the number of wired telephone calls, cellular telephone calls, instant messages, e-mail messages, and so on. For each instance, also inventory the total time spent, who the call was to, and the purpose of the call. Have each person also document his or her demographic and relevant personal information (e.g., age, gender, relationship status, children, and so on). Combine the results of all team members and discuss patterns and anomalies.

Answers to the Self-Study Questions

1. C, p. 130	**2.** E, p. 130	**3.** A, p. 138	**4.** A, p. 139	**5.** D, p. 141
6. B, p. 143	**7.** A, p. 144	**8.** D, p. 150	**9.** A, p. 154	**10.** C, p. 165

case ❶

Films Go Digital at the Sundance Film Festival

For independent films, the Sundance Film Festival is what film festivals in Cannes or Berlin are for more mainstream movies. This annual festival is sponsored by the (nonprofit) Sundance Institute based in Sundance, Utah, and was founded by actor Robert Redford more than 20 years ago. As other film festivals, the Sundance Film Festival chooses the best feature and short films in a variety of categories.

For the first time in Sundance history, in 2006 all entries in the short films category were available on the festival Web site. In fact, to date, Sundance is the only film festival to premiere films online. This new feature was so popular that after the films first aired online, there were over 40,000 e-mails expressing gratitude for the free screening.

Airing films online is not the only way the Sundance Film Festival uses information systems in innovative ways. The festival offers many filmmakers workshops and training sessions, and in 2006, a majority of the training was on digital technology since 30 percent of all films produced that year were in digital format. For many independent filmmakers, digital technology has opened vast opportunities, as it allows producing studio-quality films without having to rely on expensive lighting, film development, and postproduction facilities. Thus, people who could never afford all the necessary equipment can now produce movies digitally. Further, digital cameras and projectors and advances in software have made the transition from celluloid to digital more attainable for filmmakers who until recently used traditional technology. It is no surprise that sponsors for the 2006 Sundance Film Festival included tech giants Hewlett Packard, Sprint, Adobe Systems, and Sony.

Increasingly, independent movie producers see the Web as a powerful distribution tool. In 2006, for example, entries for the Sundance Festival's online film category totaled nearly 300, creating the need to further divide this category into the subcategories of animation, live action, and interactive.

The success of the online presentations of the 2006 Sundance Film Festival proves that movie aficionados appreciate the opportunity to watch films on Web sites as well as in theaters or on home TV sets, and that digital creation and distribution of movies is here to stay.

Questions

1. What other industries/events that currently are not posting creative content on the Web could benefit by following Sundance's lead?
2. Choose the perspective of either the artist or the general public and argue who benefits most from posting content onto the Web.
3. List the pros and cons for posting creative content on the Web.

Sources: Michelle Meyers, "Tech Plays Supporting Role at Sundance Festival," *CNet News* (January 18, 2006), http://news.com.com/Tech+plays+supporting+role+at+Sundance+festival/2100-1025_3-6028354.html?part=rss&tag=6028354&subj=news

Gwendolyn Mariano, "Sundance to Roll Film on Web Festival," *CNet News* (December 15, 2000), http://news.com.com/Sundance+to+roll+film+on+Web+festival/2100-1023_3-249997.html?tag=nl

http://festival.sundance.org/2006/

case ②

e-Enabling the Air Transport Industry: Managing the Information Systems Infrastructure

The air transport industry has always been about reaction time. Acquiring and utilizing the most accurate and timely information is a key to success. To be most effective, large amounts of data from a variety of sources must be collected, analyzed, and shared in real time, using a variety of different infrastructure components. To get the right information to the right person at the right time is a huge challenge given the variety of people who need timely information to be most effective at their jobs.

For example, pilots must have the most up-to-date information about their aircraft, the weather, and the status of air traffic control in order to fly as efficiently and safely as possible. Mechanics need to know what condition the airplanes coming to their sites are in and how best to address any problems those airplanes might have. Airline flight operations centers need to know that they will have the aircraft and crew necessary in the right places at the right times for upcoming flights. Ground operations need to know where to bring fuel and catering items to service airplanes as they arrive at their gates. And passengers need to know what they are supposed to do if their flights are delayed or rerouted. The information

technology revolution has gone a long way in helping bring all the information generated in the air transport enterprise to bear in order to increase safety, security, and efficiency. In fact, over the past several years, there have been vast improvements in the collection and dissemination of accurate and timely information throughout the various processes for supporting and operating an airplane. Nevertheless, the current systems and capabilities still have major shortcomings.

Specifically, the airplane itself, the prime generator of revenue and the prime consumer of operating funds, regularly unplugs from the rest of the information enterprise for as much as 14 hours at a time while in flight. Pilots have to navigate on the basis of weather reports that are hours old. Mechanics can't diagnose problems and implement solutions until the airplane is parked at the gate. Airline operations centers don't know whether an aircraft might have a mechanical problem or lack a crew for the next flight until it's time for that next flight. And passengers on delayed or rerouted flights have to scramble to locate new gates or rush to make connections.

Clearly, there are major gains to be made with improved data collection, analysis, and sharing. Because of this opportunity, the Boeing Company recently unveiled its e-Enabled Advantage, an effort to tie the entire air transport system into a seamless IS infrastructure that shares applications and data. As discussed in earlier chapters, e-Enabling creates a common onboard information and communication infrastructure for the benefit of passengers, flight and cabin crews, airline operations, system performance, and the overall industry. Indeed, Boeing's newest airliner, the 787, was code-named 7E7, and "e-Enabled" is one of the concepts addressed in the "E." But customers don't have to wait for the 787 to take advantage of the e-Enabled air transport system. Key infrastructure components of the e-Enabled Advantage, such as the Jeppesen Electronic Flight Bag or Airplane Health Management, are in production today.

In order to make e-Enablement possible, many different data needs have to be satisfied (see Figure on page 173). On the flight deck, for example, the Jeppesen Electronic Flight Bag (EFB) gives flight crews a sharper strategic picture of where they are, where they are going, and what waits over the horizon. The EFB offers the most up-to-date navigational information, live weather reports, instant access to flight

The Boeing 787 Dreamliner.

Source: http://www.boeing.com/companyoffices/gallery/images/commercial/787/k63304-2.html.

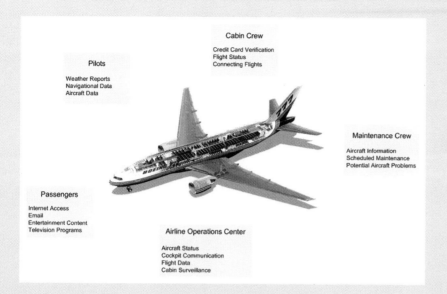

Data needs of operating a modern aircraft.

and aircraft data, airport surface positional awareness, cabin–to–flight deck surveillance, and more. In the airline operations center, various systems and data can be integrated to give managers and planners advance knowledge of possible schedule disruptions and a wide range of options to mitigate any problems. For example, each airplane contains an onboard data server that can be coupled with Boeing's Communication Navigation Surveillance/Air Traffic Management applications, various simulation and analysis products, crew management applications, and Boeing's Integrated Airline Operations Center to produce forward-looking plans to maximize operational performance. Likewise, various systems provide flight attendants with access to detailed information on their customers' needs, helping to give passengers a more enjoyable flight. In addition, the airline cabin can be connected to the airline's credit card verification systems on the ground, freeing flight attendants from having to carry thick wads of cash for beverage service, duty-free shopping, or other transactions. Catering and duty-free inventories will be updated automatically, ensuring that airlines can keep control of their

stocks, improve oversight, and make sure every flight has the cabin items it needs.

Airlines such as Hong Kong's Cathay Pacific and Etihad Airways of the United Arab Emirates use Boeing's Airplane Health Management (AHM) program to monitor airframe systems information across the entire fleet in real time using high-bandwidth information flows. With AHM, engineers and maintenance personnel are able to examine system behavior while the airplane is in flight, quickly determine whether repairs can be deferred until the next scheduled maintenance, and inform the airline operations center whether necessary repairs can be completed at the destination without disrupting the flight schedule. In fact, AHM helps determine if a problem is developing over time and allows the airline to fix critical systems before they break, avoiding costly delays and potential catastrophes.

The e-Enabled air transport system is Boeing's vision of a day when the airplane is just another node on an enterprise-wide information network, ensuring that everyone in the system has all the information they need to react at the

very best moment. The variety of different interrelated components of the e-Enabled Advantage require a solid underlying communication infrastructure to link the airplane to the airline enterprise. However, connecting a moving object to a communications infrastructure has never been an easy feat, and especially since Boeing has decided to discontinue the Connexion project (see Chapter 1), other ways have to be found to connect the airplanes to the ground systems. One way to enable this communication is through the use of ground-based networks, such as existing cell phone networks, or dedicated ground-based systems. However, for communications taking place while traveling across the oceans, this solution is not feasible. Thus, satellite-based systems have to be used. For example, telecommunications provider OnAir uses capacity on Inmarsat satellites to establish connections between the airplanes and their ground networks. As most aircraft are already equipped with Inmarsat communication systems, OnAir's systems can piggyback on these existing infrastructures.

Questions

1. What other infrastructure components could be important for e-Enabling an airline? Which infrastructure components would be most important?
2. Identify, from your own experience, ways that e-Enabling will improve your flight experience.
3. Identify several ways that an airline could market its adoption of the e-Enabled Advantage to current and potential customers.

Sources: http://www.boeing.com/news/frontiers/archive/2003/august/i_ca1.html

Boeing's Airplane Health Management to Monitor Cathay Pacific's 777 and 747 Fleets (2006), http://www.boeing.com/news/releases/2006/q2/060427b_nr.html

chapter 5

Enabling Commerce Using the Internet

preview> This chapter focuses on how companies are conducting business electronically with their customers, business partners, and suppliers, which is referred to as electronic commerce (e-commerce, or EC). The Internet and World Wide Web are extremely well suited for conducting business electronically on a global basis. Web-based EC has introduced unprecedented opportunities for the marketing of products and services, accompanied by features, functionality, and innovative methods to serve and support consumers. After reading this chapter, you will be able to do the following:

1. Describe electronic commerce, how it has evolved, and the strategies that companies are adopting to compete in cyberspace.

2. Explain the differences between extranets and intranets as well as show how organizations utilize these environments.

3. Describe the stages of business-to-consumer electronic commerce and understand the keys to successful electronic commerce applications.

4. Describe emerging trends in consumer-to-consumer e-commerce and the key drivers for the emergence of mobile commerce.

5. Explain different forms of e-government as well as regulatory threats to e-commerce.

With EC representing a growing proportion of overall retail sales, an understanding of EC can be a powerful tool in your arsenal. People with EC skills are in high demand in the marketplace; therefore, the more you know about EC, the more valuable you will become.

Managing in the Digital World: eBay Under Attack

You or someone you know has probably seen the phishing line. It comes in the form of an e-mail message from eBay on "stationery" that is an exact replica of the design eBay uses. The salutation says something like, "Dear eBay account holder." That's the first clue that the message did, in fact, not originate with eBay. (eBay always addresses account holders by their eBay user ID.) The message goes on to say that your eBay account will be canceled unless you send in some missing information, including credit card numbers and passwords. The scammer provides a link to a fake eBay site where you are asked to fill in the personal information. Don't do it. It's not from eBay; it's from a scam artist hoping to get personal information that will allow him or her to steal from you. The scam is called "phishing," and it has bedeviled eBay and its account holders for too long.

Since approximately 100 million people in 26 countries have eBay accounts, even a few responses to a phishing scam can be extremely profitable for crooks. In 2006, for example, six phishing scammers stole £200,000 (approximately $372,000) from unsuspecting eBay users in London. The gang sent e-mails identifying themselves as eBay management and, as in the tactics described previously, needed the eBay account holders to visit the eBay Web site to provide missing information. The scammers provided links that closely mimicked eBay's site. When the users signed on to the fraudulent site, the thieves stole personal information. The scammers then assumed the identities of the legitimate users and sold nonexisting products such as Rolexes and laptops. The thieves disappeared when the money arrived, and "winners" of the phony auctions were also losers.

eBay repeatedly warns users not to respond to such e-mail since the company has an internal messaging system to eliminate the need for sending most e-mail to its registered users. Still the scam continues. A variation of the "verify account information" scam sends victims to a valid Web site where they are then routed to a phony eBay site and asked to "verify" or provide account information. eBay phishing scams continue to increase despite the company's best efforts to prevent them. (eBay admits it is becoming increasingly harder to tell phony phishing e-mail from legitimate eBay messages.)

One method eBay uses to help buyers and sellers separate legitimate users from criminals is a rating system that lets customers rate transactions as positive, neutral, or negative, thus establishing a feedback score. Feedback scores allow prospective customers to see a buyer's or seller's rating and thus choose whether to proceed with a transaction. eBay also offers a form of buyer insurance—up to $500 in purchase coverage—at no additional cost. This

FIGURE 5.1

Many eBay customers are victims of phishing attacks.

service is available for those eBay users that conduct transactions through PayPal's system.

As with all forms of Internet crime, however, eBay cannot offer absolute protection for its customers. For instance, in 2003 the Salt Lake City Police arrested a 31-year-old man who was accused of perpetrating one of the biggest scams in eBay history. Hundreds of customers complained that they sent $1,000 to a company called Liquidation Universe for laptop computers they never received. Early in the investigation, police determined that the suspect scammed over 1,000 eBay customers to the tune of $1 million in just a few weeks. eBay worked with the victims of the scam to help them get their money back, but the company does not reimburse customers for items not received. In other cases, crooks were offering counterfeited products—anything from collectables to software—on eBay; by the time a buyer finds out, the seller's account is often closed. In fact, in 2005, over 16,000 entries offering pirated products were closed by the Business Software Alliance.

Unfortunately, since eBay is a popular, successful Web site, criminals who prowl the Internet will continue to target it. The best hope for honest users is that technology designed to thwart scam artists can keep up.

After reading this chapter, you will be able to answer the following:

1. What are the strengths and weaknesses of eBay's online auction model of electronic commerce versus a more traditional company Web site?

2. What are the various payment options for conducting business-to-consumer or consumer-to-consumer electronic commerce?

3. What are the threats to consumer-based electronic commerce?

Sources:

Bob Sullivan, "Man Arrested in Huge eBay Fraud," *MSNBC* (June 12, 2003), **http://msnbc.msn.com/id/3078461/**

Anonymous, "eBay Urged to Tackle Fraud Better, *BBC News* (February 26, 2006), **http://news.bbc.co.uk/1/hi/uk/4749806.stm**

http://pages.ebay.com/aboutebay/trustandsafety.html

http://news.com.com/eBay+scrambles+to+fix+phishing+bug/2100-1002_3-5600372.html

https://reporting.bsa.org/fraud/add.aspx

Electronic Commerce Defined

The Internet now provides a set of interconnected networks for individuals and businesses to complete transactions electronically. We define **electronic commerce** very broadly as the online exchange of goods, services, and money[1] among firms, between firms and their customers, and between customers. The Census Bureau of the Department of Commerce reported that annual online retail sales were up by 23 percent and that e-commerce accounted for 2.7 percent of total retail sales in the second quarter of 2006, resulting in revenues of more than $24.8 billion for that quarter (see Figure 5.2). With this much money at stake, it is little wonder that no other information systems issue has captured as much attention as has EC. Although EC was being used as far back as 1948 during the Berlin Airlift (Zwass, 1996), the emergence of the Internet and Web has fueled a revolution in the manner in which products and services are marketed and sold. Their far-reaching effects have led to the creation of an electronic marketplace where a virtually limitless array of new services, features, and functionality can be offered. As a result, a presence on the Web has become a strategic necessity for companies.

Contrary to popular belief, EC goes beyond merely buying and selling products online. EC can involve the events leading up to the purchase of a product as well as customer service after the sale. Furthermore, EC is not limited to transactions between businesses and consumers, which is known as **business-to-consumer (B2C)** EC. EC is also used to conduct business with business partners such as suppliers and intermediaries. This form of EC is commonly referred to as **business-to-business (B2B)** EC. Some companies use both forms for conducting business, such as the clothing and home furnishing retailer Eddie Bauer, while other firms concentrate solely in B2C or B2B. Some forms of EC happen between businesses and their employees; these are referred to as **business-to-employee (B2E)**. Some forms of EC do not even involve business firms, as would be the case with an online auction site such as eBay; these forms of EC are referred to as **consumer-to-consumer (C2C)**. Finally, there are forms of electronic commerce that involve a country's government and its citizens (*government-to-citizen [G2C]*), businesses (*government-to-business [G2B]*), and other governments (*government-to-government [G2G]*). These seven basic types of EC are summarized in Table 5.1.

Furthermore, there is a wide variety of ways to conduct business in each arena. In the following section, we examine the reasons that Web-based EC is revolutionizing the way business is being done. This is followed by an in-depth analysis of how companies are utilizing EC in their daily operations.

Internet and World Wide Web Capabilities

Technological forces are driving business, and the Internet and Web emerged as a strong new agent of change. The resulting technological revolution has essentially broken down the barriers to entry, leveled the playing field, and propelled commerce into the electronic

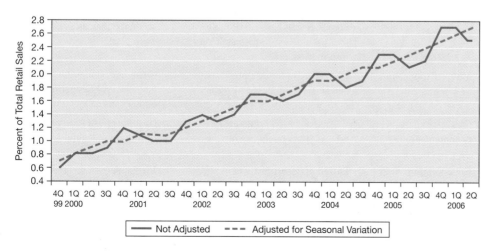

FIGURE 5.2

Electronic commerce continues to grow rapidly.

Source: http://www.census.gov/mrts/www/data/html/06Q2.html.

---

[1]EC can also include the physical distribution of digital products such as software, music, movies, and digital images.

TABLE 5.1 Types of Electronic Commerce

Type of EC	Description	Example
Business-to-consumer (B2C)	Transactions between businesses and their customers	A person buys a book from Amazon.com
Business-to-business (B2B)	Transactions among businesses	A manufacturer conducts business over the Web with its suppliers
Business-to-employee (B2E)	Transactions between businesses and their employees	An employee uses the Web to make a change in his or her health benefits
Consumer-to-consumer (C2C)	Transactions between people not necessarily working together	A person purchases some memorabilia from another person via eBay.com
Government-to-citizen (G2C)	Transactions between a government and its citizens	A person files his or her income taxes online
Government-to-business (G2B)	Transactions between a government and businesses	A government purchases supplies using an Internet-enabled procurement system
Government-to-government (G2G)	Transactions among governments	A foreign government uses the Internet to access information about U.S. federal regulations

domain (Looney and Chatterjee, 2002). Companies are exploiting the capabilities of the Web to reach a wider customer base, offer a broader range of products, and develop closer relationships with customers by striving to meet their unique needs. These wide-ranging capabilities include global information dissemination, integration, mass customization, interactive communication, collaboration, and transactional support (Chatterjee and Sambamurthy, 1999; Looney and Chatterjee, 2002; see Table 5.2).

TABLE 5.2 Capabilities of the Web

Web Capability	Description	Example
Global information dissemination	The ability to market products and services over vast distances.	Almost anyone can access Amazon.com
Integration	Web sites can be linked to corporate databases to provide real-time access to personalized information.	Customers can check account balances at www.alaskaair.com
Mass customization	Firms can tailor their products and services to meet a customer's particular needs.	Customers can build their own messenger bag on www.timbuk2.com
Interactive communication	Companies can communicate with customers, improving the image of responsiveness.	Customers can receive real-time computer support from www.geeksquad.com
Collaboration	Different departments of a company can use the Web to collaborate.	Virgin megastores uses a collaboration site to improve managers' efficiency
Transactional support	Clients and businesses can conduct business online without human support	Customers can build and purchase their own PC online without human interaction on www.dell.com

Information Dissemination The powerful combination of Internet and Web technologies has given rise to a global platform where firms from across the world can effectively compete for customers and gain access to new markets. EC has wide geographical potential, given that many countries have at least some type of Internet access. The worldwide connectivity of the Internet enables **global information dissemination**, a relatively economical medium for firms to market their products and services over vast distances. This increased geographical reach has been facilitated by virtual storefronts that can be accessed from every Web-enabled computer in the world.

Integration Web technologies also allow for **integration** of information via Web sites, which can be linked to corporate databases to provide real-time access to personalized information. No longer must customers rely on old information from printed catalogs or account statements that arrive in the mail once a month. For example, when Alaska Airlines (www.alaskaair.com) updates fare information in their corporate database, customers can access the revisions as they occur simply by browsing the company's Web site. As with nearly every other major airline, the Web allows Alaska Airlines to disseminate real-time fare pricing. This is particularly important for companies operating in highly competitive environments such as the air transport industry. Furthermore, Alaska Airlines offers their valued customers the ability to check the balances of their frequent flier accounts, linking customers to information stored on the firm's corporate database (see Figure 5.3). Customers do not have to wait for monthly statements to see if they are eligible for travel benefits and awards.

Mass Customization Web technologies are also helping firms realize their goal of mass customization. **Mass customization** helps firms tailor their products and services to meet a customer's particular needs on a large scale. For instance, bag manufacturer Timbuk2

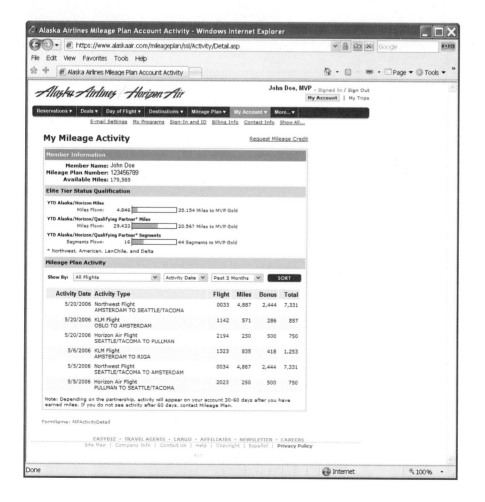

FIGURE 5.3

Alaska Airlines' mileage plan Web site.

FIGURE 5.4

Timbuk2 bags can be customized in a variety of ways.

(www.Timbuk2.com) has developed an application called Custom Messenger Bag Builder, which allows customers to create a virtual bag that is modeled just for them (see Figure 5.4). Customers can configure the virtual bag based on a number of criteria such as size, fabrics, colors, accessories, and even use (e.g., for carrying a laptop). The virtual model application also assists Timbuk2 in tracking customers' preferred styles and colors, allowing them to target marketing efforts to individual customers.

Interactive Communication **Interactive communication** via the Web enables firms to build customer loyalty by providing immediate communication and feedback to/from customers, which can dramatically improve the firm's image through demonstrated responsiveness. Many firms are augmenting telephone-based ordering and customer support with Web-based applications and electronic mail. In some cases, online chat applications are provided to allow customers to communicate with a customer service representative in real time through the corporate Web site.

Best Buy, for example, has entered into the computer repair and support business with their brand Geek Squad (see Figure 5.5). Traditionally, customers having computer problems would have to take their computer to a Best Buy store for repair. Geek Squad online (www.geeksquad.com) has implemented a feature whereby customers can contact customer support representatives at any time of the day to receive real-time online support. Support options include operation system diagnostics, software installation issues, and computer optimization, and interactive communication agents aid the customers online in real time. This feature allows the customer service agent to walk the customer through the troubleshooting process step-by-step while the customer is at home. This customer-driven approach far outdistances traditional, nonelectronic means in terms of tailoring and timeliness.

FIGURE 5.5

Geek Squad offers 24-hour computer support.

Collaboration Web technologies can also enable **collaboration**. The entertainment media company Virgin Entertainment Group, which runs 23 megastores throughout the United States, selling music, DVDs, and books, was looking for a way to maximize the time managers would spend selling products on the floor or training employees (see Figure 5.6). Before they decided to implement a Web-based collaboration system, managers would spend countless hours trying to locate inventory information for the head office, while at the same time employees in the head office would respond to literally hundreds of e-mails asking the same questions. After the introduction of Microsoft SharePoint, a Web-based collaboration suite, Virgin's managers can now spend up to 20 percent more of their time on efforts to sell products, while at the same time employees at the head office have substantially more time to devote to operational oversight or strategic planning (Microsoft, 2004).

FIGURE 5.6

Virgin megastores offer music, DVDs, books, and more.

Ethical Dilemma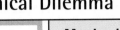

Monitoring Productive Employees

"**Y**ou have zero privacy; get over it," Scott McNeely, cofounder and long-time chief executive officer of Sun Microsystems, once said. He was speaking about privacy expectations of Internet users in general, but the quote can also apply to privacy expectations of employees in the workplace.

If you work for a company where Internet connectivity is provided, it is legal for that company to track your computer use, including e-mails sent and received, Web sites visited, and downloads to your workstation computer. The question of whether such surveillance is ethical, however, is still under debate. The essence of the debate is this: employers want employees to do a good job without abusing computer resources. Employees don't want their every keystroke and Web site visit tracked.

New technologies make it possible for employers to monitor employees' activities on the job, especially telephone use, electronic and voice mail, computer terminals, and Internet use. To date, such monitoring is unregulated; thus, your employer can listen to, watch, and read most of your on-the-job communications.

An American Management Association (AMA) survey in 2005 found that 75 percent of the employers surveyed monitor their employees' Internet use in order to prevent inappropriate surfing. Sixty-five percent use software to block employees' access to inappropriate Web sites. Approximately 30 percent track keyboard strokes and amount of time spent at the keyboard. Over 50 percent review and retain employee e-mail messages. Eight percent of the companies surveyed disclose their monitoring practices to employees. In most cases, new employees are asked to sign the privacy practice disclosure and agree to abide by its provisions.

Increasingly, companies are vigorously enforcing technology policies. The AMA survey reported that 26 percent of survey respondents had fired employees for misusing the Internet. Another 25 percent had fired employees for e-mail abuses.

While employee monitoring practices may be legal, are they ethical? On the employee side of the monitoring debate is the argument that when employers spy on employees, they are violating the individuals' privacy rights. Employers say they monitor to increase productivity but also to prevent liability. For instance, since employers are expected to maintain a workplace environment free of sexual harassment, shouldn't they be allowed to monitor e-mail messages that could implicate them in a sexual harassment suit?

Some legal experts argue that ethical questions about employee monitoring come down to the issue of contract. David D. Friedman, an economist and law professor at the University of Southern California, has said, "There isn't an agreement that is morally right for everybody. The important thing is what the parties agree to. If the employer gives a promise of privacy, then that should be respected." If, on the other hand, Friedman continues, the employer reserves the right to read e-mail or monitor Web browsing, the worker can either accept those terms or look elsewhere for employment. Friedman's comments do not address the issue of low-income employees who have no choice but to accept any job offered, regardless of employers' privacy policies.

In any case, business law and ethics experts agree that employers who monitor should do so only if the surveillance serves a legitimate purpose, should follow clear procedures to protect a worker's personal life, and should inform workers about monitoring practices.

Sources: AMA ePolicy Institute Research, "2005 Electronic Monitoring and Surveillance Survey," http://www.amanet.org/research/pdfs/EMS_summary05.pdf

"Employee Monitoring: Is There Privacy in the Workplace?," http:// www.privacyrights.org/fs/fs7-work.htm

Miriam Schulman, "Little Brother Is Watching You," *Issues in Ethics* 9, no. 2 (spring 1998), http://www.scu.edu/ethics/publications/iie/v9n2/brother.html

Transaction Support By providing ways for clients and firms to conduct business online without human assistance, the Internet and Web have greatly reduced transaction costs while enhancing operational efficiency. Many companies, such as Dell Computer Corporation, are utilizing the Web to provide automated **transaction support** (see Figure 5.7). Dell began selling computers on the Web in mid-1996. By early 1998, Dell was experiencing around $2 million in online sales per day. Dell derives about 90 percent of its overall revenues from sales to medium-size and large businesses, yet more than half of its Web-based sales have been from individuals and small businesses that typically buy one computer at a time. As a result, Dell is experiencing significant cost savings per sale by reducing the demand for phone representatives on the smaller purchases. Individual customers can access product information at any time from anywhere, benefiting not only the end consumer but also Dell. Customer service representatives can focus on lucrative corporate customers, reducing labor costs involved in servicing small-ticket items.

By streamlining operations and greatly increasing sales through both online and traditional channels, Dell has grown into one of the world's largest personal computer manufacturers, with revenue of nearly $55 billion annually for the fiscal year 2006. This phenomenon of cutting out the "middleman" and reaching customers more directly and efficiently is known as **disintermediation**.

Electronic Commerce Business Strategies

Given the vast capabilities of the Internet, the Web has transformed traditional business operations into a hypercompetitive electronic marketplace. Companies must strategically position themselves to compete in the new EC environment. At one extreme, companies following a **brick-and-mortar business strategy** choose to operate solely in the traditional physical markets. These companies approach business activities in a traditional manner by operating physical locations such as department stores, business offices, and manufacturing plants. In other words, the brick-and-mortar business strategy does

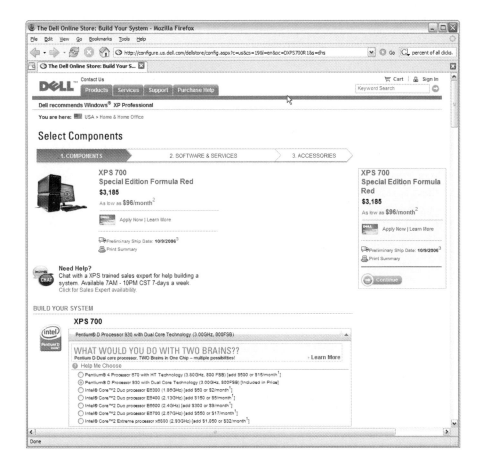

FIGURE 5.7

Customers can build their own computers at www.dell.com.

not include EC. In contrast, companies following a **click-only business strategy** (i.e., **virtual companies**) conduct business electronically in cyberspace. These firms have no physical store locations, allowing them to focus purely on EC. An example of a click-only company might be the popular eBay.com trading and exchange Web site, which does not have a physical storefront in the classic sense. While both brick-and-mortar and click-only companies would be considered "pure play companies," each focusing on one distinct way of doing business, other firms choose to straddle the two environments, operating in both physical and virtual arenas. These firms operate under the **click-and-mortar business strategy** approach (also referred to as the **bricks-and-clicks business strategy**). The three general approaches are depicted in Figure 5.8 (Looney and Chatterjee, 2002).

The Click-and-Mortar Strategy The greatest impact of the Web-based EC revolution has occurred in companies adopting the click-and-mortar approach. Click-and-mortars continue to operate their physical locations and have added the EC component to their business activities. With transactions occurring in both physical and virtual environments, it is imperative that click-and-mortars learn how to fully maximize commercial opportunities in both domains. Conducting physical and virtual operations presents special challenges for these firms, as business activities must be tailored to each of these different environments in order for the firms to compete effectively.

Another challenge for click-and-mortars involves increasing information system complexity. Design and development of complex computing systems are required to support each aspect of the click-and-mortar approach. Furthermore, different skills are necessary to support Web-based computing, requiring substantial resource investments. Companies must design, develop, and deploy systems and applications to accommodate an open computing architecture that must be globally and persistently available. For instance, with total client assets of over $1 trillion, hundreds of thousands of daily trades by customers, a variety of ways that global customers use their Web site, and a dynamic, fast-changing set of online products and services, the click-and-mortar brokerage firm Charles Schwab has a large, complex information systems staff and set of interrelated information systems (see Figure 5.9).

The Click-Only Strategy Click-only companies can often compete more effectively on price since they do not need to support the physical aspects of the click-and-mortar approach. Thus, these companies can reduce prices to rock-bottom levels (although a relatively small click-only firm may not sell enough products and/or may not order enough from suppliers to be able to realize economies of scale and thus reduce prices). Click-only firms, such as Amazon.com or eBay.com, also tend to be highly adept with technology and can innovate very rapidly as new technologies become available. This can enable them to stay one step ahead of their competition. However, conducting business in cyberspace has some problematic aspects. For example, it is more difficult for a customer to return a product to a purely online company than simply to return it to a local department

FIGURE 5.8

General approaches to electronic commerce.

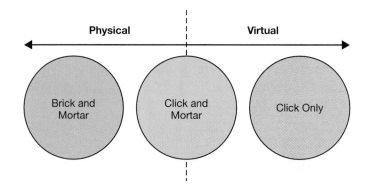

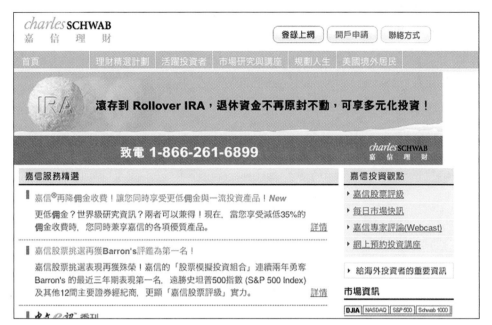

FIGURE 5.9

Brokerage firm Charles Schwab offers a variety of services online to meet the needs of its global customers.

store. In addition, some consumers may not be comfortable making purchases online. Individuals may be leery about the security of giving credit card numbers to a virtual company.

You must also develop a sound business model to be successful with EC. A **business model** is a summary of how a company will generate revenue, identifying its product offering, value-added services, revenue sources, and target customers. In other words, a business model reflects the following:

1. What does a company do?
2. How does a company uniquely do it?
3. In what way (or ways) does the company get paid for doing it?
4. How much gross margin does the company earn per average unit sale?

Laudon and Traver (2007) identified eight ingredients of a business model (see Table 5.3). Perhaps the most important ingredient for EC is a firm's revenue model. A **revenue model**

TABLE 5.3 Eight Ingredients of a Business Model

Components	Key Questions
Value proposition	Why should the customer buy from you?
Revenue model	How will you earn money?
Market opportunity	What marketspace do you intend to serve, and what is its size?
Competitive environment	Who else occupies your intended marketspace?
Competitive advantage	What special advantages does your firm bring to the marketspace?
Market strategy	How do you plan to promote your products or services to attract your target audience?
Organizational development	What types of organizational structures within the firm are necessary to carry out the business plan?
Management team	What kinds of experiences and background are important for the company's leaders to have?

Source: Adapted from Laudon/Traver, *E-Commerce: Business, Technology, Society,* 2007. Reprinted by permission of Pearson Education, Inc. Publishing as Pearson Addison Wesley.

TABLE 5.4 Five Common Revenue Models for Electronic Commerce

Revenue Model	Examples	Revenue Source
Advertising	Yahoo.com, MySpace.com	Fees from advertisers in exchange for advertisements
Subscription	WSJ.com, consumerreports.com	Fees from subscribers in exchange for access to content or services
Transaction fee	eBay.com, E-trade.com	Fees (commissions) for enabling or executing a transaction
Sales	Amazon.com, Gap.com, iTunes.com	Sales of goods, information, or services
Affiliate	MyPoints.com	Fees for business referrals

Source: Adapted from Laudon/Traver, *E-Commerce: Business, Technology, Society,* 2007. Reprinted by permission of Pearson Education, Inc. Publishing as Pearson Addison Wesley.

describes how the firm will earn revenue, generate profits, and produce a superior return on invested capital. Table 5.4 describes five common revenue models for EC, including advertising, subscription, transaction fee, sales, and affiliate.

As you can see, firms can conduct EC in a variety of ways. In the next section, we describe in greater detail how firms have evolved toward using the Internet and Web to support internal operations and to interact with each other.

Business-to-Business Electronic Commerce: Extranets

In order to communicate proprietary information with authorized users outside organizational boundaries, a company can implement an **extranet**. An extranet enables two or more firms to use the Internet to do business together. Using the Internet to support business-to-business (B2B) activities has become one of the best ways for organizations to gain a positive return on their technology-based investments. For example, aerospace giant The Boeing Company launched an extranet that can be accessed by over 1,000 authorized business partners. One of Boeing's business partners, aluminum supplier Alcoa, accesses the extranet to coordinate its shipments to Boeing as well as to check Boeing's raw materials supply to ensure appropriate inventory levels. Customers, such as the U.S. Department of Defense, log in to Boeing's extranet to receive status updates on the projects Boeing is working on for them. Overall, countless organizations are gaining benefits from B2B electronic commerce with nearly all Fortune 1000 companies deploying some type of B2B application.

Interestingly, there is a long history of organizations using proprietary networks to share business information. In this section, we will examine the evolution to the present-day extranet and review how organizations are utilizing extranets to improve organizational performance and gain competitive advantage.

The Need for Organizations to Exchange Data

Prior to the introduction of the Internet and Web, business-to-business EC was facilitated using **Electronic Data Interchange (EDI)**. These systems are generally limited to large corporations that can afford the associated expenses. The Internet and Web have provided an economical medium over which information can be transmitted, enabling small to mid-sized enterprises to participate in B2B markets. Companies have devised a number of innovative ways to facilitate B2B transactions using these technologies. Web-based B2B systems range from simple extranet applications to complex trading exchanges where multiple buyers and sellers come together to conduct business. In the following sections, we examine the stages under which modern B2B EC is done, shedding light on the different approaches and their suitability for different business requirements.

How EDI Works

EDI is the forefather of modern B2B EC and continues to maintain a stronghold in B2B computing. Forrester, an independent technology research company, estimates that U.S. companies continue to buy hundreds of billions of dollars worth of goods and services electronically each year via EDI networks and that EDI will continue to be the most widely used standard for B2B activity for several more years (Vollmer, 2003). EDI refers to the digital, or electronic, transmission of business documents and related data between organizations via telecommunications networks. More specifically, these telecommunications networks commonly take the form of **value-added networks (VANs)**, which provide a direct link over which data can be transmitted (see Technology Briefing 4—Networking). VANs are telephone communication lines that are leased from telecommunications providers, creating a secure, dedicated circuit between a company and its business partners. Figure 5.10 depicts a typical EDI system architecture using VANs to connect a company with its suppliers and customers.

EDI Streamlines Business Processes Companies use EDI to exchange a wide variety of business documents, including purchase orders, invoices, shipping manifests, delivery schedules, and electronic payments. The exchange of data in EDI follows a set of formatting standards that specify how information is transmitted electronically. EDI began in the mid-1960s as an initiative to reduce paperwork. Although EDI has never totally eliminated paper, it does help reduce the number of times business documents need to be handled. EDI provides many efficiencies because it helps to streamline business processes. By reducing the number of times documents need to be handled, business partners can exchange data faster and with fewer errors. EDI shortens the time spent producing and delivering business documents from days to seconds, allowing companies to process and update information faster. Having up-to-date information at the company's disposal allows it to make more accurate forecasts and decisions.

EDI Reduces Errors EDI helps to reduce errors by providing a single point of entry. For example, in a paper-based environment, a supplier must enter an invoice into its own system, print it, and send the invoice via surface mail to its customer. When the customer receives the invoice, someone must reenter it into the customer's system so that the invoice can be processed. In this situation, errors can occur at the original point of entry in the supplier's system as well as the point of re-entry in the customer's system. EDI eliminates dual entry. By using EDI, the supplier enters the invoice into its system and transmits the invoice to the

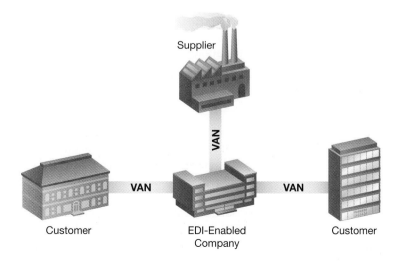

FIGURE 5.10

A typical EDI system architecture.

customer electronically. The customer's computer automatically receives the invoice via EDI and updates the system accordingly, eliminating reentry and a potential source of error.

EDI enabled RJR Nabisco to reduce the cost of processing a paper-based purchase order from $70 to less than $1. However, the cost associated with EDI-based systems has limited its usefulness to large companies. EDI is costly to implement and maintain. Software and hardware required to enable EDI can cost upward of $100,000, and monthly telecommunications charges associated with VANs can approach several thousand dollars, depending on the number of communication lines necessary to connect the company with its business partners.

Large enterprises can afford the enormous costs associated with EDI. They can justify the costs since EDI has created such dramatic efficiencies for their organizations. Yet EDI has proved to be beyond the reach of smaller enterprises. Before the introduction of the Internet and Web, a viable, economical alternative to EDI was unavailable, preventing small to midsized firms from participating in B2B markets. To make matters worse, some large corporations and government agencies had gone so far as to refuse business to companies that were not EDI-enabled. What small and midsized companies needed was a technology that would level the playing field, making B2B affordable and accessible. This leads us to the next generation of Internet-based B2B architectures.

Exchanging Organizational Data Using Extranets

EDI has been used for over four decades to conduct business between organizations. However, the trend in business today is to use the Web as the vehicle for business-to-business EC. The global accessibility and economics afforded by the Internet have enabled small to midsized firms to participate in B2B markets once reserved for large corporations. With the entrance of buyers and suppliers of all shapes and sizes, the mass adoption of these technologies has propelled B2B into the forefront of modern commerce. To use the Web for business-to-business EC, companies are creating extranets, which can be regarded as a private part of the Internet that is cordoned off from ordinary users. In other words, although the content is "on the Web," only authorized users can access it after logging on to the company's extranet Web site.

Benefits of Extranets

Extranets, as well as *intranets* (discussion to follow), benefit corporations in a number of ways, so it is no surprise that firms have readily and rapidly adopted these technologies.

Information Timeliness and Accuracy First and foremost, extranets can dramatically improve the timeliness and accuracy of communications, reducing the number of misunderstandings within the organization as well as with business partners and customers. In the business world, very little information is static; therefore, information must be continually updated and disseminated as it changes. Extranets facilitate this process by providing a cost-effective, global medium over which proprietary information can be distributed. Furthermore, they allow central management of documents, thus reducing the number of versions and amount of out-of-date information that may be stored throughout the organization. While security is still thought to be better on proprietary networks, the Internet can be made to be a relatively secure medium for business.

Technology Integration Web-based technologies are cross-platform, meaning that disparate computing systems can communicate with each other provided that standard Web protocols have been implemented. For example, an Apple iMac can request Web pages from a Linux Apache Web server. Even though the computers are running under different operating systems, they can communicate with each other over the Internet. The cross-platform nature of the Web makes implementing extranets extremely attractive as a way to connect disparate computing environments.

Low Cost–High Value In addition, extranets do not require large expenditures to train users on the technologies. Since many employees, customers, and business partners are familiar with the tools associated with the Web, they do not require special training to familiarize them with extranet interfaces. In other words, extranets look and act just like public Web sites. As long as users are familiar with a Web browser, they can utilize extranets with little difficulty.

Above all, extranets impact a company's bottom line. A company can use them to automate business transactions, reducing processing costs and achieving shortened cycle times. Extranets can also reduce errors by providing a single point of data entry from which the information can be updated on disparate corporate computing platforms without having to reenter the data. Management can then obtain real-time information to track and analyze business activities. Extranets are incredibly powerful and intensely popular. We describe in the following sections how they work and how they are being effectively utilized.

Extranet System Architecture

An extranet looks and acts just like a typical Internet-based application, using the same software, hardware, and networking technologies to communicate information (see Figure 5.11). However, an extranet uses the Internet infrastructure to connect two or more business partners and, thus, requires an additional component. Organizations can connect their internal intranet infrastructures (see discussion of intranets to follow) together using a *virtual private network,* or *VPN,* to facilitate the secured transmission of proprietary information between

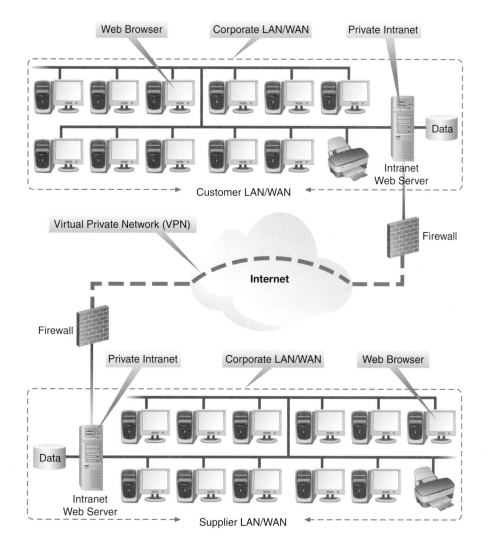

FIGURE 5.11

Typical extranet system architecture.

business partners. You will learn more about VPNs in Chapter 6—Securing Information Systems. To access information on an extranet, authorized business partners access their business partner's main extranet Web page using their Web browsers.

Extranet Applications

As the use of extranets has increased, a common set of applications has been found to be particularly beneficial to organizations. The primary use of extranets in organizations is for managing their supply chains; in other words, organizations exchange data and handle transactions with their suppliers or organizational customers. One way to handle transactions with suppliers and buyers is the use of enterprise portals, through which a business partner accesses secured, proprietary information from an organization. We will discuss different portals as well as emerging technologies enabling B2B EC in detail in Chapter 8—Building Organizational Partnerships Using Enterprise Information Systems.

Business-to-Employee Electronic Commerce: Intranets

Once organizations realize the advantage of using the Internet and Web to communicate public information outside corporate boundaries, Web-based technologies can also be leveraged to support proprietary, internal communications within an organization through the implementation of an **intranet**,[2] or business-to-employee (B2E) electronic commerce. Like an extranet, an intranet consists of a private network using Web technologies to facilitate the secured transmission of proprietary information *within* an organization. Intranets take advantage of standard Internet and Web protocols to communicate information to and from authorized employees. As was the case with extranets, intranets provide many benefits to the organization, including improved information timeliness and accuracy, global reach, cross-platform integration, low-cost deployment, and a positive return on investment.

As with the use of the Internet to support business-to-business activities, using the Internet to support internal organizational communication and processes—business-to-employee—is also rapidly expanding. For example, like their use of the Internet to support B2B activities, The Boeing Company also operates an intranet with more than 1 million pages registered with its internal search engine, serving nearly 200,000 employees. The intranet has become pervasive, impacting every department within the organization. Employees rely on the intranet to assist them in their daily business activities, ranging from tracking vacation benefits to monitoring aircraft production. In the remainder of this section, we examine the characteristics of an organizational intranet as well as the types of applications being deployed.

Intranet System Architecture

An intranet looks and acts just like a publicly accessible Web site and uses the same software, hardware, and networking technologies to communicate information. As with an extranet, users access their company's intranet using their Web browser. However, intranets use *firewalls* to secure proprietary information stored within the corporate LAN and/or WAN so that the information can be viewed only by authorized users. Firewalls with specialized software are placed between the organization's LAN or WAN and the Internet, preventing unauthorized access to the proprietary information stored on the intranet (you will learn more about firewalls in Chapter 6). In the simplest form of an intranet, communications take place within the confines of organizational boundaries and do not travel across the Internet. However, increases in employees' mobility necessitate that an intranet be accessible from anywhere. Thus, most companies allow their employees to use VPNs (see Chapter 6) to connect to the company's intranet while on the road or working from home (i.e., telecommuting). Figure 5.12 depicts a typical intranet system architecture.

---

[2]It can be argued that, on a technological level, intranets and extranets are variants of the same thing in that both employ firewalls to cordon off ordinary users. However, given that intranets and extranets have very different purposes from a business point of view, we chose to distinguish between the two.

Employees Using Company Networks Can Affect Liability

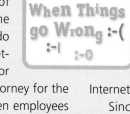

Illegal downloading and file sharing of movies and songs is common on the Internet. When a company's employees do this on the company's computers and network, the company could be held liable. For example, in September 2005, the U.S. attorney for the Central District of California charged seven employees of a cable company for illegally copying and distributing *Star Wars Episode III: Revenge of the Sith* before it was released. An eighth individual who stole a copy of an Academy Award "screener" for the film from the production company where he worked was charged with copyright infringement. In early 2006, all those charged pled guilty. The seven cable company employees faced sentences of one year in prison and $100,000 in fines. The eighth individual faced three years in prison.

"Screeners" are movie copies distributed to reviewers and voters for award programs prior to the official release of the film. When the production company employee stole a copy of *Star Wars Episode III: Revenge of the Sith,* he loaned it to a friend who took it to his workplace and allowed his coworkers to upload it onto the company's intranet. From there, several others accessed the movie or copied it to DVD. Another person uploaded the movie to the peer-to-peer file sharing network BitTorrent, where it could be accessed on the Internet the night before its official release.

Since screeners usually contain forensic markers (similar to digital watermarks) that allow identification of illegal copies and the origin of the copies, authorities quickly discovered where the distribution of the movie began. Although the movie was distributed on a company's intranet, no charges were brought against the company. The Motion Picture Association of America, however, is zealous in its efforts to protect movie copyright, and the possibility exists that in the future companies may be held liable for criminal acts perpetrated on proprietary intranets.

Sources: Laurie Sullivan, "Seven Plead Guilty to Pirating Star Wars Film," *TechNews* (January 26, 2006), http://www.informationweek.com/industries/showArticle.jhtml?articleID=177104184

Motion Picture Association of America, "U.S. Attorney Charges Star Wars Movie Thieves & Academy Award Screener," http://www.mpaa.org/ press_releases/2005_09_27b.pdf

Intranet Applications

Organizations are deploying a variety of common intranet applications to leverage their EC investments. In this section, we briefly review a few of the most significant: training, application integration, online entry of information, real-time access to information, and collaboration.

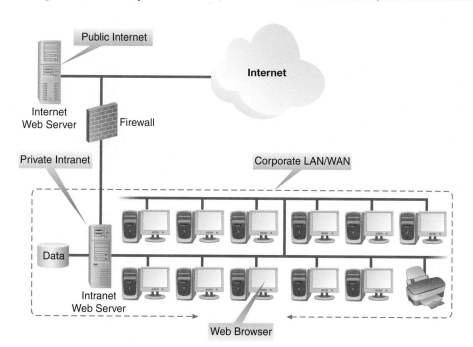

FIGURE 5.12

Intranet architecture.

Training Using its intranet, The Boeing Company offers training for nearly 200,000 of its employees (see Figure 5.13). In addition to intranet-based training about quality standards and procedures using a system called "Quality eTraining," employees can choose from a wide range of course offerings, including educational programs or supervisor training. Boeing's intranet contains an online catalog summarizing course offerings and provides a feature that allows employees to register for courses using their Web browsers. Once registered for a course, users can access multimedia content, including video lectures, presentation slides, and other course materials, directly from their desktops.

Boeing's intranet-based training initiative has led to dramatic business improvements and cost reductions. The intranet helped eliminate redundant courses and standardize course material. It virtually eliminated travel costs associated with sending employees to training sites. In addition, employees can take courses on a time-permitting basis, meaning that they can learn at a pace that accommodates their work schedule. At Boeing, employee training is no longer subject to the physical and time constraints associated with traditional forms of education.

Application Integration Many organizations have invested substantial sums of money and resources in a variety of software applications such as *enterprise resource planning, customer relationship management, sales force automation,* and various other packages to support internal operations (see Chapter 8). Often these disparate applications are installed on different computing platforms where each may be running under a different operating system, using a different database management system, and/or providing a different user interface. Because of these disparate environments, it may be difficult for, say, a salesperson to consolidate information from different systems in order to answer a customer request. Intranets can be used to alleviate this problem by providing application integration.

For example, by installing a product such as Netegrity's SiteMinder on the intranet Web server, information from separate applications can be consolidated and presented to the user through a single Web browser interface (see Figure 5.14). Now, when the salesperson needs information related to sales calls and customer support activities, the request is routed to the intranet Web server running SiteMinder, which accesses the relevant data from various applications. The intranet server consolidates the information and delivers it to the salesperson, displaying all the information necessary to make business decisions in a single Web page.

FIGURE 5.13

Only Boeing employees can access their secure intranet site.

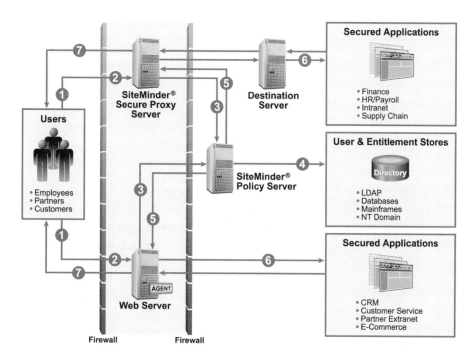

FIGURE 5.14

Application integration using
Netegrity SiteMinder.

Source: http://www.netegrity.com.

Online Entry of Information Companies can use intranets to streamline routine business processes because an intranet provides a Web browser interface to facilitate online entry of information. Microsoft has implemented an intranet-based expense reporting application called MSExpense, that allows employees from across the world to submit expense reports online, dramatically reducing the inefficiencies and expenses associated with paper-based expense report processing.

Prior to MSExpense, 136 different expense report templates existed within the corporation, and information such as mileage rates was often outdated. These issues cost Microsoft employees precious time and effort in locating the appropriate template and ensuring that the expenses they were submitting were accurate. With MSExpense, expense report templates and expense rates are centrally managed on the intranet Web server, where modifications can be made instantaneously as conditions change. Now, Microsoft employees submit the appropriate template electronically with the assurance that they have used the correct version and up-to-date expense rates.

The implementation of the MSExpense intranet application reduced the cost of processing employee expense reports by over $4.3 million per year (or from $21 to $8 per expense report), shortened expense reimbursements from three weeks to three days, and dramatically reduced error rates by providing a single point of entry (Microsoft, 2002). Furthermore, applications such as MSExpense provide management with accurate, up-to-date information to track and analyze the costs associated with key business activities as well as a way to enforce business policies to take advantage of reduced corporate rates offered by airlines, rental car companies, and hotels.

Real-Time Access to Information Unlike paper-based documents, which need to be continually updated and distributed to employees when changes occur, intranets make it less complicated to manage, update, distribute, and access corporate information.

Boeing disseminates corporate news using multimedia files distributed over the company's intranet. Formerly, news releases were produced on videotape, duplicated, and distributed via surface mail to each corporate office around the world. With the intranet-based solution, the company has eliminated the videotape reproduction process by allowing employees to view digital copies of company news releases as they occur, from the convenience of their desktops. Boeing can now disseminate news in a more timely fashion while, in the process, saving millions annually in distribution costs.

Brief Case

IM at Work

You know the drill. You download the software necessary for instant messaging (IM) from a popular public Internet service such as Microsoft's Windows Live Messenger, Jabberd, Google Talk, Yahoo! Messenger, Skype, ICQ, or AOL Instant Messenger, and you're off. You can then invite your contacts to participate, and if they have downloaded IM software from a compatible service and accept your invitation, they can contact you and vice versa—all in real time. It's a convenient and fast way to communicate directly with friends and family.

Companies have also found IM a great way to hold interactive conversations and share information with their customers and colleagues. In fact, the real-time communication environment created by IM has proven especially adaptable to organizations. The predominant business advantage to IM is that it saves time in that organizational IM users know immediately if a contact is available as opposed to playing "telephone or e-mail tag" or, worse, waiting for snail-mail deliveries. Furthermore, text and graphic files can be instantly transported for perusal during an IM conversation—a process that is more unwieldy and inconvenient via fax or e-mail.

Since the secure transport of information is vital to corporations, alternatives to using the public Internet for business IM are usually the preferred choice. Organizations can establish their own IM network, using software designed specifically for that purpose. Organizations can choose among a variety of IM protocols for establishing an IM network, but any protocol selected should fit business-use requirements, which include the following:

1. The secure transfer of messages.
2. The ability to handle hundreds or even thousands of employee accounts.
3. Client software for platforms used within the organization, such as Windows, Linux, and BSD (hybrid desktop environment).
4. Access from outside the WAN.
5. The use of the existing user data to ensure proper access rights.

Alternatives to establishing one's own IM system within a corporation include use of the public Internet and using an IM hosting service. Disadvantages to using the public Internet for business IM communication are clear:

1. Security cannot be enforced based on the corporation's needs.
2. Data resides on the provider's servers and in some cases becomes its property.
3. The corporation cannot block access to the network based on its needs.
4. The corporation has no control over the stability and availability of the network. (Major public IM networks such as ICQ have blocked access to entire countries at times.)
5. The corporation cannot automate processes such as adding new employees to existing rosters.

The second alternative of the two listed here—using an IM-hosting service—is better from security and availability standpoints than using the public Internet, but such services can be costly, and there are additional disadvantages:

- Data still resides on the provider's servers and is only as secure as the provider decides to make it.
- Privacy concerns may arise when the provider has access to all conversations.
- Although automation is possible, it will not be as flexible.

A face-to-face visit may still be the preferred method of doing business, but business IM is running a close second. In fact, increasingly, workers are exchanging instant messaging IDs with business contacts instead of or before exchanging e-mail addresses and telephone numbers.

Questions

1. How can IM be used to better manage a distributed workforce?
2. If you were the owner of a small company, would you allow your employees to use IM while working? If so, what rules would you impose? If not, why?

Sources: Oktay Altunergil, "Company-Wide Instant Messaging with Jabberd" (October 6, 2005), http://www.onlamp.com/pub/a/onlamp/2005/10/06/jabberd.html

Wikipedia, "Instant Messaging," http://en.wikipedia.org/wiki/Instant_messaging

With intranet-based solutions such as those deployed at Boeing, up-to-date, accurate information can be easily accessed on a company-wide basis from a single source that is both efficient and user friendly. Companies can become more flexible with resources required to create, maintain, and distribute corporate documents, while in the process employees become more knowledgeable and current about the information that is important to them. Employees develop a sense of confidence and become self-reliant, reducing time spent dealing with employment-related issues and allowing them to focus on their work responsibilities.

Collaboration One of the most common problems occurring in large corporations relates to the communication of business activities in a timely fashion across divisional areas of the organizations. For instance, Boeing uses its intranet to facilitate collaborative efforts, such as in the process of designing new aircraft components. In this process, three-dimensional digital models of aircraft designs frequently need to be shared between aerospace engineers. Using Boeing's intranet, an engineer can send a drawing to another engineer at a remote location; the second engineer revises the drawing as necessary and returns the updated drawing using the intranet. The Boeing intranet provides the company with the capability of reducing product development cycles as well as the ability to stay abreast of current project, corporate, and market conditions.

Business-to-Consumer Electronic Commerce

The Internet and Web have evolved with mind-boggling quickness, achieving mass acceptance faster than any other technology in modern history. The widespread availability and adoption of the Internet and Web, which are based on an economical, open, ubiquitous computing platform, have made Internet access affordable and practical, allowing consumers to participate in Web-based commerce. In addition, a great number of businesses have similarly benefited from the revolution and have implemented Web-based systems in their daily operations. This heightened level of participation by both consumers and producers has made the emergence of business-to-consumer (B2C) EC economically feasible. Unlike B2B, which concentrates on business-to-business relationships at the wholesale level, or B2E, which focuses on internal organizational communication and processes, B2C focuses on retail transactions between a company and end consumers. Table 5.5 provides a high-level comparison between these three approaches to utilizing Internet technologies.

Stages of Business-to-Consumer Electronic Commerce

With millions of B2C-oriented Web sites in existence, Web sites range from passive to active. At one extreme are the relatively simple, passive Web sites that provide only product information and the company address and phone number, much like a traditional brochure would do. At the other extreme are the relatively sophisticated, active Web sites that enable customers to see products, services, and related real-time information and actually make purchases online. As shown in some early, pioneering research on EC (Quelch and Klein, 1996; Kalakota, Olivia, and Donath, 1999), companies usually start out with an

TABLE 5.5 Characteristics of the Internet, Intranet, and Extranet

	Focus	Type of Information	Users	Access
The Internet	External communications	General, public, and "advertorial" information	Any user with an Internet connection	Public and not restricted
Intranet	Internal communications	Specific, corporate, and proprietary information	Authorized employees	Private and restricted
Extranet	External communications	Communications between business partners	Authorized business partners	Private and restricted

Source: Szuprowicz, 1998; Turban et al., 2004.

FIGURE 5.15

Stages of business-to-consumer electronic commerce.

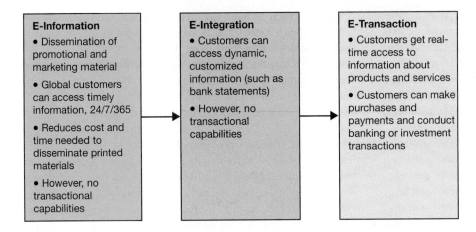

E-Information
• Dissemination of promotional and marketing material
• Global customers can access timely information, 24/7/365
• Reduces cost and time needed to disseminate printed materials
• However, no transactional capabilities

E-Integration
• Customers can access dynamic, customized information (such as bank statements)
• However, no transactional capabilities

E-Transaction
• Customers get real-time access to information about products and services
• Customers can make purchases and payments and conduct banking or investment transactions

electronic brochure and pass through a series of stages as depicted in Figure 5.15, adding additional capabilities as they become more comfortable with EC. These stages can be classified as **e-information** (i.e., providing electronic brochures and other types of information for customers), **e-integration** (i.e., providing customers with the ability to gain personalized information by querying corporate databases and other information sources), and **e-transaction** (i.e., allowing customers to place orders and make payments).

Just a few years ago, integrating transactional capabilities into a company's Web site was very difficult, especially for smaller companies on a tight budget. Now, search engines such as Yahoo! and online stores such as Amazon.com offer small businesses the possibility to sell their goods and services online without having to invest large sums in an e-transaction infrastructure. Two major categories of e-transactions are the online sales of goods and services (or *e-tailing*) and financial transactions (such as *online banking*). These two categories will be discussed next.

E-tailing: Selling Goods and Services in the Digital World

The online sales of goods and services, or **e-tailing**, can take many forms. On the one hand, using the Internet, bricks-and-clicks retailers such as Walmart.com or click-only companies such as Amazon.com sell products or services in ways similar to traditional retail channels. On the other hand, virtual companies such as Priceline.com have developed innovative ways of generating revenue. Priceline.com offers consumers discounts on airline tickets, hotel rooms, rental cars, new cars, home financing, and long-distance telephone service. The revolutionary aspect of the Priceline.com Web site lies in its **reverse pricing system** called *Name Your Own Price*. Customers specify the product they are looking for and how much they are willing to pay for it. This pricing scheme transcends traditional **menu-driven pricing**, in which companies set the prices that consumers pay for products. After a user enters the product and price, the system routes the information to appropriate brand-name companies, such as United Airlines and Avis Rent-a-Car, that either accept or reject the consumer's offer. In a recent business quarter, Priceline.com sold 4.2 million hotel room nights and 1.6 million rental car days (Priceline.com, 2006). E-tailing has both benefits and drawbacks, which are examined next.

Benefits of E-tailing Using the marketing concepts of product, place, and price, e-tailing can provide many benefits over traditional brick-and-mortar retailing.

PRODUCT BENEFITS. Web sites can offer a virtually unlimited number and variety of products because e-tailing is not limited by physical store and shelf space restrictions. For instance, e-tailer Amazon.com offers millions of book titles on the Web, compared to a local brick-and-mortar–only book retailer, which can offer "only" a few thousand titles in a store because of the restricted physical space.

For online customers, comparison shopping is much easier on the Web. In particular, a number of comparison shopping services that focus on aggregating content are available to consumers. Some companies fulfilling this niche are AllBookstores (www.allbookstores.com), BizRate (www.bizrate.com), or SideStep (www.sidestep.com). These comparison shopping sites can literally force sellers to focus on relatively low prices in order to be successful. If sellers do not have the lowest price, they must be able to offer better quality, better service, or some other advantage. These comparison shopping sites generate revenue by charging a small commission on transactions, by charging usage fees to sellers, and/or through advertising on their site.

PLACE BENEFITS. As company storefronts (virtually) exist on every computer that is connected to the Web, e-tailers can compete more effectively for customers, giving e-tailers an advantage. Whereas traditional retailing can be accessed only at physical store locations during opening hours, e-tailers can conduct business anywhere at any time.

The ubiquity of the Internet has enabled companies to sell goods and services on a global scale. Consumers looking for a particular product are not limited to merchants from their own country; rather, they can search for the product where they are most likely to get it or where they may get the best quality. For example, if you're looking for fine wines from France, you can order directly from the French site www.chateauonline.fr. This truly shows how the Internet has fueled globalization.

PRICE BENEFITS. E-tailers can also compete on price effectively since they can turn their inventory more often because of the sheer volume of products and customers who purchase them. Companies can sell more products, reducing prices for consumers while at the same time enhancing profits for the company. Further, virtual companies have no need to rent expensive retail space, allowing them to further reduce prices.

The Long Tail Together, these benefits of e-tailing have enabled a form of business model centered on "The Long Tails." Coined by Chris Anderson (2004, 2006), the concept of the **Long Tail** refers to a focus on niche markets, rather than purely on mainstream products. The distribution of consumers' needs and wants can be compared to a statistical normal distribution, where there are people with very diverse needs and wants on the tails (and very few people want the same products or services) and many people with "mainstream" needs and wants in the center of the distribution (see Figure 5.16). Due to high storage and distribution costs, most traditional brick-and-mortar retailers and service providers are forced to limit their product offerings based on the needs and wants of the mainstream customers in the center of the distribution. For example, most independent movie productions are not shown at local cinemas, as they are unlikely to draw a large enough audience to cover the movie theater's costs to show the movie. Similarly, record stores only carry CDs of which a certain number of copies will be sold each year, to cover the costs for shelf space, sales personnel and so on. Given the limited local reach of brick-and-mortar stores, this ultimately limits the stores' product selection.

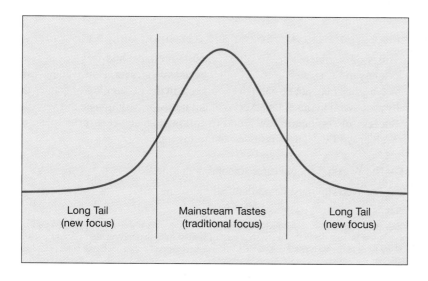

FIGURE 5.16

The Long Tails.

In contrast, made possible by their extended reach, many e-tailers can focus on the "Long Tails," that is, on products outside the mainstream tastes. Whereas a local Blockbuster store is unlikely to have a large selection of documentaries (due to a lack of local demand), Netflix can afford to have a very large selection of rather unpopular movies, and still make a profit with it. Rather than renting a few "blockbusters" to many people, many (fewer mainstream) titles are rented to a large number of people spread out on the "Long Tails." Similarly, online bookseller Amazon.com can carry a tremendous selection of (often obscure) titles, as the costs for storage are far less than those of their offline competitors. In fact, more than half of Amazon's book sales are titles that are *not* carried by the average physical bookstores, not even by megastores such as Barnes & Noble. In other words, focusing on those titles that are on the "Long Tails" of the distribution of consumers' wants can lead to a very successful business model in the digital world. A similar strategy is the mass-customization strategy pursued by Dell, which offers customized computers based on people's diverse needs and wants.

Drawbacks to E-tailing Despite all the recent hype associated with e-tailing, there are some downsides to this approach, in particular, issues associated with product delivery and the inability to adequately experience the capabilities and characteristics of a product prior to purchase.

PRODUCT DELIVERY DRAWBACKS. Excepting products that you can download directly, such as music or an electronic magazine, e-tailing requires additional time for products to be delivered. If you have run out of ink for your printer and your research paper is due this afternoon, chances are that you will drive to your local office supply store to purchase a new ink cartridge rather than ordering it online. The ink cartridge purchased electronically needs to be packaged and shipped, delaying use of the product until it is delivered. Other issues can also arise. The credit card information that you provided online may not be approved, or the shipper may try to deliver the package when you are not home.

DIRECT PRODUCT EXPERIENCE DRAWBACKS. Another problem associated with e-tailing relates to a lack of sensory information, such as taste, smell, and feel. When trying on clothes with your virtual model at Lands' End, how can you be sure that you will like the feel of the material? Or what if you discover that the pair of size 9 EE in-line skates you just purchased online fits you like an 8 D? Products such as fragrances and foods can also be difficult for consumers to assess via the Web. Does the strawberry cheesecake offered online actually taste as good as it looks? How do you know if you will really like the smell of a perfume without actually sampling it? Finally, e-tailing eliminates the social aspects of the purchase. Although growing in popularity, e-tailers won't soon replace the local shopping mall because going to the mall with some friends is still an important social experience that cannot be replicated online.

E-Commerce Web Sites: Attracting and Retaining Online Customers

The basic rules of commerce are to offer valuable products and services at fair prices. These rules apply to EC as well as to any other business endeavor. However, having a good product at a fair price may not be enough to compete in the EC arena. Companies that were traditionally successful in the old markets will not necessarily dominate the new electronic markets. Successful companies are found to follow a basic set of principles, or rules, related to Web-based EC.[3] These rules are the following:

Rule 1—The Web site should offer something unique.

Rule 2—The Web site must be aesthetically pleasing.

---

[3]Note that these rules apply mainly to how to make a Web site more successful. Realize that the underlying business model must be sound and that there are a host of similar rules that information systems personnel must follow to ensure that (1) the Web site works well, (2) it interacts properly with back-end business information systems, and (3) the site is secure.

Net Stats

E-Business is BIG Business

Statistics show that increasing numbers of consumers are shopping online. According to a report by Shop.org, a network for online retailers, and published by Forrester Research, online retail revenues totaled $176.4 billion in 2005 and were expected to reach $211.4 billion by the end of 2006 (see Table 5.6).

Source: Enid Burns, "Online Revenues to Reach $200 Billion" (June 5, 2006), http://www.clickz.com/stats/sectors/retailing/article.php/3611181

TABLE 5.6 E-Business Projected Revenues by Product Category, 2006

Product Category	Projected Revenues
Travel	$73.4 billion
Computer hardware and software	$16.8 billion
Autos and auto parts	$15.9 billion
Apparel, accessories, and footware	$15.8 billion
Cosmetics and fragrances	$800 million
Pet supplies	$500 million

Rule 3—The Web site must be easy to use and *fast*.

Rule 4—The Web site must motivate people to visit, to stay, and to return.

Rule 5—You must advertise your presence on the Web.

Rule 6—You should learn from your Web site.

RULE 1—THE WEB SITE SHOULD OFFER SOMETHING UNIQUE. Providing visitors with information or products that they can find nowhere else leads to EC profitability. Many small firms have found success on the Web by offering hard-to-find goods to a global audience at reasonable prices. Such niche markets can be in almost any category, be it delicacies (see Figure 5.17), arts supplies, or hard-to-find auto parts.

RULE 2—THE WEB SITE MUST BE AESTHETICALLY PLEASING. Successful firms on the Web have sites that are nice to look at. People are more likely to visit, stay at, and return to a Web site that looks good. Creating a unique look and feel can separate a Web site from its competition. Aesthetics can include the use of color schemes, backgrounds, and high-quality images. Furthermore, Web sites should have a clear, concise, and consistent layout, taking care to avoid unnecessary clutter.

RULE 3—THE WEB SITE MUST BE EASY TO USE AND *FAST*. As with nearly all software, Web sites that are easy to use are more popular. If Web surfers have trouble finding things at the site or navigating through the site's links or have to wait for screens to download, they are not apt to stay at the site long or to return. In fact, studies suggest that the average length of time that a Web surfer will wait for a Web page to download on his screen is only a couple of seconds. Rather than presenting a lot of information on a single page, successful Web sites present a brief summary of the information with hyperlinks, allowing users to "drill down" to locate the details they are interested in.

RULE 4—THE WEB SITE MUST MOTIVATE PEOPLE TO VISIT, TO STAY, AND TO RETURN. Given the pervasiveness of e-tailing, online consumers can choose from a vast variety of vendors for any (mainstream) product they are looking for, and are thus less likely to be

FIGURE 5.17

The Salami.com Web site.

Source: www.salami.com.

loyal to a particular e-tailer. Rather, people go to the Web sites that offer the lowest prices, or visit Web sites with whom they have built a relationship such as one that provides useful information and links, or offers free goods and services that they value. For instance, one of the reasons that Microsoft's Web site is popular is that users can download free software. Other firms motivate visitors to visit their Web sites by enabling them to interact with other users who share common interests. These firms establish an online community where members can build relationships, help each other, and feel at home. For example, at GardenWeb (www.gardenweb.com), visitors can share suggestions and ideas with other gardeners, post requests for seeds and other items, and follow electronic links to other gardening resources. At this Web site, the participants communicate and carry out transactions with one another, returning over and over for more (see Figure 5.18). E-tailers such as Amazon.com try to "learn" about their customers' interests in order to provide customized recommendations and build virtual relationships.

RULE 5—YOU MUST ADVERTISE YOUR PRESENCE ON THE WEB. Like any other business, a Web site cannot be successful without customers. Companies must draw, or pull, visitors to their Web sites. This strategy is known as pull marketing. Unlike push marketing, which actively pushes information at the consumer whether it is wanted or not (e.g., television commercials), pull marketing is a passive method used to attract visitors to your site and away from the thousands of other sites they could be visiting. The predominant method of pull marketing involves advertising the Web site. The first way to advertise your firm's presence on the Web is to include the Web site address on all company materials, from business cards and letterheads to advertising copy. It is now common to see a company's URL listed at the end of its television commercials.

In addition to advertising its URL on company materials, a firm can advertise its Web site on other commerce sites or Web sites containing related information. Advertising your presence on other popular Web sites, such as that of *USA Today* (www.usatoday.com), can cost as much as $20,000 to $30,000 per month, but they can promise that more than a million users a day will visit their sites. Given the high cost of advertising on these sites and the fact that many of those Web surfers do not even look at the online ads, the trend in Web advertising is moving away from high, fixed, monthly charges to a **pay-per-click** scheme. Under this type of pricing scheme, the firm running the advertisement pays only when a Web surfer actually clicks on the advertisement (usually between $0.01 and $0.50 per

Key Enabler

Photonic Crystal Fibers

In the distant past, before computers and the Internet, good old twisted copper wire served our telecommunication needs well. Then came computers and the Internet. Copper wire could no longer satisfy telecommunication demands. Enter optic fibers. Optic fibers are hair-thin, flexible, transparent tubes usually made of glass, used for transmitting light. A bundle of optic fibers encased together by a *cladding* layer, a buffer layer, and an outer jacket layer form strong fiber-optic cables used to carry telecommunications data at the speed of light. Fiber-optic cable has 150 times the carrying capacity of old copper-wire cables.

Just as many highways in the United States have reached traffic carrying capacity, fiber-optic cable is reaching its data transfer carrying capacity as telecommunications needs multiply. Enter photonic crystal fiber.

Photonic crystal fibers (PCF) make up a new type of fiber-optic cable based on the characteristics of photonic crystals. The key to the large data-carrying capacity of photonic crystal fibers is the fact that photonic crystals allow the fiber to contain light in a hollow core, which is not possible with conventional fiber optics. Because of this lack of confinement, conventional fiber optics need materials to hold in the light. This process of confining the light to the core is called "cladding." The lack of cladding for individual PCF fiber allows for higher-powered lasers to emit information. The PCF process offers data transmission speeds greater than 1,000 times the current fiber capacity.

PCFs have been developed to transmit signals using a broad range of light bands, making PCFs easily connectable to any fiber-optic equipment without needing any signal translation. In other words, this breakthrough will not only increase capacity but also speed transmission by eliminating the signal translation process. As with the past, when PCF capacity reaches its limits, undoubtedly technology will be ready with a replacement.

Sources: Wikipedia, "Photonic Crystal Fiber," http://en.wikipedia.org/wiki/Photonic-crystal_fiber

"Fiber Optic Cable v. Copper Wire Transmission," http://www.amherst.edu/~jkmacione/Web4.html

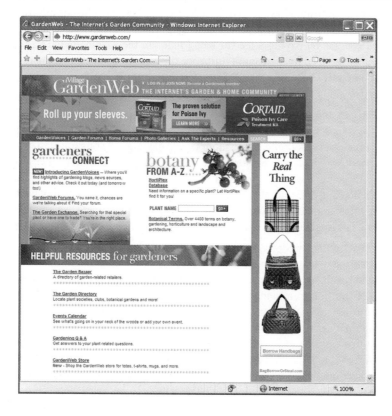

FIGURE 5.18

The GardenWeb Web site.

Source: www.GardenWeb. com.

click). Today, **affiliate marketing** allows individual Web site owners to post companies' ads on their pages; the Web site owner can earn money from referrals or ensuing sales. However, such pay-per-click models can also be abused by repeatedly clicking on a link to inflate revenue to the host or increase the costs for the advertiser; this is known as **click fraud**. The first form of click fraud is called **network click fraud**, where a site hosting an advertisement creates fake clicks in order to get money from the advertiser. In other cases, a person—competitor, disgruntled employee, and so on—inflates an organization's online advertising costs by repeatedly clicking on an advertiser's link; this is called **competitive click fraud**. In addition to using advertising or affiliate marketing, companies use *Search engine marketing* (discussed later) to increase traffic to their web sites.

RULE 6—YOU SHOULD LEARN FROM YOUR WEB SITE. Smart companies learn from their Web sites. A firm can track the path that visitors take through the many pages of its Web site and record the length of the visits, page views, common entry and exit pages, and even the users' region or Internet service provider (ISP), among other statistics. The company can then use this information to improve its Web site. If 75 percent of the visitors leave the company's site after visiting a certain page, the company can then try to find out why the surfers leave and redesign the page to incent the users to stay. Similarly, pages that go unused can be eliminated from the site, reducing maintenance and upkeep. This process of analyzing Web surfers' behavior in order to improve Web site performance (and, ultimately, maximize sales) is known as **Web analytics**.

Search Engine Marketing

To be successful, companies must advertise their presence on the Web. Traditionally, companies would advertise their products and services in regional or national newspapers or place listings in the yellow pages. With the advent of the Internet and the growth of search engines, Web surfers are using other ways to find information. A common way to find a company is to just enter the name of a product into a search engine and then visit the resulting pages. However, given the incredible numbers of results that are present for common searches such as "apparel," "sportswear," or "digital camera," most surfers visit only the first few links that are presented and rarely go beyond the first results page. Thus, companies are trying to increase their visibility in search engine results, a practice known as **search engine marketing**. However, when a Web site is first launched, it may take a while until it is included in a search engine's results. With most search engines, companies can speed up that process by paying a fee for being listed in the search engine's results (**paid inclusion**); however, a company cannot influence the ranking of its site on the results page. Therefore, companies turn to other forms of search engine marketing, such as *search engine advertising* and *search engine optimization;* these techniques are discussed next.

Search Engine Advertising   A way to ensure that your company's site is the first result users see when searching for a specific term is using **search engine advertising** (or **sponsored search**). For example, using Google's "AdWords," a company can bid for being listed in the sponsored search results of the results for the search for "televisions" (see Figure 5.19). Depending on the amount of the bid, the company's Web site is listed in the sponsored results, and the search engine receives revenue on a pay-per-click basis. As you can imagine, this can quickly become very expensive for advertisers, especially when the sponsored link is associated with a popular search term. Therefore, companies are looking for less expensive ways to improve their site's position in the search results.

Search Engine Optimization   Internet search engines such as Google, Yahoo!, and MSN order the results of a user's search according to complex, proprietary formulas, and the position of the link to a company's Web site on a search results page is outside the control of the company (see Figure 5.20). However, although the exact formulas for a Web site's location on a search engine's results page are kept as trade secrets, the major search engines give tips on how to optimize a site's ranking. The methods to improve a site's ranking are referred to as **search engine optimization** and include having other pages link to one's site, keeping the content updated, and including key words a user may query for. In other words, if a Web site is frequently updated, has content relevant to the search term,

FIGURE 5.19

Companies pay per click for being included in the sponsored listings.

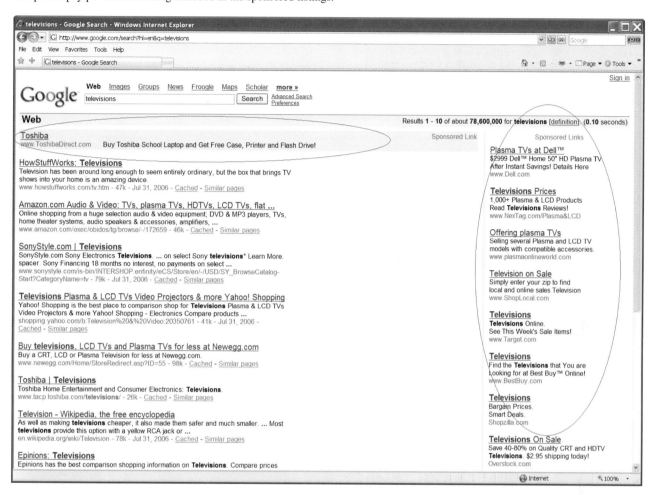

and is popular (as indicated by other pages linking to it), chances are that it will be positioned higher in the search results.

There are a multitude of companies promising to improve a page's ranking, but because search engines' algorithms are usually proprietary and there can be literally hundreds of factors influencing a site's rank, the success of using such services is often limited. Further, search engines such as Google try to figure out whether a site is using unethical "tricks" (such as "hidden" keywords) to improve its ranking and ban such sites from the listing altogether.

Securing Payments in the Digital World

In addition to increasing the visibility of their Web sites, companies have to ensure that consumers can make transactions on the Web site. However, one factor that still keeps people from engaging in online shopping, online banking, or online investing is the transfer of money. Recent polls revealed that 90 percent of all adult Internet users have changed their online behavior because of fears of threats like *identity theft* (see Chapter 10), and about a third of those who do purchase goods or services online have decided to cut back on their online purchasing (Princeton Survey, 2005). These and other factors (such as impatience, lengthy checkout procedures, or comparison shopping) lead shoppers to frequently abandon their shopping carts and to not follow through with a purchase—reports show that more than half of the online shopping carts are abandoned. Traditionally, paying for goods

FIGURE 5.20

It is hard to influence the ranking
of your company's page.

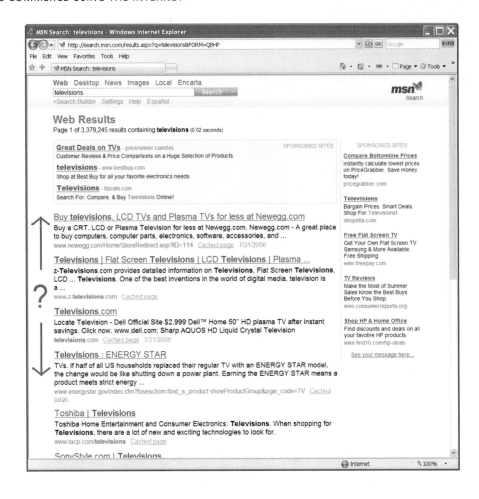

and services was limited to using credit and debit cards, but now different companies offer
payment services for buying and selling goods or services online. These different forms of
online payment will be discussed next.

Credit and Debit Cards   Credit and debit cards are still among the most accepted forms
of payment in B2C e-commerce. For customers, paying online using a credit card is easy;
all the customer needs to do is to enter his or her name, billing address, credit card number,
and expiration date to authorize a transaction. In many cases, the customer is also asked to
provide the so-called **Customer Verification Value (CVV2)**, a three-digit code located on
the back of the card (see Figure 5.21). This is one way to combat fraud in online purchases,
as the code is used for authorization by the card-issuing bank. As the CVV2 is not included
in the magnetic strip information, a person using a credit card for online transactions has to
physically possess the actual credit card (see Table 5.7 for other guidelines on how to
conduct safe transactions on the Internet).

FIGURE 5.21

The three-digit Customer
Verification Value (CVV2) is
printed on the back of a credit
card.

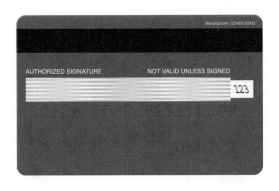

TABLE 5.7 Ways to Protect Yourself When Shopping Online

Tip	Example
Use a secure browser	Make sure that your browser has the latest encryption capabilities; also, always look for the padlock icon in your browser's status bar before transmitting sensitive information
Check the site's privacy policy	Make sure that the company you're about to do business with does not share any information you would prefer not to be shared
Read and understand the refund and shipping policies	Make sure that you can return unwanted/defective products for a refund
Keep your personal information private	Make sure that you don't give out information, such as your Social Security number, unless you know what the other entity is going to do with it
Give payment information only to businesses you know and trust	Make sure that you don't provide your payment information to fly-by-night operations
Keep records of your online transactions and check your e-mail	Make sure that you don't miss important information about your purchases
Review your monthly credit card and bank statements	Make sure to check for any erroneous or unauthorized transactions

Source: Adapted from Federal Trade Commission, "A Consumer's Guide to E-Payments," http://www.ftc.gov/bcp/conline/pubs/online/payments.htm.

However, for each transaction, an online customer has to transmit much personal information to a (sometimes unknown) merchant, and many Internet users (sometimes rightfully) fear being defrauded by an untrustworthy seller or falling victim to some other form of computer crime (see Chapter 10). Further, the use of credit cards limits ordinary people to making payments—to receive payments, one has to open up a merchant account to accept credit card payments. For people who are only once in a while selling things online (such as on the online auction site eBay—see the discussion later in this chapter), this is not a good option. To combat these problems, online shoppers (and sellers) are increasingly using third-party payment services. These are discussed next.

Payment Services Concerns for security have led to the inception of independent payment services such as PayPal (owned by eBay) or, recently, Google Checkout. These services allow online customers to purchase goods online without having to give much private information to the actual sellers. Rather than paying a seller by providing credit card information, an online shopper can simply pay by using his or her account with the payment service. Thus, the customer only has to provide the (sensitive) payment information to the payment service, which keeps this information secure (along with other information such as e-mail address or purchase history), and does not share it with the online merchant. Google linked its payment service to the search results so that Internet users looking for a specific product can immediately see whether a merchant offers this payment option; this is intended to ease the online shopping experience for consumers, thus reducing the number of people abandoning their shopping carts.

Another payment service, PayPal, goes a step further by allowing anyone with an e-mail address to send and receive money. In other words, using this service, you can send money to your friends or family members, or you can receive money for anything you're selling. This easy way to transfer money has been instrumental in the success of the online auction eBay, where anyone can sell or buy goods from other eBay users (see the discussion of consumer-to-consumer e-commerce later in this chapter). In contrast to PayPal, which is completely virtual, the electronic currency e-gold (www.e-gold.com) is backed by real gold, also allowing for person-to-person transfers (see Figure 5.22).

FIGURE 5.22

The virtual currency e-Gold is backed by real gold.

Managing Financial Transactions in the Digital World

One special form of services frequently offered online is managing financial transactions. Whereas traditionally consumers had to visit their bank to conduct financial transactions, they can now manage credit card, checking, or savings accounts online using **online banking** or paying their bills using **electronic bill pay** services. However, concerns about security of online transactions have worried many online users.

In addition to online banking, **online investing** has seen steady growth over the past several years. The Internet has changed the investment landscape considerably; now, people use the Internet to get information about stock quotes or manage their portfolios. For example, many consumers turn to sites such as MSN Money, Yahoo! Finance, or CNN Money to get the latest information about stock prices, firm performance, or mortgage rates. Then they can use online brokerage firms to buy or sell stocks.

Consumer-to-Consumer E-Commerce

Consumer-to-consumer (C2C) commerce has been with us since the start of commerce itself. Whether it was bartering, auctions, or tendering, commerce has always included consumer-to-consumer economics. According to the American Life Project, 17 percent of online American adults, or 25 million people, have used the Internet to sell things. C2C relationships can be categorized based on the number of sellers (one or many) and the number of buyers (one or many) involved, giving four distinct categories of C2C e-commerce (see Figure 5.23). This electronically facilitated interaction creates unique opportunities (such as a large pool of potential buyers) and unique problems (such as the potential of being defrauded; see Table 5.8). This section will discuss the different electronic mechanisms that consumers use to buy, sell, and trade with other consumers. Also, we will outline the current trends in consumer-to-consumer electronic commerce, including *e-auctions, online communities,* and *online publishing.*

E-Auctions

As seen throughout this text, the Internet has provided the possibility to disseminate information and services that were previously unavailable in many locations. This dissemination can be seen clearly in the emergence of electronic auctions, or **e-auctions**. E-auctions provide a

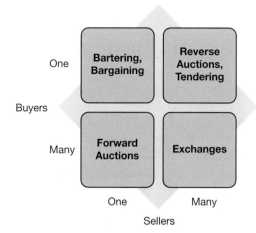

FIGURE 5.23

Types of consumer-to-consumer e-commerce.

Source: Adapted from Turban, E., King, D., Viehland, D., and Lee, J. 2006. *Electronic Commerce 2006: A Managerial Perspective.* Upper Saddle River, NJ: Prentice Hall.

place where sellers can post goods and services for sale and buyers can bid on these items. This method of transaction is called **forward auction**, where the highest bid wins. A **reverse auction** is where buyers post a *request for quote (RFQ)*, which is similar to a request for proposal (RFP) (for more on RFPs, see Chapter 9—Developing Information Systems) in that the sellers respond with bids (and the seller with the lowest bid wins), rather than posting items or services for auction. Auctions are typically characterized as dynamic and competitive environments where market forces set the prices.

The largest e-auction site you probably know is eBay (www.ebay.com). Its revenue model is based on small fees that are associated with posting items for auction, but these small fees quickly add up so that in 2006 eBay's gross revenue exceeded $6 billion. Although eBay does offer reverse auctions, the majority of the listings on its site are for forward auctions; reverse auctions are often used in B2B transactions, such as when DaimlerChrysler wants to purchase large quantities of high-quality steel. For some examples of consumer-to-consumer auction sites and what their target markets are, see Table 5.9.

TABLE 5.8 Opportunities and Threats of Consumer-to-Consumer e-Commerce

Opportunities	Problems
Consumers can buy and sell to broader markets	No quality control
Eliminates the middleman that increases the final price of products and services	Higher possibility of fraud
Always available for consumers, 24/7/365	Harder to use traditional methods to pay (checks, cash, ATM cards)
Market demand is an efficient mechanism for setting prices in the electronic environment	
Increases the numbers of buyers and sellers who can find each other	

TABLE 5.9 Examples of E-Auction Sites

Auction Model	Example
Large forward auction sites, fee-based	eBay.com auctions.yahoo.com uBid.com
Reverse auction sites	Priceline.com eWanted.com
Specialty forward auction sites	Egghead.com (books) WineBid.com (wine) TicketMaster.com (tickets)

Change Agents

Meg Whitman, President and Chief Executive Officer, eBay, Inc.

Meg Whitman's varied business experience made her especially well suited to become the president and chief executive officer (CEO) of eBay, the world's largest auction Web site, in 1998.

Margaret C. Whitman was born on August 4, 1956, and grew up on Long Island, New York. She earned a bachelor degree from Princeton and an MBA from Harvard University. Prior to eBay, Whitman was general manager of Hasbro Inc.'s Preschool Division, responsible for global management and marketing of two of the world's best-known children's brands, Playskool and Mr. Potato Head. From 1995 to 1997, Whitman was president and CEO of Florists Transworld Delivery (FTD), the world's largest floral products company. While at FTD, she oversaw its transition from a florist-owned association to a for-profit, privately owned company.

Before FTD, Whitman served as president of the Stride Rite Corporation's Stride Rite Division, where she was responsible for the launch of the highly successful Munchkin baby shoe line and the

FIGURE 5.24

Meg Whitman, president and chief executive officer, eBay, Inc.

repositioning of the Stride Rite brand and retail stores. Whitman spent 1989 to 1992 at the Walt Disney Company as senior vice president of marketing for the Disney Consumer Products Division. She also worked for eight years at Bain & Company's San Francisco office, where she was a vice president. Whitman began her career at Procter & Gamble in Cincinnati, where she worked in brand management from 1979 to 1981.

Whitman has kept eBay strong and profitable through stiff competition from Yahoo!, Lycos, and, most recently, Google. She has also triumphed over computer systems failures, hoax auction items such as human body parts or live babies, phishing scamsters, and countless other adversities, all the while maintaining eBay's customer base and support. She has also expanded to 53 country specific sites, making eBay an even bigger global player in the EC arena. Recently, while she was at the helm, eBay purchased Skype, and launched a variety of innovative sites such as rent.com (where people can search for apartments, homes, or roommates), kijiji (a site for online classifieds), or eBay Express (an online shopping mall enabling consumers to purchase new goods from multiple eBay merchants), many of which are targeted at existing online businesses.

Married to a neurosurgeon and raising two sons, Whitman seeks stress relief in fly-fishing and retreating to her husband's family farm in Tennessee.

Sources: http://www.time.com/time/digital/digital50/05.html
http://pages.ebay.com/aboutebay/thecompany/executiveteam.html#Whitman
http://www.businessweek.com/2000/00_20/b3681011.htm

According to the National Fraud Information Center & Internet Fraud Watch (NFIC/IFW), e-auctions are marred with more fraud than any commerce activity conducted over the Internet (Fraud.org, 2006). E-auction fraud accounted for 42% of all Internet-fraud related complaints filed with the NFIC/IFW, with an average loss of $1,155 in 2005. There are several different types of e-Auction fraud:

- *Bid Luring.* Luring bidders to leave a legitimate auction to buy the same item at a lower price
- *Reproductions.* Selling something that is said to be an original, but it turns out to be a reproduction

- *Bid Shielding.* Using another account to bid on one's own item, thereby artificially inflating the price of the item
- *Shipping Fraud.* Charging irregular shipping and handling fees, far above actual cost
- *Payment Failure.* Buyers not paying for item after auction conclusion
- *Nonshipment.* Sellers failing to ship item after payment has been received

Social Online Communities

Among the more interesting uses for the Internet over the past few years has been the explosion of consumer-to-consumer **social online communities** (i.e., Web sites enabling social networking) and social computing. MySpace.com exemplifies this trend, being the Web site with the highest market share, accounting for 4.5 percent of all Internet site visits in the United States in mid-2006 (Hitwise, 2006). Reportedly, MySpace now has over 100 million users, growing at about 230,000 users on a typical day. MySpace.com originally was designed to provide users with information regarding their favorite bands and a place where users were allowed to view other users' favorite bands and link to these users, thus creating a social network based on musical interests. Soon after its release, however, the actual use of MySpace changed significantly from its original purpose. Typical users are teens and young adults who utilize MySpace to link to friends, having little or nothing to do with musical interest. MySpace.com and other similar social community Web sites, such as Facebook and LinkedIn, have created unique and prolific electronic business opportunities. In fact, MySpace has been so successful that in 2005, it was purchased by Rupert Murdoch's NewsCorp for $580 million. Cyworld (see Figure 5.25) is another successful social online community that is vastly popular, especially in Asia; in South Korea, Cyworld's per capita penetration is greater than that of MySpace in the United States (Schonfeld, 2006).

These online social communities have created a large underground economy based on social networking. T-shirts, jeans, and various items are being sold because of MySpace associations. Although the likes of MySpace or Cyworld do not make money from this trade, they do have significant profits. In the case of MySpace, targeted ads generate about $2.17 per user per year (Schonfeld, 2006). Cyworld's revenue comes from the sale of virtual items that can be used within the site to improve its look and feel. Sales are estimated at nearly $300,000 a day, or more than $7 per user per year.

FIGURE 5.25

Cyworld, the next-generation social online community where users can buy virtual items.

Self-Publishing

Publishing has gone from a strictly business-to-consumer domain to a viable consumer-to-consumer practice, allowing consumers to voice their thoughts or opinions with little or no editorial review (a practice known as **self-publishing**). Because of the global flattening discussed in Chapter 2—Fueling Globalization Using Information Systems, consumers can now write, edit, and even publish without ever leaving their home. This is another example of a business model focusing on the "Long Tails." Rather than focusing on the mass market, people can publish work that may or may not appeal to the mainstream. There are two distinct types of online self-publishing, printing-on-demand and blogging, which will be examined next.

Printing-On-Demand   Traditionally, self-publishing refers to the publishing of original material (such as books) by the author. With increasingly sophisticated text editing and typesetting software targeted at the consumer market, **print-on-demand**, which refers to customized printing that is done is small batches, is becoming increasingly popular. As open-source versions of the software needed are available for free on the Internet, and the cost of print-on-demand is fixed per unit produced, almost anyone can publish his or her own books. This makes printing-on-demand particularly attractive to first-time authors who want to sell books but also for people who want to produce a professional looking book of recipes, wedding pictures, or travel diaries to place on their own coffee table or give away as a present. The leading print-on-demand companies include BookSurge, Lulu, and Blurb (see Figure 5.26 for an example of the online publishing Web site Lulu.com), and many print-on-demand services also offer distribution services. BookSurge (owned by Amazon.com) provides this end-to-end service where authors can submit their manuscript, and the online publisher will edit, format, print, and sell the work. These services are provided for a small sales commission; the rest of the revenue is returned to the author.

Blogging   A second form of self-publishing, **blogging** (or **Weblogging**) is the process of creating an online text diary (i.e., a blog, or Web log) made up of chronological entries that comment on everything from one's everyday life to wine and food to computer problems (see Figure 5.27). Rather than trying to produce physical books to sell or use as gifts, bloggers (i.e., the people maintaining blogs) merely want to share stories about their lives or voice their opinions, without receiving any monetary rewards in return. **Vlogging**, or video

FIGURE 5.26

Online publishing company Lulu's Web site.

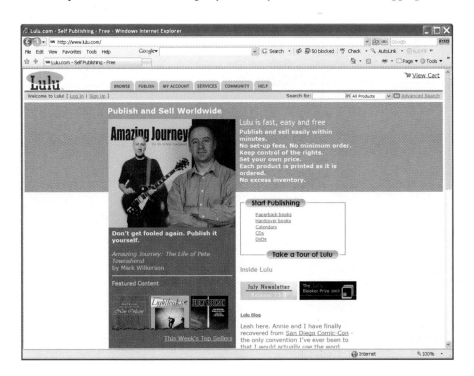

FIGURE 5.27

Anyone can publish their own topics of interest on a Web log.

blogging, has also become a popular means of commentary. Blogging originally started out as a novice's way of expressing their views using very simple pages. Now blogging has become a significant way of commentary. One such example of the power of blogging is the 2004 election scandal known as "Rathergate." Dan Rather, appearing on *60 Minutes,* reported on some suspect findings concerning President George W. Bush's record of military service. Bloggers soon after (correctly) reported that the documents used in this news story were falsified. Without the bloggers' visibility, this misrepresentation could have gone unnoticed. However, because of blogging, Dan Rather resigned from *60 Minutes,* and some say that this eventually caused his dismissal from CBS News.

Emerging Topics in Electronic Commerce

Although electronic commerce is only a little over a decade old, radical developments in technology and systems have brought e-commerce from a fringe economic activity to one of the most prevalent in today's global economy. This innovation has not slowed down and has opened some promising new areas within electronic commerce. This section will outline some emerging topics within electronic commerce. This will include innovations in *mobile commerce* (or *m-commerce*) and a special form, *location-based m-commerce,* as well as *crowdsourcing.* Also included in this section are descriptions of two exploding trends, *online entertainment* and *e-government.* Both have grown from concepts to implementation in a short period of time.

The Rise in M-Commerce

One exciting new form of e-commerce is mobile electronic commerce, or **m-commerce**. M-commerce is defined as any electronic transaction or information interaction conducted using a wireless, mobile device and mobile networks (wireless or switched public network) that leads to transfer of real or perceived value in exchange for information, services, or goods (MobileInfo, 2006).

TABLE 5.10 Some Popular Technologies for M-Commerce

Popular Handheld Product Lines	Browsers
• RIM Blackberry	• Phone.com UP.Browser
• Handspring Treo	• Nokia browser
• HP iPaq	• MS Mobile Explorer
• Samsung SCH	
• Motorola MP	

Operating Systems	Bearer Networks
• Symbian (EPOC)	• GSM
• PalmOS	• GSM/GPRS
• Pocket PC	• TDMA
	• CDMA
	• CDPD

Data Presentation Standards	
• SMS	
• WML	
• HDML	
• i-Mode	
• SyncML	
• XTML	

Common wireless mobile devices used for m-commerce include "smart" mobile phones and personal digital assistants. Technology Briefing 1—Information Systems Hardware describes these and other handheld devices. Table 5.10 lists some popular devices, operating systems, data presentation formats, browsers, and networks for m-commerce. One of the more common platforms for m-commerce is the use of powerful "smart phones" with high-speed data transfer and "always-on" connectivity over high-speed cellular networks that provide a wide variety of services and capabilities in addition to voice communication, such as multimedia data transfer, video streaming, video telephony, and full Internet access. In Table 5.11, we list some sample m-commerce applications.

Location-Based M-Commerce One form of m-commerce is **location-based services**, which are highly personalized mobile services based on a user's location. Location-based services are sent to consumers via the cellular network, via global positioning system (GPS) functionality—now built into most modern cell phones—or by using personal area

TABLE 5.11 Some M-Commerce Applications

Purchasing and Other Financially-Related Transactions

- On-line Purchasing of Goods or Services
- In-Store Purchases
- Directory/Store-Finder Services
- M-Wallets
- Vending Machine Purchases
- Stock Trading and Other Investments
- Paying Bills
- On-line Banking

Reserving and/or Booking

- Reserving and/or Purchasing Tickets for Airlines, Movies, Concerts, or Sporting Events
- Reservations for Restaurants or Hotels

Entertainment and Information

- Downloading and Playing Games
- Streaming Media for Movies or Music
- General Information such as News and Weather

network technologies such as Bluetooth. When using Bluetooth, consumers must be within range of a transmitter sending content to all available devices. Using Bluetooth, a city can provide directions to popular locations (e.g., restaurants), provide current movie listings, or any other information that might be valued. Also, businesses can use this technology to provide information about current products or sales as consumers pass by a shop. Whereas some of these applications are pull-based (e.g., the consumer trying to find information about restaurants, ATMs, or movie listings), others are push-based, providing the consumer with (sometimes unwanted) information based on his or her current location (such as information about a sales event). However, current anti-spam legislation has put a damper on push-based marketing using location-based services in some countries.

These and other location based capabilities can be provided via one or more networking technologies. For more detail on Bluetooth, cellular networks, or GPS technology, see Technology Briefing 4—Networking. One example of a very useful GPS-enabled location-based service is **e911**, or *enhanced* 911 (which is part of a federal mandate to improve the effectiveness and reliability of the 911 emergency service). When someone in distress would dial 911 from an older cell phone, the call would most likely be routed to the wrong 911 dispatch center, and the dispatcher would have no way to find out the location of the caller. GPS-enabled location-based services enable correct routing of 911 calls and also provide dispatchers with location information on the wireless 911 calls. This includes information on the phone number used to call and GPS information that would indicate where the cell phone is located within 50 meters. Another popular GPS-enabled location-based service is the phone locator, which uses GPS phone tracking capabilities. This service, offered by all major U.S. and European wireless providers, allows for users to log on to Web sites and view the location of family members' cell phones. Marketed as tracking capability built for family safety, phone locator applications can include everything from maps of a person's current location to messaging systems that alert parents when their child leaves a certain area (see Figure 5.28).

FIGURE 5.28

Parents can track their children's movements using cell phones.

TABLE 5.12 GPS-Enabled Location-Based Services

Service	Example
Location	Determining the basic geographic position of the cell phone
Mapping	Capturing specific locations to be viewed on the phone
Navigation	The ability to give route directions from one point to another
Tracking	The ability to see another person's location

In addition to these location-based services, there is now a variety of consumer oriented phone software that uses GPS and Bluetooth functionalities in cell phones. Table 5.12 lists a sample of GPS-enabled applications.

Social activities are another area that is supported by GPS technology in cell phones. With the success of Facebook.com and MySpace.com, many innovators are looking to social networks and cell phone technology to be the next big thing. Already several Web sites are proliferating with social networking cell service. This includes Dodgeball.com, which is a social networking cell phone pioneer. Dodgeball.com offers a service that allows users to view location information regarding friends and social gatherings. So if you have a buddy who is having a burger at the local burger joint, an SMS text message will be sent automatically letting the user know the location of the restaurant and who is all in attendance. Many predict that within two years, 5 percent of all text messages will be cell phone social networking related. Not bad considering that the current SMS market is annually close to $3 billion.

Key Drivers for M-Commerce Several factors have led to the rapid rise of m-commerce. First, there is exponential growth of consumer interest in and adoption of the Internet and e-commerce in general. Second, there is now development and deployment of real-time transfer of data over 3G and soon 4G cellular networks that have enabled faster data transmission and "always-on" connectivity, resulting in tremendous growth in mobile telephony and availability of powerful wireless, handheld devices. We describe these types of cellular networks in detail in Technology Briefing 4.

Through a convergence of Internet and wireless technologies, m-commerce promises to propel business by enabling the electronic exchange of capital, goods, and commercial information via mobile, untethered computing devices (Looney, Jessup, and Valacich, 2004). Indeed, the m-commerce market is predicted to grow to over $250 billion by 2007 (emarketing.com).

Crowdsourcing

Another emerging topic in e-commerce is crowdsourcing. When companies look for cheap labor, many immediately think about outsourcing work to different countries, such as India, China, or Russia (see Chapter 2). However, companies have now found a way to use everyday people as cheap labor force, a phenomenon called **crowdsourcing**, which is enabled by information technology.

For example, up until a few years ago, book publishers such as Pearson Prentice Hall had to rely on so-called stock photography for many of a book's images; in other words, publishers had to pay large sums for pictures taken by professional photographers. Clearinghouses for stock photography had to charge high fees just to cover their expenses (as they had to purchase pictures from professional photographers). Today, high-quality digital cameras can be had for far less than $1,000, and, with the right editing software, amateur photographers can create images that almost match those of professional photographers. Amateur photographers can upload their pictures to image sharing sites such as iStockphoto.com, where interested parties can license and download the images for $1-$5 per image, which is a fraction of the price of a regular stock photo. Given overhead costs that are almost negligible, iStockphoto can make a profit while still sharing parts of the revenue with the pictures' creators.

Similarly, pharmaceutical giant Eli Lilly created a site called InnoCentive, where companies can post scientific problems, and everybody can take a shot at solving the problem. Usually, a reward is paid to a successful solver. This way, an ad-hoc R&D network is created, and companies have to rely less on a dedicated R&D department, or on hiring specialists to solve a certain problem. At the same time, people can use their spare time and expertise to solve problems and earn rewards for their contributions.

As you can see, for companies, crowdsourcing is an innovative way to use people's expertise, while reducing costs. Similar to grid computing (see Chapter 4), a person's "idle time" is used for a certain business task, and many people are willing to provide their resources in exchange for a relatively small amount of money. Just imagine that you could pay for your textbooks using the money you earned from the collection of digital pictures you've taken, all for almost no extra effort. Another emerging trend is *e-lancing*. Traditionally, companies have used self-employed freelancers to work on individual projects or provide content. E-lancing takes this concept a step further by enabling people to work in more flexible ways on a variety of Internet-related projects.

Online Entertainment Industry

With consumers increasingly using e-commerce as viable alternatives for traditional commerce, the entertainment industry has no choice but to embrace the Internet as a distribution medium. This transformation for the entertainment industry has undergone a very public and very controversial scrutiny. This controversy centers on **digital rights management (DRM)**, which is a technological solution that allows publishers to control their digital media (music, movies, and so on) to discourage, limit, or prevent illegal copying and distribution. DRM restrictions include which devices will play the media, how many devices the media will play on, and even how many times the media can be played. If you ever downloaded a song or video from Apple's iTunes, then you have experienced DRM, which includes prohibiting users from copying the media or even playing the media on other (non-Apple) devices. Further, the digital content can be **watermarked** so that any illegal copy can be traced to the original purchaser. Electronic watermarking is similar in concept to watermarks placed on paper currency to prevent counterfeiting.

The entertainment industry argues that DRM allows copyright holders to minimize sales losses by preventing unauthorized duplication. Critics refer to DRM as "digital restriction management," stating that publishers are arbitrary on how they enforce DRM. Further, critics argue that DRM enables publishers to infringe on existing consumer rights and to stifle innovation.

Another e-commerce innovation in the entertainment industry involves media dissemination. With the advent of products such as **Slingbox** and TiVo, the entertainment industry, including the major U.S. network television stations and the major Hollywood studios, have no choice but to adopt the Internet as a viable dissemination medium. These industry players are now making their TV shows and movies available via Apple's iTunes and youTube.com, responding to innovations such as Slingbox (see Figure 5.29). A Slingbox,

FIGURE 5.29

Slingbox.

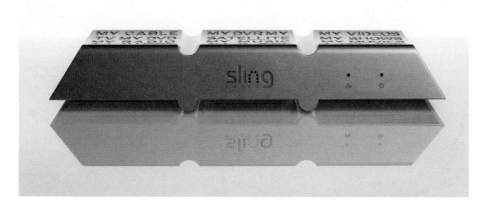

connected to a user's set-top box, acts as a personal media server and "placeshifts" television content to any Internet-enabled device. In other words, the television signal is received in the user's house and then relayed via the Internet so that the users can access TV shows or movies while traveling, being in the office, or sitting in the backyard.

E-Government

E-government is the use of information systems to provide citizens, organizations, and other governmental agencies with information about public services and to allow for interaction with the government. E-government has become more widespread since the 1998 Government Paperwork Elimination Act. Similar to the e-commerce business models, electronic government involves three distinct relationships (see Figure 5.30).

Government-to-Citizens The first form of e-government is known as **government-to-citizen (G2C)** e-commerce. This category allows for interactions between federal, state, and local governments and their constituents. The Internal Revenue Service's Internet tax filing, or *e-filing,* is one of the more recognizable government-to-citizen tools. Another e-government tool in wide use today is grants.gov. Of the over 2,200 funding opportunities for federal discretion, 54 percent were available for online submission (www.whitehouse.gov). Some states have begun working on e-voting initiatives, allowing citizens to vote online.

Government-to-Business **Government-to-business (G2B)** is similar to G2C, but this form of EC involves businesses' relationships with all levels of government. This includes e-procurement, in which the government streamlines its supply chain by purchasing materials directly from suppliers using its proprietary Internet-enabled procurement system. Also included in G2B initiatives are forward auctions, which allow businesses to

FIGURE 5.30

Local e-government initiatives.

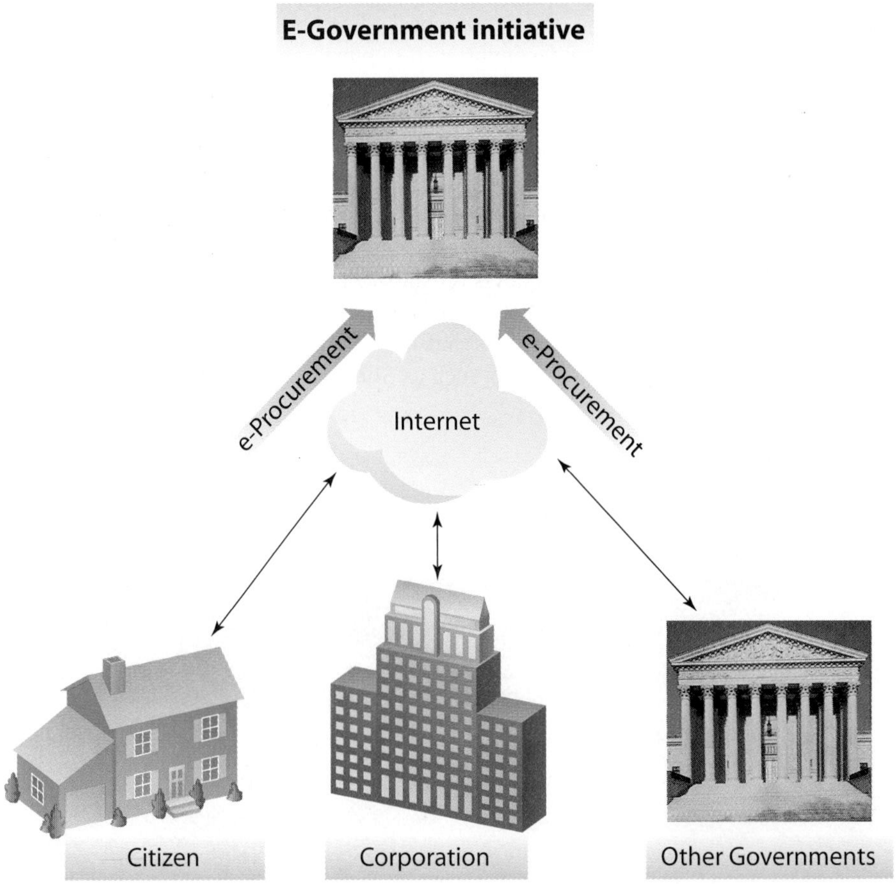

buy seized and surplus government equipment. Similar to eBay.com, the government launched auctionrp.com to provide a marketplace for real-time auctions for surplus and seized goods. Other G2B services include online application for export licenses, verification of employees' Social Security numbers, and online tax filing.

Government-to-Government Finally, **government-to-government (G2G)** EC is used for electronic interactions that take place between countries or between different levels of government within a country. Since 2002, the U.S. government has provided comprehensive e-government tools that allow foreign entities to find government-wide information related to business topics. This includes Regulations.gov and Export.gov; both allow information to be accessed regarding laws and regulations relevant to federal requirements. In addition, e-government has aligned its electronic capabilities with world issues. For example, the Consolidated Health Informatics Initiative has adopted electronic standards to allow worldwide health organizations to share information securely with government agencies. Other G2G transactions relate to the intergovernmental collaboration at the local, state, federal, and tribal levels.

Threats to E-Commerce

Although electronic commerce is now a viable and well-established business practice, there are issues that have changed the landscape for businesses and consumers and continue to do so. These threats to the current electronic business models typically take the form of policy changes. This section outlines the major factors influencing these legal developments. This includes such subjects as the USA PATRIOT Act, Internet taxation, Net neutrality, and censorship, all of which are outlined next.

The USA PATRIOT Act The **USA PATRIOT Act** (officially known as *Uniting and Strengthening America by Providing Appropriate Tools to Intercept and Obstruct Terrorism*) was introduced shortly after the 9/11 terrorist attacks in 2001. The intent of this law is to give law enforcement agencies, at the local, state, and federal levels, broader ranges of power to aid in the protection of Americans. There have been several critics of this law, including the American Civil Liberties Union, who have expressed grave concerns, including (1) reduced checks and balances on surveillance, (2) lack of focus on terrorism, and (3) surveillance on Americans by U.S. intelligence agencies. For some examples of elements included in the USA PATRIOT Act, see Table 5.13.

TABLE 5.13 Examples of the Provisions Allowed by the USA PATRIOT Act

Provision	Description
View electronic messages	Permits authorities to intercept communications to and from a trespasser within a computer system
Permits "roving" surveillance	Court orders omitting the identification of the particular instrument, facilities, or place where the surveillance is to occur
Pen register	Authorizes pen register and trap and trace device orders for e-mail as well as telephone conversations
Tangible items inclusion	Sanctions court ordered access to any tangible item rather than only business records held by lodging, car rental, and locker rental businesses
Banking regulations	Establishing minimum new customer identification standards and record keeping and recommending an effective means to verify the identity of foreign customers
Counterfeiting	Increases the penalties for counterfeiting
Finding terrorists	Increases the rewards for information in terrorism cases

Source: Congressional Research Service, *Intelligence and Related Issues,* 2006.

TABLE 5.14 Arguments For and Against Internet Taxation

For	Against
Loss in tax income of local, state, and federal governments	Slows e-commerce growth and opportunity
Unfair advantage for e-tailers over brick-and-mortar stores	Creates an opportunity for consumer fraud
Creates accountability for e-tailers	Creates a nongeographic economy where poorer states could grow
	Drives e-commerce businesses to other countries

Taxation Although this issue is a relatively old one, it remains controversial within the American legal system. With e-commerce global transaction increasing at an exponential rate, many governments are concerned that sales made via electronic sales channels have to be taxed in order to make up for the lost revenue in traditional sales methods. As people shop less in local retail stores, cities, states, and even countries are now seeing a decrease in their sales tax income because of electronic commerce. Table 5.14 highlights issues associated with Internet taxation.

THE INTERNET TAX FREEDOM ACT. Starting in 1998, the **Internet Tax Freedom Act**, passed by the U.S. Senate, created a moratorium on EC taxation in the hopes of creating incentives for EC business. According to this tax law (in addition to other provisions, such as a ban on Internet access or e-mail taxes), sales on the Internet were to be treated the same way as mail-order sales. As with mail-order sales, a company was required to collect sales tax only from consumers residing in a state where the business had substantial presence. In other words, if an EC business had office facilities or a shipping warehouse in a certain state (say, California), it would have to collect sales tax only on sales to customers from that state (in that case, California). Many EC businesses thus strategically selected their home bases to offer "tax-free shopping" to most customers. For example, Jeff Bezos, the founder of Amazon.com, closely examined several states before choosing the state of Washington for Amazon.com's head office. This way, initially only the 6 million Washington State residents had to pay tax on Amazon.com purchases. Likewise, as Amazon.com expands, it continues to be very selective in where it locates shipping facilities and warehouses. For example, Amazon.com selected Reno, Nevada to serve the Californian market in order to allow its 36 million potential customers to avoid paying sales tax on purchases. Currently, only customers located in Kansas, Kentucky, North Dakota, and Washington are charged sales tax on Amazon.com purchases. Wal-Mart, on the other hand, will have to charge taxes on all of their U.S. EC transactions, as they are physically present in every U.S. state.

USE TAX. However, the situation is not as easy as it seems. Even if you did not have to pay sales tax on goods or services purchased outside your home state, you are still liable for paying "use tax" (usually equal to your state's sales tax) on those goods and services. For example, if residents of California do not pay sales tax on an out-of-state purchase, they are asked to report that purchase and mail a check for the tax amount to the state. Other states have started adding a line for the use tax on their state income tax returns, and people have to report the taxes they owe on out-of-state purchases and face stiff penalties for misrepresenting their tax liabilities.

THE STREAMLINED SALES TAX PROJECT. With the tremendous growth in e-commerce, many states have proposed that EC businesses should be forced to collect the appropriate use tax from their customers. However, this poses tremendous problems because of local differences in taxation. For example, in Washington, fruit juice made from 100 percent juice is tax free, whereas in New York, the threshold is 70 percent juice. In some states, taxation even differs from county to county. If an EC business were to collect use tax from all its customers, it would have to know these differences in taxation to charge the correct amount to the customers' bills. Thus, over 40 states have joined efforts to propose new laws (such as the **Streamlined Tax Project**) to simplify the tax codes and make it mandatory for out-of-state sellers to collect taxes. It may not be too long until you will have to pay taxes on every purchase you make on the Internet.

Net Neutrality Columbia University professor Tim Wu originally coined the term **Net neutrality**. The underlying concept is that data that is sent over the Internet using the Internet Protocol (see Technology Briefing 5—The Internet and World Wide Web) is routed and handled in a neutral matter, regardless of the content of the data. In other words, all traffic over the Internet must be treated the same way, and your e-mail is sent, routed, and received no differently than an Amazon.com Web page or even a streaming video from Comedy Central. To view some of the approaches to Net neutrality, see Table 5.15.

Proponents of Net neutrality have asked for the Internet to be a service similar to a utility, such as power. When you are using power, it does not matter what you use your power for; the usage is metered, and you are charged accordingly. Many ISPs and telephone companies, however, have asked the U.S. government to change the nature of the Internet to allow for a prioritizing of particular applications. They believe that several large Internet companies are abusing the Internet (e.g., for bandwidth-hungry applications such as video over IP) and that this abuse causes problems for traditional Internet traffic. Their solution involves a two-tiered Internet where data is either sped up or slowed down, depending on what the data is being used for. For example, YouTube.com, the wildly popular Web site that streams millions of videos a day to users around the world, would be targeted. Telephone companies and ISPs would argue that YouTube.com causes problems for other traffic and therefore should either pay more or be "deprioritized."

Censorship **Censorship** is another hot-button issue that has gained importance. Censorship refers to governmental attempts to control Internet traffic, thus preventing some material from being viewed by a country's citizens. Several countries, including China and North Korea, have strict guidelines on what can be viewed by their citizens. Certain key words and topics are not permitted for one reason or another.

TABLE 5.15 Approaches to Net Neutrality

Approach	Description
Most favored nation	Operators must offer transit to all companies and on equal terms and cannot discriminate between them.
Separate provisioning of neutral Internet	Operators must provide Internet in accordance with the neutrality of the IP transport layer protocol but may offer other services, appropriately labeled.
Radical bit antidiscrimination	Operators must pass all packets blindly and never make any decisions based on information specific to any packet.
Enough and as good	If operators prioritize bandwidth, they must leave enough and as good bandwidth to permit nonprioritized services to reach consumers.
Tiering only	Operators may discriminate between their customers but must offer the same services to content, application, and service providers.
Police what you own	Operators may exercise discrimination with respect to entirely private networks but not Internetworks.

Source: Wikipedia.com, 2006.

Within the United States, there is also a concerted effort to censor content, specifically the content children can view. The **Child Online Protection Act (COPA)** exemplifies this approach. This law requires Internet users to verify their age before being able to view content that is deemed inappropriate for minors. In addition to concerns about explicit material that children view, there is concern with hate sites. Although difficult to do, the advocates of censorship argue that it is the ISP's responsibility to control the user's content. Many ISPs have embraced this point of view, including AOL, which strictly censors any hate sites or serial killer enthusiasts' sites.

Industry Analysis

Online Travel

Spring break is coming, and you've decided to go to Puerto Vallarta this year. Chances are, your first step will be to check the Expedia, Travelocity, and Orbitz Web sites for flights to and hotels in your chosen destination. (Expedia's 2005 fourth-quarter report showed that 75 percent of the U.S. travel customers they surveyed visit the Expedia Web site before making an online travel purchase.)

We all know the big three online travel agencies (OTAs). In today's digital world, they dominate the travel industry. They took the old brick-and-mortar travel industry and turned it into an online service where you can click to book flights and hotel reservations, change or cancel flights, reserve rental cars—even plan a vacation. In cyberspace terms, you can think of the big three as still being in Online Travel 1.0. But technology marches relentlessly on, and Online Travel 2.0 is in the works.

Travel service providers and travel customers—airlines, hotels, and car rental companies—pay fees to online travel agencies. And travel service providers selling through OTAs do not have the opportunity to build customer relationships. Therefore, some providers, including JetBlue and InterContinental Hotels, would rather have customers book directly from them. That way, they (and their customers) avoid OTA fees, and they are better able to satisfy customers since they can provide up-to-the-minute information.

Enter Online Travel 2.0—the travel search engines. They don't book travel services for you, but they locate and list URLs for hundreds of suppliers, and when you choose one, you can then click the link to the supplier's Web site. Travel search engines becoming increasingly popular with online consumers include SideStep, Kayak, Mobissimo, and Yahoo!'s FareChase.

If you want to book a travel package, especially to an international destination, OTAs may be the best choice. But if you can navigate travel services yourself, are in a hurry, or want to deal directly with travel service providers, travel search engines can fill the bill.

Questions

1. Do you use online travel agencies for assisting you with travel plans? If so, which service provider do you use, and why did you make this choice? If not, why not?
2. Forecast the future of traditional travel agencies. What electronic commerce business strategy would you recommend? Why?

Source: Brian Smith, "Yahoo's FareChase: The Stealth Disruptor?," *SearchEngineWatch* (April 27, 2006), http://searchenginewatch.com/searchday/article.php/3601971

Key Points Review

1. *Describe electronic commerce, how it has evolved, and the strategies that companies are adopting to compete in cyberspace.* Electronic commerce is the online exchange of goods, services, and money between firms and between firms and their customers. Although EC was being used as far back as 1948 during the Berlin Airlift, the emergence of the Internet and World Wide Web has fueled a revolution in the manner in which products and services are marketed and sold. Their far-reaching effects have led to the creation of an electronic marketplace that offers a virtually limitless array of new services, features, and functionality. As a result, a presence on the Internet and Web has become a strategic necessity for companies. The powerful combination of Internet and Web technologies has given rise to a global platform where firms from across the world can effectively compete for customers and gain access to new markets. EC has no geographical limitations. The global connectivity of the Internet provides a relatively economical medium for marketing products over vast distances. This increased geographical reach has been facilitated by storefronts located on every Web-enabled computer in the world. Unlike the situation with traditional storefronts, time limitations are not a factor, allowing firms to sell and service products seven days a week, 24 hours a day, 365 days a year to anyone, anywhere. A larger customer base creates increased sales volumes, ultimately saving consumers money since firms can offer their products at lower prices. Companies are exploiting one or more of the capabilities of the Web to reach a wider customer base, offer a broader range of product offerings, and develop closer relationships with customers by striving to meet their unique needs. These wide-ranging capabilities include global information dissemination, integration, mass customization, interactive communication, collaboration, and transactional support. The Web has transformed the traditional business operation into a hypercompetitive electronic marketplace. Companies must strategically position themselves to compete in the new EC environment. At one extreme, companies known as brick-and-mortars choose to operate solely in the traditional, physical markets. These companies approach business activities in a traditional manner by operating physical locations such as department stores, business offices, and manufacturing plants. In other words, the brick-and-mortar business strategy does not include EC. In contrast, click-only (or virtual) companies conduct business electronically in cyberspace. These firms have no physical locations, allowing them to focus purely on EC. Other firms choose to straddle the two environments, operating in both physical and virtual arenas. These firms operate under the click-and-mortar (or bricks-and clicks) business approach. Companies must also select a specific business model that defines how they will earn money, which markets they intend to serve, whom they will compete with, what competitive advantage they will have, how they will market themselves, and so on. Firms in cyberspace must also define a revenue model that can be based on advertising revenue, subscription revenue, transaction fee revenue, sales revenue, or some combination.

2. *Explain the differences between extranets and intranets and show how organizations utilize these environments.* Extranets enable two or more firms to use the Internet to engage in business-to-business (B2B) electronic commerce. Extranets provide timely and accurate information, allow for technology integration, and provide high value at low cost. Also referred to as business-to-employee (B2E) electronic commerce, an intranet refers to the use of the Internet within an organization to support internal business processes and activities. Examples of the types of processes or activities that might be supported include things such as training, application integration, online entry of information, real-time access to information, and employee collaboration. Both extranets and intranets provide significant benefits to organizations and are being very widely adopted by firms both big and small.

3. *Describe the stages of business-to-consumer electronic commerce and understand the keys to successful electronic commerce applications.* Business-to-consumer (B2C) electronic commerce focuses on retail transactions between a company and end consumers. Business Web sites can be relatively simple or very sophisticated and can be classified as e-information, e-integration, or e-transaction types of sites. E-information sites simply provide electronic brochures and other types of information for customers. E-integration sites provide the customers with the ability to gain personalized information by querying corporate databases and other information sources. E-transaction sites allow customers to place orders and make payments. For successful

e-commerce applications, companies should follow several rules. The basic rules of commerce are to offer valuable products and services at fair prices. These rules apply to EC as well as to any business endeavor. However, having a good product at a fair price may not be enough to compete in the EC arena. Companies that were traditionally successful in the old markets will not necessarily dominate the new electronic markets. In addition to having a sound business model and plan for generating revenue, successful companies are found to follow a basic set of principles, or rules, related to Web-based EC. These rules include having a Web site that offers something unique, is aesthetically pleasing, is easy to use, and is fast and that motivates people to visit, to stay, and to return. A company should also advertise its presence on the Web (e.g., using search engine marketing) and should try to learn from its Web site (using Web analytics).

4. *Describe emerging trends in consumer-to-consumer e-commerce and the key drivers for the emergence of mobile commerce.* The Internet has fueled the development of a variety of ways people can trade goods, socialize, or voice their thoughts and opinions. Specifically, e-auctions allow private people to sell goods to large markets. Social online communities enable the formation of huge social networks related to interests, locations, or friendships. Blogging and on-demand printing allow people to publish online diaries or printed books.

Mobile electronic commerce, or m-commerce, enables people to take full advantage of the Internet on portable, wireless devices, such as smart phones. M-commerce is rapidly expanding with the continuing expansion of worldwide Internet adoption as well as the continued evolution of faster cellular networks, more powerful handheld devices, and more sophisticated applications. Location-based services, based on GPS technology, are a key driver enabling even more creative m-commerce applications.

5. *Explain different forms of e-government as well as regulatory threats to e-commerce.* E-government is a government's use of information systems to provide a variety of services to citizens, businesses, and other governmental agencies. Depending on the services, e-government can be targeted at citizens (government-to-citizens), businesses (government-to-business), or other governmental agencies (either within a country or between countries; government-to-government). Governments' attempts to regulate electronic commerce have created some threats to EC. Most notably, the USA PATRIOT Act limits civil liberties by loosening restrictions on electronic surveillance, the Streamlined Sales Tax Project attempts to make tax collection mandatory for all out-of-state sellers (both online and offline), opponents of Net neutrality attempt to prioritize the delivery of online data depending on its use, and censorship (both outside and within the United States) attempts to limit the nature of content Internet users can view.

Key Terms

affiliate marketing   202
bid luring   208
bid shielding   209
blogging   210
brick-and-mortar business
   strategy   183
bricks-and-clicks business
   strategy   184
business model   185
business-to-business (B2B)   177
business-to-consumer (B2C)   177
business-to-employee (B2E)   177
censorship   219
Child Online Protection Act
   (COPA)   220

click fraud   202
click-and-mortar business
   strategy   184
click-only business strategy   184
collaboration   181
competitive click fraud   202
consumer-to-consumer (C2C)   177
crowdsourcing   214
Customer Verification Value
   (CVV2)   204
digital rights management
   (DRM)   215
disintermediation   183
e911   213
e-auctions   206

e-government   216
e-information   196
e-integration   196
electronic bill pay   206
electronic commerce (EC)   177
Electronic Data Interchange
   (EDI)   186
e-tailing   196
e-transaction   196
extranet   186
forward auction   207
global information
   dissemination   179
government-to-business
   (G2B)   216

Review Questions

1. What is electronic commerce (EC), and how has it evolved?
2. How have the Web and other technologies given rise to a global platform?
3. Compare and contrast two electronic commerce business strategies.
4. Explain the differences between the Internet, an intranet, and an extranet. What is the common bond among all three?
5. List and explain three benefits of using extranets.
6. What are the three stages of business-to-consumer electronic commerce?
7. List and describe six elements of or rules for a good Web site.
8. List and describe three emerging trends in consumer-to-consumer e-commerce.
9. Explain the different forms of online auctions.
10. Describe m-commerce and explain how it is different from regular e-commerce.
11. What are the primary forms of e-government? Provide examples for each.
12. What type of regulations can be considered threats to e-commerce?

Self-Study Questions

Note: Visit the Interactive Study Guide on the text Web site for additional Self-Study Questions: www.prenhall.com/Jessup.

1. Electronic commerce is the online exchange of _____ between firms and between firms and their customers.
   A. goods
   B. services
   C. money
   D. all of the above
2. _____ are those companies that operate in the traditional, physical markets and do not conduct business electronically in cyberspace.
   A. brick-and-mortars
   B. click-onlys
   C. both A and B
   D. dot-coms
3. A _____ is a summary of how a company will generate revenue, identifying its product offering, value-added services, revenue sources, and target customers.

A. profit-and-loss statement
B. revenue model
C. business model
D. annual report

4. According to the text, the three stages of Web sites include all of the following except _____.
   A. e-tailing
   B. e-integration
   C. e-transaction
   D. e-information
5. The revolutionary aspect of the Priceline.com Web site lies in its _____ system called Name Your Own Price. Customers specify the product they are looking for and how much they are willing to pay for it.
   A. immediate pricing
   B. menu-driven pricing
   C. forward pricing
   D. reverse pricing

6. A type of e-auction fraud where bidders are lured to leave a legitimate auction in order to buy the same item at a lower price.
   A. bid luring
   B. product luring
   C. customer luring
   D. low-price luring

7. A Web site should _____.
   A. be easy to use and fast
   B. offer something unique and be aesthetically pleasing
   C. motivate people to visit, to stay, and to return
   D. all of the above

8. Trying to "outsmart" a search engine to improve a page's ranking is known as _____.
   A. rank enhancement
   B. search engine optimization
   C. search engine hacking
   D. google fooling

9. C2C e-commerce can be categorized according to _____.
   A. the number of goods sold
   B. the number of buyers and sellers
   C. the payment methods accepted
   D. all of the above

10. Blogging is _____.
   A. the process of creating an online text diary
   B. a popular means to express oneself
   C. highly visible
   D. all of the above

Answers are on page 226.

Problems and Exercises

1. Match the following terms with the appropriate definitions:
   i. Electronic Data Interchange
   ii. Electronic commerce
   iii. Web analytics
   iv. Paid inclusion
   v. E-transaction
   vi. Self-publishing
   vii. Digital rights management
   viii. Search engine optimization
   ix. E-government
   x. E-integration
   a. The online exchange of goods, services, and money between firms and between firms and their customers
   b. The online sale of goods and services between firms with proprietary networks that the firms have developed and paid for entirely themselves
   c. Technologies that allow publishers to better control their digital media to limit or prevent illegal copying and distribution
   d. A stage that takes the e-integration stage one step further by adding the ability for customers to enter orders and payments online
   e. A stage in which Web pages are created on the fly to produce tailored information that addresses the particular needs of a consumer
   f. The use of information systems to provide citizens and organizations with handy information about public services
   g. Methods used to improve a site's ranking
   h. A consumer-to-consumer practice allowing people to publish original work with no or little editorial review
   i. The practice of paying a fee to be included in a search engine's listing
   j. The process of analyzing Web surfers' behavior to improve Web site performance

2. Visit Alaska Airlines' Web site (www.alaskaair.com) for real-time pricing and test the custom messenger bag builder at www.timbuk2.com. How have Internet technologies improved over the years?

3. Search the Web for a company that is purely Web based. Next, find the Web site of a company that is a hybrid (i.e., they have a traditional brick-and-mortar business plus a presence on the Web). What are the pros and cons of dealing with each type of company?

4. Do you feel that e-commerce will help or hurt shipping companies such as FedEx and UPS? Have you purchased anything over the Internet? If so, how was it delivered?

5. Do you receive advertisements through e-mail? Are they directed toward any specific audience or product category? Do you pay much attention or just delete them? How much work is it to get off an advertising list?

6. What is it about a company's Web site that draws you to it, keeps you there on the site longer, and keeps you coming back for more? If you could summarize these answers into a set of criteria for Web sites, what would those criteria be?

7. Visit the following services for comparison shopping: BestBookBuys (www.bestwebbuys.com/books/), Bizrate (www.bizrate.com), and mySimon (www.mysimon.com). These companies focus on aggregating content for consumers. What are the advantages of these Web sites?

8. Compare three different search engines. What tips do they provide to improve a page's rankings? How much does it cost to advertise a page on their results pages? If you were a company, could you think of any situation where you would pay almost any amount to have the first listing on the first results page?

9. Describe your experiences in online shopping. How did you pay for your purchases? What information did you have to reveal to the merchant? Did you feel comfortable giving out that information?

10. Visit popular social online communities (such as www.myspace.com or www.facebook.com). What features would entice you to visit such sites over and over again? Do you have a page in an online community? If yes, why? If no, what is keeping you from having such a site? Is there any content you definitely would or would not post on such page?

11. Have you ever used a mobile, wireless device such as a smart phone? If so, what do you like or dislike about it?

In what ways could your use of that device be made better? If you are not using one, what is preventing you from using one? What would have to happen before you would begin using such a device?

12. Discuss the pros and cons of digital rights management. Do you think a publisher should restrict how its content can be used? Do you think the measures taken by the entertainment industry can help contain illegal copying of music or videos?

13. Visit www.firstgov.gov. What kind of services do you see that would help you? What services would you use? What areas are missing?

14. When you shop online, is sales tax a criterion for you? Do you try to purchase goods where you do not have to pay sales tax? If you would have to pay sales tax for everything you buy online, would that change your online shopping behavior?

Application Exercises

 Note: The existing data files referenced in these exercises are available on the Student Companion Web site: **www.prenhall.com/jessup.**

 Spreadsheet Application: Analyzing Server Traffic

Campus Travel has recently found that their Internet connections between offices are becoming slow, especially during certain periods of the day. Since all the online traffic is maintained by another company, an increase in capacity requires a formal approval from the general manager. The IS manager has proposed to increase the capacity of the company's network; in a few days, he has to present the business case for this proposal at the weekly meeting of the department heads. You are asked to prepare graphs for the presentation to support the IS manager's business case. In the file ServerLogs.csv, you will find information about the network traffic for a one-week period. Prepare the following graphs:

1. Total bandwidth used for each day (line graph)
2. Bandwidth used per day, by time period (line graph)
3. Average bandwidth used in each two-hour period (line graph)

Format the graphs in a professional manner and print out each graph on a separate page (Hint: If you are using Microsoft Excel's Chart Wizard, select "Place chart: As New Sheet" in step 4).

 Database Application: Tracking Network Hardware

As Campus Travel is new to e-commerce, the management suggests following a stepwise approach for using the Internet to conduct business. Before using the Internet for conducting transactions, the managers recommend setting up a site that provides information to customers. Part of this informational site is an agency locator that shows the services each agency has. You have been asked to create a new database. This includes creating relationships in the current database. To create this new database, do the following:

1. Create a database called "agency."
2. Create a table called "agencies" and include agency ID, street address, city, state, ZIP code, phone number, number of service agents, and working hours for fields.
3. Create a table called "services" that includes service ID, name (i.e., type of service) and description.
4. Create a third table, called "agencyservices" that includes the agency ID field from the agencies table, and the service ID field from the services table.
5. Once these tables are created, go to the relationship view and connect the agencies (one side) and agencyservices (many side) tables, and the services (one side) and agencyservices (many side) tables using two one-to-many relationships (i.e., each agency can offer many services; each service can be offered by many agencies).

Team Work Exercise: So Many Books, So Little Time . . .

Have you ever bought books online? Compare and contrast your experiences with your classmates. What types of books have you purchased? Which Web sites did you use? How did you like your online purchase experience? Do you tend to stick with the same online bookstore, or do you shop around for the best bargains? Discuss strategies the different stores use to keep you from switching to another bookstore. If you have not yet bought books online, visit the Web sites of Amazon.com and Barnes & Noble as well as comparison sites, such as www.allbookstores.com, and evaluate their offerings. Summarize the benefits and drawbacks of purchasing books online.

Answers to the Self-Study Questions

1. D, p. 177
2. A, p. 184
3. C, p. 185
4. A, p. 196
5. D, p. 196
6. A, p. 208
7. D, p. 198
8. B, p. 202
9. B, p. 207
10. D, p. 210

case

IBM's Intranet: One of the World's Top 10

In 2005, IBM's intranet—known inside the company as the "w3 On Demand Workplace"—was rated one of the world's 10 best by the Nielsen Norman Group, a user experience research company. IBM was the only information technology firm to make the 2005 list.

Commenting on IBM's intranet, usability expert Jacob Nielsen said, "Designers took an aggressive yet realistic approach, creating and enforcing meticulous intranet design standards to maintain a consistent design, and using personalization to ensure the right information reaches the right people."

The Nielsen Norman Group recognized the following "best" features of IBM's intranet:

1. Personalization of News. Based on self-created profiles, employees receive internal and external news tailored to their jobs and interests.
2. Role-Specific Portlets. Job-specific portlets—that is, portal components that are specific to a person's job

(e.g., news about a customer)—are available for employees in finance, sales, and management. This means that all the tools and applications these employees need for their particular function are available directly from their IBM intranet home page.
3. Employee Directory. "If the average employee directory is a hill, the IBM BluePages would be the Matterhorn . . . with a plethora of features and pertinent information, the IBM BluePages is probably the most robust intranet employee directory we have ever encountered," Nielsen Norman's report says. BluePages facilitates collaboration by allowing IBMers to find each other more easily. Using this tool, IBMers can even search for other employees based on their areas of expertise.
4. Blogging. Through BlogCentral, IBM employees can create their

own blogs or subscribe to each other's blogs via RSS.
5. Accessibility. The intranet is designed to be easy for disabled people to use, including older users and users with motor-related disabilities, memory or literacy issues, or low vision.

Brian Truskowski, vice president and chief information officer at IBM, had this to say about the w3 On Demand Workplace when Nielsen's report came out: "[It] is a powerful productivity and collaboration tool for 329,000 IBM employees in 75 countries. Our intranet has evolved into an integrating platform that accelerates the speed with which we can find resources and knowledge to help our clients innovate and succeed."

Intranets are a vital source of information and communication for any business, and IBM's award-winning w3 On Demand Workplace is a worthy example for any organization to follow.

Questions

1. Search the Web for "intranet best practices" and list five characteristics of an effective intranet site.
2. If your university were to create a student intranet site, what online resources should be included?
3. Describe several ways that a company could measure the value of its investment in deploying an intranet.

Sources: IBM Press Release, "IBM's Intranet One of the World's Top Ten" (January 26, 2006), http://www.marketwire.com/mw/release_html_b1?release_id=107490

case

e-Enabling the Air Transport Industry: Enabling Commerce Using the Internet

For Boeing, helping their primary customers, the airlines, survive was a primary concern when developing the e-Enabled Advantage vision. In the wake of the September 11, 2001, terrorist attacks, Boeing saw several airlines file for bankruptcy protection, but at the same time, several low-cost carriers showed that the right operating structure could help airlines in their struggle for survival. In such models, reducing operating costs was one of the most important components. Most important, the low-cost airlines tried to keep their primary revenue generators, the aircraft, in the air as much as possible, as any extra minute an aircraft spends on the ground is lost revenue. In addition to shortening the times an aircraft is parked at the gate, airlines try to optimize their flight routes to save fuel or minimize the time spent waiting on permission to land at the flight's destination airport. This way, aircraft of low-cost carriers can generate revenue for up to 12 hours each day, as opposed to less than eight hours for a traditional carrier. Boeing felt that their expertise could help airlines reduce their operating costs, which would ultimately help the airlines survive.

Thus, the components of the e-Enabled Advantage program were geared at reducing operating costs. For example, the electronic flight bag helps to optimize an airplane's route, depending on weather and traffic conditions.

SBS crew scheduling software helps airlines to more effectively use available crews. The Airplane health management system helps to more easily diagnose problems with an aircraft, thus reducing turnaround times at the gate. These and other solutions could help the airlines cut operating costs in times of rising fuel prices, congestion at the airports, and worried passengers.

Throughout most of its history, Boeing has focused primarily on designing and selling products, not services. As the products offered by the main airline manufacturers (Boeing and Airbus) became more and more interchangeable, services were seen as a way to differentiate and create competitive advantage. Further, because Boeing had a long history of selling to airlines, often having decade-long relationships with their customers, they were uniquely positioned to identify services of great value. Thus, Boeing has high hopes for its e-Enabled Advantage program. Additionally, because many of these systems and services required the real-time exchange of data and information, both airlines and customers would benefit from high-speed connectivity to ground-based networks. Given this vision of the future, Boeing created its Connexion subsidiary in 2000 to develop ways to provide this high-speed connectivity. After a few years of development, it was able to roll out a variety of customer and operations focused products and services.

For Connexion by Boeing, supporting the B2B components of the e-Enabled Advantage was only one component. Primarily, providing high-speed connectivity to airplanes would enable passengers to surf the Web, access their e-mail, or access entertainment content at speeds comparable to a DSL connection, an idea that was supported by market research. For example, market research by the Boeing Company found that 50 percent of air travelers (in all classes) have a strong interest in in-flight e-mail and Internet access, with three in five saying they would be willing to pay for it. Half of those who were willing to pay said they would be willing to pay $20 or more for in-flight connectivity.

In order to get a better idea of the potential market for in-flight Internet service and to develop a solid business case, Connexion by Boeing conducted a more thorough market analysis and found the following:

- Seventy-five percent of the business travelers carried laptops on flights.
- Sixty-two percent of U.S. frequent business travelers were either "extremely" or "very" interested in in-flight broadband services.
- About one-fifth of the different airlines' frequent fliers were willing to pay as much as $35 per

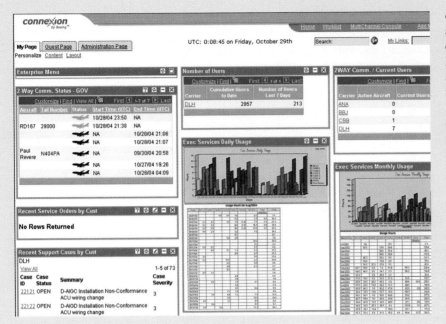

offering in-flight high-speed Internet access will provide an airline with a strong competitive advantage over its rivals. Further, the airlines could obtain vast amounts of valuable usage data to better target their customers (see Figures).

In addition to the increasing dependence on the Internet for work and our personal lives, advances in aircraft technology are also expected to contribute to an increased demand for in-flight connectivity. For example, Singapore airline recently launched an 18-hour nonstop flight from New York to Singapore using Airbus's newest long-haul plane. While many passengers—especially business travelers—are choosing nonstop flights because it can save valuable time and reduce the risk of lost luggage and missed connections, being on a long flight also means not being able to connect to the office or not being able to answer important e-mail messages. For most business travelers, such extensive isolation from the rest of the world comes at a cost—ever-growing mountains of e-mail, missed opportunities, less productive time at the destination, and valuable hours or days lost in catch-up work on return. In-flight Internet access could provide business travelers with a variety of services to maintain connection with their clients or offices, making it much more likely that customers on long-haul flights will subscribe to in-flight service.

flight for a high-speed service offering (equal to the cost of about a 3.5-minute in-flight telephone call).
- Three percent of the frequent fliers would be extremely likely to switch carriers for broadband Internet access.
- Six percent would even abandon frequent flier programs in order to obtain connectivity.

For an airline offering high-speed Internet service, such a service could attract and retain a large number of customers. An increase in a reasonable number of business travelers for an airline will translate into a huge increase in revenue. For example, an average increase of a single passenger per international flight for an international carrier equates to approximately $1 million in additional revenue annually. Consequently, Connexion believed that

In terms of potential revenues, Connexion estimated the market for in-flight connectivity at about $8 billion to $10 billion a year by the year 2012 and expected to be able to serve about half of this market, thereby generating revenues in the range of $4 billion to $5 billion annually.

However, providing in-flight Internet access meant, for Boeing, marketing directly to the end customers, namely, the airlines' passengers. Given that Boeing had formerly dealt with only a few customers, namely, the airlines, this was completely new territory for the company. While trying to persuade airlines to install the necessary infrastructure on their aircraft, Connexion also had to market the services to the passengers, who had to pay fees to access the Internet while aboard the aircraft. In addition, Boeing's move to the B2C

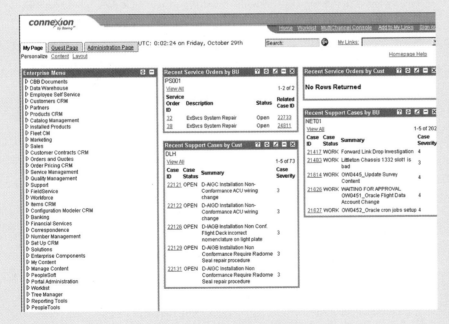

market entailed providing not only the connectivity but also content via customized portals. As neither of these areas fell into Boeing's core competencies, market acceptance of Connexion's services was slow. Below-expectation revenues and continuing fear of terrorist attacks finally led Boeing to decide to discontinue their short B2C endeavor.

Questions

1. What were the primary factors leading to the demise of Connexion by Boeing?
2. How can a company operating primarily in the B2B sector become successful in the B2C market?
3. What could Connexion have done differently to survive in the B2C market?

chapter 6
Securing Information Systems

p r e v i e w > As organizations become more dependent on information systems for enabling organizational strategy, they also become more vulnerable to a catastrophic security disaster. Because of this, organizations are focusing more of their attention on information systems security. In this chapter, we explain how you can manage the security of information systems and the critical information they hold. After reading this chapter, you will be able to do the following:

1. Explain what is meant by the term "information systems security" and describe the primary threats to information systems security and how systems are compromised.

2. Describe both technological and human-based safeguards for information systems.

3. Discuss how to better manage information systems security and the process of developing an information systems security plan.

Managing in the digital world requires careful attention to information systems security. Having thorough plans for dealing with information systems security attacks and natural disasters is critical for effectively managing information systems resources within organizations.

Managing in the Digital World: Drive-by-Hacking

How did businesses and individuals do without wireless networks before they became widely available? We can check e-mail messages while waiting in airports, access the Web using laptops in classrooms, keep a business running while attending conventions and meetings worldwide, and perform any number of additional tasks via wireless networks. A downside to the ease of communicating wirelessly, however, is that hackers have also migrated to wireless networks. Lax security on wireless networks has allowed hackers to join the network and launch malicious attacks. Recent surveys show that between 60 and 80 percent of wireless corporate networks do not use security. (A shocking statistic, considering the prevalence of destructive hacker attacks.) Thus, hackers have instituted a new type of pursuit called "war driving," whereby they drive around densely populated areas looking for unsecured networks and usually finding literately hundreds of unsuspecting victims.

Until recently, hackers were focused on discovering new ways to bypass firewalls and other security measures used to protect wired networks. Now, however, with the increasing availability of insecure wireless networks (Wi-Fi), hackers have found a new playground.

One of the more common attacks that war drivers perpetrate is called "war spamming," where hackers link into an e-mail server of an unsecured Wi-Fi network and send out millions of junk e-mails without the network administrators' knowledge. War spamming costs companies millions in bandwidth fees but is difficult to trace, so spammers are seldom caught. Some businesses are fighting back by using a technology that generates thousands of bogus wireless network access points, thus stymieing hackers trying to access personal or corporate Wi-Fi networks. Software tools called wireless camouflage, such as FakeAP, offer such protection by confusing war drivers so that they are not able to locate the "real" access point among the thousands of bogus ones. However, using network scanners such as Netstumbler or Kismet and even some of Windows XP's built-in tools, one can distinguish between genuine access points and the thousands of bogus access points. While organizations can use network scanners to find holes in their protection, most war drivers also use these to find open networks (see Figure 6.1).

All wireless access points have built-in security in the form of Wired Equivalent Privacy (WEP). WEP uses a 64-bit key to encrypt the wireless signals, which, theoretically, allows only those network users with the 64-bit code to use the Wi-Fi signal. WEP, however, has documented security flaws. These flaws allow hackers to circumvent the security and easily access the Wi-Fi network. Recently, the

FIGURE 6.1

Tools like Netstumbler find all available wireless access points, helping war drivers find open networks and network administrators to better monitor and secure their networks.

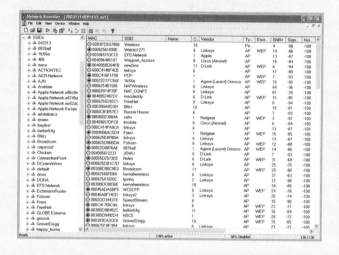

engineering security community within the IEEE (Institute of Electrical and Electronics Engineers) has worked to fix WEP security flaws by adopting "Fast Packet Keying," which is designed to repair security flaws and to finally create a truly secure wireless network.

As with all new technologies, however, there are problems with Fast Packet Keying. For instance, it is difficult to administer and deploy. Network administrators must choose between allowing users easy access and thus compromising security or installing Fast Packet Keying, which tightens security but makes day-to-day network operations more difficult.

After reading this chapter, you will be able to answer the following:

1. How can organizations better secure their wireless networks to reduce security vulnerabilities?

2. Is using a wireless network without the owner's permission wrong? If so, why? If not, why not? Are there any ethical issues associated with "piggybacking" on your neighbor's unsecured wireless network?

3. Some believe that all wireless networks should be "open" to anyone. What are the pros and cons of this perspective?

Sources:

http://news.bbc.co.uk/1/hi/sci/tech/1639661.stm

http://news.zdnet.co.uk/internet/0,39020369,2121857,00.htm

Information Systems Security

How do you secure information systems from viruses and other threats? The rule of thumb for deciding whether an information system is at risk is simple: all systems connected to networks are vulnerable to security violations from outsiders as well as insiders and to virus infections and other forms of computer crime. Threats to information systems can come from a variety of places inside and external to an organization. **Information systems security** refers to precautions taken to keep all aspects of information systems (e.g., all hardware, software, network equipment, and data) safe from unauthorized use or access. That means that you have to secure not only the personal computers on people's desks but also the notebook computers, the handhelds, the servers, all levels of the network, and any gateways between the network and the outside world.

As use of the Internet and related telecommunications technologies and systems has become more pervasive, use of these networks now creates a new vulnerability for organizations. These networks can be infiltrated and/or subverted in a number of ways. As a result, the need for tight computer and network security has increased dramatically. Fortunately, there are a variety of managerial methods and security technologies that can be used to manage information systems security effectively. In the remaining sections of this chapter, we address this new reality.

Primary Threats to Information Systems Security

Everyone who uses an information system knows that disasters can happen to stored information or to computer systems. Some disasters are accidents, caused by power outages, inexperienced computer users, or mistakes, while others are caused on purpose by malicious crackers (see Chapter 10—Information Systems Ethics and Crime). The primary threats to the security of information systems include the following (see Figure 6.2):

FIGURE 6.2

Threats to information systems security.

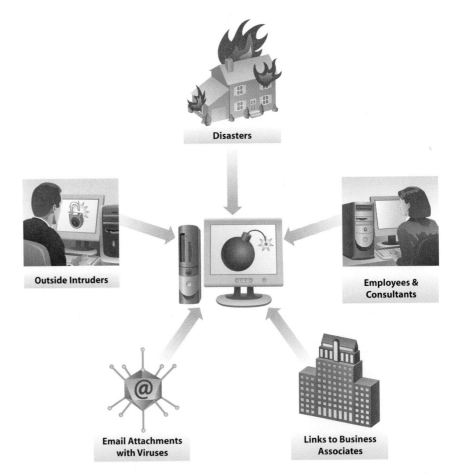

Disasters

Outside Intruders

Employees & Consultants

Email Attachments with Viruses

Links to Business Associates

- *Accidents and Natural Disasters.* Power outages, inexperienced or careless computer operators, cats walking across keyboards, and so on
- *Employees and Consultants.* People within an organization who have access to electronic files
- *Links to Outside Business Contacts.* Electronic information can be at risk when it travels between or among business affiliates as part of doing business
- *Outsiders.* Hackers and crackers who penetrate networks and computer systems to snoop or to cause damage (Viruses, currently rampant on the Internet, are included in this category.)

Information systems are most often compromised through one or more of the following: unauthorized access, information modification, denial of service, and viruses, as well as spam, spyware, and cookies. Next, each of these is examined.

Unauthorized Access An **unauthorized access** attack takes place whenever people who are not authorized to see, manipulate, or otherwise handle information look through electronically stored information files for interesting or useful data, peek at monitors displaying proprietary or confidential information, or intercept electronic information on the way to its destination.

Unauthorized access can be achieved by physically stealing computers, stealing storage media (e.g., removable flash drives, CD-ROMs, or backup tapes), or simply opening files on a computer that has not been set up to limit access. When computer information is shared by several users, as in an organization, in-house system administrators can prevent casual snooping or theft of information by requiring correct permissions. Further, administrators can log attempts by unauthorized individuals to obtain access. Determined attackers, however, will try to give themselves system administrator status or to otherwise elevate their permission level—sometimes by stealing passwords and logging on to a system as authorized users (see Figure 6.3).

One common way to gain access to a password-protected system is using a brute-force approach, i.e., trying a tremendous number of different passwords (usually in an automated fashion) until a match is found. Some systems attempt to combat this by increasing the wait time required after an unsuccessful log-in attempt, or by using CAPTCHAS. A **CAPTCHA** (Completely Automated Public Turing Test to tell Computers and Humans Apart) usually is a distorted image displaying a combination of letters and/or numbers a user has to input into a form (in addition to other required information) before submitting it. As the image is distorted, (currently) only humans can interpret the letters/numbers, and thus it can be avoided that an automated mechanism is repeatedly attempting to submit the form to gain access to a system (see Figure 6.4).

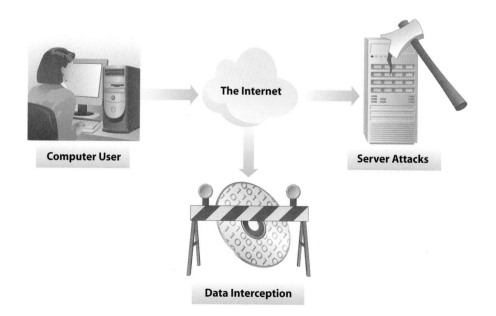

FIGURE 6.3

Unauthorized access attacks.

FIGURE 6.4

A CAPTCHA is used to prevent
unauthorized access attempts.

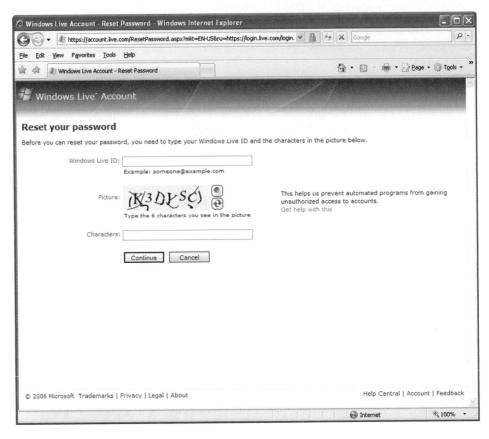

FIGURE 6.4

A CAPTCHA is used to prevent
unauthorized access attempts.

Information Modification **Information modification** attacks occur when someone
accesses electronic information and then changes the information in some way, such as
when employees give themselves electronic raises and bonuses or when crackers hack into
government Web sites and change information (see Figure 6.5).

Denial of Service **Denial of service** attacks occur when electronic intruders deliberately
attempt to prevent legitimate users of a service from using that service. To execute such
attacks, intruders often use **zombie computers**, with no (or weak) security that are located
in homes, schools, and businesses, by infecting them with viruses or worms (discussed later

FIGURE 6.5

Information modification attack.

Employee Increases salary

**Employee Accesses
Salary information**

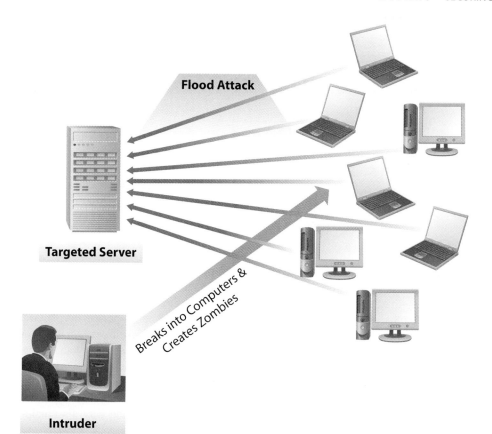

FIGURE 6.6

Denial of service attack.

in this chapter). Zombies are created when computer users who connect to the Internet don't use firewalls and antivirus software to protect themselves and are, therefore, open to attacks. The virus infiltrates unprotected computers, without users' knowledge or consent, and uses them to spread the virus to other computers and to launch attacks on popular Web sites. The Web site servers under attack crash under the barrage of bogus computer-generated visitors, causing a *denial of service* to those Internet users who are legitimately trying to visit them (see Figure 6.6). For example, MyDoom was able to recruit an army of zombies that bombarded Microsoft's Web site and literally locked out legitimate customers. (Microsoft is a popular target for virus writers, and the company must constantly provide downloadable patches to those using its software in order to prevent unauthorized intrusion.)

Computer Viruses **Viruses** are extensively discussed in Chapter 10, but they are mentioned here because they pose one of the greatest risks to computer security (see Figure 6.7). Viruses corrupt and destroy data, and they require large amounts of company and individual time, money, and resources to repair the damage they do. Viruses consist of destructive code that can erase a hard drive, seize control of a computer, or otherwise do damage. **Worms**, a variation of a virus, take advantage of security holes in operating systems and other software to replicate endlessly across the Internet, thus causing servers to crash, denying service to Internet users. For example, the Ida Code Red worm took advantage of known security vulnerabilities in the Microsoft Web server that allowed the worm to ultimately send a flood of data packets to the www.whitehouse.gov domain, overloading servers and causing a denial of service attack, bringing down the U.S. White House Web site.

Spyware, Spam, and Cookies Three additional ways in which information systems can be threatened is by spyware, spam, and cookies.

SPYWARE. Spyware is any software that covertly gathers information about a user through an Internet connection without the user's knowledge. Spyware is sometimes hidden within freeware or shareware programs. In other instances, it is embedded within a Web site and is downloaded to the user's computer, without the user's knowledge, in order to track data

FIGURE 6.7

Anatomy of a virus attack.

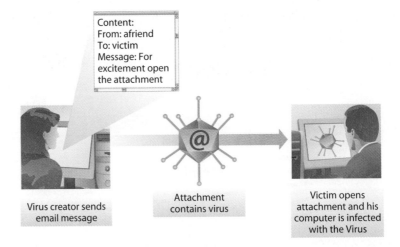

Content:
From: afriend
To: victim
Message: For excitement open the attachment

Virus creator sends email message

Attachment contains virus

Victim opens attachment and his computer is infected with the Virus

about the user for marketing and advertisement purposes. Spyware can monitor your activity and transmit that information in the background to someone else. E-mail addresses, passwords, credit card numbers, and Web sites you have visited are among the various types of information that spyware can gather. From a telecommunications perspective, spyware presents problems because it uses your computer's memory resources, eats network bandwidth as it sends information back to the spyware's home base via your Internet connection, and causes system instability or, worse, system crashes. A special type of spyware, called **adware**, collects information about a person in order to customize Web browser banner advertisements. It is important to note that spyware is not currently illegal, although there is ongoing legislative hype about regulating it some way. Fortunately, firewalls and spyware protection software can be used to scan for and block spyware.

SPAM. Another prevalent form of network traffic that invades our e-mail is spam. **Spam** is electronic junk mail or junk newsgroup postings, usually for the purpose of advertising for some product and/or service (see Figure 6.8). In addition to being a nuisance and wasting our time, spam also eats up huge amounts of storage space and network bandwidth. Some spam consists of hoaxes, asking you to donate money to nonexistent causes or warning you of viruses and other Internet dangers that do not exist. Other times, spam includes attachments that carry destructive computer viruses. As a result, Internet service providers and those who manage e-mail within organizations often now use firewalls to fight spam. For example, Washington State University utilizes the Barracuda Spam Firewall 600 (see Figure 6.9), which filters for spam and other email threats such as directory harvest attacks, phishing attacks, viruses, and more. The Barracuda Spam Firewall leverages open source spam and virus solutions in conjunction with ten defense layers. This architecture helps to reduce the amount of spam processed by the central e-mail servers and delivered to users' inboxes. The

Net Stats

Spyware Lurks on Most PCs

According to Webroot, a company that produces software to scan for and eliminate spyware, 66 percent of all Webroot-scanned personal computers are infected with at least 25 spyware programs. While statistics show that incidents of spyware found on personal computers are declining slightly, it is still a disturbing presence. "Even if it is a totally opt-in ad with consent, it adds to resource demand," explains Richard Steinnon, Webroot's vice president of threat research. "If you have five to seven [adware programs], the average we are finding, your system is not going to work."

Sources: Enid Burns, "Spyware Lurks on Most PCs" (May 6, 2005), http://www.clickz.com/stats/sectors/security/article. php/3503156

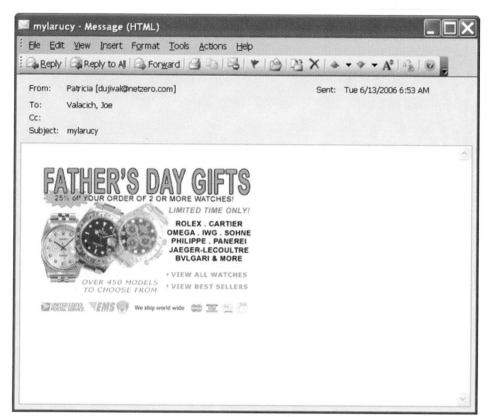

FIGURE 6.8

Spam is rampant and consumes an enormous amount of human and technology resources.

Barracuda Spam Firewall 600 can handle 3,000 to 10,000 active e-mail users. The IT administrator sets the parameters for spam filtering, and can determine how aggressively e-mail will be filtered. E-mail that is suspect to be spam can be blocked outright or sent to a quarantine folder (if the IT administrator enables the quarantine function) that is managed by the e-mail owner through a web interface. The IT administrator also has a log of all messages that are received, even those that are blocked outright, and can release messages if any are blocked unintentionally. Such instances are known as false positives, when a legitimate e-mail is inadvertently identified as spam and blocked. The Barracuda Spam Firewall has one of the lowest false positive ratings in the industry. If quarantine is enabled, users are notified on a regular interval via e-mail if any e-mail has been placed in their quarantine folder. The user then visits their quarantine folder periodically and quickly marks and deletes spam messages. Because the Barracuda Spam Firewall learns over time—through a process known as Bayesian analysis, one of the ten defense layers utilized by the Barracuda Spam Firewall—any future messages from known sources of spam are automatically blocked by the firewall.

Some spam e-mail includes **phishing** (or spoofing), which are attempts to trick financial account and credit card holders into giving away their authorization information, usually by sending spam messages to literally millions of e-mail accounts (i.e., attackers are "phishing" [fishing] for victims). These phony messages contain Web links that duplicate legitimate sites to capture account information. For example, most e-mail users regularly get phishing attacks from various spoofed banks, eBay, or PayPal (see Figure 6.10). In Chapter 10, we extensively discuss phishing and other computer crimes.

FIGURE 6.9

The Barracuda Spam Firewall 600 handles over 15 million e-mail messages a day and blocks both spam and viruses.

FIGURE 6.10

A phishing e-mail message.

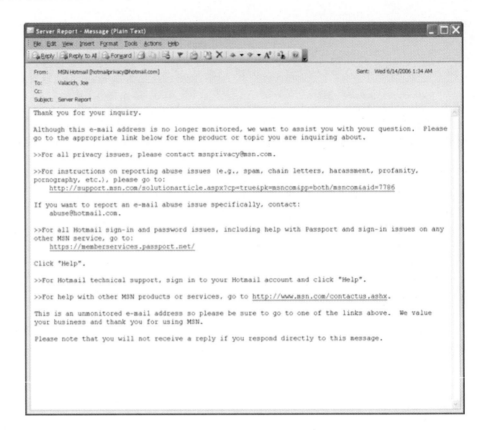

It is important to stress that it is never advisable to reply to a spam message—although if it might feel good to do so at the moment—even if the message contains instructions for removing your e-mail address from the recipients list. Replying to the message can actually be counterproductive because the spammer, or the person who sent the spam, may simply note that someone actually responded and mark your address for future mailings. In addition to e-mail–based spam, spam over instant messaging—called **spim**—is becoming increasingly used. Spim is particularly tricky because messages—typically a Web site link and some text saying how great the site is—are formatted to mimic communication chat sessions.

COOKIES. Another nuisance in Internet usage are cookies. A **cookie** is a message passed to a Web browser on a user's computer by a Web server. The browser then stores the message in a text file, and the message is sent back to the server each time the user's browser requests a page from that server.

Cookies are normally used for legitimate purposes, such as identifying a user in order to prepare a customized Web page for them, or for authentication purposes. For example, when you enter a Web site using cookies, you might be asked to fill out a form providing your name and interests or to simply provide your ZIP code. This information is packaged into a cookie, which is sent via your Web browser to be stored on your computer for later use. The next time you go to the same Web site, your browser will send the cookie to the Web server so that it can then present you with a custom-made Web page based on your name and interests, or perhaps the Web server triggers off your ZIP code and provides you with local news and weather forecasts. Often, cookies store information provided by users on a Web form (e.g., when ordering products). In such cases, cookies may contain sensitive information (such as credit card numbers) and pose a security risk in case unauthorized persons gain access to the computer.

Specific cookie management or cookie killer software can be used to manage cookies, but an even simpler way to manage cookies is through the settings in your Web browser. In the settings for the Internet Explorer Web browser, for example, you can set levels of restrictions on the use of cookies, you can stop the use of them altogether, and if you do allow them, you can go in periodically and delete them from your computer. (In Chapter 10 we talk about the ethical concerns over spyware, spam, and cookies, particularly as an invasion of privacy.)

Ethical Dilemma

To Cookie or Not to Cookie

Most online businesses use "cookies" to collect data about consumers visiting their Web sites. Cookies are bits of code that let each Web site you visit store information about you and your interests. The Internet may be a shopper's and researcher's paradise, but the downside is that every time you fill out an order form or otherwise give out personal data online, you are leaving digital footprints that marketers can trace back to you. Cookies are stored on the hard disk of your computer, usually without your knowledge or consent, so that the next time you visit a site, you are recognized and possibly even greeted by name. Unfortunately, the personal information you provide a Web site often is included in mailing lists that are sold to other marketers.

Users of most browsers can opt not to accept cookies or to have the browser warn them before accepting cookies. The downside is that if you ask to be warned, the warning will constantly pop up as you surf the Internet. And if you refuse to accept cookies, many of the Web sites you visit will not function correctly. For example, if you have asked for stock market reports or otherwise customized home pages and other information you receive, this information will no longer be available unless you again accept cookies at those sites. If you have entered passwords and IDs to use sites such as the *New York Times,* you will not be able to access the site if cookies on your hard drive have been deleted. In addition, most shopping sites will not function correctly, as online shopping carts usually work with cookies.

It was recently discovered that the Web site of the National Security Agency (NSA) installed cookies on visitors' machines. The NSA was told that this was against federal government procedures, and the Web site administrator quickly responded that the cookie placement option was a default setting on one of their Web site servers. The NSA site discontinued the practice.

Although cookies are not harmful in themselves, some privacy advocates consider them unethical. If you read a Web site's privacy policy, you may discover how the cookies for that site are used, the cookie's content, and the expiration date for the cookie.

Source: http://www.eweek.com/article2/ 0,1759,1906693,00.asp

Other Threats to Information Systems Security Many times, computer security is breached simply because organizations and individuals do not exercise proper care in safeguarding information. Some examples follow:

- Employees keep passwords or access codes on slips of paper in plain sight.
- Individuals have never bothered to install antivirus software, or they install the software but fail to keep it up to date.
- Computer users within an organization continue to use default network passwords after a network is set up instead of passwords that are more difficult to break.
- Employees are careless about letting outsiders view computer monitors, or they carelessly give out information over the telephone.
- Organizations fail to limit access to company files and system resources.
- Organizations fail to install effective firewalls or intrusion detection systems, or they install an intrusion detection system but fail to monitor it regularly.
- Proper background checks have not been done on new hires.
- Employees are not properly monitored, and they steal company data or computer resources.
- Fired employees are resentful and install harmful code, such as viruses, worms, or Trojan horses, when they leave the company.

While there are many threats to computer security, there are also ways to combat those threats. Next, we discuss safeguards organizations and individuals can use to improve information systems security.

Change Agents

Anne Mulcahy, Chief Executive Officer and Chairman of the Xerox Corporation

Among those who were surprised when Anne Mulcahy rose to the position of chief executive officer (CEO) and chairman of the Xerox Corporation in 2002 was Anne Mulcahy herself. After all, she had not received formal training to become a CEO and had graduated from college as long ago as 1974 not with a degree in business but with a B.A. in English and journalism from Marymount College in Tarrytown, New York.

Mulcahy, born on October 21, 1952, joined Xerox in 1976 as a field sales representative. Over the years, she also served as vice president of human resources, chief staff officer, corporate senior vice president, staff officer for customer operations, and, most recently, president of general markets operations, president, and chief operating officer. Mulcahy's years of experience with Xerox had familiarized her with every aspect of Xerox Corporation's business and ultimately earned her valuable credibility and respect both with clients and among employees and colleagues.

An immediate priority for CEO Mulcahy was to alleviate Xerox Corporation's $17 billion debt, which had not only raised the specter of company bankruptcy and subsequent closure but also undermined the morale of employees. With the help of Paul Allaire, director of Xerox since 1986, Mulcahy restructured the company. This was accomplished primarily by cutting expenses by $1.7 billion, selling noncore assets for $2.3 billion, and emphasizing clients. The straightforward Mulcahy also worked to improve morale among employees by straightening out accounting problems that had alerted the Securities and Exchange Commission and by logging 100,000 airline miles her first year as CEO to visit employees in far-flung Xerox locations. One year after Mulcahy took the helm, Xerox showed a profit for the first time in several years.

Not only is Mulcahy the first female CEO of Xerox Corporation, she is also the wife of a retired Xerox sales manager and the mother of two teenage sons. She currently holds member positions on the boards of Catalyst, Citigroup, Fuji Xerox, and Target Corporation.

Sources: http://www.xerox.com/go/xrx/template/ inv_rel_newsroom.jsp?ed_name=Anne_Mulcahy&app=Ne wsroom&format=biography&view=ExecutiveBiography& Xcntry=USA&Xlang=en_US

http://www.forbes.com/lists/2005/11/VI6W.html

http://www.time.com/time/photoessays/2006/ india_hospital/

http://www.businessweek.com/technology/content/ may2003/tc20030529_1642_tc111.htm

FIGURE 6.11

Anne Mulcahy, CEO and chairman of the Xerox Corporation.

Safeguarding Information Systems Resources

Any good approach to securing information systems begins first with a thorough audit of all aspects of those systems, including hardware, software, data, networks, and any business processes that involve them. By doing this, you can then decide which aspects of the various systems within the organization are most vulnerable to break-ins by unauthorized users and/or misuse by authorized users. After such an audit, you can then design and implement a security plan that makes the best use of the available resources in order to protect the systems and guard against (or at least minimize) any problems. People within the information systems department are usually responsible for implementing the security measures chosen, though people from throughout the organization should participate in the systems security audit. Some organizations even go so far as to pay an external consulting firm to attempt to break in and breach their systems so that vulnerabilities will be uncovered and fixed.

It would not make sense to spend literally millions of dollars a year to protect an asset whose loss would cost the organization only a few thousand dollars. As a result, organizations frequently conduct information systems audits. As discussed in Chapter 4—Managing the Information Systems Infrastructure, one critical component of a good information systems audit is also a thorough risk analysis. **Risk analysis** is a process in which you assess the value of the assets being protected, determine their likelihood of being compromised, and compare the probable costs of their being compromised with the estimated costs of whatever protections you might have to take. People in organizations often perform risk analyses for their systems to ensure that information systems security programs make sense economically (Panko, 2007).

Risk analysis then enables us to determine what steps, if any, to take to secure systems. There are basically three ways to react:

1. *Risk Reduction.* Taking active countermeasures to protect your systems, such as installing firewalls like those described later in this chapter
2. *Risk Acceptance.* Implementing no countermeasures and simply absorbing any damages that occur
3. *Risk Transference.* Having someone else absorb the risk, such as by investing in insurance or by outsourcing certain functions to another organization with specific expertise

Large organizations typically use a balance of all three approaches, taking steps in **risk reduction** for some systems, accepting risk and living with it in other cases (i.e., **risk acceptance**), and also insuring all or most of their systems activities as well (i.e., **risk transference**). There are two general categories of safeguards for reducing risk—technological- and human-based approaches—and any comprehensive security plan will include both.

Technological Safeguards

There are five general methods in which technology is employed to safeguard information systems:

- Physical access restrictions
- Firewalls
- Encryption
- Virus monitoring and prevention
- Audit-control software

Within any type of safeguard, there are a variety of ways in which it can be deployed. Next, we briefly review each general method.

Physical Access Restrictions Organizations can prevent unauthorized access to information systems by keeping stored information safe and allowing access only to those employees who need it to do their jobs. Of course, organizations can protect computers and data resources using *brute force* methods, such as physically securing computers to desks or requiring users to lock hard drives with keys when leaving a computer unattended. However, most organizations don't go to such lengths and require some form of **authentication** to control access. The most common form of authentication is the use of passwords, which are effective only if chosen carefully and changed frequently. Besides passwords, employees may be asked to provide an ID combination, a security code sequence, or personal data, such as a mother's maiden name. Employees authorized to use computer systems may also be issued keys to physically unlock a computer, photo ID cards, smart cards with digital ID, and

FIGURE 6.12

A smart card.

other physical devices allowing computer access. In sum, access is usually limited by making it dependent on one of the following:

- *Something You Have.* Keys, picture identification cards, smart cards, or smart badges that contain memory chips with authorization data on them (see Figure 6.12)
- *Something You Know.* Passwords, code numbers, PIN numbers, lock combinations, or answers to secret questions (your pet's name, your mother's maiden name, and so on)
- *Something You Are.* Unique attributes, such as fingerprints, voice patterns, facial characteristics, or retinal patterns (called *biometrics*)

Some measures that limit access to information are more secure than others. For example, smart cards and smart badges, passwords, lock combinations, and code numbers can be stolen. Biometric devices are difficult to fool, but determined intruders may sometimes devise ways to bypass them. Any of the previously mentioned single items can be used, but it is safer to use combinations of safeguards, such as a password and a smart card. Next, we examine various methods for implementing physical access control.

BIOMETRICS. **Biometrics** is one of the most sophisticated forms of restricting computer user access. Biometrics is a form of authentication used to govern access to systems, data, and/or facilities. With biometrics, employees may be identified by fingerprints, retinal patterns in the eye, body weight, or other bodily characteristics before being granted access to use a computer (see Figure 6.13). Once users have been authenticated, they are allowed to access certain

FIGURE 6.13

Biometric devices are used to verify a person's identity.

©AP/Wide World Photos.

Key Enabler

Voiceprint

On May 20, 1976, an unidentified person made a telephone call to a dispatcher at the Augusta, Maine, Police Department and stated that a bomb was going to go off at the Augusta State Airport. The Augusta police recorded the call. An Augusta Police Department officer listened to the tape recording and recognized the voice of the person telephoning. Later that day, at the request of the police, the identified individual came to the Augusta police station and read aloud a rough transcript of the threatening telephone call previously received and recorded at the police station. With the suspect's agreement, a tape recording was made of the reading. The police submitted both the tape recording of the threatening telephone call and the recording of the suspect's reading to two experts for voice identification analysis.

At trial, several voice identification experts presented voice spectrograms (voiceprints) showing that the defendant's voice and the voice heard making the bomb threat telephone call were made by the same individual. The defendant was found guilty of terrorism. He appealed his conviction on grounds that using voiceprints as evidence was too new to be reliable. However, the judge in the case ruled (1) that voiceprint identification had enough scientific acceptance and reliability to warrant its admissibility as evidence and (2) that the experts whose opinions were sought as evidence during trial were qualified to assist the jury in its determinations.

This case, *State of Maine v. Thomas Williams* (388 A.2d 500 [Me. 1978]), has been cited as legal precedent in many voiceprint analysis trials. (Precedent is an example used to justify similar occurrences at a later time.)

Voice identification has been used in a variety of criminal cases, including murder, rape, extortion, drug smuggling, wagering and gambling investigations, political corruption, money laundering, tax evasion, burglary, bomb threats, terrorist activities, and organized crime activities. It is

an effective method of identifying individuals for law enforcement or security purposes because each person's voice has unique characteristics that cannot be duplicated or mimicked by anyone else. Because voiceprint analysis has proved reliable, from 1967 to 2006 more than 5,000 law enforcement voice identification cases have used voiceprint analysis as evidence.

Voices can be compared visually by using a sound spectrograph to analyze complex speech waveforms into a pictorial display known as a spectrogram. The spectrogram displays the speech signal with the time along the horizontal axis, frequency on the vertical axis, and relative amplitude indicated by the degree of gray shading on the display. The resonance of the speaker's voice is displayed in the form of vertical signal impressions or markings for consonant sounds and horizontal bars or formants for vowel sounds. The visible configurations displayed are characteristic of the articulation involved for the speaker producing the words and phrases. The spectrograms serve as a permanent record of the words spoken and facilitate the visual comparison of similar words spoken between an unknown and a known speaker's voice.

Security systems also use voiceprint analysis to prevent unauthorized access to protected facilities or data. For example, banking has embraced voiceprint technology as an additional layer of security to foil potential thefts. When account holders telephone banks, a voiceprint can ensure that the caller is a legitimate account holder who should be given access to his or her account.

Voiceprint analysis is yet another example of how information systems technology benefits the wider world.

Sources: Court decision: http://www.law.harvard.edu/publications/evidenceiii/cases/williams2.htm
Steve Cain, Lonnie Smrkovski, and Mindy Wilson, "Voiceprint Identification" (October 8, 2006), http:// expertpages.com/news/voiceprint_identification.htm

systems, computers, data, and/or facilities with specified privileges. After the hijackings and attacks on September 11, 2001, the use of better security methods became a high priority for airports, large corporate buildings, and computers. Biometrics has the promise of providing very high security while at the same time authenticating people extremely efficiently, so the U.S. government and many companies are investigating how best to use this technology.

ACCESS-CONTROL SOFTWARE. Special software can also be used to help keep stored information secure. **Access-control software**, for example, may allow computer users access only to those files related to their work and may allow read-only access, which means the user can read files but cannot change them. The user might even be restricted to these resources only at certain times or for specified periods of time, and the user can be restricted to being able to only read a file, to read and edit the file, to add to the file, and/or to delete the file. Many common business systems applications now build in these kinds of security features so that you do not have to have additional, separate access-control software running on top of your applications software. Whether you are restricting user access within the application software or with the help of additional access-control software, the common approach is to authenticate that the user is indeed who he or she claims to be by requiring something that the user knows (e.g., a password) together with something that the user physically carries or has access to (e.g., an identification card or file).

WIRELESS LAN CONTROL. Given how easy and inexpensive wireless local area networks (LANs) are to install and use, their use has skyrocketed, leaving many systems open to attack. Whereas traditional LANs use physical transmission media such as copper wire and optical fiber, wireless LANs use radio waves for transmission. As a result, while traditional LANs operate by sending signals through wires or fibers in cables, wireless LANs spread their signals widely over the airwaves, allowing attackers to access the network and intercept messages relatively easily. Unauthorized people can thus easily "steal" company resources (e.g., by surfing the Web for free, which is illegal in many countries) or do considerable damage to the network. A new form of attack known as **drive-by hacking** has arisen (see the chapter-opening case), where an attacker accesses the network, intercepts data from it, and even uses network services and/or sends attack instructions to it without entering the home, office, or organization that owns the network (see Figure 6.14).

As described in more detail in Technology Briefing 4—Networking, the main standard for wireless LANs is the IEEE 802.11 family of standards. The 802.11 signals can travel up to several hundred feet away from the wireless access point that generates the signals. These LANs can be extended to cover entire buildings by placing multiple access points around the premises. Unfortunately, covering great distances in this way can also give attackers easy access both within and external to the organization. When using wireless LANs, whether in the home or in the office, it is important to configure the wireless access points such that they

FIGURE 6.14

Drive-by hacking is on the rise given the proliferation of unsecured wireless LANs.

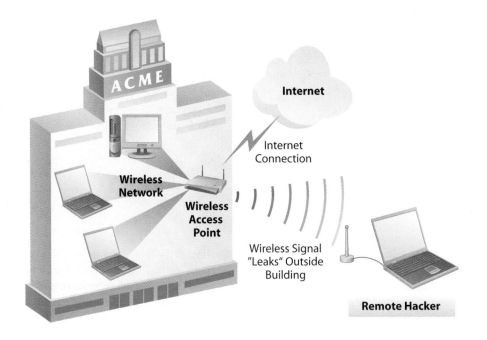

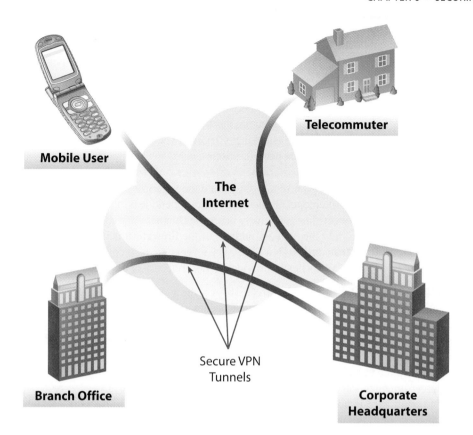

FIGURE 6.15

A virtual private network (VPN) allows remote sites and users to connect to organizational network resources using a secure tunnel.

do not allow open access. Many of these access points can be configured, for example, to allow access only to computers using preauthorized wireless network interface cards.

VIRTUAL PRIVATE NETWORKS. A **virtual private network (VPN)** is a network connection that is constructed dynamically within an existing network—often called a secure tunnel—in order to connect users or nodes (see Figure 6.15). For example, a number of companies and software solutions enable you to create virtual private networks within the Internet as the medium for transporting data. These systems use authentication and encryption (discussed later) and other security mechanisms to ensure that only authorized users can access the network and that the data cannot be intercepted and compromised; the practice of creating an encrypted "tunnel" to send secure (private) data over the (public) Internet is known as **tunneling**. For example, Washington State University requires VPN software to be used for performing e-mail communication over the Internet when connected remotely to the campus network or when using the on-campus wireless LAN.

Firewalls A **firewall** is a system designed to detect intrusion and prevent unauthorized access to or from a private network. Think of a firewall essentially as a security force inside the perimeter of the organization that spots any intruders that penetrate the organization's outer defenses.

Firewalls can be implemented in hardware, in software, or in a combination of both. Firewalls are frequently used to prevent unauthorized Internet users from accessing private networks connected to the Internet, especially private corporate intranets, described in Chapter 5—Enabling Commerce Using the Internet. All messages entering or leaving the intranet pass through the firewall, which examines each message and blocks those that do not meet the specified security criteria. Firewalls employ several different approaches:

- ■ *Packet Filter.* A firewall may examine each data packet entering or leaving the network and then accept or reject each packet based on predefined rules. **Packet filtering** is fairly effective and is transparent to users, but it takes more time to set up and may slow the network.

■ *Application-Level Control.* A firewall might perform certain security measures only on specific applications, such as file transferring. **Application-level control** is also fairly effective but may degrade performance for those applications that are monitored by the firewall.

■ *Circuit-Level Control.* A firewall may be used to detect when a certain type of connection (or "circuit") has been made between specified users or systems on either side of the firewall. Once the connection has been made, packets can flow between the two entities without further checking. **Circuit-level control** is effective for targeted types of connections that need fast, unrestricted network performance once they are connected.

■ *Proxy Server.* A firewall can serve as or create the appearance of an alternative (or "proxy") server that intercepts all messages entering and leaving the network. The use of the **proxy server** thus effectively hides the true network addresses, and potential attackers "see" only the network address of the firewall (this is also known as **network address translation [NAT]**). Proxy servers are also commonly used to locally store (cache) Web sites to provide for faster access of popular sites.

FIREWALL ARCHITECTURE. In Figure 6.16, we show a variety of different **firewall architectures** that depict how firewalls can be used within a network. Figure 6.16a depicts a basic firewall for a home network, where the firewall is implemented as software on the single computer being used. Figure 6.16b depicts a firewall router being used for either a small office or a home office. Here the firewall is implemented as hardware, but the firewall is limited to a fairly inexpensive router. Figure 6.16c depicts a firewall architecture for a larger organization that encompasses a single site (Panko, 2007).

The point here is not that you can decipher the details in these network architecture diagrams; rather, the point is to show you how the complexity and power of the firewall solution change as the situation gets more complex. At home, your firewall might simply be based in software. If you are connected to the Internet via DSL or cable, your router is likely to have a firewall built in. In the small office or home office, a router with firewall capabilities is used. For the larger organization at a single site, you might have multiple layers and types of firewalls working in concert. For large, distributed organizations spanning multiple sites, you would have even more complex layers of defense.

Encryption In any discussion of systems security, the problem of unauthorized eavesdroppers arises. Organizations can use secure channels not available to computer users outside their networks, but the Internet and public telephone lines and airwaves are not subject to the same restricted use. Most of us send e-mail around the globe; call friends, family, and colleagues on wireless telephones; and trust our desktop, notebook, and server computers with all manner of personal, financial, and corporate secrets. Until recent years, we may have felt secure in our activities. Now, however, news stories about corporate spies, malicious hackers, curious neighbors and coworkers, and suspicious government agencies have us wondering if every transfer of information is somehow subject to unseen eavesdroppers.

When you do not have access to a secure channel for sending information, encryption is the best bet for keeping snoopers out. **Encryption** is the process of encoding messages before they enter the network or airwaves, then decoding them at the receiving end of the transfer so that the intended recipients can read or hear them (see Figure 6.17). The process works because if you scramble messages before you send them, eavesdroppers who might intercept them cannot decipher them without the decoding key. (The science of encryption is called *cryptography*.)

Encryption software allows users to ensure the following:

■ *Authentication.* The ability to prove one's identity. The primary forms of host-to-host authentication on the Internet today are name based or address based, both of which are subject to falsification and are, therefore, not secure.

■ *Privacy/Confidentiality.* Ensuring that no one can read the message except the intended recipient.

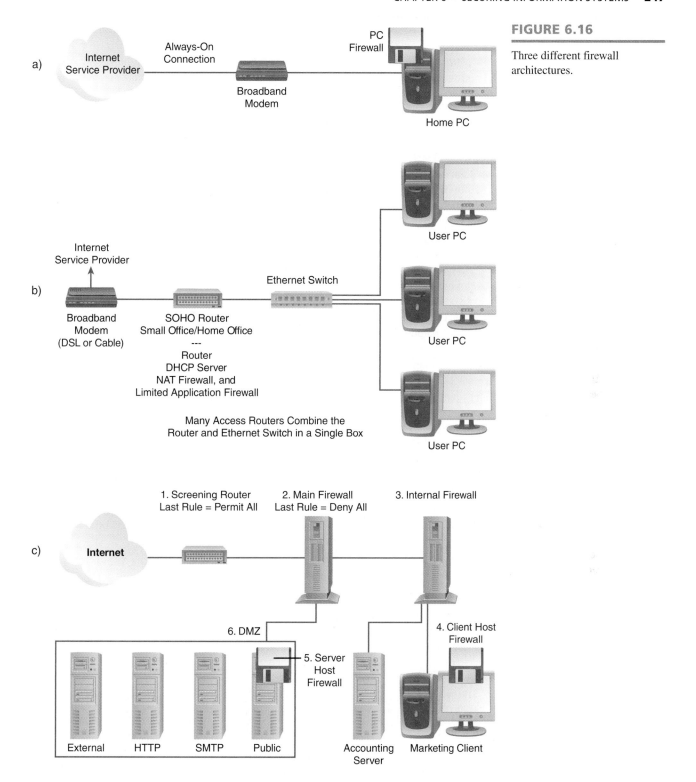

FIGURE 6.16

Three different firewall architectures.

FIGURE 6.17

Encryption is used to encode information so that unauthorized people cannot understand it.

■ *Integrity.* Assuring the recipient that the received message has not been altered in any way from the original that was sent.

■ *Nonrepudiation.* The use of a **digital signature**, available through most browsers, to prove that a message did, in fact, originate from the claimed sender.

We now have access to encryption software that scrambles text and voice messages and also allows us to send digital signatures that guarantee we are who we say we are when we send a message.

HOW ENCRYPTION WORKS. All encryption systems use a key—the code that scrambles and then decodes messages. When both sender and recipient use the same key, this is called a **symmetric secret key system**. This method of encrypting messages was used for centuries. One problem with symmetric secret key encryption is that, since both sender and recipient must keep their key secret from others, key management can be a problem. If too many people use the same key, the system can soon become ineffective. If different keys are used for sending messages to different people, the number of keys can become unmanageable.

Key management problems of secret key encryption systems were eliminated with the development of **public key** technology. Public-key encryption is asymmetric since it uses two keys—a private key and a public key (see Figure 6.18). An eccentric former hacker and researcher from the Massachusetts Institute of Technology (MIT) named Whit Diffie is credited with first envisioning the possibility of using two keys—public and private—to encrypt and decode messages. He and two coworkers published their concept in 1976. Each person has his own key pair: a public key that is freely distributed and a private key that is kept secret. Say you want to send a message to Jane using this encryption system. First, you get Jane's public key, which is widely available, and you use it to scramble your message. Now even you cannot decode the encrypted message. When Jane receives the message, she uses her private key, known only to her, to unscramble it. Public key systems also allow you to authenticate messages. If you encrypt a message using your private key, you have "signed" it. A recipient can verify that the message came from you by using your public key to decode it.

Implementing public-key encryption on a large scale, such as on a busy Web site, requires a more sophisticated solution. Here, a third party, called a **certificate authority**, is used. The certificate authority acts as a trusted middleman between computers and verifies that a Web site is a trusted site. The certificate authority knows that each computer is who

FIGURE 6.18

How keys are used to encrypt and decrypt information.

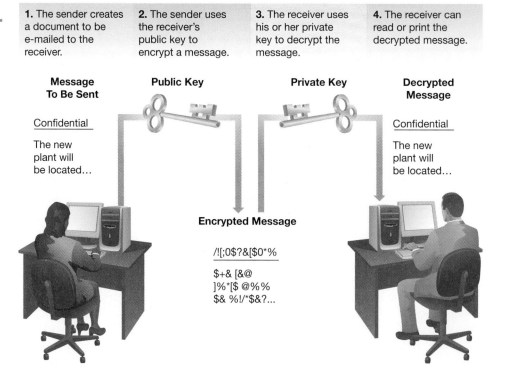

1. The sender creates a document to be e-mailed to the receiver.

2. The sender uses the receiver's public key to encrypt a message.

3. The receiver uses his or her private key to decrypt the message.

4. The receiver can read or print the decrypted message.

Message To Be Sent   Public Key   Private Key   Decrypted Message

Confidential

The new plant will be located...

Confidential

The new plant will be located...

Encrypted Message

/![;0$?&[$0*%

$+& [&@]%*[$ @%% $& %!/*$&?...

it says it is and provides the public keys to each computer. **Secure Sockets Layer (SSL)**, developed by Netscape, is a popular public-key encryption method used on the Internet.

OTHER ENCRYPTION APPROACHES. Other encryption breakthroughs followed Diffie's public–private key revelation. In 1977, three MIT professors, Ron Rivest, Adi Shamir, and Len Adleman, created RSA (named for the surname initials of the inventors), a system based on the public–private key idea. They licensed the technology to several companies, including Lotus and Microsoft, but federal laws against exporting encryption technology kept companies from incorporating RSA into their software. In 1991, Phil Zimmermann devised Pretty Good Privacy (PGP), a versatile encryption program that he gave away free to anyone who wanted to try it. It soon became the global favorite for encrypting messages.

While innovative encryption aficionados were mainstreaming the encryption concept, the government fought to keep control over keys that would allow its agents to decode communications deemed suspicious. There is great fear by legitimate governments that encryption technology will fall into the wrong hands, making it very difficult to monitor illegal activity or rogue governments. Consequently, in 1993, President Bill Clinton endorsed the Clipper Chip, a chip that could generate uncrackable codes. The catch was that also the U.S. government would have the key to decode any messages scrambled via the Clipper Chip. Opponents criticized the idea as a threat to personal liberty. But when a flaw was found in the chip, which under certain conditions would allow users to take advantage of the chip's strong encryption capabilities without giving the government the key, the Clipper Chip idea was scrapped before it could become reality.

The government finally loosened its control over encryption technology when, in 1999, federal regulations were written allowing the export of strong encryption programs. This paved the way for software developers to build encryption options into their products and made it easier for any computer user to take advantage of encryption technology. Nevertheless, the U.S. government has maintained Department of Commerce regulations against the export of strong encryption programs, but in 2003 President George W. Bush's administration promised not to enforce some of the encryption regulations that might stifle encryption research. This has solved problems some encryption researchers have had when they wanted to distribute codes for widespread use on the Internet, but future presidents' administrations may decide to strictly enforce encryption export regulations, at which time cryptography researchers may again find themselves wrangling with the federal government.

THE EVOLUTION OF ENCRYPTION. Private security and encryption researchers are working to develop products that can serve military as well as civilian needs without violating the privacy rights of individuals. Future encryption programs will provide the following:

- *Strong Security.* Generally, the larger the key used for encryption, the more secure it is. But larger keys also work at slower speeds; therefore, the trend has been toward shorter keys, which are easier to break.
- *High Speed.* Encryption is not effective if it works so slowly that it is noticeable.
- *Usable on Any Platform.* Encryption programs designed for computers have not been transferable to cellular telephones and other electronic devices. New encryption must work on a variety of platforms, such as PCs, workstations, high-end main-frames, cellular telephones, and personal digital assistants (PDAs).

While encryption cannot solve all privacy issues, such as the trading of consumer information collected on the Web or deliberately leakage of e-mail messages the sender intended to be kept private, it is definitely effective in keeping snoopers out when both senders and receivers desire privacy. Perhaps eventually encryption will protect medical records, credit histories, credit card databases, and other information that should be marked "keep out" to unauthorized viewers.

Virus Monitoring and Prevention **Virus prevention**, which is a set of activities for detecting and preventing computer viruses, has become a full-time, important task for information systems departments within organizations and for all of us with our personal

FIGURE 6.19

Virus monitoring software.

computers. While viruses often have colorful names—Melissa, I Love You, Naked Wife—they can be catastrophic from a computing perspective. Here we describe some precautions you can take to ensure that your computer is protected:

- Purchase and install antivirus software (see Figure 6.19), then update frequently to be sure you are protected against new viruses. These programs can actively scan your computer, locate viruses, inform you of the presence of viruses, destroy and/or neutralize viruses, and keep your computer updated with the most up-to-date anti-virus protection. This software is available relatively inexpensively from several software vendors and can be downloaded over the Internet from their Web sites, and updates are typically also available over the Internet as well.
- Do not use flash drives, disks, or shareware from unknown or suspect sources and be equally careful when downloading material from the Internet, making sure that the source is reputable.
- Delete without opening any e-mail message received from an unknown source. Be especially wary of opening attachments. It is better to delete a legitimate message than to infect your computer system with a destructive germ.
- If your computer system contracts a virus, report the infection to your school or company's IT department so that appropriate measures can be taken and inform people listed in your e-mail address book in case the virus has sent itself to everyone on your e-mail list. If forewarned, individuals listed in your address book can sometimes delete the infectious message before it infects their computers.

Information systems security—especially issues of unauthorized computer access, sending spam e-mail, deploying spyware, or spreading computer viruses—is at a minimum an ethical issue and at most a computer crime. (In Chapter 10, we will continue this discussion by exploring the ethical and legal implications of information systems security and use.)

Audit-Control Software **Audit-control software** is used to keep track of computer activity so that auditors can spot suspicious activity and take action. The software is designed so that any user—authorized or unauthorized—leaves electronic footprints that auditors can trace. The record showing who has used a computer system and how it was used is called an *audit trail*. For the software to effectively protect security, of course, auditors within an organization—most often someone in the IT department or information security department—must monitor and interpret results.

Other Technological Safeguards Absolute protection against security breaches remains out of reach, but here are a few additional safeguards organizations can employ:

- *Backups.* Organizations and individual computer users should perform **backups** of important files to removable flash drives, CDs, or tapes at regular intervals. Some systems can be set to perform automatic backups at specified intervals, such as at the end of a working day. Information maintained in current databases and transferred to backup tapes should be encrypted so that if crackers enter databases or thieves steal tapes, the information is useless to them.
- *Closed-Circuit Television (CCTV).* While installation and monitoring a CCTV system is costly, the systems can monitor for physical intruders in data centers, server rooms or collocation facilities. Video cameras display the physical interior and/or exterior of a facility and record all activity on tape. In-house security personnel or an outside security service can watch computer monitors and immediately report suspicious activity to the police. Digital video recording can be used to store this information digitally, even from remote cameras connected to the system via a company's intranet, wireless LANs, or the Internet.
- *Uninterruptible Power Supply (UPS).* A UPS does not protect against intruders, but it protects against power surges and temporary power failures that can cause information loss.

Clearly, there are a broad range of technological-based approaches for securing information systems. A comprehensive security plan will include numerous technological methods. Next, we examine human-based methods.

Human Safeguards

In addition to the technological safeguards, there are various human safeguards that can help to safeguard information systems, specifically, ethics, laws, and effective management (see Figure 6.20). Information systems *ethics,* discussed thoroughly in Chapter 10, relates to a broad range of standards of appropriate conduct by users. Educating potential users at an early age as to what constitutes appropriate behavior can help, but unethical users will undoubtedly always remain a problem for those wanting to maintain information systems security.

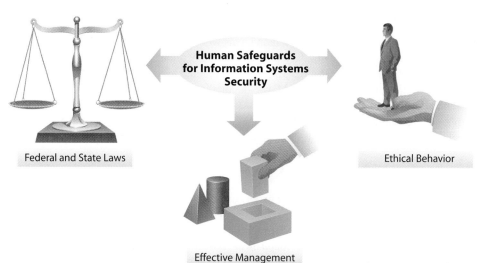

Federal and State Laws

Human Safeguards for Information Systems Security

Ethical Behavior

Effective Management

FIGURE 6.20

Human safeguards for information systems security.

Brief Case ⊙

Is Big Brother Watching You?

If you think you're the only one reading your private e-mail, we have some bad news for you. Ever since the inception of employer–employee relationships, employers have been trying to control whether the employees are doing their jobs. Traditionally, offices have been equipped with surveillance equipment, used mostly for security purposes. Information technology has taken employee monitoring to a whole new level. Using the right software, your employer can read your e-mails, monitor your Web-surfing behavior, and even log the keystrokes on your computer.

In addition, technologies such as radio frequency identification (RFID) tags and the global positioning system (GPS) can be used to track employee movements throughout a company's buildings or worldwide.

An RFID tag is a small object that can be attached to or incorporated into an animate or inanimate object. Such tags contain silicon chips and antennas to enable them to receive and respond to radio-frequency queries from an RFID transceiver. Passive tags require no internal power source; active tags require a power source (see Chapter 8—Building Organizational Partnerships Using Enterprise Information Systems).

The global positioning system is a satellite navigation system. The system consists of more than two dozen GPS satellites that broadcast precise timing signals by radio to GPS receivers, allowing them to accurately determine their location (longitude, latitude, and altitude) in any weather, day or night, anywhere on Earth.

Furthermore, someone using GPS technology could locate anyone anywhere in the world if, for example, they are using their employer's company vehicle. With the current legal environment, a company has the right to collect almost any information about what its employees are doing while on the job. Often, companies use this freedom to collect sensitive data under the disguise of attempting to safeguard the companies' data or equipment. While these tactics may help to avoid potential wrongdoings of a few errant employees or thieves, many privacy rights groups question the right of employers to violate an employee's personal privacy.

If you think you're not affected by this, think again. Consider this scenario. You're sitting at a computer in your university's library using the machine for private activities not directly related to your studies. Although you believe this to be a perfectly legitimate activity, you might already be violating your school's appropriate use policies. In fact, since you are using your university's (organization's) computing/network resources, they have the legal right to monitor what you're doing.

In today's technological environment, Big Brother truly is watching.

Questions

1. Do you feel that your employer has the right to track your movement and behavior while at work?
2. Given the availability of inexpensive and widely available surveillance technologies, as well as the use of electronic payment systems, is privacy as we know it over?

Sources: Geoffrey James, "Can't Hide Your Prying Eyes: New Technologies Can Monitor Employee Whereabouts 24/7, but CIOs Must Be Prepared for the Backlash," *Computerworld* (March 1, 2004), http://www.computerworld.com/securitytopics/security/privacy/story/0,10801,90518,00.html
"Radio Frequency Identification," http://en.wikipedia.org/ wiki/Rfid

Additionally, there are numerous federal and state *laws* against unauthorized use of networks and computer systems. Unfortunately, individuals who want unauthorized access to networks and computer systems usually find a way to exploit them; often, after the fact, laws are enacted to prohibit that activity in the future. This topic is explored in more detail in Chapter 10.

Additionally, beyond ethics and laws, the quality of information security in any organization depends on *effective management*. Managers must continuously check for security problems, recognize that holes in security exist, and take appropriate action. We discuss methods for effectively managing information systems security next.

Managing Information Systems Security

Very often some of the best things that people can do to secure their information systems are not necessarily technical in nature. Instead, they may involve changes within the organization and/or better management of people's use of information systems. For example, one of the outcomes of the systems security risk analysis described here may well be a set of computer and/or Internet use policies (sometimes referred to as **acceptable use policies**) for people

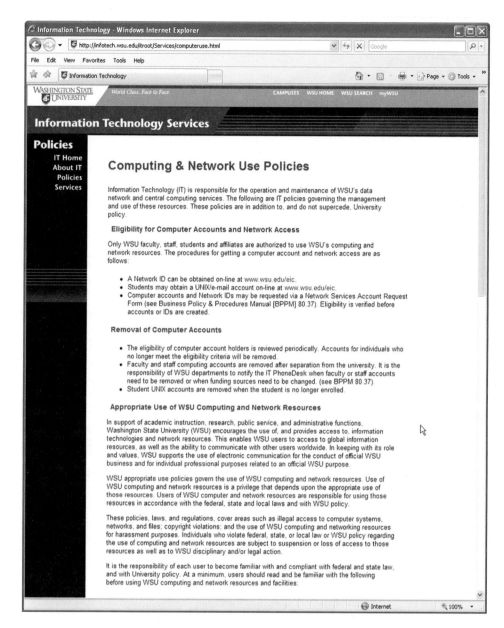

FIGURE 6.21

Most organizations provide employees or customers with an acceptable use policy.

within the organization, with clearly spelled out penalties for noncompliance (see Figure 6.21). More fundamental to security than management techniques such as these is that you make every effort to hire trustworthy employees and treat them well. Trustworthy employees who are treated well are less likely to commit offenses associated with unauthorized access.

Developing an Information Systems Security Plan

All organizations should develop an information systems security plan. An **information systems security plan** involves assessing risks, planning ways to reduce risk, plan implementation, and ongoing monitoring. This planning process should be ongoing and include these five steps:

1. ***Risk Analysis.*** Organizations should do the following:
   a. Determine the value of electronic information
   b. Assess threats to confidentiality, integrity, and availability of information
   c. Determine which computer operations are most vulnerable to security breaches
   d. Assess current security policies
   e. Recommend changes to existing practices and/or policies that will improve computer security

2. *Policies and Procedures.* Once risks are assessed, a plan should be formulated that details what action will be taken if security is breached. Policies and procedures related to computer security generally include the following:

a. *Information Policy.* How sensitive information will be handled, stored, transmitted, and destroyed.

b. *Security Policy.* Explains technical controls on all organizational computer systems, such as access limitations, audit-control software, firewalls, and so on.

c. *Use Policy.* Outlines the organization's policy regarding appropriate use of in-house computer systems. May mandate no Internet surfing, use of company computer systems only for employment-related purposes, restricted use of e-mail, and so on.

d. *Backup Policy.* Explains requirements for backing up information.

e. *Account Management Policy.* Lists procedures for adding new users to systems and removing users who have left the organization.

f. *Incident Handling Procedures.* Lists procedures to follow when handling a security breach.

g. *Disaster Recovery Plan.* Lists all the steps an organization will take to restore computer operations in case of a natural or deliberate disaster. Each department within the organization generally has its own disaster recovery plan. Such plans may include remote replication of key infrastructure items (see Chapter 4).

3. *Implementation.* Once policies and plans are established, organizations can decide which security mechanisms to use and train personnel regarding security policies and measures. During this phase, network security mechanisms, such as firewalls, are put in place, as are intrusion detection systems, such as antivirus software, manual and automated log examination software, and host- and network-based intrusion detection software. Encryption information, passwords, and smart cards and smart badges are also disseminated and explained during this phase. The information technology department is usually responsible for instituting security measures.

4. *Training.* Personnel within an organization should know the security policy and the plan for disaster recovery and be prepared to perform assigned tasks in that regard—both routinely on a daily basis and disaster related.

5. *Auditing.* Auditing is an ongoing process that assesses policy adherence, the security of new projects, and whether the organization's computer security can be penetrated. Penetration tests are conducted in-house and/or by an outside contractor to see how well the organization's computer security measures are working. Can the intrusion detection system detect attacks? Are incident response procedures effective? Can the network be penetrated? Is physical security adequate? Do employees know security policies and procedures?

Responding to a Security Breach

Organizations that have developed a comprehensive information systems security plan, as outlined previously, will have the ability to rapidly respond to any type of security breach to their information systems resources or if a natural disaster occurs. Common responses include restoring lost data using backups, performing a new risk audit, and implementing a combination of additional (more secure) safeguards (as described previously). Additionally, when intruders are discovered, organizations can contact local law enforcement agencies and the FBI for assistance in locating and prosecuting them. Several online organizations issue bulletins to alert organizations and individuals to possible software vulnerabilities or attacks based on reports from organizations when security breaches occur.

For example, the Computer Emergency Response Team, Coordination Center (CERT/CC), was established by the U.S. federal government in 1988 as a major center of Internet security expertise, located at the Software Engineering Institute (www.sei.cmu.edu), a federally funded research and development center operated by Carnegie Mellon University (www.cmu.edu). CERT was started in 1988 by the U.S. Defense Advanced Research Projects Agency after the Morris worm disabled approximately 10 percent of all computers connected to the Internet. CERT/CC is still very active, studying Internet security vulnerabilities, providing services to organizations whose Web sites have been attacked, publishing security alerts, conducting and publishing research, and providing training to incident response professionals. Their Web site is at www.cert.org.

Similarly, the Computer Security Division (CSD) is one of eight divisions within the U.S. National Institute of Standards and Technology's Information Technology Laboratory. The mission of NIST's CSD is to improve information systems security by doing the following:

- Raising awareness of IT risks, vulnerabilities, and protection requirements, particularly for new and emerging technologies
- Researching, studying, and advising agencies of IT vulnerabilities and devising techniques for the cost-effective security and privacy of sensitive federal systems
- Developing standards, metrics, tests, and validation programs to promote, measure, and validate security in systems and services, to educate consumers, and to establish minimum security requirements for federal systems
- Developing guidance to increase secure IT planning, implementation, management, and operation

The Web site of the CSD of the NIST is at csrc.nist.gov; it is also a very helpful resource for those who are concerned about information systems security. Computer security is important to governments, organizations, and individuals because it can help maintain confidentiality of information, ensure reliability and availability of systems, and sometimes report and pur-

Backhoe Cyber Threat

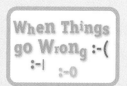

When you hear the word "cyberthreat," what comes to mind? Is it strictly digital threats, such as worms? Worms, viruses, and Trojan horses are, indeed, serious cyberthreats. A case in point is the MSBlaster worm, which spread to the far reaches of the Internet in 2003 and infected countless computers, causing damage estimated at up to $1.3 billion.

A less obvious type of cyberthreat, however—a threat usually considered only by security experts—is the threat to the hard infrastructure of the Internet. For instance, in early 2006, workers burying a TV cable in Arizona mistakenly dug up an unmarked fiber-optic cable. The workers had dutifully called the "call before you dig" number provided at the site and were given the go-ahead to bury the TV cable. This mishap had widespread consequences since the cable was part of the huge Internet backbone. Even though the cable was part of a self-healing ring, many Internet and cell phone users were immediately disconnected. Adding to the problem was the fact that other parts of the ring had been damaged earlier during a mudslide in California.

The fact that over 675,000 incidents have been reported in only one year, in which telephone lines, fiber-optic cables, water lines, or gas pipelines were accidentally damaged, illustrates how vulnerable the telecommunications infrastructure is. Even more worrisome, since information about the location of the infrastructure is publicly available, is the possibility for terrorists to exploit this vulnerability using nothing more than a backhoe.

The ease with which one could attack the telecommunications infrastructure was demonstrated by a graduate student who, for his dissertation, mapped the major fiber-optic cables across the United States. Interestingly, he found that most of the cables are buried along major interstate highways and railroads and that there are only two routes through which most of the Internet traffic flows. His dissertation soon got attention from the Department of Homeland Security, which realized that it would be disastrous if it fell into the wrong hands. (On the other hand, publicizing this type of information might have helped to sensitize the public as well as the authorities about how vulnerable the telecommunications infrastructure really is and what can be done to protect it.)

Sources: http://www.wired.com/news/technology/1,70040-0.html
http://www.washingtonpost.com/ac2/wp-dyn/A23689-2003Jul7?language=printer

sue those intruders operating unethically and illegally. Our pervasive reliance on the Internet for both personal and professional uses has brought with it the disadvantage that the Internet, as a network of networks, has security weaknesses that must be aggressively managed.

The State of Systems Security Management

We continue to hear and read about cases where a breach of computer security was catastrophic and/or had potentially dire consequences. For example, a stolen laptop computer in May 2006 reportedly put 26.5 million U.S. military personnel at risk for *identity theft* because it contained a large database that included Social Security numbers, birth dates, and other personal information. Nevertheless, even with these highly publicized incidents, systems security measures are paying off for most organizations. According to the annual Computer Security Institute (CSI)/FBI Computer Crime and Security Survey (2006), the total financial losses resulting from cybercrime are decreasing. Key findings from their survey include the following:

- Computer virus attacks result in the greatest financial losses for organizations; other significant costs were due to unauthorized access and denial of service attacks.
- Relatively few organizations (about 25 percent) utilize cyberinsurance (to cover losses incurred from attacks), even though it is widely available.
- Relatively few organizations (about 20 percent) report computer intrusions to law enforcement due to various fears such as how negative publicity would hurt stock values or how competitors might gain an advantage over news of a security incident.
- Most organizations do not outsource security activities.
- Nearly all organizations (nearly 90 percent) conduct routine and ongoing security audits.
- The majority of organizations believed security training of employees is important, but most respondents said their organization did not spend enough on security training.

In addition to these findings, organizations use a broad variety of security technologies (see Figure 6.22). Clearly, because malicious crackers won't become complacent anytime soon, it is encouraging that organizations appear to be gaining ground to guard against attacks. The lesson learned here is that we need to continue to implement vigilant approaches to better manage systems security in the digital world.

FIGURE 6.22

Security technologies used by CSI/FBI Computer Crime and Security Survey respondents (2006).

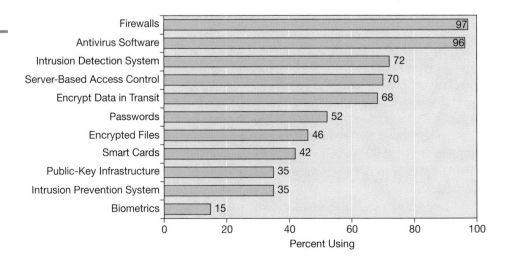

Industry Analysis

Banking Industry

Like many other industries moving into the Internet age, the banking business is changing. Since the nineteenth century, banks in the United States have been heavily regulated. Federal and state laws passed in the 1800s and the 1930s have limited banks to certain geographic locations and have determined the services they could offer. For example, in many states each bank could maintain locations for accepting deposits in only one state, and in some states they were allowed to maintain offices in just one county. Banks could offer traditional banking services, including deposits and loans, but little more. Insurance services were banned, and securities underwriting was limited. The many banking laws and regulations were intended to limit the number of bank failures after the Great Depression and to make banks safer, but they also limited services that banks could provide to customers and prevented them from competing with stockbrokers and insurance companies.

Nearly all these banking restrictions were eased or eliminated from the 1970s to the present, when banking deregulation took place. Deregulation resulted in increased acquisitions and consolidations, integration across state lines, and a larger market share for better-run banks as they gained ground over their less efficient rivals. As a result, banks could offer more customer services at lower prices, benefiting the country's overall economy.

Today, the Internet provides banks with another way to serve customers and another venue for competition. Banks can now offer customers the convenience and security of online banking services—from account management to loan applications and certificate of deposit purchases. No longer do customers judge banks simply according to hours open, ATM locations, fees charged, or travel distance to a brick-and-mortar site. Now banks offering online services can also expect potential customers to judge them according to the following:

1. The degree to which the online banking experience can be personalized
2. Ease of use
3. Responsiveness of the site

Technological and global changes will undoubtedly change the banking industry further as the twenty-first century progresses.

Questions

1. Do you use online banking; if so, what capabilities do you use most or find most useful? If not, why not?
2. Deregulation of the banking industry allowed banks to more freely operate across state lines; should international banks be allowed to operate in domestic markets? Why or why not?

Sources: http://stlouisfed.org/news/speeches/1999/01_12_99.html

http://www.microsoft.com/presspass/features/2005/nov05/11-15Banking.mspx

Philip E. Strahan, "The Real Effects of Banking Deregulation," http://research.stlouisfed.org/publications/review/03/07/Strahan.pdf

Key Points Review

1. ***Explain what is meant by the term "information systems security" and describe the primary threats to information systems security and how systems are compromised.*** Information systems security refers to precautions taken to keep all aspects of information systems (e.g., all hardware, software, network equipment, and data) safe from unauthorized use or access. The primary threats to information systems include accidents and natural disasters, employees and consultants, links to outside business contacts, and outsiders. Information systems are most often compromised through one or more of the following: unauthorized access, information modification, denial of service, and viruses, as well as spam, spyware, and cookies.

2. *Describe both technological- and human-based safeguards for information systems.* There are five general categories of technological safeguards: physical access restrictions, firewalls, encryption, virus monitoring and protection, and audit-control software. Physical access restrictions restrict unauthorized access using authentication through something a person has (e.g., identification card), something a person knows (e.g., password), or something a person is (e.g., unique human attribute). Many organizations use some combination of methods to best control information systems assets. A variety of technologies can be deployed to enhance system security, including firewalls, biometrics, virtual private networks, encryption, and virus protection tools. Firewalls are hardware or software that is used to detect intrusion and prevent unauthorized access to or from a private network. Biometrics is a technology used to better authenticate users by matching fingerprints, retinal patterns in the eye, body weight, or other bodily characteristic before granting access to a computer. Virtual private networks use authentication and encryption to provide a secure tunnel within a public network such as the Internet so that information can pass securely between two computers. Encryption—the process of encoding messages before they enter the network or airwaves—is very useful for securing information when you do not have access to a secure telecommunications channel. Virus monitoring and protection utilizes a set of hardware and software to detect and prevent computer viruses. Audit-control software is used to keep track of computer activity so that auditors can spot suspicious activity and take action if necessary. Other technological safeguards include backups, closed-circuit television, and uninterruptible power supplies. Human safeguards include ethical standards, federal and state laws, and effective management. Organizations typically utilize a combination of both technological and human safeguards when protecting their information systems resources.

3. *Discuss how to better manage information systems security and the process of developing an information systems security plan.* Because no system is 100 percent secure, organizations must utilize all available resources for implementing an effective information systems security plan. The planning process includes a risk analysis, the development of policies and procedures, implementation, training, and ongoing auditing. A number of organizations are available to help with systems security, including the Computer Emergency Response Team, Coordination Center (CERT/CC), and also the National Institute of Standards and Technology, Computer Security Division (CSD). They provide resources, solutions, alerts, research results, and training related to information systems security in addition to improved management approaches.

Key Terms

acceptable use policies   252

access-control software   244

adware   236

application-level control   245

audit-control software   250

authentication   241

backups   251

biometrics   242

CAPTCHA   233

certificate authority   248

circuit-level control   246

confidentiality   246

cookie   238

denial of service   234

digital signature   248

drive-by hacking   244

encryption   246

firewall   245

firewall architectures   246

information modification   234

information systems security   232

information systems security plan   253

integrity   257

network address translation (NAT)   246

nonrepudiation   248

packet filtering   245

phishing   237

privacy   246

proxy server   246

public key   248

risk acceptance   241

risk analysis   241

risk reduction   241

risk transference   241

Secure Sockets Layer (SSL)   249

spam   236

spim   238

spyware   236

symmetric secret key system   248

tunneling   245

unauthorized access   233

virtual private network (VPN)   245

viruses   235

virus prevention   249

worms   235

zombie computers   234

Review Questions

1. List and describe the primary threats to information systems security.

2. List and describe how information systems are most often compromised.

3. Describe risk analysis as it relates to information systems security and explain three ways to approach systems security risk.
4. What are physical access restrictions, and how do they make an information system more secure?
5. What is a firewall?
6. Describe encryption and how it helps to secure information.

7. Describe several methods for preventing and/or managing the spread of computer viruses.
8. What is audit-control software?
9. Describe three human-based approaches for safeguarding information systems.
10. What is an information systems security plan and what are the five steps for developing such a plan?

Self-Study Questions

Visit the Interactive Study Guide on the text Web site for additional Self-Study Questions: **www.prenhall.com/jessup**.

1. What is the common rule for deciding if an information system has a security risk?
   A. Only desktop computers are at risk.
   B. Only network servers are at risk.
   C. All systems connected to networks are vulnerable to security violations.
   D. Networks have nothing to do with computer security.
2. Primary threats to the security of electronic information include which of the following?
   A. small children and household pets
   B. defective power connections
   C. accidents and natural disasters
   D. none of the above
3. Which of the following does *not* pose a threat to electronic information?
   A. unauthorized access
   B. denial of service
   C. unauthorized information modification
   D. all of the above can compromise information
4. Information modification attacks occur when _____.
   A. an authorized user changes a Web site address
   B. a Web site crashes
   C. the power is cut off
   D. someone who is not authorized to do so changes electronic information
5. Technical safeguards used to protect information include _____.
   A. laws
   B. effective management
   C. firewalls and physical access restrictions
   D. ethics
6. Limiting access to electronic information usually involves _____.
   A. something you have
   B. something you know
   C. something you are
   D. all of the above

7. Which of the following is the process of determining the true, accurate identity of a user of an information system?
   A. audit
   B. authentication
   C. firewall
   D. virtual private network
8. Which of the following approaches to information systems security is aimed at assessing the value of the assets being protected, determining their likelihood of being compromised, and comparing the probable costs of their being compromised?
   A. keeping stored information safe with passwords and allowing access only to those employees who need it to do their jobs
   B. using biometrics that may include fingerprints and retinal scans or other bodily characteristics
   C. making every effort to hire good employees and treat them well
   D. conducting a risk analysis
9. A(n) _____ is a system composed of hardware, software, or both that is designed to detect intrusion and prevent unauthorized access to or from a private network.
   A. encryption
   B. firewall
   C. alarm
   D. logic bomb
10. _____ is the process of encoding messages before they enter the network or airwaves, then decoding them at the receiving end of the transfer so that recipients can read or hear them.
    A. encryption
    B. biometrics
    C. authentication
    D. disaster recovery

Answers are on page 261.

Problems and Exercises

1. Match the following terms to the appropriate definitions:
   i. Acceptable use policy
   ii. Authentication

   iii. Biometrics
   iv. Encryption
   v. Firewall

    vi. Phishing

    vii. Risk analysis

    viii. Spyware

    ix. Unauthorized access

    x. Zombie computer

      a. A type of security that grants or denies access to a computer system through the analysis of fingerprints, retinal patterns in the eye, or other bodily characteristics

      b. Specialized hardware and software that are used to keep unwanted users out of a system, or to let users in with restricted access and privileges

      c. The process of encoding messages before they enter the network or airwaves, then decoding them at the receiving end of the transfer so that recipients can read or hear them

      d. The process of identifying that the user is indeed who they claim to be, typically by requiring something that the user knows (e.g., a password) together with something that the user carries with him or her or has access to (e.g., an identification card or file)

      e. Computer and/or Internet use policy for people within an organization, with clearly spelled-out penalties for noncompliance

      f. A process in which you assess the value of the assets being protected, determine their likelihood of being compromised, and compare the probable costs of their being compromised

      g. An e-mail that attempts to trick financial account and credit card holders into giving away their private information

      h. A computer that has been infected with a virus allowing an attacker to control it without the knowledge of the owner

      i. Software that covertly gathers information about a user through an Internet connection with the knowledge of the owner

      j. Accessing a computer system by a person who does not have the authority to do so

2. There are many brands of software firewalls, with ZoneAlarm, Norton's Internet Security, and McAfee's Personal Firewall being three popular choices. Search for these products on the Web and learn more about how a firewall works and what it costs to give you this needed protection; prepare a one-page report that outlines what you have learned.

3. Search for further information on encryption. What is the difference between 128-bit and 40-bit encryption? What level of encryption is used in your Web browser? Why has the U.S. government been reluctant to release software to other countries with higher levels of encryption?

4. What levels of user authentication are used at your school and/or place of work? Do they seem to be effective? What if a higher level of authentication were necessary? Would it be worth it, or would the added steps cause you to be less productive?

5. Search for more information on the Computer Emergency Response Team, Coordination Center, and the Computer Security Division of the U.S. National Institute of Standards and Technology's Information Technology Laboratory. What role do you envision they will continue to play in the development of better information systems security? Do either of these seem to be organizations you might want to work for? Are they hiring?

6. Should the encryption issue be subject to ethical judgments? For instance, if an absolutely unbreakable code becomes feasible, should we use it with the knowledge that it may help terrorists and other criminals evade the law? Should governments regulate which encryption technology can be used so that government law enforcement agents can always read material generated by terrorists and other criminals? Explain your answer. Should the government continue to regulate the exportation of encryption technology to foreign countries, excluding those that support terrorism as it does now? Why or why not?

7. Assess and compare the security of the computers you use regularly at home, work, and/or school. What measures do you use at home to protect security? What measures are taken at work or school to protect security? (If possible, interview IT/IS personnel at work and/or at school to determine how security is protected in the workplace and in classrooms.) Describe any security vulnerabilities you find and explain how they might be corrected.

8. Take a poll of classmates to determine who has had personal experience with computer virus infections, identity theft, or other computer/information intrusions. How did victims handle the situation? What are classmates who have not been victimized doing to secure computers and personal information?

9. Research the statistics for the number of unauthorized intrusions into computer systems last year. Which type was most prevalent? Which groups committed the highest number of intrusions—hackers, employees, and so on?

10. What is the outlook for computer security in the future? Are there new techniques/laws and so on that will improve security?

11. Visit the Web site for the Computer Emergency Response Team at www.cert.org/tech_tips/denial_of _service.html and answer the following:

    a. What are the three basic types of denial of service attacks?

    b. What impact can denial of service attacks have on an organization?

    c. What other devices or activities within an organization might be impacted by denial of service attacks?

    d. Name three steps organizations might take to prevent denial of service attacks.

If the previously given URL is no longer active, conduct a Web search for "denial of service attacks." Other active links can provide answers to the questions.

Application Exercises

 The existing data files referenced in these exercises are available on the Student Companion Web site: **www.prenhall.com/jessup.**

 Spreadsheet Application: Tracking Web Site Visits at Campus Travel

Campus Travel has recently started selling products on the Internet; the managers are eager to know how the company's Web site is accepted by the customers. The file CampusTravel.csv contains transaction information for the past three days, generated from the company's Web server, including IP addresses of the visitors, whether or not a transaction was completed, and the transaction amount. You are asked to present the current status of the e-commerce initiative. Use your spreadsheet program to prepare the following graphs:

1. A graph highlighting the total number of site visits and the total number of transactions per day
2. A graph highlighting the total sales per day

   Make sure to format the graphs in a professional manner, including headers, footers, and the appropriate labels, and print each graph on a separate page (Hint: To calculate the total number of site visits and the total number of transactions, use the "countif" function to count the number of Yes answers).

 Database Application: Creating Forms at Campus Travel

After helping Campus Travel to a good start with their databases, you have decided that they should enter in data using forms rather than doing it from tables. From your experience, you know that employees have an easier time being able to browse, modify, and add records from a form view. As this can be implemented using your existing database, you decide to set up a form. You can accomplish this by doing the following:

1. Open the employees database (employeeData.mdb).
2. Select the employee table in the database window.
3. Create a form using the table (Hint: This can be done by selecting the Autoform Wizard in the Forms view).
4. Save the form as "employees."

Team Work Exercise: Should Security Upgrades Be Made Available for Pirated Software?

Microsoft and other software producers make free upgrades available to legitimate buyers of applications when security risks are exposed. You probably have firsthand experience with updating Microsoft's products as new security risks are identified; only those who purchased and registered the software are eligible to receive these free downloads. Unfortunately, some people use pirated copies of Microsoft software and are, of course, not eligible to receive security downloads. The argument has been made that these security upgrades should be free to everyone because individuals using software with security vulnerabilities are a threat to everyone using the Internet since their computers are more easily converted to zombies that can spew spam in ever-increasing numbers and they are more likely to contract and spread viruses. Those who argue that security patches should be available to everyone say that there will always be pirated software in use—especially in those countries that have no laws against it or weak laws against it—so if we are ever to tighten security on the Internet, software manufacturers must provide security patches as a public service. Do you agree that security patches for popular software should be available free to everyone, no questions asked? Explain your answer. Do you agree that software vulnerable to security breaches threatens all computer users? Why or why not? In your opinion, is it possible for the Internet community to solve this problem without asking software developers to give away their product? Explain your answer.

Answers to the Self-Study Questions

1. C, p. 232	**2.** C, p. 232	**3.** D, p. 233	**4.** D, p. 234	**5.** C, p. 241
6. D, p. 242	**7.** B, p. 241	**8.** D, p. 253	**9.** B, p. 245	**10.** A, p. 246.

case ①

Under Attack

By now you know the scam. You receive an e-mail from eBay or maybe from PayPal, American Express, or your bank or credit card company that says they are "updating" your account information. The e-mail letterhead looks legitimate, so you read on. If you will just use the Web site address provided, the problem can be remedied, and your account won't be canceled. If you visit the URL provided, the site looks legitimate—that is, it's been "spoofed" to fool you—but it was posted by the scam artists to steal your account information. By now you probably also know better than to respond to such a request. The scam is called "phishing"—meaning to "fish" for user information—and it's akin to identity theft. If you are conned into revealing account numbers, the scam artists will use that information to steal from you.

Phony e-mail is just one version of the phishing scam. Others include the following:

- Phishing via instant message, whereby users are sent a link to click on. Similar to the e-mail phishing, the user is directed to a fraudulent Web site that asks for sensitive information.
- Phishing via malware. Malware (short for "malicious software") is a malicious program that is installed on an unsuspecting user's computer via a virus or Trojan horse. This *malware* then runs in the background waiting for the user to go to, for example, a financial site. As soon as the *malware* detects the user going to a prime site, a pop-up window appears asking for sensitive information. This pop-up cannot be blocked since it is generated from the infected PC, not the Web server.

All three types of phishing are a significant problem for Internet businesses and consumers. Over 57 million Americans were reportedly exposed to e-mail phishing in 2005, and 5 percent of those e-mail recipients were victimized. The scam has grown from a nuisance to a $1-billion-a-year problem in the United States. What is even more troublesome is the fact that 101 brands have been high jacked or spoofed with over 92 percent of these occurring in the financial sector. (PayPal is the country's number one financial victim, and American Express is number 2.) Clearly, phishing thieves are not only persistent but often successful at gaining access to users' sensitive information.

In an effort to defeat phishers, PayPal has stopped using e-mail to contact account holders. Instead, PayPal has its own proprietary messaging system that handles all transactions. If PayPal needs to contact you regarding your account, they will send a single e-mail message saying that there is a message waiting on the Web site messaging system. This procedure may further complicate access for an account holder, but it also adds a necessary layer of security.

Questions

1. What types of companies are most susceptible to phishing attacks?
2. Assume you have replied to a phishing e-mail; research on the Web what steps you should follow to limit any possible consequences.
3. Research on the Web for the telltale signs of a phishing message.

Sources: Antiphishing Work Group, http://www.antiphishing.org

American Express Phishing, http://www10.americanexpress.com/sif/cda/page/0,1641,21372,00.asp

case ②

e-Enabling the Air Transport Industry: Securing Information Systems

Information systems are at the heart of today's latest-generation aircraft. Pioneered by Airbus, many commercial aircraft now use so-called fly-by-wire systems, where the aircraft's control surfaces, such as rudders or elevators, are controlled using electrical systems rather than more traditional hydromechanical systems, which use a combination of mechanic and hydraulic circuits to steer an airplane. However, monitoring aircraft operations is becoming increasingly complex, and the airplane's systems and pilots rely on tremendous amounts of data from the engines, flight controls, landing gear, cabin environment, and so on. Thus, newest-generation aircraft, such as the Boeing 787 or the Airbus A380, take the fly-by-wire concept a step further and use Ethernet technology (see Technology Briefing 4) for all internal data communications networks. In addition to onboard data communication, air-to-ground connections (such as for air traffic control or for an airline's

In-flight entertainment systems are transmitted using standard networking technologies.

business operations, such as Boeing's Airplane Health Management) also increasingly use Internet Protocol (IP) technology to satisfy the tremendous data transfer needs.

Thus far, IP-based networks have been used primarily for in-flight entertainment, such as seat-back televisions. In its A380, Airbus uses IP-based networks not only for the transfer of in-flight entertainment but also for the avionics network (i.e., all electronic systems that are used in an aircraft, such as systems for communication or navigation). In such next-generation aircraft, data are transferred between different avionic equipment, crew management systems, in-flight entertainment systems, and multiple onboard and off-board (i.e., ground-based) networks.

Ethernet-based protocols have proven reliable in a wide variety of circumstances and are thus very well suited for the use on aircraft, with its high demands on reliability. For aircraft manufacturers, the use of the standard IP means that the systems are usable and upgradable for years to come. Further, many of the airlines' ground-based networks are based on Ethernet standards, so using IP onboard aircraft and for communication between aircraft and ground control centers allows for seamless integration of the systems. However, the use of such standards also means that the e-Enabled aircraft can be vulnerable to a variety of threats, such as "back doors" allowing intruders to access and compromise a system, viruses, worms, denial of service attacks, shutdown of an aircraft's

support systems, or content exploitation (such as revealing critical flight, crew, or passenger data).

Any interruption to such systems (be it due to human user, application, network, or end-system disruption or failure) can have a variety of consequences, ranging from mere annoyances to potentially grave consequences. For example, failure of in-flight entertainment systems are often merely an annoyance but can also have some consequences related to an airline's future revenues due to disgruntled passengers. In contrast, failure of onboard avionics systems can have grave consequences for the operation of an aircraft. Thus, securing these networks is of utmost concern for air traffic safety.

Risk analyses can help to identify the areas where vulnerability is highest and where the potential consequences of an attack are most severe. To secure the IP-based networks used aboard aircraft as well as the networks linking an aircraft to the ground, issues such as authentication, access control, data confidentiality and integrity, countermeasures, and system recovery have to be taken into account. Various vulnerabilities of operating systems or Web browsers serve as a constant reminder that there are numerous hackers attempting to gain access to different systems. However, at this time, a common, coherent set of solutions for aviation security is nonexistent, and aircraft manufacturers as well as manufacturers of avionics equipment have to scramble to find ways to best secure their systems.

Questions

1. By relying on established standards for data communication, potential vulnerabilities are introduced that can impact air traffic security. Identify and contrast the trade-offs between the need to transmit data and the potential to compromise security.
2. Given the possibility that a hacker onboard an aircraft could break into airline systems, propose arguments for and against allowing passengers to use computers while in flight.
3. Based on the information provided in the chapter, what security measures can be taken to protect the IP-based networks discussed in the case?

Source: C. A. Wargo and C. Dhas, "Security Considerations for the e-Enabled Aircraft," *Proceedings of the 2003 IEEE Aerospace Conference* 4 (2003): 1533–50.

chapter 7

Enhancing Business Intelligence Using Information Systems

preview > Every day, the capabilities of many information systems are expanding, making it difficult to make clear-cut distinctions between the capabilities and the focus of some systems. Nevertheless, it is important to understand that organizations comprise different levels and functions, each performing various business processes. Additionally, these different levels, functions, and processes require different types of information system capabilities to provide the business intelligence necessary for effective management. Consequently, this chapter describes several types of information systems and where and how each is used in organizations. Some of the systems described are relatively new, while others have been mainstays in organizations since the 1960s. After reading this chapter, you will be able to do the following:

1. Describe the characteristics that differentiate the operational, managerial, and executive levels of an organization.

2. Explain the characteristics of the three information systems designed to support each unique level of an organization: transaction processing systems, management information systems, and executive information systems.

3. Describe the characteristics of seven information systems that span the operational, managerial, and executive levels: decision support systems, intelligent systems, data-mining and visualization systems, office automation systems, collaboration technologies, knowledge management systems, and functional area information systems.

This chapter focuses on how organizations are using and applying specific types of information systems to best support *internal* business processes. In Chapter 8—Building Organizational Partnerships Using Enterprise Information Systems, we focus on systems that support business processes that span multiple organizational functions as well as potentially multiple organizations, critical in today's competitive global environment.

Managing in the Digital World: Amazon.com—They Wrote the Book on Gaining Business Intelligence from Information Systems

In 12 years since the company's inception in 1994, Amazon.com, founded and headed by Jeff Bezos, has grown from a garage-based online book reseller to one of the world's largest retailers for music, DVDs, videos, computer and video games, photography equipment, toys, software, tools and hardware, wireless products, electronics, and kitchen and housewares. In fact, Amazon is a world of online commerce, boasting nearly 35 million customers worldwide (see Figure 7.1).

Amazon's commitment to be "customer-centric" has resulted in a satisfied, returning customer base unequaled in the dot-com marketplace. Among the innovations that make customers smile and keep coming back are the following:

- The Amazon.com Web site greets you by name each time you visit.
- The site remembers your recent purchases and recommends similar products you might like.
- At the top of Amazon.com's home page, a "gold box," tailored for each individual returning customer, contains books, music, video and DVDs he or she might want to buy—all at deep discounts. Offers are good for one hour each day and are changed as customers revisit the site. Gold box items are determined by customer behavior, including how fast or slow the user clicks, whether the user is browsing in general or looking for specific items, which categories are searched, and so on.
- At the bottom of Amazon's home page are bargains a returning customer might like to investigate.

All these features are based on previous behavior that customers exhibited while on the site. How does Amazon.com manage this degree of personalization? Data warehousing and mining is the key for gaining business intelligence. "We work hard to refine our technology, which allows us to make recommendations that make shopping more convenient and enjoyable," explains Diane N. Lye, Amazon.com's senior manager for worldwide data mining. Amazon has teamed up with SAS Software to achieve advanced statistical analysis of its data. For example, Amazon uses SAS software to obtain and test the different types of page layout and information presentation and sequencing, and SAS software also provides effective fraud protection.

The tracking techniques Amazon.com uses to prevent fraud include the following:

- Checking shipping addresses against billing addresses—Usually, people perpetrating a fraud don't

FIGURE 7.1

Amazon.com utilizes information systems to gain business intelligence for selling books, a diverse range of products, and combating fraud.

ship products to their homes, so they will use different shipping and billing addresses.
- Checking method of shipment—People intending to somehow defraud Amazon usually request the fastest possible shipping method.
- Checking credit card sources—Dishonest customers may use credit cards issued by small banks that do not have the capability to immediately authorize transactions.

Amazon uses many unique tools to help attract and retain customers. For example, the "one-click" feature available on Amazon.com lets returning customers check out with one click, avoiding filling in shipping and credit card information each time products are purchased. This feature further improves the customer experience—a factor that is always at the forefront of Amazon.com's stated purpose. (Some competitors have copied this feature, and Amazon-filed lawsuits against them were pending as of early 2007.)

Other unique Amazon programs include the following:

1. The Amazon Advantage program allows vendors to use Amazon as a platform for retail selling.
2. The Amazon Associates program allows Web site owners to refer visitors to Amazon's Web site; the Web site owners earn a fee each time a referral makes a purchase.

3. The Amazon Marketplace feature lets individuals sell items from the Amazon Web site, much like eBay, but items for sale are restricted to products Amazon carries.
4. The Web Services program provides developers free hosting space and some basic application programming interfaces (APIs) to develop applications that can be integrated with Amazon's Web site.

Amazon.com's use of information systems to gain business intelligence has clearly facilitated the online retailer's phenomenal success.

After reading this chapter, you will be able to answer the following:

1. Why is data warehousing and mining a key element for gaining business intelligence within a company like Amazon.com?

2. How does Amazon.com learn from their customers and design its Web site accordingly?

3. What customer service and support capabilities are offered by Amazon.com that help to attract and retain customers?

Sources:

http://www.sas.com/success/amazon_personalization.html

http://news.com.com/2100-1017-237332.html

http://www.sas.com/images/email/c3456/2005_11_23.pdf

Decision-Making Levels of an Organization

Every organization is composed of decision-making levels, as illustrated in Figure 7.2. Each level of an organization has different responsibilities and, therefore, different informational needs. In this section, we describe each of these levels.

Operational Level

At the **operational level** of a firm, the routine, day-to-day business processes and interactions with customers occur. Information systems at this level are designed to automate repetitive activities, such as sales transaction processing, and to improve the efficiency of business processes and the customer interface. Managers at the operational level, such as foremen or supervisors, make day-to-day decisions that are highly structured and recurring. **Structured decisions** are those in which the procedures to follow for a given situation can be specified in advance. For example, a supervisor may decide when to reorder supplies or how best to allocate personnel for the completion of a project. Because structured decisions are relatively straightforward, they can be programmed directly into operational information systems so that they can be made with little or no human intervention. For example, an inventory management system for a shoe store in the mall could keep track of inventory and issue an order for additional inventory when levels drop below a specified level. Operational managers within the store would simply need to confirm with the inventory management system that the order for additional shoes was needed. Figure 7.3 summarizes the general characteristics of the operational level.

Managerial Level

At the **managerial level** of the organization, functional managers (e.g., marketing managers, finance managers, manufacturing managers, and human resource managers) focus on monitoring and controlling operational-level activities and providing information to higher levels of the organization (see Figure 7.3). Managers at this level, referred to as midlevel managers, focus on effectively utilizing and deploying organizational resources to achieve the strategic objectives of the organization. Midlevel managers typically focus on problems within a specific business function, such as marketing or finance. Here, the scope of the decision usually is contained within the business function, is moderately complex, and has a time horizon of a few days to a few months. For example, a marketing manager at Nike may decide how to allocate the advertising budget for the next business quarter or some other fixed time period.

FIGURE 7.2

Organizations are composed of levels, with each using information technology to automate activities or assist in decision making.

FIGURE 7.3

Different levels of an organization use different information systems to support different users, performing different business processes, with different objectives.

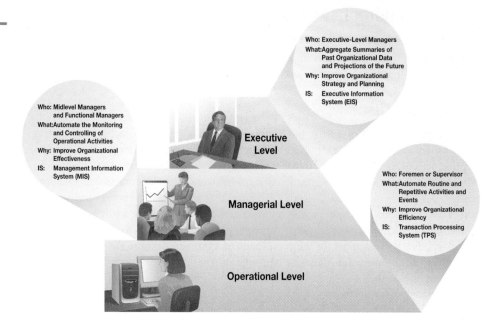

Managerial-level decision making is not nearly as structured or routine as operational-level decision making. Managerial-level decision making is referred to as semistructured decision making because solutions and problems are not clear-cut and often require judgment and expertise. For **semistructured decisions**, some procedures to follow for a given situation can be specified in advance but not to the extent where a specific recommendation can be made. For example, an information system could provide a production manager at Nike with summary information about sales forecasts for multiple product lines, inventory levels, and overall production capacity. The manager could use this information to create multiple production schedules. With these schedules, the manager could examine inventory levels and potential sales profitability, depending on the order in which manufacturing resources were used to produce each type of product.

Executive Level

At the **executive level** of the organization, managers focus on long-term strategic issues facing the organization, such as which products to produce, which countries to compete in, and what organizational strategy to follow (see Figure 7.3). Managers at this level include the president and chief executive officer (CEO), vice presidents, and possibly the board of directors and are referred to as "executives." Executive-level decisions deal with complex problems with broad and long-term ramifications for the organization. Executive-level decisions are referred to as unstructured decisions because the problems are relatively complex and nonroutine. In addition, executives must consider the ramifications of their decisions in terms of the overall organization. For **unstructured decisions**, few or no procedures to follow for a given situation can be specified in advance. For example, top managers may decide to develop a new product or discontinue an existing one. Such a decision may have vast, long-term effects on the organization's levels of employment and profitability. To assist executive-level decision making, information systems are used to obtain aggregate summaries of trends and projections of the future.

In summary, most organizations have three general levels: operational, managerial, and executive. Each level has unique activities and business processes, each requiring different types of information. The next section examines various types of information systems designed to support each organizational level.

Net Stats

The Growing Blogosphere

It's huge, and it's constantly growing, much like the puddle of slime in the old movie *The Blob*. It's the *blogosphere*—that segment of cyberspace where millions of students, professional journalists, company employees, and just plain ordinary people post their blogs. Blogs started out as smatterings of personal feelings, observations, likes, and dislikes—much like daily journals that contained anything a blogger felt like posting for others to read. That trend continues, but professional journalists, novelists, physi-

cians, professors, and others in various occupations have also joined the blogosphere to produce, perhaps, a more considered, educated, precise, and focused online journal (or not). Although the blogosphere is not the monster that will eat the Internet, it clearly is one of the fastest-growing phenomena in the digital world (see Figure 7.4).

Sources: Dave Sifry, "State of the Blogosphere...," Technorati (February 6, 2006), http://www.clickz.com/img/Weblogs_Cumulative_March2003_April2006.html

FIGURE 7.4

The growing blogosphere.

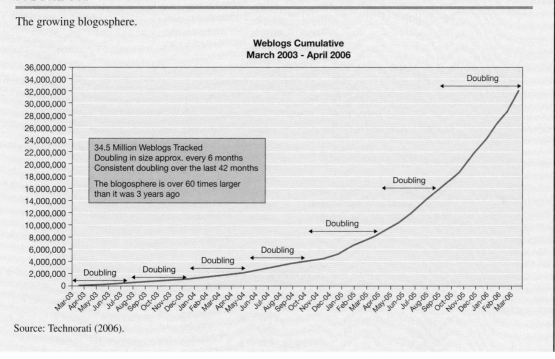

Source: Technorati (2006).

General Types of Information Systems

An easy way to understand how all information systems work is to use an input, process, and output model—the basic systems model (for a thorough discussion, see Checkland, 1981), which can be used to describe virtually all types of systems. As an example, Figure 7.5 shows elements of a payroll system decomposed into input, process, and output elements. The inputs to a payroll system include time cards and employee lists as well as wage and salary information. Processing transforms the inputs into outputs that include paychecks, management reports, and updated account balances. The remainder of this section uses the basic systems model to describe various information systems.

FIGURE 7.5

Payroll system shown as an instance of the basic systems model.

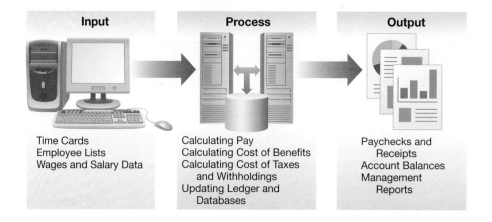

Transaction Processing Systems

Many organizations deal with repetitive activities. Grocery stores scan groceries at the checkout counter. Banks process checks drawn on customer accounts. Fast-food restaurants process customer orders. All these repetitive activities are examples of **transactions** that occur as a regular part of a business's day-to-day operations. A **transaction processing system (TPS)** is a special class of information system designed to process business events and transactions. Consequently, TPSs often reside close to customers, at the operational level of the organization (see Figure 7.3). The goal of transaction processing systems is to automate repetitive business processes within organizations to increase speed and accuracy and to lower the cost of processing each transaction—that is, to make the organization more efficient. Because TPSs are used to process large volumes of information, organizations have spent considerable resources designing them. A TPS can reduce or eliminate people from the process, thereby reducing transaction costs and reducing the likelihood of data entry errors. Examples of business processes supported by TPS include the following:

- Payroll processing
- Sales and order processing
- Inventory management

FIGURE 7.6

Architecture of a transaction processing system using the basic systems model.

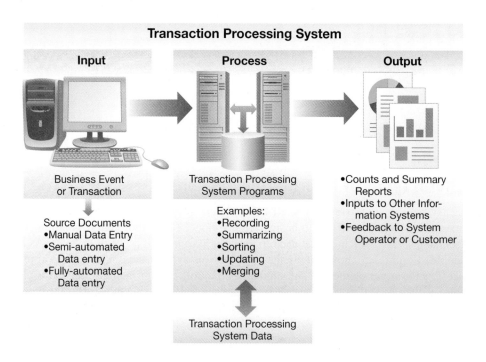

TABLE 7.1 Examples of Online and Batch Transaction Processing Systems

Online TPS	Batch TPS
University class registration processing	Students final grades processing
Airline reservation processing	Payroll processing
Concert/sporting event ticket reservation processing	Customer order processing (for example, insurance forms)
Grocery store checkout processing	Bank check processing

- Product purchasing, receiving, and shipping
- Accounts payable and receivable

Architecture of a TPS   The basic architecture of a TPS is shown in Figure 7.6 When a business transaction occurs, source documents describing the transaction are created. **Source documents**, paper or electronic, serve as a stimulus to a TPS from some external source. For example, when you fill out a driver's license application, it serves as a source document for a TPS that records and stores all licensed drivers in a state. Source documents can be processed as they are created—referred to as online processing—or they can be processed in batches—referred to as batch processing. **Online processing** of transactions provides immediate results to the system operator or customer. For example, an interactive class registration system that immediately notifies you of your success or failure to register for a class is an example of an online TPS. **Batch processing** of transactions occurs when transactions are collected and then processed together as a "batch" at some later time. Banks often use batch processing when reconciling checks drawn on customer accounts. Likewise, your university uses batch processing to process end-of-term grade reports—all inputs must be periodically processed in batches to calculate your grade-point average. Online processing is used when customers need immediate notification of the success or failure of a transaction. Batch processing is used when immediate notification is not needed or is not practical. Table 7.1 lists several examples of online and batch transaction processing systems. Additionally, as summarized in Table 7.2, information can be entered into a TPS in one of three ways: **manual data entry** (i.e., information entered by hand), **semiautomated data entry** (i.e., information entered using some type of data capture device), or **fully automated data entry** (i.e., information entered without human intervention).

The characteristics of a TPS are summarized in Table 7.3. Inputs to a TPS are business events or transactions. The processing activities of a TPS include recording, summarizing,

TABLE 7.2 Ways Information can be Entered into a Transaction Processing System

Data Entry Method	Description	Example
Manual	Having a person enter the source document information by hand.	When applying for a new driver's license, a clerk manually enters information about you into a driver's license recording system, often copying the information from a form that you filled out by hand.
Semiautomated	Capturing data using a device such as a grocery store checkout scanner to speed the entry and processing of the transaction.	When purchasing products online, your order goes directly to an order fulfillment system without any additional human intervention.
Fully automated	Computer-to-computer communication without any human intervention.	When the inventory of a car manufacturer falls below a certain level, the manufacturer's inventory system automatically notifies the supplier's system that more materials are needed.

TABLE 7.3 Characteristics of a Transaction Processing System

Inputs	Business events and transactions
Processing	Recording, summarizing, sorting, updating, merging
Outputs	Counts and summary reports of activity; inputs to other information systems; feedback to system operators or customers
Typical users	Operational personnel and supervisors

sorting, updating, and merging transaction information with organizational databases. Outputs from a TPS include summary reports, inputs to other systems, and operator notification of processing completion. People who are very close to day-to-day operations most often use TPSs. For example, a checkout clerk at the grocery store uses a TPS to record your purchases. Supervisors may review transaction summary reports to control inventory, to manage operations personnel, or to provide customer service. Additionally, inventory management systems may monitor transaction activity and use this information to manage inventory reordering. This is an example of the output from a TPS being the input to another system.

Information Systems Problems at the Tokyo Stock Exchange

As the Internet age marches on, it's becoming increasingly apparent that a business is only as solvent as its information systems are current. In fact, outdated information systems can cause unprecedented economic disasters.

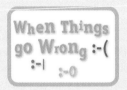

In December 2005, the Tokyo Stock Exchange, the second-largest stock exchange in the world, received an order to sell 610,000 shares of J-Com Co. stock for 1 yen (U.S.$0.009) per share. At that time, the newly listed company's stock was trading at 610,000 yen (U.S.$5,310) per share, and 610,000 shares were 40 times more than the number of shares that had been issued. The order should have been to sell one share, but a software glitch garbled the transaction, and the order could not be canceled even after the mistake was discovered. Misuho Securities Co. lost billions of yen (approximately U.S.$350 million) as a result of the erroneous transaction.

The Tokyo Stock Exchange's software woes continued in January 2006, when it was forced to end trading early because its computer system, installed in 1999, was close to capacity. The system was designed to handle 4.5 million trades daily, and just after 2:00 P.M. on January 18, the number of trades had reached 4 million, forcing the TSE to shut down. The heavy trading on that day came as the result of published allegations of wrongdoing at Livedoor Co., a major Japanese Internet portal, and lower profit announcements at Yahoo! and Intel. Trading had been steadily increasing, however, because of TSE's heavily promoting online trading, despite the fact that capacity was limited by outdated information systems.

Even before the trading error in December, the TSE was experiencing difficulty with its software. In November 2005, trading was suspended when an erroneously installed software patch caused the exchange's computer system to crash. System vendor Fujitsu Limited took responsibility for that error.

Fearful that the entire Japanese economy would suffer, after the January shutdown, TSE announced plans to immediately increase trade capacity to 5 million per day—the same number handled by the New York Stock Exchange's computer system. By the end of 2006, the TSE hoped to have an information system in place that would handle 7 million to 8 million trades and 14 million orders in a day.

Clearly, when outdated information systems can affect a business's solvency and a nation's economy, it behooves IT managers to keep up with changing technology.

Sources: Martyn Williams, "Tokyo Stock Exchange Faces More IT Worries," *Computerworld* (January 18, 2006), http://www.computerworld.com/managementtopics/management/story/0,10801,107828,00.html
Justin McCurry, "Tokyo Stock Exchange Acts to Avoid New Debacle," *The Guardian* (January 21, 2006), http:// business.guardian.co.uk/story/0,1691603,00.html

Management Information Systems

Management information system (MIS) is a term with two meanings. It describes the field of study that encompasses the development, use, management, and study of computer-based information systems in organizations. It also refers to a specific type of information system that is used to produce **reports** (i.e., organized compilations of data from a database) to support the ongoing, recurring business processes associated with managing an entire business or a functional area within a business. Such reports usually take the form of either **scheduled reports** (i.e., reports produced at predefined intervals) or **ad hoc reports** (i.e., reports created due to unplanned information requests). Consequently, an MIS often resides at the managerial level of the organization, as shown in Figure 7.3. We will discuss the reports produced by an MIS later in this section.

Whereas TPSs automate repetitive information-processing activities to increase efficiency, an MIS helps midlevel managers make more effective decisions. MISs are designed to get the right information to the right people in the right format at the right time to help them make better decisions. MISs can be found throughout the organization. For example, a marketing manager for Nike may have an MIS that contrasts sales revenue and marketing expenses by geographic region so that he or she can better understand how regional marketing for the "Tiger Woods Golf" promotions are performing. Examples of the types of business processes supported by MISs include the following:

- Sales forecasting
- Financial management and forecasting
- Manufacturing planning and scheduling
- Inventory management and planning
- Advertising and product pricing

Architecture of an MIS The basic architecture of an MIS is shown in Figure 7.7. At regular intervals, managers need to review summary information of some organizational activity. For example, a sales manager at a Ford dealership may review the weekly performance of all his sales staff. To aid his review, an MIS summarizes the total sales volume of each salesperson in a report. This report may provide a plethora of information about each person, including the following:

- What are this salesperson's year-to-date sales totals?
- How do this year's sales figures compare with last year's?

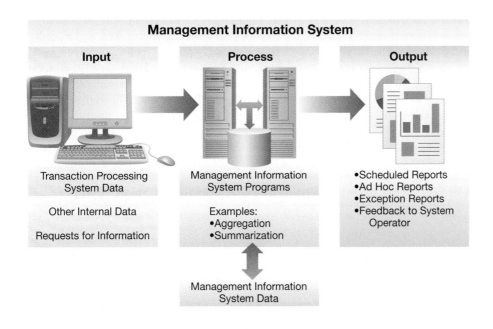

FIGURE 7.7

Architecture of a management information system using the basic systems model.

TABLE 7.4 Common Reports Produced by Management Information Systems

Report	Description
Scheduled reports	Reports produced at predefined intervals—daily, weekly, or monthly—to support routine decisions
Key-indicator reports	Reports that provide a summary of critical information on a recurring schedule
Exception reports	Reports that highlight situations that are out of the normal range
Drill-down reports	Reports providing greater detail as to why a key indicator is not at an appropriate level or an exception occurred
Ad hoc reports	Reports providing unplanned information requests to support a nonroutine decision

- What is the average amount per sale?
- How do sales change by the day of the week?

Imagine the difficulty of producing these weekly reports manually for an organization that has 50 salespeople, 500 salespeople, or even 5,000 salespeople! It would be very difficult if not impossible to create these detailed reports on each salesperson without an MIS. In addition to scheduled and ad hoc reports, an MIS typically also produces **drill-down reports**, **exception reports**, and **key-indicator reports** (see Table 7.4).

The characteristics of an MIS are summarized in Table 7.5. In general, inputs to an MIS are transaction processing data produced by a TPS, other internal data (such as sales promotion expenses), and ad hoc requests for special reports or summaries. The processing aspect of an MIS focuses on data aggregation and summary. Outputs are formatted reports that provide scheduled and nonrecurring information to midlevel managers. For example, a store manager can use an MIS to review sales information to identify products that are not selling and are in need of special promotion.

Executive Information Systems

In addition to operational personnel and midlevel managers, top-level managers or executives can use information technology to support day-to-day business processes such as cash and investment management, resource allocation, and contract negotiation. An information system designed to support the highest organizational managers is called an **executive information system (EIS)** (see Figure 7.3). An EIS (sometimes referred to as an *executive support system*) consists of technology (hardware, software, data, and procedures) and the people needed to consolidate information and support users to assist executive-level decision making. An EIS provides information to executives in a highly aggregated form so that they can scan information quickly for trends and anomalies. For example, executives may track various market conditions—such as the Dow Jones Industrial Average—to assist in making investment decisions. Although EISs are not as widely used as other types of information systems, this trend is rapidly changing because more and more executives are becoming comfortable with information technology and because an EIS can provide

TABLE 7.5 Characteristics of a Management Information System

Inputs	Transaction processing data and other internal data; scheduled and ad-hoc requests for information
Processing	Aggregation and summary of data
Outputs	Scheduled, exception, and ad-hoc reports; feedback to system operator
Typical Users	Midlevel managers

Brief Case ⊙

Ministry of Sound

Twenty years ago, the Ministry of Sound was a small dance club in London. Today, that once small club is a well-known brand in dance culture and one of the largest entertainment companies in the United Kingdom. The club's expansion began in the 1990s when its house music attracted a new generation of fans. Today, the Ministry of Sound's global dance franchise includes a record label, licensed products, tours, clubs, events, and—cell phones. Ministry of Sound has teamed up with 3 Mobile in the United Kingdom to offer a branded video phone. The phone not only aesthetically captures the dance culture but also is loaded with Ministry of Sound music, and users can load new music and video.

Ministry of Sound's product and service lines were not always the envy of the entertainment industry. "The Ministry" once had problems with its information systems implementation strategy and especially with data management as the company grew. Data management problems eventually led to customer dissatisfaction and lost sales.

Specifically, lack of integration across the company's business units caused problems with simple reporting functions. For example, customers were entered into several different databases, which meant that when a customer changed addresses, all databases had to reflect the change. Quite frequently, not all databases were changed correctly, and the result was duplicate mailings, incorrect market and sales information, and sometimes a complete loss of customer information.

The Ministry of Sound turned to information systems consultants to help with their data management problems. The key to this process was to consolidate the various databases so that every business unit could update, access, and retrieve customer information from a single source. Existing databases were reorganized through elimination of duplicate records, correcting data anomalies, standardizing data attributes, and incorporating sales and customer data from the company's e-commerce site. The data reorganization tasks were vital to retaining customer information it had taken the Ministry of Sound 15 years to collect (see Technology Briefing 3—Database Management).

Through use of a central data warehouse, the Ministry of Sound was able to standardize the data for future data mining. These information systems changes paved the way for the Ministry of Sound's global expansion.

Questions

1. If you were the manager of the Ministry of Sound Web site, specifically describe the reports you would need to effectively manage the site.
2. Given that the Ministry of Sound has ample data on its customers' preferences, describe a new highly personalized product offering that would appeal to their customers.

Sources: www.ministryofsound.com

http://www.esato.com/news/article.php/id=722

http://www.brandrepublic.com/bulletins/media/article/538394/ministry-snaps-gmgs-hed-kandi-enterprise-records/

http://members.microsoft.com/customerevidence/search/evidencedetails.aspx?evidenceid=13636&languageid=1

---

substantial benefits to the executive. Business processes supported by an EIS include the following:

- Executive-level decision making
- Long-range and strategic planning
- Monitoring of internal and external events and resources
- Crisis management
- Staffing and labor relations

An EIS can deliver both "soft" and "hard" data to the executive decision maker. **Soft data** include textual news stories or other nonanalytical information. **Hard data** include facts and numbers. While lower-level TPSs and MISs generate much of the hard data provided by an EIS, providing timely soft information to executive decision makers has been much more of a challenge. For example, deciding how to get the late-breaking news stories and information to the system in a format consistent with the EIS philosophy was a significant challenge to organizations. Many investment organizations, for example, subscribe to online services such as Dow Jones as a source for their stock market data. However, executives typically want to view only data that are aggregated and summarized in a user-friendly format. To get the right information into the hands of the executives, personnel or specially designed systems select appropriate information and translate the information into a user-friendly format.

The Internet has made it much easier to gather soft data to support executive decision making. The use of numerous Web-based news portals such as FOXNews.com, CNN.com, ABCNews.com, and MSNBC.com allow users to easily customize news content so that assistants can quickly summarize and evaluate information for viewing by executives. In addition, online streaming media—video and audio—is radically changing how many executives gain soft information. Various subscription-based services from RealNetworks, Yahoo!, CNN, and others provide customized content on almost any subject or industry, virtually as it hits the newswires. Figure 7.8 shows an example of the range of content available from RealNetworks. Two very powerful features of these services make them particularly attractive for gathering soft data. First, these services can be customized to filter information so that they deliver only the information deemed relevant to the executive. For example, if an executive is interested in the software, Internet/online, and telecommunications industries, these industries can be specifically tracked. Second, these services will deliver this information to virtually any device, literally tracking you until you receive the message. For example, they can be customized so that important information is sent to a computer (using e-mail, instant messaging, or a Web link), a cell phone (via voice or text message), or a blackberry. The goal is to get the right information to a customer, using the most convenient medium.

FIGURE 7.8

RealNetworks provides a broad range of content that can be integrated into applications or sent to a variety of devices.

Key Enabler

Nanotubes

By now you probably recognize "nano" as a preface indicating that something is beyond small—it's microscopic. Nanotechnology, for instance, refers to a field of science the goal of which is to control individual atoms and molecules to create computer chips and other devices that are thousands of times smaller than current technologies permit. Nanotechnologists work at the level of the nanoscale—8 to 10 atoms span 1 nanometer (nm). The human hair is approximately 70,000 to 80,000 nm thick.

A "nanotube," you can surmise, is a microscopic tube. Nanotubes, also called buckytubes, are constructed of a sequence of carbon 60 (C60) atoms. They are extremely strong and resilient and are pure conductors of electricity. Nanotubes are used in resistors, capacitors, inductors, diodes, and transistors.

The C60 used to create nanotubes is a new, pure form of carbon first synthesized in the early 1980s. Just two other pure forms of carbon exist in nature—graphite, the slippery material used in pencils, and diamonds. Since this third form of pure carbon consists of C60 molecules linked together to form a ball much like a microscopic soccer ball, it was called a "buckyball," after R. Buckminster Fuller, who designed the first geodesic dome (think Epcot Center at Disney World in Orlando, Florida).

The buckyball is the only molecule of a single atom that forms a hollow sphere. Furthermore, it spins at over 100 million times per second and can bounce back undamaged from high-speed collisions. Compressed to 70 percent of its original size, the buckyball is harder than diamonds.

Nanotubes are similar to buckyballs but are cylindrical instead of spherical in shape. Nanotubes are formed from one single layer of graphite rolled into a tube (single walled) or from two or more layers of graphite rolled inside one another (double walled). Nanotubes form carbon fibers that share the characteristics of buckyballs described previously—super-strength and resilience—and are excellent conductors of electricity. NASA has led the field in developing uses for nanotubes in the space program, and practical uses in many fields have evolved from that research. Not only do nanotubes have the potential to revolutionize the storage and transport of energy, but they can be used to build stronger, lighter materials for use in everything from automobiles to the space shuttle to drug delivery systems and diagnostic equipment in medicine and more.

Sources: "The Buckyball," http://www.insite.com.br/rodrigo/bucky/buckyball.txt

"Nanotube," *Webopedia*, http://webopedia.com/TERM/n/nanotube.html

"Nanotubes and Buckyballs," *Nanotechnology News* (June 15, 2006), http://www.nanotech-now.com/nanotube-buckyball-sites.htm

http://en.wikipedia.org/wiki/Nanotubes

http://www.personal.rdg.ac.uk/~scsharip/tubes.htm

Architecture of an EIS The architecture of an EIS is shown in Figure 7.9. Inputs to an EIS are all internal data sources and systems, external data sources such as Dow Jones and CNN that contain information on competitors, financial markets, news (local, national, and international), and any other information the executive deems important in making day-to-day decisions. An EIS could "overload" the executive with too much information from too many sources. Systems designers use filtering software to customize the EIS so that only key information is provided, in its most effective form, to executives. Also, system designers provide output information to executives in a highly aggregated form, often using graphical icons to make selections and bar and line charts to summarize data, trends, and simulations. Multiple monitors are often used to display the information so that it is easier to view. The characteristics of an EIS are summarized in Table 7.6.

Digital Dashboards Both managers and executives view summary information to make decisions. Such summary information is often presented in the form of a **digital dashboard** (see Figure 7.10). Within systems like an EIS, digital dashboards deliver information, possibly from multiple sources, to provide warnings, action notices, and

FIGURE 7.9

Architecture of an executive
information system using the
basic systems model.

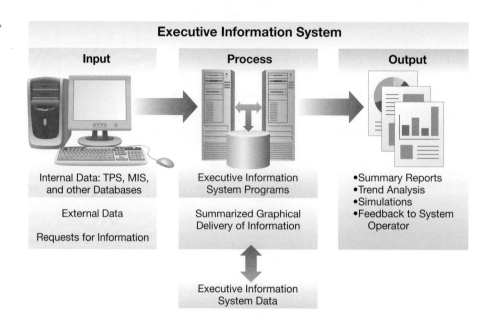

FIGURE 7.9

Architecture of an executive
information system using the
basic systems model.

TABLE 7.6 Characteristics of an Executive Information System

Inputs	Aggregate internal and external data
Processing	Summarizing, graphical interpreting
Outputs	Summary reports, trends, and simulations; feedback to system operator
Typical Users	Executive-level managers

summaries of business conditions. Although data are typically provided in a very
highly aggregated form, the executive also has the capability to drill down and see the
details if necessary. For example, suppose a digital dashboard within an EIS
summarizes employee absenteeism, and the system shows that today's numbers are
significantly higher than normal. The executive can see this information in a running

FIGURE 7.10

A digital dashboard.

Source: http://www.dundas.com/
Dashboards/index.aspx?.

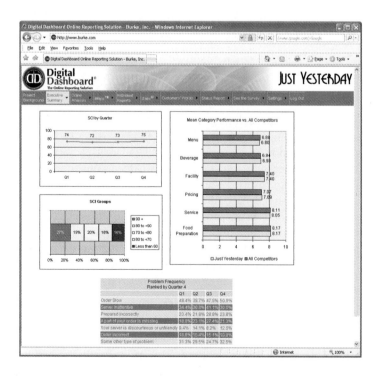

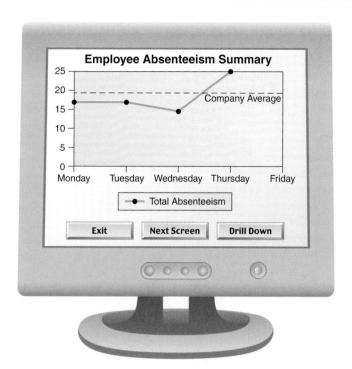

FIGURE 7.11

A digital dashboard showing a
total employee absenteeism
line chart.

line chart, as illustrated in Figure 7.11. If the executive wants to understand why
absenteeism is so high, a selection on the screen can provide the details behind the
aggregate numbers, as shown in Figure 7.12. By drilling down into the data, the
executive can see that the spike in absenteeism was centered in the manufacturing area.
Also, the digital dashboard can connect the data in the system to the organization's
internal communication systems (e.g., electronic or voice mail) so that the executive
can quickly send a message to the appropriate managers to discuss solutions to the
problem discovered in the drill-down.

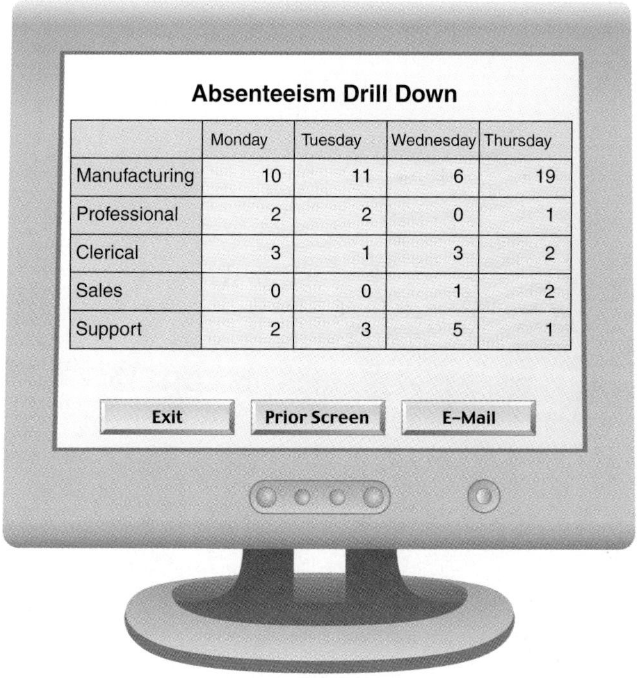

Absenteeism Drill Down

	Monday	Tuesday	Wednesday	Thursday
Manufacturing	10	11	6	19
Professional	2	2	0	1
Clerical	3	1	3	2
Sales	0	0	1	2
Support	2	3	5	1

Exit   Prior Screen   E–Mail

FIGURE 7.12

Drill-down numbers for
employee absenteeism.

Information Systems That Span Organizational Boundaries

The preceding section examined three general classes of information systems within specific hierarchical levels in the organization. There are also systems that span all levels of the organization (see Figure 7.13). Seven types of boundary-spanning systems are the following:

- Decision support systems
- Intelligent systems
- Data mining and visualization systems
- Office automation systems
- Collaboration technologies
- Knowledge management systems
- Functional area information systems

This section describes each of these in more detail. Systems designed to support the business processes that go outside the boundaries of an organization are examined in Chapter 8.

Decision Support Systems

A **decision support system (DSS)** is a special-purpose information system designed to support organizational decision making. A DSS is designed to support the decision making related to a particular recurring problem in the organization through the combination of hardware, software, data, and procedures. DSSs are typically used by managerial-level employees to help them solve semistructured problems such as sales and resource forecasting, yet a DSS can be used to support decisions at virtually all levels of the organization. With a DSS, the manager uses decision analysis tools such as Microsoft Excel—the most commonly used DSS environment—to either analyze or create meaningful information to support the decision making related to nonroutine problems. A DSS is designed to be an "interactive" decision aid, whereas the systems described previously—TPS, MIS, and EIS—primarily present the outputs from the system in a passive way.

FIGURE 7.13

Organizational boundary-spanning information systems.

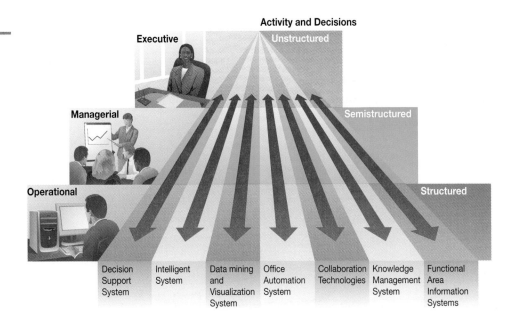

A DSS augments human decision-making performance and problem solving by enabling users to examine alternative solutions to a problem via "what-if" analyses. A **what-if analysis** allows you to make hypothetical changes to the data associated with a problem (e.g., loan duration or interest rate) and observe how these changes influence the results. For example, a cash manager for a bank could examine what-if scenarios of the effect of various interest rates on cash availability. Results are displayed in both textual and graphical formats.

Architecture of a DSS Like the architecture of all systems, a DSS consists of input, process, and output components as illustrated in Figure 7.14 (Sprague, 1980). Within the process component, models and data are utilized. The DSS uses **models** to manipulate data. For example, if you have some historic sales data, you can use many different types of models to create a forecast of future sales. One technique is to take an average of the past sales. The formula you would use to calculate the average is the model. A more complicated forecasting model might use time-series analysis or linear regression. See Table 7.7 for a summary of the models used to support decision making in organizations. Data for the DSS can come from many sources, including a TPS or an MIS. The user interface is the way in which the DSS interacts with the user by collecting inputs and displaying output and results.

Table 7.8 summarizes the characteristics of a DSS. Inputs are data and models. Processing supports the merging of data with models so that decision makers can examine alternative solution scenarios. Outputs are graphs and textual reports. The next section discusses an example of a DSS that you might use at home.

Using a DSS to Buy a Car When you buy a new car, you must decide how to pay for it. Will you pay cash? Will you finance most or part of the purchase price? Organizations face the same decisions every day when performing common business processes, such as purchasing supplies, raw materials, and capital equipment: Should they pay cash or finance these purchases? What information do they need to make this decision? The tools that organizations use are relatively simple and readily available to you. After going through the car purchasing example, you will have a better understanding of how organizations use decision support technology to improve the business intelligence when making day-to-day decisions.

Assume that the selling price of the car you decided to purchase is $22,500 and that you make a $2,500 down payment, leaving you with a monthly payment of about $400.

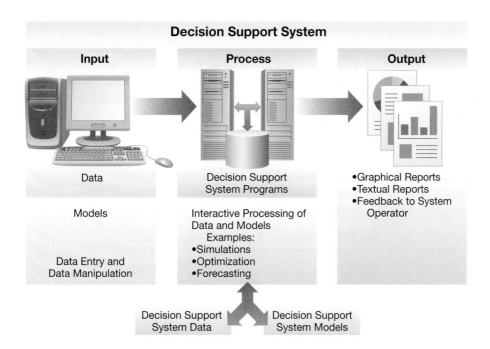

Decision Support System

Input	Process	Output

Data

Models

Data Entry and Data Manipulation

Decision Support System Programs

Interactive Processing of Data and Models
Examples:
•Simulations
•Optimization
•Forecasting

•Graphical Reports
•Textual Reports
•Feedback to System Operator

Decision Support System Data   Decision Support System Models

FIGURE 7.14

Architecture of a decision support system using the basic systems model.

TABLE 7.7 Common DSS Models for Specific Organizational Areas

Area	Common DSS Models
Accounting	Cost analysis, discriminant analysis, break-even analysis, auditing, tax computation and analysis, depreciation methods, budgeting
Corporate Level	Corporate planning, venture analysis, mergers and acquisitions
Finance	Discounted cash flow analysis, return on investment, buy or lease, capital budgeting, bond refinancing, stock portfolio management, compound interest, after-tax yield, foreign exchange values
Marketing	Product demand forecast, advertising strategy analysis, pricing strategies, market share analysis, sales growth evaluation, sales performance
Human Resources	Labor negotiations, labor market analysis, personnel skills assessment, employee business expense, fringe benefit computations, payroll and deductions
Production	Product design, production scheduling, transportation analysis, product-mix, inventory level, quality control, plant location, material allocation, maintenance analysis, machine replacement, job assignment, material requirements planning
Management Science	Linear programming, decision trees, simulation, project evaluation and planning, queuing, dynamic programming, network analysis
Statistics	Regression and correlation analysis, exponential smoothing, sampling, time-series analysis, hypothesis testing

TABLE 7.8 Characteristics of a Decision Support System

Inputs	Data and models; data entry and data manipulation commands (via user interface)
Processing	Interactive processing of data and models; simulations, optimization, forecasts
Outputs	Graphs and textual reports; feedback to system operator (via user interface)
Typical Users	Midlevel managers (although a DSS could be used at any level of the organization)

You want to see how different financing options from your credit union might influence your monthly payments. As you can see from Table 7.9, interest rates vary depending on the duration of your loan—lower rates for a shorter duration, higher rates for a longer duration. You now have all the information you need to analyze your financing options.

To conduct this analysis, you can use Microsoft Excel's loan analysis template (Excel uses the term "template" to refer to models). In this template, you enter the loan amount, annual interest rate, and length of the loan, as shown in Figure 7.15. With this information, the loan analysis DSS automatically calculates your monthly payment, the total amount paid, and the amount of interest paid over the life of the loan. You can change any of the input amounts to examine what-if scenarios—"What if I finance the loan over four years rather than five?" This is exactly how your college or university examines its financing options when it makes capital equipment purchases. Using this DSS tool, you decide to purchase your new vehicle over five years (see Table 7.10 for a loan analysis summary).

TABLE 7.9 Interest Rates and Loan Duration

Interest Rate	Loan Duration
4% per year	3 years
6% per year	4 years
8% per year	5 years

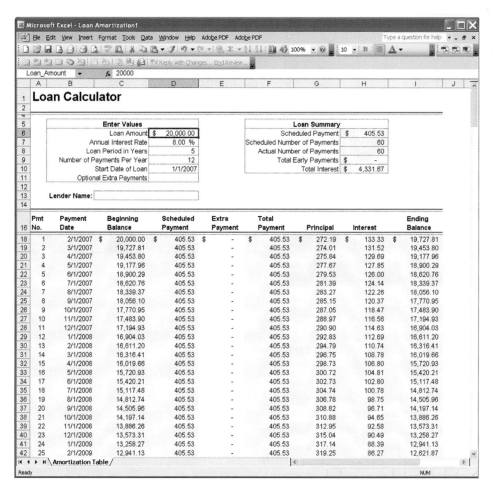

FIGURE 7.15

Loan analysis template in Microsoft Excel.

The next section discusses intelligent systems, a class of organizational information systems that is closely related to DSSs.

Intelligent Systems

Artificial intelligence (AI) is the science of enabling information technologies—software, hardware, networks, and so on—to simulate human intelligence, such as reasoning and learning, as well as gaining sensing capabilities, such as seeing, hearing, walking, talking, and feeling. AI has had a strong connection to science fiction writers where AI-enabled technologies aid humans (e.g., Mr. Data in *Star Trek: The Next Generation*) or attempt world domination (e.g., *The Matrix*) (Figure 7.16). The current reality of AI is that it is lagging far behind the imagination of most science fiction writers, but, nevertheless, great strides have been made. Most notably, the developments of several types of intelligent systems are having great successes for a variety of applications. An **intelligent system**—comprised of sensors, software, and computers embedded in machines and devices—emulates and enhances human capabilities. Intelligent systems are having

TABLE 7.10 Loan Analysis Summary

Interest Rate	Loan Duration	Monthly Payment	Total Paid	Total Interest	Feasible Payment
4% per year	3 years	$590.48	$21,257.27	$1,257.27	No
6% per year	4 years	$488.26	$23,436.41	$3,436.41	No
8% per year	5 years	$405.53	$24,331.67	$4,331.67	Yes

FIGURE 7.16

Artificial intelligence in the real world lags behind the imagination of science fiction writers.

Source: http://world.honda.com/ ASIMO/.

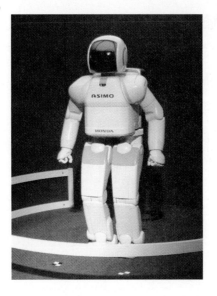

tremendous impacts in a variety of areas, including banking and financial management, medicine, engineering, and the military. Three types of intelligent systems—expert systems, neural networks, and intelligent agents—are particularly relevant in business contexts and are discussed next.

Expert Systems   An **expert system (ES)** is a type of intelligent system that uses reasoning methods based on knowledge about a specific problem domain in order to provide advice, much like a human expert. ESs are used to mimic human expertise by manipulating knowledge (understanding acquired through experience and extensive learning) rather than simply manipulating information (for more information, see Turban, Aronson, and Liang, 2005). Human knowledge can be represented in an ES by facts and rules about a problem coded in a form that can be manipulated by a computer. When you use an ES, the system asks you a series of questions, much as a human expert would. It continues to ask questions, and each new question is determined by your response to the preceding question. The ES matches the responses with the defined facts and rules until the responses point the system to a solution. A **rule** is a way of encoding knowledge, such as a recommendation, after collecting information from a user. Rules are typically expressed using an "if-then" format. For example, a rule in an expert system for assisting with decisions related to the approval of automobile loans for individuals could be represented as follows: *If* personal income is $50,000 or more, *then* approve the loan.

FUZZY LOGIC.   Given that most experts make decisions with limited information as well as use general categories of information when making judgments, researchers have developed **fuzzy logic** to broaden the capabilities of ESs and other intelligent systems. Specifically, fuzzy logic allows ES rules to be represented using approximations or subjective values in order to handle situations where information about a problem is incomplete. For example, a loan officer when assessing a customer's loan application may generally categorize some of the customer's financial information, such as income and debt level, as high, moderate, or low rather than using precise amounts. In addition to numerous business applications, fuzzy logic is used to better control antilock braking systems and household appliances as well as when making medical diagnoses or filtering offensive language in chat rooms (see Figure 7.17).

The most difficult part of building an ES is acquiring the knowledge from the expert and gathering and compiling it into a consistent and complete form capable of making recommendations. ESs are used when expertise for a particular problem is rare or expensive, such as in the case of a complex machine repair or medical diagnosis. Using fuzzy logic, ESs are also utilized when knowledge about a problem is incomplete.

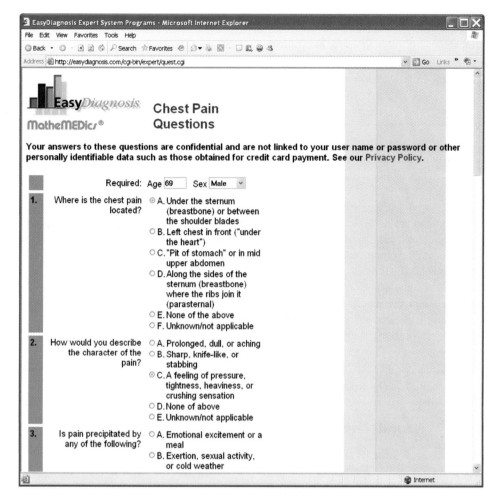

FIGURE 7.17

Expert system to make a medical recommendation.

ARCHITECTURE OF AN EXPERT SYSTEM. As with other information systems, the architecture of an ES (and other intelligent systems) can be described using the basic systems model (see Figure 7.18). Inputs to the system are questions and answers from the user. Processing is the matching of user questions and answers to information in the knowledge base. The processing in an expert system is called **inferencing**, which consists of matching facts and rules, determining the sequence of questions presented to the user,

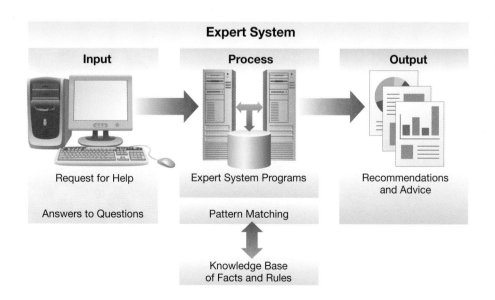

FIGURE 7.18

Architecture of an expert system using the basic systems model.

TABLE 7.11 Characteristics of an Expert System

Inputs	Request for help, answers to questions
Processing	Pattern matching and inferencing
Outputs	Recommendation or advice
Typical Users	Midlevel managers (although an expert system could be used at any level of the organization)

and drawing a conclusion. The output from an ES is a recommendation. The general characteristics of an ES are summarized in Table 7.11.

Neural Network System A **neural network** attempts to approximate the functioning of the human brain. Typically, a neural network is *trained* by having it categorize a large database of past information for common patterns. Once these patterns are established, new data can be compared to these learned patterns and conclusions drawn. For example, many financial institutions use neural network systems to analyze loan applications. These systems compare a person's loan application data with the neural network containing the *intelligence* of the success and failure of countless prior loans, ultimately making a loan acceptance (or rejection) recommendation (see Figure 7.19).

FIGURE 7.19

Neural networks approximate the functioning of the brain by creating common patterns in data and then compare new data to learned patterns to make a recommendation.

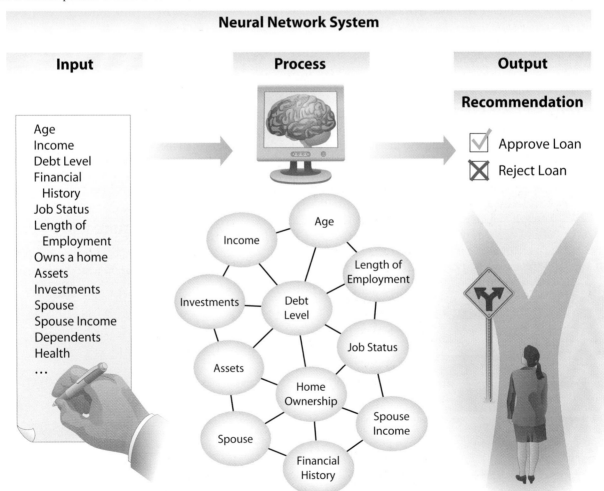

Intelligent Agent Systems An **intelligent agent**, or simply *an agent* (also called a **bot**—short for "software robot"), is a program that works in the background to provide some service when a specific event occurs. There are several types of agents for use in a broad range of contexts, including the following:

1. **Buyer Agents (Shopping Bots)** Agents that search to find the best price for a particular product you wish to purchase
2. **User Agents**. Agents that automatically perform a task for a user, such as automatically sending a report at the first of the month, assembling customized news, or filling out a Web form with routine information
3. **Monitoring and Sensing Agents**. Agents that keep track of key information such as inventory levels or competitors' prices, notifying the user when conditions change
4. **Data-Mining Agents**. Agents that continuously analyze large data warehouses to detect changes deemed important by a user, sending a notification when such changes occur
5. **Web crawlers** Agents that continuously browse the Web for specific information (e.g., used by search engines)—also known as **Web spiders**
6. **Destructive Agents**. Malicious agents designed by spammers and other Internet attackers to farm e-mail addresses off Web sites or deposit spyware on machines

In sum, there are ongoing developments to make information systems *smarter* so that organizational decision makers gain business intelligence. Although systems such as ESs, neural networks, and intelligent agents have yet to realize the imagination of science fiction writers, they have taken great strides in helping information systems better support business decision making.

Data-Mining and Visualization Systems

Data mining, as described in Chapter 4—Managing the Information Systems Infrastructure, refers to methods for better analyzing vast data warehouses to better understand customers, products, markets, or any other aspect of a business for which data have been captured. Data mining applies sophisticated statistical techniques to perform what-if analyses, to make predictions, and to facilitate decision making. Data-mining capabilities can be embedded into a broad range of managerial, executive, and functional area information systems (see the following discussion) as well as within decision support and intelligent systems. Results for these analyses can be provided on digital dashboards, paper reports, Web portals, e-mail alerts (using monitoring or data-mining agents), and mobile devices as well as a variety of information systems (see Figure 7.20).

In addition to performing complex analyses of vast amounts of data, these systems also have the ability to provide powerful visualizations of this data. Specifically, **visualization** refers to the display of complex data relationships using a variety of graphical methods. For example, Figure 7.21 shows the visualization of a massive weather system approaching the east coast of the United States. Once represented visually, analysts can perform what-if analyses to better forecast the locations and magnitude of the storm in order to better execute evacuation and recovery plans. In similar ways, organizations around the world are utilizing visualization technologies to enhance business intelligence.

A variation of data mining is text mining. **Text mining** refers to analytical techniques for extracting information from textual documents. As networking and processing speeds continue to increase, creative analytical approaches are being developed to gain business intelligence from sources previously not possible. Text mining can be applied to a variety of documents, from Web sites to transcripts, customer calls, and student college applications. For example, eBay could use text mining to analyze distinct groups of vendors according to their textual profiles rather than just product offerings, volume, and other analytics common within data-mining applications.

To extract information from the Internet, for example, a web crawler would gather sites and documents that matched some prespecified criteria and place this information in a massive document warehouse. Once collected, the text-mining system would apply a variety of analytical techniques to produce reports that analysts could review to gain additional insights beyond what is typically gained using data-mining analytics alone (see Figure 7.22).

FIGURE 7.20

Data-mining results can be delivered to users in a variety of ways.

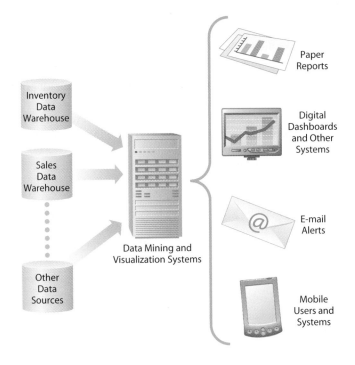

Office Automation Systems

The **office automation system (OAS)** is the third type of system that spans organizational levels. OASs are a collection of software and hardware for developing documents, scheduling resources, and communicating. Document development tools include word processing and desktop publishing software as well as the hardware for printing and producing documents. Scheduling tools include electronic calendars that help manage human and other resources, such as equipment and rooms. For example, "smart" electronic calendars can examine multiple schedules to find the first opportunity when all

FIGURE 7.21

Visualization is the display of complex data relationships using a variety of graphical methods.

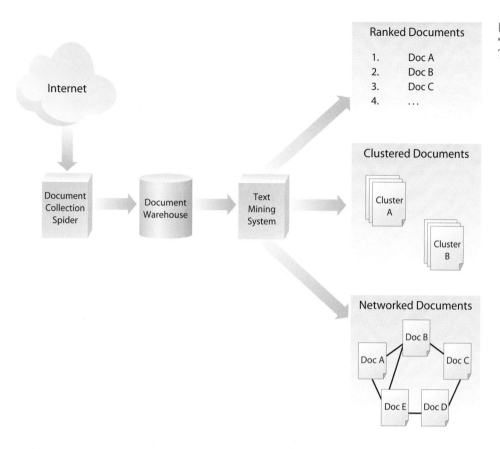

FIGURE 7.22

Text mining the Internet.

resources (people, rooms, and equipment) are available. Communication technologies include electronic mail, voice mail, fax, videoconferencing, and groupware. Examples of the types of business processes supported by an OAS include the following:

- Communication and scheduling
- Document preparation
- Analysis and merging of data
- Consolidation of information

Architecture of an Office Automation System The architecture of an OAS is shown in Figure 7.23. The inputs to an OAS are documents, schedules, and data. The processing of this information involves storing, merging, calculating, and transporting these data. Outputs include messages, reports, and schedules. The general characteristics of an OAS are summarized in Table 7.12.

Collaboration Technologies

To be competitive, organizations constantly need to bring together the right combinations of people who have the appropriate set of knowledge, skills, information, and authority to solve problems quickly and easily. Traditionally, organizations have used task forces, which are temporary work groups with a finite task and life cycle, to solve problems that cannot be solved well by existing work groups. Unfortunately, traditional task forces, like traditional organizational structures, cannot always solve problems quickly. Structure and logistical problems often get in the way of people trying to get things done quickly.

Organizations need flexible teams that can be assembled quickly and can solve problems effectively and efficiently. Time is of the essence. Membership on these **virtual teams** is fluid, with teams forming and disbanding as needed, with team size fluctuating as necessary, and with team members coming and going as they are needed. Employees may, at times, find themselves on multiple teams, and the life of a team may be very short. In

FIGURE 7.23

Architecture of an office
automation system using the
basic systems model.

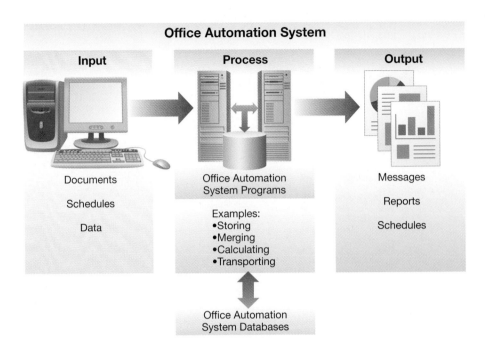

addition, team members must have easy, flexible access to other team members, meeting contexts, and information. Think of these virtual teams as dynamic task forces.

Traditional office technologies, such as telephones or emails, are of some use to members of virtual teams but are not well suited to support the types of collaboration described previously. Telephones and pagers are not useful for rich, rapid, multiple-person team collaboration. This technology is best suited for person-to-person communication. E-mail is a useful technology for teams, but it does not provide the structure needed for effective multiperson interactive problem solving. Companies need technologies that enable team members to interact through a set of media either at the same place and time or at different times and in different locations, with structure to aid in interactive problem solving and access to software tools and information. A number of technologies, described in the following sections, fit the bill.

Videoconferencing In the 1960s, at Disneyland and other theme parks and special events, the picturephone was first being demonstrated to large audiences. The phone companies estimated that we would be able to see a live picture with our phone calls in the near future. It took another 30 years, but that prediction has come true within many organizations. Many organizations are conducting **videoconferencing** to replace traditional meetings, using either desktop videoconferencing or dedicated videoconferencing systems that can cost from a few thousand dollars up to $500,000 (see Figure 7.24).

Desktop Videoconferencing **Desktop videoconferencing** has been enabled by the growing power of processors powering personal computers and faster Internet connections. A desktop videoconferencing system usually comprises a fast personal computer, a

TABLE 7.12 Characteristics of an Office Automation System

Inputs	Documents, schedules, data
Processing	Storing, merging, calculating, transporting
Outputs	Messages, reports, schedules
Typical Users	All organizational personnel

FIGURE 7.24

Polycom's Executive Collection videoconferencing unit with dual 50-inch displays.

Photo courtesy of Polycom, Inc. ©2004.

Web cam (i.e., a small camera, often with fixed focus, though zooming and panning features are available) (see Figure 7.25), a speaker telephone or separate microphone, videoconferencing software (e.g., Skype, Yahoo! Messenger, or Windows Live Messenger), and a high-speed Internet connection.

Future of Desktop Videoconferencing As computer components and fast connections to the Internet get less and less expensive, you can expect to see more desktop videoconferencing performed with your personal computer. In fact, some notebook computers are now manufactured and sold with video cameras built in. However, one of the most intriguing new technologies for desktop videoconferencing that we have seen is Microsoft Office RoundTable 2007, a communications device that incorporates a 360-degree camera and unified communications software with a built in microphone (see Figure 7.26). This system allows all meeting content to be recorded, indexed, and stored for later playback. When combined with Microsoft Office Communications Server 2007,

FIGURE 7.25

Logitech's popular QuickCam.

FIGURE 7.26

Microsoft Office RoundTable
2007.

Source: Microsoft Office
RoundTable Fact Sheet–June 2006,
http://microsoft.com/presspass/
presskits/uc/images/image 001.jpg

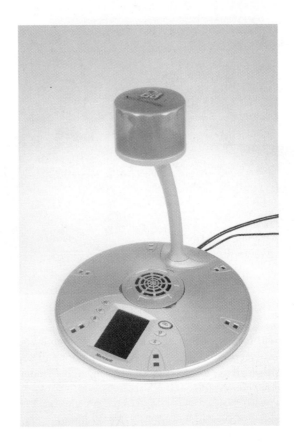

RoundTable provides meeting participants from remote locations a panoramic view of
everyone in the conference room plus close-up views triggered by voice activation.
Originally developed as a prototype in Microsoft Research, RoundTable is now being
further developed for commercialization by Microsoft Corp's Unified Communications
Group.

Dedicated Videoconferencing Systems   Dedicated videoconferencing systems are
typically located within organizational conference rooms, facilitating meetings with
customers or project team members across town or around the world. These systems can
be highly realistic—as if you are almost co-located with your colleagues—and extremely
expensive, costing up to $500,000. Alternatively, systems can be relatively inexpensive
costing only a few thousand dollars. No matter what type of dedicated videoconferencing
system utilized by an organization, this collaboration technology has come a long ways
from the demonstration at Disneyland in the 1960s, becoming mainstream in most modern
organizations.

Groupware   The term **groupware** refers to a class of software that enables people to
work together more effectively. As mentioned previously, groupware and other
collaboration technologies are often distinguished along two dimensions:

1. Whether the system supports groups working together at the same time (synchronous
   groupware) or at different times (asynchronous groupware)
2. Whether the system supports groups working together face-to-face or distributed

Using these two dimensions, groupware systems can be categorized as being able to support four types of group interaction methods as shown in Figure 7.27. With the increased
use of group-based problem solving and virtual teams, there are many potential benefits of
utilizing groupware systems. These benefits are summarized in Table 7.13.

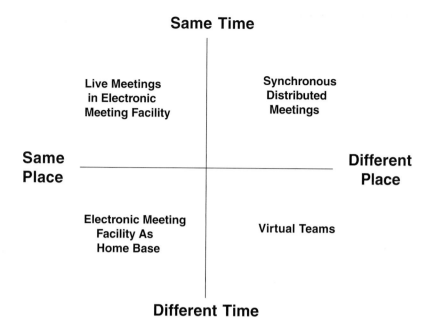

FIGURE 7.27

Groupware supports same and different time, as well as same and different place, group interaction.

ASYNCHRONOUS GROUPWARE. A large number of asynchronous groupware tools are becoming commonplace in organizations, including e-mail, newsgroups and mailing lists, work flow automation systems, intranets, group calendars, and collaborative writing tools. One of the most popular groupware systems—and arguably the system that put groupware into the mainstream—appeared in 1989 when Lotus Development released its Notes software product (today, Lotus is owned by IBM). In recent years, many new groupware products have emerged, most of which work through or with the Internet. Even with all these alternative asynchronous groupware systems available, Notes continues to be an industry leader and is widely deployed throughout the world (see Figure 7.28).

TABLE 7.13 Benefits of Groupware

Benefits	Examples
Process structuring	Keeps the group on track and helps it avoid costly diversions (e.g., doesn't allow people to get off topic or the agenda)
Parallelism	Enables many people to speak and listen at the same time (e.g., everyone has an equal opportunity to participate)
Group size	Enables larger groups to participate (e.g., brings together broader perspectives, expertise, and participation)
Group memory	Automatically records member ideas, comments, votes (e.g., allows members to focus on content of discussions, rather than on recording comments)
Access to external information	Can easily incorporate external electronic data and files (e.g., plans and proposal documents can be collected and easily distributed to all members)
Spanning time and space	Enables members to collaborate from different places at different times (e.g., reduces travel costs or allows people from remote locations to participate)
Anonymity	Member ideas, comments and votes are not identified to others (if desired) (e.g., can make it easier to discuss controversial or sensitive topics without fear of identification or retribution)

FIGURE 7.28

Lotus Notes is an award-winning groupware application with an installed base of millions of users worldwide.

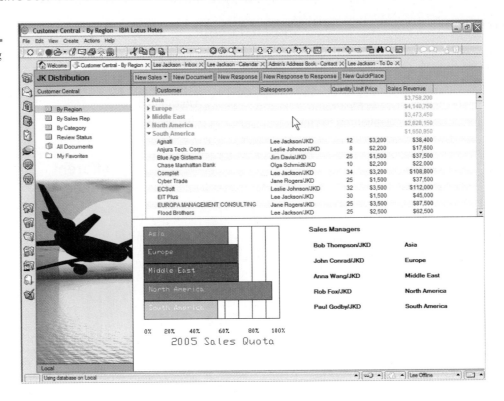

SYNCHRONOUS GROUPWARE. Like asynchronous groupware, there are also many forms of synchronous groupware available to support a wide variety of activities, including shared whiteboards, online chat, electronic meeting support systems, and, of course, video communication systems (discussed previously). Although many forms of groupware can be used to help groups work more effectively, one category of groupware focuses on helping groups have better meetings. These systems are commonly referred to as an **electronic meeting system (EMS)**. An EMS is essentially a collection of personal computers networked together with sophisticated software tools to help group members solve problems and make decisions through interactive electronic idea generation, evaluation, and voting. Some typical uses for an EMS include strategic planning sessions, marketing focus groups, brainstorming sessions for system requirements definition, business process management, and quality improvement. EMSs have traditionally been housed within a dedicated meeting facility, as shown in Figure 7.29. However, EMSs are also being implemented with notebook computers so that the system can be taken on the road. Additionally, Web-based implementations are supporting distributed meetings where group members access the EMS software from their computers in their offices or from home. While EMS and related software have been around for quite some time, organizations are now beginning to discover how useful these tools can be to support e-meetings and other forms of teamwork. Evidence that groupware has become mainstream is the recent media blitz for Microsoft Live Meeting and WebEx online meeting software (where Lily Tomlin says, "We have to start meeting this way!").

Knowledge Management Systems

Knowledge management, as described in Chapter 4, refers to the processes an organization uses to generate value from its knowledge assets (Awad and Ghaziri, 2004). Recall that *knowledge assets* are the set of skills, routines, practices, principles, formulas, methods, heuristics, and intuitions (whether *explicit* or *tacit*), used by organizations to improve efficiency, effectiveness, and profitability. All databases, manuals, reference works, textbooks, diagrams, displays, computer files, proposals, plans, and any other artifacts in

FIGURE 7.29

A computer-supported meeting facility, complete with networked PCs and electronic meeting system software.

Courtesy of Groupsystems.com.

Ethical Dilemma

Too Much Intelligence? RFID and Privacy

Radio frequency identification (RFID) tags are the latest in technological tracking devices. Each tag generates a signature signal that an RFID reader can identify. The identification is then sent to the information system that can identify the product that was tagged. For example, the pharmaceutical industry has recently begun tagging certain drugs in large quantities, such as 100-pill bottles of Viagra and Oxycontin, in order to track them as they move through the supply chain and prevent counterfeits from reaching the public.

As is true with all electronic tracking devices, privacy advocates are concerned about misuse. Since, theoretically, RFID tags can be read by anyone who has an RFID reader, the tags have the potential of revealing private consumer information. For example, if you buy a product that has an RFID tag, someone with an RFID reader can possibly identify where you bought the product and how much you paid for it. The amount of information imprinted on an RFID tag is limited, however, and since few retail businesses have

purchased RFID writers, readers, or the erasers that can clear information from the tags before they leave a store, the likelihood of privacy abuse is currently slim. Although pharmaceutical companies use RFID tags to track certain products, drug company spokespersons say it is highly unlikely that consumers will take home tracking devices with their heart medications or birth control pills.

An 18-year-old federal law mandates that drugs be tracked every time they change hands from the factory to the pharmacy, but the U.S. Food and Drug Administration (FDA) has put off enforcing the requirement until RFID technology becomes more widely used. As the technology becomes more widely used, consumer protection laws and policies will undoubtedly need to be in place.

Sources: Randy Dotinga, "Viagra Tag Could Be Bitter Pill," *Wired News* (January 18, 2006), http://www.wired.com/news/technology/0,70033-0.html?tw=wn_tophead_15 Anonymous, "FDA to Require Drug Tracking Via RFID," *Newsfactor Magazine Online* (June 13, 2006), http://www.newsfactor.com/story.xhtml?story_id=40435

which both facts and procedures are recorded and stored are considered knowledge assets (Winter, 2001). Additionally, as many companies are beginning to lose a large number of baby boomers to retirement, companies are using knowledge management systems to capture these crucial knowledge assets (Leonard, 2005). Clearly, effectively managing knowledge assets will enhance business intelligence.

Given the diversity of knowledge assets, there is no single technology that represents a comprehensive knowledge management system. In essence, a *knowledge management system* is a collection of technology-based tools that include communication technologies—e-mail, groupware, instant messaging, and the like—as well as information storage and retrieval systems—database management systems, data warehouses, and data mining and visualization—to enable the generation, storage, sharing, and management of knowledge assets.

Benefits and Challenges of Knowledge Management Systems Many potential benefits can come from organizations' effectively capturing and utilizing their tacit knowledge assets (Santosus and Surmacz, 2001) (see Table 7.14). For example, innovation and creativity may be enhanced by the free flow of ideas throughout the organization. Also, by widely sharing best practices, organizations should realize improved customer service, shorter product development, and streamlined operations. Enhanced business operations not only will improve the overall organizational performance but also will enhance employee retention rates by recognizing the value of employees' knowledge and rewarding them for sharing it. Thus, organizations can realize many benefits from the successful deployment of a knowledge management system.

Although there are many potential benefits for organizations that effectively deploy knowledge management systems, to do so requires that several substantial challenges be overcome (Table 7.14). First, effective deployment requires employees to agree to share their personal tacit knowledge assets and to take extra steps to utilize the system for identifying best practices. Therefore, to encourage employee buy-in and also to enable the sharing of knowledge, organizations must create a culture that values and rewards widespread participation. Second, experience has shown that a successful deployment must first identify what knowledge is needed, why it is needed, and who is likely to have this knowledge. Once an organization understands "why, what, and who," identifying the best technologies for facilitating knowledge exchange is a much easier task. In other words, the best practices for deploying knowledge management systems suggest that organizations save the "how"—that is, what collaboration and storage technologies to use—for last.

Third, the successful deployment of a knowledge management system must be linked to a specific business objective. By linking the system to a specific business objective and coupling that with the use of an assessment technique such as return on investment, an organization can then identify costs and benefits and also be sure that the system is providing value in an area that is indeed important to the organization. Fourth, the knowledge management system must be easy to use, not only for putting knowledge

TABLE 7.14 Benefits and Challenges of Knowledge Management Systems

Benefits	Challenges
• Enhanced innovation and creativity	• Getting employee buy-in
• Improved customer service, shorter product development, and streamlined operations	• Focusing too much on technology
	• Forgetting the goal
• Enhanced employee retention	• Dealing with knowledge overload and obsolescence
• Improved organizational performance	

in but also for getting knowledge out. Similarly, the system cannot overload users with too much information or with information that is obsolete. Just as physical assets can erode over time, knowledge, too, can become stale and irrelevant. Therefore, an ongoing process of updating, amending, and removing obsolete or irrelevant knowledge must occur, or the system will fall into disarray and will not be used. In sum, to gain the greatest benefits from an investment in a knowledge management system, the organization must take care to overcome various challenges.

How Organizations Utilize a Knowledge Management System   The people using a knowledge management system will be working in different departments within the organization, doing different functions, and will likely be located in different locations around the building, city, or even the world. Each person—or group of people—can be thought of as a separate island that is set apart from others by geography, job focus, expertise, age, and gender. Often, a person on one island is trying to solve a problem that has already been solved by another person located on some other island. Finding this "other" person is often a significant challenge (see Figure 7.30). The goal of a successful knowledge management system is to facilitate the exchange of needed knowledge between these separate islands.

Once organizations have collected their knowledge into a repository, they must find an easy way to share it with employees (often using an intranet), customers and suppliers (often with an extranet), or the general public (often using the Internet). These **knowledge portals** can be customized to meet the unique needs of their intended users. For example, the FDA is responsible for keeping the public (e.g., citizens, researchers, and industry) informed on the most up-to-date information related to food (e.g., information on mad cow disease or product recalls) and drugs (e.g., the status of a drug trial). At the FDA Web site, they use a Google *search appliance*—a special type of computer that analyzes and indexes information within a Web site—so that visitors can quickly search and find needed information using the popular Google interface within the FDA's more than 1 million documents (see Figure 7.31).

In addition to the FDA, countless other organizations, such as Ford Motor Company, Eli Lilly, Wal-Mart, and Dell Computers, are also rapidly deploying knowledge management

"I wonder who knows?"

FIGURE 7.30

In a large or global organization, finding the person with the right knowledge can be a significant challenge.

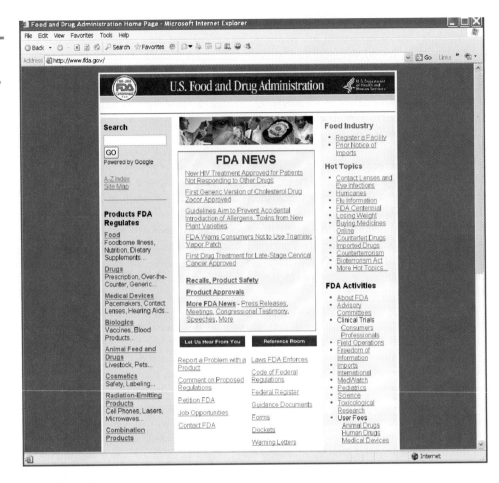

systems. We are learning from these deployments that all organizations, whether for-profit or nonprofit, struggle to get the right information to the right person at the right time. Through the use of a comprehensive strategy for managing knowledge assets, organizations are much more likely to gain a competitive advantage and a positive return on their information systems investments.

Functional Area Information Systems

A **functional area information system** is a cross-organizational-level information system designed to support the business processes of a specific functional area (see Figure 7.32). Such systems may be any of the types described previously—TPS, MIS, EIS, DSS, ES, and OAS. A functional area represents a discrete area of an organization that focuses on a specific set of activities. For example, people in the marketing function focus on the activities that promote the organization and its products in a way that attracts and retains customers. People in accounting and finance focus on managing and controlling capital assets and financial resources of the organization. Table 7.15 lists various organizational functions, describes the focus of each one, and lists examples of the types of information systems used in each functional area.

One type of functional area information system that is growing in popularity is called a **geographic information system (GIS)**. A GIS is a system for creating, storing, analyzing, and managing geographically referenced information. For example, a GIS can be used by a retail company to identify the optimal location for a new store or help a farmer identify areas too wet to fertilize (see Figure 7.34). Using GIS, analysts can combine geographic, demographic, and other data for locating target customers, finding optimal site locations, or determining the right product mixes at different locations; additionally, GIS can perform a

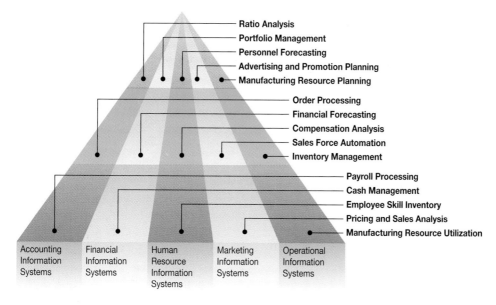

FIGURE 7.32

Business processes supported by various functional area information systems.

variety of analyses, such as market share analysis and market competitive analysis. Cities, counties, and states also use GIS for aiding in infrastructure design and zoning issues (e.g., where should the new elementary school be located?). Clearly, GIS, like all the systems described in this chapter, are providing organizations with business intelligence to better compete in the digital world.

TABLE 7.15 Organizational Functions and Representative Information Systems

Functional Area	Information System	Examples of Typical Systems
Accounting and Finance	Systems used for managing, controlling, and auditing the financial resources of the organization	• Inventory management • Accounts payable • Expense accounts • Cash management • Payroll processing
Human Resources	Systems used for managing, controlling, and auditing the human resources of the organization	• Recruiting and hiring • Education and training • Benefits management • Employee termination • Workforce planning
Marketing	Systems used for managing new product development, distribution, pricing, promotional effectiveness, and sales forecasting of the products and services offered by the organization	• Market research and analysis • New product development • Promotion and advertising • Pricing and sales analysis • Product location analysis
Production and Operations	Systems used for managing, controlling, and auditing the production and operations resources of the organization	• Inventory management • Cost and quality tracking • Materials and resource planning • Customer service tracking • Customer problem tracking • Job costing • Resource utilization

Change Agents

Jeff Bezos, Founder and Chief Executive Officer of Amazon.com

"If you can't feed a team with two pizzas it's too large," Jeff Bezos, chief executive officer (CEO) of Amazon.com, one of the largest electronic retailers on the Internet, once told a group of his company's managers. Long a believer in a decentralized, uncomplicated company where small groups of employees can innovate to their hearts' content, Bezos, born on January 12, 1964, has become *the* example of how to succeed in e-commerce.

Jeff Bezos founded Amazon.com in 1994 in Seattle, Washington, and remains the company's CEO. (He chose "Amazon" as the company's name simply because he wanted a name that would come up quickly in search engines.) When the Barnes & Noble book barons opened a competing Web site in 1997, Forrester Research chief George Colony made his famous prediction that Amazon.com would be "Amazon.toast."

Against all odds, however, and contrary to Colony's prediction, Bezos deftly steered Amazon.com through the Internet boom and bust, in the process creating a stable yet innovative company that strives above all to be "customer-centric." What started as a Web site to provide a million book titles, some of them rare and out of print (critics said it was an impossible dream), has become a virtual superstore carrying products that range from bed linens to electronics, clothing, and gourmet food.

Bezos graduated from Princeton in 1986 with a degree in electrical engineering and computer science, then went to work for FITEL, a high-tech start-up company in New York. Two years later, Bezos began working for Bankers Trust Company, a Wall Street financial firm, where he developed computer systems and became the company's youngest vice president in 1990. From 1990 to 1994, Bezos worked for D. E. Shaw & Co. in New York, where he helped build a technologically sophisticated Wall Street hedge fund. Bezos left his vice president position at Shaw to start Amazon.com. The company first turned a profit in 2003 and today is worth some $17 billion. Bezos and his wife, Mackenzie, and two sons still live in Seattle.

Sources: Jeff Bezos, chairman and CEO, Amazon.com
http://www.askmen.com/men/may00/26c_jeff_bezos.html
http://www.fastcompany.com/magazine/85/bezos_1.html

FIGURE 7.33

Jeff Bezos, founder and chief executive officer of Amazon.com.

Source: http://www.newmediamusings.com/photos/web2/cover-image-jeff_bezos.jpg.

FIGURE 7.34

A geographic information system aids in analyzing geographically referenced information.

Source: http://www.esri.com/software/arcgis/extensions/businessanalyst/graphics/ba_gravity_model_chicago.gif.

Industry Analysis

Internet Protocol Television

Imagine this: You decide to watch *The Graduate*, a popular movie from 1967, via your television set. When the movie is over, you watch a 1979 episode of *The Dukes of Hazzard* TV series, then you go online to play "Doom." Next you catch up on your e-mail, do research for a paper that's coming due, and call your parents in a distant city. These activities are not extraordinary, but the fact that you performed every one of them on your TV is.

The technology that will deliver the TV features described here—and more—is called Internet Protocol television (IPTV). This current trend in the television industry takes programming control away from the cable companies and puts it directly under consumers' control. IPTV is transported over whatever method someone connects to the Internet, including wireless and mobile devices.

High-definition television (HDTV), whereby cable subscription services provide digital TV service using the Internet Protocol, communicated over the companies' broadband connection, is popular in metropolitan areas. This service provides full-duplex connections that can offer such features as video on demand, Web access, and voice access. IPTV, however, will provide more services and content—such as access to extensive video and film libraries—than HDTV and will be offered in more areas of the country.

Availability of IPTV, to date, has been spotty, while improvements are made to the telecommunications transport infrastructure. As of May, 2006, 1,200 IPTV channels have been offered free of charge in the United States, deliverable to Internet-enabled devices such as iPods, HDTVs connected to computers, and 3G cell phones. Programming is now available via iTunes downloads, including such television series as *Lost* and *Desperate Housewives*, and Comedy Central offers streaming programming via the Internet.

Europe and Asia currently lead the world in IPTV revenue because of telecommunications delivery infrastructure that includes faster and more numerous broadband connections. Nevertheless, the United States is expected to catch up by 2009, when revenue from IPTV is predicted to reach $44 billion.

Questions

1. With the possibility of various technologies converging, which industry is in the best position to capitalize on IPTV?
2. How will IPTV help to fuel globalization?

Sources: Roy Mark, "IPTV a $44B Market by 2009," *Internet News* (May 9, 2006), http://www.internetnews.com/infra/article.php/3604891

http://www.telecommagazine.com/newsglobe/article.asp?HH_ID=AR_2057

http://www.technologynewsdaily.com/node/2712

Key Points Review

1. *Describe the characteristics that differentiate the operational, managerial, and executive levels of an organization.* At the operational level of the firm, the routine day-to-day business processes and interaction with customers occur, and information systems are designed to automate repetitive activities, such as sales transaction processing. Operational-level managers such as foremen or supervisors make day-to-day decisions that are highly structured and recurring. At the managerial level of the organization, functional managers focus on monitoring and controlling operational-level activities and providing information to higher levels of the organization. Midlevel or functional managers focus on effectively utilizing and deploying organizational resources to achieve the organization's strategic objectives. At this level, the scope of the decisions usually is contained within the business function, is moderately complex, and has a time horizon of a few days to a few months. At the executive level of the organization, decisions are often very complex problems with broad and long-term ramifications for the organization. Executive-level decisions are often referred to as being messy or unstructured because executives must consider the ramifications for the overall organization.

2. *Explain the characteristics of the three information systems designed to support each of the unique levels of an organization: transaction processing systems, management information systems, and executive information systems.* Transaction processing systems are designed to process business events and transactions and reside close to customers at the operational level of the organization. These systems are used to automate repetitive information-processing activities to increase speed and accuracy and to lower the cost of processing each transaction—that is, to make the organization more efficient. Management information systems reside at the managerial level and are designed to produce regular and ad hoc reports to support the ongoing, recurring decision-making activities associated with managing an entire business or a functional area within a business. These systems are used to help midlevel managers make more effective decisions. Executive information systems are used to provide information to executives in a very highly aggregate form so that information can be scanned quickly for trends and anomalies. Executives use these systems to provide a one-stop shop for a lot of their informational needs.

3. *Describe the characteristics of the seven information systems that span the organizational, managerial, and executive levels: decision support systems, intelligent systems, data mining and visualization, office automation systems, collaboration technologies, knowledge management systems, and functional area information systems.* Decision support systems (DSS) support organizational decision making and are typically designed to solve a particular recurring problem in the organization. DSSs are most commonly used to support semistructured problems that are addressed by managerial-level employees. A DSS is designed to be an interactive decision aid. Intelligent systems such as expert systems, neural networks, and intelligent agents work to emulate and enhance human capabilities. Expert systems (ESs) apply knowledge within some topic area to provide advice by mimicking human expertise (understanding acquired through experience and extensive learning). ESs are used when expertise for a particular problem is rare or expensive. Neural networks attempt to approximate the functioning and decision making of the human brain by comparing patterns in new data versus complex patterns learned from prior data. Intelligent agents are programs that can be applied to a broad variety of situations, typically operating in the background to provide some service when a special event occurs or when a request is made. Data-mining and visualization systems aid in analyzing vast data warehouses to better understand business conditions and present this information using various types of graphical representations. Office automation systems are technologies for developing documents, scheduling resources, and communicating. Collaboration technologies such as videoconferencing, groupware, and electronic meeting systems are used to support the communication and teamwork of virtual teams. Knowledge management systems are a collection of technology-based tools that enable the generation, storage, sharing, and management of knowledge assets. Functional areas represent discrete areas of organizations and typically include accounting and finance, human resource management, marketing, and production and operations management. Functional area information systems are designed to support the unique requirements of specific business functions.

Key Terms

ad hoc reports   273

artificial intelligence (AI)   283

batch processing   271

bot   287

buyer agents   287

data-mining agents   287

decision support system
   (DSS)   280

desktop videoconferencing   291

destructive agents   287

digital dashboard   277

drill-down reports   274

electronic meeting system
   (EMS)   294

exception reports   274

executive information system
   (EIS)   294

executive level   268

expert system (ES)   284

fully automated data entry   271

functional area information
   system   298

fuzzy logic   284

geographic information system
   (GIS)   299

groupware   292

hard data   275

inferencing   285

intelligent agent   287

intelligent system   283

key-indicator reports   274

knowledge portals   298

management information system
   (MIS)   273

managerial level   267

manual data entry   271

models   281

monitoring and sensing
   agents   287

neural network   286

office automation system
   (OAS)   290

online processing   271

operational level   267

reports   273

rule   284

scheduled reports   273

semiautomated data entry   271

semistructured decisions   268

soft data   275

source documents   271

structured decisions   267

text mining   288

transaction processing system
   (TPS)   270

transactions   270

unstructured decisions   268

user agents   287

videoconferencing   291

virtual teams   290

visualization   288

Web cam   292

Web crawlers   287

Web spiders   287

what-if analysis   281

Review Questions

1. Compare and contrast the characteristics of the operational, managerial, and executive levels of an organization.
2. What is the difference between "hard" and "soft" data?
3. Describe the differences between online processing and batch processing. Give examples of each.
4. What are the three methods used for inputting data into a transaction processing system? Provide examples of each.
5. List three different types of reports and tell where or how the information from each is used.
6. How does a management information system differ from a transaction processing system in terms of purpose, target users, capabilities, and so forth?
7. Describe and give examples of two types of data entry.
8. How does an executive information system "drill down" into the data?

9. What are the seven types of information systems that traditionally span the boundaries of organizational levels?
10. Explain the purpose of a model within a decision support system.
11. What is the difference between a decision support system and an expert system?
12. Describe four types of intelligent agents. How can they be used to benefit organizations?
13. How can data mining and visualization be used to gain business intelligence and improve decision making?
14. What is groupware, and what are the different types?
15. Compare and contrast stand-alone videoconferencing and desktop videoconferencing.
16. What is a knowledge management system, and what types of technologies make up a comprehensive system?
17. Provide some examples of functionally specific information systems and needs within an organization.

Self-Study Questions

Visit the Interactive Study Guide on the text Web site for additional Self-Study Questions: **www.prenhall.com/jessup**.

1. At the _____ level of the organization, functional managers (e.g., marketing managers, finance managers, manufacturing managers, and human resource managers) focus on monitoring and controlling operational-level activities and providing information to higher levels of the organization.

A. operational

B. managerial

C. organizational

D. executive

2. Examples of the types of activities supported by management information systems include all of the following except

A. inventory management and planning

B. manufacturing planning and scheduling

C. financial management and forecasting

D. sales and order processing

3. A(n) _____ report provides a summary of critical information on a recurring schedule.

A. scheduled

B. exception

C. key-indicator

D. drill-down

4. Examples of the types of activities that can be supported by expert systems include all of the following except _____.

A. payroll calculations

B. financial planning

C. machine configuration

D. medical diagnosis

5. A supervisor's having to decide when to reorder supplies or how best to allocate personnel for the completion of a project is an example of a _____ decision.

A. structured

B. unstructured

C. automated

D. delegated

6. The types of boundary-spanning systems include all of the following except _____.

A. decision support systems

B. resource planning systems

C. office automation systems

D. expert systems

7. _____ processing of transactions provides immediate results to the system operator or customer.

A. online

B. batch

C. fully automated

D. semiautomated

8. A marketing manager for Nike may have a(n) _____ system that contrasts sales revenue and marketing expenses by geographic region so that he can better understand how regional marketing for the "Tiger Woods Golf" product line promotions are performing.

A. transaction

B. expert

C. office automated

D. management information

9. In a(n) _____ data entry system, a data capture device such as a grocery store checkout scanner speeds the entry and processing of the transaction.

A. manual

B. semiautomated

C. fully automated

D. expert

10. What is true about knowledge management?

A. As baby boomers retire at an increasing rate, knowledge management is helping organizations capture their knowledge.

B. A knowledge management system is not a single technology but a collection of technology-based tools.

C. Finding the right technology to manage knowledge assets is much easier than identifying what knowledge is needed, why it is needed, and who has this knowledge.

D. All of the above are true.

Answers are on page 307.

Problems and Exercises

1. Match the following terms with the appropriate definitions:

   i. Operational level

   ii. Transactions

   iii. Virtual teams

   iv. Source document

   v. Online processing

   vi. Management information system

   vii. Expert system

   viii. Inferencing

   ix. Transaction processing system

   x. Decision support system

   a. An information system designed to process day-to-day business event data at the operational level of an organization

   b. A special-purpose information system designed to mimic human expertise by manipulating knowledge (understanding acquired through experience and extensive learning) rather than simply information

   c. The bottom level of an organization, where the routine day-to-day interaction with customers occurs

d. A special-purpose information system designed to support organizational decision making primarily at the managerial level of an organization

e. Processing of information immediately as it occurs

f. Repetitive events in organizations that occur as a regular part of conducting day-to-day operations

g. An information system designed to support the management of organizational functions at the managerial level of the organization

h. A document created when a business event or transaction occurs

i. The matching of facts and rules, as well as determining the sequence of questions presented to the user, and drawing a conclusion

j. Teams forming and disbanding as needed, with team size fluctuating as necessary and with team members coming and going as they are needed

2. Visit guide.real.com on the Web. RealNetworks provides information on almost any subject or industry, virtually as it hits the newswires. What types of "hard" and "soft" data can you find?

3. Do you feel that, as much as possible, transaction processing systems should replace human roles and activities within organizations? Why or why not? How much cost savings will there be if these humans are still needed to run the systems? What if you were the person being replaced? Will all errors necessarily be eliminated? Why or why not?

4. Imagine that your boss has asked you to build an inventory transaction system that would enable the receiving and shipping clerks to enter inventory amounts for purchases and sales, respectively. Discuss the pros and cons of building this system as an online processing system versus a batch processing system. Which would you recommend to your boss?

5. The national sales manager for ABC Corp. is interested in purchasing a software package that will be capable of providing "accurate" sales forecasts for the short term and the long term. She has asked you to recommend the best type of system for this purpose. What would you recommend? Do you have any reservations about such a system? Why or why not?

6. Visit MSN Money (www.moneycentral.msn.com/investor/calcs/n_expect/main.asp) on the Web to determine your life expectancy using a decision support system. What did you learn? Is there a difference between life expectancies for different genders? If you browse MSN Money, what other interesting stuff do you find? Also check out www.bigcharts.com.

7. Interview a top-level executive within an organization with which you are familiar and determine the extent to which the organization utilizes executive information systems (or information aggregation technologies like digital dashboards). Does this individual utilize an executive information system in any way? Why or why not? Which executives do utilize an executive information system?

8. Based on your experiences with transaction processing systems (in everyday life and/or in the workplace), which ones use online processing and which use batch processing? Do these choices fit the system, the information, and the environment? Would you make any adjustments? Why or why not?

9. Using any program you choose or using the Web site www.moneycentral.com, find or create a template that you could use in the future to determine monthly payments on car or home loans. Compare your template with the one at www.bankrate.com/brm/calculators/autos.asp. Would you have categorized the program you used to create this template as a decision support system before doing this exercise?

10. Describe your experiences with expert systems, or go to www.exsys.com or www.easydiagnosis.com on the Web and spend some time interacting with their demonstration systems. Now choose a problem that you know a lot about and would like to build your own expert system for. Describe the problem and list the questions you would need to ask someone in order to make a recommendation.

11. Go out onto the Web and compare three shopping bot intelligent agents for a product you are interested in (e.g., www.bottomdollar.com, www.mysimon.com, www.shopzilla.com, www.shopping.com, or www.pricegrabber.com). Did the different agents find the same information, or were there any differences? Did you prefer one over the others? Why?

12. Choose an organization with which you are familiar that utilizes office automation systems; which systems does it use? Which functions have been automated, and which have not been? Why have some functions not been automated? Who decides which office automation system to implement?

13. Have you seen or used ad hoc, exception, key-indicator, and/or drill-down reports? What is the purpose of each report? Who produces and who uses the reports? Do any of these reports look or sound familiar from your work experience?

14. Interview an information systems manager within an organization at a university or workplace. Of the three categories of information systems—transaction processing, management, and executive—which do people utilize most in this organization? Why? Have any of these areas experienced an increase or decrease in the last few years? What predictions does this manager have regarding the future of traditional information systems? Do you agree? Prepare a 10-minute presentation to the class on your findings.

15. Describe how various systems described in this chapter might enable employees to work from home rather than at the company's office. What technologies in particular might these employees utilize and how? Will companies look favorably on this use of technology? Why or why not?

16. For your university, identify several examples of various knowledge assets and rate these assets on their value to the university on a 10-point scale (1 = low value to 10 = high value).

17. Examine your university Web site to identify examples where a knowledge management system could be used (or is being used) to help provide improved services to students.

18. Pick an organization you are familiar with and describe what could be contained in separate knowledge portals for customers, suppliers, employees, and the general public.

Application Exercises

 The existing data files referenced in these exercises are available on the Student Companion Web site: **www.prenhall.com/ jessup**.

 Spreadsheet Application: Travel Loan Facility

A new aspect of the business has been added to Campus Travel. Students can apply for a loan to help pay for their travels. However, loans for travel are available only to students who are traveling outside the country for at least two weeks. Since the costs for this type of international travel differ depending on how you travel, where you stay, and what you do at the destination, different loan packages are available. For a month in Europe, you have decided to take out a loan. You have already taken a look at several offers but are unsure whether you can afford it. Set up a spreadsheet to calculate the payments per month for the following situations:

1. Two weeks in Eastern Europe; Price: $2,000; Percentage Rate: 5.5%; Time: one year

2. Two weeks in Western Europe; Price: $3,000; Percentage Rate: 6.0%; Time: one year

3. Three weeks in Eastern Europe; Price: $3,000; Percentage Rate: 6.5%; Time: two years

4. Three weeks in Western Europe; Price: $3,500; Percentage Rate: 5.5%; Time: two years

5. Four weeks in Eastern Europe; Price: $4,000; Percentage Rate: 6.0%; Time: two years

6. Four weeks in Western Europe; Price: $5,000; Percentage Rate: 6.5%; Time: three years

Once you have calculated the payments, calculate the total amount to be paid for each option as well as the total interest you would pay over the course of the loan. Make sure to use formulas for all calculations and print out a professionally formatted page displaying the results and a page displaying the formulas (Hint: In Microsoft Excel, use the "PMT" function in the category "Financial" to calculate the payments. Use Ctrl + ` [grave accent] to switch between formula and data views).

 Database Application: Tracking Regional Office Performance at Campus Travel

The general manager wants to know which offices were most profitable during the previous year and asks you to prepare several reports. In the file FY2006.mdb, you find information about the offices, sales agents, and destinations. Use the report wizard to generate the following reports:

1. List of all sales agents grouped by office (including total number of agents per office)

2. List of sales agents for each destination (grouped by destination, including total number of agents)

3. Destinations sold by each sales agent (including total number of destinations)

Team Work Exercise: What's the Hot Topic?

Visit a Web site of an information systems–related content provider, such as *InformationWeek, Computerworld, CIO*, or *NewsFactor*, and scan the current headlines. You can find these online resources at www.informationweek.com, www.computerworld.com, www.cio.com, and www.news

factor.com. After having scanned the headlines, get together with your team and discuss your findings. What is the focus of the different sites? What are the hot technologies and related issues? Which seem to be most important to business managers? Prepare a brief presentation for your classmates.

Answers to the Self-Study Questions

1. B, p. 267 **2.** D, p. 273 **3.** C, p. 274 **4.** A, p. 284 **5.** A, p. 267
6. B, p. 280 **7.** A, p. 271 **8.** D, p. 273 **9.** B, p. 271 **10.** D, p. 294

case

Home Depot's Quandary

Home Depot, the world's largest home improvement retailer, sells thousands of products in each of its 1,900 stores across the United States. By 2001, the 342 service organizations responsible for placing those products in each Home Depot retail store had become a problem. Since each service representative worked for one organization, on commission, and service representatives were not organized or supervised, they could place products anywhere they wanted inside the stores. The result was that chaos reigned. A service representative might move a competitor's product to an inaccessible corner or place his or her own organization's products closer to the checkout stations, relegating competitors' products to the back of the store. The stores' policy of placing like products together—doors next to doorknobs and doorbells—fell apart.

In 2000, Home Depot hired a new CEO, Bob Nardelli, to modernize store operations and help the company better compete with Lowe's and other home improvement super stores. Under Nardelli's leadership, merchandise managing was centralized under the direction of the company's department of vendor services, and merchandise service representatives no longer had unrestrained freedom. Nardelli and his vice president and director of vendor services wanted to involve the Home Depot IT department, but IT department managers were reluctant to depart from past policies and operations. The decision was made, therefore, to outsource the project.

Home Depot awarded EnfoTrust Networks the contract to develop a custom system for the company's vendor management. Since the project did not involve managing which products to move into the showroom but rather focused on controlling and guiding vendors inside the showroom, supply chain software was ruled out. Nardelli and his project group named their vendor management system the "In-Store Service Initiative." The technology consisted of the use of thousands of handheld computers and an EnfoTrust server.

The In-Store Service Initiative was initially implemented just within the electric and lighting department of Home Depot, but within two years the system was expanded to include every department except plants and garden supplies. The new vendor system required each service representative to sign in to a showroom, then place products being assisted by a handheld terminal. The system guided each representative through a series of yes-or-no questions about product classification, product placement, location of the product on the showroom floor, and display tags. The system also assisted representatives with moving inventory, returning damaged items, and replacing missing labels. When the representative left the showroom, he or she was asked to sign out. The vendor company could then analyze the data, looking for numbers of negative answers to questions within the system, and then make the required changes for compliance with Home Depot guidelines.

Each handheld terminal was equipped with a camera so that service representatives could take photos before and after completing their work. The photos served as a convenient form of documentation should disputes among vendors arise.

Quality of the handheld computers used was, at first, a challenge for Home Depot. Since handhelds are usually made for clean office environments and not for rugged use, they had to be modified for Home Depot's use at significant cost. In addition, vendors had to be persuaded to purchase the handhelds.

Early challenges were overcome, and EnfoTrust now reports that the Home Depot account involves handling nearly 340,000 photographs from approximately 11,500 handhelds. In the near future, Home Depot plans to use a Wi-Fi network that will let service representatives send data to the EnfoTrust server directly from the showroom.

Questions

1. What type of system would you categorize the In-Store Service Initiative system? Why?
2. What types of reports could Home Depot generate from the data captured by the In-Store Service Initiative system?
3. Imagine you are a store manager for Home Depot. Design a digital dashboard for the data generated by the In-Store Service Initiative system. Make sure you list your assumptions and define each type of data within your dashboard.

Sources: Jeffry Schwartz, "Home Depot Renovates Its Data Warehouse," *VarBusiness* (November 22, 2002), http://www.varbusiness.com/sections/customer/customer.jhtml;jsessionid=RWHPUF13VKNUQQSNDBCSKH0CJUMEKJVN?articleId=18829496&_requestid=16963

Carmen Nobel, "Home Depot Tackles Network Challenge," *eWeek* (November 22, 2005), http://www.eweek.com/article2/0,1895,1887081,00.asp

case ②

e-Enabling the Air Transport Industry: Enhancing Business Intelligence Using Information Systems

For commercial airlines, maximizing operational efficiency and market presence can be the key for survival. As discussed in earlier cases, the Boeing Company has envisioned the e-Enabled Advantage, which uses integrated information and communications systems to improve the ways an airline can run its business, as a way to help airlines achieve this goal. Drawing on resources of the entire company, Boeing hoped to give the air transport industry a future in which people, airplanes, assets, information systems, knowledge applications, and decision support tools work together seamlessly across an airline's functional areas and hierarchical levels. In the near future, Jeppesen Electronic Flight Bag, SBS International Crew Scheduling and Management software, and Boeing Airplane Health Management will be seamlessly integrated, and airborne and ground-based operations will be linked in real time to enable people to achieve the airlines' goals.

The infrastructure necessary to e-Enable a commercial airplane is a complex system of systems that channels the wealth of information generated by airplane avionics, the airline operations centers, airport and air traffic managers, weather services, and regulatory agencies directly to the people who use the information at the instant when that information is most useful. In addition to integrating existing information systems, a new generation of visualization tools and decision aids is currently under development to create robust flight plans, revise and optimize schedules in real time, and all but eliminate unscheduled maintenance.

For any commercial airline, the most important revenue-generating business function is flight operations. In order to increase efficiency before, during, and after the flight, Boeing's subsidiary Jeppesen has developed a system that makes all features of a traditional paper-based flight bag available electronically to the pilot and the crew. This Electronic Flight Bag (EFB) is a software and data services solution that offers airlines advanced information management capabilities and delivers more accurate performance calculations, thus creating significant savings of time and money while increasing safety and streamlining the management of flight information. Using information technology, airlines can realize the "paperless cockpit," in which most paper documents are eliminated. Revisions to electronic documents are made electronically, and computations are rapid and more precise. In addition to reducing the paper trail associated with flight planning and execution, the EFB also integrates security-relevant features, such as cabin video surveillance, which also helps an airline comply with security mandates for video and EFB functionality in a single system. Finally, certain EFB applications, such as Taxi Position Awareness, can contribute to a reduction or elimination of runway incursions. Enhanced position awareness and decreased pilot workload mitigate one of the top safety concerns in aviation today while also helping to improve the efficiency of ground operations.

In contrast to traditional paper-based flight documentation, the EFB can increase efficiency and effectiveness by providing accurate and timely performance calculations, such as precise, real-time calculation of takeoff and landing performance, including maximum takeoff and landing weights and engine power settings. The paperless cockpit also helps to create cost savings, as the electronic distribution of information can directly reduce support costs associated with receiving, reviewing, and distributing paper documents such as electronic navigation charts, electronic airplane and flight operations manuals, and electronic aircraft logbooks. In addition to offering superior search and retrieval functions, these electronic documents also help to reduce an aircraft's takeoff weight because of the reduced need for bulky paper-based documents.

Crew scheduling is an important supporting function to sustain an airline's flight operations. To provide airlines with a seamlessly integrated solution, Boeing decided to acquire SBS International, a company specializing in crew management solutions. These software tools help an airline monitor crew assignments in real time and help increase efficient use of resources by providing timely and accurate information, helping to optimize crew scheduling and avoid rule-violation penalties that can adversely affect an airline's operating costs. In addition to the mere scheduling, these systems were even designed to amend hotel and ground transportation arrangements to the schedules, maintain detailed master records, and communicate with payroll systems. Using an aircraft's data transmission infrastructure, these systems can be accessed in flight, maximizing the potential for last-minute schedule, or ground transportation or accommodation changes, if necessary. For the crew, this real-time access to the latest information means less uncertainty and can increase the crew's satisfaction with their jobs. At the same time, the real-time availability helps the employees at the managerial levels of an airline, as crew members can accept or decline schedule change requests in a more timely manner, helping to reduce uncertainty and aiding in the crew-scheduling process.

Another important support function for an airline's flight operation is aircraft maintenance. Boeing's Airplane Health Management (AHM) is a system designed to reduce delays, cancellations, air turnbacks, and diversions through the innovative use of existing data. Made possible by advances in data processing, transmission, and analysis, AHM integrates remote collection, monitoring, and analysis of airplane data to determine the status of an airplane's current and future serviceability. These data are converted into information airlines can use to make the operational or fix-or-fly decisions that can make the difference between profit and loss since minimizing aircraft downtime is a very important factor in reducing operating costs and improving profitability.

When a fault occurs in flight, AHM allows airlines to make operational decisions immediately and, if maintenance is required, to make arrangements for the people, parts, and equipment sooner rather than later. It is also designed to aid in forecasting and fixing problems before failure, a process referred to as "prognostics." Problems that might have initiated unplanned maintenance can be performed on a planned basis, helping the employees on the managerial level schedule the aircraft's availability. Real-time information availability can help to reduce schedule interruptions and trim the number of delays by sending data directly from air to ground so that repair teams can begin work on a solution before the plane lands. The ground maintenance crews can directly access the aircraft's systems and diagnose the problem, and mechanics can work on fixing the problem as soon as the aircraft arrives at the gate. This helps to get the aircraft back into the air as soon as possible, in turn helping to minimize costs associated with delays, rescheduling, or flight cancellations.

As for any other company, information is only as valuable as the ability to act on it. The e-Enabled Advantage integrates powerful visualization tools and decision aids to help an airline incorporate the latest information from throughout the network into dynamic planning (see Figure). Using the e-Enabled Advantage's integrated systems, an airline can interrupt the cascade of unforeseen events before they become costly schedule disruptions. On the flight deck, the EFB gives flight crews a sharper strategic picture of where they are, where they are going, and what is waiting beyond the horizon.

An airline command center.

Questions

1. Briefly discuss the various features of Boeing's e-Enabled airplane vision. How could the systems mentioned in the case be integrated with the different systems in other business functions (e.g., accounting, finance, and sales and marketing) of an airline? Explain.
2. Which other features necessary to sustain an airline's flight operation could be integrated into the e-Enabled Advantage? Look up potential solutions at www.boeing.com.
3. How can the information generated at the operational and managerial level be used at the executive level of an airline?

Sources: www.boeing.com/commercial/ams/mss/brochures/airplane_health_brochure.html

www.boeing.com/commercial/e-Enabled/index.html

www.jeppesen.com

www.sbsint.com

chapter 8

Building Organizational Partnerships Using Enterprise Information Systems

preview > This chapter describes how companies are deploying enterprise-wide information systems to build and strengthen organizational partnerships. Enterprise systems help to integrate various business activities, to streamline and better manage interactions with customers, and to coordinate better with suppliers in order to meet changing customer demands more efficiently and effectively. After reading this chapter, you will be able to do the following:

1. Describe what enterprise systems are and how they have evolved.

2. Describe enterprise resource planning systems and how they help to improve internal business processes.

3. Describe customer relationship management systems and how they help to improve downstream business processes.

4. Describe supply chain management systems and how they help to improve upstream business processes.

5. Understand and utilize the keys to successfully implementing enterprise systems.

Large companies continue to find that they need systems that span their entire organization and tie everything together. As a result, an understanding of enterprise systems is critical to succeed in today's competitive and ever-changing digital world.

Managing in the Digital World: Customer Relationship Management and Major League Baseball

In 2004, the Boston Red Sox baseball team won the World Series. Twelve hours later, the Web site for major league baseball—MLB.com—had sold $3 million worth of Boston Red Sox gear. Three million dollars worth of sales in a 12-hour period is still a record for MLB.com. How can an information system handle this many customers while still offering services such as live video feeds, ring tones, and game tickets? Major League Baseball Advanced Media (MLBAM), the company that creates and serves the content for all 30 MLB teams, as well as the Web site MLB.com, has the answer: Since MLBAM became Major League Baseball's (MLB's) provider of customer relationship management (CRM) in 2001, the focus for the Web site has always been the customer. Services that attract and retain MLB.com customers include the following:

- Team merchandise
- Live audio and video streaming of 97 percent of all MLB games to more than 1 million subscribers, generating a reported $12 million to $16 million in revenue per year
- Fantasy baseball
- Ring tones, wallpaper, and other mobile content for cell phones
- Game tickets for all 30 MLB teams

Every one of these services has been lucrative for MLB.com. For example, the Web site has sold more than 1.5 million ring tones, mobile phone wallpaper, and other mobile content at prices ranging from 99 cents to $2.99. MLB.com is also *the* place for any baseball stat and story, including live online stats for all the 4860 games played in any given season.

MLBAM clearly identifies mobile phone content as an area for profit and growth. MLBAM mobile content is a billion-dollar industry that also includes statistical services and video feeds. MLB gave away their statistics until MLBAM convinced the 100-year-old corporation to charge for the service. Now any Web site that wants to publish MLB statistics has to buy a license through MLBAM.

MLBAM also runs MiLB.com for minor league baseball, which offers similar services as MLB.com for over 100 teams in three different countries, as part of MLB's strategy to promote baseball inside and outside of the United States. The World Baseball Classic is an example of baseball's expansion and has opened up another outlet for MLBAM to sell merchandise, tickets, and other services at the World Baseball Classic's Web site: www. worldbaseballclassic.com. In fact, the World Baseball Classic's Web site sold more merchandise during the three-

week tournament than it sold during any prior World Series. Over 50 percent of sales were to customers outside the United States.

MLBAM has not always been the darling of CRM applications. For instance, after taking over from Sportsline.com, MLBAM refused to accept advertising in any form on the MLB.com site. Instead, the organization concentrated on becoming the largest online baseball store. This angered many big-name corporate clients who then pulled their traditional advertising from MLB ballparks around the country. While the move seemed risky at first, it resulted in a clean, content-oriented CRM data collection and storage site that now reaps the rewards of this decision.

Another decision looming as a deal breaker for MLBAM is that of entering the $1 billion industry of fantasy sports. Yahoo! and Microsoft also offer fantasy baseball sites, and MLBAM threatens them by requiring all fantasy baseball sites to license players' names and statistics from them. The threat of "pay the licensing fee or shut down" may have a negative impact on MLB.com by alienating those who made the site so highly successful.

Clearly, however, MLBAM is committed to offering baseball fans a wide variety of baseball merchandise and services through use of a comprehensive and appropriately used CRM. The commitment—and the access to customer data—will surely continue to pay off in the future.

After reading this chapter, you will be able to answer the following:

1. In what ways do MLB.com's front-office systems provide data for back-office systems?

2. How does MLB.com operationalize sales force automation capabilities within their Web site?

3. Which of MLB.com's customer service and support capabilities attract and retain customers? What might frustrate customers?

Sources:

Ryan Nairane, "Baseball Goes beyond Baseball Diamond," *Internet News* (May 5, 2004), http://www.internetnews.com/bus-news/article.php/3349891

Jon Surmacz, "In a League of Its Own," *CIO,* http://www.cio.com/archive/041505/baseball.html

Enterprise Systems

Companies use information systems to support their various business processes and activities for internal operations such as manufacturing, order processing, and human resource management. Companies can also use information systems to support external interactions with customers, suppliers, and business partners. Businesses have leveraged information systems to support business processes and activities for decades, beginning with the installation of applications to assist companies with specific business tasks such as issuing paychecks. Often these systems were built on different computing platforms, such as mainframes and midrange computers, each operating in unique hardware and software environments. Applications running on different computing platforms are difficult to integrate, as custom interfaces are required in order for one system to communicate with another.

Utilizing different applications on separate computing platforms can create tremendous inefficiencies within organizations because data cannot readily be shared between the systems. To utilize this data to facilitate business processes and decision making, information must be reentered from one system to the next or be consolidated by a third system. Additionally, the same pieces of data may also be stored in several versions throughout the organization. **Enterprise-wide information systems** (or **enterprise systems**), thus, are information systems that allow companies to integrate information across operations on a company-wide basis. Rather than storing information in separate places throughout the organization, enterprise systems provide a central repository common to all corporate users. This, along with a common user interface, allows personnel to share information seamlessly no matter where the data is located or who is using the application (see Figure 8.2).

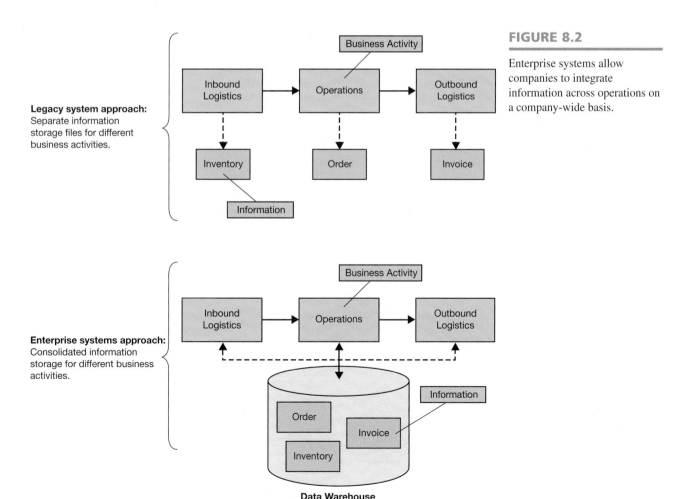

Legacy system approach: Separate information storage files for different business activities.

Enterprise systems approach: Consolidated information storage for different business activities.

Data Warehouse

FIGURE 8.2

Enterprise systems allow companies to integrate information across operations on a company-wide basis.

The emergence of the Internet and Web has resulted in the globalization of customer and supplier networks, opening up new opportunities and methods to conduct business. Customers have an increasing number of options available to them, so they are demanding more sophisticated products that are customized to their unique needs. They also expect higher levels of customer service. If companies cannot keep their customers satisfied, the customers will not hesitate to do business with a competitor. Companies need to provide quality customer service and develop products faster and more efficiently to compete in global markets. Enterprise systems can be extended to streamline communications with customers and suppliers. Rather than focusing only on internal operations, these systems can also focus on business activities that occur outside organizational boundaries. Enterprise systems can help companies find innovative ways to increase accurate on-time shipments, avoid (or at least anticipate) surprises, minimize costs, and ultimately increase customer satisfaction and the overall profitability of the company.

Enterprise systems come in a variety of shapes and sizes, each providing a unique set of features and functionality. When deciding to implement enterprise solutions, managers need to be aware of a number of issues. One of the most important involves selecting and implementing applications that meet the requirements of the business as well as of its customers and suppliers. In the following sections, we examine the ways in which information systems can be leveraged to support business processes. This is followed by an in-depth analysis of how enterprise systems have evolved and how companies are using these systems to support their internal and external operations.

Supporting Business Activities

As we talked about in Chapter 3—Valuing Information Systems Investments, information systems can be used to increase competitive advantage by supporting and/or streamlining business processes (Porter and Millar, 1985). For example, an information system could be used to support a billing process in such a way that it reduces the use of paper and, more important, the handling of paper, thus reducing material and labor costs. This system can help managers keep track of that same billing process more effectively because they will have more accurate, up-to-date information about the billing process, enabling them to make smart, timely business decisions.

Information systems can be used to support either internally or externally focused business processes. **Internally focused systems** support functional areas, business processes, and decision making *within* an organization. These activities can be viewed as a series of links in a chain along which information flows within the organization. At each stage (or link) in the process, value is added in the form of the work performed by people associated with that process, and new, useful information is generated. Information begins to accumulate at the point of entry and flows through the various links, or business processes, within the organization, progressing through the organization with new, useful information being added every step of the way (see Figure 8.3).

FIGURE 8.3

Information flow for a typical order.

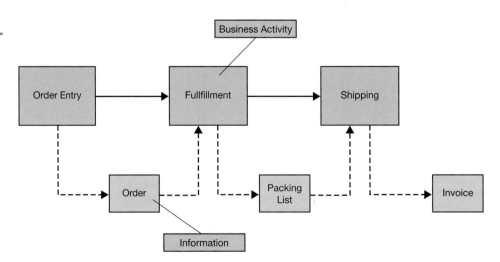

In contrast, **externally focused systems** coordinate business activities with customers, suppliers, business partners, and others who operate *outside* an organization's boundaries. A system that communicates across organizational boundaries is sometimes referred to as an **interorganizational system (IOS)** (Kumar and Crook, 1999). The key purpose of an IOS is to streamline the flow of information from one company's operations to another's (e.g., from a company to its potential or existing customers).

Competitive advantage can be accomplished here by integrating multiple business processes in ways that enable a firm to meet a wide range of unique customer needs. Sharing information between organizations helps companies to adapt more quickly to changing market conditions. For instance, should consumers demand an additional component to be added to a product, a company can gain this information from its information systems that support sales and pass it along to its component suppliers in real time. Information systems allow the company and its suppliers to satisfy the needs of customers efficiently since changes can be identified and managed immediately, creating a competitive advantage for companies that can respond quickly. We can view processes and information flows across organizations just as we previously viewed the processes and information flows within an organization. At each stage (or link) in the process, value is added by the work performed, and new, useful information is generated and exchanged between organizations (see Figure 8.4). Using IOS, one company can create information and transmit it electronically to another company.

Internally Focused Applications

Because companies within certain industries operate their businesses differently, one of the first challenges an organization must face is to understand how it can use information systems to support its unique internal business activities. Generally, the flow of information through a set of business activities is referred to as a *value chain* (Porter and Millar, 1985), in which information flows through functional areas that facilitate the internal activities of the business. Figure 8.5 depicts the value chain framework. In Chapter 3, we spoke of the strategic value of analyzing a value chain; now, we show you how to use value chain analysis to implement enterprise systems.

Functional areas can be broken down into core and support activities. *Core activities* are functional areas within an organization that process inputs and produce outputs. *Support activities* are those activities that enable core activities to take place. In the following sections, we focus on core activities and then turn our attention to the support activities that make them possible.

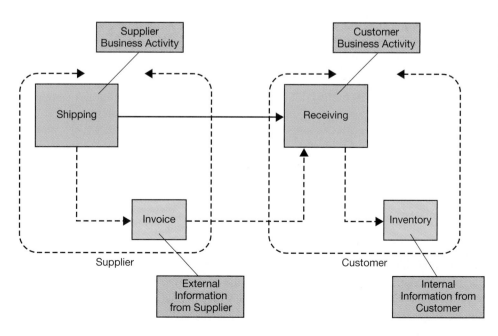

FIGURE 8.4

Information flow for a typical shipment across organizational boundaries.

FIGURE 8.5

Value chain framework.

Source: Porter and Millar (1985).

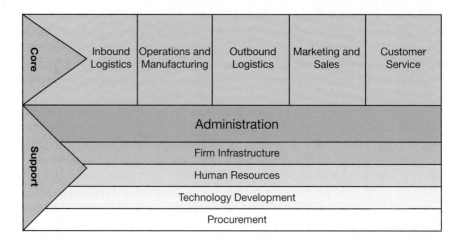

Core Activities Core activities include inbound logistics, operations and manufacturing, outbound logistics, marketing and sales, and customer service. These activities may differ widely, depending on the unique requirements of the industry in which a company operates, although the basic concepts hold in most organizations.

INBOUND LOGISTICS ACTIVITIES. Inbound logistics involves the business activities associated with receiving and stocking raw materials, parts, and products. For example, inbound logistics at Cisco Systems involves the receipt of electronic components that go into making their end products, such as routers. Shippers deliver electronic components to Cisco, where employees unwrap the packages and stock the components in the company's inventory. Cisco can automatically update inventory levels at the point of delivery, allowing purchasing managers to access real-time information related to inventory levels and reorder points.

OPERATIONS AND MANUFACTURING ACTIVITIES. Once the components have been stocked in inventory, the functional area of operations and manufacturing takes over. Operations and manufacturing can involve such activities as order processing and/or manufacturing processes that transform raw materials and/or component parts into end products. Companies such as Dell Computers utilize Web-based information systems to allow customers to enter orders online. This information is used to coordinate the manufacturing of a customized personal computer in which the component parts are gathered and assembled to create the end product. During this process, inventory levels from inbound logistics are verified; if the appropriate inventory exists, workers pick the components from existing supplies and build the product to the customer's specifications. When components are picked, items are deducted from inventory; once the product is assembled, inventory levels for the final product are updated.

OUTBOUND LOGISTICS ACTIVITIES. The functional area of outbound logistics mirrors that of inbound logistics. Instead of involving the receipt of raw materials, parts, and products, outbound logistics focuses on the distribution of end products. For example, outbound logistics at Amazon.com involves the delivery of books that customers have ordered. Orders that have been processed by the operations area are forwarded to outbound logistics, which picks the products from inventory and coordinates delivery to the customer. At that point, items are packaged and deducted from the company's inventory, and an invoice is created that will be sent to the customer. Amazon.com can automatically update sales information at the point of distribution, allowing managers to view inventory and revenue information in real time.

MARKETING AND SALES ACTIVITIES. The marketing and sales functional area facilitates the presales (i.e., before the sale) activities of the company. These include such things as creation of marketing literature, communication with potential and existing customers, and pricing of goods and services. As discussed in Chapter 5—Enabling Commerce Using the

Internet, many companies support the business activity of marketing and sales by creating an e-brochure. Other companies, such as Amtrak, a U.S. passenger train service, use information systems to update pricing information and schedules. This information is entered directly into the pricing and scheduling systems, allowing the information to become immediately accessible throughout the organization and to end consumers through the organization's Web site.

CUSTOMER SERVICE ACTIVITIES. Whereas marketing and sales focus on presales activities, customer service focuses on the postsales (i.e., after the sale) activities. Customers may have questions and need help from a customer service representative. Many companies, such as Hewlett-Packard (HP), are utilizing information systems to provide customer service. These applications allow customers to search for and download information related to the products that they have purchased. For example, HP customers may need to install drivers for the printers they have just purchased. Rather than calling a customer service representative, customers can help themselves through a self-service customer support application.

Companies can use information systems to track service requests. When a customer calls in for repairs to a product, customer service representatives can access a bevy of information related to the customer. For instance, an agent can access technical information concerning the specific product as well as review any problems the customer has encountered in the past. This enables customer service representatives to react quickly to customer concerns, improving the customer service experience.

Support Activities Support activities are business activities that enable the primary activities to take place. Support activities include administrative activities, infrastructure, human resources, technology development, and procurement.

ADMINISTRATIVE ACTIVITIES. Administrative activities focuses on the processes and decision making to orchestrate the day-to-day operations of an organization, particularly those processes that span organizational functions and levels. Administration includes systems and processes from virtually all functional areas—accounting, finance, marketing, operations, and so on—as well as both the executive and the managerial level.

INFRASTRUCTURE ACTIVITIES. Infrastructure refers to the hardware and software that must be implemented to support the applications that the primary activities use. An order entry application requires that employees who enter orders have a computer and the necessary software to accomplish their business objective. In turn, the computer must be connected via the network to a database containing the order information so that the order can be saved and recalled later for processing. Infrastructure provides the necessary components to facilitate the order entry process (see Chapter 4—Managing the Information Systems Infrastructure).

HUMAN RESOURCE ACTIVITIES. Human resources involves the business activities associated with employee management, such as hiring, interview scheduling, payroll, and benefits management. Human resources is classified as a support activity since the primary activities cannot be accomplished without the employees to perform them. In other words, all the primary activities use the human resource business activity. For example, if a company needs a new customer service representative to serve the growing volume of customers, the request is processed through the human resource function, which creates the job description and locates the appropriate person to fill the job.

TECHNOLOGY DEVELOPMENT ACTIVITIES. Technology development includes the design and development of applications that support the primary business activities. If you are planning on pursuing a career in the management information systems field, the technology business activity is likely where you will find a job. Technology can involve a wide array of responsibilities, such as the selection of packaged software or the design and development of a custom application to meet a particular business need. Many companies are leveraging the technology business activity to build Internet, intranet, and extranet applications for these purposes. As seen in previous chapters, companies use these systems to support a wide variety of primary business activities.

Brief Case ⊘

Outsourcing Your McDonald's Order

Dial the customer service telephone number for countless companies, and chances are you will speak to a representative based in India, the Dominican Republic, Thailand, or another offshore location. The practice of outsourcing is becoming increasingly prominent in our lives: Customer service and catalog sales representatives are often located offshore. More than 50 percent of U.S. income tax returns are prepared outside the United States. And the latest major industry to outsource? Surprisingly, it's fast food. Since outsourcing lends itself to services and products not used or consumed where they are purchased, fast-food drive-through kiosks have proved the perfect opportunity for outsourcing.

McDonald's, one of America's largest success stories, is synonymous with fast food. Founded in 1948 in San Bernardino, California, the company has parlayed its original 15-cent hamburgers and 10-cent French fries into a worldwide, $20 billion business. The company strives for uniformity in its 31,000 locations around the globe. That is, if a customer orders a quarter-pounder with fries in Tokyo, the meal should be of the same quality as the quarter-pounder with fries ordered in Moscow, Shanghai, or Chicago (see Figure 8.6).

As McDonald's became increasingly globalized, it made financial sense for the company to search for outsourcing possibilities. The drive-through service seemed especially well suited because of the repetitive nature of the service and the fact that it is difficult to retain staff in the low-paying drive-through positions.

McDonald's was not interested in investing millions in a new drive-through ordering system to facilitate outsourcing. Any changes made in technology had to be easy and cheap, and outsourcing fit the bill. McDonald's restaurants everywhere were already connected to the Internet since daily sales were downloaded to corporate offices and price changes uploaded to retail outlets. Therefore, the software was updated to allow for orders to be processed overseas and be entered into McDonald's food management queue. It didn't matter if the order was taken 20 feet or 20,000 miles away; the process was the same—only the network was different.

FIGURE 8.6

McDonald's can be found in most places in the world.

Like most organizations, the Internet and information technology are vital in allowing McDonald's to improve its business processes. Now your McDonald's order might be going from router to router at light speed and arriving at a foreign destination, to be relayed back to the local McDonald's where your order will actually be served. For McDonald's, the end goal is the same as it was over 55 years ago—customers will receive the same quality product at any McDonald's restaurant, but their orders may be routed to the Dominican Republic, India, or Thailand before they are filled and the food is served.

Questions

1. From the perspective of both McDonald's and its customers, what are the pros and cons for outsourcing drive-through ordering?
2. What risks does a local McDonald's restaurant assume when utilizing outsourced drive-through service? How can these risks be minimized?

Source: Brian R. Hook, "Technology Beefs Up Restaurant Drive Through Experience," *CRMBuyer* (April 11, 2005), http://www.crmbuyer.com/story/41938.html

PROCUREMENT ACTIVITIES. Procurement refers to the purchasing of goods and services that are required as inputs to the primary activities. Allowing each functional area to send out purchase orders can create problems for companies, such as maintaining relationships with more suppliers than necessary and not taking advantage of volume discounts. The procurement business activity can leverage information systems by accumulating purchase

Change Agents

Larry Ellison, Founder and Chief Executive Officer, Oracle Corporation

He's known as "the other software billionaire." He's outspoken, highly competitive, a fashionable dresser, and not averse to risk. He's Larry Ellison, the founder and chief executive officer of Oracle Corporation, second only to Microsoft in software sales.

Ellison was born on August 17, 1944, in New York City to a 19-year-old, unmarried mother who could not care for him. When he was nine months old, Ellison's great-aunt and great-uncle, hardworking Russian immigrants, adopted him. He did not find out he was adopted until he was 12 years old but says, "I don't attribute very much of my personality to my adoption. I attribute an awful lot to my relationship with my father, who was a Russian immigrant. He came here and was very, very poor. He dearly loved this country as only an immigrant can, loved our government as only an immigrant can. He was a bomber pilot in World War II. He really had the philosophy of 'my country,

FIGURE 8.7

Larry Ellison, founder and chief executive officer, Oracle Corporation.

Source: http://e,-wikipedia.org/wiki/Image:Larry_ellison_portrait.jpg.

right or wrong.' He never questioned the government's policies, never questioned authority, and he didn't want me to question authority."

Whatever his father's wishes might have been, Ellison grew up questioning authority and taking risks—traits that have served him well in business. A college dropout who used programming skills to further his career, Ellison earned a reputation as an impeccable business man who can anticipate software needs and who spurs his employees to sometimes deliver what others consider impossible. For example, he has promised potential customers software features that didn't exist, then returned to his development teams for results that justify the sales pitch. Furthermore, he has hired employees for impressive character traits who were so unskilled that they needed manuals to do their jobs.

Asked in a 2005 interview about his worst business experience, Ellison said it was in 1990, when Oracle was 20 years old and showed a first-quarter loss for the first time ever. He said he realized when the numbers came in that the management team that was efficient in running a $5 million company was no longer efficient in running a $1 billion company. "I had to fire people," he said of that time. "That was the most difficult thing I had to do in business, asking a bunch of people to leave Oracle."

Ellison tells interviewers that his idea of happiness is to live an "intelligent life," which includes altruism, for the self-gratification it brings; working with intelligent people; and pursuing activities such as sailing and flying for the challenge and the "adrenaline rush."

Ellison serves on Apple Computer's board and on the board for the Dian Fossey Gorilla Fund. The many honors and awards he has received include Entrepreneur of the Year from Harvard Business School.

"If the Internet turns out not to be the future of computing, we're toast," Ellison said early in his career. "But if it is, we're golden." By anyone's business standards, Oracle, Ellison's creation, is "golden."

Sources: Academy of Achievement Interview with Ellison (May 22, 1997), http://www.achievement.org/autodoc/page/ell0int-1

http://www.askmen.com/men/may00/24_larry_ellison.html

orders from the different functional areas within the corporation. By having this information at their disposal, procurement personnel can combine multiple purchase orders containing the same item into a single purchase order. Ordering larger volumes from its suppliers means that the company can achieve dramatic cost savings through volume discounts. Procurement receives, approves, and processes requests for goods and services from the primary activities and coordinates the purchase of those items. This allows the primary activities to concentrate on running the business rather than adding to their workload.

Externally Focused Applications

The flow of information can be streamlined not only within a company but outside organizational boundaries as well. A company can create additional value by integrating internal applications with suppliers, business partners, and customers. Companies accomplish this by connecting their internal value chains as a **value system** (Porter and Millar, 1985), in which information flows from one company's value chain to another company's value chain. Figure 8.8 depicts the value system framework. In this diagram, three companies are aligning their value chains to form a value system. First, company A processes information through its value chain and forwards the information along to its customer, company B, which processes the information through its value chain and sends the information along to its customer, company C, which processes the information through its value chain. Adding additional suppliers, business partners, and customers can create complex value systems. However, for our purposes, we simply view an organization's information systems as a value chain that interacts with the value chains of other organizations.

Externally focused systems can be used to coordinate a company's value chain with another company's value chain or with consumers (such as in business-to-consumer electronic commerce). Any information that feeds into a company's value chain, whether its source is another company's value chain or an end consumer, is considered part of the value system.

The value system can be viewed as a river of information that flows from a source to an ultimate destination. Like a river, at any particular point there is a flow coming from upstream and progressing downstream. Value systems comprise upstream and downstream information flows. An **upstream information flow** consists of information that is received from another organization, whereas a **downstream information flow** relates to the information that is produced by a company and sent along to another organization. For instance, using the value system depicted in Figure 8.8 as an example, the upstream and downstream information flows for company B become quite evident. In this case, company B receives information from its upstream supplier, processes the information through its internal

---

FIGURE 8.8

Value system framework.

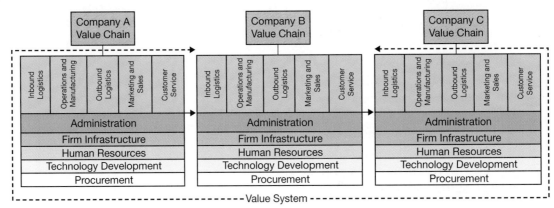

Source: Porter and Millar (1985).

value chain, and subsequently passes information downstream to its distributors and/or customers. These flows of external information into and from a company can be leveraged to create additional value and competitive advantage.

The Rise of Enterprise Systems

Software programs come in two forms—packaged and custom. **Packaged applications** are software programs written by third-party vendors for the needs of many different users and organizations, whereas **custom applications** are software programs that are designed and developed exclusively for a specific organization. Packaged applications that you are likely familiar with are Microsoft Money and Quicken, which are software packages users can purchase off the shelf to help them with their financial matters. Packaged systems are highly useful for standardized, repetitive tasks such as making entries in a check register. They can be quite cost effective since the vendor that builds the software application can spread out development costs through selling to a large number of users.

Yet packaged applications may not be well suited for tasks that are unique to a particular business. In these cases, companies may prefer to develop (or have developed for them) custom applications that can accommodate their particular business needs. The development costs of custom systems are much higher than for packaged applications because of the time, money, and resources that are required to design and develop them. Furthermore, applications need to be maintained internally when changes are required. With packaged applications, the vendor makes the changes and distributes new versions to its customers. In all, there are trade-offs when choosing between the packaged and custom application routes. Managers must consider whether packaged applications can meet the business requirements and, if not, conduct a cost-benefit analysis to ensure that taking the custom application approach will prove worthwhile to the company.

Figure 8.9 provides a high-level overview of how enterprise systems typically evolve. As companies begin to leverage information systems applications, they typically start out by fulfilling the needs of particular business activities in a particular department within the organization. Systems that focus on the specific needs of individual departments are not

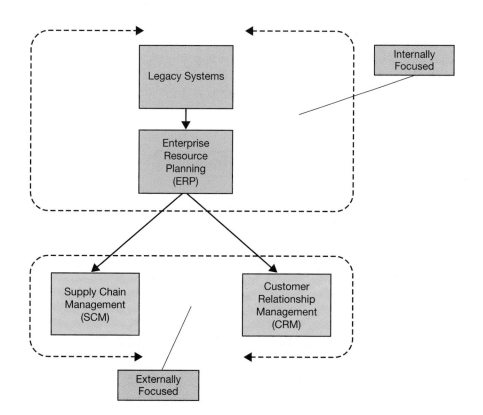

FIGURE 8.9

Stages of enterprise systems evolution.

designed to communicate with other systems in the organization and are, therefore, referred to as **stand-alone applications**. Stand-alone applications usually run on a variety of computing hardware platforms, such as mainframes and midrange computers. Together, stand-alone applications and the computers they run on are often referred to as **legacy systems**, given that they are typically older systems that are either fast approaching or beyond the end of their useful life within the organization. Legacy systems tend to require substantial resources to maintain them to accommodate emerging business needs.

Legacy Systems When companies first use information systems to support business activities, they usually begin by implementing systems in various departments rather than starting with a single application that can accommodate all aspects of the business. Each department implements applications to assist it with its daily business activities, which are optimized for its unique needs and the manner in which personnel in a particular unit accomplish job tasks. These applications tend to be infrastructure specific, meaning that they run on particular hardware and software platforms. As a result, each department normally has its own computing system that runs its necessary applications. Although departmental systems enable departments to conduct their daily business activities efficiently, these systems often are not very helpful when people from one part of the firm need information from another part of the firm (e.g., people in manufacturing need forecasts from sales).

Given that these older systems were not necessarily designed to communicate with other applications beyond departmental boundaries, they are classified as "legacy" systems, or systems that operate within the confines of a particular business need. Legacy systems and their associated stand-alone applications can prove problematic when information from multiple departmental systems is required to support business processes and decision making (as is often the case). For example, if the applications for inbound logistics and operations are not integrated, companies will lose valuable time in accessing information related to inventory levels. When an order is placed through operations, personnel need to verify that the components are available in inventory before the order can be processed.

If the inventory and order-entry systems are not integrated, personnel may have to access two separate applications or use a custom interface that pulls information from both systems. Figure 8.10 provides an example of how information flows through legacy systems within an organization. As the diagram depicts, information is generated by the inbound logistics business activity, but it does not flow through to the next business activity, in this case operations. Since the inbound logistics and operations departments use different legacy systems, information cannot readily flow from one business activity to

FIGURE 8.10

Information flows using legacy systems.

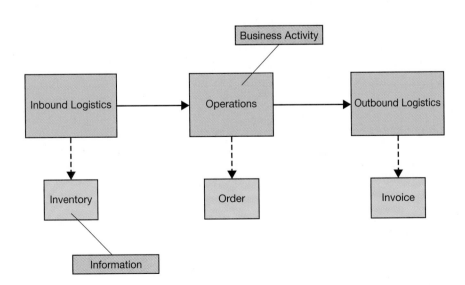

another. Understandably, this creates a highly inefficient process for operations personnel, who must have access to two systems or a common interface that pulls information together in order to get both the order entry and the inventory information. In some cases, inventory information may be stored on both systems, creating the potential for inaccuracies. Should data be updated in one system but not the other, the data becomes outdated and inaccurate. In addition, there are further, unnecessary costs associated with entering, storing, and updating data redundantly.

The Need for Integrated Enterprise Systems Companies can gain several advantages by integrating and converting legacy systems so that information stored on separate computing platforms can be consolidated to provide a centralized point of access. The process of **conversion** transfers information stored on legacy systems to a new, integrated computing platform, which typically comes in the form of *enterprise resource planning (ERP)* applications (discussed later in this chapter). Although such applications do an excellent job of serving the needs of internal business operations on an organization-wide basis, they are not necessarily designed to completely accommodate the communication of information outside the organization's boundaries.

Systems that facilitate interorganizational communications focus on either the upstream or the downstream information flows. Since these systems coordinate business activities across organizational boundaries, they are classified as externally focused applications. *Customer relationship management* applications concentrate on the downstream information flows, integrating the value chains of a company and its distributors or customers (discussed later). In contrast, *supply chain management* applications operate on the upstream information flows, integrating the value chains of a company and its suppliers (also discussed later).

Improving Business Processes through Enterprise Systems Because all companies are different, no packaged software application will exactly fit the unique requirements of a particular business. Likewise, enterprise systems come in a variety of shapes and sizes, each designed to accommodate certain transaction volumes, industries, and business processes. Thus, ERP vendors provide different **modules**, which are components that can be selected and implemented as needed. The modules provided by different vendors may vary in the specific business processes they support as well as what they are called (see Tables 8.1 and 8.2 for examples of modules and key capabilities of the mySAP business suite).

VANILLA VERSUS CUSTOMIZED SOFTWARE. As the naming and capabilities differ between the ERP vendors, it is critical for managers to understand the vendors' naming conventions and software modules to gain an understanding of how these features can be implemented to meet the company's business processes. The features and modules that an enterprise system comes with out of the box are referred to as the **vanilla version**. If the vanilla version does not support a certain business process, the company may require a customized version. **Customization** either provides additional software that is integrated with the enterprise system or direct changes to the vanilla application itself. SAP, for example, includes literally thousands of elements in their various enterprise systems that can be customized and also offers many industry-specific versions that have already been customized for a particular industry based on SAP's perceptions of the best way to do things (i.e., best practices). Companies must take special care when dealing with customization issues. Customizations can be extremely costly, and maintaining and upgrading customizations can be troublesome. For example, a customization made to the

TABLE 8.1 Key Components of the mySAP Business Suite

mySAP Customer Relationship Mgmt	mySAP Supplier Relationship Mgmt
mySAP ERP	mySAP Supply Chain Mgmt
mySAP Product Lifecycle Mgmt	

TABLE 8.2 Key Capabilities of mySAP ERP

Capability	Explanation
Business analysis	Enables you to evaluate your business performance by taking advantage of functionality for analyzing your workforce, operations, and supply chain.
Financial and management accounting	Allows you to manage corporate finance functions by automating financial supply chain management, financial accounting, and management accounting. This capability is enabled by mySAP ERP Financials.
Human capital management	Gives you the tools you need to maximize the profitability potential of your workforce, with functionality for employee transaction management and employee life-cycle management. This capability is enabled by mySAP ERP Human Capital Management.
Operations management	Empowers you to streamline operations with integrated functionality for managing end-to-end logistics processes—while expanding your collaborative capabilities in supply chain management, product life-cycle management, and supplier relationship management. This capability is enabled by mySAP ERP Operations.
Corporate services management	Allows you to optimize centralized and decentralized services for managing real estate, corporate travel, and incentives and commissions. This capability is enabled by mySAP ERP Corporate Services.
Self-services	Provides an employee-centric portal that enables both employees and managers to create, view, and modify key information. Uses a broad range of interaction technologies, including Web browser, voice, and mobile devices, for easy access to internal and external business content, applications, and services.

vanilla version will need to be reprogrammed when a new release of the system is implemented because subsequent releases of the software will not include the previous customizations. In other words, new vanilla versions must be continually upgraded to accommodate the company-specific customizations. This process can involve a substantial investment of time and resources.

BEST PRACTICES–BASED SOFTWARE. One of the major hurdles posed to companies that implement enterprise systems involves changing business processes to accommodate the manner in which the software works. Enterprise system implementations are often used as a catalyst for overall improvement of underlying business processes. As with SAP, most enterprise systems are designed to operate according to industry-standard business processes, or best practices. In fact, most enterprise system vendors build best practices into their applications to provide guidelines for management to identify business activities within their organizations that need to be streamlined. Implementations and future upgrades to the system will go more smoothly when companies change their business processes to fit the way the enterprise system operates.

Many organizations have spent many years developing business processes that provide them with a competitive advantage in the marketplace. Adopting their industry's best practices may force these companies to abandon their unique ways of doing business, putting them on par with their industry competitors. In other words, companies can potentially lose their competitive advantages by adopting the best practices within their industry. Best practices is an area that managers must carefully consider before selecting any type of enterprise system because some enterprise system vendors tightly integrate best practices into the software, and companies that reject best practices are in for a long and time-consuming implementation. Other vendors provide a series of options that companies select before implementing the software, allowing them some (but not complete) flexibility in changing their business processes to accommodate the enterprise system modules. Given the importance and difficulty of changing business processes with enterprise and other systems implementations, we now briefly describe business process management.

BUSINESS PROCESS MANAGEMENT. Since the first publishing of *The Principles of Scientific Management* by Fredrick Taylor in 1911, organizations have focused on improving business processes. Over the years, various forms of business process improvement have been developed (see Table 8.3). Given the magnitude of change that an enterprise system can impose on an organization's business processes, understanding the role of business process management in the implementation of an enterprise system is necessary. **Business process management (BPM)** is a systematic, structured improvement approach by all or part of an organization whereby people critically examine, rethink, and redesign business processes in order to achieve dramatic improvements in one or more performance measures, such as quality, cycle time, or cost. BPM became very popular in the 1990s (and was then called **business process reengineering [BPR]**) when Michael Hammer and James Champy published their best-selling book *Reengineering the Corporation.*

Hammer and Champy and their proponents argued that radical redesign of an organization was sometimes necessary in order to lower costs and increase quality and that information systems were the key enabler for that radical change. The basic steps in BPM can be summarized as follows:

1. Develop a vision for the organization that specifies business objectives, such as reducing costs, shortening the time it takes to take products to market, improving quality of products and/or services, and so on
2. Identify the critical processes that are to be redesigned
3. Understand and measure the existing processes as a baseline for future improvements
4. Identify ways that information systems can be used to improve processes
5. Design and implement a prototype of the new process(es)

BPM is like quality improvement approaches such as *total quality management* and *continuous process improvement* in that they are intended to be cross-functional approaches to improve an organization. BPM differs from these quality improvement approaches, however, in one fundamental way. These quality improvement approaches tend to focus on incremental change and gradual improvement of processes, while the intention behind BPM is radical redesign and drastic improvement of processes.

When BPR was introduced in the 1990s, many efforts were reported to have failed. These failures occurred for a variety of reasons, including the lack of sustained management commitment and leadership, unrealistic scope and expectations, and resistance to change. In fact, BPR gained the reputation of being a nice way of saying "downsizing."

Nevertheless, BPR (and its successors such as BPM) lives on today and is still a popular approach to improving organizations. No matter what it is called, the conditions that appear to lead to a successful business process improvement effort include the following:

TABLE 8.3 Some Other Terms Closely Related to Business Process Management

Business activity modeling	Business process redesign
Business activity monitoring	Business process reengineering (BPR)
Business architecture modernization (BAM)	Functional process improvement
Business process improvement (BPI)	Workflow management

- Support by senior management
- Shared vision by all organizational members
- Realistic expectations
- Participants empowered to make changes
- The right people participating
- Sound management practices
- Appropriate funding

In any event, it is clear that successful business process change, especially involving enterprise systems, requires a broad range of organizational factors to occur that are far beyond the technical implementation issues. Next, we examine the three most popular forms of enterprise systems.

Enterprise Resource Planning

When companies realize that legacy systems can create dramatic inefficiencies within their organizations, the next step is to integrate legacy information on a company-wide basis. As previously described, applications that integrate business activities across departmental boundaries are often referred to as **enterprise resource planning (ERP)** systems. In the 1990s, we witnessed companies' initial push to implement integrated applications, as exhibited by skyrocketing ERP sales at that time. Be aware that the terms "resource" and "planning" are somewhat misnomers, meaning that they do not accurately describe the purpose of ERP since these applications do very little in the way of planning or managing resources. The reason for the term "enterprise resource planning" is that these systems evolved in part during the 1990s from material requirements planning (MRP) and manufacturing resource planning (MRP II) packages. Do not get hung up on the words "resource" and "planning." The key word to remember from the acronym ERP is "enterprise."

Integrating Data to Integrate Applications

ERP takes stand-alone applications a step further by providing a common data warehouse and similar application interfaces that service the entire enterprise rather than portions of it. Information stored on legacy systems is converted into large, centralized data repositories known as data warehouses (see Chapter 4—Managing the Information Systems Infrastructure for more information on data warehouses). Data warehouses are databases that store information related to the various business activities of an organization. Data warehouses alleviate the problems associated with multiple computing platforms by providing a single place where all information relevant to the company and particular departments can be stored and accessed, as depicted in Figure 8.11.

In contrast to legacy systems, where it is difficult to share information between business activities, ERP applications make accessing information easier by providing a central information repository. Where an ERP solution is used, both inbound logistics and operations have access to inventory data because both business activities have access to the same pieces of information. Rather than information flowing from one department to the next, data can be accessed and updated at will, meaning that the next business activity can access information in the data warehouse whenever it needs to. This gives personnel access to accurate, real-time information. The beauty of ERP lies in the fact that information can be shared throughout the organization. For example, inventory information is accessible not only to inbound logistics and operations but also to accounting and customer service personnel. If a customer calls in wondering about the status of an order, customer service representatives can find out by accessing the data warehouse through the ERP application. Prior to the emergence of ERP, customer service representatives may have had to retrieve information from two or more separate computing systems, making their job extremely difficult while potentially resulting in dissatisfied customers. Storing data in a single place and making it available to everyone within the organization empowers everyone in the organization to be aware of the current state of business and to perform their jobs better.

FIGURE 8.11

Information storage using an ERP solution.

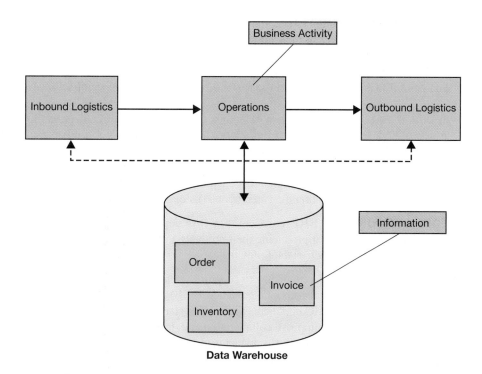

Data Warehouse

ERP applications that access the data warehouse are designed to have the same look and feel, regardless of the unique needs of a particular department. Inbound logistics and operations personnel will use a common user interface to access the same pieces of information from the data warehouse. Although the inbound logistics screens and the operations screens will have different features tailored to the unique needs of the business activity, the screens will look comparable, with similar designs, screen layouts, menu options, and so on. The Microsoft Office products provide a useful analogy. Microsoft Word and Microsoft Excel are designed to serve separate functions (word processing and spreadsheets, respectively), but overall the products look and feel very similar to one another. Word and Excel have similar user interfaces and simply differ in the features and functionality that each application offers.

Choosing an ERP System

When selecting an appropriate ERP application for an organization, management needs to take many factors into careful consideration. ERP applications come as packaged software, which means a one-size-fits-all strategy. However, businesses have unique needs even within their own industries. In other words, like snowflakes, no two companies are exactly alike. Management must carefully select an ERP application that will meet the unique requirements of the particular company. Companies must consider a number of factors in the ERP selection. Among the most prevalent issues facing management are ERP control and ERP business requirements.

ERP Control ERP control refers to the locus of control over the computing systems and decision making regarding these systems. Companies typically either opt for centralized control or allow particular business units to govern themselves. In the context of ERP, these decisions are based on the level of detail in the information that must be provided to management. Some corporations want to have as much detail as possible made available at the executive level, whereas other companies do not require such access. For instance, an accountant in one company may want the ability to view costs down to the level of individual transactions, while an accountant in another company may want only summary information. Another area related to control involves the consistency of policies and procedures. Some companies prefer that policies and procedures remain consistent throughout an organization. Other companies want to allow each business unit to develop its own policies and procedures to accommodate the unique ways that they do business. ERP applications vary widely in their allowance for control, typically assuming either a corporate or a business-unit locus of control. Some ERP applications allow users to select or customize the locus of control. In either case, management must consider the ERP's stance on control to ensure it will meet the business requirements of the company.

ERP Business Requirements When selecting an ERP system, organizations must choose which modules to implement from a large menu of options—most organizations only adopt a subset of the available ERP components. There are two major categories of ERP components—ERP *core* components and ERP *extended* components (see Figure 8.12). Most ERP vendors provide components that are tailored to specific industry best practices and, of course, allow customization if desired by the customer.

ERP CORE COMPONENTS. **ERP core components** support the important *internal* activities of the organization for producing their products and services. These components support internal operations, such as the following:

1. *Financial Management.* Components to support accounting, financial reporting, performance management, and corporate governance.
2. *Operations Management.* Components to simplify, standardize, and automate business processes in order to improve collaboration and decision making.
3. *Human Resource Management.* Components to support employee recruitment, assignment tracking, performance reviews, payroll, and regulatory requirements.

ERP EXTENDED COMPONENTS. **ERP extended components** support the primary *external* activities of the organization for dealing with suppliers and customers. Specifically, ERP extended components primarily focus on customer relationship management and supply chain management. Both are discussed in detail later in this chapter.

ERP Limitations

While ERP helps companies to integrate systems across the organization, it falls short in communicating across organizational boundaries (Larson and Rogers, 1998). Since ERP applications are designed to service internal business activities, they tend not to be well suited for managing value system activities. Companies wanting to integrate their value chains with the business activities of their suppliers, business partners, and customers typically choose to implement systems other than (or in addition to) ERP to manage the

FIGURE 8.12

An ERP system consists of core and extended components.

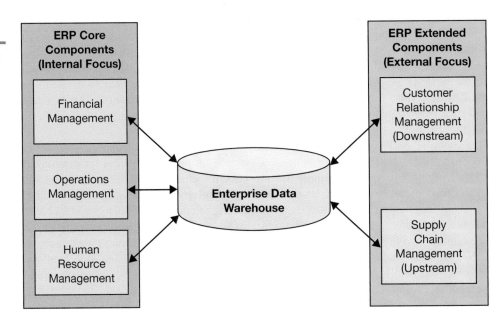

upstream and/or downstream flows of information. These types of applications, designed to coordinate activities outside organizational boundaries, are discussed in the following sections.

Customer Relationship Management

With the changes introduced by the Web, in most industries a company's competition is simply a mouse click away. It is increasingly important for companies not only to generate new business but also to attract repeat business from existing customers (see Figure 8.13). This means that to remain competitive, companies must keep their customers satisfied. In today's highly competitive markets, customers hold the balance of power because if they become dissatisfied with the levels of customer service they are receiving, they have many alternatives readily available. The global nature of the Web has affected companies worldwide in virtually all industries. An economic transformation is taking place, shifting the emphasis from conducting business transactions to managing relationships. Marketing researchers have found that the cost of trying to get back customers that have gone elsewhere can be up to 50 to 100 times as much as keeping a current one satisfied. Thus, companies are finding it imperative to develop and maintain customer satisfaction and develop deeper relationships with their customers in order to compete effectively in their markets.

Customer relationship management (CRM) is a corporate-level strategy to create and maintain, through the introduction of reliable systems, processes, and procedures, lasting relationships with customers by concentrating on the downstream information flows. Applications focusing on downstream information flows have two main objectives—to attract potential customers and create customer loyalty. The appropriate CRM technology combined with business process management of sales-related business processes can have tremendous benefits to an organization (see Table 8.4). To pursue customer satisfaction as a basis for achieving competitive advantage, organizations must be able to access information and track customer interactions throughout the organization, regardless of where, when, or how the interaction occurs. This means that companies need to have an integrated system that captures information from retail stores, Web sites, call centers, and various other ways that organizations communicate downstream within their value chain. More

FIGURE 8.13

Organizations must work harder than ever to attract and retain customers where comparison shopping is the norm and competitors are just a click away.

TABLE 8.4 Benefits of a Customer Relationship Management System

Benefit	Examples
Enables 24/7/365 operation	Web-based interfaces provide product information, sales status, support information, issue tracking, and so on.
Individualized service	Learn how each customer defines product and service quality so that customized product, pricing, and services can be designed or developed collaboratively.
Improved information	Integrate all information for all points of contact with customer—marketing, sales, and service—so that all who interact with customers have the same view and understand current issues.
Speeds problem identification/resolution	Improved record keeping and efficient methods of capturing customer complaints help to identify and solve problems faster.
Speeds processes	Integrated information removes information handoffs, speeding both sales and support processes.
Improved integration	Information from the CRM can be integrated with other systems to streamline business processes and gain business intelligence as well as making other cross-functional systems more efficient and effective.
Improved product development	Tracking customer behavior over time helps to identify future opportunities for product and service offerings.
Improved planning	Provides mechanisms for managing and scheduling sales follow-ups to assess satisfaction, repurchase probabilities, time frames, and frequencies.

important, managers need the capability to monitor and analyze factors that drive customer satisfaction as changes occur according to prevailing market conditions.

CRM applications come in the form of packaged software that is purchased from software vendors. CRM applications are commonly integrated with a comprehensive ERP implementation to leverage internal and external information to better serve customers. Like ERP, CRM applications come with various features and modules. Management must carefully select a CRM application that will meet the unique requirements of their business processes.

Companies that have successfully implemented CRM can experience greater customer satisfaction and increase productivity in their sales and service personnel, translating into dramatic enhancements to the company's profitability. CRM allows organizations to focus on driving revenue as well as streamlining costs as opposed to emphasizing only cost cutting. Cost cutting tends to have a lower limit because there are only so many costs that companies can streamline, whereas revenue generation strategies are bound only by the size of the market itself. The importance of focusing on customer satisfaction is emphasized by findings from the National Quality Research Center, which estimates that a 1 percent increase in customer satisfaction can lead to a threefold increase in a company's market capitalization.

Developing a CRM Strategy

To develop a successful CRM strategy, organizations must do more than simply purchase and install CRM software. A successful CRM strategy must include enterprise-wide changes, including the following:

- *Policy and Business Process Changes.* Organizational policies and procedures need to reflect a customer-focused culture.
- *Customer Service Changes.* Key metrics for managing the business need to reflect customer-focused measures for quality and satisfaction as well as process changes to enhance the customer experience.

Misusing CRM Data

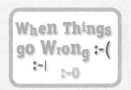

Many companies have difficulty understanding and connecting with their customers, possibly because sales, marketing, service, operations, and finance data are stored in separate locations. Customer relationship management (CRM) systems can help improve customer targeting and thus improve the results of marketing campaigns, but only if the system is used correctly. Sometimes the CRM system itself increases company liability.

For example, in the early 2000s, when mad cow disease was frequently in the news and consumers were cautioned not to buy tainted meat, meat containing parts of a cow that had contracted bovine spongiform encephalopathy (BSE, or mad cow disease) was distributed in Washington State. Over 10,000 pounds of potentially infected meat ended up in supermarkets before it could be recalled. A customer of the Kroger-owned QFC grocery chain purchased ground beef from the affected batch and served her family a taco dinner before she learned that she might have purchased tainted meat. The worried customer asked her local QFC supermarket to check her loyalty card data to find out if the meat she purchased was indeed part of the recalled batch. When she was informed that she did purchase potentially affected beef, she sued the grocery store chain for not informing her of the recall. The company had extensive customer information stored in the CRM system but made no attempt to notify customers of the meat recall. The retailer might not have been able to alert customers to the meat recall quickly enough since meat is a perishable product, but, in this case, apparently the fact that the company did not try led to the customer's lawsuit.

An often-heard argument against installing a CRM program is that they are a waste of money since companies are not apt to use the information the program offers to contact customers or even to make customer and marketing analyses. Those critics who say CRM systems must be used correctly in order to avoid privacy infractions were given fuel for their argument in 2004 when grocery giant Albertsons faced charges of using their customers' data in improper ways. In a big marketing campaign, individuals called and mailed Albertsons' pharmacy customers, encouraging those customers to refill prescriptions for certain drugs or, in some cases, to switch prescriptions. Employees who called customers posed as pharmacists or pharmacy technicians, but they were, in fact, marketing personnel attempting to market higher-priced drugs. The pharmaceutical companies who would profit from the campaign provided the screening criteria and even wrote the letters to be sent out to customers of Albertsons. For cooperating, Albertsons received from the pharmaceutical companies involved in the campaign up to $4.50 per letter, up to $15 per phone call, and incentive payments for drugs sold. A group called the Privacy Rights Clearinghouse then sued Albertsons for misuse of private customer information.

Clearly, the individualized information stored in a well-done CRM program is extremely powerful. That means that companies using such systems must be aware of privacy laws and must be ever vigilant to prevent allegations of privacy abuses.

Sources: Evan Schuman, "Retail CRM: Does Data Create a Duty?," *eWeek* (July 12, 2004), http://www.eweek.com/article2/0,1895,1623538,00.asp

Evan Schuman, "Albertsons Learns the Legal Dangers of CRM," *eWeek* (September 13, 2004), http://www.eweek.com/article2/0,1895,1645491,00.asp?rsDis=Albertsons_Learns_the_Legal_Dangers_of_CRM-Page001–135208

Anonymous, "Solution Lines, Customer Relationship Management," http://www.sas.com/solutions/crm/index.html?sgc=u

■ ***Employee Training Changes.*** Employees from all areas—marketing, sales, and support—must have a consistent focus that values customer service and satisfaction.

■ ***Data Collection, Analysis, and Sharing Changes.*** All aspects of the customer experience—prospecting, sales, support, and so on—must be tracked, analyzed, and shared to optimize the benefits of the CRM.

In sum, the organization must focus and organize its activities to provide the best customer service possible (see Figure 8.14). Additionally, successful CRM strategy must carefully consider ethical and privacy concerns of customers' data (discussed later in this chapter).

FIGURE 8.14

A successful CRM strategy
requires enterprise-wide changes.

Architecture of a CRM

A comprehensive CRM system provides three primary components:

1. *Operational CRM.* Systems for automating the fundamental business processes—marketing, sales, and support—for interacting with the customer
2. *Analytical CRM.* Systems for analyzing customer behavior and perceptions (e.g., quality, price, and overall satisfaction) in order to provide business intelligence
3. *Collaborative CRM.* Systems for providing effective and efficient communication with the customer from the entire organization

Operational CRM is commonly referred to as a **front-office system** because it enables direct interaction with customers. In contrast, analytical CRM is commonly referred to as a **back-office system** because it provides the analysis necessary to more effectively manage the sales, service, and marketing activities. Additionally, all systems that are not accessible or visible to the customer, including inventory management, producing goods and services, and other supply chain activities, are referred to as back-office systems. Finally, collaborative CRM provides the communication capabilities of the CRM environment (see Figure 8.15). Next, we examine each of these architecture components.

Operational CRM **Operational CRM** includes the systems used to enable customer interaction and service. With an effective operational CRM environment, organizations are able to provide personalized and highly efficient customer service. Customer-focused personnel are provided complete customer information—history, pending sales, and service requests—in order to optimize interaction and service. It is important to stress that the operational CRM environment provides *all* customer information regardless of the touch point. This means that marketing, sales, and support personnel see *all* prior and current interactions with the customer regardless of where it occurred within the organization. To facilitate the distinct parts of the operational CRM, three separate systems are utilized (see Figure 8.16).

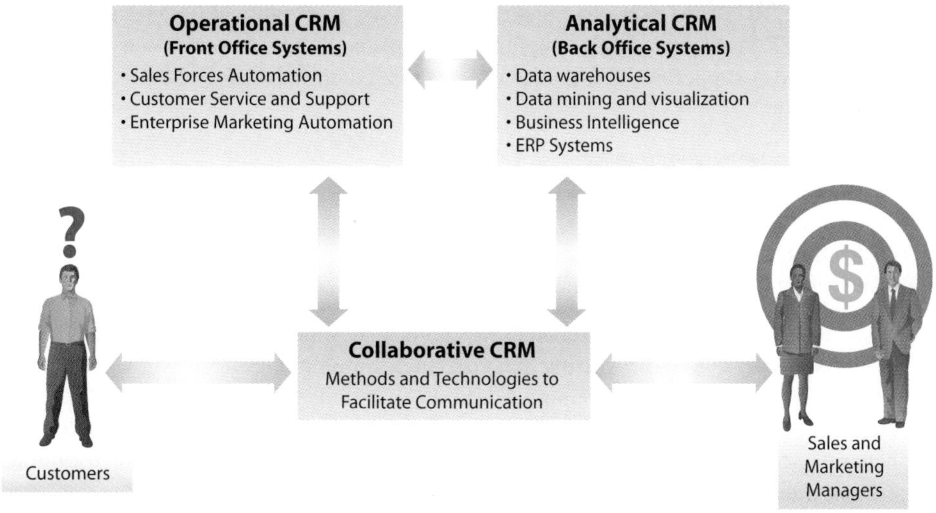

Operational CRM
(Front Office Systems)
• Sales Forces Automation
• Customer Service and Support
• Enterprise Marketing Automation

Analytical CRM
(Back Office Systems)
• Data warehouses
• Data mining and visualization
• Business Intelligence
• ERP Systems

Collaborative CRM
Methods and Technologies to
Facilitate Communication

Customers

Sales and
Marketing
Managers

FIGURE 8.15

A comprehensive CRM
environment provides
operational, analytical, and
collaborative components.

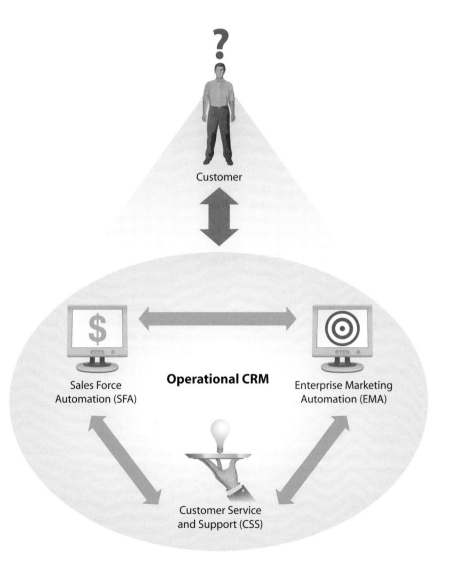

Customer

Operational CRM

Sales Force
Automation (SFA)

Enterprise Marketing
Automation (EMA)

Customer Service
and Support (CSS)

FIGURE 8.16

An operational CRM is used to
enable customer interaction and
service.

SALES FORCE AUTOMATION. The first component of an operational CRM is **sales force automation (SFA)**. SFA refers to systems to support the day-to-day sales activities of an organization. SFA supports a broad range of sales related business processes, including the following:

- Order processing and tracking
- Contact development, assignment, and management
- Customer history, preferences (product and communication), and management
- Sales forecasting and performance analyses
- Sales administration

SFA systems provide advantages for sales personnel, sales managers, and marketing managers. For sales personnel, SFA helps them use their time more efficiently and ultimately focus more on selling than on paperwork and other nonselling tasks (see Table 8.5). Likewise, for sales managers, the SFA system provides improved information, allowing for better day-to-day management of the sales function and improved forecasting of future events (see Table 8.6). For example, SFA allows sales managers to track a plethora of sales performance measures, including the following:

- Revenue per sales person, per territory, or as a percentage of sales quota
- Margins by product category, customer segment, or customer
- Number of calls per day, time spent per contact, revenue per call, cost per call, or ratio of orders to calls
- Number of lost customers per period or cost of customer acquisition
- Percentage of goods returned, number of customer complaints, or number of overdue accounts

Finally, SFA improves the effectiveness of the marketing function by providing an improved understanding of market conditions, competitors, and products. This enhanced information will provide numerous advantages for the management and execution of the marketing function. Specific advantages include the following:

- Improved understanding of markets, segments, and customers
- Improved understanding of competitors

TABLE 8.5 Advantages of Sales Force Management Systems for *Sales Personnel*

Advantages	Examples
Less paperwork	Customer contact information is recorded using e-forms that automatically provide known customer data; fill-in-the-blanks forms are used to capture new information.
Fewer handoffs	Information is automatically routed to other team members and managers.
Fewer errors	e-forms ensure that customer data is automatically entered; forms can require necessary updates to be entered before saving and sharing.
Better information	Sales personnel has accurate, up-to-date, complete information on all interactions with customers as well as higher-quality sales leads.
Better training	Common systems ensure that sales personnel follows common processes and procedures.
Improved teamwork	Automatically sharing all sales-related information facilitates successful team selling and the sharing of best practices.
Improved morale	Improved training and less "busywork" allows a greater focus on selling and revenue generation.
Higher sales	Streamlined selling processes and improved communications allow sales personnel to focus more on selling than on nonselling activities.

TABLE 8.6 Advantages of Sales Force Management Systems for *Sales Managers*

Advantages	Examples
Improved information	Sales performance data is automatically tabulated and presented in easy-to-understand tables, charts, and graphs.
Improved time usage	Less time summarizing and tracking information allows greater time for advising and coaching sales personnel.
Better planning and forecasts	Improved accuracy and timeliness of information leads to better forecast and plans.
Improved scheduling	Accurate and real-time data allows managers to more effectively deploy sales personnel.
Improved coordination	Accessible information allows better coordination with marketing, production, and finance.
Better sales force tracking	Systems allow managers to track a greater number of up-to-date measures, leading to improved management and faster response when problems arise.

- Enhanced understanding of your organization's strengths and weaknesses
- Better understanding of the economic structure of your industry
- Enhanced product development
- Improved strategy development and coordination with the sales function

In sum, the primary goals of SFA are to identify potential customers, streamline selling processes, and improve managerial information. Next, we examine systems for improving customer service and support.

CUSTOMER SERVICE AND SUPPORT. The second component of an operation CRM system is **customer service and support (CSS)**. CSS refers to systems that automate service requests, complaints, product returns, and information requests. In the past, organizations had *help desks* and *call centers* to provide customer service and support. Today, organizations are deploying a **customer interaction center (CIC)**, using multiple communication channels to support the communication preferences of customers, such as the Web, face-to-face contact, telephone, fax, and so on (see the section "Collaborative CRM" later in this chapter). The CIC utilizes a variety of communication technologies for optimizing customers' communications with the organization. For example, automatic call distribution systems forward calls to the next available person; while waiting to connect, customers can be given the option to use key or voice response technologies to check account status information. In essence, the goal of the CSS is to provide great customer service—anytime, anywhere, and through any channel—while at the same time keeping service and support costs low. Customers can log service requests or gain updates to pending support requests using a variety of self-service or assisted technologies (see Figure 8.17). Successful CSS systems enable faster response times, increased first-contact resolution rates, and improved productivity for service and support personnel. Managers can utilize digital dashboards to monitor key metrics such as first-contact resolution and service personnel utilization, allowing improved management of the service and support functions (see Chapter 7—Enhancing Business Intelligence Using Information Systems).

ENTERPRISE MARKETING AUTOMATION. The third component of an operational CRM system is **enterprise marketing automation (EMA)**. An EMA system provides a comprehensive view of the competitive environment, including competitors, industry trends, and a broad range of environmental factors (see Table 8.7). Understanding these factors can help to assess the attractiveness of a particular market as well as provide insights for tailoring marketing strategies for differing markets. Marketing managers can use this information to gain business intelligence, leading to improved marking strategies and plans.

FIGURE 8.17

A customer interaction center allows customers to use a variety of self-service and assisted technologies to interact with the organization.

Analytical CRM **Analytical CRM** focuses on analyzing customer behavior and perceptions in order to provide the business intelligence necessary to identify new opportunities and to provide superior customer service. Organizations that effectively utilize analytical CRM can more easily customize marketing campaigns from the segment level to even the individual customer. Such customized campaigns help to increase cross- or up-selling (i.e., selling more or more profitable products) as well as retaining customers by having accurate, timely, and personalized information.

Key technologies within analytical CRM systems include data mining, decision support, and other business intelligence technologies that attempt to create predictive models of various customer attributes (see Chapter 7). These analyses can focus on enhancing a broad range of customer focused business processes, including the following:

- Marketing campaign management and analysis
- Customer campaign customization
- Customer communication optimization
- Customer segmentation and sales coverage optimization
- Pricing optimization and risk assessment and management
- Price, quality, and satisfaction analysis of competitors
- Customer acquisition and retention analysis

TABLE 8.7 An Enterprise Marketing Automation System Tracks Many Environmental Factors That Shape the Competitive Environment

Factor	Example of Data
Economic	Gross national product or gross domestic product per capita and growth Unemployment and inflation Consumer and investor confidence Currency exchange rates and trade balance Financial and political health of trading partners
Governmental and public policy	Political stability and risk Budget deficit or surplus Corporate and personal tax rates Import tariffs, quotas, and export restrictions Environmental protection laws Intellectual property and patent laws Laws that favor/impede business investment
Technology and infrastructure	Efficiency of public infrastructure (e.g., roads, ports, and airports) Industrial productivity and potential partners/competitors Any new technology that could impact the company Cost and accessibility of electrical power
Ecology	Ecological concerns that affect the firms' production processes or customers' buying habits Ecological concerns that affect customers' perception of the company or product
Cultural	Demographic factors such as population size, age, education, income, ethnic origin, and religion Attitudes toward materialism, capitalism, free enterprise, individualism/collectivism, role of family, role of government, consumerism, environmentalism, importance of work, and pride of accomplishment Cultural views toward health, diet and nutrition, and housing conditions
Suppliers	Quality, quantity, and stability of labor Wage expectations, strikes, and labor relations Quality, quantity, competitiveness, and stability of suppliers

- Customer satisfaction and management
- Product usage, life cycle analysis, and product development
- Product and service quality tracking and management

Once these predictive models are created, they can be delivered to marketing and sales managers using a variety of visualization methods, including digital dashboards and other reporting methods. To gain the greatest value from the analytical CRM process, data collection and analysis must be continuous so that all decision making reflects the most accurate, comprehensive, and up-to-date information.

Collaborative CRM **Collaborative CRM** refers to systems for providing effective and efficient communication with the customer from the entire organization. The heart of a collaborative CRM is the CIC (as described previously), which enables customers to utilize the communication method they prefer when interacting with the organization. Additionally, a collaborative CRM supports customer communication and collaboration with the entire organization. In other words, collaborative CRM integrates the communication related to all aspects of the marketing, sales, and support processes in order to better serve and retain customers. Collaborative CRM enhances communication in the following ways:

- *Greater Customer Focus.* Understanding customer history and current needs helps to focus the communication on issues important to the customer.
- *Lower Communication Barriers.* Customers are more likely to communicate with the organization when personnel have complete information and utilize the communication methods and preferences of the customer.

■ *Increased Information Integration.* All information about the customer as well as all prior and ongoing communication is given to all organizational personnel interacting with the customer; customers can get status updates from any organizational touch point.

In addition to these benefits, collaborative CRM environments are flexible such that they can support both routine and nonroutine events.

Ethical Concerns with CRM

Although CRM has become a strategic enabler for developing and maintaining customer relationships, it is not viewed positively by those who feel it invades customer privacy and facilitates coercive sales practices. Proponents of CRM warn that relying too much on the "systems" profile of a customer, based on statistical analysis of past behavior, may categorize customers in a way that they will take exception to. Additionally, given that a goal of CRM is to better meet the needs of customers by providing highly *personalized* communication and service, at what point does the communication get *too* personal? It is intuitive to conclude that when customers feel the system knows too much about them, personalization could backfire on a company. Clearly, CRM raises several ethical concerns in the digital world (see Chapter 10—Information Systems Ethics and Crime for a comprehensive discussion of information privacy). Nevertheless, as competition continues to increase in the digital world, CRM will be a key technology for attracting and retaining customers.

Ethical Dilemma 🔽

Targeting or Discriminating? Ethical Pitfalls of Customer Relationship Management

Customer relationship management (CRM) systems could be called a marketer's dream. CRM systems promise companies the capability of getting to know their customers and maximizing the benefit gained from every customer. Through the use of sophisticated features, CRM software can let companies take a close look at customer behavior, drilling down to smaller and smaller market segments. Once so segmented, customers can be targeted with very specific "special offers" or promotions. For the company, this process reaps the greatest returns from marketing efforts since only those customers are targeted who are likely to respond to the marketing campaign.

From a consumer's perspective, CRM systems seem like a great idea. Finally, you stop receiving advertisements for reams of stuff that doesn't interest you. But what if a company uses their CRM software in a more discriminating way? Where do companies draw the line between using CRM data to offer certain clients customized deals and unethically discriminating against other customers? For example, banks, which have the ability to segment their customers according to their creditworthiness, might use this credit risk data to target customers having a low credit rating. Although these customers are more risky for the banks, the higher fees and interest for credit make these customers especially lucrative.

A fine line exists between using CRM data for targeted marketing purposes and using such data to take advantage of certain groups. Companies using CRM systems must develop ethical principles for using the data collected from customers, inform customers about how data will be used, and refrain from stepping over the ethical/unethical line.

Source: Alain Jourdier, "Too Close for Comfort," *CIO* (May 1, 2002), http://www.cio.com/archive/050102/reality.html

Supply Chain Management

In the previous section, we looked downstream at CRM applications. Now we turn our attention upstream. Getting the raw materials and components that a company uses in its daily operations is an important key to business success. When deliveries from suppliers are accurate and timely, companies can convert them to finished products more efficiently. Coordinating this effort with suppliers has become a central part of companies' overall business strategies, as it can help them reduce costs associated with inventory levels and get new products to market more quickly. Ultimately, this helps companies drive profitability and improve their customer service since they can react to changing market conditions swiftly. Collaborating, or sharing information, with suppliers has become a strategic necessity for business success. In other words, by developing and maintaining stronger, more integrated relationships with suppliers, companies can more effectively compete in their markets through cost reductions and responsiveness to market demands.

What Is Supply Chain Management?

The term **supply chain** is commonly used to refer to the producers of supplies that a company uses. Companies often procure specific raw materials and components from many different suppliers. These suppliers, in turn, work with their suppliers to obtain goods; their suppliers work with additional suppliers and so forth. The further out in the supply chain one looks, the more suppliers are involved. As a result, the term "chain" becomes somewhat of a misnomer since it implies one-to-one relationships facilitating a chain of events flowing from the first supplier to the second to the third and so on. A more descriptive term to describe the flow of materials from suppliers to a company is **supply network** because multiple suppliers are involved in the process of servicing a single organization (see Figure 8.18).

FIGURE 8.18

A typical supply network.

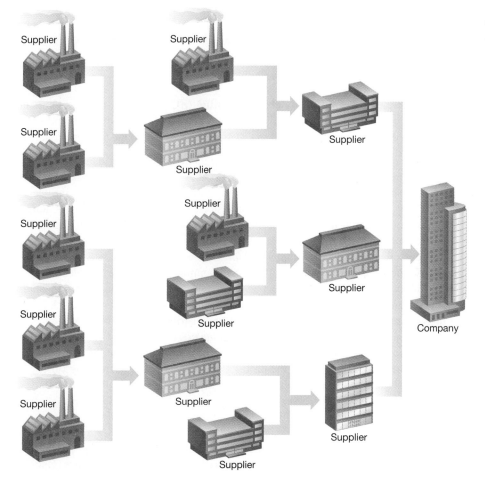

Several problems can arise when firms within a supply network do not collaborate effectively. Information can easily become distorted as it moves from one company down through the supply network, causing a great deal of inefficiency. Problems such as excessive inventories, inaccurate manufacturing capacity plans, and missed production schedules can run rampant, causing huge ripple effects that lead to degradations in profitability and poor customer service by everyone within the supply network. Implementing integrated business processes allows a company to better coordinate the entire supply network.

Information systems focusing on improving upstream information flows have two main objectives—to accelerate product development and to reduce costs associated with procuring raw materials, components, and services from suppliers. These systems, called **supply chain management (SCM)**, improve the coordination of suppliers, product or service production, and distribution. When executed successfully, SCM helps in not only reducing inventory costs but also enhancing revenue through improved customer service. SCM is often integrated with ERP to leverage internal and external information in order to better collaborate with suppliers. Like ERP and CRM applications, SCM packages are delivered in the form of modules (see Table 8.8) that companies select and implement according to their differing business requirements.

As discussed previously, ERP and CRM are primarily used to optimize (reengineer) business processes *within* the organization, whereas SCM is used to improve business processes that *span* organizational boundaries. Given its scope, SCM is adopted primarily by large organizations with a large and/or complex supplier network. To reap the greatest benefits from the SCM processes and systems, organizations need to extend the system to include all trading partners regardless of size, providing a central location for information integration and common processes so that all partners benefit.

SCM Architecture

An SCM system includes more than simply hardware and software; it also integrates business processes and supply chain partners. As shown in Table 8.8, an SCM system consists of many modules or applications. Each of these applications supports either supply chain planning or supply chain execution. Both are described next.

Supply Chain Planning **Supply chain planning (SCP)** involves the development of various resource plans to support the efficient and effective production of goods and services (see Figure 8.19). Four general types of plans are developed within the SCP process:

1. ***Demand Planning and Forecasting.*** SCP begins with product demand planning and forecasting. To develop these plans, SCM modules examine historical data to develop the most accurate forecasts possible. The accuracy of these plans will be influenced greatly by the stability of the data. When historic data is stable, plans can be longer in duration, whereas if historic data shows unpredictable fluctuations in demand, the forecasting time frame must be narrowed. Demand planning and forecasting leads to the development of the overall *demand forecast.*
2. ***Distribution Planning.*** Once final product planning forecasts are complete, plans for moving products to distributors can be developed. Specifically, distribution planning focuses on delivering products or services to consumers as well as the warehousing, delivering, invoicing, and payment collection. Distribution planning leads to the development of the overall *transportation schedule.*
3. ***Production Scheduling.*** Production planning focuses on the coordination of all activities needed to create the product or service. When developing this plan, analytical tools are used to optimally utilize materials, equipment, and labor. Production also involves product testing, packaging, and delivery preparation. Production scheduling leads to the development of the *production plan.*
4. ***Procurement Planning.*** Procurement planning focuses on the development of inventory estimates using inventory simulations and other analytical techniques. Once

TABLE 8.8 Functions that Optimize the Supply Network

Module	Key Uses
Supply chain collaboration	Share information and integrate processes up and down the supply chain
	Provide Internet-enabled processes such as collaborative planning, forecasting, and replenishment (CPFR) and vendor-managed inventory
Collaborative design	Streamline product design processes across supply chain partners to reduce time to market
	React quickly to changing market conditions, such as product launches and new customer segments
Collaborative fulfillment	Commit to delivery dates in real time
	Fulfill orders from channels on time with order management, transportation planning, and vehicle scheduling
	Support the entire logistics process, including picking, packing, shipping, and international activities
Collaborative demand and supply planning	Develop a one-number forecast of customer demand by sharing demand and supply forecasts instantaneously across multiple tiers
	Enable suppliers and vendors to use shared forecasts and real-time demand signals to replenish stock automatically
Collaborative procurement	Provide global visibility into direct material spending
	Allow partners to leverage buying clout and reduce ad hoc buying
Production planning	Support both discrete and process manufacturing
	Optimize plans and schedules while considering resource, material, and dependency constraints
Supply chain event management	Monitor every stage of the supply chain process, from price quotation to the moment the customer receives the product, and issue alerts when problems arise
	Capture data from carriers, vehicle on-board computers, GPS systems, and other sources
Supply chain exchange	Create an online supply chain community that enables partners to collaborate on design, procurement, demand and supply management, and other supply chain activities
Supply chain performance management	Report key measurements in the supply chain, such as filling management rates, order cycle times, and capacity use
	Integrate planning and execution functions with competitive information and market trends

Source: www.sap.com.

inventory levels are estimated, suppliers are chosen who contractually agree to preestablished delivery and pricing terms. *Inventory simulation* is a key element of the procurement planning process.

As suggested, various types of analytical tools—such as statistical analysis, simulation, and optimization—are used to forecast and visualize demand levels, distribution and warehouse locations, resource sequencing, and so on. Once these plans are developed, they are used to guide supply chain execution. Additionally, it is important to note that SCM planning is an ongoing process—as new data are obtained, plans are updated.

Supply Chain Execution **Supply chain execution (SCE)** is the execution of supply chain planning. Essentially, SCE puts the SCM planning into motion and reflects the processes involved in improving the collaboration of all members of the supply chain—suppliers,

FIGURE 8.19

Supply chain planning is used to create demand forecasts, inventory simulations, manufacturing plans, and transportation schedules.

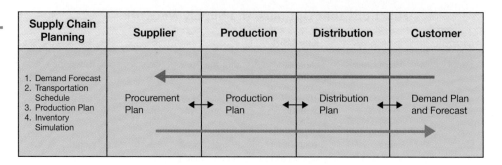

producers, distributors, and customers. SCE involves the management of three key elements of the supply chain: product flow, information flow, and financial flow (see Figure 8.20). Each of these flows is discussed next.

THE PRODUCT FLOW. **Product flow** refers to the movement of goods from the supplier to production, from production to distribution, and from distribution to the consumer. Although product flow is thought to flow primarily in one direction, an effective SCM system will also automate product returns. Effectively processing returns and customer refunds is a critical part of supply chain execution. Thus, an SCM system should support not only the physical product production process but also the necessary processes in place to efficiently receive excessive or defective products from customers (e.g., ship replacements or credit accounts).

THE INFORMATION FLOW. **Information flow** refers to the movement of information along the supply chain, such as order processing and delivery status. Like the product flow, information flows can also move up or down the supply chain as needed. The key element to the information flow is the complete removal of paper documents. Specifically, all orders, fulfillment, billing, and consolidation information is shared electronically. These paperless information flows save not only paperwork but also time and money. Additionally, because the SCM system uses a central database to store information, all supply chain partners have access to all the current information at all times.

THE FINANCIAL FLOW. **Financial flow** refers primarily to the movement of financial assets throughout the supply chain. Financial flows also include information related to payment schedules, consignment and ownership of products and materials, and other relevant information. Linkages to electronic banking and financial institutions allow payments to automatically flow into the accounts of all members within the supply chain.

Developing an SCM Strategy

When developing a supply chain management strategy, an organization must consider a variety of factors that will affect the efficiency and effectiveness of the supply chain. **Supply chain efficiency** is the extent to which a company's supply chain is focusing on minimizing procurement, production, and transportation costs, sometimes by reducing

FIGURE 8.20

Supply chain execution focuses on the efficient and effective flow of products, information, and finances along the supply chain.

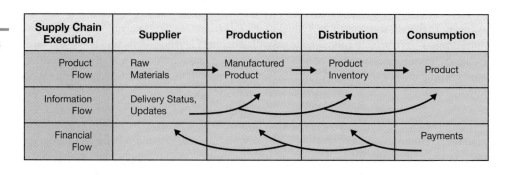

Key Enabler

Three-Dimensional Fabrication

Traditionally, manufacturing prototypes—cars, specialized machinery, prostheses, and the like—has been a slow and arduous process. No more. Prototyping for many products is now fast and precise because of a process called "fabbing," also know as three-dimensional (3-D) printing.

Although 3-D printing has been in use since 1988, it was not commercially viable until recently. New technology in printing allows for creating 3-D, usable, moving parts instead of simply block models as in the past.

Three-dimensional printing is accomplished by using two printer heads. The first printer head lays down a fine powder, and the second head is a gluing agent. With each pass of the printer heads, another thin layer of glued powder is laid down. As each layer is added, a 3-D image emerges.

Not only is fabbing now more applicable, but it has also increased in speed. The process has gone from taking days to create a prototype to finishing a model in hours, allowing engineers to produce several models in a short period of time.

Hewlett-Packard (HP) has been a leader in developing 3-D printers. Once priced at $100,000, a 3-D HP printer now sells for $1,000. Engineers, IS personnel, hardware vendors, and consumers have benefited from the development, refinement, and availability of 3-D printers since designs can now be more quickly transformed into computer products.

Source: http://www.wired.com/news/technology/0,1282,59648,00.html

---

customer service. In contrast, **supply chain effectiveness** is the extent to which a company's supply chain is focusing on maximizing customer service, regardless of procurement, production, and transportation costs. In other words, the design of the supply chain must consider natural trade-offs between a variety of factors and should reflect the organization's competitive strategy. For example, an organization utilizing a low-cost provider competitive strategy would likely focus on a supply chain efficiency. Alternatively, an organization focusing on a superior customer service differentiation strategy would opt for a supply chain effectiveness strategy. Of course, it is also likely that, because of the availability and locations of major suppliers and customers, hybrid strategies would be implemented. Nevertheless, organizations must match their overall supply chain strategy to their overall competitive strategy to reap the greatest benefits (see Figure 8.21).

Supply Chain Strategy	Procurement	Production	Transportation
Effectiveness	More Inventory Multiple Inventory Sources …	General Purpose Facilities More Facilities Higher Excess Capacity …	Fast Delivery Times More Warehouses …
↕	↕	↕	↕
Efficiency	… Single Inventory Source Less Inventory	Less Excess Capacity Fewer Facilities Special Purpose Facilities	… Fewer Warehouses Longer Delivery Times

FIGURE 8.21

A supply chain strategy requires a balancing between supply chain efficiency and effectiveness.

Emerging SCM Trends

As is the case with all technologies, SCM is evolving. One key trend is the development of enterprise portals, providing an alternative to proprietary supply linkages. In addition, new technologies are helping to add greater value to SCM. These topics are briefly examined next.

Enterprise Portals Most SCM systems are tightly integrated with a relatively small number of suppliers or customers. The goal of SCM is to optimize the flow rather than minimize costs or maximize revenue. For example, it may make sense for an organization to have a close, proprietary relationship with suppliers of rare, unique, or critical components to a product. However, for other more standard components, it may be more advantageous to utilize some form of business-to-business (B2B) marketplace. These B2B marketplaces are referred to as **enterprise portals**. Portals, in the context of B2B supply chain management, can be defined as access points (or front doors) through which a business partner accesses secured, proprietary information from an organization. Enterprise portals provide a single point of access to this type of information, which may be dispersed throughout an organization. Enterprise portals can provide substantial productivity gains and cost savings by creating a single point of access where the company can conduct business with any number of business partners.

Enterprise portals come in two basic forms: distribution portals and procurement portals. Distribution portals automate the business processes involved in selling or distributing products from a single supplier to multiple buyers. On the other end of the spectrum, procurement portals automate the business processes involved in purchasing or procuring products between a single buyer and multiple suppliers (see Figure 8.22). Distribution and procurement portals can vary depending on the number of buyers and suppliers that utilize the portal. For example, the "big three" automotive industry giants Ford Motor Company, DaimlerChrysler, and General Motors have teamed up to create a procurement portal that suppliers to the big three can access. Similarly, a few companies can share distribution portals to purchase products from many suppliers. When the balance between buyers and sellers nears a point of equilibrium, these systems are classified as **trading exchanges**.

Distribution portals, procurement portals, and trading exchanges commonly service specific industries or groups of firms that rely on similar products or services. Tailoring products and services to particular companies creates a **vertical market**, or a market that services the needs of a specific sector. Vertical markets can create tremendous efficiencies for companies since they bring together numerous participants along the supply network.

DISTRIBUTION PORTALS. **Distribution portals** are designed to automate the business processes that occur before, during, and after sales have been transacted between a supplier and multiple customers. In other words, distribution portals provide efficient tools for customers to manage all phases of the purchasing cycle, including product information, order entry, and customer service. Dell Computers services business customers through its distribution portal Premier.Dell.com (see Figure 8.23).

PROCUREMENT PORTALS. **Procurement portals** are designed to automate the business processes that occur before, during, and after sales have been transacted between a buyer and multiple suppliers. Procurement portals provide efficient tools for suppliers to manage all phases of the distribution cycle, including dissemination of product information,

FIGURE 8.22

Distribution portals, trading exchanges, and procurement portals.

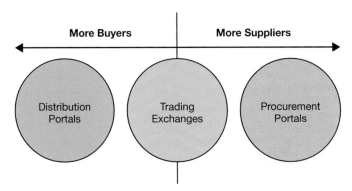

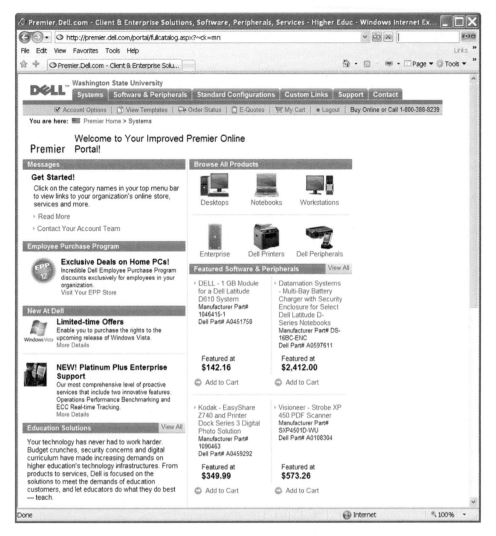

FIGURE 8.23

Distribution portal
Premier.Dell.com.

Source: http://www.dell.com.

purchase order processing, and customer service. Ford Motor Company has implemented a procurement portal called Ford Supplier Portal, where suppliers come to share information and conduct business with Ford (see Figure 8.24).

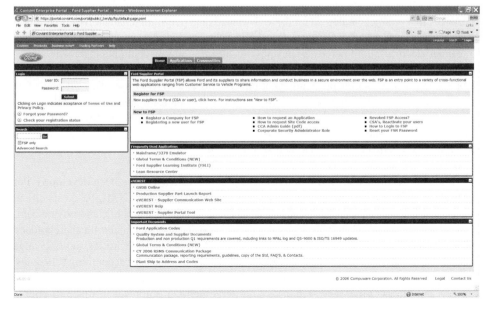

FIGURE 8.24

Ford supplier procurement portal.

Source: https://portal.covisint.com/portal/public/_l:en/tp/fsp.

Trading Exchanges

Enterprise portals tend to be beyond the reach of small to midsize businesses because of the costs involved in designing, developing, and maintaining this type of system. Many of these firms do not have the necessary monetary resources or skilled personnel to develop large-scale SCM applications on their own. To service this market niche, a number of trading exchanges, or electronic marketplaces, have sprung up. Trading exchanges are operated by third-party vendors, meaning that they are built and maintained by a particular company. These companies generate revenue by taking a small commission for each transaction that occurs, by charging usage fees, by charging association fees, and/or by generating advertising revenues. Unlike distribution and procurement portals, trading exchanges allow many buyers and many sellers to come together, offering firms access to real-time trading with other companies in their vertical markets. Some of the most popular trading exchanges include www.e-steel.com and www.scrapsite.com (steel), www.paperspace.com (paper), and www.neoforma.com and www.sciquest.com (medical equipment).

Key Technologies for Enhancing SCM Several new technologies are helping organizations gain even more from their investments in SCM systems. In this section, we briefly review two that are providing significant benefits to managing supply chains.

EXTENSIBLE MARKUP LANGUAGE (XML). **Extensible Markup Language (XML)** is a data presentation standard first specified by the World Wide Web Consortium, an international consortium of companies whose purpose is to develop open standards for the Web. XML allows designers of Web documents to create their own customized tags, enabling the definition, transmission, validation, and interpretation of data between applications and between organizations (see Technology Briefing 2—Information Systems Software for more on XML).

XML does not specify any particular formatting; rather, it specifies the rules for tagging elements. A **tag** is a command that is inserted in a document in order to specify how the document or a portion of the document should be formatted and/or used. As a result, XML is a powerful, tailorable information tagging system that can be used for sharing similar data across applications over the Web.

As described in Technology Briefing 2, hypertext markup language (HTML) instructs a Web browser how data on a Web page should be laid out cosmetically on a user's screen. XML also uses tags in Web documents much like HTML, but they go well beyond HTML. XML instructs systems as to how information should be interpreted and used. For example, by using XML, you can tag a string of numbers and text on a Web page as an invoice or a set of images in a product catalog. With these advanced data definition characteristics built into Web applications, you can then use the Web as the worldwide network for business-to-consumer electronic commerce and business-to-business supply chain management.

Many people think that XML is on its way to becoming the standard for automating data exchange between business information systems and may well replace all other formats for electronic data interchange (EDI). Companies can, for example, use XML to create an application for doing Web-based ordering, for checking on and managing inventory, for signaling to a supplier that more parts are needed, for alerting a third-party logistics company that a delivery is needed, and so on and then have all these various applications working together using the common language of XML.

XML is customizable, and a number of variations of XML have been developed. For example, **Extensible Business Reporting Language (XBRL)** is an XML-based specification for publishing financial information. XBRL makes it easier for public and private companies to share information with each other, with industry analysts, and with shareholders. XBRL includes tags for data such as annual and quarterly reports, Securities and Exchange Commission filings, general ledger information, and net revenue and accounting schedules.

XML is not, however, a panacea for SCM. Support for and use of XML is growing rapidly, but all the necessary standards and agreements are not yet in place to enable

XML-based applications to work seamlessly with all other applications and systems. Further, while nearly anyone can learn to use a text editor to create a basic HTML document, XML is far more complex and requires not only knowledge of XML but also expertise in distributed database design and management. Nevertheless, XML holds great promise for managing supply chains by its ability to inject more information into the process.

RADIO FREQUENCY IDENTIFICATION. Another exciting technology now being used within a SCM system is **radio frequency identification (RFID)**, which is starting to replace standard bar codes you find on almost every product. RFID is the use of the electromagnetic or electrostatic coupling in the RF portion of the electromagnetic spectrum in order to transmit signals. An RFID system uses a transceiver and antenna to transfer information to a processing device, or **RFID tag**.

RFID tags can be used just about anywhere that a unique identification system might be needed, such as on clothing, pets, cars, keys, missiles, or manufacturing parts. RFID tags can range in size from being a fraction of an inch and inserted beneath an animal's skin up to several inches across and fixed on a shipping container (see Figure 8.25). The

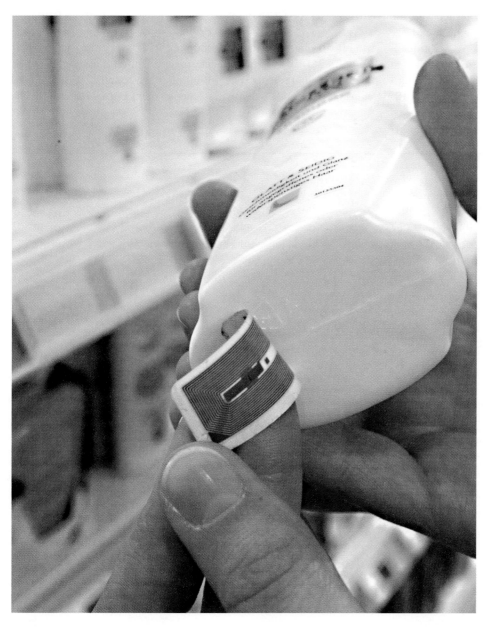

FIGURE 8.25

An RFID is small but contains a lot of information.

Source: http://www.future-store.org/ servlet/PB/-s/15tbdle1hnkm0j13 ganj31cza8nf1e6vrsr/menu/ 1007260_l2_yno/index.html.

tag can carry information as simple as the name of the owner of the pet or as complex as how a product is to be manufactured on the shop floor.

RFID systems offer advantages over standard bar-code technologies in that RFID eliminates the need for line-of-sight reading. RFID also does not require time-consuming hand scanning, and RFID information is readable regardless of the entity's position or whether the tag is plainly visible. RFID tags can also contain more information than bar codes. It is possible to retrieve information about an entity's version, origin, location, maintenance history, and other important information and to manipulate that information on the tag. RFID scanning can also be done at greater distances than can bar-code scanning. *Passive tags* are small and relatively inexpensive (less than $1) and typically have a range up to a few feet. *Active tags,* on the other hand, cost upward of $5, include a battery, and can transmit hundreds of feet.

RFID systems offer great opportunities for managing supply chains. For example, airlines are strapped for cash and think a lot about those metal, rolling serving carts that are used on airplanes and that can cost as much as $1,000 each. "We've heard horrific stories of airlines losing up to 1,500 of these things in three months," says Tony Naylor, vice president of in-flight solutions for eLSG.SkyChefs, a technology provider for the airline catering industry, based in Irving, Texas (Edwards, 2003). To keep tabs on their vanishing carts, eLSG.SkyChefs now uses an RFID system with an RFID tag on each cart.

Additionally, virtually all major retailers are adopting RFID to better manage their supply chains (see Figure 8.26), as are governments for tracking military supplies and weapons, drug shipments and ingredients (i.e., for eliminating counterfeit drugs), and citizens with RFID chips on passports. While RFID's deployment is growing rapidly, the

Net Stats

RFID on the Rise

The market for radio frequency identification (RFID) tags, those high-tech devices that let businesses keep track of certain products via radio frequency transmitters and receivers, is exploding. According to industry estimates, the total RFID market (including related services) is expected to grow from $2.7 billion in 2006 to $12.3 billion in 2010, making RFID tags the hottest wireless item since cell phones first came out. Experts predict that supply chain elements, such as shipping cartons and labels, will account for most of the growth. The second-largest segment of growth will be consumer items—everything from drug containers to clothing (see Table 8.9).

Source: Dylan McGrath, "RFID Market to Grow 10 Fold by 2016, Firm Says," *EE Times* (January 26, 2006), http://www.eetimes.com/news/latest/showArticle.jhtml?articleID=177104240

TABLE 8.9 RFID Market Sectors by Percent of Total Revenues, 2004

Sector	Revenues (%)
Security/access control/purchasing	62.6 (includes RFID in automotive keys)
Animals (pigs, dogs, cows, etc.)	28.2
Cartons/supply chain	4.9
Consumer products	0.78
Large freight	0.64
Humans	0.34
Other	2.5

Note: Table does not total to 100% because of rounding.

Source: In-Stat (found at: http://www.clickz.com/showPage.html?page=3460851).

FIGURE 8.26

A pallet of inventory being processed as it passes through an RFID gate.

Source: http://www.future-store.org/servlet/PB/-s/ 15tbdle1hnkm0j13ganj31cza8nf1e6vr sr/menu/1007260_l2_yno/index.html.

systems are still relatively expensive, there isn't yet a clear set of data standards, and global radio frequencies differ between countries. Fortunately, these hurdles are being overcome by cooperation between vendors. In any event, RFID is clearly a valuable new technology for managing supply chains.

The Formula for Enterprise System Success

To summarize, the main objective of enterprise systems is to create competitive advantage by streamlining business activities within and outside a company. However, many implementations are more costly and time consuming than originally envisioned. It is not uncommon to have projects that run over budget, meaning that identifying common problems and devising methods for dealing with these issues can prove invaluable to management. A recent survey suggested that 40 to 60 percent of companies that undertake enterprise system implementations do not fully realize the results that they had hoped for (Langenwalter, 2000). Companies that have successfully installed enterprise systems are found to follow a basic set of recommendations related to enterprise system implementations (Koch, Slater, and Baatz, 2000). Although the following list is not meant to be comprehensive, these recommendations will provide an understanding of some of the challenges involved in implementing enterprise systems:

> *Recommendation 1.* Secure executive sponsorship
>
> *Recommendation 2.* Get help from outside experts
>
> *Recommendation 3.* Thoroughly train users
>
> *Recommendation 4.* Take a multidisciplinary approach to implementations

Secure Executive Sponsorship

The primary reason that enterprise system implementations fail is believed to be a direct result of lack of top-level management support. Although executives do not necessarily need to make decisions concerning the enterprise system, it is critical that they buy into the decisions made by project managers. Many problems can arise if projects fail to grab the attention of top-level management. In most companies, executives have the ultimate authority regarding the availability and distribution of resources within the organization. If executives do not understand the importance of the enterprise system, this will likely result in delays or stoppages because the necessary resources may not be available when they are needed.

A second problem that may arise deals with top-level management's ability to authorize changes to the way the company does business. When business processes need to be changed to incorporate best practices, these modifications need to be completed. Otherwise, the company will have a piece of software on its hands that does not fit the way people accomplish their business tasks. Lack of executive sponsorship can also have a trickle-down effect within the organization. If users and midlevel management perceive the enterprise system to be unimportant, they are not likely to view it as a priority. Enterprise systems require a concentrated effort, and executive sponsorship can propel or stifle the implementation. Executive management can obliterate any obstacles that arise.

Get Help from Outside Experts

Enterprise systems are complex. Even the most talented information systems departments can struggle in coming to grips with ERP, CRM, and SCM applications. Most vendors have trained project managers and consultants to assist companies with installing enterprise systems. Using consultants tends to move companies through the implementation more quickly and tends to help companies train their personnel on the applications more effectively. However, companies should not rely too heavily on consultants and should plan for the consultants leaving once the implementation is complete. When consultants are physically present, company personnel tend to rely on them for assistance. Once the application goes live and the consultants are no longer there, users have to do the job themselves. A key focus should be facilitating user learning.

Thoroughly Train Users

Training is often the most overlooked, underestimated, and poorly budgeted expense involved in planning enterprise system implementations. Enterprise systems are much more complicated to learn than stand-alone systems. Learning a single application requires users to become accustomed to a new software interface, but enterprise system users regularly need to learn a new set of business processes as well. Once enterprise systems go live, many companies experience a dramatic drop-off in productivity. This issue can potentially lead to heightened levels of dissatisfaction among users, as they prefer to accomplish their business activities in a familiar manner rather than doing things the new way. By training users before the system goes live and giving them sufficient opportunities to learn the new system, a company can allay fears and mitigate potential productivity issues.

Take a Multidisciplinary Approach to Implementations

Enterprise systems affect the entire organization; thus, companies should include personnel from different levels and departments in the implementation project (Kumar and Crook, 1999). In CRM and SCM environments in which other organizations are participating in the implementation, it is critical to enlist the support of personnel in their organizations as well. Project managers need to include in the implementation personnel from midlevel management, the information systems department, external consultants, and, most important, end users.

Failing to include the appropriate people in the day-to-day activities of the project can prove problematic in many areas. From a needs analysis standpoint, it is critical that all the business requirements be sufficiently captured before selection of an enterprise solution. Since end users are involved in every aspect of daily business activities, their insights can be invaluable. For instance, an end user might make salient a feature that no one on the project team had thought of. Having an application that does not meet all the business's requirements can result in poorly fitting software or customizations. Another peril in leaving out key personnel is the threat of alienation. Departments and/or personnel that do not feel included may develop a sense of animosity toward the new system and view it in a negative light. In extreme cases, users will refuse to use the new application, resulting in conflicts and inefficiencies within the organization.

Although these expansive enterprise system implementations are often cumbersome and difficult, the potential payoff is huge. As a result, organizations are compelled to

Industry Analysis

The Comics Industry: Digital Distribution to the Rescue

Not too many generations ago, comic books were a major source of entertainment. Kids sequestered in their rooms, hidden in tree houses, or lying in tents on campouts read piles of them. There was Superman, Spiderman, Wonder Woman, Batman, the Fantastic Four, The Hulk, G.I. Joe, Betty Boop, Little Audrey, and more. Kids saved allowances to buy their favorites and traded them even up with other comic book aficionados (see Figure 8.27).

Then along came television cartoons and shows for kids, followed by computer games and Xbox, Nintendo, and PlayStation game players. Technology trumped static comic books, and the comics industry dwindled. In 1998, Marvel Comics, creator of 5,000 beloved comic book characters and the largest player in the industry, was bankrupt; DC Comics, the second-largest comic book producer, was also on its last legs. Many smaller comic companies were no longer in business.

The comic industry revived, however, when it dawned on comic company executives that technology was the answer. Superman, Spiderman, Batman, the Fantastic Four, and other comic book heroes weren't dead—they simply needed to make the transition from the printed page to the big screen and to digital media.

Thanks to the global Internet, comic fans can now log on to Web sites to rediscover their favorite comic book characters. Marvel.com, for example, lets users access more than 30 older comics. Users can read the first five pages and then are asked to log in or register. Marvel has found that 82 percent of online comic book readers are more likely to purchase comic books in stores than those who have not logged on to Marvel.com.

Cell phones are another new distribution channel for the comic industry. In Japan, especially, comics read via cell phones are big business. There are now 181 Japanese comic titles transported to the cell phone platform, all of which can be downloaded for 40 yen, or about 50 U.S. cents. This market has estimated yearly revenues of 4.5 billion yen ($400 million in U.S. dollars).

Licensing comic book characters has also helped revive the industry. In the past, licensing comic book characters used in movies and on apparel has been a low-income generator for the industry even though consumer demand has been high. For example, Marvel licensed the *Men in Black* characters in 1997 for movies for about $1 million, while the first *Men in Black* movie generated close to $560 million in worldwide sales. The risk was low for Marvel, but so were the rewards. In fact, Marvel received less than 1 percent in licensing fees for 12 of their characters used in movies that generated approximately $3.6 billion worldwide.

Comic companies have seen the profit-to-be-made light and are now developing their own studios to produce their characters' films. This move is not without risk—making movies is a risky business—but could eventually lead to comic companies once again becoming dominant players in the entertainment industry.

Questions

1. If you were an adviser to the comics industry, what distribution methods should be developed next? Is there anyone you should partner with? Why or why not?

2. What is unique/common about the comics industry when compared to other industries impacted by the changes brought on by the digital world?

Sources: Susanna Hamner, "Marvel Comics Leaps into Movie-Making," *Business 2.0* (June 1, 2006), http://money.cnn.com/magazines/business2/business2_archive/2006/05/01/8375925/index.htm
Anonymous, "Marvel Successful with Dot Comics" (May 4, 2006), http://www.tmcnet.com/usubmit/2006/05/04/1637788.htm
Anonymous, "Comic on Mobiles?" *Business Guide* (May 9, 2006), http://www.jinbn.com/2006/05/09100016.html

FIGURE 8.27

The comics industry is undergoing tremendous change in the digital world.

implement these systems. Further, given the popularity and necessity of such systems, you are likely to find yourself involved in the implementation and/or use of such a system. We are confident that after reading this chapter, you will be better able to understand and help with the development and use of such systems.

Key Points Review

1. *Describe what enterprise systems are and how they have evolved.* Enterprise systems are information systems that span the entire organization and can be used to integrate business processes, activities, and information across all the functional areas of a firm. Enterprise systems can be either prepackaged software or custom-made applications. The implementation of enterprise systems often involves business process management, a systematic, structured improvement approach by all or part of an organization that critically examines, rethinks, and redesigns processes in order to achieve dramatic improvements in one or more performance measures, such as quality, cycle time, or cost. Enterprise systems evolved from legacy systems that supported distinct organizational activities by combining data and applications into a single comprehensive system.

2. *Describe enterprise resource planning (ERP) systems and how they help to improve internal business processes.* ERP systems evolved from "material requirements planning" systems during the 1990s and are, for the most part, used to support internal business processes. ERP systems allow information to be shared throughout the organization through the use of a large data warehouse, helping to streamline business processes and improve customer service. When selecting an ERP system, organizations must choose which modules to implement from a large menu of options—most organizations adopt only a subset of the available ERP components. ERP core components support the major internal activities of the organization for producing their products and services, while ERP extended components support the primary external activities of the organization for dealing with suppliers and customers.

3. *Describe customer relationship management (CRM) systems and how they help to improve downstream business processes.* CRM is a corporate-level strategy to create and maintain lasting relationships with customers by concentrating on the downstream information flows through the introduction of reliable systems, processes, and procedures. Applications focusing on downstream information flows have two main objectives—to attract potential customers and create customer loyalty. To develop a successful CRM strategy, organizations must do more than simply purchase and install CRM software; they must also make changes to policy and business processes, customer service, employee training, and data utilization. A CRM consists of three primary components: operational CRM, analytical CRM, and collaborative CRM. Operational CRM focuses on front-office activities that deal directly with customers. Analytical CRM focuses on back-office activities that aid managers in analyzing the sales and marketing functions. Finally, collaborative CRM provides effective communication capabilities within the organization and externally with customers.

4. *Describe supply chain management (SCM) systems and how they help to improve upstream business processes.* SCM systems focus on improving upstream information flows and have two main objectives—to accelerate product development and to reduce costs associated with procuring raw materials, components, and services from suppliers. SCM consists of supply chain planning (SCP) and supply chain execution (SCE) components. SCP involves the development of various resource plans to support the efficient and effective production of goods and services. SCE puts the SCM planning into motion and reflects the processes involved in improving the collaboration of all members of the supply chain—suppliers, producers, distributors, and customers. SCE involves the management of three key elements of the supply chain: product flow, information flow, and financial flow. When developing a supply chain management strategy, an organization must consider a variety of factors that will affect the efficiency and effectiveness of the supply chain. Specifically, organizations must match their overall supply chain strategy to their overall competitive strategy to reap the greatest benefits.

5. *Understand and utilize the keys to successfully implementing enterprise systems.* Experience with enterprise system implementations suggest that there are some common problems that can be avoided and/or should be managed carefully. Organizations can avoid common implementation problems by (1) securing executive sponsorship, (2) getting necessary help from outside experts, (3) thoroughly training users, and (4) taking a multidisciplinary approach to implementations.

Key Terms

analytical CRM   332
back-office system   332
business process management
    (BPM)   325
business process reengineering
    (BPR)   325
collaborative CRM   332
conversion   323
custom applications   321
customer interaction center
    (CIC)   335
customer relationship management
    (CRM)   329
customer service and support
    (CSS)   335
cutomization   323
distribution portals   344
downstream information
    flow   320
enterprise marketing automation
    (EMA)   335
enterprise portals   344

enterprise resource planning
    (ERP)   326
enterprise systems   313
enterprise-wide information
    systems   313
ERP core components   328
ERP extended components   328
Extensible Business Reporting
    Language (XBRL)   346
Extensible Markup Language
    (XML)   346
externally focused systems   315
financial flow   342
front-office system   332
information flow   342
internally focused systems   314
interorganizational system
    (IOS)   315
legacy systems   322
modules   323
operational CRM   332
packaged applications   321

procurement portals   344
product flow   342
radio frequency identification
    (RFID)   347
RFID tag   347
sales force automation (SFA)   334
stand-alone applications   322
supply chain   339
supply chain effectiveness   343
supply chain efficiency   342
supply chain execution
    (SCE)   341
supply chain management
    (SCM)   340
supply chain planning (SCP)   340
supply network   339
tag   346
trading exchanges   344
upstream information flow   320
value system   320
vanilla version   323
vertical market   344

Review Questions

1. Describe what enterprise systems are and how they have evolved.
2. Contrast internally and externally focused systems.
3. What are the core and support activities of a value chain?
4. Give an example of upstream and downstream information flows in a value system.
5. Compare and contrast customized and packaged applications as well as vanilla versions versus best practices–based software.
6. What are the core components of an enterprise resource planning system?
7. What is a customer relationship management system, and what are its primary components?

8. What is supply chain management, and how does supply chain planning differ from supply chain execution?
9. How does customer relationship management differ from supply chain management?
10. Contrast distribution portals, procurement portals, and trading exchanges.
11. What is XML, and how will it impact supply chain management?
12. What is RFID, and how will it impact supply chain management?
13. What are the keys to successfully implementing an enterprise system?

Self-Study Questions

Visit the Interactive Study Guide on the text Web site for additional Self-Study Questions: **www.prenhall.com/jessup.**

1. _____ are information systems that allow companies to integrate information support operations on a company-wide basis.
    A. customer relationship management systems
    B. enterprise systems

C. WANs
D. interorganizational systems
2. Which of the following is a core activity according to the value chain model?
    A. firm infrastructure
    B. customer service

C. human resources

D. procurement

3. According to the value chain model, which of the following is a support function?

A. technology development

B. marketing and sales

C. inbound logistics

D. operations and manufacturing

4. All of the following are true about legacy systems except _____.

A. they are stand-alone systems

B. they are older software systems

C. they are enterprise resource planning systems

D. they may be difficult to integrate into other systems

5. A comprehensive customer relationship management system includes all but what of the following components?

A. operational CRM

B. analytical CRM

C. diagnostic CRM

D. collaborative CRM

6. Sales force automation is most closely associated with what?

A. enterprise resource planning

B. customer relationship management

C. supply chain management

D. legacy systems

7. Which of the following is commonly used to refer to the producers of supplies that a company uses?

A. procurement

B. sales force

C. supply network

D. customers

8. Which type of flow does supply chain execution not focus on?

A. procurement flow

B. product flow

C. information flow

D. financial flow

9. RFID tags are used for _____.

A. tracking military weapons

B. eliminating counterfeit drugs

C. tracking passports

D. all of the above

10. _____ is a systematic, structured improvement approach by all or part of an organization that critically examines, rethinks, and redesigns processes in order to achieve dramatic improvements in one or more performance measures such as quality, cycle time, or cost.

A. systems analysis

B. business process management

C. customer relationship management

D. total quality management

Answers are on page 356.

Problems and Exercises

1. Match the following terms with the appropriate definitions:
   i. Enterprise systems
   ii. Legacy systems
   iii. Supply chain
   iv. ERP extended components
   v. Customer relationship management
   vi. Customer interaction center
   vii. Supply chain management
   viii. Business process management
   ix. Enterprise portal
   x. RFID

   a. Components that support the primary *external* activities of the organization for dealing with suppliers and customers

   b. Information systems that provide a single point of access to secured, proprietary information, which may be dispersed throughout an organization

   c. The use of the electromagnetic or electrostatic coupling in the RF portion of the electromagnetic spectrum in order to transmit signals

   d. Older systems that are not designed to communicate with other applications beyond departmental boundaries

   e. Information systems that allow companies to integrate information on a company-wide basis

   f. Applications that concentrate on downstream information flows, integrating the value chains of a company and its distributors or customers

   g. Commonly used to refer to the producers of supplies that a company uses

   h. A systematic, structured improvement approach by all or part of an organization whereby people critically examine, rethink, and redesign business processes in order to achieve dramatic improvements in one or more performance measures such as quality, cycle time, or cost

   i. The use of multiple communication channels to support the communication preferences of customers

   j. Applications that operate on upstream information flows, integrating the value chains of a company and its suppliers

2. Find an organization that you are familiar with and determine how many software applications it is utilizing concurrently. Is the company's information system cohesive, or does it need updating and streamlining?

3. What part does training users in an ERP system play, and how important is it in job satisfaction? What productivity problems can result in an ERP implementation?

4. What are the payoffs in taking a multidisciplinary approach to an ERP implementation? What departments are affected, and what is the typical time frame? Research an organization that has recently implemented an ERP system. What could the company have done better, and what did it do right?

5. What companies are using data warehouses? Research this question and determine the cost and size of a data warehouse. What are the advantages and disadvantages of data warehouses, especially for implementing enterprise systems? What is the typical time frame for implementation?

6. Based on your own experiences with applications, have you used customized or off-the-shelf applications? What is the difference, and how good was the system documentation?

7. Search the Web for the phrase "best practices," and you will find numerous sites that summarize the best practices for a variety of industries and professions. Choose one and summarize these best practices into a one-page report.

8. Choose a company you are familiar with and examine how efficiently or effectively they have designed the procurement, production, and transportation aspects of their businesses.

9. Assume you are a sales manager. What sales performance measures would you want the customer relationship management system to provide you in order to

better manage your sales force? For each measure, describe how you would you use it and at what interval you would need to update this information.

10. Find an organization that is utilizing customer relationship management (visit vendor Web sites for cases studies or industry journals such as *CIO Magazine* or *ComputerWorld*). Who within the organization is most involved in this process, and who benefits?

11. Discuss the ethical trade-offs between using large databases that profile and categorize customers so that companies can more effectively market their products. Think about products that are "good" for the consumer versus those that are not.

12. Search the Web for recent articles on business process management and related approaches (e.g., business process reengineering) for improving organizations. What is the current state of the art for these approaches? To what extent are these "headlines" about information systems implementations, especially regarding enterprise systems?

13. Use the Web to visit a distribution portal, procurement portal, and trading exchange. What do they have in common? What do they have that is unique?

14. Search the Web for recent stories about the use of XML within supply chain management. To what extent does it appear that XML is becoming a standard?

15. What applications other than those mentioned in the chapter are there for RFID tags? What must happen in order for the use of RFID to become more widespread?

Application Exercises

 The existing data files referenced in these exercises are available on the Student Companion Web site: **www.prenhall.com/jessup**.

 **Spreadsheet Application: Choosing an ERP System at Campus Travel**

Campus Travel is interested in integrating their business processes to streamline processes such as purchasing, sales, human resource management, and customer relationship management. Because of your success in implementing the e-commerce infrastructure, the general manager asks you for advice on what to do to streamline operations at Campus Travel. Use the data provided in the file ERPSystems.csv to make a recommendation about which ERP system to purchase. The file includes ratings of the different modules of the systems and the weights assigned to these ratings. You are asked to do the following:

1. Determine the product with the highest overall rating (Hint: Use the SUMPRODUCT formula to mul-

tiply each vendor's scores with the respective weights and add the weighted scores).

2. Prepare the necessary graphs to compare the products on the different dimensions and the overall score.

3. Be sure to professionally format the graphs before printing them out.

Database Application: Managing Customer Relations at Campus Travel

Not all frequent fliers accumulate large amounts of miles. There are many who never travel for years but have frequent flier accounts. As manager of sales and marketing, you want to find out how to target these individuals better with promotions and special offers. To acomplish this task, you will need to create the following reports:

1. A report displaying all frequent fliers, sorted by distance traveled

2. A report displaying all frequent fliers, sorted by the total amount spent on air travel.

In the file InfrequentFliers.mdb, you find travel data of the members of a frequent flier program for the year 2007.

Prepare professionally formatted printouts of all reports, including headers, footers, dates, and so on. (Hint: Use the report wizard to create the reports; use queries to sum up the fares and distances for each traveler before creating the respective reports.)

Team Work Exercise ERP, CRM, and SCM

Work in a small group with classmates and use a search engine such as Google to search the Web for sites with information on ERP, CRM, and SCM. What types of Web sites are you finding? Choose a particular software package related to ERP, CRM, or SCM and split up your group to research the company's site as well as related articles on the system at an online magazine such as *InformationWeek* or *Computerworld*. Get back together with your group and discuss your findings. How is the system portrayed by the company/vendors and by the magazines? Does the product seem to deliver what the company promises? Prepare a brief presentation of your findings.

Answers to the Self-Study Questions

1. B, p. 313	**2.** B, p. 315	**3.** A, p. 317	**4.** C, p. 322	**5.** C, p. 332
6. B, p. 334	**7.** C, p. 339	**8.** A, p. 341	**9.** D, p. 347	**10.** B, p. 335

case

Using the Internet to Improve Upstream and Downstream Information Flow

Networks have continually evolved to better serve all patrons of the Internet and will undoubtedly continue to play a large part in online company development. In fact, most large organizations have been utilizing the Internet as a key part of the enterprise-wide information system strategy for several years, and virtually all medium-sized to large organizations have Web sites today. Additionally, a 2006 survey of Fortune 500 businesses by the Computer Technology Industry Foundation reported that 74 percent use the Internet to enable business-to-business activities, up from just 31 percent in 2005. Clearly, for large organizations, the Internet is being used for much more than an electronic brochure.

A powerful example of how a company can utilize the Internet to leverage its investment in enterprise-wide information systems is FedEx. For example, when you mail a package via FedEx, you get a tracking number that allows you to follow your package as it moves to its destination. Through the Web, you can enter your tracking number and locate any package still in its system. Also located on the company's Web site is their shipping service, which IT experts call a stroke of genius. In a single session, you enter all the information needed to prepare a shipper form, obtain a tracking number, print the form, and schedule a pickup. By using the Internet, FedEx is getting their customers to do some of their work for them. With this linkage between internal information systems and customers through the Internet, FedEx has lowered costs yet increased customer control and satisfaction—and inspired hundreds of other companies to copy them.

In addition to FedEx's innovative implementation of the Internet, other practical uses include the following:

- Private newsgroups that companies use to share ideas and experiences in utilizing FedEx's services
- Groupware in which several companies collaborate to create new products and services
- Training programs or other educational services that companies develop and share
- Shared catalogs accessible only to those within a common industry or trade
- Project management and control for companies that are part of a shared project

Large companies have, indeed, discovered the value of the Internet. One segment that has struggled to leverage these benefits have been small companies, especially those without a dedicated technology staff. To address this situation, Microsoft has recently made the Internet much more accessible and powerful for a broader range of organizations with the creation of Office Live, a Web site creation application for users of the Microsoft Office Suite. In June 2006, introductory ads for the product stated, "Microsoft Office Live Basics provides your company with its own domain name, hosting, Web site, and e-mail accounts for free." The service included the following:

- Company domain name (e.g., www.northwindtraders.com)
- Five Web mail accounts (2 GB storage each)
- Easy-to-use Site Builder to create your own Web site (30 MB storage space)
- Web site traffic reports to help you track your site's performance

While Office Live allows a small company to create an online Web site without hiring staff to maintain it, the system can be much more than an electronic brochure. Companies using Microsoft's Office Suite not only can create, share, and manage documents using the existing Office applications but also can create complex systems such as customer relationship management or accounts payable systems that link company employees, customers, and vendors to a single site through a secure business-to-business extranet. Microsoft undoubtedly saw the potential for adding future upgrade sales to Office Live as well as the Office Suite by the release of these user-friendly but powerful services.

One disadvantage to Office Live is that only those companies that have adapted Microsoft's Office Suite of applications gain the full power of the site. Companies who do not use the Office Suite cannot easily adapt Office Live. In addition, Office Live–constructed Web sites can be hosted only by Microsoft—a practice Microsoft critics see as typically monopolistic.

Questions

1. Develop a list of corporate best practices from some of the Web sites you use to buy products. Which of these practices require the Web site to access information from a database to provide the service?
2. For a small business that you are familiar with, list and describe some of their upstream and downstream information flows that could be facilitated through a Web site like Office Live.
3. From both Microsoft's and a customer's perspective, list the pros and cons to Microsoft's Office Live requirements of customers having to use the Microsoft Office Suite software to gain the full power of the Office Live environment and having Microsoft host the customer's Web site.

Sources: Anonymous, "Businesses Rely Heavily on Extranet Web Sites for E-Commerce," *BtoB Online* (April 25, 2006), http://www.btobonline.com/article.cms?articleId=27787

Mark S. Merkow, "Extraordinary Extranets," *Webreference,* http://www.webreference.com/content/extranet/

Anonymous, "Microsoft Office Live," *Microsoft Corporation,* http://officelive.microsoft.com/OfficeLiveBasic.aspx#10

case ②

e-Enabling the Air Transport Industry: Building Organizational Partnerships Using Enterprise Information Systems

For many airlines, constantly striving to reduce operating costs may well be the key for survival. Over the past years, airlines have faced a difficult economic environment, especially as operating costs skyrocketed because of increasing fuel prices and costs for airport security. In addition, schedule interruptions and canceled flights due to security threats can cost airlines millions of dollars in lost revenues and generate huge unforeseen operating costs. For example, following the August 10, 2006, terror threat, British Airways had to pay for 10,000 hotel rooms for stranded passengers and lost nearly $95 million in revenue because of canceled flights.

While factors such as rising gas prices temporarily created additional demand for air travel, translating into additional revenue for the airlines, the situation is far from optimal. In fact, most industry analysts agree that this is the hardest economic crisis ever for the air transport industry. As a result, many airlines are canceling orders for new airplanes as they fight for survival. Needless to say, the health of the air transport industry is a critical concern for aircraft manufacturers such as Boeing and Airbus.

In an attempt to aid the air transport industry and find new revenue streams, both Boeing and Airbus have started offering enterprise-wide information systems to help airlines better manage their operations. As discussed in prior chapters, Boeing's e-Enabled Advantage program includes components such as the Jeppesen Electronic Flight Bag, Aircraft Health Management, and SBS Crew Scheduling Solutions. These systems are intended to help airlines increase reliability and efficiency as well as integrate information to improve operations and decision making. Similarly, competitor Airbus offers several systems such as its Class 3 Electronic Flight Bag, AIRMAN aircraft fault management tool, and ADOC electronic aircraft documentation. Although each of these tools is designed to save costs for the airlines, it is only through the application of *integrated* solutions that significant cost reductions can be realized. Of course, flight operations are only one aspect of an airline's business. There are many other areas where savings can be obtained.

For example, to survive in today's highly turbulent world, airlines have to analyze every aspect of their business, including marketing and frequent flier programs, route profitability, catering, and support processes, such as human resources, purchasing, or financials. In sum, all business processes must be streamlined and made as efficient as possible. Further, two factors differentiate one airline from another: price and customer service. While many—especially low-cost—carriers differentiate in terms of price, customer service quality can secure customer loyalty, especially in the higher-paying (i.e., business class and first class) segments. Thus, any systems that help to not only control costs but also enhance customer service are making inroads into this industry.

Consequently, enterprise-wide software giant SAP has started offering ERP solutions, targeted directly at the aerospace and defense industry (SAP A&D). These systems allow airlines to integrate various legacy systems, helping to streamline business processes and improve decision making. For instance, SAP's human resources module offers the capabilities for managing recruiting,

training, payroll processing, and benefits for the airline's employees, helping airlines to lower various operating costs. Using the SAP NetWeaver Portal technology, every employee can access tailored information using a Web interface, which is especially important for those employees who are constantly on the move as part of their job, such as pilots or crew members.

Specific to the air transport industry, SAP also provides tools for analyzing route profitability. Given that most of today's airlines have a portfolio of both profitable and less profitable routes, such insights can provide needed information on which routes to add, eliminate, or modify (e.g., use a smaller-capacity airplane). Additionally, because many low-cost carriers try to focus exclusively on the most profitable routes, these routes become increasingly more competitive. Therefore, there is a need to continuously analyze route profitability as the dynamics of various markets fluctuate. Because most airlines simply cannot afford to keep unprofitable routes, understanding the profitability of each route can help airlines to more proactively manage their business.

In addition to these components, airlines can use SAP A&D's operational, analytical, and collaborative CRM components to provide customized services to their passengers, increasing customer service and loyalty. By collecting customer data at each point of the service encounter, airlines are able to create targeted marketing campaigns, leading to improved frequent flier programs and a greater return on marketing investments. Additionally, SAP's CRM components include capabilities to manage help desk operations, complaint processing, or customer satisfaction and loyalty analysis.

Clearly, today is a very difficult time for the air transport industry. Airlines that are best able to effectively manage all aspects of their supply chain have the greatest chance for survival. Like other industries that operate in highly competitive environments, the air transport industry is turning to enterprise-wide information systems. These systems are being developed by both existing software companies and the airline manufactures. As this industry increasingly adopts and deploys these systems, best practices will emerge, ultimately leading to a stronger and healthier industry.

Airlines have to integrate a variety of systems to survive in turbulent times.

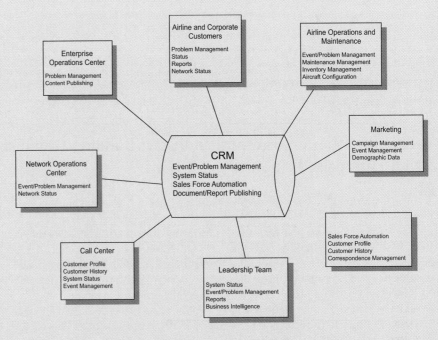

Questions

1. With the airlines' increasing needs for systems integration, how can the different solutions offered by the aircraft manufacturers and software vendors such as SAP be integrated?
2. Which components mentioned in the case do you see as most important for an airline's survival? Why?
3. Research the Web for the history of frequent flier programs. Where do you see such programs heading? How can CRM systems be used for frequent flier programs?

Sources: K. Tchorek and M. Fletcher, "British Air, Ryanair Cancel Flights on Security Delay," retrieved August 22, 2006, from http://www.bloomberg.com/apps/news?pid=20601102&sid=aG_UAkveYoc4&refer=uk

SAP, "Powerful Solutions for Enterprise-Wide Airline Management," retrieved August 22, 2006, from available at http://www.sap.com/industries/aero-defense/pdf/BWP_Powerful_Sol_Ent_Airline_Mgt.pdf

chapter 9
Developing Information Systems

preview > As you have read throughout this book and have experienced in your own life, information systems are of many different types, including decision support systems, executive information systems, group support systems, and electronic commerce systems. Just as there are different types of systems, different approaches have been found to be more appropriate for developing some types of systems and less appropriate for others. Learning all the possible ways to develop or acquire a system and, more important, how to identify the optimal approach takes years of study and experience. To this end, this chapter has several objectives. After reading this chapter, you will be able to do the following:

1. Understand the process used by organizations to manage the development of information systems.

2. Describe each major phase of the systems development life cycle: systems identification, selection, and planning; system analysis; system design; system implementation; and system maintenance.

3. Describe prototyping, rapid application development, object-oriented analysis, and design methods of systems development, along with each approach's strengths and weaknesses.

4. Understand the factors involved in building a system in-house, along with situations in which it is not feasible.

5. Explain three alternative systems development options: external acquisition, outsourcing, and end-user development.

If you are a typical business student, you might be wondering why we have a chapter on building and acquiring information systems. The answer is simple: no matter what area of an organization you are in—such as marketing, finance, accounting, human resources, or operations—you will be involved in the systems development process. In fact, research indicates that the IS spending in most organizations is controlled by specific business functions. What this means is that even if your career interests are in something other than IS, it is very likely that you will be involved in the IS development process. Understanding all available options is important to your future success.

Managing in the Digital World: Online Gaming

Are you familiar with *Pacman*? If you haven't played this simple, classic computer game from the 1980s, maybe you've been hiding out in a jungle somewhere or just pulling a Rip Van Winkle for the past 20 years. If you aren't familiar with the game, this is how it works. Using the arrow keys on your computer keyboard, you move the round yellow figure with the big open mouth around a course resembling a maze. The object is for the Pacman character to "eat" as many white dots as possible, all the while avoiding evil ghosts Blinky, Pinky, Inkey, and Clyde, who will devour Pacman if they catch him. Graphics were primitive and clunky in early computer games, and strategy was simple—players with the quickest reflexes racked up the highest scores (see Figure 9.1).

Computer games have come a long way since *Pacman*. Today, graphics are sophisticated; players often need logic, strategy, and puzzle-solving skills; and choices are plentiful. Several genres, or types, of games are also available on CDs or online, including the following:

- Action. Usually involve a single shooter who moves through several graphic scenarios pursuing an enemy. Examples include *Doom, Quake, Star Trek Voyager, Rune,* and *Tribes.*
- Adventure. Narrative-based video games that require puzzle solving and interaction with other characters rather than reflex reaction. *Zork, King's Quest, The Secret of Monkey Island,* and *Myst* are examples.
- Role Playing. Require a player to take on a fictitious persona who progresses to higher levels within the game by improving the character's skills. *Hellfire, Diablo, Lands of Lore, Torment, The Vampire,* and *Masquerade* are role-playing games.
- Simulators. Involve allowing the player to control helicopters, cars, airplanes, or other machines and strive to provide a realistic environment for operating the machines. Can require players to learn many procedures and control features. Examples include *Microsoft Flight Simulator, Microsoft Combat,* and *Re-volt.*
- Strategy. Involves creating a character and a strategy for winning the game. Examples are *Sacrifice, Age of Empires II, Black & White,* and *Homeworld.*
- Arcade. Coin-operated games usually installed in businesses, such as restaurants, bars, or mall areas. Most arcade games are redemption (reward players for skill, usually with tickets to play more games), pinball machines, or video games.
- Platform or Performer. Require players to move an object or character up or down, right or left, while collecting certain items. Examples include *Pacman, Super Mario Brothers,* and *Castlevania.*

FIGURE 9.1

The classic game *Pacman*. (You can play Pacman and more 1980s computer games at http://www.80smusiclyrics.com/games/#null.)

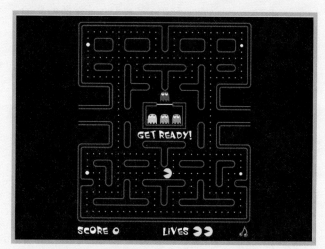

- Puzzle or Maze. Emphasize puzzle solving and involve logic, strategy, pattern recognition, and sometimes pure luck. *Tetris, Lumenis, Bomberman,* and *The Incredible Machine* are puzzle games.

The game genres listed here can be further categorized as single player or multiplayer. (Some of those listed can be both.) Single-player games are restricted to one player at a time, but there are usually many levels of increasing difficulty that a player can progress through. In single-player games, a player usually is pitted against the computer, called a virtual opponent. Sometimes many people take turns at playing one single-player game to see who can score the highest. The person who is playing the game at any time is referred to as being in the "hot seat."

Multiplayer games involve more than one player, and the levels of difficulty do not change unless all players have progressed to another level. Unlike a single-player game, a multiplayer game allows two or more players to play the game at the same time, competing against each other or possibly teaming up to achieve a common goal.

A special category of multiplayer games dubbed "massively multiplayer" let a large number of players interact simultaneously to create a complex virtual scene. There are two main categories for massively multiplayer games: MMORPG (massively multiplayer online role-playing game) and MMORTS (massively multiplayer online real-time strategy).

In order for multiple players to play in the same virtual environment, their computers have to be connected to each other via a LAN (local area network) or over the Internet. When computers are connected via a LAN, the gaming location is referred to as a "LAN party." Since LANs provide much faster connection speeds than the Internet, players have more control over the gaming environment, and the game sequences progress correctly. Slow Internet connection speeds cause delays that can slow the game down to the point of frustration or boredom and can cause lags that affect players' actions. For example, if you shoot an enemy in an action game, latency caused by a slow connection can slow the action to the point that the enemy you thought you shot dodges the bullet. Most advanced gamers test the network speeds before starting a game to ensure that all actions take place on time.

Gaming is a profitable and competitive industry. Some of the famous producers of computer games are Nintendo, Sony, Electronic Arts, and Microsoft. The gaming industry consists of game developers and game publishers. The developers usually consist of programmers, artists, sound engineers, and editors. Similar to textbooks, games usually have publishers who back the entire production of a game. Game development usually takes from anywhere between a year to three years for completion. The games today require an extensive amount of programming, story line and plot, action sequence, sound and other effects, and multiple levels of game difficulty along with multiplayer capability. There are games that are still created by single programmers, but most of the popular ones are by big companies and take a lot of developmental time. The cost of development has made big game publishers look at international markets, such as India, to acquire game development talent.

As games get more intense and involve more player attention, the consequences of extended exposure to games become a concern. There are numerous games that are very violent or sexually explicit. Many countries have started using game rating systems and in cases have banned certain games altogether. The online gaming environment is a very conducive place for like-minded people to meet while gaming. Most games now have the capability to provide alternate communication channels among players so that they can coordinate themselves against an attack or plan a strategy. This functionality has promoted certain games to cult status with a large loyal fan base.

Most multiplayer online games have their own economy and trading system. Players can buy and sell goods they have created or acquired. There are internal markets and policies whereby players are allowed to barter goods. This process brings the playing environment to another level. However, cheating exists even in the gaming world. There are numerous ways cheating is carried out, such as modifying certain system characteristics, understanding code bugs that were unintended by the game developers, and buying cheat codes from other, more experienced gamers. The usual victims of cheating are inexperienced gamers with a lot of greed.

After reading this chapter, you will be able to answer the following:

1. What process would you use if you were designing a new computer game?

2. How would the development process differ if you were designing a new payroll system versus a new game?

3. How important is system testing for an online game versus a traditional type of software, such as a payroll system? Justify your answer.

Sources:

http://www.newsfactor.com/story.xhtml?story_id=40592

http://www.newsfactor.com/story.xhtml?story_id=39369

http://www.outsource2india.com/why_india/articles/game-development.asp

http://blogs.mercurynews.com/aei/2005/07/profile_indias_.html

http://www.macrovision.com/pdfs/Best%20Practices_Games_June2004.pdf

http://en.wikipedia.org/wiki/Online_gaming

The Need for Structured Systems Development

The process of designing, building, and maintaining information systems is often referred to as **systems analysis and design**. Likewise, the individual who performs this task is referred to as a **systems analyst**. (This chapter uses "systems analyst" and "programmer" interchangeably.) Because few organizations can survive without effectively utilizing information and computing technology, the demand for skilled systems analysts is very strong. Organizations want to hire systems analysts because they possess a unique blend of managerial and technical expertise—systems analysts are not just "techies." In fact, systems analysts remain in demand precisely because of this unique blend of abilities, but it was not always this way.

The Evolution of Information Systems Development

In the early days of computing, systems development and programming was considered an art that only a few technical "gurus" could master. Unfortunately, the techniques used to construct systems varied greatly from individual to individual. This variation made it difficult to integrate large organizational information systems. Furthermore, many systems were not easily maintainable after the original programmer left the organization. As a result, organizations were often left with systems that were very difficult and expensive to maintain. Many organizations, therefore, underutilized these technology investments and failed to realize all possible benefits from their systems.

To address this problem, information systems professionals concluded that system development needed to become an engineering-like discipline (Nunamaker, 1992). Common methods, techniques, and tools had to be developed to create a disciplined approach for constructing information systems. This evolution from an "art" to a "discipline" led to the use of the term **software engineering** to help define what systems analysts and programmers do. Transforming information systems development into a formal discipline would provide numerous benefits. First, it would be much easier to train programmers and analysts if common techniques were widely used. In essence, if all systems analysts had similar training, it would make them more interchangeable and more skilled at working on the systems developed by other analysts. Second, systems built with commonly used techniques would be more maintainable. Both industry and academic researchers have pursued the quest for new and better approaches for building information systems.

Options for Obtaining Information Systems

Organizations can obtain new information systems in many ways. One option, of course, is for the members of the organization to build the information system themselves. Organizations can also buy a prepackaged system from a software development company or consulting firm. Some information systems that are commonly used in many organizations can be purchased for much less money than what it would cost to build a new one. Purchasing a prepackaged system is a good option as long as its features meet the needs of the organization. For example, a payroll system is an example of a prepackaged system that is often purchased rather than developed by an organization because tax laws, wage calculations, check printing, and accounting activities are highly standardized. Figure 9.2 outlines several sources for information systems.

A third option is to have an outside organization or consultant custom-build a system to an organization's specifications. This is generally referred to as having the development outsourced. This is a good option when an organization does not have adequate systems development resources or expertise. A final option is to let individual users and departments build their own custom systems to support their individual needs. This is referred to as end-user development. Most organizations allow end-user development to be used to construct only a limited range of systems. For example, systems that span organizational boundaries or perform complex changes to corporate databases are typically not candidates for end-user development. In contrast, a common application that

FIGURE 9.2

There are a variety of sources for information systems.

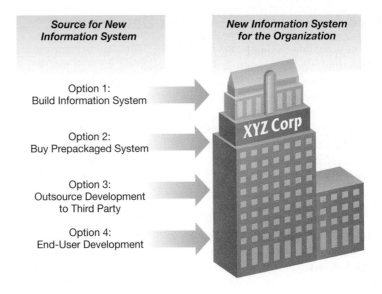

might be constructed using end-user development is a data analysis system using a spreadsheet application such as Microsoft Excel. Regardless of the source of the new information system, the primary role of managers and users in the organization is to make sure that any new system will meet the organization's business needs. This means that managers and users must understand the systems development process to ensure that the system will meet their needs.

Information Systems Development in Action

The tools and techniques used to develop information systems are continually evolving with the rapid changes in information systems hardware and software. As you will see, the information systems development approach is a very structured process that moves from step to step. Systems analysts become adept at decomposing large, complex problems into many small, simple problems. They can then easily solve each simple problem by writing a relatively short computer program. The goal of the systems analyst is to build the final system by piecing together the many small programs into one comprehensive system. This process of decomposing a problem is outlined in Figure 9.3. An easy way to think about

FIGURE 9.3

Problem decomposition makes solving large, complex problems easier.

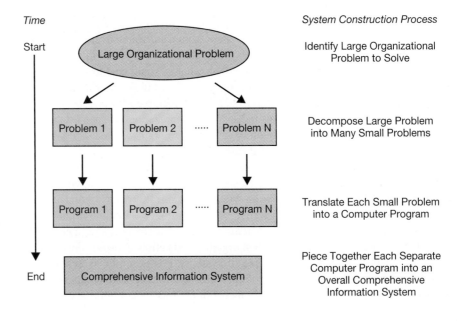

this is to think about using Lego blocks for building a model house. Each individual block is a small, simple piece that is nothing without the others. When put together, the blocks can create a large and very complex design. When systems are built in this manner, they are much easier to design, program, and, most important, maintain.

The Role of Users in the Systems Development Process

Most organizations have a huge investment in transaction processing and management information systems. These systems are most often designed, constructed, and maintained by systems analysts within the organization, using a variety of methods. When building and maintaining information systems, systems analysts rely on information provided by system users, who are involved in all phases of the system's development process. To effectively participate in the process, it is important for all members of the organization to understand what is meant by systems development and what activities occur. A close, mutually respectful working relationship between analysts and users is a key to project success. Now that you understand the history and need for systems development, it is time to consider some of the relevant techniques that are used in systems development.

Conquering Computer Contagion

Blue Security, an Israel-based Internet security company start-up, thought it had the answer to spammers. For every unwanted spam message that the half million clients of the company's service, Blue Frog, received, a message was returned to the advertiser. As a result, six of the top 10 spammers were inundated by the opt-out messages and were forced to eliminate Blue Frog's clients from their mailing list. One spamming company, however, decided to fight back.

According to Blue Security, PharmaMaster responded by sending so many spam messages to Blue Frog's clients that several Internet service provider servers crashed.

Under PharmaMaster's threat of continuing and expanded attacks, on May 2, 2006, Blue Security folded. "We cannot take the responsibility for an ever-escalating cyberwar through our continued operations," Eran Reshef, chief executive officer (CEO) and founder of Blue Security, was quoted in a May 17, 2006, article by Robert Lemos, published online at Security Focus.com.

As PharmaMaster, so have all authors of malware (destructive computer code such as viruses, Trojan horses and worms, and intrusive pop-up and spam ads) continued to flout efforts to cleanse the Internet of their disruptive and exasperating wares, as evidenced by statistics gathered for just one month in 2006. The top 10 viruses reported to Sophos, an Internet security firm, in April 2006 is shown in Table 9.1.

Unfortunately, the battle against malware will probably rage as long as the Internet exists. On the plus side, however, the battle has given rise to new enterprises dedicated solely to protecting Internet users—the "white knights" who will continue to come to the rescue as long as the malware threat exists.

TABLE 9.1 Top 10 Viruses (April 2006)

Rank	Virus	Percent of Reports
1	W32/NETSKY-P	18.5
2	W32/ZAFI-B	16.9
3	W32/NYXEM-D	8.5
4 (TIE)	W32/MYDOOM-AJ	3.9
4 (TIE)	W32/NETSKY-D	3.9
5	W32/MYTOB-FO	3.6
6	W32/MYTOB-C	2.8
7	W32/MYTOB-Z	2.6
8	W32/DOLEBOT-A	2.2
9	W32/MYTOB-AS	1.3
	Others	35.8

Source: Sophos Plc (2006).

Sources: http://www.securityfocus.com/news/11392

http://www.clickz.com/stats/sectors/email/article.php/3609201

Steps in the Systems Development Process

Just as the products that a firm produces and sells follow a life cycle, so do organizational information systems. For example, a new type of tennis shoe follows a life cycle of being introduced to the market, being accepted into the market, maturing, declining in popularity, and ultimately being retired. The term **systems development life cycle (SDLC)** describes the life of an information system from conception to retirement (Hoffer, George, and Valacich, 2008). The SDLC has five primary phases:

1. System identification, selection, and planning
2. System analysis
3. System design
4. System implementation
5. System maintenance

Figure 9.4 is a graphical representation of the SDLC. The SDLC is represented as four boxes connected by arrows. Within the SDLC, arrows flow in both directions from the top box (system identification, selection, and planning) to the bottom box (system implementation). Arrows flowing down represent that the flow of information produced in one phase is being used to seed the activities of the next. Arrows flowing up represent the possibility of returning to a prior phase, if needed. The system maintenance arrow connecting the last phase to the first is what makes the SDLC a cycle.

Phase 1: System Identification, Selection, and Planning

The first phase of the SDLC is **system identification, selection, and planning**, as shown in Figure 9.5. Understanding that it can work on only a limited number of projects at a given time because of limited resources, an organization must take care that only those projects that are critical to enabling the organization's mission, goals, and objectives are undertaken. Consequently, the goal of system identification and selection is simply to identify and select a development project from all possible projects that could be performed. Organizations differ in how they identify and select projects. Some organizations have a formal **information systems planning** process whereby a senior manager, a business group, an IS manager, or a steering committee identifies and assesses all possible systems development projects that an organization could undertake. Others follow a more ad hoc process for identifying potential projects. Nonetheless, after all possible projects are identified, those deemed most likely to yield significant organizational benefits, given available resources, are selected for subsequent development activities.

It is important to note that different approaches for identifying and selecting projects are likely to yield different organizational outcomes (see Table 9.2). For example,

FIGURE 9.4

The systems development life cycle defines the typical process for building systems.

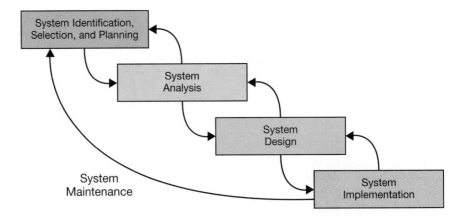

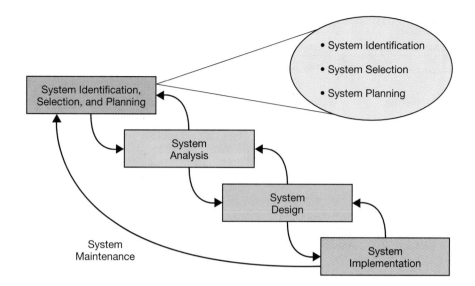

FIGURE 9.5

Phase 1 of the SDLC focuses on system identification, selection, and planning.

projects identified by top management more often have a strategic organizational focus, and projects identified by steering committees more often reflect the diversity of the committee and therefore have a cross-functional focus. Projects identified by individual departments or business units most often have a narrow, tactical focus. Finally, the typical focus of projects identified by the development group is the ease with which existing hardware and systems can be integrated with the proposed project. Other factors—such as project cost, duration, complexity, and risk—are also influenced by the source of a given project. The source of projects has been found to be a key indicator of project focus and success.

Just as there are often differences in the source of systems projects within organizations, there are often different evaluation criteria used within organizations when classifying and ranking potential projects. During project planning, the analyst works with the customers—the potential users of the system and their managers—to collect a broad range of information to gain an understanding of the project size, potential benefits and costs, and other relevant factors. After collecting and analyzing this information, the analyst can bring it together into a summary planning document that can be reviewed and compared with other possible projects. Table 9.3 provides a sample of the criteria often used by organizations. When reviewing a potential development project, organizations may focus on a single criterion but most often examine multiple criteria to make a decision to accept or reject a project. If the organization accepts the project, system analysis begins.

Phase 2: System Analysis

The second phase of the SDLC is called **system analysis**, as highlighted in Figure 9.6. One purpose of the system analysis phase is for designers to gain a thorough under-

TABLE 9.2 Sources of Systems Development Projects and Their Likely Focus

Project Source	Primary Focus
Top management	Broad strategic focus
Steering committee	Cross-functional focus
Individual departments and business units	Narrow, tactical focus
Systems development group	Integration with existing information systems focus

Source: Adapted from McKeen, Guimaraes, and Wetherbe (1994).

TABLE 9.3 Possible Evaluation Criteria for Classifying and Ranking Projects

Evaluation Criteria	Description
Strategic alignment	The extent to which the project is viewed as helping the organization achieve its strategic objectives and long-term goals.
Potential benefits	The extent to which the project is viewed as improving profits, customer service, and so forth, and the duration of these benefits.
Potential costs and resource availability	The number and types of resources the project requires and their availability.
Project size/duration	The number of individuals and the length of time needed to complete the project.
Technical difficulty/ risks	The level of technical difficulty involved in successfully completing the project within a given time and resource constraint.

Source: Hoffer, George, and Valacich (2008).

standing of an organization's current way of doing things in the area for which the new information system will be constructed. The process of conducting an analysis requires that many tasks, or subphases, be performed. The first subphase focuses on determining system requirements. To determine the requirements, an analyst works closely with users to determine what is needed from the proposed system. After collecting the requirements, analysts organize this information using data, process, and logic

Net Stats

Personalities of Broadband Users

Connecting to the Internet using a high-speed broadband connection is becoming increasingly common. Although all broadband users share the ability to rapidly download music or surf the Web, Netpop Research has found that these users have distinct personalities, including:

1. **The Content King.** These users are typically younger and focused on accessing entertainment content such as movies, music, and games.
2. **The Social Clicker.** These users can be young or old, utilizing the web for communication. Younger users are active at social networking sites like MySpace.com and like to chat with friends using Yahoo! or MSN Messenger; older users primarily socialize via e-mail.

3. **The Online Insider.** These users are both producers and consumers of online user created content that can be found on blogs, community discussion boards, and chat rooms.
4. **The Fast Tracker.** These users voraciously seek information and news on politics, sports, weather, and virtually any other topic of interest.
5. **The Everyday Pro.** These users focus on leveraging online tools to improve their personal productivity, utilizing tools like online banking and shopping.

Clearly, there are different types of broadband users. Fortunately, there is ample room for everyone on the Web. What type of user are you?

Source: http://www.clickz.com/showPage.html?page= 3623965

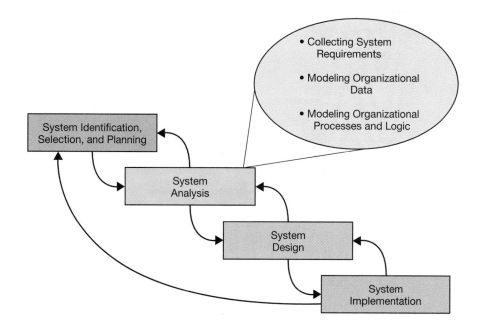

FIGURE 9.6

Phase 2 of the SDLC focuses on collecting requirements and modeling data, processes, and logic.

modeling tools. These elements will be illustrated and discussed later in the chapter (see Figure 9.10).

Collecting System Requirements The collection and structuring of system requirements is arguably the most important activity in the systems development process because how well the information system requirements are defined influences all subsequent activities. The old saying "garbage in, garbage out" very much applies to the system building process. **Requirements collection** is the process of gathering and organizing information from users, managers, business processes, and documents to understand how a proposed information system should function. Systems analysts use a variety of techniques for collecting system requirements, including the following (Hoffer et al., 2008):

- ■ *Interviews.* Analysts interview people informed about the operation and issues of the current or proposed system.
- ■ *Questionnaires.* Analysts design and administer surveys to gather opinions from people informed about the operation and issues of the current or proposed system.
- ■ *Observations.* Analysts observe workers at selected times to see how data are handled and what information people need to do their jobs.
- ■ *Document Analysis.* Analysts study business documents to discover issues, policies, and rules as well as concrete examples of the use of data and information in the organization.

In addition to these techniques, there are contemporary approaches for collecting system requirements that include the following:

- ■ *Critical Success Factors Methodology.* A **critical success factor (CSF)** is something that must go well to ensure success for a manager, department, division, or organization. To understand an organization's CSFs, a systems analyst interviews people throughout the organization and asks each person to define his or her own personal CSFs. After the analyst collects these individual CSFs, he or she can merge, consolidate, and refine them to identify a broad set of organization-wide CSFs, as shown in Figure 9.7. Table 9.4 summarizes the strengths and weaknesses of the CSF approach.

FIGURE 9.7

Merging individual CSFs to represent organization-wide CSFs.

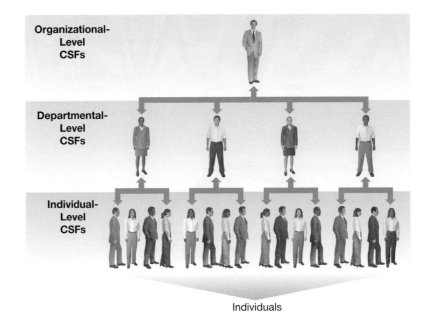

■ *Joint Application Design.* **Joint application design (JAD)** is a special type of a group meeting in which all (or most) users meet with the analyst at the same time. During this meeting, the users jointly define and agree on system requirements or designs. This process has resulted in dramatic reductions in the length of time needed to collect requirements or specify designs. The JAD meeting can be held in a normal conference room or special-purpose JAD room (see Figure 9.8). Table 9.5 summarizes the strengths and weaknesses of the JAD approach.

Modeling Organizational Data Data are facts that describe people, objects, or events. A lot of different facts can be used to describe a person: name, age, gender, race, and occupation, among others. To construct an information system, systems analysts must understand what data the information system needs in order to accomplish the intended tasks. To do this, they use data modeling tools to collect and describe the data to users to confirm that all needed data are known and presented to users as useful information. Figure 9.9 shows an entity-relationship diagram (ERD), a type of data model describing students, classes, majors, and classrooms at a university. Each box in the diagram is referred to as a data entity. Each data entity may have one or more attributes that describe it. For example, a "student" entity may have attributes such as ID, Name, and Local Address. Additionally, each data entity may be "related" to other data entities. For example, because students take classes, there is a relationship between students and classes: "Student Takes

TABLE 9.4 Strengths and Weaknesses of the CSF Approach

Strengths	Weaknesses
Senior managers intuitively understand the approach and support its usage.	High-level focus can lead to an oversimplification of a complex situation.
Provides a method for understanding the information needs of the organization in order to make effective decisions.	Difficulty in finding analysts trained to perform the CSF process that requires both understanding information systems and being able to communicate effectively with senior executives.
	Method is not user centered but analyst focused.

Source: Boynton and Zmud (1994).

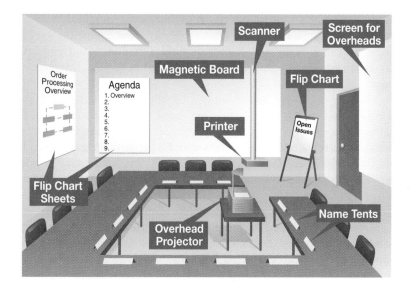

FIGURE 9.8

A JAD room.

Source: Adapted from J. Wood and D. Silver, *Joint Application Design* (New York: John Wiley & Sons, 1989).

TABLE 9.5 Strengths and Weaknesses of the JAD Approach

Strengths	Weaknesses
Group-based process enables more people to be involved in the development effort without adversely slowing the process.	Very difficult to get all relevant users to the same place at the same time to hold a JAD meeting.
Group-based process can lead to higher levels of system acceptance and quality.	Requires high-level executive sponsor to ensure that adequate resources are available in order to allow widespread participation.
Group involvement in the design and development process helps to ease implementation, user training, and ongoing support.	

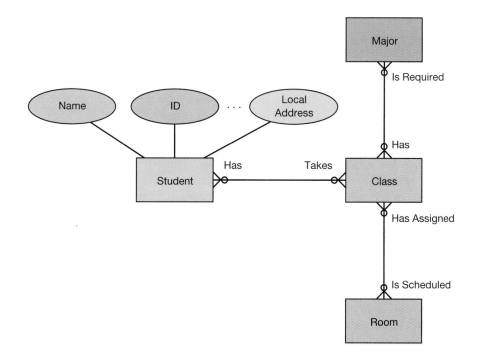

FIGURE 9.9

A sample ERD for students.

Class(es)" and "Class Has Student(s)." Relationships are represented in the diagram by lines drawn between related entities. Data modeling tools enable the systems analyst to represent data in a form that is easy for users to understand and critique. For more information on databases and data modeling, see Technology Briefing 3—Database Management.

Modeling Organizational Processes and Logic As the name implies, **data flows** represent the movement of data through an organization or within an information system. For example, your registration for a class may be captured in a registration form on paper or on a computer terminal. After it is filled out, this form probably flows through several processes to validate and record the class registration, as shown as "Data Flows" in Figure 9.10. After all students have been registered, a repository of all registration information can be processed for developing class rosters or for generating student billing information, which is shown as "Data" in Figure 9.10. **Processing logic** represents the way in which data are transformed. For example, processing logic is used to calculate students' grade-point averages at the conclusion of a term, as shown in the "Processing Logic" section in Figure 9.10.

After the data, data flow, and processing logic requirements for the proposed system have been identified, analysts develop one or many possible overall approaches—sometimes called designs—for the information system. For example, one approach for the system may possess only basic functionality but have the advantage of being relatively easy and inexpensive to build. An analyst might also propose a more elaborate approach for the system, but it may be more difficult and more costly to build. Analysts evaluate alternative system approaches with the knowledge that different solutions yield different benefits and different costs. After a system approach is selected, details of that particular system approach can be defined.

Phase 3: System Design

The third phase of the SDLC is **system design**, as shown in Figure 9.11. As its name implies, it is during this phase that the proposed system is designed; that is, the details of the chosen approach are developed. As with analysis, many different activities must occur during system design. The elements that must be designed when building an information system include the following:

- Forms and reports
- Interfaces and dialogues
- Databases and files
- Processing and logic

Designing Forms and Reports A **form** is a business document containing some predefined data and often including some areas where additional data can be filled in. Figure 9.12 shows a computer-based form taken from Yahoo! Using this form, customers can create a Yahoo! account in order to take advantage of instant messaging, e-mail, and other services.

A report is a business document containing only predefined data. In other words, reports are static documents that are used to summarize information for reading or viewing. For example, Figure 9.13 shows a report summarizing regional sales performance for several salespeople.

Designing Interfaces and Dialogues Just as people have different ways of interacting with other people, information systems can have different ways of interacting with people. A system interface might be text based, communicating with you through text and forcing you to communicate with it the same way. Alternatively, a system interface could use graphics and color as a way to interact with you, providing you with color-coded windows and special icons. A system dialogue could be developed that does nothing and waits for you to type in a command. Or it could ask you questions to

FIGURE 9.10

Four key elements to
development of a system:
Requirements, Data, Data Flows,
and Processing Logic.

Requirements

Data

Name	Class	GPA
Patty Nicholls	Senior	3.7
Brett Williams	Grad	2.9
Mary Shide	Fresh	3.2

Data Flows

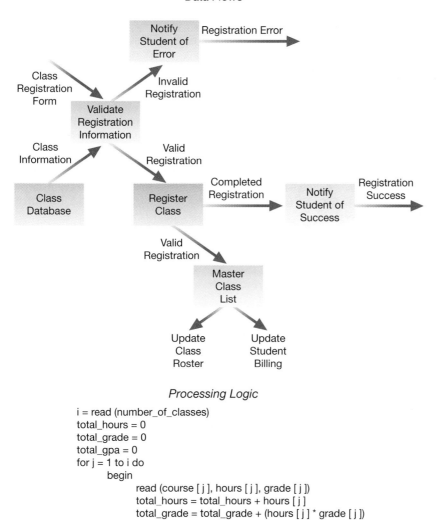

Processing Logic

```
i = read (number_of_classes)
total_hours = 0
total_grade = 0
total_gpa = 0
for j = 1 to i do
        begin
                read (course [ j ], hours [ j ], grade [ j ])
                total_hours = total_hours + hours [ j ]
                total_grade = total_grade + (hours [ j ] * grade [ j ])
        end
current_gpa = total_grade / total hours
```

which you respond by typing in commands or present you with menus of choices from
which you select your desired options. It could even do all these things. Over the past
several years, standards for user interfaces and dialogues have emerged, making things
easier for both designers and users. For example, both the Mac and the Windows
operating systems use interfaces that enable the user to select pictures, icons, and menus

FIGURE 9.11

Phase 3 of the SDLC focuses on developing the details of the chosen approach.

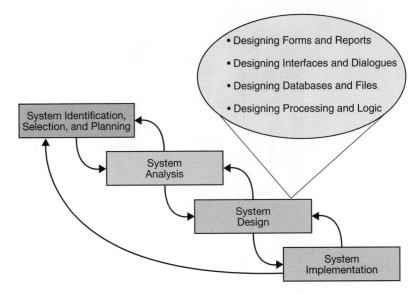

to send instructions to the computer; such interface is referred to as being a **graphical user interface (GUI)** (Figure 9.14). (See Technology Briefing 2—Information Systems Software for more on GUIs.)

Designing Databases and Files To design databases and files, a systems analyst must have a thorough understanding of an organization's data and informational needs. As described previously, a systems analyst often uses data modeling tools to first gain a comprehensive understanding of all the data used by a proposed system. After the conceptual data model has been completed, typically using an entity-relationship diagram, it can be easily translated into a physical data model in a database management system. For example, Figure 9.15 shows a physical data model to keep track of student information in a Microsoft Access database. The physical data model is more complete (shows each attribute of the student) and more detailed (shows how the information is formatted) than a

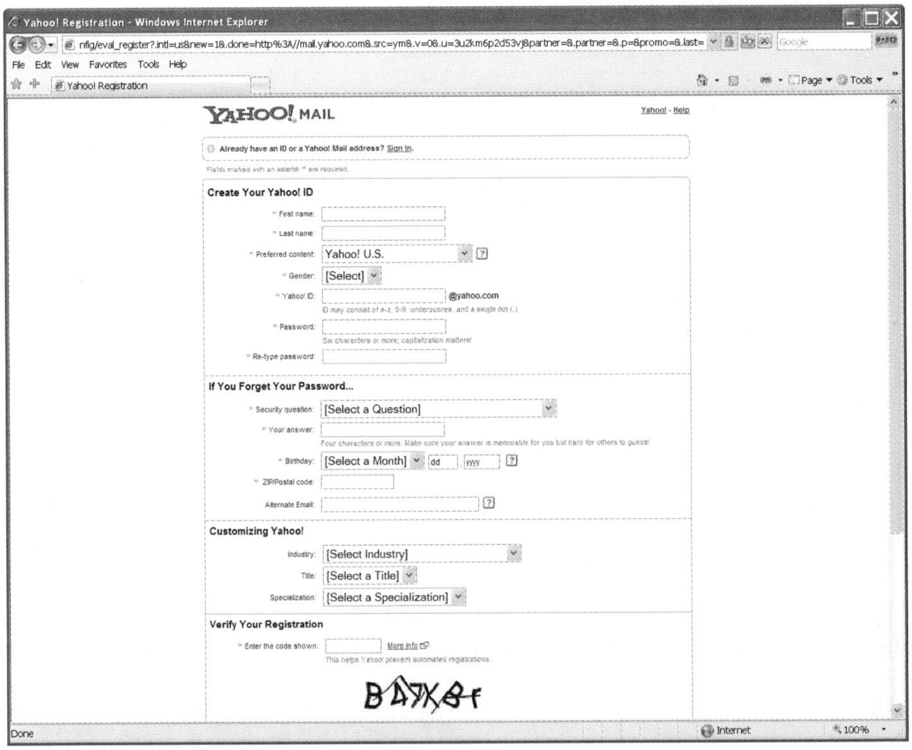

FIGURE 9.12

Yahoo! account registration form.

FIGURE 9.13

Sales summary report.

Ascend Systems Incorporated
SALESPERSON ANNUAL SUMMARY REPORT 2007

			QUARTERLY ACTUAL SALES			
REGION	SALESPERSON	SSN	FIRST	SECOND	THIRD	FOURTH
Northwest and Mountain						
	Wachter	999-99-0001	16,500	18,600	24,300	18,000
	Mennecke	999-99-0002	22,000	15,500	17,300	19,800
	Wheeler	999-99-0003	19,000	12,500	22,000	28,000
Midwest and Mid-Atlantic						
	Spurrier	999-99-0004	14,000	16,000	19,000	21,000
	Powell	999-99-0005	7,500	16,600	10,000	8,000
	Topi	999-99-0006	12,000	19,800	17,000	19,000
New England						
	Speier	999-99-0007	18,000	18,000	20,000	27,000
	Morris	999-99-0008	28,000	29,000	19,000	31,000

conceptual data model. For example, contrast Figure 9.15 with the student information contained in the conceptual data model in Figure 9.9.

Designing Processing and Logic The processing and logic operations of an information system are the steps and procedures that transform raw data inputs into new or modified information. For example, when calculating your grade-point average, your school needs to perform the following steps:

1. Obtain the prior grade-point average, credit hours earned, and list of prior courses
2. Obtain the list of each current course, final grade, and course credit hours
3. Combine the prior and current credit hours into aggregate sums
4. Calculate the new grade-point average

The logic and steps needed to make this calculation can be represented in many ways. One method, referred to as writing pseudocode—a textual notation for describing programming code—enables the systems analyst to describe the processing steps in a manner that is similar to how a programmer might implement the steps in an actual programming language.

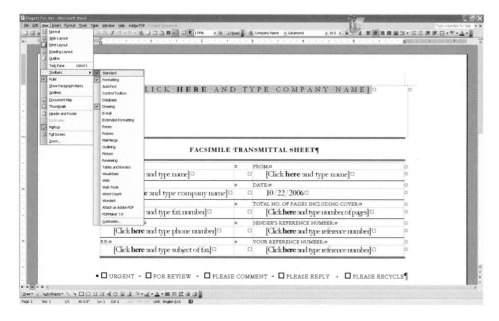

FIGURE 9.14

Most Windows-based programs follow a standard that governs the naming and placement of menus that makes it easier for users and for designers.

Key Enabler

The Brain-Wave Interface

Brain-wave interfaces might seem like something out of *Star Trek* where a person can think of an action via some computer interface and it happens, but this sci-fi technology is actually in the works. The fact is that some companies' research and development departments are working on this futuristic concept for use in consumer products.

Honda is one of the companies looking at this new technology, hoping to eventually use it to link someone's thoughts with machines such as automobiles. The technology may be most useful in the medical field, however, to help patients who have lost the use of their limbs through spinal injuries or amputations to move again.

A case in point is Jesse Sullivan, a 59-year-old former power company lineman in Tennessee whose body coursed with 7,200 volts of electricity when he mistakenly made contact with a live wire in the ground. When Sullivan awoke from a coma one month after the accident, both arms had been amputated. Sullivan's doctors found

him a desirable candidate for medical research, and he was "rewired" so that his computerized artificial arms and hands move in response to his thoughts. "All I have to do is want to do it and I do it," Sullivan told Keith Oppenheim of CNN in March 2006. Further research is needed to allow for Sullivan and others using similar artificial limbs to make more complex movements.

Brain-wave typing is presently closest to becoming a viable consumer-level application of the brain-wave interface concept. This technology uses a combination of brain waves, facial expression, and eye movements to control typing for persons with disabilities. Although pure brain-wave interfaces are still futuristic, they are definitely promising as key enablers in interface technology with astounding prospects for the future.

Sources: http://www.cnn.com/2006/US/03/22/btsc. oppenheim.bionic/index.html

http://www.wired.com/news/wireservice/0,70982-0.html? tw=wn_index_9

FIGURE 9.15

The physical data model for student information from an Access database.

C:\MSOFFICCE\ACCESS\STUDENT.MDB	Saturday, June 23, 2007
Table: Students	Page: 1

Properties

Date Created:	6/23/07 10:35:41 PM	Def. Updatable:	Yes
Last Updated:	6/23/07 10:35:43 PM	Record Count:	0

Columns

Name	Type	Size
StudentID	Number (Long)	4
FirstName	Text	50
MiddleName	Text	30
LastName	Text	50
ParentsNames	Text	255
Address	Text	255
City	Text	50
State	Text	50
Region	Text	50
PostalCode	Text	20
PhoneNumber	Text	30
EmailName	Text	50
Major	Text	50
Note	Memo	-

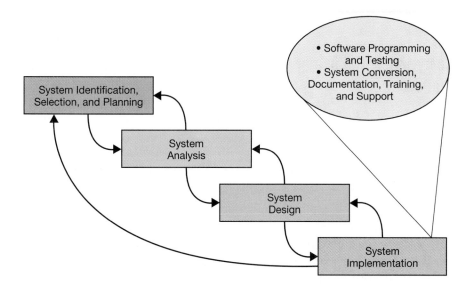

FIGURE 9.16

Phase 4 of the SDLC focuses on programming, testing, conversion, and support.

The "Processing Logic" in Figure 9.10 is an example of pseudocode. Other tools used by systems analysts during this activity include structure charts and decision trees. Converting pseudocode, structure charts, and decision trees into actual program code during system implementation is a relatively straightforward process.

Phase 4: System Implementation

Many separate activities occur during **system implementation**, the fourth phase of the SDLC, as highlighted in Figure 9.16. One group of activities focuses on transforming the system design into a working information system that can be used by the organization. These activities include software programming and testing. A second group of activities focuses on preparing the organization for using the new information systems. These activities include system conversion, documentation, user training, and support. This section briefly describes what occurs during system implementation.

Software Programming and Testing Programming is the process of transforming the system design into a working computer system. During this transformation, both processing and testing should occur in parallel. As you might expect, a broad range of tests are conducted before a system is complete, including **developmental testing**, **alpha testing**, and **beta testing** (see Table 9.6).

System Conversion, Documentation, Training, and Support **System conversion** is the process of decommissioning the current system (automated or manual) and installing the new system in the organization. Effective conversion of a system requires not only that the new software be installed but also that users be effectively trained and supported. System conversion can be performed in at least four ways, as shown in Figure 9.18.

TABLE 9.6 General Testing Types, Their Focus, and Who Performs Them

Testing Type	Focus	Performed by
Developmental	Testing the correctness of individual modules and the integration of multiple modules	Programmer
Alpha	Testing of overall system to see whether it meets design requirements	Software tester
Beta	Testing of the capabilities of the system in the user environment with actual data	Actual system users

Change Agents

William (Bill) Henry Gates III, Chairman and Chief Software Architect, Microsoft Corporation

Bill Gates, born October 28, 1955, founded Microsoft Corporation with his lifelong friend, Paul Allen, in 1974. The rest is history.

As schoolmates at Lakeside Academy in Seattle, Washington, Gates and Allen spent every available moment studying computers and programming and practicing on time-share computers wherever Lakeside Academy could buy time. The two became so adept at programming that they were often hired to debug programs and to write business-specific programs.

Gates left for Harvard University in 1973, enrolling in prelaw. Allen stayed behind in Washington, but he and Gates remained in close contact, often discussing the possibility of starting a software company of their own. In 1974, Allen saw an article in *Popular Electronics* about the Altair 8080

computer, touted in the magazine as the "World's First Microcomputer Kit to Rival Commercial Models." Allen saw the inherent opportunity and rushed to Harvard to show Gates. The two immediately called Altair's parent company, Micro Instrumentation and Telemetry Systems (MITS), and told a spokesperson that they had written a program for the Altair called BASIC. (They had not yet written a line of code, however, and had never touched an Altair.) Altair was interested in the program, so Allen and Gates managed to simulate an Altair setup in Harvard's computer lab and wrote a program that performed well on the stand-in. The two programmers nervously demonstrated BASIC on the Altair for company executives and were delighted (and amazed) when the program worked perfectly. MITS struck a deal with Allen and Gates to purchase the rights to BASIC, and the two decided the time was right to start their software company. Gates dropped out of Harvard, programmers (mostly friends of Gates and Allen) were hired, and Microsoft was off and running.

Today,

- Both Bill Gates and Paul Allen are multi-billionaires.
- Gates has written two books: *The Road Ahead* (1995) and *Business @ the Speed of Thought* (1999).
- Bill and his wife, Melinda, fund a foundation ($28.8 billion) dedicated to improving health and education around the world.
- Microsoft, based in Redmond, Washington, is one of the largest companies in the world, employing more than 71,000 workers full time.
- Microsoft has revenues of more than $44 billion.
- Microsoft has subsidiaries in more than 100 countries and regions and has branched out into other business segments such as entertainment and gaming.

Sources: http://ei.cs.vt.edu/~history/Gates.Mirick.html

http://www.microsoft.com/billgates/bio.asp

FIGURE 9.17

William (Bill) Henry Gates III, chairman and chief software architect, Microsoft Corporation.

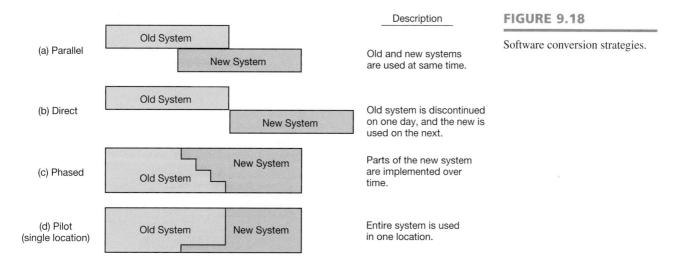

FIGURE 9.18

Software conversion strategies.

Many types of documentation must be produced for an information system. Programmers develop system documentation that details the inner workings of the system to ease future maintenance. A second type of documentation is user-related documentation, which is typically written not by programmers or analysts but by users or professional technical writers. The range of documents can include the following:

- User and reference guides
- User training and tutorials
- Installation procedures and troubleshooting suggestions

In addition to documentation, users may also need training and ongoing support to use a new system effectively. Different types of training and support require different levels of investment by the organization. Self-paced training and tutorials are the least expensive options, and one-on-one training is the most expensive. Table 9.7 summarizes various user training options.

Besides training, providing ongoing education and problem-solving assistance for users is also necessary. This is commonly referred to as system support, which is often provided by a special group of people in the organization who make up an information center or help desk. Support personnel must have strong communication skills and be good problem solvers in addition to being expert users of the system. An alternative option for a system not developed internally is to outsource support activities to a vendor specializing in technical system support and training. Regardless of how support is provided, it is an ongoing issue that must be managed effectively for the company to realize the maximum benefits of a system.

TABLE 9.7 User Training Options

Training Option	Description
Tutorial	One person taught at one time by a human or by paper-based exercises
Course	Several people taught at one time
Computer-aided instruction	One person taught at one time by the computer system
Interactive training manuals	Combination of tutorials and computer-aided instruction
Resident expert	Expert on call to assist users as needed
Software help components	Built-in system components designed to train users and troubleshoot problems
External sources	Vendors and training providers to provide tutorials, courses, and other training activities

FIGURE 9.19

Mapping of maintenance to
SDLC.

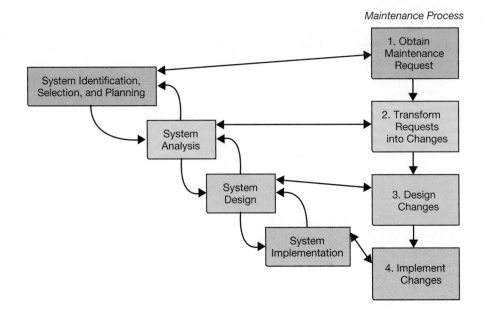

Maintenance Process

Phase 5: System Maintenance

After an information system is installed, it is essentially in the maintenance phase of the SDLC, in which an information system is systematically repaired and/or improved. In the maintenance phase, one person within the systems development group is responsible for collecting maintenance requests from system users. After they are collected, requests are analyzed so that the developer can better understand how the proposed change might alter the system and what business benefits and necessities might result from such a change. If the change request is approved, a system change is designed and then implemented. As with the initial development of the system, implemented changes are formally reviewed and tested before installation into operational systems. The **system maintenance** process parallels the process used for the initial development of the information system, as shown in Figure 9.19. Interestingly, it is during system maintenance that the largest part of the system development effort occurs.

The question must be, then, Why does all this maintenance occur? It is not as if software wears out in the physical manner that cars, buildings, or other physical objects do. Correct? Yes, but software must still be maintained. The types of maintenance are summarized in Table 9.8.

As with **adaptive maintenance**, both **perfective maintenance** and **preventive maintenance** are typically a much lower priority than **corrective maintenance**. Over the life of

TABLE 9.8 Types of Software Maintenance

Maintenance Type	Description
Corrective maintenance	Making changes to an information system to repair flaws in the design, coding, or implementation
Adaptive maintenance	Making changes to an information system to evolve its functionality to accommodate changing business needs or to migrate it to a different operating environment
Perfective maintenance	Making enhancements to improve processing performance or interface usability or adding desired but not necessarily required system features (in other words, "bells and whistles")
Preventive maintenance	Making changes to a system to reduce the chance of future system failure

a system, corrective maintenance is most likely to occur after initial system installation or after major system changes. This means that adaptive, perfective, and preventive maintenance activities can lead to corrective maintenance activities if they are not carefully designed and implemented.

As you can see, there is more to system maintenance than you might think. Lots of time, effort, and money are spent in this final phase of a system's development, and it is important to follow prescribed, structured steps. In fact, the approach to systems development described in this chapter—from the initial phase of identifying, selecting, and planning for systems to the final phase of system maintenance—is a very structured and systematic process. Each phase is fairly well prescribed and requires active involvement by systems people, users, and managers. It is likely that you will have numerous opportunities to participate in the acquisition or development of a new system for an organization for which you currently work or will work in the future. Now that you have an understanding of the process, you should be better equipped to make a positive contribution to the success of any systems development project.

Brief Case ⊘

Hackers, Patches, and Reverse Engineering

Microsoft dominates the market for operating systems, which is good news and bad news for the company. It's good news for the business's bottom line but bad news in that the company's prominence has made its software a popular target for hackers (those who break into computer systems for the purpose of stealing or manipulating data) and other computer criminals. When security experts discover a breach, Microsoft releases a code "patch" to plug security holes. Downloading and installing these patches has become a regularly performed ritual for Windows users.

You might reasonably expect that after an operating system, browser, or other application has been on the market for several years, all security holes will have been detected and closed. Not so. Unfortunately, there are invariably hackers who find new holes that have not yet been detected.

How do hackers find security holes? Smart hackers may study an application until they recognize an entrance hole, while not-so-smart hackers simply "free ride" on the efforts of others by following "recipes" posted on hacker Web sites.

Lately, the frequent release of patches has provided hackers another means of discovering security holes that requires less time and effort than studying a program's code. When Microsoft, Firefox, or other software producers release a security patch, hackers use special software tools to backtrack or reverse engineer the patch. Once they determine the location of the security hole for which the patch was issued, they work on ways to circumvent the patch and exploit the security hole in a new, unpatched way. (Reverse engineering is not always destructive and may be legally used to improve a program, but use of the term here implies using the process for unauthorized entry into a computer system.)

Thus, the dilemma for software manufacturers and security companies is this: if they do not release patches, hackers can exploit security holes; if they do release patches, more people will know about the security holes and will attempt to exploit them. Yet consumers using software with security holes expect patches to be issued. The solution? Microsoft tries to prevent hackers from reverse engineering by withholding detailed information about patches for security holes for three months after discovery of the hole, but that strategy does not usually deter hackers. There will always be hackers looking for security holes in software, but, fortunately, there will also always be software engineers, programmers, and security experts who can foil hackers' attempts to breach security. Solutions may come after the fact, but they do arrive.

Questions

1. Explain what type(s) of maintenance Microsoft is performing when fixing security holes and releasing patches to its customers.
2. Are there situations where it is justified for hackers to find and exploit security holes in software? If so or if not, explain.

Sources: http://www.techweb.com/wire/security/175803256, retrieved June 5, 2006

http://www.techweb.com/wire/security/175803652, retrieved June 5, 2006

Other Approaches to Designing and Building Systems

The SDLC is one approach to managing the development process and is a very good approach to follow when the requirements for the information system are highly structured and straightforward—for example, for a payroll or inventory system. Today, organizations need a broad variety of information systems, not just payroll and inventory systems, for which requirements either are very hard to specify in advance or are constantly changing. For example, an organization's Web site is likely to be an information system with constantly changing requirements. How many Web sites have you visited in which the content or layout seemed to change almost every day? For this type of system, the SDLC might work as a development approach, but it would not be optimal. In this section, we describe three approaches for developing flexible information systems: prototyping, rapid application development, and object-oriented analysis and design.

Prototyping

Prototyping is a systems development methodology that uses a trial-and-error approach for discovering how a system should operate. You may think that this does not sound like a process at all; however, you probably use prototyping all the time in many of your day-to-day activities, but you just do not know it. For example, when you buy new clothes, you likely use prototyping—that is, trial and error—by trying on several shirts before making a selection.

Figure 9.20 diagrams the prototyping process when applied to identifying/determining system requirements. To begin the process, the system designer interviews one or several

FIGURE 9.20

The prototyping process uses a trial-and-error approach to discovering how a system should operate.

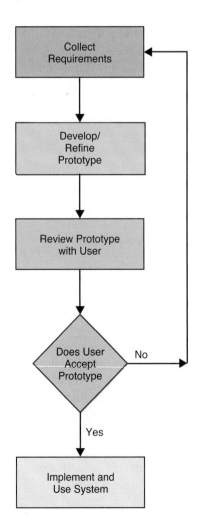

users of the system, either individually or as a group, using a JAD session. After the designer gains a general understanding of what the users want, he or she develops a prototype of the new system as quickly as possible to share with the users. The users may like what they see or ask for changes. If the users request changes, the designer modifies the prototype and again shares it with them. This process of sharing and refinement continues until the users approve the functionality of the system.

Rapid Application Development

Rapid application development (RAD) is a four-phase systems development methodology that combines prototyping, computer-based development tools, special management practices, and close user involvement (Martin, 1991; McConnell, 1996; Hoffer et al., 2008). RAD has four phases: (1) requirements planning, (2) user design, (3) construction, and (4) the move to the new system. Phase 1, requirements planning, is similar to the first two phases of the SDLC, in which the system is planned and requirements are analyzed. To gain intensive user involvement, the RAD methodology encourages the use of JAD sessions to collect requirements. Where RAD becomes radical is during phase 2, in which users of the information system become intensively involved in the design process. Computer-aided software engineering (CASE) and other advanced development tools (see Technology Briefing 2) are used to structure requirements and develop prototypes quickly. As prototypes are developed and refined, they are continually reviewed with users in additional JAD sessions. Like prototyping, RAD is a process in which requirements, designs, and the system itself are developed via iterative refinement, as shown in Figure 9.21. In a sense, with the RAD approach the people building the system and the users of that system keep cycling back and forth between phase 2 (user design) and phase 3 (construction) until the system is finished. As a result, RAD requires close cooperation between users and designers to be successful. This means that management must actively support the development project and make it a priority for everyone involved. Table 9.9 illustrates the strengths and weaknesses of the three approaches to IS development discussed in this section.

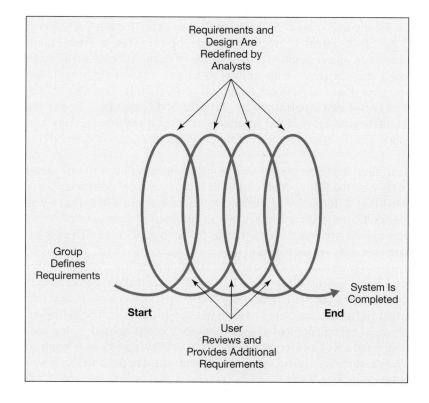

FIGURE 9.21

Iterative refinement is a key to the success of RAD.

TABLE 9.9 Strengths and Weaknesses of Prototyping, RAD, and Object-Oriented Analysis and Design Approaches

Approach	Strengths	Weaknesses
Prototyping	Develops close working relationship between designer and users; works well for messy and hard-to-define problems	Not practical with a large number of users; system may be built too quickly, which could result in lower quality
Rapid Application Development	Active user involvement in design process; easier implementation due to user involvement	Systems are often narrowly focused—limits future evolution; system may be built too quickly, which could result in lower quality
Object-Oriented Analysis and Design	Integration of data and processing during design should lead to higher-quality systems; reuse of common modules makes development and maintenance easier	More difficult to train analysts and programmers on the object-oriented approach; unnecessary re-creation of common objects across different systems

Object-Oriented Analysis and Design

Object-Oriented Analysis and Design (OOA&D) is another alternative approach to developing a system (see George, Batra, Valacich, and Hoffer, 2007). In the conventional SDLC approach, analysts model data and processes separately; the outputs of these modeling processes are handed over to a programmer, who writes the program code and implements the database. In contrast, rather than thinking separately about data and processes, the analyst using an OOA&D approach thinks in terms of common modules (called objects), which combine the "what" (the data) and the "how" (the operations to be performed), as he or she defines the relevant system components. An example of an object would be a specific student, who has a name, an address, date of birth (i.e., the "what"), but can also perform certain operations, such as register for a class (the "how"). Thus, with the tight coupling between the methods and data and between the conceptual model of the system and its actual implementation, OOA&D can turn every programmer into an analyst and every analyst into a programmer. Additionally, analysts typically use somewhat different diagramming methods when performing OOA&D to better integrate various aspects of the system (see Figure 9.22). Furthermore, if an object-oriented programming language is being used, it enables the design and implementation of the objects to happen quickly and simultaneously, as oftentimes, pre-existing objects can be reused or adapted. In sum, OOA&D is a more integrative systems development process than the SDLC approach, in which data and operations on the data are modeled separately at a conceptual level and are later implemented and brought together in a subsequent phase of the systems development process.

This section has described other popular information systems development approaches beyond the SDLC. Additionally, there are even more approaches for designing and constructing information systems beyond those discussed here (e.g., Agile Methodologies, EXtreme Programming, and so on). Each of these alternative methodologies focuses either on overcoming the limitations to the traditional SDLC or on finding ways to optimize some unique aspect of the development process (see Hoffer et al., 2008). Thus, the wise organization and the skilled analyst often utilize multiple methods when developing a single system. What should be clear to you is that no approach is perfect and that all have strengths and weaknesses (see Table 9.9); a skilled systems developer, much like a skilled craftsman, has many tools at his or her disposal. The skilled craftsman chooses the most appropriate tool and approach for the task at hand. Using one systems development approach or tool for all systems and problems is akin to using only a hammer to build a house. Building a house with just a hammer might be possible, but it would probably be a strange-looking house.

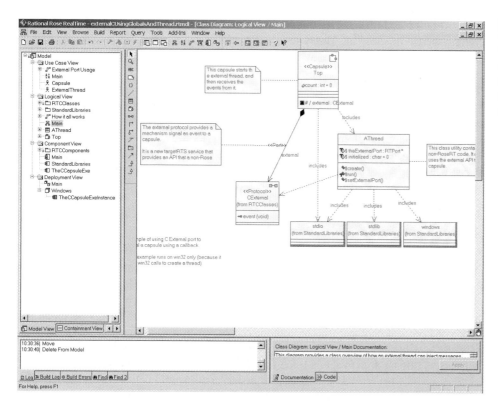

FIGURE 9.22

When performing object-oriented analysis and design, analysts use diagramming methods that integrate all aspects of the system.

Need for Alternatives to Building Systems Yourself

Building systems in-house with the IS staff is always an option to consider. Many times, however, this is not a feasible solution. The following are four situations in which you might need to consider alternative development strategies.

Situation 1: Limited IS Staff

Often, an organization does not have the capability to build a system itself. Perhaps its IS staff is small or deployed on other activities, such as maintaining a small network and helping users with problems on a day-to-day basis. This limited staff may simply not have the capability to take on an in-house development project without hiring several analysts or programmers, which is very expensive in today's labor market.

Situation 2: IS Staff Has Limited Skill Set

In other situations, the IS staff may not have the skills needed to develop a particular kind of system. This has been especially true with the explosion of the Web; many organizations are having outside groups manage their sites. For example, Walt Disney contracted the development and management of its Web site and the sites of many of its subsidiaries, including ABC News and ESPN, to a company called Starwave.com. Starwave was founded by Paul Allen, one of Bill Gates's initial partners at Microsoft and owner of the Portland Trailblazers, Seattle Seahawks, and numerous other companies (www.paulallen.com). This relationship continued until 1998, when Disney purchased Starwave and transformed it into the Walt Disney Internet Group (Court, 1998). In essence, Disney did not initially have the right set of skills to move onto the Internet, so it had an outside organization develop and manage its Web sites. Once it realized the strategic importance of the Internet, Disney purchased this expertise by buying Starwave. In sum, although the existing IS staff at Disney was highly skilled at producing and managing traditional applications, the sudden call for Web-based systems required that Disney seek outside help. It is not as if the IS director can tell the CEO that Disney cannot build a new Web site because the IS staff does not have the necessary skills to build it. Fortunately, there are alternatives to having the IS staff build the system; the IS director can simply tap into specialized skills that are not present within the existing IS staff but that are available on the open market.

Situation 3: IS Staff Is Overworked

In some organizations, the IS staff may simply not have the time to work on all the systems that the organization requires or wants. Obviously, the number of people dedicated to new development is not infinite. Therefore, you must have ways to prioritize development projects. In most cases, systems that are of strategic importance or that affect the whole organization are likely to receive a higher priority than those that offer only minor benefits or affect only one department or a couple of people in a department. Nonetheless, the IS manager must find a way to support all users, even when the IS staff may be tied up with other "higher-priority" projects.

Situation 4: Problems with Performance of IS Staff

Earlier in this book we discussed how and why systems development projects could sometimes be risky. Often the efforts of IS departments are derailed because of staff turnover, changing requirements, shifts in technology, or budget constraints. Regardless of the reason, the result is the same: another failed (or flawed) system. Given the large expenditures in staff time and training as well as the high risk associated with systems development efforts, the prudent manager tries to limit the risk of any project as much as possible. What if it were possible to see the completed system to know what it looked like before development began? Being able to see into the future would certainly help you learn more about the system and whether it would meet your needs, and it would help to lower the risk of a project. When building a system in-house, it is obviously not possible to see into the future. However, using some of the alternative methods described in this chapter, you can, in fact, see what a completed system might look like. These methods will enable you to know what you are buying, which greatly lowers the risk of a project.

Common Alternatives to In-House Systems Development

Any project has at least four different systems development options. Previously, we discussed the first option: building the system in-house with your IS staff. The other options are the following:

- External acquisition
- Outsourcing
- End-user development

The following sections examine each of these options in closer detail to see how one or more of them might fit the four situations described in the preceding section.

External Acquisition

Purchasing an existing system from an outside vendor such as IBM, EDS, or Accenture is referred to as **external acquisition**. How does external acquisition of an information system work? Think about the process that you might use when buying a car. Do you simply walk into the first dealership you see, tell them you need a car, and see what they try to sell you? You had better not. Probably you have done some up-front analysis and know how much money you can afford to spend and what your needs are. If you have done your homework, you probably have an idea of what you want and which dealership can provide the type of car you desire.

This up-front analysis of your needs can be extremely helpful in narrowing your options and can save you a lot of time. Understanding your needs can also help you sift through the salespeople's hype that you are likely to encounter from one dealer to the next as each tries to sell you on why his or her model is perfect for you (see Figure 9.23). After getting some information, you may want to take a couple of promising models for a test

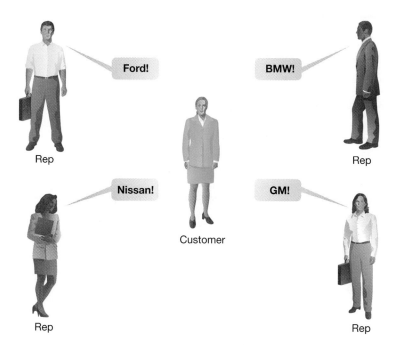

FIGURE 9.23

Multiple car dealers canvass a prospective car buyer.

drive, actually getting behind the wheel to see how well the car fits you and your driving habits. You might even talk to other people who have owned this type of car to see how they feel about it. Ultimately, you are the one who has to evaluate all the different cars to see which one is best for you. They may all be good cars; however, one may fit your needs just a little better than the others.

The external acquisition of an information system is very similar to the purchase of a car. When you acquire an IS, you should do some analysis of your specific needs. For example, how much can you afford to spend, what basic functionality is required, and approximately how many people will use the system? Next, you can begin to "shop" for the new system by asking potential vendors to provide information about the systems that they have to offer. After you evaluate this information, it may become clear that several vendors have systems that are worth considering. You may ask those vendors to come to your organization and set up their systems so that you and your colleagues are able to "test-drive" them. Seeing how people react to the systems and seeing how each system performs in the organizational environment can help you "see" exactly what you are buying. By seeing the actual system and how it performs with real users, with real or simulated data, you can get a much clearer idea of whether that system fits your needs. When you take a car for a test-drive, you learn how the car meets your needs. By seeing how the system meets your needs before you buy, you can greatly reduce the risk associated with acquiring that system.

Steps in External Acquisition   In many cases, your organization will use a competitive bid process for making an external acquisition. In the competitive bid process, vendors are given an opportunity to propose systems that meet the organization's needs. The goal of the competitive process is to help the organization ensure that it gets the best system at the lowest possible price. Most competitive external acquisition processes have at least five general steps:

1. System identification, selection, and planning
2. Systems analysis
3. Development of a request for proposal
4. Proposal evaluation
5. Vendor selection

You have already learned about the first two steps because they apply when you build a system yourself as well as when you purchase a system through an external vendor. Step 3,

FIGURE 9.24

Sample RFP document for an
information systems project.

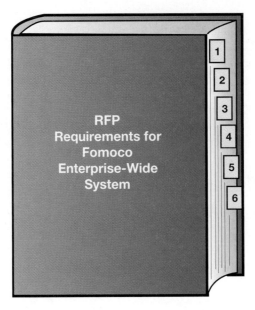

1. Summary of existing
   systems and applications
2. Reliability, backup, and
   service requirements
3. System performance
   and features
4. Evaluation criteria
5. Timetable
6. Budget

development of a request for proposal, is where the external acquisition process differs
significantly from in-house development.

Development of a Request for Proposal A **request for proposal (RFP)** is simply a
report that is used to tell vendors what your requirements are and to invite them to provide
information about how they might be able to meet those requirements (see Figure 9.24).
An RFP is sent to vendors who might potentially be interested in providing hardware
and/or software for the system.

Among the areas that may be covered in an RFP are the following:

- A summary of existing systems and applications
- Reliability, backup, and service requirements
- Requirements for system performance and features
- The criteria that will be used to evaluate proposals
- Timetable and budget constraints (how much you can spend)

The RFP is then sent to prospective vendors along with an invitation to present their
bids for the project. Eventually, you will likely receive a number of proposals to evaluate.
If, on the other hand, you do not receive many proposals, it may be necessary to rethink the
requirements—perhaps the requirements are greater than the budget limitations or the
timetable is too short. In some situations, you may first need to send out a preliminary
request for information simply to gather information from prospective vendors. This will
help you determine whether, indeed, the desired system is feasible or even possible. If you
determine that it is, you can then send out an RFP.

Proposal Evaluation The fourth step in external acquisition is to evaluate proposals
received from vendors. This evaluation may include viewing system demonstrations,
evaluating the performance of those systems, and examining criteria important to the
organization and judging how the proposed systems "stack up" to those criteria.
Demonstrations are a good way to get a feel for the different systems' capabilities. Just as
you can go to the showroom to look over a new car and get a feel for whether it meets your
needs, it is also possible to screen various systems through a demonstration from the
vendor. During a demonstration, a sales team from the vendor gives an oral presentation
about their system, its features, and cost, followed by a demonstration of the actual system.
In some cases, this may take place at your location; other times, it may take place at the
vendor's facility or at one of the vendor's clients, particularly when the system is not easily

transportable. Although such demonstrations are often useful in helping you understand the features of different systems being proposed, they are rarely enough in and of themselves to warrant purchasing the system without further evaluation.

One of the ways you can better evaluate a proposed system is through **systems benchmarking**, which is the use of standardized performance tests to facilitate comparison between systems. Benchmark programs are sample programs or jobs that simulate your computer workload. You can have benchmarks designed to test portions of the system that are most critical to your needs, based on your systems analysis. A benchmark might test how long it takes to calculate a set of numbers, how long it takes to access a set of records in a database, or how long it would take to access certain information given a certain number of concurrent users. Some common system benchmarks include the following:

- Response time given a specified number of users
- Time to sort records
- Time to retrieve a set of records
- Time to produce a given report
- Time to read in a set of data

In addition, vendors may also supply benchmarks that you can use, although you should not rely solely on vendor information. For popular systems, you may be able to rely on system benchmarks published in computer trade journals such as *PC Magazine* or on industry web sites such as cnet.com. However, in most cases, demos and benchmarks alone do not provide all the information you need to make a purchase. The systems analysis phase should have revealed some specific requirements for the new system. These requirements may be listed as criteria that the organization can use to further evaluate vendor proposals. Depending on what you are purchasing—hardware, software, or both—the criteria you use will change. Table 9.10 provides examples of commonly used evaluation criteria.

Vendor Selection In most cases, more than one system will meet your needs, just as more than one car will usually meet your needs. However, some probably "fit" better than others. In these cases, you should have a way of prioritizing or ranking competing proposals. One way of doing this is by devising a scoring system for each of the criteria and benchmarking results. For example, an organization might create a scoring system in which benchmarking results are worth 100 total points, while online help features are worth only 50 points. All the points for each criterion are then summed to give an overall score for each system. Then the system with the highest score (or one of the systems among several with the highest scores) is selected. Figure 9.25 shows an example of a form that could be used to evaluate systems and choose a vendor using this method.

In the example shown in Figure 9.25, system A looks like the best solution because it scored highest. Using such an evaluation method, it is possible that scoring low on a given criterion might exclude otherwise outstanding systems from being purchased. You can see

TABLE 9.10 Commonly Used Evaluation Criteria

Hardware Criteria	Software Criteria	Other Criteria
Clock speed of CPU	Memory requirements	Installation
Memory availability	Help features	Testing
Secondary storage (including capacity, access time, and so on)	Usability	Price
	Learnability	
Video display size	Number of features supported	
	Training and documentation	
Printer speed	Maintenance and repair	

FIGURE 9.25

Sample system evaluation form with subset of criteria.

Criterion	Max Points (or weight)	Systems Being Evaluated (Score)		
		A	B	C
Disk capacity	20	10	17	12
Compatibility	50	45	30	25
Usability	30	12	30	20
Vendor Support	35	27	16	5
Benchmark Results	50	40	28	30
(add as needed...)				
Total	185	134	121	92

that systems B and C fared very poorly on the vendor support criterion. It is possible that those systems do not have very good vendor support. However, it is also possible that the vendor did not adequately communicate its commitment to support, perhaps because it did not realize it was such an important issue. Therefore, it is very important for you to communicate with vendors about the evaluation process and which criteria you value most highly.

Companies may use other, less formalized approaches to evaluate vendors. Sometimes they use simple checklists; other times they use a more subjective process. Regardless of the mechanism, eventually a company completes the evaluation stage and selects a vendor, ending the external acquisition process.

Outsourcing

A related but different alternative to purchasing an existing system is outsourcing. With the external acquisition option, an organization typically purchases a single system from an

Ethical Dilemma

Software Vendors and Clients

Assume you are a software consultant, advising business clients about the most appropriate, effective, and affordable software they can purchase. Now assume that a software vendor you know has referred a business client to you, expecting you to recommend their software to the business client. In your opinion, however, this vendor's software is not the correct choice for the business referred. You have an ethical dilemma: if you recommend the vendor's software, you will not be serving the client well, but if you don't, you may alienate the vendor. What to do? Mike Sisco, a consultant and former CEO, offers the following guidelines for resolving such issues, published online at techrepublic.com:

1. It is probably impractical, from a business standpoint, for you to have no alliances with software vendors, and if your consulting company has formed alliances with certain vendors, you are ethically obligated to honor them.

2. You are also ethically obligated to recommend the best software fit to business clients. The key to serving both business clients and software vendor alliances well is to remember that the software you recommend needs to collect and analyze the businesss data effectively and as economically as possible.

"The bottom line," Sisco sums up, "is that we all have preferences for software products, just as we do for automobiles, for example. Driving a Chevy versus a Ford may not be your first recommendation, but they'll both get you to the destination in relatively the same manner. Software products that address the same set of business issues are very similar."

Source: http://techrepublic.com/5100-6333-5034737. html#

outside vendor. Outsourcing is the practice of turning over responsibility for some or all of an organization's information systems development and operations to an outside firm. Outsourcing includes a variety of working relationships. The outside firm, or service provider, may develop your information systems applications and house them within their organization, they may run your applications on their computers, or they may develop systems to run on existing computers within your organization. Anything is fair game in an outsourcing arrangement. Today, outsourcing has become a big business and is a very popular option for many organizations (see Chapter 1 for more information on outsourcing).

Why Outsourcing?

A firm might outsource some (or all) of its information systems services for many reasons. Some of these are old reasons, but some are new to today's environment (Applegate, Austin, and McFarlan, 2007):

- *Cost and Quality Concerns.* In many cases it is possible to achieve higher-quality systems at a lower price through economies of scale, better management of hardware, lower labor costs, and better software licenses on the part of a service provider.
- *Problems in IS Performance.* IS departments may have problems meeting acceptable service standards because of cost overruns, delayed systems, underutilized systems, or poorly performing systems. In such cases, organizational management may attempt to increase reliability through outsourcing.
- *Supplier Pressures.* Perhaps not surprisingly, some of the largest service providers are also the largest suppliers of computer equipment (e.g., IBM or Hewlett-Packard). In some cases, the aggressive sales forces of these suppliers are able to convince senior managers at other organizations to outsource their IS functions.
- *Simplifying, Downsizing, and Reengineering.* Organizations under competitive pressure often attempt to focus on only their "core competencies." In many cases, organizations simply decide that running information systems is not one of their core competencies and decide to outsource this function to companies such as IBM and EDS, whose primary competency is developing and maintaining information systems.
- *Financial Factors.* When firms turn over their information systems to a service provider, they can sometimes strengthen their balance sheets by liquidating their IT assets. Also, if users perceive that they are actually paying for their IT services rather than simply having them provided by an in-house staff, they may use those services more wisely and perceive them to be of greater value.
- *Organizational Culture.* Political or organizational problems are often difficult for an IS group to overcome. However, an external service provider often brings enough clout, devoid of any organizational or functional ties, to streamline IS operations as needed.
- *Internal Irritants.* Tension between end users and the IS staff is sometimes difficult to eliminate. At times this tension can intrude on the daily operations of the organization, and the idea of a remote, external, relatively neutral IS group can be appealing. Whether the tension between users and the IS staff (or service provider) is really eliminated is open to question; however, simply having the IS group external to the organization can remove a lingering thorn in management's side.

Managing the IS Outsourcing Relationship McFarlan and Nolan (1995) argue that the ongoing management of an outsourcing alliance is the single most important aspect of the outsourcing project's success. Their recommendations for the best management are as follows:

1. A strong, active chief information officer (CIO) and staff should continually manage the legal and professional relationship with the outsourcing firm.
2. Clear, realistic performance measurements of the systems and of the outsourcing arrangement, such as tangible and intangible costs and benefits, should be developed.
3. The interface between the customer and the outsourcer should have multiple levels (e.g., links to deal with policy and relationship issues and links to deal with operational and tactical issues).

Managing outsourcing alliances in this way has important implications for the success of the relationship. For example, in addition to making sure a firm has a strong CIO and staff, McFarlan and Nolan recommend that firms assign full-time relationship managers and coordinating groups lower in the organization to "manage" the IS outsourcing project. This means that as people within the IS function are pulled away from traditional IS tasks such as systems development, they are moved toward new roles and organized into new groups. The structure and nature of the internal IS activities change from exclusively building and managing systems to including managing relationships with outside firms that build and manage systems under legal contract.

Not All Outsourcing Relationships Are the Same Most organizations no longer enter into a strictly legal contract with an outsourcing vendor but rather into a mutually beneficial relationship with a strategic partner. In such a relationship, both the firm and the vendor are concerned with—and perhaps have a direct stake in—the success of the other. Yet other types of relationships exist, meaning that not all outsourcing agreements need to be structured the same way (Fryer, 1994). In fact, at least three different types of outsourcing relationships can be identified:

- Basic relationship
- Preferred relationship
- Strategic relationship

A basic relationship can best be thought of as a "cash-and-carry" relationship in which you buy products and services on the basis of price and convenience. Organizations should try to have a few preferred relationships in which the buyer and supplier set preferences and prices to the benefit of each other. For example, a supplier can provide preferred pricing to customers that do a specified volume of business. Most organizations have just a few strategic relationships in which both sides share risks and rewards.

We have now discussed two systems development alternatives that rely on external organizations to alleviate, either completely or partially, the burden of managing IS development projects in-house. In some cases, however, it may not be possible or convenient to rely on agencies outside the organization for development. In these cases, organizations may rely on another option for systems development projects.

End-User Development

In many organizations, the growing sophistication of users within the organization offers IS managers a fourth alternative for systems development. This fourth alternative is **end-user development**—having users develop their own applications. This means that the people who are actually going to use the systems are also those who will develop those systems. End-user development, then, is one way IS departments can speed up application development without relying on external entities such as vendors or service providers. However, end-user development also has risks associated with it. This section outlines the benefits of having end users develop their own applications as well as some of the drawbacks of this approach.

Benefits of End-User Development To help you better understand the benefits of end-user development, you should quickly review some of the problems with conventional development that are suggested by the four situations presented earlier in this chapter:

- *Cost of Labor.* Conventional systems development is labor intensive. Over the past several decades, software costs have increased while hardware costs have declined, as shown in Figure 9.26. As you can see from the figure, it becomes much cheaper for IS managers to substitute hardware for labor by giving users their own equipment. An IS manager can significantly reduce the cost of application development simply by giving end users the tools they need and enabling them to develop their own applications. Better yet, the various departments within the organization can purchase their own equipment, and the IS staff can simply provide guidance and other services.

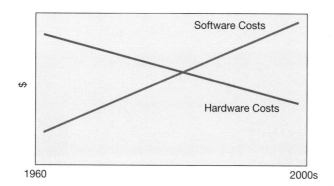

FIGURE 9.26

Rising software costs versus declining hardware costs.

- *Long Development Time.* New systems can take months or even years to develop, depending on the scale and scope of the new system and the backlog of systems waiting to be developed. As a result, users' needs may significantly change between when a system is initially proposed and when it is actually implemented. In these cases, the system may be virtually obsolete before it has even been implemented. End-user–developed systems can "skip" the queue of systems waiting to be developed by the IS organization, resulting in more rapidly developed systems.
- *Slow Modification or Updates of Existing Systems.* Related to the time it takes to develop new systems is the problem of maintaining existing systems. Often, updates to existing systems are given a lower priority than developing new systems. Unfortunately, this can result in systems that are unable to keep pace with changing business needs, becoming antiquated and underused. When end users develop their own systems, the users have the responsibility of maintaining and updating applications as needed. Also, when systems are implemented, they often cause changes to the underlying business processes. These changes may necessitate further change or modification to the application, as highlighted in Figure 9.27. Rather than rely on IS staff to make these changes, users are able to modify the application in a timely manner to reflect the changed business process.

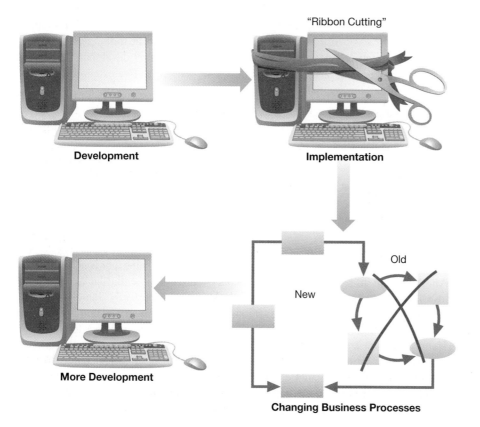

FIGURE 9.27

Continuous cycle of development. A system is developed and implemented. However, it eventually becomes inadequate, and new development takes place.

FIGURE 9.28

Shifting systems development workload as end-user development has become more prevalent.

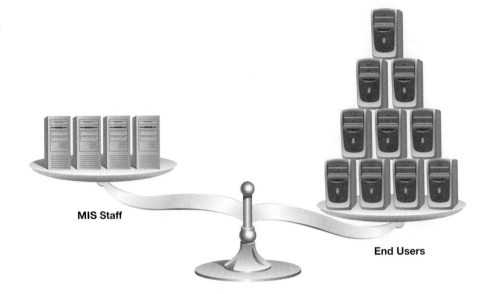

MIS Staff

End Users

- *Work Overload.* One reason for long development times and slow modifications is that IS departments are often overloaded with work. When you leverage the talents of end-user developers, you can, in effect, increase the size of the development staff by shifting some of the workload normally handled by IS professionals to end users, as depicted in Figure 9.28.

End-user development can radically decrease the development workload in the IS department. However, such a shift may cause other areas within IS, such as a help desk, to become flooded with requests for assistance. Nonetheless, end-user development can be an excellent option for organizations faced with some of the problems previously described.

Encouraging End-User Development End-user development sounds great, but how can organizations encourage and enable users to develop their own systems? Fortunately, the availability of easy-to-use, fourth-generation development tools (see Technology Briefing 2—Information Systems Software) has enabled end-user development to become more practical today than in the early to mid-1980s. There are five categories of fourth-generation tools that are summarized in Table 9.11.

End-User Development Pitfalls This chapter has painted a pretty rosy picture of end-user development so far. However, it is important to understand that along with the benefits come some problems, as illustrated in Figure 9.29. The information systems and computer science professions have established software development standards and generally accepted practices that are used throughout different organizations and across different types of systems. Unfortunately, users may not be aware of these standards, such as the need for adequate documentation, built-in error checking, and testing procedures. In small, personal applications, not adhering to the standards may not present a problem. However, if the system manages or interconnects with important business data, then lack of adherence to sound principles can quickly become a big problem if data becomes corrupted or is not secure.

Another problem for end-user–developed systems is a potential lack of continuity. Suppose James develops a new system that meets his needs perfectly. James understands the system and uses it every day. However, one day James is transferred and is replaced by Jordan, a new hire to the company. The system that was intuitive for James to use may not be so intuitive for Jordan. Jordan may quickly abandon James's system or may be forced to develop her own system. This example shows how end-user development can easily result in a lack of continuity among applications, leading to redundant development efforts and a lot of wasted productivity in the organization. In organizations where turnover is frequent, a lot of time can be lost "reinventing the wheel" simply because systems that are in place

TABLE 9.11 Categories of Fourth-Generation Programming Tools

Fourth-Generation Programming Tools	Description
Personal computer tools	Tools—including spreadsheets, database management systems, and graphics programs—enabling users to build their own applications using macro languages or embedded tools within the software
Query languages/report generators	Capabilities within database systems and other applications enabling users to search a database by entering various search criteria or to produce various types of textual and graphical reports
Graphics generators	Tools allowing users to extract relevant information from databases to generate pie charts, line graphs, area plots, or other types of graphics
Decision support or modeling tools	Spreadsheets and other dedicated decision support tools enabling the analysis of routine and more complex, multidimensional problems
Application generators	Tools for developing small customized systems where the user specifies what analysis is to be done in a relatively user-friendly language rather than in the more tedious commands of a lower-level programming language

FIGURE 9.29

End-user development can sometimes be problematic.

Industry Analysis

The "New" Web

When the dot-com bubble burst in 2001, many believed the Web's usefulness as a business vehicle was over. Time would quickly show, however, that in most cases dot-com failures simply eliminated concepts not well suited to the online business community (remember sites for buying groceries and pet food?) and made room for those that were. And those dot-com businesses that survived the shake-up had certain traits in common:

1. *The Web Is the Business Platform.* Businesses uniquely suited to the Web environment, such as Amazon and Google, sell products or offer services consumers can't find in a brick-and-mortar competitor (e.g., out-of-print books).
2. *The Sites Leverage All Customers, from Small to Large.* For example, highly successful eBay enables even the smallest customer transactions, while dot-com sites that leveraged only the largest customer transactions generally failed.
3. *Increased Use Automatically Improves the Service.* While some Web business sites must add servers as business increases, others take advantage of users' resources as traffic increases. For example, peer-to-peer music download sites allow users to network directly, using the site itself as an intermediary.
4. *The Hyperlink Feature Inherent in Web Design Is Used to the Fullest.* Yahoo!, for example, was originally a catalog of links, and Google based its revolutionary search platform on PageRank, a system that used the link structure of the Web rather than document characteristics to search data.
5. *Lightweight Programming.* The use of such scripting languages as Perl, Python, PHP, and Ruby is supported, which facilitates an open-source philosophy, allowing users to contribute and change content. Wikipedia, for example, is a collection of definitions contributed by users.

When the dot-com fallout settled, industry observers categorized Web businesses that survived as "Web 2.0," a term coined in 2001 at a brainstorming session between O'Reilly Media and MediaLive International. Participants in the session contrasted specific "Web 1.0" and "Web 2.0" businesses as a starting point for determining those characteristics that are unique to enterprises that succeed online (see Table 9.12).

Out of this brainstorming session, the annual Web 2.0 Conference was born. (The third annual conference was held November 7–9, 2006, in San Francisco, California.) Although the term was coined in 2001, Web 2.0 uses many older technologies to offer interactive business environments, such as the following:

- *Web services* (from 1998) to allow organizations to communicate data without intimate knowledge of each other's systems behind the firewall
- *Ajax* (from 1998) to allow Web applications to make fast changes to the user interface without reloading the entire browser page
- *Web content syndication* (from 1997) to allow data such as news feeds, events, stories, and other Web content to be seamlessly published on another site

Such "older" technologies are now incorporated in many current Web technologies, such as wikis (Web sites that allow users to add, change, or remove content), podcasts (a method for distributing multimedia files, such as audio and video, over the Internet), **RSS** feeds (short for "Really Simple Syndication," a set of standards for sharing updated Web content such as news and sports scores across sites), blogs (short for "Web log," a Web-based publication consisting of chronologically posted articles), and social networks (Web sites that provide a virtual community for people interested in a particular subject).

All the major players in the Web search business have used these dynamic technologies to enhance their online presence. One such example is Microsoft with its launch of Live.com, based on Ajax technology, allowing users access to functionality usually reserved for desktop applications. Now with Live.com, users can right-click objects

TABLE 9.12 Contrasting Web 1.0 to Web 2.0

Web 1.0	Web 2.0
DoubleClick	Google AdSense
Ofoto	Flickr
Akamai	BitTorrent
mp3.com	Napster
Britannica Online	Wikipedia
Personal websites	Blogging
Evite	Upcoming.org and EVDB
Domain name speculation	Search engine optimization
Page views	Cost per click
Screen scraping	Web services
Publishing	Participation
Content management systems	Wikis
Directories (taxonomy)	Tagging ("folksonomy")
Stickiness	Syndication

Source: http://www.oreillynet.com/pub/a/oreilly/tim/news/2005/09/30/what-is-web-20.html, retrieved June 5, 2006.

such as e-mail, drag and drop elements to create customized home pages, and even use keyboard shortcuts, such as copying and pasting, in the Web environment.

Google has gone one step further and allowed any programmer to build on Google applications using Web services. Some of the more interesting applications developed using Google Web services include the Craigslist-developed dynamic map of all available apartments in the United States (www.housingmaps.com). Similarly, the city of Chicago uses Google Map's Web services to create a dynamic map of crime locations within the city, including maps of different types of crimes and even crimes taking place on any given bus route (www.chicagocrime.org).

The evolution of Web 2.0 businesses and the previously mentioned Web industry advances have made possible desktop-like applications on the Web (e.g., Microsoft's Live.com) and the customized application of current technologies (e.g., various Google tools and applications). In short, business models for Web 2.0 that employ the previously listed traits for surviving in the "new" Web have the best chance for success.

Questions

1. Envision and describe general features of Web 3.0 applications. What do you think is coming next for the Web?

2. Describe an application or service you would like to be able to do on the Web today that is not yet possible. Describe the potential market for this application or service. Forecast how long you believe it will take before this will occur or be possible.

Sources: http://www.oreillynet.com/pub/a/oreilly/tim/news/2005/09/30/what-is-web-20.html, retrieved June 5, 2006

http://en.wikipedia.org/wiki/AJAX, retrieved June 5, 2006

http://web2.wsj2.com/the_best_web_20_software_of_2005.htm, retrieved June 5, 2006

http://www.web2con.com/, retrieved June 5, 2006

are undocumented and cannot easily be used by new employees. Likewise, end users in different parts of an organization might create systems for handling similar tasks, unbeknownst to each other, leading to redundant efforts.

Related to the continuity problem is the question of whether users and managers should be spending their time on IS development. That is, the organization has hired individuals to be financial managers, production managers, marketers, or salespeople. The organization expects these employees to add value to the organization based on the skills that they have to offer. If their time and energy are diverted to developing new systems, then the organization loses out on the potential productivity these individuals have to offer in other ways. Also, individual motivation, morale, and performance might suffer if the employee is unable to concentrate on his or her area of expertise and instead spends too much time worrying about developing new systems.

Fortunately, organizations that have been successful in moving to end-user development are aware of many of these problems and have established some controls to avoid them. One control mechanism is an information center (IC), which is charged with encouraging end users to develop their own applications while at the same time providing some management oversight. The IC staff can assist or train end users in proper development techniques or standards, prevent redundancy in application development, and ensure that systems are documented properly. IC staff are often not functional-area experts but are typically experts in using the fourth-generation tools. Working together, end users and the IC staff can develop useful systems for an organization.

Key Points Review

1. *Understand the process used by organizations to manage the development of information systems.* The development of information systems follows a process called the systems development life cycle (SDLC). The SDLC is a process that first identifies the need for a system and then defines the processes for designing, developing, and maintaining an information system. The process is very structured and formal and requires the active involvement of managers and users.

2. *Describe each major phase of the SDLC: systems identification, selection, and planning; system analysis; system design; system implementation; and system maintenance.* The SDLC has five phases: system identification, selection, and planning; system analysis; system design; system implementation; and system maintenance. Systems identification, selection, and planning is the first phase of the SDLC, in which potential projects are identified, selected, and planned. System analysis is the second phase of the SDLC, in which the current ways of doing business are studied and alternative replacement systems are proposed. System design is the third phase of the SDLC, in which all features of the proposed system are described. System implementation is the fourth phase of the SDLC, in which the information system is programmed, tested, installed, and supported. System maintenance is the fifth and final phase of the SDLC, in which an information system is systematically repaired and improved.

3. *Describe prototyping, rapid application development, and object-oriented analysis and design methods of systems development, along with each approach's strengths and weaknesses.* Prototyping is an iterative systems development process in which requirements are converted into a working system that is continually revised through a close working relationship between analysts and users. The strengths of prototyping are that it helps develop a close working relationship between designers and users and that it is a good approach for hard-to-define problems. Its weaknesses are that it is not a practical approach for a large number of users and that it can at times lead to a lower-quality system if the system is built too quickly. Rapid application development (RAD) is a systems development methodology that combines prototyping, computer-based development tools, special management practices, and close user involvement. The strength of RAD is that users are actively involved in the design process, making system implementation much easier. The weaknesses of RAD are that systems are sometimes narrowly focused—which might limit future evolution—and that quality problems might result if a system is designed and built too quickly (as is the case with prototyping). Object-oriented analysis and design (OOA&D) is a systems development approach that focuses on modeling objects—data and operations bundled together—rather than on modeling these separately. The strengths of OOA&D are the integration of data and processing during the design phase, which should lead to higher-quality systems, and the reuse of common objects, which should make development and maintenance easier. The weaknesses of OOA&D are that it is more difficult to train analysts and programmers in the object-oriented approach and that analysts often re-create common objects.

4. *Explain the factors involved in building a system in-house, along with situations in which it is not*

feasible. It is not feasible for an organization to build a system in-house in at least four situations. First, some organizations have limited IS staffing and, therefore, do not have the capability to build a system themselves. Second, an organization may have IS staff with a limited skill set. Existing IS staff may be highly skilled at producing traditional applications but not have the skills to build new types of systems or systems that require emerging development tools. Third, in many organizations, the IS staff does not have the time to work on all the systems that the organization desires. Fourth, some organizations have performance problems with their IS staff whereby staff turnover, changing requirements, shifts in technology, or budget constraints have resulted in poor results. In any of these situations, it may be advantageous to an organization to consider an alternative to in-house systems development.

5. *Explain three alternative systems development options: external acquisition, outsourcing, and end-user development.* External acquisition is the process of purchasing an existing information system from an external organization or vendor.

External acquisition is a five-step process. Step 1 is system identification, selection, and planning, which focuses on determining whether a proposed system is feasible. Step 2 is systems analysis, which focuses on determining the requirements for the system. Step 3 is the development of a request for proposal (RFP). An RFP is a communication tool indicating an organization's requirements for a given system and requesting information from potential vendors on their ability to deliver such a system. Step 4 is proposal evaluation, which focuses on evaluating proposals received from vendors. This evaluation may include viewing system demonstrations, evaluating the performance of those systems, and examining criteria important to the organization and the ways the proposed systems meet those criteria. Step 5 is vendor selection, which focuses on choosing the vendor to provide the system. Outsourcing refers to the turning over of partial or entire responsibility for information systems development and management to an outside organization. End-user development is a systems development method whereby users in the organization develop, test, and maintain their own applications.

Key Terms

adaptive maintenance   380

alpha testing   377

beta testing   377

corrective maintenance   388

critical success factor (CSF)   369

data flows   372

developmental testing   377

end-user development   392

external acquisition   386

form   372

graphical user interface (GUI)   374

information systems planning   366

joint application design (JAD)   370

object-oriented analysis and design (OOA&D)   384

perfective maintenance   380

preventive maintenance   380

processing logic   372

prototyping   382

rapid application development (RAD)   383

request for proposal (RFP)   388

requirements collection   369

RSS   396

software engineering   363

system analysis   367

system conversion   377

system design   372

system identification, selection, and planning   366

system implementation   377

system maintenance   380

systems analysis and design   363

systems analyst   363

systems benchmarking   389

systems development life cycle (SDLC)   366

Review Questions

1. What are the five phases of the systems development life cycle (SDLC)?

2. List and describe six techniques used in requirements collection.

3. What are the four major components/tasks of the system design phase of the SDLC?

4. What are the four options for system conversion? How do they differ from each other?

5. Compare and contrast the four types of system maintenance.

6. What are three alternative approaches to the SDLC for designing and building systems?

7. What are the advantages and disadvantages of prototyping?

8. List and define the four phases of rapid application development.

9. What is object-oriented analysis and design, and what are its strengths and weaknesses?

10. Define outsourcing and list three major types.

11. What is system benchmarking, and what are some common benchmarks?

12. What are some of the reasons outsourcing is more popular than ever?

13. What are the three recommendations made in this chapter for managing an outsourcing IS relationship?

14. Describe five categories of fourth-generation tools.

15. End-user developers have what advantages and disadvantages?

Self-Study Questions

Visit the Interactive Study Guide on the text Web site for additional Self-Study Questions: **www.prenhall.com/jessup.**

1. Which of the following is not one of the five phases of the systems development life cycle?
A. system analysis
B. system implementation
C. system design
D. systems resource acquisition

2. _____ is the process of gathering and organizing information from users, managers, business processes, and documents to understand how a proposed information system should function.
A. requirements collection
B. systems collection
C. systems analysis
D. records archiving

3. Which of the following is the correct order of phases in the systems development life cycle?
A. maintenance, analysis, planning, design, implementation
B. analysis, planning, design, implementation, maintenance
C. planning, analysis, design, implementation, maintenance
D. maintenance, planning, analysis, design, implementation

4. In the systems design phase, the elements that must be designed when building an information system include all of the following except _____.
A. reports and forms
B. questionnaires
C. databases and files
D. interfaces and dialogues

5. _____ maintenance involves making enhancements to improve processing performance or interface usability or adding desired (but not necessarily required) system features (in other words, "bells and whistles").

A. preventive
B. perfective
C. corrective
D. adaptive

6. Which of the following is an alternative to building a system in-house?
A. external acquisition
B. end-user development
C. outsourcing
D. all of the above

7. A _____ is a report that an organization uses to tell vendors what its requirements are and to invite them to provide information about how they might be able to meet those requirements.
A. request letter
B. vendor request
C. request for proposal
D. payables request

8. Which of the following is not a type of outsourcing?
A. basic
B. elite
C. strategic
D. preferred

9. Which of the following factors is a good reason to outsource?
A. problems in IS performance
B. supplier pressures
C. financial factors
D. all of the above

10. Most competitive external acquisition processes have at least five general steps. Which of the following is not one of those steps?
A. vendor selection
B. proposal evaluation
C. development of a request for proposal
D. implementation

Answers are on page 402.

Problems and Exercises

1. Match the following terms with the appropriate definitions:
  i. Request for proposal
  ii. Systems benchmarking
  iii. Alpha testing
  iv. Systems development life cycle

  v. End-user development
  vi. Prototyping
  vii. Pilot conversion
  viii. Systems analysis
  ix. Outsourcing
  x. External acquisition

    xi. Data flows

    xii. Requirements collection

       a. The movement of data through an organization or within an information system

       b. Term that describes the life of an information system from conception to retirement

       c. The second phase of the systems development life cycle

       d. The process of gathering and organizing information from users, managers, business processes, and documents to understand how a proposed information system should function

       e. Performed by software testers to assess whether the entire system meets the design requirements of the users

       f. When the entire system is used in one location but not in the entire organization

       g. A systems development methodology that uses a trial-and-error approach for discovering how a system should operate

       h. The practice of turning over responsibility for some or all of an organizations information systems development and operations to an outside firm

       i. Users developing their own applications

       j. Purchasing an existing system from an outside vendor

       k. A way to evaluate a proposed system by testing a portion of it with the system workload

       l. A report that is used to tell vendors what your requirements are and to invite them to provide information about how they might be able to meet those requirements

2. Explain the differences between data and data flows. How might systems analysts obtain the information they need to generate the data flows of a system? How are these data flows and the accompanying processing logic used in the system design phase of the life cycle? What happens when the data and data flows are modeled incorrectly?

3. When Microsoft posts a new version of Internet Explorer on its Web site and states that this is a beta version, what does it mean? Is this a final working version of the software, or is it still being tested? Who is doing the testing? Search the Web to find other companies that have beta versions of their products available to the public. You might try Corel (www.corel.com) or Adobe (www.adobe.com). What other companies did you find?

4. Why is the system documentation of a new information system so important? What information does it contain? For whom is this information intended? When will the system documentation most likely be used?

5. Conduct a search on the Web for "systems development life cycle," using any search engine. Check out some of the hits. Compare them with the SDLC outlined in this chapter. Do all these life cycles follow the same general path? How many phases do the ones you found on the Web contain? Is the terminology the same or different? Prepare a 10-minute presentation to the class on your findings.

6. Choose an organization with which you are familiar that develops its own information systems. Does this organization follow a SDLC? If not, why not? If so, how many phases does it have? Who developed this life cycle? Was it someone within the company or was the information system adopted from somewhere else?

7. Describe your experiences with information systems that were undergoing changes or updates. What kind of conversion procedure was being used? How did this affect your interaction with the system as a user? Who else was affected? If the system was down altogether, for how long was it down? Do you or any of your classmates have horror stories, or were the situations not that bad?

8. Compare and contrast RAD and object-oriented methodologies. What are the strengths and weaknesses of each? Visit Object FAQ at www.objectfaq.com/oofaq2/.

9. Conduct a search on the Web for "object-oriented analysis and design" using any search engine you wish. Check out some of the hits. You should have found numerous articles regarding OOA&D's use by IS departments. Are these articles positive or negative regarding OOA&D? Do you agree with the articles? Prepare a 10-minute presentation to the class on your findings.

10. Interview an IS manager within an organization with which you are familiar. Determine whether the organization uses methodologies such as prototyping, RAD, and/or OOA&D for system projects. Who chooses the methodology? If the organization has not used a methodology, is it because of choice or because of a lack of need, understanding, or capability of using the methodology?

11. Choose an organization with which you are familiar and determine whether it builds its applications in-house. How many IS staff members does the organization have, and how large is the organization they support?

12. Think about the requirements of a career in IS. Do IS positions generally require people to work 40 hours a week or more if a project has a deadline? Do positions in the IS department require people skills? To find these answers, visit the IS department at your university, a local business, or an online clearinghouse of jobs, such as hotjobs.yahoo.com or www.job-hunt.org.

13. Find an organization, either on the Internet at www.computerworld.com or www.infoworld.com or a company you may want to work for in the future, that outsources work. What are the managerial challenges of outsourcing, and why is this a popular alternative to hiring additional staff?

Application Exercises

 The existing data files referenced in these exercises are available on the Student Companion Web site: **www.prenhall.com/jessup.**

Spreadsheet Application: Outsourcing Information Systems at Campus Travel

Campus Travel wants to increase its customer focus and wants to be able to better serve its most valued customers. Many members of the frequent flyer program have requested the ability to check on the status of their membership online; furthermore, the frequent flyers would welcome the opportunity to book reward flights online. As you know that there are a number of companies specializing in building such transactional systems, you have decided to outsource the development of such system. The following weights are assigned to evaluate the different vendors' systems:

- Online booking capability: 20 percent
- User friendliness: 25 percent
- Maximum number of concurrent users: 20 percent
- Integration with current systems: 10 percent
- Vendor support: 10 percent
- Price: 15 percent

To evaluate the different offers, you need to calculate a weighted score for each vendor using the data provided in the Outsourcing.csv spreadsheet. To calculate the total points for each vendor, do the following:

1. Open the file outsourcing.csv
2. Use the SUMPRODUCT formula to multiply each vendor's scores with the respective weights and add the weighted scores
3. Use conditional formatting to highlight all vendors falling below a total of 60% and above a total of 85% to facilitate the vendor selection.

Database Application: Building a Special Needs Database for Campus Travel

In addition to international travel, travel reservations for people with special needs is an area of specialty of Campus Travel. However, to be able to recommend travel destinations and travel activities you should know what facilities are available at each destination. Therefore, you have been asked to create a database of the destinations and the type of facilities that are available for people with special needs. In order to make the system as useful as possible for all, you need to design reports for the users to retrieve information about each destination. Your manager would like to have a system that contains the following information about the destinations:

- Location
- Availability of facilities for physically handicapped
- Distance to medical facilities
- Pet friendliness

Each location may have one or more handicap facility (e.g., hearing, walking, sight, and so on). A type of handicap facility can be present at multiple locations. Also, each location has to have one pet friendly accommodation/activity and may also have accommodation for different type of pets (dogs, cats, and so on). After designing the database, please design three professionally formatted reports that (1) list the locations in alphabetical order, (2) list all locations that have the handicap facilities for those that find it difficult to walk, and (3) list all locations that have a cat-friendly policy.

Hint: In Microsoft Access, you can create queries before preparing the reports. Enter a few sample data sets and print out the reports.

Team Work Exercise: Determining a Development Approach

You have just been hired by an organization, and you have been charged with purchasing 10 new standard desktop computers. Compile a list of criteria you will use to evaluate the vendor to choose. Having determined the different criteria, discuss the importance of these factors and rank them accordingly. Prepare a report explaining the criteria and rankings.

Answers to the Self-Study Questions

1. D, p. 366
2. A, p. 369
3. C, p. 366
4. B, p. 372
5. B, p. 380
6. D, p. 386
7. C, p. 388
8. B, p. 392
9. D, p. 391
10. D, p. 387

case

The Emergence of Open Source Software

You're probably well aware, by now, that some software, such as the Linux operating system and the Firefox browser, is *open source*. That is, creators of the programs made the source code available so that anyone could program changes to improve the application's performance.

The Open Source Initiative (OSI), a nonprofit organization dedicated to promoting open-source software, was formed in 1998 by Bruce Perens and Eric S. Raymond, two prominent proponents of open-source software. The OSI formulated an *open-source definition* to determine whether software can be considered for an open-source license. An open-source license is a copyright license for software that specifies that the source code is available for redistribution and modification without programmers having to pay the original author. OSI conditions for meeting the open source definition include the following:

1. The software can be redistributed for free.
2. Source code is freely available.
3. Redistribution of modifications must be allowed.
4. Licenses may require that modifications be available only as patches.
5. Rights attached to the program must apply to all to whom the program is redistributed.
6. No one who wants to modify the code can be locked out.
7. Commercial software users cannot be excluded.
8. License may not be restricted to a specific product.
9. Licenses cannot specify that any other software distributed with the licensed software must also be open code.
10. Licenses must be technology neutral; that is, no click-wrap acceptance of the license shall be required. (The term "click-wrap" is a takeoff on the license enclosed with packaged software that informs users that opening the shrink wrap around the software implies acceptance. Click-wrap clauses are so named because they appear when software is downloaded and require computer users to click on "I accept" or "I decline.")

One category of open-source software that meets these criteria and that has gained widespread acceptance is operating systems, including the following:

- Linux (www.linux.org/). The most used Unix-like operating system on the planet. Versions have been run on anything from handheld computers and regular PCs to the world's most powerful supercomputers. For a list of popular Linux distributions, see www.linuxiso.org.
- FreeBSD (www.freebsd.org/), OpenBSD (www.openbsd.org/), and NetBSD (www.netbsd.org/). The BSDs are all based on the Berkeley Software Distribution of the Unix operating system, developed at the University of California, Berkeley. Another BSD-based open-source project is *Darwin* (http://developer.apple.com/opensource/index.html), which is the base of Apple's Mac OS X.

In addition, many of the router boxes and root DNS servers that keep the Internet working are based on one of the BSDs or on Linux. Microsoft also uses BSD to keep their Hotmail and MSN services working.

Furthermore, in addition to the operating software described here, much of the software that keeps the Internet working is also open source, including the following:

- Apache (www.apache.org/), which runs over 70 percent of the world's Web servers (see www.security space.com/s_survey/data/200609/index.html).
- BIND (www.isc.org/index.pl?/sw/bind/), the software that provides the DNS (domain name service) for the entire Internet.
- Sendmail (www.sendmail.org/), the most important and widely used e-mail transport software on the Internet.
- Firefox (www.mozilla.com/firefox), the open-source redesign of the Netscape Browser, is recovering ground lost by Netscape in the "browser wars." (Netscape's legal fight with Microsoft over the dominance of Internet Explorer). With each new release, Firefox added functionality, stability, and cross-platform consistency that is not available from any other browser, and many of the popular features (such as tabbed browsing) have since been copied by its competitors.
- OpenSSL (www.openssl.org/) is the standard for secure communication (strong encryption) over the Internet.

The Internet has clearly taken advantage of the open-source concept and will undoubtedly continue to do so.

Questions

1. What are the pros and cons of having so much open-source software enabling the Internet?
2. For what types of applications do you think open-source is better than non–open-source software? When is it worse?
3. Find a for-profit company that is distributing open-source software. What is the software? How does the company make money? Is its revenue model sustainable?
4. Do you use any open-source software on your personal computer, such as the Linux operating system or the Firefox browser? Why or why not?

Sources: http://www.opensource.org/docs/products.php
http://en.wikipedia.org/wiki/Open_Source_Definition
http://en.wikipedia.org/wiki/Open_source

case ②

e-Enabling the Air Transport Industry: Information Systems Development and Acquisition

In the late 1990s, a vision to take broadband Internet access to the sky was formed. While the technologies to make this vision possible already existed, no company had taken on the challenge to integrate the wide variety of technologies necessary—satellite communications, state-of-the-art antenna technology, large-scale networking technology, and mobile communications—to provide high-speed Internet access to airplane passengers. In addition to overcoming various technical hurdles, the Boeing Company needed to clearly establish that indeed there was adequate demand for such a system.

To gain an understanding of market potential, research was conducted that found that, initially, 62 percent of U.S. frequent business travelers were either "extremely" or "very" interested in broadband services and that 18 percent of U.S.-based frequent flyers and nearly 20 percent of European-based frequent flyers would pay $35 per flight for high-speed Internet service. Of the U.S. frequent flyers surveyed, 3 percent said they were extremely likely to switch carriers for such a service. These numbers clearly demonstrated a huge market potential for the airlines, as an average increase of a single passenger per international flight is worth approximately $1 million in additional airline revenue annually. These promising numbers were seen as an excellent basis to form the business case for the proposed system. Throughout the project identification phase of the project, several rounds of revisions were made to the business case before getting the final approval by Boeing's executives to launch the Connexion by Boeing system.

In order to maximize the revenue-generating potential of this business idea, Connexion's systems analysts worked closely with its marketing unit to understand the system features that would be necessary to meet the needs of their potential customers. Having established the key features of the proposed system, Connexion's marketing and sales team

engaged several major airlines to identify the mandatory versus the desired features of the system. For example, many airlines were concerned with the time needed for the installation of the system, as any hour an aircraft does not spend in the air directly translates into lost revenue. Similarly, many airlines were concerned with the

cost of installing the communications equipment and the pricing of the service for customers. The requirements collection phase produced the marketing requirements document, which then became the top-level business and systems requirements document. This document became the blueprint the systems analysts

Connexion One test equipment.

used to develop their top-level specifications on how to design the final system.

Once the detailed system design and product service development was completed, Connexion's systems engineering team involved all of the integrated product teams (which represented the different stakeholders of the project) to develop the lower-level subsystems necessary for providing onboard Internet access. With these specifications, the requirements could be determined down to the element level. In order to comply with aviation standards and to facilitate installation and maintenance of the system, the components had to be set up as line replaceable units, which are components of communications systems that adhere to various specifications, allowing the entire system to be easily exchanged during routine maintenance. This ensured that costs and time needed for installation and maintenance would be kept low.

The initial phases of the project went very smoothly. However, many of the assumptions of the business case were suddenly challenged by several successive events, including the first Iraq war (Desert Storm); the September 11, 2001, terrorist attacks; the SARS crisis in Southeast Asia; and overall economic downturn. Together, these events contributed to a significant downturn within the travel industry that very negatively impacted most commercial airlines. As a result, many of the airlines that had initially been interested in installing the system were forced to withdraw their commitment because of increased costs to comply with new security standards and reduced demand for air travel. For Connexion, the withdrawal of the commercial airline market required that the business case be reexamined. Given these dramatic changes, Connexion shifted its focus to the governmental and private-jet market segments in order to keep the business case viable. Nevertheless, although the commercial airline market was not currently interested in installing the system, Connexion managed to continue to involve 16 of the world's leading airlines in the process to identify and refine system features and services.

The airlines' involvement, critiques, and clarified requirements proved invaluable for Connexion, as it helped to refine the system specifications to meet the airlines' evolving market situation. Additionally, it also slowly provided the airlines with the opportunity to buy in to the system that they were helping to design and review. As the design evolved, industry partners continued to work closely with Connexion in the evaluation of new services and system features.

Having finished the design phase, Connexion then started initial testing of the system. Aboard a specially equipped Boeing 737—the Connexion One—airplane, systems engineers thoroughly tested the functionality of the system. Using the test equipment installed aboard this aircraft, Connexion's engineers demonstrated that both wired and wireless modes could be operated safely without harmful interference with the airplane's communications, avionics, and navigations systems. Consequently, Connexion received approval for the system from the U.S. Federal Aviation Administration as well as the certification by regulatory authorities in the United Kingdom (CAA) and Germany (LBA), which granted certifications to Boeing and Lufthansa Technik that allowed the use of wireless laptops and PDAs (personal digital assistants) on select flights during the initial testing aboard commercial airliners.

In early 2003, the first demonstrations of the technology aboard commercial aircraft started on a Lufthansa flight between Frankfurt and Washington, D.C. For the next three months, passengers successfully used Connexion's services aboard certain scheduled Lufthansa and British Airways transatlantic flights. These demonstrations helped to increase the number of other airlines interested in the service. Following Lufthansa, airlines such as SAS, Japan Airlines, and ANA signed definite agreements to equip all or parts of their fleets with Connexion's systems.

While the system has been proven to work in commercial airline operations, Connexion's systems engineers continued working on refining the system. Because of the demand by international airlines, Connexion decided to extend the coverage of its services to the transpacific routes as well as to South America and Africa. As many long-range international flights use routes via Greenland or northern Siberia or Alaska, the need to develop a next-generation antenna arose. Connexion's first-generation antenna worked very well on routes up to a certain latitude; however, airplanes flying further up north were not able to connect to the geostationary satellites orbiting around the equator. In cooperation with Mitsubishi Electric Corporation, Connexion developed the next-generation antenna, which helped to overcome these shortcomings and enable broadband Internet access at an even greater number of routes.

During the systems analysis and design process, Connexion experienced several setbacks, primarily because of major international events. However, by refining the system specifications on the basis of changing requirements, Connexion weathered these crises and, in 2003, commercially rolled out high-speed in-flight Internet access across private, governmental, and commercial sectors.

However, all efforts ultimately proved to be in vain, as airlines only sluggishly adopted the services, and the installed base lagged far below what Connexion had hoped for. In addition to this, uncertainty about the regulatory environment grew with recurring terrorist threats. Most notably, in August 2006, a terror plot to use electronics equipment to ignite liquid explosives onboard a number of aircraft was foiled by British law enforcement; shortly thereafter, carrying electronic equipment such as laptops, cell phones, or MP3 players onboard was severely restricted on routes between Great Britain and the United States. For many airlines, this showed just how quickly the regulatory environment could change, and in the wake of these events, Boeing decided to discontinue the Connexion service offering.

Questions

1. Briefly describe the systems analysis and design process at Connexion.
2. In what ways did Connexion follow the standard SDLC process as described in the chapter? Where did Connexion deviate from this process?
3. How can a company such as Connexion deal with changes in the external environment? How could Boeing's efforts have been salvaged?

chapter *10*

Managing Information Systems Ethics and Crime

p r e v i e w > Given that computers and information systems are now a fundamental part of doing business, opportunities for misusing and abusing information, computers, and systems now abound. This digital world we live in causes us to ask some important new ethical questions. Who owns information, particularly information about us? Who is responsible for the accuracy of information? Should guidelines be set for how business organizations and business professionals use information, computers, and information systems, and, if so, what should these guidelines be? What penalties should be assessed for computer crime and abuses? After reading this chapter you will be able to do the following:

1. Describe the advent of the information age and how computer ethics impact the use of information systems.

2. Discuss the ethical concerns associated with information privacy, accuracy, property, and accessibility.

3. Define computer crime and list several types of computer crime.

4. Describe and explain the differences between cyberwar and cyberterrorism.

This chapter focuses on the last major topic related to managing in the digital world, specifically, various issues associated with information systems ethics and computer crime. Both of these topics are becoming increasingly important to successfully managing information systems.

Managing in the Digital World: BitTorrent

In 1999, Shawn Fanning, a student at Northeastern University in Boston, thought he had a groundbreaking idea for a Web site. Tired of searching IRC or Lycos to find music, Fanning devised a *peer-to-peer* file sharing system that allowed users to exchange music files directly. Under Fanning's unique system, files were not stored on a central server but were uploaded and downloaded from the hard drives of users' computers. For example, if a user wanted to download a Ricky Martin song, he or she could search among other users to locate that song and then download the tune from another user's computer.

Fanning called his service Napster, and it was phenomenally successful since users could download hit tunes as MP3 files without buying CDs loaded with "filler" songs and could locate and download hard-to-find songs not available anywhere else. The trouble was, the Motion Picture Association of America (MPAA) and the Recording Industry Association of America soon discovered the site and filed copyright-infringement suits against Fanning. Heavy metal band Metallica and rapper Dr. Dre also brought copyright violation suits against Fanning. The courts sided with the music industry and shut Napster down in 2001. As part of the court's decision, Fanning paid music creators and copyright holders $26 million in damages.

Napster filed for bankruptcy in 2001 and was sold. The site continues to exist as a free service for users to listen to music selections, but users who want to download tunes must pay (see www.napster.com).

The hugely successful peer-to-peer file sharing system Fanning originated did not disappear with the demise of Napster. The latest star in the file sharing constellation is BitTorrent. The difference between Napster and BitTorrent is that BitTorrent is not a program or a file server. BitTorrent is a protocol designed for transferring files. This protocol lets users connect to ad hoc peer-to-peer networks, allowing users to communicate directly with each other to send and receive files. Although there is a central server called a tracker, it simply manages the connection and does not have any knowledge of the files being transported between users.

BitTorrent's key concept is that users can upload at the same time they are downloading by breaking data down into smaller, more easily transferred chunks. This feature lets users connect to several other users and either helps others download or uses the combined bandwidth of a group of users to download large files at lightning-fast speeds, thus optimizing available bandwidth. The protocol is designed to work better with more users on the network. Supportive sharing has built-in growth since each new user brings supply as well as demand.

FIGURE 10.1

Napster is synonymous with music downloading.

BitTorrent technology has contributed new catchwords to the computer lexicon. For example, "leechers" are users who download content without sharing that content with anyone else. "Seeders" are users who not only download content but also provide content to be downloaded using their hard drives and bandwidth. Many users will not allow their content to be downloaded by leechers and will block leechers when they see them.

Why hasn't this service been stopped via lawsuits? Primarily because BitTorrent servers only manage the BitTorrent protocol connection and do not store files for downloading. The software that allows for users to download and upload files is not associated with BitTorrent. In other words, anyone can create a BitTorrent program, and many developers have.

Surprisingly, the MPAA has embraced BitTorrent's strategy instead of fighting it. Warner Brothers Home Entertainment Group recently launched a legal peer-to-peer service in Germany called In2Movies. Subscribers use Warner Brothers' client-based software that, in turn, uses the BitTorrent network protocol to manage connections among Warner Brothers' clients. Subscribers can download films on the same day the product is released. The business model is simple: users will pay a certain fee for each movie they download. In turn, as an incentive, users receive bonus points for sharing movies they downloaded using In2Movies, and can use these bonus points to "pay" for downloading additional content. The consumers "download to own" the movies (i.e., they can watch the movies as often as they desire), but cannot play burnt copies using a standalone DVD player.

Warner Brothers' strategy is considered revolutionary since the entertainment industry considers the file sharing battle a lost cause. Warner Brothers' strategy not only shows how to reduce distribution costs by maximizing network effectiveness but also provides a speedy download experience for the consumer. This move allows Warner Brothers not only positive press and exposure to the music sharing communities, but it allows them to save millions in their digital distribution.

Another company using BitTorrent technology to its advantage is Blizzard entertainment. Blizzard's hit game title *World of Warcraft* uses the BitTorrent protocol for patches and update information. When gamers update or patch their current *World of Warcraft* installation, they do not download the necessary files from Blizzard's servers. Instead, they connect using the BitTorrent protocol to other users worldwide to download the files. Thus, they use a combined bandwidth and service space to accomplish digital distribution. With over 3 million users, *World of Warcraft* is a widely profitable title for Blizzard. And since Blizzard uses the BitTorrent distributed file sharing technology, scalability costs are marginal.

After reading this chapter, you will be able to answer the following:

1. What ethical issues do technologies like BitTorrent raise?

2. Debate the ethics of seeders versus leechers.

3. If you were a popular performer in the music industry, how would you feel about file sharing?

Sources:

http://en.wikipedia.org/wiki/Napster

http://en.wikipedia.org/wiki/Bittorrent

http://www.bittorrent.com/introduction.html

http://online.wsj.com/public/article/SB113858875415059685BRDbFwW653bFI5_3EHCWikZeZd8_20070130.html?mod=blogs

Information Systems Ethics

In his book *The Third Wave,* futurist Alvin Toffler describes three distinct phases, or "waves of change," that have taken place in the past or are presently taking place within the world's civilizations (see Figure 10.2). The first wave—a civilization based on agriculture and handwork—was a comparatively primitive stage that began as civilizations formed and lasted for thousands of years. The second wave of change—the industrial revolution—overlapped with the first wave. The industrial revolution began in Great Britain toward the end of the eighteenth century and continued over the next 150 years, moving society from a predominantly agrarian culture to the urbanized machine age. Where once families supported themselves by working the land or handcrafting items for sale or trade, now mothers, fathers, and children left home to work in factories. Steel mills, textile factories, and eventually automobile assembly lines replaced farming and handwork as the principal source of family income.

As the industrial revolution progressed, not only did occupations change to accommodate the mechanized society, but so did educational, business, and social and religious institutions. On an individual level, now punctuality, obedience, and the ability to perform repetitive tasks were qualities to be instilled and valued in children in public schools and, ultimately, in workers.

The Information Age Arrives

In a much shorter period of time than it took for civilization to progress past the first wave, societies worldwide moved from the machine age into the **information age**—a period of change Toffler has dubbed the "third wave." As the third wave gained speed, information became the currency of the realm. For thousands of years, from primitive times through the Middle Ages, information, or the body of knowledge known to that point, was limited. It was transmitted verbally within families, clans, and villages, from person to person and generation to generation. Then came Johann Gutenberg's invention of the printing press with movable type in the middle of the 15th century, and a tremendous acceleration occurred in the amount and kind of information available to populations. Now knowledge could be imparted in written form and sometimes came from distant locations. Information could be saved, absorbed, debated, and written about in publications, thus adding to the exploding data pool.

Computer Literacy and the Digital Divide

Most modern-day high school and university students have grown up in a computerized world. If by some chance they do not know how to operate a computer by the time they graduate from high school, they soon acquire computer skills because in today's work world knowing how to use a computer—called **computer literacy** (or information

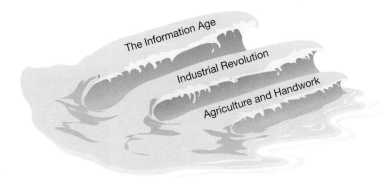

FIGURE 10.2

The information age is the biggest wave of change.

literacy)—can mean the difference between being employed and being unemployed. Knowing how to use a computer can also open up myriad sources of information to those who have learned how to use the computer as a device to gather, store, organize, and otherwise process information. In fact, some fear that the information age will not provide the same advantages to "information haves"—those computer-literate individuals who have unlimited access to information—and "information have-nots"—those with limited or no access or skills.

The first computer-related occupations have evolved as computers have become more sophisticated and more widely used. Where once we thought of computer workers primarily as programmers, data entry clerks, systems analysts, or computer repairpersons, today many more job categories in virtually all industries (see Figure 10.3) involve the use of computers. In fact, today there are few occupations where computers are not somehow in use. Computers manage air traffic, perform medical tests, monitor investment portfolios, enable online shopping, and more. Since they are especially adept at processing large amounts of data, they are used extensively by universities and public schools, in businesses of all sizes, and in all levels and departments of government. Engineers, architects, interior designers, and artists use special computer-aided design programs. Musicians play computerized instruments, and they write and record songs with the help of computers. Not only do we use computers at work, we also use them in our personal lives. We teach our children on them, manage our finances, do our taxes, compose letters and term papers, create greeting cards, send and receive electronic mail, surf the Internet, and play games on them.

Unfortunately, there are still many people in our society who are being left behind in the information age. The gap between those individuals in our society who are computer literate and have access to information resources like the Internet and those who do not is referred to as the **digital divide**. The digital divide is one of the major ethical challenges facing society today when you consider the strong linkage between computer literacy and a person's ability to compete in the information age. For example, access to raw materials and money fueled the industrial revolution, "but in the informational society, the fuel, the power, is knowledge," emphasizes John Kenneth Galbraith, an American economist specializing in emerging trends in the U.S. economy. "One has now come to see a new class structure divided by those who have information and those who must function out of ignorance. This new class has its power not from money, not from land, but from knowledge."

The good news is that the digital divide in America is rapidly shrinking, but there are still major challenges to overcome. In particular, people in rural communities, the elderly, people with disabilities, and minorities lag behind national averages for Internet access and computer literacy. Outside the United States, the gap gets even wider and the obstacles much more difficult to overcome, particularly in the developing countries, where infrastructure and financial resources are lacking. For example, most developing countries are lacking modern informational resources such as affordable Internet access or efficient

FIGURE 10.3

Computers are used in countless types of jobs and industries. (a) Benelux Press/© Getty Images, Inc. (b) B. Busco/© Getty Images, Inc. (c) Jean Louis Batt/© Getty Images, Inc. (d) © Getty Images/Eye Wire, Inc.

electronic payments methods like credit cards. Clearly, the digital divide is a major ethical concern facing the information age.

A broad range of ethical issues have emerged through the use and proliferation of computers. **Computer ethics** is used to describe the issues and standards of conduct as they pertain to the use of information systems. In 1986, Richard O. Mason wrote a classic article on the issues central to this debate—information privacy, accuracy, property, and accessibility—and these issues are still at the forefront of most ethical debates related to how information systems store and process information (see Figure 10.4). Next, we examine each of these issues.

Information Privacy

If you use the Internet regularly, sending e-mail messages and visiting Web sites, you may have felt that your personal privacy is at risk. Several Web sites where you like to shop greet you by name and seem to know which products you are most likely to buy (see Figure 10.6). Every day, the in-box in your browser's mail program is full to overflowing with messages urging you to buy something. As a result, you may feel as though eyes are on you every time you log on to your Internet service provider (ISP). **Information privacy** is concerned with what information an individual should have to reveal to others through the course of employment or through other transactions, such as online shopping.

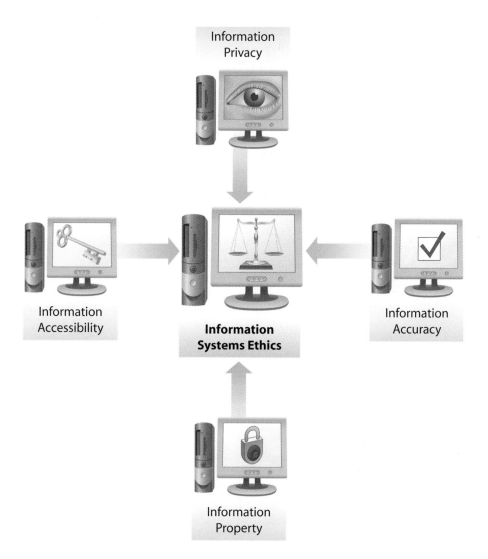

FIGURE 10.4

Information privacy, accuracy, property, and accessibility are central to most ethical concerns about information technology.

Change Agents

Judy McGrath, Chairman and Chief Executive Officer of MTV Networks

When Judy McGrath graduated from Cedar Crest College in Allentown, Pennsylvania, in 1974 with a bachelor's degree in English, her dream was to pursue a career writing about music for *Rolling Stone* magazine. Instead, she took a job writing about food for *Mademoiselle*, a women's magazine—a job she admits she was least qualified to fill. "When they hired me, I was using my oven to store my sweaters," McGrath told writer Jack Myers in May 2005. "I'm the single worst cook on the planet. For years, when our doorbell rang my daughter would yell 'the food's here.' I was in the job for a few months and I turned in a story with a recipe that included 10 pounds of lard, a slight error, so they suggested I move over to fashion. I wasn't much better; I'd wear white shoes with black stockings." But McGrath learned on the job and moved up to the position of senior writer, then moved to *Glamour* as copy chief, where she described her job as editing "stories about models' party tips and why some women like men who don't like women and why."

Four years into her job at *Glamour*, in 1981, two of McGrath's friends told her about a network they were starting called MTV. She was offered a position at the start-up as an on-air promotions writer, and she accepted.

In 1991, McGrath became responsible for all programming, music, production, and promotion at MTV. Two years later, McGrath was promoted to president of the 100-channel MTV network, which includes MTV, MTV2, VH-1, CMT, Nickelodeon, TV Land, Spike TV, Nick at Night, and Comedy Central. Twenty-three years after beginning her career with MTV, in 2004, McGrath became chairman and chief executive officer of MTV Networks.

With McGrath, 53, married and mother of a 10-year-old daughter, at the helm, the MTV Network has evolved from providing only rock-and-roll music to offering a variety of music—from rock-and-roll and heavy metal to rhythm and blues and country—and programming that includes original and sometimes controversial shows, such as *The Jon Stewart Show, The Real World, Beavis and Butthead, The Daily Show,* and, most recently, a U.S.-based 24/7 channel called LOGO, which is devoted to programs about gays and lesbians. MTV Network programming also reflects McGrath's sense of social responsibility, evident in such television campaigns as *Save the Music, Choose or Lose, Rock the Vote,* and *Fight for Your Rights.*

True to her devotion to creativity over political correctness and her belief that music enhances all cultures, McGrath provides the mostly young, antiauthoritarian, often maverick MTV Network employees the freedom and security to express ideas and maintains that controversy doesn't bother her. Rather, she has said, she is "always worried about missing a cultural beat."

FIGURE 10.5

Judy McGrath, chairman and chief executive officer, MTV Networks.

Source: http://www.broadband-accessintel.com/include/magazine/cw/040306/McGrath_Judy.jpg.

Sources: http://www.cnn.com/SPECIALS/2004/global.influentials/stories/mcgrath/
http://www.forbes.com/lists/2005/11/6J9A.html
http://www.mediavillage.com/jmlunch/2005/05/23/lam-05-23-05/

FIGURE 10.6

Amazon.com is famous for personalizing its Web site to individual customers.

Source: http://www.amazon. com.

While the information age has brought widespread access to information, the downside is that others may now have access to personal information that you would prefer to keep private. Personal information, such as Social Security numbers, credit card numbers, medical histories, and even family histories, is now available on the Internet. Using search engines, your friends, co-workers, current or future employers, or even your spouse can find out almost anything that has been posted by or about you on the Internet. For example, it is very easy to locate your personal blog, your most recent party pictures posted on MySpace.com or Facebook, or even sensitive questions you asked in a public discussion forum about drug use or mental health. Moreover, many of such pages are stored in the search engines' long-term cache, so that the stored pages remain accessible for a long time even after they have been taken off the web.

One of the fastest-growing "information" crimes in recent years has been **identity theft**. Identity theft is the stealing of another person's Social Security number, credit card number, and other personal information for the purpose of using the victim's credit rating to borrow money, buy merchandise, and otherwise run up debts that are never repaid. In some cases, thieves even withdraw money directly from victims' bank accounts. Since many government and private organizations keep information about individuals in accessible databases, opportunities abound for thieves to retrieve it. Reclaiming one's identity and restoring a good credit rating can be frustrating and time consuming for victims.

The solution to identity theft lies in the government and private sector working together to change practices used to verify a person's identity. For example, a mother's maiden name and an individual's Social Security number are too easily obtained. Other methods of personal identification, such as biometrics and encryption, may need to be used if the problem is to be solved. Methods of information security—including biometrics and encryption—were discussed in Chapter 6—Securing Information Systems.

Before moving on, it is important to distinguish between unethical behavior and a crime. Identity theft is clearly a crime. However, many "misuses" of computers and information may not be crimes but would be considered unethical by most people. As technology moves forward and allows humans to do things not possible before, existing laws often do not apply to these emerging situations. One of the ongoing debates regarding technological innovations revolves around the question, Just because it is not a crime, does that make it okay to do it?

How to Maintain Your Privacy Online When you make Web purchases, vendors are not required by law to respect your privacy. In other words, a vendor can track what pages you look at, what products you examine in detail, which products you choose to buy, what method of payment you choose to use, and where you have the product delivered. After collecting all that information, unscrupulous vendors can sell it to others, resulting in more direct-mail advertising, electronic spam in your e-mail in-box or calls from telemarketers.

When surveyed about concerns related to online shopping, most consumers list issues of information privacy as a top concern. As a result, governments have pressured vendors to post their privacy policies on their Web sites. Unfortunately, these policies do not often protect the privacy of consumers. To protect yourself, you should always review the privacy policy of all companies you do business with and refuse to do business with those that do not have a clear policy. According to the Consumer Protection Working Group of the American Bar Association at safeshopping.org, a seller's privacy policy should indicate at least the following:

- What information the seller is gathering from you
- How the seller will use this information
- Whether and how you can "opt out" of these practices

To make sure your shopping experience is a good one, you can take a few additional steps to maintain your privacy:

- *Choose Web Sites That Are Monitored by Independent Organizations.* Several independent organizations monitor the privacy and business practices of Web sites (see www.epubliceye.com or www.openratings.com).
- *Avoid Having "Cookies" Left on Your Machine.* Many commercial Web sites leave cookies on your machine so that the owner of the site can monitor where you go and what you do on the site (see Chapter 6). To enhance your privacy, you should carefully manage your browser's cookie settings or get special "cookie management" software (see www.cookiecentral.com).
- *Visit Sites Anonymously.* There are ways to visit Web sites anonymously. Using services provided by companies such as Anonymizer (www.anonymizer.com), you have total privacy from marketers, identity thieves, or even coworkers when surfing the Web.
- *Use Caution When Requesting Confirmation E-Mail.* When you buy products online, many companies will send you a confirming e-mail message to let you know that the order was received correctly. A good strategy is to have a separate e-mail account, such as one that is available for viewing via a Web browser, that you use when making online purchases.

Of course, there are no guarantees that all your online experiences will be problem free, but if you follow the advice provided here, you are much more likely to maintain your privacy.

Avoid Getting Conned in Cyberspace The Internet has fundamentally changed the way consumers gather information, shop, and do business. Unfortunately, con artists and other lawbreakers have gone high tech and are using the Internet to cheat consumers in a number of clever ways. The U.S. Federal Trade Commission has compiled advice on how not to get taken by crafty con artists on the Internet (www.ftc.gov/bcp/conline/pubs/online/dotcons.htm). Among the listed "dot-cons" were offers to let you see adult images in exchange for revealing your credit card number, auction cheats, charges for a "free" Web site appearing on telephone bills, and various investment, travel and vacation, business, and health care products scams (see Table 10.1).

Information Accuracy

The issue of **information accuracy** has become highly charged in today's wired world. Information accuracy is concerned with ensuring the authenticity and fidelity of information as well as with identifying who is responsible for informational errors that harm people. With all the computerization that has taken place, people have come to expect to receive and retrieve information more easily and quickly than ever before. In addition, because computers "never make mistakes," we have come to expect this information to be accurate. A case in point is at the bank. The combination of automated teller machines,

TABLE 10.1 Top Ten List of Dot-Cons from the Federal Trade Commission and Advice on How Not to Get Conned

The Con	The Bait	The Switch	Advice
Internet auctions	Great deals on great products.	After sending money, consumers receive inferior item or nothing at all.	Investigate the seller carefully. Use a credit card or escrow service to pay.
Internet access service	Free money, simply for cashing a check.	After cashing "free" check, consumers are locked into long-term Web service with steep penalties for early cancellation.	Read both sides of the check, the fine print, or any documentation that comes with the check.
Credit card fraud	View online adult images for free, just for sharing your credit card number to "prove" you are over 18.	Fraudulent promoters run up unauthorized charges on consumers' cards.	Share your credit card numbers only when you are buying from a company you trust. Dispute unauthorized charges (federal law limits your liability to $50).
International modem dialing	Free access to adult material by downloading "viewer" or "dialer."	Exorbitant long-distance phone bills as the viewer or dialer reconnects to an international carrier.	Do not download programs providing "free" access without carefully reading all the fine print. Dispute unauthorized charges to your account.
Web cramming	Free custom-designed Web site for 30-day trial.	Telephone is billed even when consumers do not accept offer or agree to continue service.	Review phone bill carefully, and challenge all charges you do not recognize.
Multilevel marketing plans/pyramids	Make money selling products you sell as well as those sold by people you recruit to sell.	Consumers are required to recruit other distributors, but products sold to distributors do not qualify for commissions.	Avoid programs that require you to recruit distributors, buy expensive inventory, or commit to a minimum sales volume.
Travel/vacations	Great trips for bargain prices.	Low-quality accommodations and services, often with hidden charges.	Get references and the details of the trip in writing.
Business opportunities	Be your own boss, and earn a high salary.	Consumers invest in unproven or insecure ventures.	Talk with others who have made the same investment, get all promises in writing and study the contract carefully. Consult with a lawyer or accountant.
Investments	Realize huge investment returns.	Big profits always mean big risks.	Check with state and federal securities and commodities regulators; insist on talking with other investors.
Health-care products/services	Cure serious illness or fatal health problems.	Consumers put faith in unproven solutions and put off pursuing needed health care.	Consult with health professionals to evaluate cure-alls or promises to provide fast or easy cure.

Source: www.ftc.gov/bcp/conline/pubs/online/dotcons.htm.

computerized record systems, and large, electronic client and transaction databases should provide customers with quick and accurate access to their account information. However, we continue to hear about and experience record-keeping errors at banks.

An error of a few dollars in your banking records does not seem significant. However, what if it were an error of hundreds or thousands of dollars in the bank's favor? What if the error caused one of your important payments (such as a home mortgage payment) to bounce? Bank errors can be quite important.

Now, imagine how significant a data accuracy error might be in other settings. Hospitals use similar automation and computer-intensive record keeping. Imagine what would happen if prescription information appeared incorrectly on a patient's chart and the patient became fatally ill as a result of the medicine that was mistakenly dispensed to him. The significance of such a data accuracy error could be tremendous. Furthermore, it would not be clear who was to blame. Would this be the fault of the doctor, the pharmacist, the programmer, the data entry clerk, or maybe some combination of errors by the system designer, the system analyst, the system programmer, the database administrator, and the vendor? It would be too easy simply to blame the computer; some one person would need to be found at fault.

Computer-based information systems and the data within those systems are only as accurate and as useful as they have been made to be. This suggests the need for better precautions and greater scrutiny when modern information systems are designed, built, and used. This means that everyone must be concerned with data integrity, from the design of the system, to the building of the system, to the person who actually enters data into the system, to the people who use and manage the system. Perhaps more important, when data errors are found, people should not blame the computer. After all, people designed it, built it, and entered data into it in the first place.

Wikipedia

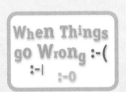

When Things go Wrong :-(

If you have ever researched a paper for a class (and who hasn't?), you undoubtedly used a Web search engine, and you more than likely were referred to Wikipedia, a free online encyclopedia with almost 4 million entries. In Wikipedia, any user can create or edit articles, but if anyone can write entries (called "Wikies," derived from the Hawaiian term "wiki wiki," which means "quick"), you might ask, Are the entries accurate?

A 2006 expert-led study reported in the journal *Nature* compared the accuracy and quality of science articles in Wikipedia with science articles published in the *Encyclopaedia Britannica*. The study found numerous errors in both encyclopedias, but in the 42 science articles compared, differences in accuracy were not alarming. The average number of inaccuracies for science articles in Wikipedia was four, three in *Britannica*.

"I'm pleased," said Jimmy Wales, cofounder of Wikipedia and president of the resource's parent organization, the Wikimedia Foundation of St. Petersburg, Florida, in *Nature*'s report. "Our goal is to get to *Britannica* quality, or better."

In some cases, however, incorrect Wikipedia entries have remained undetected for a while, until they are spotted and a new editor changes them. On other occasions, writers have used the "anyone can edit" feature to input biased information. For example, journalist John Seigenthaler found that he was linked to the assassinations of John and Robert Kennedy in his Wikipedia entry. The entry remained unchanged for over four months, until Seigenthaler alerted Wales.

In another instance, podcasting expert Adam Curry was accused of editing out references to his competitors in his Wikipedia entry. Curry said he had intended only to make the article "more accurate."

In yet another case, entries in the German Wikipedia site were copied from old East German encyclopedias. Not only did this infringe on the encyclopedias' copyrights, but many of the articles were written to conform to Marxist-Leninist ideologies, popular during the socialist regime in East Germany.

One of the most striking cases involving modified Wikipedia entries is currently being investigated by Wikipedia staff, who found that changes to entries about U.S. senators and state representatives were made from Internet addresses originating within the Senate or the House of Representatives. Changes consisted mostly of correcting spelling or grammatical flaws, but, in addition, negative comments were removed or replaced by politicians' campaign material. Clearly, opening up an encyclopedia's editing process to all may not be the best way to ensure accuracy.

Sources: http://www.nature.com/nature/journal/v438/n7070/full/438900a.html
http://www.boston.com/news/globe/ideas/articles/2005/12/18/the_wiki_effect/?page=1
http://www.tgdaily.com/2006/01/31/wikipedia_investigates_congressionaledits/
http://www.dw-world.de/dw/article/0,2144,1796407,00.html

Information Property

It happens to all of us. Nearly every day in the mail, we receive unwanted solicitations from credit card companies, department stores, magazines, or charitable organizations. Many of these envelopes are never opened. We ask the same question over and over again: "How did I get on another mailing list?" Your name, address, and other personal information were most likely sold from one company to another for use in mass mailings. You probably did not give anyone permission to buy or sell information about you, but that is not a legal issue or a matter of concern for some firms. **Information property** focuses on who owns information about individuals and how information can be sold and exchanged.

Data Privacy Statements   Who owns the computerized information about people—the information that is stored in thousands of databases by retailers, credit card companies, and marketing research companies? The answer is that the company that maintains the database of customers or subscribers legally owns the information and is free to sell it. Your name, address, and other information are all legally kept in a company database to be used for the company's future mailings and solicitations. However, the company can sell its customer list or parts of it to other companies who want to send similar mailings. This is where the problems begin. For instance, the apparel retailer The Gap (see Figure 10.7) could sell names and addresses from its customer database to companies looking for a similar customer base or buying pattern. Of course, The Gap would not likely sell parts of its list to competitors (see www.gapinc.com/public/includes/privacy-policy.shtml). Still, many people are concerned that these companies have full ownership of this purchasing and demographic data.

There are limits, however, to what a company can do with such data. For example, if a company stated at one time that its collection of marketing data was to be used strictly internally as a gauge of its own customer base and then sold that data to a second company years later, it would be unethically and illegally breaking its original promise. Companies collect data from credit card purchases (by using a credit card, you indirectly allow this) or from surveys and questionnaires you fill out when applying for a card. They also collect data when you fill in a survey at a bar, restaurant, supermarket, or mall about service quality or product preferences. By providing this information, you implicitly agree that this data can be used as the company wishes (within legal limits, of course).

What is even more problematic is the combination of this survey data with transaction data from your credit card purchases. Using the demographic data (Who am I, and where do I live?) and the psychographic data (What are my tastes and preferences?), companies can create a highly accurate profile of customers. How do you know who is accessing these

FIGURE 10.7

Companies like The Gap have online privacy policies that may or may not protect your personal information.

databases? This is an issue that each company must address at both a strategic/ethical level (Is this something that we should be doing?) and a tactical level (If we do this, what can we do to ensure the security and integrity of the data?). The company needs to ensure proper hiring, training, and supervision of employees who have access to the data and implement the necessary software and hardware security safeguards.

Spam, Cookies, and Spyware In addition to the information you knowingly share with a Web site when purchasing a product, spam, cookies, and spyware are three additional ways that information property about individuals and organizations is being collected and (ab)used on the Internet. *Spam,* discussed in Chapter 6, refers to unsolicited e-mail that promotes a product or service or makes some other type of solicitation. If you have ever signed up for a contest online, filled out a registration form for an Internet service, or even bought a book from Amazon.com, chances are your e-mail address was sold to e-marketers. Although there are federal, state, and international laws related to spam, most notably the CAN-SPAM Act of 2003, very little can be done to stop a motivated spammer (see www.spamlaws.com for more information).

Also described in Chapter 6, a *cookie* is a small text file on your computer that stores information about your Web-browsing activity at a particular site. Although you can choose to not accept the storage of cookies, you may not be able to visit the site, or it may not function properly. For example, to read the *New York Times* online, you must register by entering your name and other information. When you go through the registration process, cookies are stored on your machine. If you don't accept cookies or you delete the stored cookies, you are not allowed to access the online newspaper without reregistering. Similarly, you will have to accept cookies when purchasing from many e-tailers, as most online shopping carts require cookies to function properly. Although the use of cookies is a relatively well known mechanism for "enhancing" your surfing experience, many privacy advocates believe that it is a form of spyware. If you like the personalized touch cookies can provide, or want to be able to shop online, you will have to decide if the subsequent loss of your information property is a fair trade-off.

Spyware is any technology that is used to collect information about a person or organization without their knowledge (again, see Chapter 6). In other words, spyware is software

FIGURE 10.8

Windows Defender is a widely used spyware monitoring and removal tool.

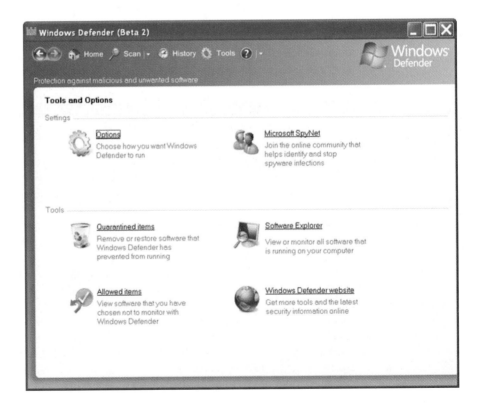

that runs on a person's computer to collect information about the user and to transmit this information to some other party. This collected information is typically used for advertising purposes (often referred to as *adware*), although it can also be used for committing various types of computer crimes. Unfortunately, most privacy advocates feel that it is unlikely that spyware will become illegal or heavily regulated anytime soon. Fortunately, there are many effective tools available to monitor and remove unwanted spyware (see Figure 10.8).

Cybersquatting Another information property issue relates to **cybersquatting**, the dubious practice of registering a domain name, then trying to sell the name for big bucks to the person, company, or organization most likely to want it. Domain names are one of the few scarce resources on the Internet, and victims of cybersquatting include Panasonic, Hertz, Avon, and numerous other companies and individuals. Fortunately, the U.S. government passed the Anti-Cybersquatting Consumer Protection Act in 1999, which made registering, trafficking in, or using a domain name to profit from the goodwill of a trademark belonging to someone else a crime. Fines for cybersquatting can reach as high as $100,000 in addition to the forfeiture of the disputed domain name. As a result, recent court cases have not been kind to squatters. Many feel, however, that it is often much easier simply to pay the cybersquatter because that will likely be much cheaper and faster in the long run than to hire a lawyer and go through the legal process. Others, such as rapper Eminem, who won a case against a company that had registered the domain name eminemmobile.com, use a fast-track procedure of the World Intellectual Property Organization of the United Nations to stop others from using their names without permission. No matter how companies or individuals deal with this problem, valuable resources of time and money will be wasted resolving these disputes.

Information Accessibility

With the rapid increase in online databases containing personal information and the influx in the use of computer-based communication between individuals, who has the right to access and monitor this information has raised many ethical concerns. **Information accessibility** focuses on defining what information a person or organization has the right to obtain about others and how this information can be accessed and used.

For example, almost everyone sends and receives electronic mail, whether or not they have a PC. All that is needed to participate is access to the Internet, whether through a home PC, a school's computer lab, a wireless phone, a handheld computer, or any of several other devices that provide Internet access. E-mail is one of the most popular software applications of all time, and projections are that its use will only continue to increase. That is why e-mail aficionados and privacy groups were chilled when the Federal Bureau of Investigation (FBI) under the Clinton administration demonstrated a software application named Carnivore to telecommunications industry representatives. Carnivore was designed to be connected to the computers of ISPs, where it would lurk undetected by ISP subscribers and eavesdrop on *all* communications delivered by the ISP, including e-mail, instant messaging, chat rooms, and visits to Internet sites. If the FBI detected communications that it decided were threatening, as in, for example, activities of terrorists, members of organized crime groups, and hackers, they could unleash Carnivore (see Figure 10.9).

In 2005, the FBI abandoned Carnivore in favor of commercially available eavesdropping software. Nevertheless, Carnivore and its successors are extremely controversial. The FBI claims that its cyberwiretaps will provide a "surgical ability" to intercept and collect only those communications that are the subject of lawful wiretaps. However, privacy advocates such as Marc Totenberg, director of the Electronic Privacy Information Center, counter that unlike police searches of cars and houses for drugs, these cyberwiretaps will allow "dragnet fishing" while sifting through all traffic on an ISP. Clearly, Carnivore and other eavesdropping technologies will be central to numerous ethical discussions.

Beyond the government's accessing information, recent court cases have not supported computer privacy for employee e-mail transmissions and Internet usage. For example, although most companies provide employees with access to the Internet and

FIGURE 10.9

How Carnivore works.

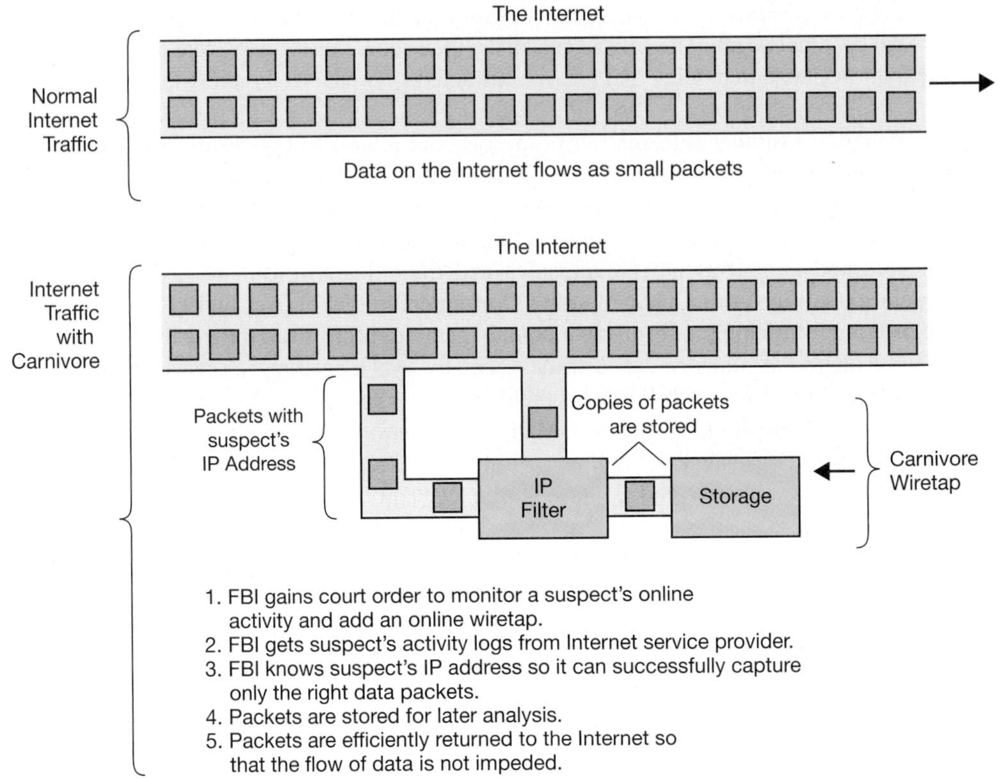
The Internet
Normal Internet Traffic
Data on the Internet flows as small packets
The Internet
Internet Traffic with Carnivore
Packets with suspect's IP Address
Copies of packets are stored
IP Filter
Storage
Carnivore Wiretap
1. FBI gains court order to monitor a suspect's online activity and add an online wiretap.
2. FBI gets suspect's activity logs from Internet service provider.
3. FBI knows suspect's IP address so it can successfully capture only the right data packets.
4. Packets are stored for later analysis.
5. Packets are efficiently returned to the Internet so that the flow of data is not impeded.

other outside e-mail systems, many periodically monitor the e-mail messages that employees send and receive. Monitoring employee behavior is nothing new, and it was to many businesses a natural extension to monitor e-mail messages.

Surprisingly, there is little legal recourse for those who support e-mail privacy. In 1986, Congress passed the Electronic Communications Privacy Act (ECPA), but it offered far stronger support for voice mail than it did for e-mail communications. This act made it much more difficult for anyone (including the government) to eavesdrop on phone conversations. E-mail privacy is, thus, much harder to protect. In addition, no other laws at the federal or state levels protect e-mail privacy. However, some states, most notably California, have passed laws that define how companies should inform their employees of this situation and in which situations monitoring is legal. Even so, this law is more of a guideline for ethical practice than a protection of privacy (Sipior and Ward, 1995).

Fortunately, the ECPA and the court case judgments thus far on e-mail monitoring suggest that companies must be prudent and open about their monitoring of e-mail messages and Internet usage. Companies should use good judgment in monitoring e-mail and should make public their policy about monitoring messages. One primary reason that employees perceive their e-mail to be private is the fact that they are never told otherwise (Weisband and Reinig, 1995). In addition, employees should use e-mail only as appropriate, based on their company's policy and their own ethical standards. Given recent actions and rulings on the capture and usage of e-mail messages over the Internet, it appears that online privacy is in jeopardy, in and out of business organizations. As a general rule, we all need to realize that what we type and send via e-mail in and out of the workplace is likely to be read by others for whom the messages were not intended. It is wise to generate only those e-mail messages that would not embarrass us if they were made public.

Net Stats

Bundled Services

In Rapid City, South Dakota, population 62,000, residents of The Lodge, an apartment complex for senior citizens, receive telephone service, cable television, and Internet connection service from one company—Prairie Wave Telecommunications. Similarly, Comcast, Cox Communications, Time Warner Cable, Sprint, Verizon, and Qwest are among those large companies offering "bundle" telecommunication deals for residents of many metropolitan areas. Most bundle providers advertise that customers can save an average of $150 to $160 a year over the price of individual subscriptions to services.

From the companies' standpoint, states a 2006 article in the *Washington Post,* "the more customers buy in bundles, the less likely they are to switch providers. That's why phone companies such as Verizon Communications Inc. are spending billions of dollars on fiber-optic lines to deliver Internet and television services—so they can lure subscribers from cable providers and wrap them up with full-service packages."

Consumers, on the other hand, are not always happy with the deal. Many buy a telecommunications bundle because the combined price is lower than purchasing each service separately. The downside, however, is that if they decide to drop one service, such as Internet, in favor of another company, it can be difficult and costly. For example, the *Washington Post* article cited here recounted the experience of one family whose first bill for a Verizon bundle totaled $305 and contained fees ($1.71 a minute for long-distance calls) they hadn't expected.

Telecommunications companies see bundled deals as the wave of the future, but the concept may have to be tailored more to the needs of individual households before it dominates the marketplace.

Source: Yuki Nogushi, "No Bundle of Joy," *Washington Post* (March 22, 2006), http://www.washingtonpost.com/wp-dyn/content/article/2006/03/21/AR2006032101734.html

The Need for a Code of Ethical Conduct

Not only has the Internet age found government playing catch-up to pass legislation pertaining to computer crime, privacy, and security, it has also created an ethical conundrum. For instance, the technology exists to rearrange and otherwise change photographs, but is the practice ethical? After all, if photographs no longer reflect absolute reality, how can we trust published images? It may not be illegal for you to "steal" computer time from your school or place of employment to do personal business, but many people would consider this unethical. Is it ethical for companies to compile information about your shopping habits, credit history, and other aspects of your life for the purpose of selling such data to others? Should guidelines be in place to dictate how businesses and others use information and computers? If so, what should the guidelines include, and who should write them? Should there be penalties imposed for those who violate established guidelines? If so, who should enforce such penalties?

Many businesses have devised guidelines for the ethical use of information technology and computer systems, and many computer-related professional groups have also published guidelines for their members. Such organizations include the Assistive Devices Industry Association of Canada, the Association for Computing Machinery, the Australian Computer Society, the Canadian Information Processing Society, the Association of Information Technology Professionals, the Hong Kong Computer Society, the Institute of Electrical and Electronics Engineers, the International Federation for Information Processing, the International Programmers Guild, and the National Society of Professional Engineers.

Most universities and many public school systems have written guidelines for students, faculty, and employees about the ethical use of computers. EduCom, a nonprofit organization of colleges and universities, has developed a policy for ethics in information technology that many universities endorse. In part, the EduCom statement concerning software and intellectual rights says,

> Because electronic information is volatile and easily reproduced, respect for the work and personal expression of others is especially critical in computer environments. Violations of authorial integrity, including plagiarism, invasion of privacy, unauthorized access, and trade secret and copyright violations, may be grounds for sanctions against members of the academic community.

Most organization and school guidelines encourage all system users to act responsibly, ethically, and legally when using computers and to follow accepted rules of online etiquette as well as federal and state laws.

Responsible Computer Use The Computer Ethics Institute is a research, education, and policy study organization with members from the IT-related professions and from academic, corporate, and public policy communities. The group studies how advances in information technology have impacted ethics and corporate and public policy and has issued widely quoted guidelines for the ethical use of computers. The guidelines prohibit the following:

- Using a computer to harm others
- Interfering with other people's computer work
- Snooping in other people's files
- Using a computer to steal
- Using a computer to bear false witness
- Copying or using proprietary software without paying for it
- Using other people's computer resources without authorization or compensation
- Appropriating other people's intellectual output

The guidelines recommend the following:

- Thinking about social consequences of programs you write and systems you design
- Using a computer in ways that show consideration and respect for others

Responsible computer use in the information age includes avoiding the types of behavior mentioned here. As a computer user, when in doubt, you should review the ethical guidelines published by your school, place of employment, and/or professional organization. Some users bent on illegal or unethical behavior are attracted by the anonymity they believe the Internet affords. But the fact is that we leave electronic tracks as we wander through the Web, and some perpetrators have been traced and successfully prosecuted when they thought they had hidden their trails. The fact is, too, that if you post objectionable material on the Internet and people complain about it, your ISP can ask you to remove the material or remove yourself from the service.

Computer Crime

Computer crime is defined as the act of using a computer to commit an illegal act. This broad definition of computer crime can include the following:

- Targeting a computer while committing an offense. For example, someone gains unauthorized entry to a computer system in order to cause damage to the computer system or to the data it contains.
- Using a computer to commit an offense. In such cases, computer users may steal credit card numbers from Web sites or a company's database, skim money from bank accounts, or make unauthorized electronic fund transfers from financial institutions.
- Using computers to support a criminal activity, despite the fact the computers are not actually targeted. For example, drug dealers and other professional criminals may use computers to store records of their illegal transactions.

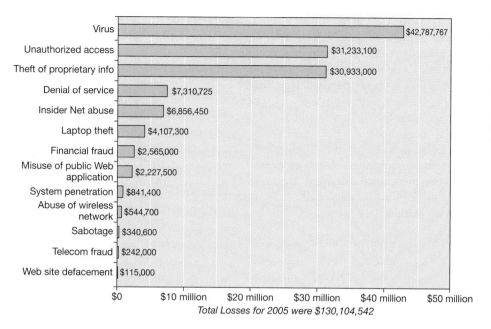

FIGURE 10.10

Type of computer crime and estimated financial losses for 639 respondents from a variety of organizations.

Source: 2006 CSI/FBI Computer Crime and Security Survey, Computer Security Institute.

According to the Computer Security Institute (CSI), the overall trend for computer crime has been declining over the past several years (CSI, 2006). Nevertheless, the reported losses for organizations can be tremendous. For example, a recent CSI survey of 700 individuals from a variety of organizations estimated that the various computer crimes cost their organizations over $130 million (see Figure 10.10). Note that this survey represents only a fraction of actual losses to the world economy, where worldwide losses for computer viruses alone were estimated to exceed $14.2 billion in 2005 (see Figure 10.11). Many organizations do not report incidents of computer crime because of fear that negative publicity could hurt stock value or provide advantages to competitors. Thus, experts believe that many incidents are never reported. It is clear that computer crime is a fact of life. In this section, we briefly introduce this topic of growing importance.

The Computer Access Debate

Traditionally, there have been two sides to the issue of computer access. On one side are liberal civil rights champions, the information industry, communications service providers, and hackers who want to prosecute computer criminals under the law but not prevent the free exchange of information. On the opposing side are privacy advocates, government agencies, law enforcement officials, and businesses that depend on the data stored in

FIGURE 10.11

Financial impact of virus attacks, 1995–2005.

Source: http://www.computereconomics.com/article.cfm?id=1090.

Financial Impact of Virus Attacks 1995–2005

Worldwide Impact (US $)	
2005	$14.2 billion
2004	17.5 billion
2003	13.0 billion
2002	11.1 billion
2001	13.2 billion
2000	17.1 billion
1999	13.0 billion
1998	6.1 billion
1997	3.3 billion
1996	1.8 billion
1995	500 million

computers who take a much stricter position, advocating the free exchange of information *only* among those with authorization for access. Anyone who breaks into a computer is trespassing, they say, and all intruders should be subject to penalties under the law.

In today's information age, however, the debate has expanded, and lines between the two sides may not be as clearly drawn. The global reach of computer networks has raised concern over copyrights, privacy, and security among all user groups. Most computer users now agree that ownership rights of those who create software and other copyrighted materials disseminated over networks must be protected. And when financial or health-related data is collected about individuals and stored on computers, that information should not be freely available to anyone who can retrieve it. Both sides of the information access argument agree that one of the major challenges of the information age will be to protect privacy and security while at the same time allowing authorized access to digitized information.

Unauthorized Computer Access

A person who gains unauthorized access to a computer system has committed a computer crime. Unauthorized access means that the person who has gained entry to a computer system has no authority to use such access. Here are a few additional examples from recent media reports:

- Employees steal time on company computers to do personal business.
- Intruders break into government Web sites and change the information displayed.
- Thieves steal credit card numbers and Social Security numbers from electronic databases, then use the stolen information to charge thousands of dollars in merchandise to victims.

Research conducted by the CSI has also found that the frequency of (successful) attacks on computer systems has been declining (see Figure 10.12). Of the 693 respondents, representing organizations large and small from a variety of industries, "only" 56 percent reported unauthorized computer use in 2005—this is down from a high of 70 percent in 2000. Although computer crime has decreased somewhat, there is increasing demand for more and broader federal and state laws to expressly prohibit various crimes, given the widespread and increasing dependence on computer and networking technologies.

Federal and State Laws

In the United States, there are two main federal laws against computer crime: the Computer Fraud and Abuse Act of 1986 and the Electronic Communications Privacy Act of 1986. The Computer Fraud and Abuse Act of 1986 prohibits the following:

FIGURE 10.12

Unauthorized computer access has been on the decline.

Source: 2005 CSI/FBI Computer Crime and Security Survey, Computer Security Institute.

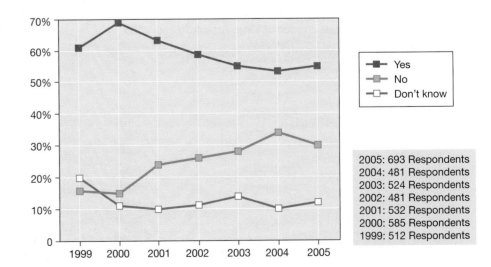

2005: 693 Respondents
2004: 481 Respondents
2003: 524 Respondents
2002: 481 Respondents
2001: 532 Respondents
2000: 585 Respondents
1999: 512 Respondents

■ Stealing or compromising data about national defense, foreign relations, atomic energy, or other restricted information

■ Gaining unauthorized access to computers owned by any agency or department of the U.S. government

■ Violating data belonging to banks or other financial institutions

■ Intercepting or otherwise intruding on communications between states or foreign countries

■ Threatening to damage computer systems in order to extort money or other valuables from persons, businesses, or institutions

In 1996, the Computer Abuse Amendments Act expanded the Computer Fraud and Abuse Act of 1986 to prohibit the dissemination of computer viruses and other harmful code.

The Electronic Communications Privacy Act of 1986 makes it a crime to break into any electronic communications service, including telephone services. It prohibits the interception of any type of electronic communications. Interception, as defined by the law, includes listening in on communications without authorization and recording or otherwise taking the contents of communications. In 2002, however, the U.S. Congress passed the USA PATRIOT Act (Patriot Act) to extend the Computer Fraud and Abuse Act (see also Chapter 5—Enabling Commerce Using the Internet). Under the prior law, investigators could not monitor voice communication—or stored voice communication—when investigating someone suspected of violating the Computer Fraud and Abuse Act. Under the Patriot Act, investigators can gain access to voice-related communications much more easily, and this makes it a very controversial law. What also raises scrutiny is that it was passed 45 days after the September 11, 2001, terrorist attacks with very little debate or public awareness. Civil libertarians feel that the Patriot Act greatly erodes many existing constitutional protections. Although the Patriot Act was scheduled to expire on December 31, 2005, it was initially extended and then reauthorized in March 2006. In this reauthorization, 14 of its 16 provisions were made into permanent law; two are slated to expire in 2010. Given the polarized views regarding the war on terror and the uneasy trade-offs between civil liberty and homeland security, it is likely that the Patriot Act will continue to be hotly debated long into the future.

In addition to the primary laws discussed here, other federal laws may apply to computer crime. Patent laws protect some software and computer hardware, and contract laws may protect trade secrets that are stored on computers. In 1980, the U.S. Copyright Act was amended to include computer software, making it a violation of this act to post online written compositions, photos, sound files, and software without the permission of the copyright holder.

The FBI and the U.S. Secret Service jointly enforce federal computer crime laws. The FBI is in charge when crimes involve espionage, terrorism, banking, organized crime, and threats to national security. The Secret Service investigates crimes against U.S. Treasury Department computers and against computers that contain information protected by the Right to Financial Privacy Act. Information protected by the Financial Privacy Act includes credit card information, credit-reporting information, and data on bank loan applications. In some federal computer crime cases, the U.S. Customs Department, the Commerce Department, or the military may have jurisdiction. In addition to federal laws against computer crime, all 50 states have passed laws prohibiting computer crime. Many foreign countries also have similar laws.

Some violations of state and federal computer crime laws are charged as misdemeanors. These violations are punishable by fines and by not more than one year in prison. Other violations are classified as felonies and are punishable by fines and by more than one year in prison. The Patriot Act converted many misdemeanors into felony-level offenses. Nevertheless, intent can often determine whether crimes are prosecuted as misdemeanors or felonies. If intruders breach computer systems with intent to do harm, they may be charged with a felony. If a break-in is classified as reckless disregard but causes no damage, the offense may be classified as a misdemeanor.

Some critics argue that laws do not go far enough to prosecute computer crimes, while others believe they should not be invoked when systems are breached but no damage is done.

Even the definition of "damage" is debatable. For instance, has damage occurred if someone gains unauthorized access to a computer system but does not steal or change information?

There are additional difficulties in legislating and enforcing laws that affect global networks. Since many countries can be involved when break-ins and other crimes occur, who has jurisdiction? Should e-mail messages be monitored for libelous or other illegal content, and, if so, who should have monitoring responsibility? Is e-mail subject to the same laws as mail delivered by the U.S. Postal Service, or is it more akin to telephone communications and the laws that apply to them?

Computer Forensics

As computer crime has gone mainstream, law enforcement has had to become much more sophisticated in their computer crime investigations. **Computer forensics** is the use of formal investigative techniques to evaluate digital information for judicial review. Most often, computer forensics experts evaluate various types of storage devices to find traces of illegal activity or to gain evidence in related but noncomputer crimes. In fact, in most missing person or murder cases today, investigators immediately want to examine the victim's computer for clues or evidence.

Computer forensics experts are extremely skilled in investigating computer crime. Likewise, many computer criminals are also experts, making the forensics process extremely difficult in some cases. Some criminals, for example, have special "booby-trap" programs running on computers to destroy evidence if someone other than the criminal uses the machine. Using special software tools, computer forensics experts can often restore data that has been deleted from a computer's hard drive. Clearly, computer forensics will continue to evolve as criminals utilize more sophisticated computer-based methods for committing and aiding criminal activities.

Hacking and Cracking

Those individuals who are knowledgeable enough to gain access to computer systems without authorization have long been referred to as **hackers**. The name was first used in the 1960s to describe expert computer users and programmers who were students at the Massachusetts Institute of Technology. They wrote programs for the mainframes they used and freely exchanged information, but they followed unwritten rules against damaging or stealing information belonging to others. They claimed that their motives for roaming freely through computer systems were based entirely on curiosity and the desire to learn as much as possible about computers.

As computer crime became more prevalent and damaging, true hackers—those motivated by curiosity and not by a desire to do harm—objected to use of the term to describe computer criminals. Today, those who break into computer systems with the intention of doing damage or committing a crime are usually called **crackers**. Some computer criminals attempt to break into systems or deface websites to promote political, or ideological goals (such as free speech, human rights, and anti-war campaigns); these hackers are referred to as **hacktivists**.

Types of Computer Criminals and Crimes

Computer crimes are almost as varied as the users who commit them. Some involve the use of a computer to steal money or other assets or to perpetrate a deception for money, such as advertising merchandise for sale on a Web auction site, collecting orders and payment, and then sending either inferior merchandise or no merchandise at all. Other computer crimes involve stealing or altering information. Some of those thieves who steal information or disrupt a computer system have demanded a ransom from victims in exchange for returning the information or repairing the damage. Cyberterrorists have planted destructive programs in computer systems, then threatened to activate them if a ransom is not paid (see more on cyberterrorism later in this chapter). Crimes in the form of electronic vandalism cause damage when offenders plant viruses, cause computer systems to crash, or deny service on a Web site.

Brief Case ⊙

Attacks on the Net

Hacking has changed since a few mainframe-knowledgeable students at the Massachusetts Institute of Technology practiced the art in the 1960s. Personal computers hadn't been invented yet, but these early hackers didn't destroy information, lock up systems, or otherwise disrupt computer operations. They simply enjoyed learning everything they could about computers, and they believed in the free exchange of information.

Unfortunately, that early innocence has been replaced by crackers with a malevolent desire to disrupt networks, hold information and computer systems hostage, or otherwise launch cyberthreats and weapons. Sometimes the motive is simply "look at me, aren't I clever?" Malicious hacking might also be perpetrated for profit, as when a computer-savvy employee is fired, holds a grudge against his employer, and demands a ransom for purloined company data or when a code writer charges for his or her ability to launch a denial of service (DoS) attack. Recall, a DoS attack occurs when electronic intruders deliberately attempt to prevent legitimate users of a service from using that service by flooding a network or server with bogus requests, thereby causing servers to crash and disrupting network traffic (see Chapter 6).

DoS attacks have become popular with cybercriminals in recent years. For instance, in February 2000, five Web giants—Yahoo!, Web retailer Amazon.com, online auction house eBay, discount retailer Buy.com, and CNN Interactive—in two separate incidents were brought down under the weight of tens of thousands of bogus messages. The FBI's National Infrastructure Protection Center investigated, and in 2005, the perpetrator, who had been a teenager using simple hacking tools when the attacks were launched, was sentenced to 18 months in prison. (Under the National Infrastructure Protection Act of 1996, DoS attacks are federal crimes punishable by prison sentences and fines.)

Questions

1. Are computer crime laws tough enough?
2. How can worldwide cooperation be gained to combat computer crime?

Sources: Joseph Lo, "Denial of Service or 'Nuke' Attacks" (March 12, 2005), http://www.irchelp.org/irchelp/nuke/
CNN Archives, "Cyber Attacks Batter Web Heavyweights" (February 9, 2000), http://archives. cnn.com/2000/TECH/computing/02/09/cyber .attacks.01/index.html

---

Use of the Internet has fostered other types of criminal activity, such as the stalking of minors by sexual predators through newsgroups and chat rooms. Those who buy, sell, and distribute pornography have also found in the Internet a new medium for carrying out their activities.

Who Commits Computer Crimes? When you hear the term "cracker" or computer criminal, you might imagine a techno-geek, someone who sits in front of his or her computer all day and night attempting to break the ultra-super-secret security code of one of the most sophisticated computer systems in the world, perhaps a computer for the U.S. military, a Swiss bank, or the Central Intelligence Agency. While this fits the traditional profile for a computer criminal, there is no clear profile today. More and more people have the skills, the tools, and the motives to hack into a computer system. A modern-day computer criminal could be a disgruntled, middle-aged, white-collar worker sitting at a nice desk on the fourteenth floor of the headquarters building of a billion-dollar software manufacturer. Computer criminals have been around for decades. For the most part, we associate hackers and crackers with their pranks and crimes involving security systems and viruses. Nevertheless, hackers and crackers have caused the loss of billions of dollars' worth of stolen goods, repair bills, and lost goodwill with customers.

Studies attempting to categorize computer criminals show that they generally fall into one of four groups. These groups are listed next, from those who commit most infractions to those who commit the fewest number of infractions:

1. Current or former employees who are in a position to steal or otherwise do damage to employers—World Security Corporation reported in 2004 that 85 to 95 percent of theft from businesses was perpetrated internally, while just 5 to 15 percent involved forced entry.

Ethical Dilemma

Ethical Hacking

Some hackers who are skilled in "unauthorized computer access" have found that it makes more economic sense to be paid for their computer skills than to continue to operate outside the law. Marc Maiffret, cofounder of a computer security firm, is a case in point.

Maiffret says he has always been interested in figuring out how things work. When he was small, he took apart various household items to see how they worked, then "tried" to put them back together. He came relatively late to computers, however, getting his first machine when he was 15. "I was very curious to figure out how this machine worked, what made it tick," Maiffret recalls.

Maiffret soon discovered the online hacker culture and was "captivated by their way of thinking." It seemed, Maiffret says, that hackers "were the great thinkers of our society, especially when it comes to pushing the limits and understanding things." The progression for him was to go from "understanding software and systems" to "learning how to make them do things they shouldn't normally do—how to break them."

By the ripe old age of 17, Maiffret knew, through experience, that there were few, if any, computer systems that could keep him out. He had dropped out of high school and was looking for work when he was introduced to Jordanian businessman Firas Bushnaq, then the chief executive officer of eCompany, a software firm. Maiffret offered Bushnaq a deal—if he could break into Bushnaq's corporate network, Bushnaq would hire him as a security expert. Bushnaq agreed, and Maiffret cracked (broke into) eCompany's network in less than an hour. Bushnaq hired Maiffret and taught him how to write commercial software and, perhaps most important, how to run a business.

Today, 24-year-old Maiffret and Bushnaq run their own company, eEye Digital Security. The company finds holes in different types of software for its software-vendor clients. It then devises and sells software to prevent unauthorized visitors from breaching a client's system. "We sell software that can identify all the ways a hacker is able to break into your computer system and network, and we offer preventative information on how to resolve those vulnerabilities," Maiffret sums up. When asked to reveal some of the techniques he uses to discover software vulnerabilities, Maiffret's standard reply is, "I could tell you, but I would have to kill you."

Maiffret's insights into the hacker culture have contributed to his business success. "There is a beautiful subculture that is the computer underground," Maiffret explains, "where differences are accepted far more often than in the 'real' world. It's a different way of thinking, especially in relation to the business world. And nine times out of ten you'll find that the really technical hackers who are the best of the best don't have a lot of formal education."

Maiffret's title at eEye is "Chief Hacking Officer," and the company's Web site address is www.eEye.com. Check out the services offered to see how one "ethical hacker" has found success in the online business world.

While Maiffret has made a success of his security business, most hackers who dream of being recognized for their skills and hired by security firms will be disappointed. For example, the president of Rent-A-Hacker, a security troubleshooting firm headquartered in Boulder, Colorado, has said he rejects job-seeking crackers every day. The company employs hackers, but not for illegal activities, and the chief executive officer of Rent-A-Hacker won't hire anyone with a criminal record. The hackers who haven't been arrested are the true experts, the man maintains, and he has employed nearly 100 of them.

Sources: E-mail interview with Maiffret, 2005

http://www.rent-a-hacker.com/

2. People with technical knowledge who commit business or information sabotage for personal gain.
3. Career criminals who use computers to assist in crimes.
4. Outside crackers simply snooping or hoping to find information of value—Crackers committed an estimated 5,700,000 intrusions during the first half of 2004, but most caused no harm. About 12 percent of cracker attacks cause damage.

Some crackers probe others' computer systems, electronically stored data, or Web sites for fun, for curiosity, or just to prove they can. Others have malicious or financial motives and intend to steal for gain or do other harm. Whatever the motives, discovery, prosecution, fines, and jail terms can result.

Data Diddling, Salami Slicing, and Other Techno-Crimes As long as computers and the data they contain are an integral part of our daily lives, criminals will devise ways to take illegal advantage of the technology. Such crimes cost society billions of dollars annually. (The exact amount can only be estimated since many businesses do not report crimes for fear of losing customers or devaluing the company's stock if the offenses became public.) Over the years, colorful jargon has evolved to label the many types of computer crime, as summarized in Table 10.2. Additionally, technology enables many traditional types of crimes such as harassment (i.e., where individuals with grudges send threatening e-mail, post names and addresses of adversaries on Web sites, and so on) or the victimization of children and adults through stalking and other predatory practices.

Software Piracy

Software developers and marketers want you to buy as many copies of their products as you want, of course. But commercial software vendors do not want you or anyone else to buy one copy, then bootleg additional copies to sell or to give to others. Vendors also take a dim view of companies that buy one copy of a software application, then make many copies to distribute to employees. In fact, the practice is called **software piracy**, and it is illegal.

When you buy commercial software, it is legal for you to make one backup copy for your own use. It is also legal to offer shareware or public domain software for free through bulletin boards and other Web sites. But **warez** peddling—offering stolen proprietary software for free over the Internet—is a crime. ("Warez" is the slang term for such stolen software.)

Both patent and copyright laws can apply to software. Copyright laws covering software include the 1980 Computer Software Copyright Act, a 1992 act that made software piracy a felony, and the 1997 No Electronic Theft (NET) Act, which made copyright infringement a criminal act even when no profit was involved.

Software piracy has become a problem because it is so widespread, costing the commercial software industry billions of dollars a year. The crime is difficult to trace, but some individuals and companies have been successfully prosecuted for pirating software. Many companies are trying to limit software piracy by requiring the users to enter license keys, or verifying the key before allowing the customer to register or update the software. With its new operating system Windows Vista, Microsoft went even further. When a user first installs the software, and on every subsequent update to the operating system, the system attempts to validate itself in order to confirm that the software has been successfully registered. If the software has not been successfully registered, the user will have 30 days to enter a valid license key. After such time, Vista will switch into a *reduced functionality mode,* severely limiting what can be done on the computer. For example, a user will only be able to use the web browser for one hour before being logged off, will not be allowed to use Microsoft Office tools to view or edit documents, and will only receive the most critical security updates. Some view Microsoft's new

TABLE 10.2 Types of Computer Crimes

Type of Crime	Description	Recent Examples
Carding	Stealing credit card information for one's own use or to sell	A carder code-named Smak sells a CD with 100,000 credit card numbers to undercover law enforcement agents.
Cloning	Using scanners to steal wireless transmitter codes for cell phones, then duplicating the phone for illegal use	The practice was so prevalent in New York City in the mid-1990s that the mayor, police commissioner, and a city council member were victims.
Data diddling	Changing electronic data before or after it is entered on computers	A payroll clerk in a large company credits overtime hours to her own account, allowing her to steal hundreds of thousands of dollars from the company and her fellow employees.
Dumpster diving	Scouring wastebaskets and dumpsters for credit card receipts and other information, then using the information illegally or selling it	A young man in California impersonated telephone employees to gain access to equipment. He was so successful that he started his own telephone service before he was caught.
Phishing or spoofing	Attempting to trick financial account and credit card holders into giving away their authorization information, usually by posting false Web sites that duplicate legitimate sites	Many account holders at eBay, the popular auction Web site, were duped by a false Web site into giving up account numbers.
Phreaking	Breaking into telephone systems to make free long-distance calls or for other purposes	Kevin Mitnick, who served prison time in California under computer crime statutes, allegedly impersonated telephone employees to get free telephone service.
Piggybacking or shoulder-surfing	Looking over a person's shoulder while he or she is using an automated teller machine, cell phone, or other device in order to steal access information	At the Port Authority Terminal in New York City, computer fraud officers have often arrested people using binoculars to filch codes from telephone calling cards.
Salami slicing	Stealing small amounts of money from a large number of financial accounts	A bank employee transfers one penny from the balance of thousands of accounts every day and puts the money in an account she has set up for herself. She accumulates hundreds of thousands of dollars before being discovered.
Social engineering or masquerading	Misrepresenting yourself in order steal equipment or to trick others into revealing sensitive information	A person telephones a company employee and says he is working at home and needs certain information. He is lying but has enough genuine information to trick the employee into revealing network passwords. He then cracks the network and downloads proprietary information.
Vishing	Also known as voice phishing; instead of asking users to visit a Web site, asking users to call a fake telephone number and "confirm" their account information	An e-mail asks the recipient to call a phone number to confirm his credit card information. The fake phone number has been set up using VoIP technology, and the caller transfers his information to a scammer located somewhere around the globe, who is then able to run charges on the credit card.

policy as being a bit draconian, while others feel that such aggressive measures are long overdue.

Software Piracy Is a Global Business A major international issue businesses deal with is the willingness (or unwillingness) of governments and individuals to recognize and enforce the ownership of intellectual property—in particular, software copyright. Piracy of software and other technologies is widespread internationally. The Business Software Alliance points to countries such as Vietnam, China, Indonesia, Ukraine, and Russia as those with the highest percentages of illegal software (Business Software Alliance, 2006). In these countries, more than 80 percent of the software used consists of illegal copies. Worldwide losses due to piracy exceeded $34 billion in 2005. Because technology usage varies significantly by region, average piracy levels and dollar losses greatly differ across regions (see Table 10.3).

In addition to being a crime, is software piracy also an ethical problem? Perhaps in part, but business people must acknowledge and deal with other perspectives as well. In part, the problem stems from countries' differing concepts of ownership. Many of the ideas about intellectual property ownership stem from long-standing cultural traditions. For example, the concept of individual ownership of knowledge is traditionally a strange one in many Middle Eastern countries, where knowledge is meant to be shared. Plagiarism does not exist in a country where words belong to everyone. By the same token, piracy does not exist either. This view is gradually changing; the Saudi Arabia Patent Office granted its first patents several years ago, and their piracy rates have plummeted from 79 percent in 1996 to 52 percent in 2005.

In other cases, there are political, social, and economic reasons for piracy. In many other countries, software publishers are simply not catering to the needs of consumers, who often simply do not have the funds to purchase software legitimately. This is true in many areas of South America and other regions with low per capita income. It is particularly true of students and other members of university communities whose needs are critical in some areas.

Other factors leading to piracy or infringement of intellectual property agreements throughout the world include lack of public awareness about the issue, lack of an industrial infrastructure that can produce legitimate software, and the increasingly high demand for computer and other technology products. The United States has repeatedly pressured and threatened other countries accused of pirating. It is interesting to note, however, that despite the fact that few of these cultural and economic explanations are valid in the United States, we lead the world in the sheer volume of illegal software in use. Businesses that operate in glass offices should surely not throw stones.

Computer Viruses and Other Destructive Code

Recently, one of the popular antivirus Web sites reported that 1,400 new pieces of **malware**—short for "malicious software" such as viruses, worms, and Trojan horses—were unleashed on computer users in a single month. *Viruses* are destructive programs that disrupt the normal functioning of computer systems. They differ from other types of malicious code in that they can reproduce themselves. Some viruses are intended to be harmless pranks, but more often they do damage to a computer system by erasing files on the hard drive or by slowing computer processing or otherwise compromising the system.

Viruses are planted in host computers in a number of ways (Figure 10.13). Boot sector viruses attach themselves to that section of a hard disk that lets the user boot up or

TABLE 10.3 Software Piracy Levels and Dollar Losses by Region

Region	Piracy Level	Dollar Loss (million)
North America	22%	7,686
Western Europe	35%	11,838
Asia/Pacific	54%	8,050
Latin America	68%	2,026
Middle East/Africa	57%	1,615
Eastern Europe	69%	3,095
World Wide	35%	34,297

Source: Business Software Alliance (2006).

FIGURE 10.13

How a computer virus is spread.

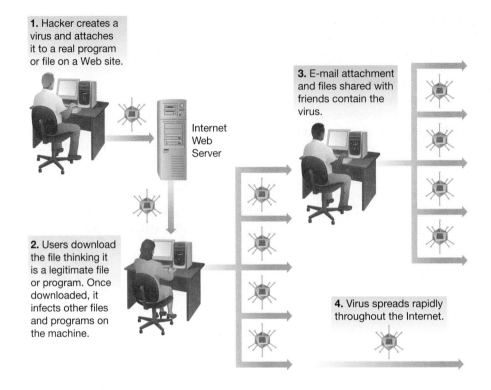

1. Hacker creates a virus and attaches it to a real program or file on a Web site.

2. Users download the file thinking it is a legitimate file or program. Once downloaded, it infects other files and programs on the machine.

Internet Web Server

3. E-mail attachment and files shared with friends contain the virus.

4. Virus spreads rapidly throughout the Internet.

start the computer. They are most often spread through malicious e-mail attachments or file downloads. File infector viruses attach themselves to files with certain extensions, such as .doc or .exe. Some viruses are a combination of boot sector and file infector viruses, and many of these can change in order to fool antivirus programs. Viruses transmitted through e-mail messages became popular in the late 1990s. When an unsuspecting recipient of an e-mail message opens the message or an attachment to the message, the virus is activated. Usually such e-mail viruses can then send copies of themselves to everyone in the victim's address book, thus spreading throughout networked computers at an alarming rate.

Worms, Trojan Horses, and Other Sinister Programs Viruses are among the most virulent forms of computer infections, but other destructive code can also be damaging. A *worm,* for example, usually does not destroy files, but, like a virus, it is designed to copy and send itself, spreading rapidly throughout networked computers. It eventually brings computers to a halt simply by clogging memory space with the outlaw code, thus preventing normal function.

Another destructive program is the **Trojan horse**. Unlike a virus, the Trojan horse does not copy itself, but, like viruses, it can do much damage. When a Trojan horse is planted in a computer, its instructions remain hidden. The computer appears to function normally, but in fact it is performing underlying functions dictated by the intrusive code. For example, under the pretext of playing chess with an unsuspecting systems operator, a cracker group installed a Trojan horse in a Canadian mainframe. While the game appeared to be proceeding normally, the Trojan horse program was sneakily establishing a powerful unauthorized account for the future use of the intruders.

Logic bombs or **time bombs** are variations of Trojan horses. They also do not reproduce themselves and are designed to operate without disrupting normal computer function. Instead, they lie in wait for unsuspecting computer users to perform a triggering operation. Time bombs are set off by specific dates, such as the birthday of a famous person. Logic bombs are set off by certain types of operations, such as entering a specific password or adding or deleting names and other information to and from certain computer files. Disgruntled employees have planted logic and time bombs on being fired, intending for the program to activate after they have left the company. In at least one instance in recent history, a former employee in Minnesota demanded money to deactivate the time bomb he had planted in company computers before it destroyed employee payroll records.

Internet Hoaxes

An **Internet hoax** is a false message circulated online about new viruses; funds for alleged victims of crime or the September 11, 2001, terrorist attacks; kids in trouble; cancer causes; or any other topic of public interest. One especially effective virus hoax that was circulated in 2004 was an e-mail message that told recipients that someone they knew had inadvertently infected their computers with a virus. To rid themselves of the infection, message recipients were told to look for a certain file and delete it, then inform everyone in their address books of the virus. The message was a hoax. The file was a legitimate component of the Microsoft Windows operating system, and people who

Key Enabler

The Liquid Lens

In the last photo you received from a camera phone, was the image poor, at best? That's par for camera phones, but image quality should soon improve as liquid lens technology becomes more widely available. Liquid lenses will let many portable devices take high-resolution images without manufacturers having to increase the size of the lens or the supporting electronics.

To date, two types of liquid lenses have been developed for consumer use:

1. *Varioptic,* a technology company based in France and founded in 2002, developed a lens based on electrowetting—the tendency of water to spread on a substrate. The lens consists of two liquids of equal density sandwiched between two windows in a conical vessel. One liquid is water, which is conductive. The other is oil. The oil acts as a lid, allowing the engineers to work with a fixed volume of water, and provides a measure of stability for the optical axis. The interface between the oil and water will change shape depending on the voltage applied across the conical structure. At 0 volts, the surface is flat, but at 40 volts, the surface of the oil is highly convex, much like the human eye.

2. A second type of lens, called *fluidlens,* is made entirely of water, looks like a contact lens, and can change shape much like the human eye.

These lenses offer several advantages, including no movable parts and therefore more durability, low power consumption, and the potential to be made extremely small. An additional advantage to both lenses is that the optical quality of liquids is better than plastic or glass, so that when they are used in camera phones and digital cameras, higher quality images can be produced. Furthermore, liquid lenses have the advantage of being very durable; they literally cannot be dented or scratched.

Liquid lens technology lets designers integrate smaller and smaller lenses into a wide array of products. Accordingly, other industries, such as automobile manufacturers and medicine, are interested in adapting the liquid lens to their products.

Sources: Louis Frenzel, "Liquid Lens Focuses On Low Cost and Power," *Electronic Design* (October 12, 2006), http://www.elecdesign.com/Articles/Index.cfm?AD=1&ArticleID=13608

William Chee, "New Patented Lens Made of Liquid Paves Way for Slimmer Digital Cameras," *RealTechNews* (August 17, 2005), http://www.realtechnews.com/posts/1670

received the hoax message deleted it and told others to delete it also. Fortunately, the file was not crucial to the Windows operating system, and most computer operators who deleted it did not suffer any consequences. The message functioned as a virus in that unsuspecting recipients quickly passed it along and recipients themselves destroyed files on hard drives.

In most cases, the consequences will be small, and your friends will just ridicule you for passing on a hoax; in other cases, spammers might "harvest" e-mail addresses from hoaxes, potentially causing your inbox to be flooded with junk mail. Several Web sites such as Hoaxbusters (hoaxbusters.ciac.org), Symantec, or McAfee publish lists of known hoaxes, and you should always check to see if a message is a hoax before you forward it to others.

Cyberwar and Cyberterrorism

Over the past several years, individual computer criminals have caused billions of dollars in losses through the use of viruses, worms, and unauthorized access to computers. In the future, many believe that coordinated efforts by national governments or terrorist groups have the potential to do hundreds of billions of dollars in damage as well as put the lives of countless people at stake (Panko, 2007). Most experts believe that cyberwar and cyberterrorism are imminent threats to the United States and other technologically advanced countries. A major attack that cripples a country's information infrastructure or power grid or even the global Internet could have devastating implications for a country's (or the world's) economic system and make transportation systems, medical capabilities, and other key infrastructure extremely vulnerable to disaster.

Cyberwar

Cyberwar refers to an organized attempt by a country's military to disrupt or destroy the information and communication systems of another country. Cyberwar is often executed simultaneously with traditional methods to quickly dissipate the capabilities of an enemy. Given that the United States and the NATO alliance is the most technologically sophisticated war machine in the world—and also the most dependent on its networking and computing infrastructure—it is also the most vulnerable to a cyberwar (or cyberterrorism) attack.

Cyberwar Vulnerabilities The goal of cyberwar is to turn the balance of information and knowledge in one's favor in order to diminish an opponent's capabilities and to also enhance those of the attacker. Cyberwar will utilize a diverse range of technologies, including software, hardware, and networking technologies, to gain an information advantage over an opponent. These technologies will be used to electronically blind, jam, deceive, overload, and intrude into an enemy's computing and networking capabilities in order to diminish various capabilities, including the following:

- Command and control systems
- Intelligence collection and distribution systems
- Information processing and distribution systems
- Tactical communication systems and methods
- Troop and weapon positioning systems
- Friend-or-foe identification systems
- Smart weapons systems

Additionally, controlling the content and distribution of propaganda and information to an opponent's civilians, troops, and government is a key part of a cyberwar strategy. One of the big challenges for governments moving forward will be to fully integrate a cyberwar strategy with overall fighting capabilities.

Cyberterrorism

Unlike cyberwar, **cyberterrorism** is launched not by governments but by individuals and organized groups. Cyberterrorism is the use of computer and networking technologies against persons or property to intimidate or coerce governments, civilians, or any segment of society in order to attain political, religious, or ideological goals. One of the great fears about cyberterrorism is that an attack can be launched from a computer anywhere in the world—no borders have to be crossed, no bombs smuggled and placed, and no lives lost in making the attack. Because computers and networking systems control power plants, telephone systems, and transportation systems, as well as water and oil pipelines, any disruptions in these systems could cause loss of life or widespread chaos (Volonino and Robinson, 2004). Just as physical terrorist attacks have physical and psychological effects, so also do cyberattacks. Dealing with the unknown—where, when, and how—of an indiscriminant terrorist attack is what leads to "terror."

What Kinds of Attacks Are Considered Cyberterrorism? Cyberterrorism could involve physical destruction of computer systems or acts that destroy economic stability or infrastructure. Cyberterrorist acts could likely damage the machines that control traffic lights, power plants, dams, or airline traffic in order to create fear and panic. Attacks launched in cyberspace could take many forms, such as viruses, denial of service, destruction of government computers, stealing classified files, altering Web page content, deleting or corrupting vital information, disrupting media broadcasts, and otherwise interrupting the flow of information. Table 10.4 summarizes several categories of attacks that experts believe cyberterrorists will try to deliver.

The goal of cyberterrorists is to cause fear, panic, and destruction. Through the power of computer technology and global networks, terrorists can gain access to critical parts of the world's infrastructure to produce both physical and virtual terror. Given the great potential for cyberterrorism, many experts believe that it will, unfortunately, become the weapon of choice for the world's most sophisticated terrorists.

How the Internet Is Changing the Business Processes of Terrorists Virtually all modern terrorist groups utilize the Internet (Weimann, 2006). Beyond using the Internet to wage cyberattacks, the Internet is a powerful tool for improving and streamlining the

TABLE 10.4 Categories of Potential Cyberterrorist Attacks

Category	Description
Coordinated bomb attacks	A number of devices—from small explosive devices to large weapons of mass destruction—that communicate with each other through the Internet or cellular phone network and are made to simultaneously detonate if one device stops communicating with the others
Manipulation of financial and banking information	To disrupt the flow of financial information with the objective of causing fear and lack of confidence in the world's or a country's financial system
Manipulation of the pharmacological industry	To make hard-to-detect changes in the formulas of medications in order to cause fear and lack of confidence in this important industry
Manipulation of transportation control systems	To disrupt airline and railroad transportation systems, possibly leading to disastrous collisions
Manipulation of the broader civilian infrastructures	To compromise the communication, broadcast media, gas lines, water systems, and electrical grids in order to cause panic and fear within the population
Manipulation of nuclear power plants	To disrupt cooling systems in order to cause a meltdown that would disperse radiation

TABLE 10.5 How Terrorists Are Using the Internet

Use	Description
Information dissemination	Web sites are developed to disseminate propaganda to current and potential supporters, to influence international public opinion, and to notify potential enemies of pending plans.
Data mining	The vast amount of information available on the Internet regarding virtually any topic aids in planning, recruitment, and numerous other endeavors.
Fund-raising	Web sites for bogus charities and nongovernmental organizations to raise funds and transfer currencies around the world.
Recruiting and mobilization	Groups can utilize Web sites to provide information for recruiting new members as well as utilizing more interactive Internet technologies, such as roaming online chat rooms and cybercafés for receptive individuals.
Networking	The Internet has enabled a less hierarchical, cell-based organizational structure that is much more difficult to combat; networking capabilities also allow different groups, with common enemies, to better share and coordinate information.
Information sharing	As events occur, the Internet provides a powerful tool for announcing events as well as sharing best practices; for example, the official Hamas Web site details how to make homemade poisons and gases.
Planning and coordinating	The communication and information dissemination capabilities ease the difficulty of designing and executing plans.
Information gathering	The use of mapping software such as Google Earth to locate potential targets for terrorist attacks.
Location monitoring	The use of public web cams to monitor and study potential attack sites (e.g., Times Square or public resources such as tunnels or power generation facilities).

business processes of the modern terrorist (see Table 10.5). Just as the Internet has fueled globalization for organizations and societies, it too has fueled global terrorism. Clearly, the Internet is transforming the "business processes" of the modern terrorist.

Assessing the Cyberterrorism Threat Some experts claim that because of the general openness of access, the Internet infrastructure is vulnerable to cyberterrorism, and such incidents are often cited by the media. For example, in a January 2000 article for *Blueprint Magazine*, "Get Ready for Cyberwar," author Sam Nunn reported the following:

- In a 1997 operation called *Eligible Receiver*, the U.S. government hired 35 hackers to test the nation's vulnerability to cyberattacks. The attackers, dubbed "Red Team," quickly obtained access to 36 of the Department of Defense's 40,000 networks. They determined that they could have shut down large segments of the nation's power grid and disrupted communications of the Pacific Command in Honolulu.
- In another systems vulnerability probe, the Defense Information Systems Agency followed the results of some 38,000 deliberate attacks. Only 5 percent of the systems administrators realized they were under attack, and only 4 percent of those reported the attacks to a higher authority.

The U.S. Department of Defense, a popular target for hackers and crackers, reported in late 2004 that it receives some 60 to 90 attacks by unauthorized intruders daily. While the majority of such attacks have not done damage, a few were alarmingly successful:

- During the Gulf War in 1991, a group of Dutch crackers stole electronic information about U.S. troop movements and offered it for sale to Iraq. The Iraqis turned down the offer, thinking it was a hoax.

- In 1998, a 20-year-old Israeli cracker, Ehud Tennebaum, also known as "The Analyzer," joined two crackers in California to disrupt U.S. troop movements by disabling computers at the Pentagon, the National Security Agency, and national labs.
- In 1999, crackers allegedly gained control of a British military communication satellite and held it for ransom. The British military denied that the satellite had ever been under the control of intruders.
- Also in 1999, during the Serbia/Kosovo war, Serb crackers allegedly gained access to NATO Web pages and flooded e-mail accounts with pro-Serb messages.
- During the 2000 presidential election in the United States, Web attacks were reported that involved intruders with various political motives. Information was changed on targeted Web sites, snooping on political sites was rampant, and many denial of service attacks were launched.
- In May 2003, Romanian crackers compromised systems that housed life support control for 58 scientists and contractors in Antarctica. FBI agents assisted in the arrest of the crackers who attempted to extort money from the research station.

While defense and security departments within the United States need to protect against cyberterrorism, the U.S. military has also researched methods of using information technology to its advantage in times of war. For example, the United States reportedly conducted its first cyberwar campaign during the 78-day Serbia/Kosovo war by establishing a team of information warriors to support its bombing campaign against Serbia. The U.S. information operation cell electronically attacked Serbia's critical networks and command and control systems.

While cyberterrorism obviously remains a threat to computer and network security, some experts point out that there are disadvantages to using acts of cyberterrorism as a weapon, including the following:

1. Computer systems and networks are complex, so cyberattacks are difficult to control and may not achieve the desired destruction as effectively as physical weapons.
2. Computer systems and networks change and security measures improve, so it requires an ever-increasing level of knowledge and expertise on the part of intruders for cyberattacks to be effective. This means that perpetrators will be required to continuously study and hone their skills as older methods of attack no longer work.
3. Cyberattacks rarely cause physical harm to victims; therefore, there is less drama and emotional appeal for perpetrators than using conventional weapons.

While cyberterrorism and cyberwar may be methods of choice for future generations with advanced computer knowledge, experts are hopeful that the increasing sophistication of computer security measures will help reduce the number of such incidents.

The Globalization of Terrorism With the proliferation and dependence on technology increasing at an astronomical rate, the threat of cyberterrorism will continue to increase. As has been true with virtually all governments and business organizations, fueled by the digitization of information and the Internet, terrorism has become a global business. To be adequately prepared, national governments along with industry partners must design coordinated responses to various attack scenarios. In addition to greater cooperation and preparedness, governments must improve their intelligence-gathering capabilities so that potential attacks are thwarted before they begin. Industry must also be given incentives to secure their information resources so that losses and disruptions in operations are minimized. International laws and treaties must rapidly evolve to reflect the realities of cyberterrorism, where attacks can be launched from anywhere in the world, to anywhere in the world. Fortunately, experts believe that the likelihood of a devastating attack that causes significant disruption in the major U.S. infrastructure systems is quite low because the attackers would need "$200 million, intelligence information, and years of preparation" to succeed (Volonino and Robinson, 2004). Nevertheless, small attacks have been occurring for years and are likely to increase in frequency and severity—even a "small" attack, like an individual suicide bomber, can cause tremendous chaos to a society. Clearly, there are great challenges ahead.

Industry Analysis

Cybercops Track Cybercriminals

The CSI (crime scene investigation) television shows have made "DNA testing" a household phrase. Virtually everyone knows that a criminal who leaves body cells or fluids—hair and skin cells, saliva, blood, semen, and so on—at the scene of a crime can be linked to the crime through DNA analysis. (DNA, or deoxyribonucleic acid, is present in all living tissue—plant or animal.) The CSI shows have helped to illustrate that just as crime laboratories have had to keep technologically current, so, too, have law enforcement officers at national, state, and local levels.

Because technological advancement has been rapid, law enforcement has lagged behind, but it is catching up. At the federal level, the Computer Crime and Intellectual Property Section within the Justice Department is devoted to combating cybercrime. In addition, the FBI has created computer crime squads in 16 metropolitan areas around the country specifically to investigate cybercrime. In Washington, D.C., the FBI's National Infrastructure Protection Center acts as a clearinghouse for information and expertise relating to cybercrime. And each federal judicial district has at least one assistant U.S. attorney, called a computer and telecommunications crime coordinator, who has received special training in how to investigate and prosecute cybercrime.

Furthermore, every state now has a computer crime investigation unit available as a resource to local law enforcement agencies, and many municipal police departments have their own computer crime investigative units.

Software tools available to law enforcement agencies have also improved. Programs such as the Software Forensic Tool Kit provide police with the ability to search and re-create deleted files on computers. Also digitized for law enforcement use are criminal identification systems, such as the Statewide Network of Agency Photos (SNAP). Law enforcement officers can search SNAP's digital database for mug shots that show a criminal's distinguishing marks, such as scars and tattoos, making criminal identification simpler. SNAP is connected to the Automatic Fingerprint Identification Systems, which electronically transmits fingerprints at the time a person is arrested.

Similarly, the Classification System for Serial Criminal Patterns, developed by the Chicago Police Department, allows detectives to look for possible patterns connecting crimes.

Radio communication has also been updated to provide a secure means of voice communication for law enforcement officers. No longer can any interested civilian buy a receiver and monitor police calls since digitalized voice communication can now be encrypted, allowing for a higher level of security.

It's an unfortunate fact that criminals have discovered how to use the Internet to their advantage. Clearly, however, law enforcement is gaining on them as officers also use technological advancement to track, arrest, and prosecute cybercriminals.

Questions

1. Today, is it harder or easier to be a criminal? Why?
2. Argue whether law enforcement can or cannot ever get ahead of criminals.

Sources: http://www.nlectc.org/justnetnews/weeklynews. html#story11

http://www.usdoj.gov/criminal/cybercrime/AGCPPSI.htm

Key Points Review

1. *Describe the advent of the information age and how computer ethics impacts the use of information systems.* The information age refers to a time in the history of civilization when information became the currency of the realm. Being successful in many careers today requires that people be computer literate since the ability to access and effectively operate computing technology is a key part of many careers. A digital divide is said to exist between people who are computer literate and those who are not. Because computer literacy is so critical in the information age, a major ethical concern for society centers on who is computer literate and who is not.

2. *Discuss the ethical concerns associated with information privacy, accuracy, property, and accessibility.* Information privacy is concerned with what information an individual should have to reveal to others through the course of employment or through other transactions, such as online shopping. Ensuring authenticity and fidelity of information, as well as identifying who is responsible for informational errors that harm people, is information accuracy. Information property focuses on who owns information about individuals and how information can be sold and exchanged. To define what information a person or organization has the right to obtain about others and how this information can be accessed and used is information accessibility. While the information age has brought widespread access to information, the downside is that others may now have access to personal information that you would prefer to keep private. Because there are few safeguards for ensuring the accuracy of information, individuals and companies can be damaged by informational errors. Additionally, because information is so easy to exchange and modify, information ownership violations readily occur. Likewise, with the rapid increase in online databases containing personal information and the increase in the use of computer-based communication between individuals, who

has the right to access and monitor this information has raised many ethical concerns.

3. *Define computer crime and list several types of computer crime.* Computer crime is defined as the act of using a computer to commit an illegal act, such as targeting a computer while committing an offense, using a computer to commit an offense, or using computers in the course of a criminal activity. A person who gains unauthorized access to a computer system has also committed a computer crime. Those individuals who are knowledgeable enough to gain access to computer systems without authorization have long been referred to as hackers. Today, those who break into computer systems with the intention of doing damage or committing a crime are usually called crackers. Hackers and crackers can commit a wide variety of computer crimes, including data diddling, salami slicing, phreaking, cloning, carding, piggybacking or shoulder-surfing, social engineering and masquerading, dumpster diving, and spoofing. Crackers are also associated with the making and distributing of computer viruses and other destructive codes. Finally, making illegal copies of software, a worldwide computer crime, is called software piracy.

4. *Describe and explain the differences between cyberwar and cyberterrorism.* Cyberwar refers to an organized attempt by a country's military to disrupt or destroy the information and communication systems of another country. The goal of cyberwar is to turn the balance of information and knowledge in one's favor in order to diminish an opponent's capabilities and also to enhance those of the attacker. Cyberterrorism is the use of computer and networking technologies by individuals and organized groups against persons or property to intimidate or coerce governments, civilians, or any segment of society to attain political, religious, or ideological goals. Now that terrorist groups are increasingly using the Internet for their purposes, one of the great fears about cyberterrorism is that an attack can be launched from a computer anywhere in the world.

Key Terms

carding 430	cybersquatting 419	hacktivists 426
cloning 430	cyberterrorism 435	identity theft 413
computer crime 422	cyberwar 434	information accessibility 419
computer ethics 411	data diddling 430	information accuracy 414
computer forensics 426	digital divide 410	information age 409
computer literacy 409	dumpster diving 430	information privacy 411
crackers 426	hackers 426	information property 417

Review Questions

1. Describe the advent of the information age and how computer ethics impacts the use of information systems.
2. What is the difference between the digital divide and computer literacy?
3. Compare and contrast information accuracy, information privacy, and information property.
4. Compare and contrast a worm, a virus, a Trojan horse, and a logic or time bomb.
5. List five dot-cons that you find interesting and give the advice suggested for avoiding these traps.
6. What is identity theft, and what is the solution according to this chapter?
7. Define cybersquatting. What year did the U.S. government pass legislation to deter this action, and what is the name of the act?
8. Define computer crime and list several types of computer crime.
9. Explain the purpose of the Computer Fraud and Abuse Act of 1986 and the Electronic Communications Privacy Act of 1986.
10. Define unauthorized access and give several examples from recent media reports.
11. Viruses that are spread via e-mail transmitted over the Internet are also frequently in the news. What are five ways to prevent these viruses?
12. Define and contrast cyberwar and cyberterrorism.

Self-Study Questions

Visit the Interactive Study Guide on the text Web site for additional Self-Study Questions: **www.prenhall.com/jessup**.

1. Being _____, or knowing how to use the computer as a device to gather, store, organize, and process information, can open up myriad sources of information.
   A. technology illiterate
   B. digitally divided
   C. computer literate
   D. computer illiterate
2. A broad definition of computer crime includes all of the following except _____.
   A. targeting a computer while committing an offense
   B. using computers in the course of a criminal activity, despite the fact the computers are not actually targeted
   C. using a computer to commit a legal act
   D. using a computer to commit an offense
3. _____ focuses on defining what information a person or organization has the right to obtain about others and how this information can be accessed and used.
   A. information accessibility
   B. information accuracy
   C. information privacy
   D. information property
4. The Computer Ethics Institute is a research, education, and policy study organization with members from the IT professions and from academic, corporate, and public policy communities. The guidelines prohibit all of the following except _____
   A. using a computer to harm others
   B. using a computer to bear false witness
   C. copying or using proprietary software without paying for it
   D. using computer resources with authorization
5. In the United States, two main federal laws have been passed against computer crime, including _____.
   A. the Computer Fraud and Abuse Act of 1986
   B. the Electronic Communications Privacy Act of 1986
   C. the E-Commerce Internet Act of 1996
   D. A and B
6. Those individuals who break into computer systems with the intention of doing damage or committing a crime are usually called _____.
   A. hackers
   B. crackers
   C. computer geniuses
   D. computer operatives
7. Which of the following copyright laws is applicable to illegal software piracy?
   A. the 1980 Computer Software Copyright Act
   B. a 1992 act that made software piracy a felony
   C. the 1997 No Electronic Theft (NET) Act, which made copyright infringement a criminal act even when no profit was involved
   D. all of the above

8. The use of computer and networking technologies by individuals and organized groups against persons or property to intimidate or coerce governments, civilians, or any segment of society in order to attain political, religious, or ideological goals is known as _____.
   A. cyberwar
   B. cybercrime
   C. cyberterrorism
   D. none of the above

9. The use of formal investigative techniques to evaluate digital information for judicial review.
   A. Data diddling
   B. Computer ethics

C. Computer forensics
D. Warez

10. Crimes committed against telephone company computers with the goal of making free long-distance calls, impersonating directory assistance or other operator services, diverting calls to numbers of the perpetrator's choice, or otherwise disrupting telephone service for subscribers is called _____.
    A. phreaking
    B. cloning
    C. carding
    D. data diddling

Answers are on page 443.

Problems and Exercises

1. Match the following terms with the appropriate definitions:
   i. Digital divide
   ii. Information privacy
   iii. Cyberwar
   iv. Information accuracy
   v. Shoulder-surfing
   vi. Identity theft
   vii. Information accessibility
   viii. Worm
   ix. Computer ethics
   x. Social engineering

   a. The stealing of another person's Social Security number, credit card number, and other personal information for the purpose of using the victim's credit rating to borrow money, buy merchandise, and otherwise run up debts that are never repaid

   b. An area concerned with what information an individual should have to reveal to others through the course of employment or through other transactions, such as online shopping

   c. The gap between those individuals in our society who are computer literate and have access to information resources such as the Internet and those who do not

   d. Code that usually does not destroy files but, like a virus, is designed to copy and send itself, spreading rapidly throughout networked computers and eventually bringing computers to a halt simply by clogging memory space with the outlaw code, thus preventing normal functioning

   e. An area concerned with ensuring the authenticity and fidelity of information as well as identifying who is responsible for informational errors that harm people

   f. Focuses on defining what information a person or organization has the right to obtain about others and how this information can be accessed and used

   g. The issues and standards of conduct as they pertain to the use of information systems

   h. Gaining information needed to access computers by tricking company employees by means of posing as magazine journalists, telephone company employees, and forgetful coworkers in order to persuade honest employees to reveal passwords and other information

   i. The act of simply standing in line behind a card user at an automated teller machine, looking over that person's shoulder, and memorizing the card's personal identification number and then placing the stolen number on a counterfeit access card and using it to withdraw cash from the victim's account

   j. An organized attempt by a country's military to disrupt or destroy the information and communication systems of another country

2. The Electronic Frontier Foundation (www.eff.org) has a mission of protecting rights and promoting freedom in the "electronic frontier." The organization provides additional advice on how to protect your online privacy. Review its suggestions and provide a summary of what you can do to protect yourself.

3. In some cases, individuals engage in cybersquatting in the hope of being able to sell the domain names to companies at a high price; in other cases, companies engage in cybersquatting by registering domain names that are very similar to their competitors' product names in order to generate traffic from people misspelling Web addresses. Would you differentiate between these practices? Why or why not? If so, where would you draw the boundaries?

4. Do you consider yourself computer literate? Do you know of any friends or relatives who are not computer literate? What can you do to improve your computer literacy? Is computer literacy necessary in today's job market? Why or why not?

5. Look at the following Web sites for tips and articles on identity theft: www.consumer.gov/idtheft/ and www.identitytheft.org/. Did you find anything that you think might help you in the future? Did you bookmark any of these tips or e-mail them to your classmates or friends?

6. Complete the computer ethics quiz at web.cs.bgsu.edu/maner/xxicee/html/welcome.htm and visit online-ethics.org/cases/robot/robot.html for more issues on computer ethics and social implications of computing. Should ethical codes apply to all professions?

7. Find your school's guidelines for ethical computer use on the Internet and answer the following questions: Are there limitations as to the type of Web sites and material that can be viewed (e.g., pornography)? Are students allowed to change the programs on the hard drives of the lab computers or download software for their own use? Are there rules governing personal use of computers and e-mail?

8. Do you believe that there is a need for a unified information systems code of ethics? Visit www.albion.com/netiquette/corerules.html. What do you think of this code? Should it be expanded, or is it too general? Search the Internet for additional codes for programmers or Web developers. What did you find?

9. Visit the Consumer Sentinel (www.consumer.gov/sentinel/) to learn about how law enforcement agencies around the world work together to fight consumer fraud. The site contains statistics on consumer complaints and sorts this data in many interesting ways. Prepare a report using the most current data on the top five complaint categories.

10. Choose an organization with which you are familiar. Determine what the company's computer ethics policy is by obtaining a written copy and reviewing it. In addition, asking questions and observing several employees may provide insight into the actual application. Does this organization adhere to a strict or casual ethics policy? Prepare a 10-minute presentation to the rest of the class on your findings.

11. Visit www.safeshopping.org and prepare a summary of its top 10 safe online shopping tips. Did you find these tips useful enough to share with a friend or classmate? Did you bookmark the site or e-mail it to a friend?

12. To learn more about protecting your privacy, visit www.cookiecentral.com, www.epubliceye.com, and www.openratings.com. Did you learn something that will help protect your privacy? Why is privacy more important than ever?

13. Should laws be passed to make spam a crime? If so, how should lawmakers deal with First Amendment rights? How would such laws be enforced?

14. Do you think that educational institutions should be allowed to monitor e-mail sent and received on school computers? Why or why not? Do you think that any e-mail messages sent or received over a computer at work should be considered company property? Why or why not?

15. Do you feel the media generate too much hype regarding hackers and crackers? Since companies such as Microsoft have been hacked into, are you concerned about your bank account or other sensitive information?

16. Review Table 10.1's list of dot-cons from the Federal Trade Commission. Have any suspicious groups contacted you or any of your friends or classmates?

17. Identity theft is a new type of theft. Visit www.fraud.org to find ways to protect yourself. Search the Internet for additional sources that provide information on identity theft and make a list of other ways to safeguard against it. What are some of the losses in addition to stolen documents and additional bills to pay that may result from identity theft?

18. Search the Internet for information about the damaging effects of software piracy and/or look at the following Web sites: www.bsa.org and www.microsoft.com/piracy. Is software piracy a global problem? What can you do to mitigate the problem? Prepare a short presentation to present to the class.

19. Check one or more of the following Web sites to see which hoaxes are currently circulating online: hoaxbusters.ciac.org, www.truthorfiction.com, or vmyths.com/news.cfm. What are five popular hoaxes now circulating online?

20. What laws should be enacted to combat cyberterrorism? How could such laws be enforced?

Application Exercises

 The existing data files referenced in these exercises are available on the Student Companion Web site: **www.prenhall.com/jessup**.

 Spreadsheet Application: Analyzing Ethical Concerns at Campus Travel

Because of the employees' increased use of IT resources for private purposes at Campus Travel, you have announced that a new IT use policy will be implemented. You have set up a Web site for the employees to provide feedback to the proposed changes; the results of this survey are stored in the file EthicsSurvey.csv. Your boss wants to use the survey results to find out what the greatest concerns in terms of ethical implications are for the employees, so you are asked to do the following:

1. Complete the spreadsheet to include descriptive statistics (mean, standard deviation, mode, minimum, maximum, and range) for each survey item. Use formulas

to calculate all statistics for the responses to the individual questions

(Hint: In Microsoft Excel, you can look up the necessary formulas in the category "Statistical.")

2. Provide a graph highlighting the means of the different items.

Make sure to professionally format the pages before printing them out.

Database Application: Tracking Software Licenses at Campus Travel

Recently, you have taken on the position of an IS manager at Campus Travel. In your second week at work, you realize that many of the software licenses are about to expire or have already expired. As you know about the legal and ethical implications of unlicensed software, you have decided to set up a software asset management system that lets you keep track of the software licenses. You have already set up a database and stored some of the information, but you want to make the system more user friendly. Using the SWLicenses.mdb database, design a form to input the following information for new software products:

- Software title
- Installation location (office)
- License number
- Expiration date

Furthermore, design a report displaying all software licenses and expiration dates (sorted by expiration dates)

(Hint: In Microsoft Access, use the form and reports wizard to create the form).

Team Work Exercise: Making Copies of Programs, Games, Music, and Videos

Have you ever gone to a friend's house with a blank CD or DVD and copied a program, a game, music, or a movie? Has anyone offered to give you a "free" copy of a program or game? Discuss the possible reasons for and against doing this with your team members. What would be the arguments of an open-source software proponent? Now that you have read this chapter, how do you feel about making an illegal copy of such items? Is it okay to let someone else copy your programs, games, music, or movies as long as your own copies are not pirated? If you had an illegal copy of your favorite musical group's latest CD, what would you say to them if they asked you why you made an illegal copy?

Answers to the Self-Study Questions

1. C, p. 409	**2.** C, p. 422	**3.** A, p. 419	**4.** D, p. 422	**5.** D, p. 424
6. B, p. 426	**7.** D, p. 429	**8.** C, p. 435	**9.** C, p. 426	**10.** A, p. 430

---

case ①

Digital Data on Government Computers a Security Concern

For whatever reason—claim to fame, curiosity, espionage, or profit—military networks and Web sites are constant targets for hackers. In fact, the U.S. Department of Defense reported that in 2005, it received 75,000 computer intrusion attempts. While the majority of such attacks have not done damage, a few were alarmingly successful. Witness these examples:

- In 2000, Dennis Moran, an 18-year-old cracker known as "Coolio," successfully hacked three U.S. Army servers, an Air Force server, and two private sector computers. An Army cybercrimes investigative unit nabbed him, and he was sentenced to a year in prison and ordered to pay $15,000 to his victims.

- In 2001–2002, Gary McKinnon, an unemployed systems administrator living in London, hacked into 97 U.S. military and NASA computers. The United States estimated that the cost of tracking and correcting the problems he allegedly caused was over $1 million. McKinnon was tracked down and arrested under the Computer Misuse Act by the U.K. National Hi-Tech Crime Unit (NHTCU) in 2002 and later that year was also indicted by the U.S. government. He posted bail but was required to sign in at his local police station every evening and to remain at his home address at night. In addition, he could not use a computer with access to the Internet. In late 2005, the United

States formally began extradition proceedings, but as of late 2006, McKinnon was still living in London and fighting extradition to the United States on grounds that his crimes were committed in the United Kingdom, not the United States. He told the media that if extradited to the United States, he feared he would be imprisoned at Guantanamo Bay.

Hackers often target military computers simply because they are a rich source of all types of information. In an incident that did not involve hackers, however, a disturbing amount of sensitive data kept on government computers was stolen. In June 2006, the U.S. Department of Defense announced that personal data for 80 percent of active military personnel had been stolen when an employee of the Department of Veterans Affairs took a laptop home from work and burglars stole the computer. While the thieves may not have realized what was on the laptop they stole, the data was an identity thief's dream and a potential threat to the safety of military personnel.

According to security experts, another worry was that the stolen information could reach foreign governments and their intelligence services or other hostile forces, allowing them to target service members and their families. "There is a global black market in this sort of information . . . and you suddenly have a treasure trove of information on the U.S. military that is available," said James Lewis, director of technology and public policy at the Center for Strategic and International Studies, in an interview for the *Washington Post*.

Also revealed in May 2006 was the fact that the stolen laptop and external hard drive contained the names, birth dates, and Social Security numbers of 26.5 million military veterans discharged from service after 1975. In June 2006, the stolen laptop and hard drive were recovered; U.S. government officials reported that the thieves quickly erased the hard drive to make the notebook more difficult to trace when selling it. Nevertheless, the Veterans Administration (VA) employee who took the sensitive data home without permission was fired. Also, his boss resigned, and another VA

official was placed on administrative leave while the FBI investigated. A coalition of veterans groups sued the VA for privacy rights violations, seeking $1,000 for each veteran affected.

Unfortunately, it is not unusual for government employees to take home sensitive data on laptops, Lewis said. "The rules we have are either chaotic or nonexistent. . . . We still have a paper rules government when we are a digital nation."

While stolen government data is a colossal concern, there are guards at the digital gate. For instance, the U.S. Army has assembled a supersecret, multi-million-dollar hacker posse that is charged with defending all Department of Defense networks. The unit, called the Joint Functional Component Command for Network Warfare (JFCCNW), is also in charge of the highly classified Computer Network Attack, a mission to be launched in the event of an all-out cyberwar. JFCCNW's capabilities are a well-kept secret, but experts believe it can destroy networks at will and penetrate enemy computers to compromise or steal sensitive data.

Questions

1. Does the government do enough to punish cyber attackers and criminals?
2. Develop a set of policies or procedures for governmental employees regarding data security.
3. Who is ultimately responsible for data on a stolen laptop? Why?

Sources: John Lasker, "U.S. Military's Elite Hacker Crew," *Wired News* (April 14, 2005), http://www.wired.com/news/privacy/0,67223-0.html?tw=wn_story_page_prev2

Ann Scott Tyson and Christopher Lee, "Data Theft Affected Most in Military," *Washington Post* (June 7, 2006), http://www.washingtonpost.com/wp-dyn/content/article/2006/06/06/AR2006060601332.html

"Gary McKinnon," http://en.wikipedia.org/wiki/Gary_McKinnon

case ❷

e-Enabling the Air Transport Industry: Managing Information Systems Ethics and Crime

The terrorist attacks against New York's World Trade Center caused huge losses in terms of human lives as well as financial losses for all companies directly or indirectly affected by the events. For the air transport industry, the revenues dropped

significantly in the aftermath of 9/11, as many of their most valued customers suddenly reduced air travel because of security concerns. Therefore, regaining the travelers' confidence was seen as a primary factor in many airlines' struggle for survival.

At the same time, the Department of Defense (DoD) and the newly created Department of Homeland Security started to combat the threat of terrorism in the United States and required the airlines to install advanced security measures aboard all commercial aircraft. One important way to minimize the threat of terrorism was to "engage terrorism abroad—to not let it cross borders—[through] preventative and proactive efforts to stop acts before they start," as one senior Boeing official stated. However, preventing terrorism from reaching the United States is a highly complex task because of the tremendous numbers of people, moving vehicles, and tons of freight that enter the United States each year. For example, 11.2 million trucks, 2.2 million rail cars, and 500,000 international flights enter the country each year (see the table).

For companies such as Boeing, homeland security is a growth area, with an addressable market of $4 billion to $6 billion a year from the Department of Homeland Security alone, along with opportunities from DoD and from abroad. Boeing also has an interest in ensuring the efficient flow of people and commerce—it is a leading U.S. exporter and one of the largest American importers and relies on the air transport industry for about half its revenues in the United States. Boeing's homeland security–related projects include technological achievements such as the national missile defense and the Future Combat Systems, as well as numerous activities to increase aviation security by developing features such as reinforced cockpit doors for their aircraft. One attempt to improve the safety and security of air travel is to improve communications to and from airplanes and

between airplanes and air marshals. Air traffic management, the Boeing commercial Airplanes Group, and Boeing's Integrated Defense Systems business unit of Space and Intelligence Systems also play a role in protecting the United States against terrorist threats.

A primary issue related to aviation security is that once an airplane has left the airport, it is largely disconnected from the rest of the world. During any flight, a variety of adverse conditions can occur, ranging from effects of extreme turbulence and medical emergencies to incidents of air rage or, in the worst case, terrorist attacks or attempted hijackings. In case any of these events occur during a flight, the flight crew has to be able to handle the situation without being able to contact anyone for help. In most cases, it is not even possible to transmit detailed reports of the situation to the airline's operations center, situation awareness centers, or Federal Aviation Administration (FAA) centers. Boeing envisions using near-real-time data transmission capabilities help to deal with this issue. While the pilot and the rest of the crew will still have to handle the onboard event on their own, improved communication systems can provide a way to enable data and voice communication between the aircraft and ground crews to exchange critical information about the event and to guide the aircraft's captain in decision making.

One such application is real-time cabin surveillance. In order to enable this application, an aircraft needs to

be equipped with several different cameras, such as cockpit door cameras or covert infrared or zoom-type cameras throughout the cabin. This system of cameras allows the crew at the flight deck to monitor any events occurring in the cabin during a flight, from the safety of the cockpit, without compromising security. The pilots can use specific software to remotely control the cameras' zoom or viewing angle to focus on certain parts of the aircraft's cabin. This video data, which is also stored in an onboard video recorder, can be accessed remotely by ground crews to improve collaborative decision making in response to threats or other nonnormal events. Furthermore, this video data can serve as evidence for law enforcement officers in cases of air rage or other passenger misbehavior, such as theft or tampering. Redundant data storage (both airborne and on the ground) for most data flows is provided to support further non-real-time analysis. In addition to its serving as a threat deterrent if the airlines advertise its use onboard the airplane, the camera system may give the passengers a sense of security during the flight, helping to strengthen the passengers' confidence in the safety of air travel.

Similarly, an aircraft's flight data can be monitored remotely, helping the ground crews detect if there are any deviations from the airplane's regular flight path (See Figure). Used as a virtual cockpit voice recorder, the system can help inform ground crews about whatever

Cross-Border Traffic and Commerce in the United States

Miles of border the United States shares with Canada and Mexico	7,500
Number of different jurisdictions	About 87,000
Number of truck, rail, or sea containers entering the United States on a typical day	69,370
Number of international air travelers entering the United States on a typical day	235,732
Number of passengers/crew arriving by ship to the United States on a typical day	71,858
Number of privately owned vehicles entering the United States on a typical day	333,226
Shipments of goods approved for entry to the United States on a typical day	79,107
Fees, duties, and tariffs collected on a typical day	$81.8 million

Source: U.S. Customs and Border Protection, "Fact Sheet: On a Typical Day. . . ,"
http://www.cbp.gov/linkhandler/cgov/newsroom/fact_sheets/typical_day.ctt/typical_day.pdf, retrieved July 15, 2006.

is happening on the flight deck and can also serve as a backup for the physical black boxes installed aboard all commercial aircraft. At the same time, ground crews can query sensors throughout the aircraft, helping to detect any chemical, explosive, or biological threats. To help the situation awareness centers in assessing an event, flight information, data recorder, and global positioning satellite data are all simultaneously "live linked" over a broadband network.

Another key feature enabled by such system is the possibility to trigger silent alarms using small key-chain transmitters. This silent alarm feature allows the aircraft's captain, air marshals, or members of the cabin crew to covertly transmit signals to the airline's operations center, FAA centers, and/or situation awareness centers. In cases where an aircraft has a situation or an event that precludes normal communications, one or more crew members activate a silent alarm, initiating an onboard sequence of events, such as automatic cockpit or cabin video/audio capture. When these silent alarms are activated, the ground personnel attempt to contact the airplane using prearranged methods that the crew acknowledges using the onboard alarm system. If an onboard event alert is triggered and verified, the ground personnel can then execute a variety of response plans. As this can happen covertly, aggressive passengers or potential hijackers or terrorists remain unaware of the alarm's being triggered, helping personnel handle the situation.

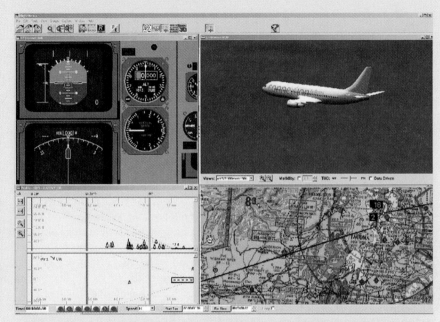

External monitoring of flight information.

Questions

1. In what other ways can high-speed data transmission capabilities be used to increase aircraft security?
2. Do you see any ethical issues related to monitoring passengers during a flight? Why or why not?
3. In severe circumstances, the ground crews might end up in a situation in which they are able to watch the situation but are not able to react appropriately. How do you see the benefits of the systems in these cases? Can you see any ethical dilemmas arising from assessing a situation remotely and providing advice on somewhat limited information?

Sources: http://www.boeing.com/news/frontiers/archive/2004/march/cover1.html

http://www.boeing.com/ids/homeland_security/ourCapabilities1.htm

http://spacecom.grc.nasa.gov/icnsconf/docs/2002/03/Session_A2-5_Miller.pdf

Technology Briefing

Information Systems Hardware

preview > If you want to purchase a computer, you have a broad range of options. Over the years, hardware has become less expensive, making it possible for individuals and organizations of all sizes to take advantage of computer-based technologies. However, large computer systems can still cost millions of dollars. Organizations must select the right hardware or risk making a costly mistake. To make an informed decision about information systems hardware, you must understand what it is and how it works. After reading this briefing, you will be able to do the following:

1. Describe key elements of information systems hardware.
2. List and describe the types of computers that are being used in organizations today.

Our approach in this technology briefing is not to bog you down with hardware facts and jargon but to provide you with a managerial overview.

Key Elements of Information Systems Hardware

Information systems hardware is classified into three types: input, processing, and output devices (see Figure TB1.1). **Input devices** are used to enter information into a computer. **Processing devices** transform inputs into outputs. The central processing unit (CPU), with the help of several other closely related devices that store and recall information, is the most important processing element of a computer. Finally, **output devices**, such as a computer monitor and printer, deliver information to you in a usable format. This section describes each of these three key elements of information systems hardware. (For a more detailed discussion, see Evan et al., 2007.)

Input Devices

For information systems hardware to perform a task, data must be input into the system. Certain types of data can be entered more easily using one type of input device than another. For example, **keyboards** are currently the primary means to enter text and numbers. Alternatively, architects and engineers can use scanners to enter their designs and drawings into computers. Graphics tablets simulate the process of drawing or sketching on a sheet of paper. A great deal of research and development are conducted to identify optimal ways to input various types of information and to build and sell new input devices (Te'eni, Carey, and Zhang, 2007). There are four general categories of input devices: entering text and numbers, pointing and selecting information, entering batch data, and entering audio and video (see Table TB1.1).

Along with the typical devices used on today's computers, there are several emerging trends in technology that have changed how we use computers by adding flexibility and utility. This is discussed next.

Keyboards Historically, entering text and numbers had to be done using a **QWERTY keyboard**. QWERTY stands for how the letters are arranged on the keyboard, with Q-W-E-R-T-Y being the first six letters going from left to right on the keyboard. Today, the keyboard is only one of many options for inputting text and numbers. Additionally, there are several different flavors of keyboards that can be used. For example, **ergonomic keyboards** resemble a widened V shape that is designed to reduce the stress placed on the wrists, hands, and arms when typing. Of course, both the standard and the ergonomic keyboards can be wireless, using either infrared or Bluetooth technologies. Infrared, the same technology as a television remote control, uses infrared light to send data; as with a remote control, both devices need to face each other in an unobstructed line of sight. In contrast, Bluetooth sends data over short-range radio waves, and thus does not require line-of-sight to communicate. Bluetooth, which is becoming increasingly popular, will be discussed more thoroughly in Technology Briefing 4—Networking.

FIGURE TB1.1

Input devices include the mouse and keyboard, and output devices include the monitor; the central processing unit transforms input into output.

TABLE TB1.1 Methods for Input to an Information System

Category	Typical Devices	Emerging Technology
Entering original text/numbers	QWERTY keyboard Ergonomic keyboard	Wireless keyboards Laser keyboards Voice-to-text
Selecting and pointing	Mouse Trackballs Joysticks Touch screen Light pen Touch pad	Eye tracking
Entering batch data	Scanners Bar-code/optical character readers	Biometric readers RFID scanners
Entering audio and video	Microphone Digital cameras	Digital video

Another type of keyboard gaining popularity is the laser keyboard. The laser keyboard, also known as the virtual laser keyboard, uses both laser and infrared technology to project a full-size QWERTY keyboard on any surface (see Figure TB1.2).

Pointing and Selecting Devices In addition to entering text and numbers, computer users use **pointing devices** to select items from menus, to point, and to sketch or draw (see Figure TB1.3). You probably use a pointing device, such as a *mouse*, when using a graphical operating environment (such as Microsoft Windows) or when playing a video game. Several of the most popular types of pointing devices are listed in Table TB1.2. An **eye-tracking device** is an innovative pointing device primarily developed for the disabled for help with computer pointing. The eye tracker is used in cases where voice and finger

FIGURE TB1.2

The virtual laser keyboard.

Source: http://www.sforh.
com/ images/keyboards/
virtual-keyboard-lg.jpg.

FIGURE TB1.3

Pointing devices: a touch screen (a), a light pen (b), a mouse (c), and a touch pad (d).

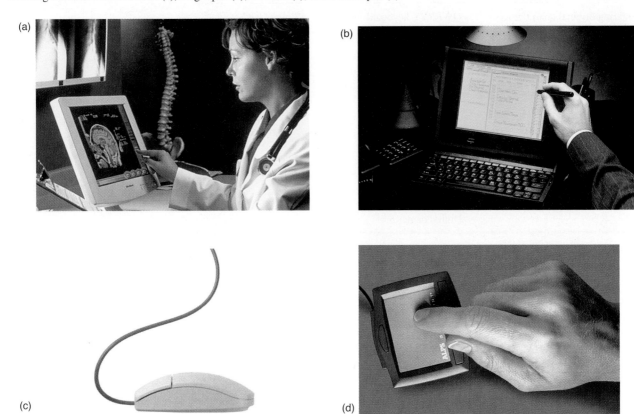

Sources: (a) Getty Images, Inc. (b) Courtesy Grid Systems Corporation. (c) Getty Images, Inc. (d) Apple Computer, Inc.

manipulation is not possible. This device is built around a monitor and tracks the eye movements of the user, moving the pointer to where the user is focusing on; a "click" is signaled by blinking for a set amount of time.

Entering Batch Data Another category of computer-based input is **batch input**. Batch input is used when a great deal of routine information needs to be entered into the computer. **Scanners** convert printed text and images into digital data. Scanners range from a small handheld device that looks like a mouse to a large desktop box that resembles a personal photocopier (see Figure TB1.4). Rather than duplicating the image on another

TABLE TB1.2 Selecting and Pointing Devices

Device	Description
Mouse	Pointing device that works by sliding a small box-like device on a flat surface; selections are made by pressing buttons on the mouse.
Trackball	Pointing device that works by rolling a ball that sits in a holder; selections are made by pressing buttons located near or on the holder.
Joystick	Pointing device that works by moving a small stick that sits in a holder; selections are made by pressing buttons located near or on the holder.
Touch screen	A method of input for which you use your finger; selections are made by touching the computer display.
Light pen	Pointing device that works by placing a pen-like device near a computer screen; selections are made by pressing the pen to the screen.

(a)

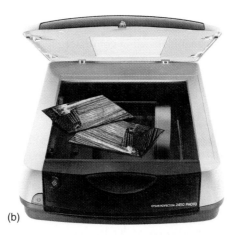

(b)

FIGURE TB1.4

Handheld (a) and flatbed
(b) scanners are a type of
batch input device.

Sources: (a) Intermec Technologies
Corporation. (b) Courtesy of Epson
America, Inc.

piece of paper, the computer translates the image into digital information that can be stored or manipulated by the computer. Special **text recognition software** can convert handwritten text into the computer-based characters that form the original letters and words. Insurance companies, universities, and other organizations that routinely process large batches of forms and documents have applied scanner technology to increase employee productivity.

When the keyboard, mouse, and typical scanner cannot handle the job of transferring data to the computer, specialized scanners may be called for. These devices, which include optical mark recognition (OMR) devices, optical character recognition (OCR) devices, bar-code readers, and magnetic ink character readers, are summarized in Table TB1.3. Also, *RFID* (radio frequency identification) scanners are a popular system input method for a variety of contexts (see Chapter 8—Building Organizational Partnerships Using Enterprise Information Systems).

Other Scanning Technologies Used in many European and Asian countries, as well as at many colleges and universities, **smart cards** are special credit card-sized cards, containing a microprocessor chip, memory circuits, and often a magnetic stripe. When issued by a school, smart cards are photo-identification cards that can also be used to unlock dormitory doors, make telephone calls, do laundry, make purchases from vending machines or student cafeterias and snack bars, and more. Some smart cards allow for contactless transmission of data using RFID technology (e.g., the Exxon Speedpass for purchasing gasoline). *Biometric devices* are also being used commercially to input data.

TABLE TB1.3 Specialized Scanners for Inputting Information

Scanner	Description
Optical mark recognition (OMR)	Used to scan questionnaires and test answer forms where answer choices are circled or clocked in using pencil or pen
Optical character recognition (OCR)	Used to read and digitize typewritten, computer-printed, and even hand-printed characters such as on sales tags on department store merchandise or patient information in hospitals
Bar-code/optical character readers	Used mostly in grocery stores and other retail businesses to read bar code data at the checkout counter; also used by libraries, banks, hospitals, utility companies, and so on
Magnetic ink character recognition (MICR)	Used by the banking industry to read data, account numbers, bank codes, and check numbers on preprinted checks
Biometric scanners	Used to scan biofeatures of users to enable everything from secure access to payment procurement

These devices read certain features, including iris, fingerprints, and hand or face geometry. Biometric devices, discussed in more detail in Chapter 6—Securing Information Systems, are being included in consumer products, such as laptops, allowing users to log on to the laptop using a fingerprint scanner rather than the traditional keyboard entry of user name and password.

Entering Audio and Video   In regards to computers, **audio** refers to sound that has been digitized for manipulation, storage, and replay. Further, audio input is helpful when a user's hands need to be free to do other tasks; it can be entered into computers via a microphone, CD, or other audio device. When audio is entered in analog (i.e., not digital) form, a sound card (discussed later) is used to "translate" the sounds for the computer. **Video** refers to still and moving images that can be recorded, manipulated, and displayed. Video has become popular for assisting in security-related applications, such as room monitoring and employee verification. It has also gained popularity for videoconferencing and chatting on the Internet, using your PC, and very inexpensive video cameras.

VOICE INPUT. Perhaps one of the easiest ways to enter data into a computer is simply to speak into a microphone. With the increased interest in such applications as Internet-based telephone calls and videoconferencing, microphones have become an important component of computer systems. A process called **speech recognition** also makes it possible for your computer to understand speech. For many disabled people, the use of the keyboard is not an option for entering in text and numbers. For this reason, researchers have developed a variety of options for the disabled users, including voice-to-text translators. **Voice-to-text software** is an application that uses a microphone to monitor a person's speech and then converts the speech into text. There are consumer versions of voice-to-text software that are relatively cheap, but the commercial software used by the disabled can be very expensive. Speech recognition technology can also be especially helpful for physicians and other medical professionals, airplane cockpit personnel, factory workers whose hands get too dirty to use keyboards, and computer users who cannot type and do not want to learn (see Figure TB1.5).

OTHER FORMS OF AUDIO INPUT. In addition to using a microphone, users can enter audio using electronic keyboards, or can transfer audio from another device (such as an audio recorder). The users can then analyze and manipulate the sounds via sound editing software for output to MP3s, CDs, or other media. Here are a few examples of how audio input, other than spoken words, might be used:

- A scientist studying the sounds made by whales enters those sounds into a computer to analyze pitch, volume, tone, and other patterns.
- Audiologists and other medical personnel enter sounds to be played back to patients during hearing tests or therapy.
- Forensic scientists use a computer to analyze a voice on a tape recorder for identification by a crime victim or witnesses.
- Filmmakers manipulate sounds to serve specific story purposes.

FIGURE TB1.5

Voice input is becoming an important way for many to interact with a computer.

Source: Peter Beck/Corbis/Stock Market.

VIDEO INPUT. A final way in which information can be entered into a computer is through video input. Digital cameras record images or short video clips in digital form, on small, removable memory cards rather than on film. Storage capacity is influenced by the resolution and size you select for pictures or the length of the recording for video. At any time, you can connect the camera to a port on a PC for downloading to the computer's memory (discussed later). Accompanying software lets you clear the memory card for later use. Digital camera technology has become so portable that it has been used in a variety of products, including cell phones and laptops. High-quality digital cameras are generally more expensive than film-based cameras, ranging in price from $150 to $10,000 or more. However, they offer three main advantages. You can record digital images without using a scanner, you can take photographs without having film developed, and you can record video. Presently, photos taken with high-end digital cameras are suitable for professional-quality photos, but for video recordings, specialized digital video (DV) cameras are still the best choice (see Figure TB1.6). Since huge digital files are created when video clips are recorded, DV cameras use digital video tapes or DVDs rather than memory cards. Further, when the clips are downloaded to the computer, storage and processing requirements are demanding.

There are also lower-quality cameras that are priced from $30 to $200 (see Figure TB1.7). These devices, often referred to as webcams, have become very popular with people wanting to use the Internet for chatting with friends and family, using programs like Skype, Google Talk, Windows Live Messenger or Yahoo! Messenger. Using the input of a webcam, a PC can create **streaming video**, which is a sequence of moving images in a compressed form that can be sent over the Internet; the images are displayed on the receiver's screen as they arrive. **Streaming media** is streaming video with sound. With streaming video or streaming media, a Web user does not have to wait for the entire file to be downloaded before seeing the video or hearing the sound. Instead, the media are sent in a continuous stream that is played as it arrives. This is why streaming has become popular for real-time chatting, and it is how live broadcasts, like the news on CNN (www.cnn.com) or even baseball games (www.mlb.com), can be viewed on a computer over the Internet.

We have described numerous options for providing input to a computer. After information is entered into a computer, it can be processed, stored, and manipulated. In the next section, we describe the processing aspects of information systems hardware.

Processing: Transforming Inputs into Outputs

In this section we provide a brief overview of computer processing. To begin, we describe how data and information are represented within a computer. Next, we briefly describe the internal processing components of a desktop computer, focusing primarily on the central processing unit and data storage technologies.

FIGURE TB1.6

High-quality digital video cameras can be connected directly to a computer for storing information as well as for editing and adding special effects.

FIGURE TB1.7

Low-priced webcams are popular with people who like to chat over the Internet.

Binary Code Your brain can readily process written words, photographs, music, an instructor's lecture (at least some of the time), videos, and much more. If you grew up speaking English, your brain will process incoming information in that language only. Similarly, computers can process incoming data, but only after the words, photos, music, and other information have been translated into a language they can understand. The language that computers understand is called digital data or **binary code**, which simply means that all incoming data must be translated into the 1s and 0s of binary math. Binary, or base-2 math (2, 4, 8, 16, 32, and so on), is used by computers instead of the more familiar base 10 because it matches the way a computer's hardware works.

Binary codes make up **machine language**, the only language computers understand. The individual 1s and 0s that make up the code are called **bits**—short for binary digits. Eight bits equal a **byte**, or about one typed character, such as the letter "A" or the number "6" on the keyboard. You will often see computer storage and memory sizes expressed in multiples of bytes (see Table TB1.4).

Whereas companies such as Google already have databases far larger than a petabyte (1 quadrillion bytes), future memory and storage capacities will also include exabytes (1 quintillion bytes) and zettabytes (1 sextillion bytes). The bits in the binary code are the

TABLE TB1.4 Elements of Computer Storage

Measurement	No. of Bits	No. of Bytes	No. of Kilobytes	No. of Megabytes	No. of Gigabytes
Byte	8	1			
Kilobyte* (K)	8,192	1,024	1		
Megabyte (MB)	8,388,608	1,048,576	1,024	1	
Gigabyte (GB)	8,589,934,592	1,073,741,824	1,048,576	1,024	1
Terabyte (TB)	8,796,093,022,208	1,099,511,627,776	1,073,741,824	1,048,576	1,024

*A kilobyte equals a little more than 1,000 bytes, but the number is usually rounded to 1,000. The same is true for the number of kilobytes in a megabyte, and so on.

basic instruction units for all the work the computer does. The bits represent on/off commands for tiny electric switches inside the computer's processor. When a low-voltage current is applied to a switch, it is read as a 0, and the switch is closed. A high-voltage current is read as a 1, and the switch is opened. Similarly, positive and negative magnetized locations used to store data are represented in binary notation as 0s or 1s.

One of the biggest challenges for the computer industry has been to determine how to translate all the different types of information into digital data that a computer can understand. Early computers could not translate incoming data at all. They used paper cards on which strings of 1s and 0s were represented by punched holes. Later, computers received information from a keyboard, which was the first time a translation was made to 1s and 0s from text that computer users could understand. Today's computers can translate many types of data, including words, photos, sound, and video, to binary code, then manipulate and store it. One of the main reasons computers become so quickly outdated is that newer models keep coming out that can process more amounts and types of information.

Programs (applications) you run on your computer contain instructions. (This is software, covered in Technology Briefing 2—Information Systems Software.) Programs may tell the computer to open a specific file, move data from one location to another, open a new window on the monitor screen, add a column of figures, and so on. Before the computer can follow program instructions, however, those instructions must be converted to machine language. The central processing unit (described later) uses a special built-in program called a language translator to translate incoming data into binary code called machine language. After the processor converts incoming data to machine language, it organizes the bits into groups—for instance, 64-bit instructions—that represent specific operations and storage locations.

Once the computer receives instructions from a program, it processes the information into a form that you, the computer user, can understand. In a word processing program, for example, the letters and numbers you type are displayed on the monitor, just as they would appear on a sheet of paper if you were using an old-fashioned typewriter. But, unlike on the typewriter, when you press the "L" key, for example, on the computer keyboard, the computer is actually receiving the information as a series of 1s and 0s, specifically "01001100." As you type a letter or a term paper, the data is processed, then displayed on the monitor in a form that makes sense to you. The binary code the computer actually uses is hidden from your view (see Figure TB1.8). You see words, lines, and paragraphs. After you write a document, you can then print it out on paper, store it on the computer's hard disk, or even post it to an Internet Web site.

Other binary codes are used to relay data and instructions to and from the central processing unit. There are several different types of binary codes that have been developed. Some are in wide use, such as **ASCII (American Standard Code for Information Interchange)**, and others are used for specialized equipment (see Table TB1.5).

System Unit A computer's **system unit** is the physical box that houses all of the electronic components that do the work of the computer (see Figure TB1.9). In addition to a power button, you can access the PCs CD-ROM or DVD drives from the front of the PC;

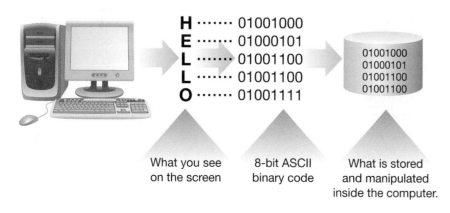

H ······· 01001000	
E ······· 01000101	01001000
L ······· 01001100	01000101
L ······· 01001100	01001100
O ······· 01001111	01001100

What you see on the screen   8-bit ASCII binary code   What is stored and manipulated inside the computer.

FIGURE TB1.8

How computers translate information into binary code so that the computer can store and manipulate the information.

TABLE TB1.5 Types of Encoding for Information Systems

Code	Name	Description	Variants
ASCII	American Standard Code for Information Interchange	Often pronounced "aski," a character encoding based on the English alphabet. ASCII codes represent symbols (letters and numbers) in binary form. Most character encodings have a historical basis in ASCII.	Extended-US-ASCII IBM367
MIME	Multipurpose Internet Mail Extensions	This is the standard coding for the Internet. Virtually all e-mail is transmitted in MIME format.	RFC 2045 8BITMIM
MAC OS Roman		This encoding is used by Mac OS to represent text. It encodes 256 characters; this includes 128 characters that are identical to ASCII.	
Unicode		This encoding has become an industry standard that was designed to allow symbols from all languages.	UTF-8 UTF-7 UCS-2

many older PCs also have a diskette drive. Through ports at the back of the system unit, you can connect peripheral hardware, such as a keyboard, a mouse, speakers, printers, and scanners. Newer multimedia PCs also have ports at the front that allow you to connect a variety of devices, such as audio or video equipment, USB devices (described later), or memory cards.

The system unit contains the following:

- Motherboard, power supply, and fan
- Central processing unit(s)
- RAM and ROM memory

FIGURE TB1.9

The system unit houses all of the electronic components that do the work of the computer.

(a)

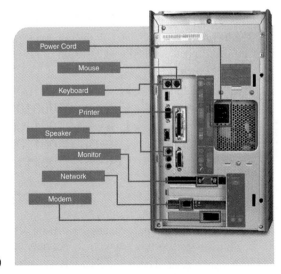

(b)

FIGURE TB1.10

A computer's motherboard holds or connects to all of the computer's electronic components.

Source: Peter Beck/Corbis/Stock Market.

- Hard drive, CD-ROM, or DVD-ROM drive
- Ports for plugging in peripherals and add-in slots for sound, video, internal LAN card, USB devices, and other cards

In all types and models of computers, the main circuit board or system board, most often called the motherboard, is the heart of the system unit.

Motherboard The **motherboard** is aptly named because it contains all of the components that do the actual processing work of the computer (see Figure TB1.10). It is a large printed plastic or fiberglass circuit board that holds or connects to all of the computer's electronic components. Plugged into or otherwise connected to the motherboard are the central processing unit (often referred to as the computer's brain), RAM and ROM memory, video and sound cards, hard disks and CD-ROM or DVD drives, all expansion slots, ports for printers and other external devices, and the power supply. All of these devices are described next.

The computer's **power supply** converts electricity from the wall socket to a lower voltage. Whereas typically, power supplied by the utility companies can vary from 110 to 240 volts AC, depending on where you are in the world, a PCs components use lower voltages—3.3 to 12 volts DC. The power supply converts the power accordingly and also regulates the voltage to eliminate spikes and surges common in most electrical systems. For added protection against external power surges, many PC owners opt to connect their systems to a separately purchased voltage surge suppressor. The power supply includes one or several fans for air cooling the electronic components inside the system unit. That low humming noise you hear while the computer is running is the fan.

Central Processing Unit The **central processing unit (CPU)** is often called the computer's brain. It is also called a microprocessor, processor, or chip, and it is responsible for performing all of the operations of the computer. Its job includes loading the operating system (e.g., Windows Vista, MAC OS X) when the machine is first turned on and performing, coordinating, and managing all the calculations and instructions relayed to it while the computer is running.

The CPU consists of two main sections: the **arithmetic logic unit (ALU)** and the **control unit**. The ALU performs mathematics, including all forms of addition, subtraction, multiplication, and division. It also performs logical operations, which involve comparing packets of data, then executing appropriate instructions. Combined in various ways, these functions allow the computer to perform complicated operations rapidly. The control unit works closely with the ALU by performing four primary functions:

1. *Fetching* the next program instruction from the computer's memory.
2. *Decoding* instructions so that the computer knows what to do next. The control unit uses separate registers (temporary storage locations inside the CPU) to store the instructions and to store information about storage location in memory.

FIGURE TB1.11

The Intel Core 2 Duo microprocessor contains more than 291 million transistors.

3. *Retrieving* the necessary data from memory and telling the ALU to execute the required instructions.
4. *Storing* results of its computations in a register or in memory.

Both the ALU and the control unit use registers because they can access them more quickly than they can access main memory, thus adding to processing speed (see the discussion of different types of memory later).

The CPU is composed of millions of tiny transistors arranged in complex patterns that allow it to interpret and manipulate data. The inner workings of a CPU are very complex. For most of us, it is easiest to think of a CPU as being a "black box" where all the processing occurs. The CPU is a small device made of silicon. For example, the Intel Core 2 Duo CPU packs more than 291 million transistors into an area about the size of a dime. These transistors are so small that you could fit a hundred inside a single human cell. The Intel Core 2 Duo CPU is packaged in a container that is bigger than a dime because additional wiring is used to connect all of these transistors of the CPU to the motherboard (see Figure TB1.11).

MOORE'S LAW. The general trend in computing is toward smaller, faster, and cheaper devices. But for how long can this trend continue? In the 1970s, Dr. Gordon Moore, then a researcher at Intel, hypothesized that computer processing performance would double every 18 months. When Moore made this bold prediction, he did not limit it to any specified period of time. This prediction became known as **Moore's Law**. Interestingly, the first CPU had 2,200 transistors, so Dr. Moore has been basically correct so far. Feature size—the size of lines on the chip through which signals pass—has been reduced from about the width of a human hair in the 1960s (20 microns—a micron is equal to 1 millionth of a meter), to the size of a bacterium in the 1970s (5 microns), to smaller than a virus today (.07 micron—the feature size on an Intel Core 2 Duo CPU). As feature size is reduced, a greater number and variety of circuits can be packed increasingly closer together. Both feature density and complexity has facilitated the continued performance increases that microprocessors have realized. Figure TB1.12 shows this trend. For more on Moore's Law, visit Intel's Web site (http://www.intel.com/technology/mooreslaw/index.htm); if you search on the Web using the phrase "Moore's Law," you will get many interesting pages to review.

Evolution of Feature Size

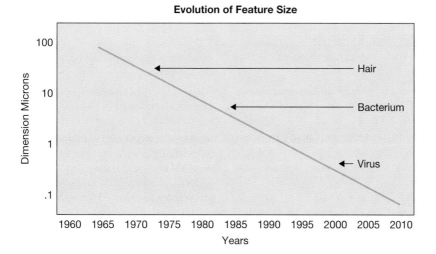

FIGURE TB1.12

Moore's Law predicted that computer processing performance would double every 18 months. To increase performance, feature size has had to shrink.

The number of transistors that can be packed into a modern CPU and the speed at which processing and other activities occur are remarkable. For example, the Intel Core 2 Duo CPU can complete hundreds of millions of operations every second. To achieve these incredible speeds, the CPU must execute instructions very rapidly. In addition to the number of transistors on the CPU, three other factors greatly influence its speed—its system clock speed, registers, and cache memory—and these are described next.

CLOCK SPEED. Within the computer, an electronic circuit generates pulses at a rapid rate, setting the pace for processing events to take place, rather like a metronome marks time for a musician. This circuit is called the **system clock**. A single pulse is a **clock tick**, and in microcomputers the processor's **clock speed** is measured in hertz (Hz). One megahertz (MHz) is 1 million clock ticks, or instruction cycles, per second. Microprocessor speeds are measured in different units, depending on the type of computer. Personal computer speeds are most often measured in gigahertz (GHz, or 1 billion hertz). Microprocessor speeds improve so quickly that faster chips are on the market about every six months. Today, most new PCs operate at faster than 3 GHz. To give you an idea of how things have changed, the original IBM PC had a clock speed of 4.77 MHz.

See Table TB1.6 for a description of computer speeds. It takes a permanent storage device such as a hard disk (described later) about 10 milliseconds to access information. Within a CPU, however, a single transistor can be changed from a 0 to a 1 in about 10 picoseconds (10 trillionth of a second). Changes inside the CPU occur about 1 billion times faster than they do in a fixed disk because the CPU operates only on electronic impulses, whereas the fixed disks perform both electronic and mechanical activities, such as spinning the disk and moving the read/write head (described later). Mechanical activities are extremely slow relative to electronic activities.

REGISTERS. Within the CPU itself, **registers** provide temporary storage locations where data must reside while it is being processed or manipulated. For example, if two numbers are to be added together, both must reside in registers, with the result placed in a register. Consequently, one factor influencing the speed and power of a CPU is the number and size of the registers.

CACHE MEMORY. A **cache** (pronounced "cash") is a small block of memory used by processors to store those instructions most recently or most often used. Just as you might keep file folders you use most in a handy location on your desktop, cache memory is located within or close to the CPU. Thanks to cache memory, before performing an operation, the processor does not have to go directly to main memory, which is farther away from the microprocessor and takes longer to reach. Instead, it can check first to see if needed data is contained in the cache. Cache memory is another way computer engineers have increased processing speed.

TABLE TB1.6 Elements of Computer Time

Name	Fraction of a Second	Description	Example
Millisecond	1/1000	One thousandth of a second	Fixed disks access information in about 10 to 20 milliseconds.
Microsecond	1/1,000,000	One millionth of a second	A 3.2-GHz CPU executes approximately 3.2 billion operations in a second, or about 3,200 operations every microsecond.
Nanosecond	1/1,000,000,000	One billionth of a second	Most type of RAM used in PCs have access times (the time needed to read information from the RAM to the CPU) from 3 to 50 nanoseconds (lower is better). Most cache memory has access times less than 20 nanoseconds.
Picosecond	1/1,000,000,000,000	One trillionth of a second	Inside a CPU, the time that it takes to switch a circuit from one state to another is in the range of 5 to 20 picoseconds.
Femtosecond	$1/10^{15}$, or 10^{-15}	One quadrillonth of a second	Used in laser technology to measure the length of the laser pulse. Used for nanosurgery.
Attosecond	$1/10^{18}$, or 10^{-18}	One quintillonth of a second	A term used in photon research. Also is the shortest amount of time scientists are able to measure.

Cache may be located inside the microprocessor—similar to registers—or outside of but close to the microprocessor. Special high-speed cache memory, called **internal cache** (also called Level 1, or L1, cache), is incorporated into the microprocessor's design. **External (or secondary) cache** (also called Level 2, or L2, cache) is usually not built into the CPU but is located within easy reach of the CPU on the motherboard. The more cache available to a CPU, the better the overall system performs because more information is readily available (although at a certain size, factors such as heat emission and power consumption become prohibitive to increasing the CPU cache).

The CPU translates input into binary data and binary data into information that can be understood by humans. To be used by the CPU, data must be stored either temporarily or permanently.

Primary Storage **Primary storage** is for current information. Computers need temporary storage space for current calculations, and this type of memory, measured in bytes, provides it. In addition to registers and cache, described previously, examples of primary storage are random-access memory and read-only memory. Both are made up of chips containing thousands of electronic circuits etched on silicon wafers. Each circuit or switch is either conducting an electrical current (on) or not conducting an electrical current (off).

Random-Access Memory **Random-access memory (RAM)** is the computer's main or **primary memory**. It consists of several chips mounted on a small circuit board and plugs into a "memory bank" of the motherboard (see Figure TB1.13). RAM stores the programs and data currently in use. RAM is so named because data stored here can easily and quickly be accessed randomly by the CPU. RAM provides temporary storage of data for

FIGURE TB1.13

Random-access memory (RAM) consists of several chips mounted on a small circuit board.

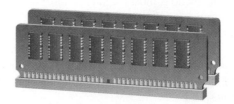

the CPU; because information is stored temporarily, it is referred to as **volatile memory**. That is, instructions and work stored in RAM are lost when the power to the computer is turned off or when new data is placed there. So if you have been working at your computer for hours on a research paper, do not trip over the power cord or otherwise accidentally turn off the power. If you do, unless you have saved your work in progress to your computer's hard disk or other secondary storage device, you will lose all your diligent work.

For the most efficient and speedy processing, the more RAM a computer has, the better. Today, the amount of RAM in most microcomputers is measured in megabytes or gigabytes. When this book went to print, most PC users considered 1 GB of RAM essential to run available software. The term **memory wall** has been used to describe the disparity between the increase in clock speed on CPU and the memory speed and size. From 1986 until 2006, memory speed has increased at an annual rate of 10 percent, with CPU speed increasing more than 50 percent annually. Tomorrow's PC users will undoubtedly have some number of gigabytes, or even terabytes, of RAM as an option.

Read-Only Memory **Read-only memory (ROM)** exists as a chip on the motherboard that can be read from but cannot be written to. That is, the CPU can read the information stored in ROM, but the computer user cannot change it. ROM is nonvolatile, which means that it does not lose its instructions when the power to the computer is shut off. ROM stores programs as instructions that are automatically loaded when the computer is turned on, such as the basic input/output system (BIOS).

A variation of ROM is erasable ROM, referred to as EEPROM (electrically erasable programmable read-only memory). You may have heard EEPROM referred to by a more user-friendly term, **flash memory**. This type of memory can be repeatedly written to and erased like RAM, but, unlike RAM, it retains its information after power is turned off. Flash memory is the storage technology behind many popular consumer devices such as digital cameras, MP3 players, and portable storage devices called **flash drives** (see Figure TB1.14).

(a)

(c)

(b)

FIGURE TB1.14

Flash memory is used as a storage technology in a variety of products.

TABLE TB1.7 Comparing Methods of Secondary Storage

Type	Speed	Method of Data Access	Relative Cost / MB
Magnetic tape	Slow	Sequential	Low
Floppy disk	Slow	Direct	Low
Fixed disk	Fast	Direct	High
Compact discs	Medium	Direct	Low
Optical disks	Fast	Direct	Medium
Flash drive	Fast	Direct	High

Because a flash drive is a removable storage technology, it is generally considered a secondary storage technology. Further, because of factors such as cost and performance, EEPROM is not well suited as a primary storage technology. Nevertheless, companies such as IBM and Samsung have developed technologies called magnetic RAM (MRAM) and phase-change RAM (PRAM), respectively, both of which are nonvolatile but equal or exceed the performance of traditional RAM. With such technology, you will one day be able to start working on your computer as soon as you have turned it on, without having to wait for it to boot up.

Secondary Storage **Secondary nonvolatile storage** is for permanently storing data to a large-capacity storage component, such as hard disk, diskette, CD-ROM disk, magnetic tape, and, of course, flash drives (see Table TB1.7). Hard disks and diskettes are magnetic media. That is, diskettes and the disks inside a hard disk drive are coated with a magnetic material. Reading data from the disks involves converting magnetized data to electrical impulses that can be understood by the processor. Writing to the disks is the reverse—converting electrical impulses to magnetized spots representing data.

Hard disk drives, diskette drives, and tapes are secondary storage devices with **read/write heads** that inscribe data to or retrieve data from hard disks, diskettes, and tapes. Hard disk, diskette, and tape drives are usually installed internally but may be externally located and attached via cables to ports on the back of the system unit. Diskettes and tapes are removable secondary storage media. That is, they must be inserted into the appropriate drive (or tape reader) to be read from or written to and are removed when these tasks are accomplished, just as a flash drive has to be plugged into a USB port on your computer.

Hard Drives Most of the software run on a computer, including the operating system, is stored on the **hard drive or hard disk**. The hard drive is a secondary storage device usually located inside the system unit of a computer. It writes data and programs to a fixed disk. The storage capacity of the hard drives for today's microcomputers is now measured in gigabytes (GB), or billions of bytes. It is not unusual for PCs currently on the market to come equipped with hard drives with 100-GB to 300-GB storage capacities. Modern supercomputers can have millions of gigabytes of storage. Most microcomputers have one hard drive, but additional drives can usually be added either internally or externally. To make sure critical data is not lost, some computers employ **RAID (redundant array of independent disks)** technology to store redundant copies of data on two or more hard drives. RAID is not typically used on an individual's computer but is very common for Web servers and many business applications. RAID is sometimes called a "redundant array of *inexpensive* disks" because it is typically less expensive to have multiple redundant disks than fewer highly reliable and expensive ones.

Hard drives consist of several disks, or platters, stacked on top of one another so that they do not touch (see Figure TB1.15). Each disk within a disk pack has an access arm with two read/write heads—one positioned close to the top surface of the disk and another positioned close to the bottom surface of the disk. (Both surfaces of each disk are used for

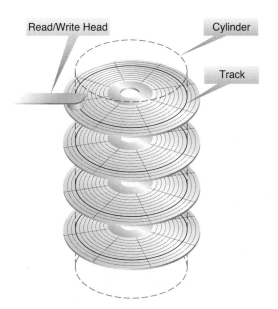

Read/Write Head

Cylinder

Track

FIGURE TB1.15

A hard drive consists of several disks that are stacked on top of one another and read/write heads to read and write information.

Source: Pfaffenberger/CIYF Brief 2003, Prentice Hall, 2003.

data storage, usually with the exception of the top surface of the top disk and the bottom surface of the bottom disk.) When reading from or writing to the disks, the read/write heads are constantly repositioned to the desired storage location for the data while the disks are spinning at speeds of 5400 to 15000 RPM. The read/write heads do not actually touch either surface of the disks. In fact, a **head crash** occurs if the read/write head for some reason touches the disk, leading to a loss of data.

Diskette Drives and Diskettes A **diskette** (or floppy disk) is a removable storage medium with a capacity of (typically) 1.44 megabytes, which can be read using a diskette drive. Because of the increase in use of relatively inexpensive flash memory having a capacity of up to eight GB or more, most personal computers do not contain diskette drives any more. This technology will soon be phased out for more practical means of data transfer and storage.

Optical Disk Storage **Optical disks**, or those using laser beam technology, have become popular as storage requirements have increased. An optical disk, coated with a metallic substance, is written to when a laser beam passing over the surface of the disk burns small spots into the disk surface, each one representing a data package. The data can be read when a laser scans the surface of the disk and a lens picks up various light reflections from the data spots. Some optical disks are read-only. That is, information is entered on them by a manufacturer. The information cannot be changed, nor can new information be written to the disk by the computer user. Other optical disks can be written to by the user. One advantage to using optical disks for storage is that they can hold much more information than diskettes: a single optical disk can record the information from hundreds of diskettes. Optical disks have made possible the huge growth in multimedia software applications for PCs.

COMPACT DISCS. For many years, **CD-ROMs (compact disc—read-only memory)**, have been the standard for distributing data; because of their low cost and their storage capacity of up to 800 MB, CD-ROMs are often used to distribute software. As CD-ROMs cannot be written to, most computers have turned to another type of optical disk that data can be written to, the **CD-R (compact disc—recordable)**. One of the problems with a CD-R is that information can only be written onto it once. A **CD-RW (compact disc—rewritable)** can be written onto multiple times using a CD-RW drive. However, many

FIGURE TB1.16

DVD 2.0. With next-generation high-capacity DVDs, users can now store huge (20 to 50 GB) amounts of data on DVDs.

users desire higher storage capacity than CD-Rs or CD-RWs can offer for multimedia (such as video) or large data backups.

DIGITAL VERSATILE DISKS. The **DVD-ROM (digital versatile disk–read-only memory)** has more storage space than a CD-ROM because DVD-ROM (or typically referred to as simply DVD) drives use a shorter-wavelength laser beam that allows more optical pits to be deposited on the disk. Like compact discs, there are recordable (DVD-R) and rewritable (DVD-RW) versions of this storage technology. DVDs used for the distribution of movies are also called **digital video disks**.

The drive to offer high-definition (HD) video content has created two new DVD formats: Blu-Ray and HD-DVD (See Figure TB1.16). Both formats offer up to 50 GB of storage but do so in very different ways, and because of the differences in technologies, HD-DVDs will not play in Blu-Ray players and vice versa. Many HD movies will be available in either or both formats, and industry experts view this development in the next-generation DVDs to be similar to the Beta-versus-VHS-format battle of the 1980s, where one technology (VHS) ended up being more popular.

Magnetic Tapes **Magnetic tapes** used for storage of computer information consist of narrow plastic tape coated with a magnetic substance. Storage tapes range from one-half inch wide, wound on a reel, to one-fourth inch wide, wound into a plastic cassette that looks much like a music cassette tape. As with other forms of magnetic storage, data are stored in tiny magnetic spots. The storage capacity of tapes is expressed as **density**, which equals the number of **characters per inch (CPI)** or **bytes per inch (BPI)** that can be stored on the tape. Mainframe computers use tape drives called stackers that wind tape from a supply reel to a take-up reel as data are read.

Magnetic tape is still used for storing large amounts of computer information, but it is gradually being replaced by high-capacity disk storage since disk storage is equally reliable. In fact, information stored on disks is easier to locate because, using disks, computers do not have to scan an entire tape to find a specific data file.

Ports To use the full functionality of a computer, you need to be able to connect various types of devices, such as mice, printers, and cameras, to the system unit. A **port** provides a

TABLE TB1.8 Common Computer Ports, Their Applications, and Description

Port Name	Used to Connect	Description
Serial	Modem, mice, keyboard, terminal display, MIDI	• Used to transfer one bit at a time • Slowest data transfer rates
Parallel	Printer	• Used to transfer several bits concurrently • Many times faster than serial
USB (Universal Serial Bus)	Printer, scanner, mice, keyboard, digital camera and camcorders, external disk drives	• A very high speed data transfer method • Up to 480 million bytes per second • Up to 127 devices simultaneously connected
IEEE 1394 ("Fire Wire")	Digital camera and camcorders, external disk drives	• Extremely high speed data transfer method • Up to 800 million bytes per second • Up to 63 devices simultaneously connected

hardware interface—plugs and sockets—for connecting devices to computers. The characteristics of various types of ports are summarized in Table TB1.8.

Now that you understand how information is input into a computer and how it is processed, we can turn our attention to the third category of hardware—output technologies.

Output Devices

After information is input and processed, it must be presented to the user. Computers can display information on a screen, print it, or emit sound. The sections that follow discuss details about how each of these output devices operates.

Video Output **Monitors** are used to display information from a computer. Traditionally, monitors consist of a cathode ray tube (CRT), which is similar to a television but with much higher resolution. Monitors can be color, black and white, or monochrome (meaning all one color, usually green or amber). Notebooks and many desktop computers use lighter and thinner **liquid crystal display (LCD)** to replace the bulky CRT monitor. Because display monitors are embedded into a broad range of products and devices, such as cell phones, digital cameras, or automobiles (e.g., to display route maps and other relevant information), they must be sturdy, reliable, lightweight, energy-efficient, and low in cost (see Figure TB1.17). Recent development in monitor technologies has thus focused on other display technologies such as organic light-emitting diodes (OLED). Finally, projectors are used for presentation to an audience. Projectors have gone from large very expensive equipment ($5,000 or more) to very small, relatively inexpensive equipment ($200). This is due primarily to the development of LCD technology as previously discussed. In fact, projectors have become so affordable that they are now a consumer-grade product that competes with regular and flat-screen TVs. No matter what type of display is used, it needs to be connected to a computer's video card. A video card (or graphics card) tells the monitor which dots to activate to produce the text or image. While for many applications video cards that are integrated into the computer's motherboard are sufficient, other applications (such as 3-D games or animation software) require the use of high-end video cards having a dedicated processor (called graphics processing unit, or GPU) and 1 GB or more of RAM.

Printers and Plotters Information can be printed in several different ways. A **plotter** (Figure TB1.18a) is used for transferring engineering designs from the computer to drafting paper, which is often as big as 34 by 44 inches. The plotter uses several pens as it draws each of the lines individually. **Dot matrix printers** (Figure TB1.18b) are older, electric typewriter–based devices for printing information on paper. Letters are formed using a series of small dots. Once the most commonly used type of printer, dot matrix

FIGURE TB1.17

Monitors display information from a computer.

printers are now mostly found printing voluminous batch information, such as periodic reports and forms. **Ink-jet printers** use a small cartridge to transfer ink onto paper. This process creates a typewriter-like image that can initially smear because the ink is wet when it is sprayed onto the paper. Ink-jet printers (Figure TB1.18c) can be designed to print both black and white and color. **Laser printers** are the most commonly used printers today.

FIGURE TB1.18

A plotter (a), a dot matrix printer (b), an ink-jet printer (c), and a laser printer (d).

(a)

(b)

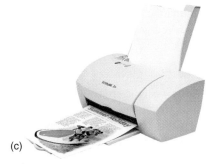

(c)

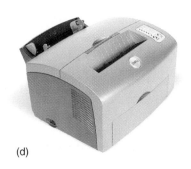

(d)

They use an electrostatic process to force ink onto the paper, literally "burning" the image onto the paper. The resulting high quality is considered necessary for almost all business letters and documents. Laser printers (Figure TB1.18d) can also produce color images, but high-end color laser printers can cost thousands of dollars.

Audio Output   In addition to transmitting text as output, almost all computers also transmit audio as output. With the use of a **sound card** and speakers, a computer can produce stereo-quality sound. The computer translates digits into sound by sending data to the sound card that interprets these data into tones. The tones are then sent to the speakers for output. Other audio output devices (such as headphones) can be plugged directly into a USB port. A sound card is also used to capture and convert audio for storage or processing.

Now that you understand how computer hardware works, we can discuss the types of computers that people and organizations typically use.

Types of Computers

Over the past 60 years, information systems hardware has gone through many radical changes. In the 1940s, almost all business and government information systems consisted of file folders, filing cabinets, and document repositories. Huge rooms were dedicated to the storage of these records. Information was often difficult to find, and corporate knowledge and history were difficult to maintain. Only certain employees knew specific information. When these employees left the firm, so did all their corporate knowledge. The computer provided the solution to the information storage and retrieval problems facing organizations up to the 1940s. Shifts in computing eras were facilitated by fundamental changes in the way computing technologies worked. Each of these fundamental changes is referred to as a distinct generation of computing. Table TB1.9 highlights the technology that defined the five generations of computing. We conclude by briefly describing the four general types of computers currently being used in organizations (see Table TB1.10).

TABLE TB1.9 Five Generations of Computing

Generation	Time Line	Major Event	Characteristics
1	1946–1958	Vacuum tubes	• Mainframe era begins • ENIAC and UNIVAC were developed
2	1958–1964	Transistors	• Mainframe era expands • UNIVAC is updated with transistors
3	1964–1990s	Integrated circuits	• Mainframe era ends • Personal computer era begins • IBM 360 with general purpose operating system • Microprocessor revolution: Intel, Microsoft, Apple, IBM PC, MS-DOS
4	1990s–2000	Multimedia and low cost PCs	• Personal computer era ends • Interpersonal computing era begins • High-speed microprocessor and networks • High-capacity storage • Low-cost, high-performance integrated video, audio, and data
5	2000–present	Widespread Internet accessibility	• Interpersonal computing era ends • Internetworking era begins • Ubiquitous access to Internet with a broad variety of devices • Prices continue to drop; performance continues to expand

TABLE TB1.10 Characteristics of Computers Currently Being Used in Organizations

Type of Computer	Number of Simultaneous Users	Physical Size	Typical Use	Memory	Typical Cost Range
Supercomputer	1–many	Like an automobile to as large as multiple rooms.	Scientific research	5,000+ GB	Low: $1 million High: more than $20 million
Mainframe	1,000+	Like a refrigerator	Large general purpose business and government	Up to 100+ GB	Low: $1 million High: $10 million
Midrange	5–500	Like a file cabinet	Midsize general purpose business	Up to 20GB	Low: $10,000 High: $100,000
Microcomputer	1	Handheld to fitting on a desktop	Personal productivity	512 MB to 2 GB	Low: $200 High: $5,000

Supercomputers

The most powerful and expensive computers that exist today are called **supercomputers**. Supercomputers are often used for scientific applications, solving massive computational problems that require large amounts of data. They can cost many millions of dollars. Rather than in clock speed (as your PC), supercomputers' processing speeds are measured in FLOPS (floating points operations per second). An example of one of the world's premier supercomputers is IBM's Blue Gene/L, which uses 131,072 processors that process information at 135.5 TFLOPS (1 TFLOP = 1,012 FLOPS). This supercomputer has been applied to several different problems, from forecasting weather to molecular modeling. To achieve this incredible speed, supercomputers are equipped with numerous fast processors that work in parallel to execute several instructions simultaneously. An extensive staff is usually required to operate and maintain supercomputers and to support the researchers and scientists using them. Supercomputers often run only one application at a time in order to dedicate all processing capabilities to a single massive application. (Figure TB1.19 shows a Cray supercomputer, one of the more popular computers in this class. In addition to Cray and IBM, leading producers of supercomputers are Hitachi, NEC, and Fujitsu.

FIGURE TB1.19

The Cray supercomputer.

Source: Cray, Inc.

Mainframes

The backbone of large corporate computing has historically been large, high-powered computers called **mainframe computers**. The general difference between a supercomputer and a mainframe is that supercomputers focus on calculation speed and are limited to one application at a time, whereas mainframes focus on input/output speed and reliability. Mainframes can be the size of a large refrigerator (and even larger), and they often cost several million dollars to purchase. Organizations normally use mainframe computers for processing large amounts of business data, and the machines are designed to support hundreds or even thousands of users simultaneously. In addition to businesses, many federal and state governments use mainframe computers to manage the massive amount of data generated by day-to-day governmental activities. Federal agencies, such as the Internal Revenue Service, have several mainframe computers to handle the massive databases related to individual and corporate payroll and tax information. Large corporations, such as Alamo Rent a Car, American Airlines, and Holiday Inn, use mainframes to perform repetitive tasks, such as processing reservations. Unisys and IBM are the largest producers of mainframes (see Figure TB1.20).

Midrange Computers

Midrange computers, often referred to as *minicomputers*, are scaled-down versions of mainframes that were created for companies that did not have the budgets for mainframes and did not need that amount of computing power. In the past few years, the distinction between large midrange computers and small mainframes has blurred in both performance and price. Nonetheless, midrange computers have become integral to many smaller and midsized organizations and typically cost tens to hundreds of thousands of dollars, supporting from five to 500 users simultaneously. As with mainframes, IBM is a leader in the midrange computer market with its System i5 model (the successor of the AS/400), but other manufacturers, such as Hewlett-Packard, also service this market. The midrange market as a whole has been declining as microcomputers have become faster and have absorbed some of the functionality once required of midrange and mainframe computers.

Microcomputers

Microcomputers, also referred to as **personal computers (PCs)**, fit on desktops, generally cost between a few hundred dollars and $5,000, and are used in homes and offices (see Figure TB1.21). Microcomputers can be relatively stationary desktop models or portable, notebook-sized computers. High-end microcomputers can cost more than $5,000 and can be used as a design workstation for engineers or as a server that manages shared resources

FIGURE TB1.20

IBM mainframe computer.

Source: Courtesy of IBM Corporate Archives.

FIGURE TB1.21

A personal computer.

Source: Apple Computer, Inc.

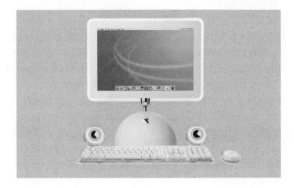

such as printers or large databases or that delivers content over the Internet. In the past few years, the popularity of microcomputers has exploded. Within organizations, microcomputers are the most commonly used computing technology for knowledge workers, and they have become as common as the telephone. In fact, more microcomputers than televisions are now sold in the United States each year. Next, we delve a bit deeper into the types of microcomputers.

Network Computers A **network computer** (sometimes called a thin client) is a microcomputer with minimal memory and storage, designed to connect to networks, especially the Internet, to use the resources provided by servers. The concept of network computing is to reduce the obsolescence and maintenance of personal computers by allowing inexpensive machines to access servers that deploy resources—software programs, printers, and so on—to all machines on the network (see Figure TB1.22).

Portable Computers When computers appeared that could fit on a desktop, users considered them the ultimate in lighter, smaller, handier machines. Then came laptop computers you could carry, but the first models were heavy and bulky. Next on the portable computer scene were notebook computers that could fit in a backpack or briefcase. Today, battery-powered laptop and notebook computers are popular for both business and personal use (see Table TB1.11 for a summary of trade-offs between desktop and portable computers). These computers are equipped with a flat display panel; fold into a small, convenient carry case; and can weigh as little as three pounds or less. With a portable computer, you can use a keyboard and a mouse as well as a trackball, touch pad, or other built-in pointing devices. Most portable computers come equipped with wireless networking capabilities and USB ports and can connect to printers, scanners, or other

FIGURE TB1.22

A Sun Microsystems network computer.

Source: Chris LaGrand/Getty Images, Inc.

TABLE TB1.11 Trade-Offs between Desktop and Portable Computers

Desktop Computer	Portable Computer
One location for use	Mobile—any location for use
Lower price	Higher price
Expandable	Very limited expandability
Better ergonomics—full-size/high-resolution color screen, large keyboard, and so on	Cramped ergonomics—small screen, small keyboard, awkward pointing device, and so on
Relatively easy to service/repair	Hard to service/repair

peripherals. Many students, employees, and others now use a portable computer as their only PC rather than buying both a desktop and a portable machine.

Portable computers can also be easily converted into a desktop machine. This is done by using a **docking station** that allows the portable computer to be easily connected to desktop peripherals, including full-sized monitors, keyboards, and mice. Docking stations are common in many businesses and university settings, as they allow fully functional desktop usability while providing for the portable computer experience. The three most popular forms of portable computers—notebooks, tablets, and handhelds—are described next.

NOTEBOOK COMPUTERS. Mobile computers once weighed 20 pounds and were portable only in the sense that they could be moved—with difficulty—from one location to another. A few years ago, machines evolved to what was referred to as a laptop, weighed around 10 pounds, and could be folded up and carried like a briefcase. The trend has been toward smaller, lighter, yet ever more powerful **notebook computers** some of which weigh only 2.5 pounds and can be easily carried in a briefcase or backpack (see Figure TB1.23).

TABLET PCS. A **tablet PC** is a type of notebook computer that accepts input from an electronic pen (called a stylus) or a keyboard. There are two types of tablet PCs: slate and convertible (see Figure TB1.24). *Slate* models contain a variety of ports for plugging in external keyboards and other devices as needed. Typically, users interact with a slate tablet PC by using the stylus, using handwriting recognition software to enter text and interpret commands. Slate models are particularly useful for applications where having a keyboard would be too bulky or it would be awkward to type. Alternatively, *convertible* models are quite similar to existing notebook computers but also have displays that swivel and fold flat to cover their keyboard. When converted into a tablet PC, they resemble a "fat" slate tablet PC.

Both slate and convertible models have a special type of screen that captures the movement of the stylus. Because tablet PCs have been designed to support mobile professionals in the work environment, all typically have built-in wireless Ethernet access for

FIGURE TB1.23

Notebook computers are very portable and typically weigh less than five pounds.

FIGURE TB1.24

Tablet PCs are designed to support mobile professionals.

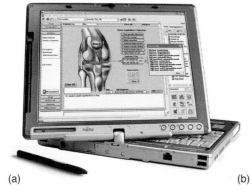

(a)

(b)

connecting to the Internet. To date, there are mixed reviews as to how effectively first-generation tablet PCs are performing in the workplace. Some feel that tablet PCs are still too heavy, that their batteries do not last long enough, and that the text recognition capabilities are adequate at best. Nevertheless, experts feel that these limitations will be quickly overcome so that tablet PCs will become a clear alternative to traditional notebook computers.

HANDHELD COMPUTERS. The first handheld computers were introduced around 1994, but they failed to live up to expectations, perhaps because consumers had expected that they would replace PCs. Then in 1996, Palm introduced a handheld computer that was never intended to replace the PC but performed some essential computing tasks so well that users could often leave their laptop and notebook computers at home. Since then, billed first as information appliances, then as **personal digital assistants (PDAs)**, handheld computers have filled a niche in the portable computer market. Today, the capabilities of many PDAs are beginning to rival the functionality of desktop PCs. For example, HP's iPAQ Pocket PC allows users to send and receive e-mail, work on documents and spreadsheets, surf the Web, and perform countless other activities. Handheld technologies are also being integrated into cell phones with many companies developing the PDA/cell phone. The most popular PDA/cell phones are made by RIM, which makes the Blackberry (see Figure TB1.25), and Palm, which manufactures the Treo.

FIGURE TB1.25

Personal digital assistants allow you to have a very powerful computer in the palm of your hand.

As you can see, information systems hardware is rapidly evolving. In most organizations today, an information systems infrastructure includes a diverse range of computing hardware, from supercomputers, mainframes, and midrange computers to personal computers and personal digital assistants. Chapter 4—Managing the Information Systems Infrastructure discusses the trends and solutions used by organizations facing the task of integrating a broad variety of hardware components. For individuals, computers have become common, with many families having several. Using history as a guide, it is a good bet that computing hardware will continue to evolve at a rapid pace, having some intended and unforeseen consequences for us all.

Key Points Review

1. *Describe key elements of information systems hardware.* Information systems hardware is classified into three types: input, processing, and output technologies. Input hardware consists of devices used to enter information into a computer. Processing hardware transforms inputs into outputs. The central processing unit is the device that performs this transformation, with the help of several other closely related devices that store and recall information. Finally, output-related hardware focuses on delivering information in a usable format to users.

2. *List and describe the types of computers that are being used in organizations today.* Computers come in all shapes, sizes, degrees of power, and prices. The four general classes of computers are supercomputer, mainframe, midrange, and microcomputer. A supercomputer is the most expensive and most powerful kind of computer; it is used primarily to assist in solving massive research and scientific problems. A mainframe is a very large computer that is the main, central computing system for major corporations and governmental agencies. Midrange computers offer lower performance than mainframes but higher performance than microcomputers and are typically used for engineering and midsized business applications. A microcomputer is used for personal computing, for small business computing, and as a workstation attached to large computers or to other small computers on a network. Portable computers—notebook computers, tablet PCs, and handheld computers—are a special type of microcomputer designed to support mobility.

Key Terms

Review Questions

1. Information systems hardware is classified into what three major types?
2. Describe various methods for entering data into and interacting with a computer.
3. How do computers represent internal information, and how is this different from the ways in which humans typically communicate information to each other?
4. Describe the system unit and its key components.
5. What determines the speed of a CPU?
6. How do a computer's primary storage, secondary storage, ROM, and RAM interact?
7. Compare and contrast the different types of secondary data storage.
8. What are output devices? Describe various methods for providing computer output.
9. Describe the different types of computers and their key distinguishing characteristics.

Self-Study Questions

Visit the Interactive Study Guide on the text Web site for additional Self-Study Questions: **www.prenhall.com/jessup.**

1. A system unit contains all of the following except _____.
   A. CD-ROM
   B. central processing unit
   C. power supply
   D. monitor
2. Which of the following is not an input device?
   A. biometric scanner
   B. touch screen
   C. sound board
   D. light pen
3. Which of the following is an example of hardware?
   A. an operating system
   B. Microsoft Suite
   C. system software
   D. central processing unit
4. Which of the following is an output device?
   A. laser printer
   B. touch screen
   C. video camera
   D. keyboard
5. _____ can convert handwritten text into computer-based characters.
   A. scanners
   B. bar-code/optical character readers
   C. text recognition software
   D. audio/video
6. A _____ card is a special credit card with a microprocessor chip and memory circuits.
   A. smart
   B. master
   C. universal
   D. proprietary
7. Which of the following has the largest storage, along with video capacity?
   A. CD-ROM
   B. floppy disk
   C. DVD-ROM
   D. cache memory
8. Which of the following types of computer can use a docking station?
   A. supercomputer
   B. microcomputer
   C. portable computer
   D. mainframe
9. A _____ is the most powerful and expensive computer today.
   A. HAL
   B. mainframe
   C. personal digital assistant
   D. supercomputer
10. A type of tablet PC is called a _____.
    A. hardtop
    B. convertible
    C. sportster
    D. pickup

Answers are on page 476.

Problems and Exercises

1. Match the following terms with the appropriate definitions:
   i. Cache memory
   ii. Batch input
   iii. Smart card
   iv. Audio
   v. DVD-ROM
   vi. Motherboard
   vii. Streaming video
   viii. Network computer
   ix. Flash memory
   x. Memory wall

   a. A special type of credit card with a magnetic stripe that includes a microprocessor chip and memory circuits
   b. A small block of memory used by the central processor to store those instructions most recently or most often used
   c. An optical storage device that has more storage space than a diskette or CD-ROM disk and uses a shorter wavelength laser beam, which allows more optical pits to be deposited on the disk
   d. A sequence of moving images, sent in a compressed form over the Internet and displayed on the receiver's screen as the images arrive
   e. The slow innovation in memory speed as compared to processor speed
   f. A large printed plastic or fiberglass circuit board that contains all of the components that do the actual processing work of the computer and holds or connects to all of the computer's electronic components
   g. A type of input for large amounts of routine information
   h. A microcomputer with minimal memory and storage designed to connect to networks to use the resources provided by servers
   i. Memory that can be repeatedly written to and erased like RAM, but unlike RAM it retains its information after power is turned off
   j. Sound that has been digitized for storage and replay on the computer

2. Imagine that you have decided it is time to purchase a new computer. Analyze your purchase options with regard to using this computer for personal productivity versus business productivity. What differences might your potential usage make on your hardware choices? Why?

3. Imagine that you have just informed your supervisor that you will need to purchase new computers for yourself and three fellow employees. Your supervisor states that she has heard in the news that computer prices are dropping constantly, and she feels that you should wait a bit before making this purchase. She adds that you can still be 100 percent effective with your current computer and software. Develop a counterargument explaining why you should make the purchase now instead of waiting. Will this be a hard sell? Why or why not?

4. Go visit a computer shop or look on the Web for mice or touch pads. What is new about how these input devices look or how they are used? What are some of the advantages and disadvantages of each device?

5. What types of printers are most common today? What is the cost of a color printer versus a black-and-white one? Compare and contrast laser and ink-jet printers in terms of speed, cost, and quality output. What kind of printer would you buy or have you bought?

6. What happens when a computer runs out of RAM? Can more RAM be added? Is there a limit? How does cache memory relate to RAM? Why is RAM so important in today's modern information systems world? Search the Web for RAM retailers. Compare their prices and options.

7. Do you feel that floppy disks will be obsolete sometime in the near future? Why or why not? What storage and retrieval options are available in addition to CD-ROMs and floppy disks? What are you currently using, and what would you like to purchase?

8. Back in the 1970s, rockets were sent to the moon with less than the amount of computing power found in today's microcomputers. Now, these microcomputers seem to be outdating themselves every two years. Will this era of continuous improvement end? Why or why not? If so, when?

9. Do you have a Palm handheld or some other type of PDA (personal digital assistant) or know of someone who does? What functions do PDAs offer? Look on the Web or go to the mall to shop for one. Are the prices decreasing? At what point do you plan to purchase one?

10. Interview an IS manager within an organization that you are familiar with. Determine what issues played a role in the latest information systems hardware purchase this person made. Other than budget, what issues do you think should be considered?

11. Based on your experiences with different input devices, which do you like the best and least? Why? Are your preferences due to the devices' design or usability, or are they based on the integration of the device with the entire information system?

12. Visit a company that uses several different types of computers. Which types do they use? What categories of computers are used at this company (e.g., microcomputers)? Does the company have any plans to expand its computer usage to another category? Why or why not?

13. In simple language, explain what happens with the keystrokes that you type into a computer using a keyboard. Be sure to discuss memory, processing, and inputs. Draw any diagrams that may help you with this explanation.

14. Check the Web for information on different types of Apple computers. What is new? What brands of Windows-compatible computers have you used or purchased? What are you currently using? What influences your computer purchasing decisions?

15. Choose a few of the computer hardware vendors that sell computers to the general public. These include Dell, HP, Lenovo, Gateway, Apple, and many lesser-known brands. Using each company's home page on the Web, determine what options these vendors provide for input devices, processing devices, and output devices. Does it seem that this company has a broad range of choices for its customers? Is there something that you did not find available from this company? Present your findings in a 10-minute presentation to the rest of the class.

Answers to the Self-Study Questions

1. D, p. 455	**2.** C, p. 448	**3.** D, p. 457	**4.** A, p. 466	**5.** C, p. 451
6. A, p. 451	**7.** C, p. 464	**8.** C, p. 471	**9.** D, p. 468	**10.** B, p. 471

Technology Briefing
Information Systems Software

preview >

Software directs the functions of all computer hardware. Without software, the biggest, fastest, most powerful computer in the world is nothing more than a fancy paperweight. After reading this briefing, you will be able to do the following:

1. Describe the common functions of systems software.
2. Describe the various types of application software.
3. Describe the characteristics of various types of programming languages and application development environments.

If you use an automated teller machine (ATM) to withdraw money, word processing to prepare papers, or e-mail to communicate with your classmates and professors, you rely on software to execute instructions. Software is also intertwined with all types of products and services—toys, music, appliances, health care, and countless other products. As a result, the term *software* can be confusing because it is used in many different ways. We will unravel this confusion in the next section by describing the different types of software that are used in today's organizations.

Key Information Systems Software Components

Software consists of programs, or sets of instructions, that tell the computer to perform certain processing functions. Software's job is to provide instructions that allow all the hardware components in your computer system to speak to each other. The two basic types of information systems software are systems software and application software. In the next section, we discuss systems software and how it supports the overall operation of the computer hardware.

Systems Software/Operating System

Systems software is the collection of programs that control the basic operations of computer hardware. The most prominent type of systems software, the **operating system**, coordinates the interaction between hardware devices (e.g., the central processing unit [CPU] and the monitor), peripherals (e.g., printers), application software (e.g., a word processing program), and users, as shown in Figure TB2.1. Additionally, given that microprocessors are embedded in countless devices including cell phones, digital video recorders like TiVo, and automobiles, you are likely interacting with operating systems more than you realize. For example, the I-Drive system utilized within luxury BMW automobiles is enabled by a Microsoft operating system. Likewise, the onboard passenger entertainment systems within many aircraft are powered by the Linux operating system.

Operating systems are often written in assembly language, a very low-level computer programming language that allows the computer to operate quickly and efficiently. The operating system is designed to insulate you from this low-level language and make computer operations unobtrusive. The operating system performs all of the day-to-day operations that we often take for granted when using a computer, such as updating the system clock, printing documents, or saving information to a disk. Just as our brain and nervous system control our body's breathing, heartbeat, and senses without our conscious realization, the systems software controls the computer's basic operations transparently.

FIGURE TB2.1

Operating systems coordinate the interaction between users, application software, hardware, and peripherals.

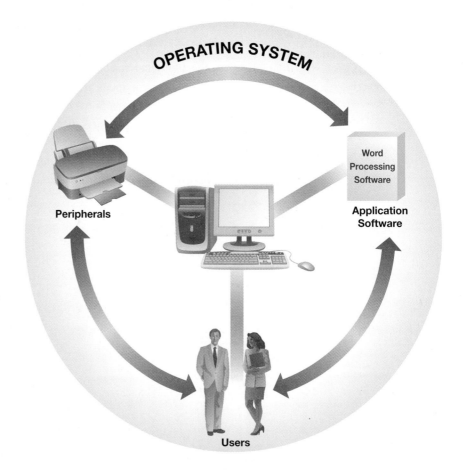

Common Systems Software Functions Many tasks are common to almost all computers. These include getting input from a keyboard or mouse, reading from and/or writing to a storage device (such as a hard disk drive), and presenting information to you via a monitor. Each of these tasks is performed by the operating system, just as a manager of a firm oversees people and processes (as depicted in Figure TB2.2). For example, if you want to copy a word processing file from a flash drive onto your computer, operating systems make this very easy for you. Using an operating system such as Microsoft Windows, you simply use the mouse to point at a graphic icon of the word processing file on the flash drive, then click and drag it onto an icon of your hard disk. That is all it takes to copy the file from the flash drive to your hard drive. The operating system makes this process appear easy. However, underlying the icons and simple dragging operations is a complex set of coded instructions that tell the electronic components of the computer that you are transferring a set of bits and bytes located on the flash drive to a location on your internal hard disk. Imagine if you had to program those sets of instructions every time you wanted to copy a file from one place to another. The operating system manages and executes these types of system operations so that you can spend your time on more important tasks.

The operating system performs many different tasks, including the following:

- Booting (or starting) your computer
- Reading programs into memory and managing memory allocation
- Managing where programs and files are located in secondary storage
- Maintaining the structure of directories and subdirectories
- Formatting disks
- Controlling the computer monitor
- Sending documents to the printer

Interfaces: Command versus GUI The operating system is stored on the hard disk, and a portion of the operating sysem is transferred into primary memory when the computer boots up. After the operating system is in memory, it begins to manage the computer and provide an **interface**. Different operating systems and application programs use different types of user interfaces, with the most typical being command, menu, and GUI. It is through this interface that you interact with the computer. The **command-based interface** requires that you type text commands into the computer to perform basic operations. You could type the command "DELETE File1" to erase the file with the name "File1." Unix is an example of an operating system that uses a command-based user interface. A **menu interface** presents a list of options from which a user selects to invoke a command or system operation. Menus are popular because users only have to understand simple signposts and route options in order to navigate through a system.

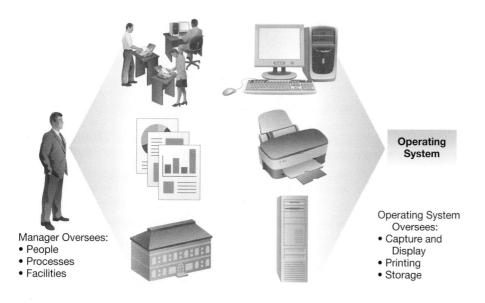

FIGURE TB2.2

A manager oversees organizational resources, whereas an operating system oversees computer resources.

Operating System

Manager Oversees:
- People
- Processes
- Facilities

Operating System Oversees:
- Capture and Display
- Printing
- Storage

The Windows operating environment uses a graphical user interface.

The most common type of interface for the PC is called a graphical user interface (GUI) (see Figure TB2.3). The GUI uses pictures, icons, and menus to send instructions from the user to the computer system. GUIs eliminate the need for users to input arcane commands into the computer and are, therefore, a popular interface. Examples of systems software using a GUI are Windows Vista and Mac OS X.

Popular Operating Systems Just as there are many kinds of computers, there are many different kinds of operating systems (see Table TB2.1). In general, operating systems—whether for large mainframe computers or for small notebook computers—perform similar operations. Obviously, large multiuser supercomputers are more complex than

TABLE TB2.1 Common Operating Systems

Operating System	Description
OS/390	A proprietary operating system developed specifically for large IBM mainframe systems.
Unix	A multiuser, multitasking operating system that is available for a wide variety of computer platforms. Commonly used because of its superior secure design.
Windows	Currently, by far the Windows desktop operating system is the most popular in the world. Variations are also used to operate large servers, small handhelds, and cell phones.
Mac OS	The first commercially graphical-based operating system, making its debut in 1984. Now it is based on the Linux operating system.
Linux	A freely distributed operating system designed in 1991 by a Finnish student. Known for providing a secure, low-cost, multiplatform operating system. Also, Linux powers about one-third of all Web servers.
Symbian OS	An open operating system designed for mobile devices that is owned by Ericsson, Nokia, Panasonic, Samsung, Siemens AG, and Sony Ericsson.

TABLE TB2.2 Common Types of Computer Software Utilities

Utility	Description
Backup	Archives files from the hard disk to tapes, flash drive, or other storage devices
File defragmentation	Converts a fragmented file stored on your hard disk (one not stored contiguously) into one that will load and be manipulated more rapidly
Disk and data recovery	Allows the recovery of damaged or erased information from hard and floppy disks
Data compression	Compresses data by substituting a short code for frequently repeated patterns of data, much like the machine shorthand used by court reporters, allowing more data to be stored on a disk
File conversion	Translates a file from one format to another, so it can be used by an application other than the one used to create it
Antivirus	Monitors and removes viruses—lines of code designed to disrupt the computer's operation and make your life miserable
Device drivers	Allows new hardware added to your computer system, such as a game controller, printer, scanner, and so on, to function with your operating system
Spam blockers	Monitors your incoming e-mail messages and filters or blocks unwanted messages from arriving
Spyware detection and removal	Monitors and removes spyware from your computer
Media players	Allows music in formats such as MP3, WMA, or WAV or video in formats such as MPEG, AVI, or ASF to be listened to or watched on a computer

small desktop systems; therefore, the operating system must account for and manage that complexity. However, the basic purpose of all operating systems is the same.

Utilities **Utilities or utility programs** are designed to manage computer resources and files. Some are included in operating systems software. Others must be purchased separately and installed on your computer. Table TB2.2 provides a sample of a few utility programs that are considered essential.

As mentioned earlier, systems software (or the operating system) is the type of software that is needed to run a computer. However, with just the systems software alone, users can perform very few (if any) important business tasks. In the next section, we discuss a second type, application software, that is used in today's information systems.

Application Software

Unlike systems software, which manages the operation of the computer, **application software** lets a user perform a specific task, such as writing a business letter, processing the payroll, managing a stock portfolio, or manipulating a series of forecasts to come up with the most efficient allocation of resources for a project. The application program interacts with the systems software, which, in turn, interacts with the computer hardware.

The two basic types of application software are the following:

- Customized, or proprietary, software—developed specifically by or for a particular organization
- Commercial software—purchased off the shelf and used by a variety of people and/or organizations to meet their specific needs

These two types of software will be discussed next.

Customized Application Software **Customized application software** is developed to meet the specifications of an organization. This software may be developed in-house by the company's own information systems staff, or it may be contracted, or outsourced, to a specialized vendor charged with developing the software to the company's contractual specifications. Customized application software has two primary advantages over commercial software:

1. **Customizability.** It can be tailored to meet unique user requirements. For example, suppose a retailer needs a kiosk in its store to help shoppers locate specific products. Many shoppers may not be familiar with computers and may be intimidated by operating a keyboard or a mouse. With customized software, the company could develop a touch screen input interface with which users could simply point at objects in a catalog. The computer could then process this information and tell the user that, for example, men's shoes are located on the first floor in the southeast corner and provide a map of the store.

2. **Problem Specificity.** The company pays only for the features specifically required for its users. For example, company- or industry-specific terms or acronyms can be included in the program, as can unique types of required reports. Such specificity is not possible in off-the-shelf programs that are targeted to a general audience.

Off-the-Shelf Application Software Although customized software has advantages, it is not automatically the best choice for an organization. **Off-the-shelf application software** (or packaged software) is typically used to support common business processes that do not require any specific tailoring. In general, off-the-shelf software is less costly, faster to procure, of higher quality, and less risky than customized software. Table TB2.3 summarizes examples of off-the-shelf application software.

Combining Customized and Off-the-Shelf Application Software It is possible to combine the advantages of customized and off-the-shelf software. Companies can purchase off-the-shelf software and then modify it for their own use. For example, a retailer may want to purchase an off-the-shelf inventory management program and then modify it to account for the specific products, outlets, and reports it needs to conduct its day-to-day business. In some cases, the company selling the off-the-shelf software makes these customized changes for a fee. Other vendors, however, do not allow their software to be modified.

Examples of Information Systems Application Software Application software is categorized by its design and by the type of application or task it supports. The task-oriented categories for application software are (1) large business systems and office automation and (2) personal productivity tools (see Table TB2.4). Applications in the business category are purchased or developed by the organization to support the central, organization-wide operations of the company. Those in the office automation or personal productivity category are tools used to support the daily work activities of individuals and small groups. We will describe and provide examples of each type of application software in the following sections.

TABLE TB2.3 Examples of Information Systems Application Software

Category	Application	Description	Examples
Business information systems	Payroll	The automation of payroll services, from the optical reading of time sheets to generating paychecks.	www.infosoftpr.com www.payroll.com
	Inventory	A system that can automate millions of pieces of merchandise in management, order processing, billing, and shipping.	www.trackingsystems.com www.realassetmgt.com
Office automation	Personal productivity	Used for individuals or groups who want to accomplish a wide range of tasks from word processing to graphics to e-mail.	www.openoffice.org www.corel.com www.microsoft.com/office

TABLE TB2.4 Examples of Productivity Software

Tool	Examples
Word processor	Microsoft Word, Corel Word Perfect, OpenOffice Writer, Microsoft Works
Spreadsheet	Microsoft Excel, OpenOffice Calc, Google Spreadsheet, Simple Spreadsheets
Database management	OpenOffice BASE, Microsoft Access, Borland Paradox, Microsoft FoxPro, IBM DB2, MySQL
Presentation software	Apple Keynote, OpenOffice Impress, Microsoft PowerPoint, Harvard Graphics
E-mail	Mozilla Thunderbird, Apple Mail, Opera M2, Microsoft Outlook and Outlook Express
Web browsers	Microsoft Internet Explorer, Mozilla Firefox, Opera Presto, Netscape Navigator
Chat	Microsoft Live Messenger, Yahoo! Messenger, Google GTalk, Trillian, IRQ
Calendar and contact management	Lotus Notes, Microsoft Outlook and Outlook Express, ACT!

Open-Source Software

Open-source software refers to systems software, applications, and programming languages in which the source code (the actual program code) is freely available to the general public for use and/or modification (see Table TB2.5). Open-source software is typically developed by a group of interested parties—individuals and organizations—who wish to improve and extend the software and share these changes with all interested parties. The open-source concept has grown out of the broader technology community as a backlash to large software companies that dominate this industry. Nevertheless, many large mainstream software companies are actively involved in the open-source community. For example, IBM is playing a leading role in evolving the Linux operating system. Likewise, Sun

TABLE TB2.5 Examples of Open-Source Software

Type of Software	Description	Examples
Operating systems	This software operates the hardware on computers.	Linux (www.linux.org)
		FreeBSD (freebsd.org)
		Amoeba (http://www.cs.vu.nl/pub/amoeba/amoeba.html)
Business information systems	A wide variety of applications used in everyday businesses.	Finance: Turbo Cash (www.turbocashuk.com)
		GIS: NASA World Wind (worldwind.arc.nasa.gov)
		Office Suite: OpenOffice (www.openoffice.org)
		Antivirus: Open Antivirus (openantivirus.org)
		Firewall: FWBuilder (fwbuilder.org)
		Web browser: Firefox (www.mozilla.com/firefox)
		E-mail: Mozilla Thunderbird (www.mozilla.com/thunderbird/)
Developer tools	These are both application development suites and database products and are used in application development.	Languages: PERL (PERL.com)
		PHP (php.net)
		Databases: MySQL (mysql.com)
		Web server: Apache (www.apache.org)
		Version control: Microsoft Codeplex (codeplex.com)

Microsystems is active in developing and extending the OpenOffice personal productivity software environment.

People and organizations that actively participate in the open-source software communities have established a certification process, called the Open Source Initiative (OSI), that verifies that software meets a set of standards. To gain OSI certification, a piece of software must meet the following criteria:

- The author or holder of the license of the source code cannot collect royalties on the distribution of the program.
- The distributed program must make the source code accessible to the user.
- The author must allow modifications and derivations of the work under the program's original name.
- No person, group, or field of endeavor can be denied access to the program.
- The rights attached to the program must not depend on the program's being part of a particular software distribution.
- The licensed software cannot place restrictions on other software that is distributed with it.

The primary goals of the OSI movement are to gain widespread participation from a broad range of programmers in order to more quickly evolve a piece of software's capabilities and to more readily find programming flaws. By having a broad and active community of programmers readily share and examine each other's work, proponents of this concept believe that improvements will happen at a faster pace. With the broad and growing success of Firefox, Linux, and OpenOffice, it is clear that open-source software is becoming a clear alternative for individuals and organizations to consider when selecting a variety of software products. You can learn more about how organizations use open-source software in Chapter 4—Managing the Information Systems Infrastructure.

Programming Languages and Development Environments

Each piece of application software we have discussed in this briefing is developed using some programming language. A programming language is the computer language the software vendor uses to write application programs. For application software such as spreadsheets or database management systems, the underlying programming language is invisible to the user. However, programmers in an organization's information systems group and, in some instances, end users can use programming languages to develop their own specialized applications. Many different types of programming languages exist, each with its own strengths and weaknesses. Popular languages used in businesses and industry today are summarized in Table TB2.6.

Compilers and Interpreters

Programs created using programming languages must be translated into code—called assembly or **machine language**—that the hardware can understand. Most programming languages are translated into machine languages through a program called a **compiler**, as depicted in Figure TB2.4. The compiler takes an entire program written in a programming language, such as C#, and converts it into a completely new program in machine language that can be read and executed directly by the computer. Use of a compiler is a two-stage process. First, the compiler translates the computer program into machine language, and then the CPU executes the machine language program. Such programs are usually compiled before they are sold to the customers, speeding up the application.

Some programming environments do not compile the entire program into machine language. Instead, each statement of the program is converted into machine language and executed "on the fly", i.e., one statement at a time, as depicted in Figure TB2.5. The type of program that does the conversion and execution is called an **interpreter**. Programming languages can be either compiled or interpreted.

TABLE TB2.6 Popular Programming Languages

Language	Application	Description
BASIC	General purpose	Beginner's All-Purpose Symbolic Interaction Code. An easy-to-learn language, BASIC works on most all PCs.
C/C++	General purpose	C++ is a newer version of C. Developed at AT&T Bell Labs. Complex languages used for a wide range of applications.
COBOL	Business	COmmon Business-Oriented Language. Developed in the 1960s, it was the first language for developing business software. COBOL is used for most business transaction processing applications on mainframes.
FORTRAN	Scientific	FORmula TRANslator. The first commercial high-level language, developed by IBM in the 1950s. Designed for scientific, mathematical, and engineering applications.
Pascal	Teaching structured programming	Named after the mathematician Blaise Pascal. Uses building-block approach to programming. Useful in developing large programs.
HTML	World Wide Web	Hypertext Markup Language. The most widely used language for developing Web pages. Markup languages simplify pages for transmission by using symbols that tell what document elements should look like when displayed.
Java	World Wide Web	An object-oriented programming language developed at Sun Microsystems in the early 1990s. It is a popular programming language for the Internet because it is highly transportable from one computer to another.
.NET Framework	World Wide Web	Microsoft offers a variety of programming languages (ASP.NET, C#, etc.) that can easily be integrated into Web applications.
LISP	Artificial intelligence	LISt Processor. Dates from the late 1950s. One of the main languages used to develop applications in artificial intelligence. Also the language for high-speed arcade graphics.

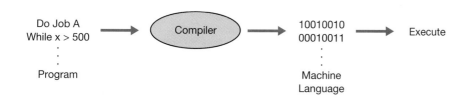

FIGURE TB2.4

A compiler translates the entire computer program into machine language, then the CPU executes the machine language program.

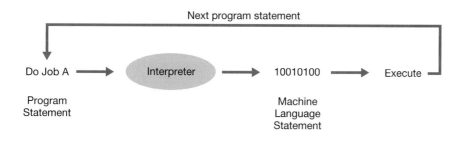

FIGURE TB2.5

Interpreters read, translate, and execute one line of source code at a time.

Programming Languages

Over the past few decades, software has evolved. In the early days of computing, programming languages were quite crude by today's standards. Initially used in the 1940s, the first generation of programming languages was called machine languages. Programmers wrote in binary code to instruct the computer exactly which circuits to turn on and which to turn off. As you might guess, machine language is very unsophisticated and therefore very difficult to write. Because it is so difficult, very few programs are actually written in machine language. Instead, programmers rely on higher-level languages. In the early 1950s, a more sophisticated method for programming was developed in which the binary codes used in machine language were replaced by symbols, called symbolic languages, which were a lot easier for humans to understand. Programs written in symbolic language or any higher-level language still need to be converted into machine language in order to run.

In the mid-1950s, the first high-level programming language, called FORTRAN, was developed by IBM. The big innovation of high-level languages was that they used English-like words to instruct the computer. Consequently, high-level languages are much easier to program in than lower-level languages. Programmers must fully understand the tasks that are to be accomplished when writing a new application in order to choose the best programming language for those tasks.

In the 1970s, several user-oriented languages, called **fourth-generation languages (4GLs)**, were created. These languages are more like English than third-generation languages in that they focus on the desired output instead of the procedures required to get that output. Fourth-generation languages, also called outcome-oriented languages, are commonly used to write and execute queries of a database. For example, the widely used database query language called Structured Query Language (SQL) is a fourth-generation language (see Technology Briefing 3—Database Management for more on SQL). See Figure TB2.6 for several lines of SQL displayed in a sentence-like statement requesting that the last and first names of people in a database called "Customer" with credit limits equal to $100 be displayed.

More recently, **fifth-generation languages (5GLs)** have been developed for use within some expert system or artificial intelligence applications. 5GLs are called natural languages because they allow the user to communicate with the computer using true English sentences. For example, Hewlett-Packard and other software vendors have developed tools for document search and retrieval and database queries that let the user query the documents or database with English-like sentences. These sentences are then automatically converted into the appropriate commands (in some cases SQL) needed to query the documents or database and produce the result for the user. If the system does not understand exactly what the user wants, it can ask for clarification. The same code shown in Figure TB2.6 might appear as shown in Figure TB2.7 if a natural language were used. Although 5GL languages are not common and are still being further developed, they have been used to forecast the performance of financial portfolios, help diagnose medical problems, and estimate weather patterns.

Of course, programming languages continue to evolve. One new characteristic for describing programming languages is whether they are object oriented. In addition, visual

FIGURE TB2.6

A 4GL query using SQL that requests that the last and first names of those who have a credit limit equal to $100 be displayed from a database called "Customer."

```
SELECT LAST FIRST
FROM CUSTOMER
WHERE CREDIT_LIMIT = 100

DIEHR GEORGE
JANKOWSKI DAVID
HAGGARTY JOSEPH
JESSUP JAMIE
VALACICH JAMES
VALACICH JORDAN
```

BEGINNING WITH THE LAST NAME ON THE FOL-
LOWING LIST OF CUSTOMERS, FIND CUSTOMERS
WHO HAVE A CREDIT LIMIT OF $100.

DIEHR GEORGE

JANKOWSKI DAVID

HAGGARTY JOSEPH

JESSUP JAMIE

VALACICH JAMES

VALACICH JORDAN

FIGURE TB2.7

A 5GL query using natural
language to request the same
information as the SQL query in
Figure TB2.6.

programming languages and Web development languages are rapidly gaining popularity.
We discuss these next.

Object-Oriented Languages

Object-oriented languages are the most recent in the progression of high-level programming languages and are extremely popular with application developers. For features of
object-oriented languages, see Table TB2.7.

Visual Programming Languages

Just as you may have found it easier to use a computer operating system with a GUI, such
as Windows Vista or Mac OS X, programmers using **visual programming languages** may
also take advantage of the GUI. For instance, programmers can easily add a command button to a screen with a few clicks of a mouse (see Figure TB2.8) instead of programming the
button pixel by pixel and using many lines of code. Visual Basic.NET and Visual C#.NET
are two popular examples of visual programming languages.

Web Development Languages

If you have been surfing the Web for a while, you probably either already have a personal Web
page or have thought of posting one. In that event, you have some experience with using a programming language. The language you used to create your Web page is called **Hypertext**

TABLE TB2.7 Features of Object-Oriented Languages

Feature	Description	Examples
Objects	These languages allow programmers to group data and program instructions together into modules, or objects, that can be manipulated by the programmer. Once programmed, objects can be reused for different programs.	An object might be a student.
Encapsulation	The process of grouping pieces of data together. When pieces of data are encapsulated, they can be isolated from other parts of the program.	Encapsulation might be the student's grades or financial aid.
Inheritance	This means that when one class of objects is defined, all other objects with the same characteristics are automatically defined by the same terms.	If "student majors" is defined as an object for a search, then, through inheritance, objects such as "English major" or "mathematics major" would fall under the same definition. Therefore, once an object is created, it can be plugged into several different applications.
Event driven	A program written with the event-driven approach does not follow a sequential logic. The programmer does not determine the sequence of execution for the program.	The user can press certain keys and click on various buttons and boxes that are presented. This triggers the code execution.

FIGURE TB2.8

Visual Basic.NET, a visual programming language, is used to create standard business forms.

Source: Hoffer, George, and Valacich, *Modern Systems Analysis and Design*, 5th ed. (Upper Saddle River, NJ: Prentice Hall, 2008).

Markup Language (HTML). HTML is a text-based file format that uses a series of codes, or tags, to set up a document. Because HTML editing programs are visually oriented and easy to use, you do not need to memorize the language to set up a Web page. The programs for creating Web pages are called **Web page builders or HTML editors**, and there are many on the market, including Microsoft FrontPage and Macromedia Dreamweaver.

In HTML, the tags used to identify different elements on a page and to format the page are set apart from the text with angle brackets (< >). Specific tags are used to mark the beginning and the ending of an element or a formatting command. For example, if you want text to appear in bold type, the HTML tag to begin bolding is . The tag to turn off bolding, at the end of the selected text, is . The "a href" command sets up a hyperlink from a word or image on the page to another HTML document. Tags also denote document formatting commands, such as text to be used as a title, sizes of text in headings, the ends of paragraphs, underlining, italics, bolding, and places to insert pictures and sound (see Table TB2.8).

A good way to learn HTML is to find a Web page you like, then use the "View Source" command on your browser to see the hypertext that created the page (see Figure TB2.9). Once you have created your Web page and saved it to disk, you can upload it to an Internet account you have created through your Internet service provider.

TABLE TB2.8 Common HTML Tags

Tag	Description
<html>. . . </html>	Creates an HTML document
<head>. . . </head>	Sets off the title and other information that is not displayed on the Web page itself
<body>. . . </body>	Sets off the visible portion of the document
. . .	Creates bold text
<a href="URL">. . . </a>	Creates a hyperlink
<a href="mailto:EMAIL">. . . </a>	Creates a mailto link
<p>. . . </p>	Creates a new paragraph
<table>. . . </table>	Creates a table

(a)

FIGURE TB2.9

A Web page and the HTML commands used to create it.

Source: Courtesy Washington State University.

(b)

Adding Dynamic Content to a Web Page Markup languages such as HTML are for laying out or formatting Web pages. If you want to add animated cartoons or other dynamic content or have users interact with your Web page other than by clicking on hypertext links, then you will need access to tools such as Java, Web services, a scripting language, and so on.

JAVA. Java is a programming language that was developed at Sun Microsystems in the early 1990s. It lets you spice up your Web page by adding active content such as circles that whirl and change colors, hamsters marching to a tune, forms to help users calculate car payments at various interest rates, or any other such dynamic content. You can do this in one of two ways: by learning Java or a similar language and programming the content you want or by downloading free general purpose **applets** from the Web to provide the content you want on your Web page. Applets are small programs that are executed within another application, such as a Web page. When a user accesses your Web page, the applets you inserted are downloaded from the server with your Web page to a Java-enabled browser running on a PC.

Later, when the user leaves your Web page, the Web page and the applets disappear from his or her computer.

MICROSOFT .NET. **Microsoft .NET** is a programming platform that is used to develop applications that are highly interoperable across a variety of platforms and devices. For example, .NET can create an application that runs on desktop computers, mobile computers, or Web-enabled phones. .NET applications can be constructed using a suite of visual programming languages including C# (pronounced as C-sharp), Java, and BASIC. To gain its interoperability, .NET utilizes Web services.

WEB SERVICES. Web services are web-based software systems used to integrate information from different applications and databases over a network. To support the interoperability from machine to machine, Web services use XML. The *Extensible Markup Language (XML)* was designed (1) to be used as a Web page construction tool when users want to create their own markup tags and (2) to build database queries. XML is a powerful language that lets users create database fields for a number of different applications. XML makes it easy for Web users or other computers to request and receive information from a variety of databases. One practical application of Web services is Microsoft's Live.com. This Web site gathers information from several sources and aggregates the content (see Figure TB2.10).

The advantages of Web services include the following:

- Web services offer interoperability between a variety of software applications that are on different operating systems.
- Web services allow software and services from different companies and locations to be shared and combined easily to provide a powerful integrated application.
- Web services, similar to object-oriented languages, allow the reuse of components.
- Web services are easily distributed, thereby facilitating a distributed approach to application integration.

SCRIPTING LANGUAGES. **Scripting languages** can also be used to supply interactive components to a Web page. These languages let you build programs or scripts directly into HTML page code. Web page designers frequently use them to check the accuracy of user-entered information, such as names, addresses, and credit card numbers. You can also use

FIGURE TB2.10

Web services are enabling powerful applications.

them to connect freestanding applets to your HTML-created Web page. Two common scripting languages are Microsoft's VBScript and Netscape's JavaScript.

JAVASCRIPT. JavaScript, created by Netscape, bears little resemblance to Java. The two are similar, however, in that both Java and JavaScript are useful component software tools for creating Web pages. That is, both allow users to add or create applets that lend dynamic content to Web pages. Both are also cross-platform programs, meaning that they can typically be used by computers running Windows, Linux, Mac OS, and other operating systems.

The development of programming languages is an ongoing process of change and innovation. These changes often result in more capable and complex systems for the user. The popularity of the Internet has spurred the creation of innovative and evolving software. From the pace of change that is occurring, it is clear that many more innovations are on the horizon.

OPEN-SOURCE TOOLS. Along with commercial products there are several open-source tools in wide use today. The most common is PHP, originally designed as a high-level tool for producing dynamic Web content. Another open-source application used frequently is MySQL, a multiuser database management system with over 6 million customers. This robust database can be used instead of commercial products such as Oracle or Microsoft's SQL server. For more information on database management systems, see Technology Briefing 3.

MACROMEDIA FLASH. Another common way to add dynamic content to Web sites is **Flash**. Using the application development suite Macromedia Flash, developers can create animation and video that can be compressed small enough for fast download speeds. When you browse the Web and see animation or complex data streams, this is usually done in Flash. Flash animation is displayed on your screen using the Adobe Flash player. Flash can also include Web services to allow data-driven animation. Some examples of data-driven flash animation on Web sites are the bag builder at Timbuk2 (www.timbuk2.com) and the live major league baseball game update at Yahoo!'s sports site (sports.yahoo.com/mlb/gamechannel).

Automated Development Environments

Over the years, the tools for developing information systems have increased both in variety and in power. In the early days of systems development, a developer was left to use a pencil and paper to sketch out design ideas and program code. Computers were cumbersome to use and slow to program, and most designers worked out on paper as much of the system design as they could before moving to the computer. Today, system developers have a vast array of powerful computer-based tools at their disposal. These tools have changed forever the ways in which systems are developed. **Computer-aided software engineering (CASE)** refers to automated software tools used by systems developers to design and implement information systems. Developers can use these tools to automate or support activities throughout the systems development process with the objective of increasing productivity and improving the overall quality of systems. The capabilities of CASE tools are continually evolving and being integrated into a variety of development environments. Next we briefly review some of the interesting characteristics of CASE.

Types of CASE Tools Two of the primary activities in development of large-scale information systems are the creation of design documents and the management of information. Over the life of a project, thousands of documents need to be created—from screen prototypes to database content and structure to layouts of sample forms and reports. At the heart of all CASE environments is a repository for managing information.

CASE also helps developers represent business processes and information flows by using graphical diagramming tools. By providing standard symbols to represent business processes, information flows between processes, data storage, and the organizational entities

FIGURE TB2.11

High-level system design diagram from a CASE tool.

Source: Hoffer, George, and Valacich, *Modern Systems Analysis and Design*, 5th ed (Upper Saddle River, NJ: Prentice Hall, 2008).

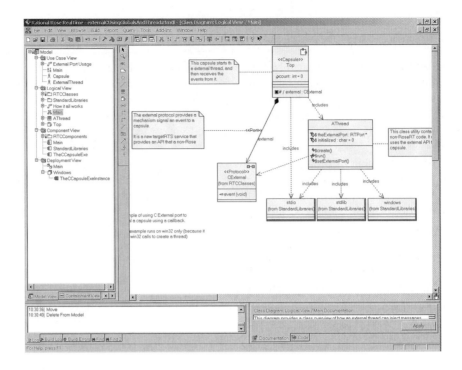

that interact with the business processes, CASE eases a very tedious and error-prone activity (see Figure TB2.11). The tools not only ease the drawing process but also ensure that the drawing conforms to development standards and is consistent with other design documents developed by other developers.

Another powerful capability of CASE is its ability to generate program source code automatically. CASE tools keep pace with contemporary programming languages and can automatically produce programming code directly from high-level designs in languages such as Java, Visual Basic.NET, and C#.NET. In addition to diagramming tools and code generators, a broad range of other tools assists in the systems development process. The general types of CASE tools used throughout the development process are summarized in Table TB2.9.

TABLE TB2.9 General Types of CASE Tools

CASE Tool	Description
Diagramming tools	Tools that enable system process, data, and control structures to be represented graphically.
Screen and report generators	Tools that help model how systems look and feel to users. Screen and report generators also make it easier for the systems analyst to identify data requirements and relationships.
Analysis tools	Tools that automatically check for incomplete, inconsistent, or incorrect specifications in diagrams, screens, and reports.
Repository	A tool that enables the integrated storage of specifications, diagrams, reports, and project management information.
Documentation generators	Tools that help produce both technical and user documentation in standard formats.
Code generators	Tools that enable the automatic generation of program and database definition code directly from the design documents, diagrams, screens, and reports.

Source: Adapted from Hoffer, George, and Valacich, 2008. *Modern Systems Analysis and Design*, 5th ed, Upper Saddle River, NJ: Prentice Hall.

Key Points Review

1. *Describe the common functions of systems software.* Systems software is the collection of programs that form the foundation for the basic operations of the computer hardware. Systems software, or the operating system, performs many different tasks. Some of these tasks include booting your computer, reading programs into memory, managing memory allocation to those programs, managing where programs and files are located in secondary storage, maintaining the structure of directories and subdirectories, formatting disks, controlling the computer monitor, and sending documents to the printer. The systems software manages the dialogue you can have with a computer using either a command-based or graphical interface. A command-based interface requires that text commands be typed into the computer, whereas a graphical user interface uses pictures and icons as well as menus to send instructions back and forth between the user and the computer system.

2. *Describe the various types of application software.* You can find a large number of computer software applications. Customized application software is developed specifically for a single organization. This kind of software is tailored to an organization's unique requirements. Off-the-shelf application software is not customized to the unique needs of one organization but is written to operate within many organizations. In general, off-the-shelf software is less costly, faster to procure, of higher quality, and less risky than customized software. Business information systems are applications developed to perform a firm's organization-wide operations, such as payroll or inventory management. Office automation or personal productivity software is designed to support activities such as word processing and electronic mail.

3. *Describe the characteristics of various types of programming languages and application development environments.* A programming language is the computer language programmers use to write application programs. In order to run on a computer, programs must be translated into binary machine language. Programming languages are translated into machine languages through special types of programs, called compilers and interpreters. Over the past several decades, programming languages have evolved. Early software used machine language, which told the computer exactly which circuits to turn on and which to turn off. Next, symbolic languages used symbols to represent a series of binary statements. This was followed by the development of high-level languages, such as FORTRAN, COBOL, C, and Java. The difference between these high-level languages and earlier languages is that the high-level languages use English-like words and commands, making it easier to write programs. Fourth-generation languages are called outcome-oriented languages because they contain even more English-like commands and tend to focus on what output is desired instead of the procedures required to get that output. Again, these languages made it even easier to program. Fifth-generation languages are called natural languages because they allow the user to communicate with the computer using true English sentences. In addition to this generational evolution, object-oriented programming, visual programming, and Web development languages are relatively new enhancements to programming languages. Object-oriented languages group together data and their corresponding instructions into manipulable objects. Visual programming languages use a graphical interface to build graphical interfaces for other programs. Web development languages are a rapidly evolving set of tools designed for constructing Internet applications and Web content. Together, object-oriented programming, visual programming, and Web development languages are making it easier for programmers to develop today's complex software systems, especially for modern Internet-based systems. Finally, computer-aided software engineering environments help systems developers construct large-scale systems more rapidly and with higher quality.

Key Terms

applets   489

application software   481

command-based interface   479

compiler   484

computer-aided software
   engineering (CASE)   491

customized application
   software   481

fifth-generation languages
   (5GLs)   486

Flash   491

fourth-generation languages
   (4GLs)   486

Hypertext Markup Language
   (HTML)   488

interface   479

interpreter   484

Java   489

JavaScript   491

machine language   484

menu interface   479

Microsoft .NET   490

object-oriented languages
   487

Review Questions

1. Define the term *software* and list several software packages and their uses.
2. Describe at least four different tasks performed by an operating system.
3. What is the difference between a command-based interface and a graphical user interface?
4. Describe the similarities and differences between at least two major operating systems in use today.
5. Name and describe four functions of utility programs.
6. Contrast using off-the-shelf application software with using customized application software.

7. Describe the evolution of programming languages as well as various contemporary programming languages in use today.
8. What is HTML, and why is it important?
9. Describe various options for adding dynamic content to a Web page.
10. What is CASE, and how can it help in the development of information systems?
11. What is open-source software? Why would business choose to implement open-source software?

Self-Study Questions

Visit the Interactive Study Guide on the text Web site for additional Self-Study Questions: **www.prenhall.com/jessup.**

1. Which of the following is an example of an operating system?
   A. Microsoft Access
   B. Microsoft Excel
   C. Microsoft Word
   D. Microsoft Windows
2. An operating system performs which of the following tasks?
   A. booting the computer
   B. managing where programs and files are stored
   C. sending documents to the printer
   D. all of the above
3. Which of the following is a popular operating system?
   A. Noodle
   B. Linux
   C. FORTRAN
   D. PowerEdge
4. Which is not an advantage of off-the-shelf application software?
   A. lower cost
   B. faster to obtain
   C. easier to use
   D. higher quality due to large customer base
5. What is the name of the programming language developed by Sun Microsystems in the 1990's?
   A. Latte
   B. Java
   C. Mocha
   D. none of the above

6. Which of the following programming languages would most likely *not* be used for Web display devices?
   A. HTML
   B. JavaScript
   C. XML
   D. Fortran
7. Automated software tools used to develop information systems that can improve the overall system quality and increase programmer productivity are called _____.
   A. computerized programming
   B. automated development
   C. computer-aided programming
   D. none of the above
8. A utility program may provide _____.
   A. antivirus protection
   B. file conversion capability
   C. file compression and defragmentation
   D. all of the above
9. Fifth-generation languages are also referred to as _____ languages.
   A. assembly
   B. natural
   C. high-level
   D. low-level
10. What were first-generation programming languages called?
    A. natural language
    B. assembly language
    C. machine language
    D. none of the above

Answers are on page 496.

Problems and Exercises

1. Match the following terms with the appropriate definitions:
   i. Operating system
   ii. Applets
   iii. Visual programming languages
   iv. Graphical user interface
   v. Object-oriented programming languages
   vi. Scripting language
   vii. Interpreter
   viii. Flash
   ix. Compiler
   x. Customized application software
      a. Translates a computer program into machine language, which is then executed by the computer
      b. Software used to create and display dynamic content on Web sites
      c. An interface that enables the user to use pictures, icons, and menus in order to send instructions to the computer
      d. Coordinates the interaction between users, applications, and hardware
      e. Programming languages that provide a graphical user interface and are generally easier to use than non-GUI languages
      f. Small software programs that can be used to provide special features to a Web site
      g. Programming languages that group together data and their corresponding instructions into manipulable objects
      h. Software developed based on specifications provided by a particular organization
      i. Translates the computer program into machine language one statement at a time
      j. Used to supply interactive components to a Web page by building programs or scripts directly into HTML page code

2. How do software programs affect your life? Give examples of software from areas other than desktop computers. Are the uses for software increasing over time?

3. In what situations would customized software be utilized? How does the cost compare with the benefit?

4. What are the implications for an organization of having more than one operating system? What might be the advantages? What are some of the disadvantages? Would you recommend such a situation? Prepare a 10-minute presentation to the rest of the class on your findings.

5. Imagine that you are in charge of procuring software applications for your division of a company. You are in need of a powerful business information systems software application that will control most of the accounting and bookkeeping functions. Based on your current knowledge of the intricacies of the accounting profession and its practices, would you be more likely to purchase this application as a customized software application or an off-the-shelf software application? Why did you select this choice? What would make you choose the other option?

6. Based on the information within this and other briefings, as well as the chapters within this textbook, discuss the importance of a single decision to purchase one software application over another—for example, purchasing Microsoft Excel instead of Lotus 1-2-3. Who will be affected? How will they be affected? What changes might occur because of the purchase?

7. Based on your own experiences with computers and computer systems, what do you like and dislike about different operating systems that you have used? Were these uses on a professional or a personal level or both? Who made the decision to purchase that particular operating system? Did you have any say in the purchase decision?

8. Choose an organization that utilizes a variety of different software applications. Are these software applications customized applications, off-the-shelf applications, or a combination of the two? Talk with some of the employees to determine how they feel about using customized versus off-the-shelf software applications.

9. Search the Web for organizations that specialize in creating customized software applications for their clients. In what specific product categories do these organizations specialize, if any? Were you able to find any pricing information directly from their home pages?

10. Have the off-the-shelf software applications you have used met your requirements? Were you able to perform the functions and routines that you needed? Did the software meet your expectations? Would you have bought this type of software if you knew then what you know today?

11. Find an organization that does a lot of in-house programming and utilizes a variety of different programming languages. Determine the generation level of these languages. Are the same personnel programming in most (or all) of the languages, or are different personnel programming in each of the languages? Is this assignment of programmers intentional or unintentional?

12. Imagine that you and a friend are at a local ATM getting some cash from your account to pay for a movie. The ATM does not seem to be working. It is giving you an error message every time you press any button. Is this most likely a software-related problem, a hardware-related problem, or a network-related problem? Why? Use the information in this and other briefings to help you make your decision.

13. Describe how you would handle resistance to implementing CASE tools by those who feel they will be replaced by technology. From whom is this resistance most likely to come? Is this fear legitimate? Why or why not?

Answers to the Self-Study Questions

1.	D, p. 480	**2.**	D, p. 479	**3.**	B, p. 480	**4.**	C, p. 482	**5.**	B, p. 485
6.	D, p. 487	**7.**	D, p. 491	**8.**	D, p. 481	**9.**	B, p. 486	**10.**	C, p. 486

Technology Briefing
Database Management

3

p r e v i e w > People in organizations rely on information about customers, products, invoices, suppliers, markets, transactions, and competitors. In large organizations, this information is stored in **databases** that can be billions (giga-) or trillions (tera-) of bytes in size. If an organization lost this data, it would have difficulties pricing and selling its products or services, cutting payroll checks for its employees, and even sending out mail. After reading this briefing, you will be able to do the following:

1. Describe why databases have become so important to modern organizations.

2. Describe what databases and database management systems are and how they work.

We begin by discussing the importance of database technology for the success of organizations. The technology briefing concludes by describing the key activities involved in designing and using modern databases.

Database Management for Strategic Advantage

Databases are collections of related data organized in a way that facilitates data searches, and are vital to an organization's success. Increasingly, we are living in an information age. Information once taken for granted or never collected at all is now used to make organizations more productive and competitive. Stock prices in the market, potential customers who meet a company's criteria for its products' target audience, and the credit rating of wholesalers and customers are all types of information. Think about this book you are reading, which is in itself information. The publisher had to know available authors capable of writing this book. The publisher also had to have information on you, the target audience, in order to determine that writing this book was worthwhile and to suggest a writing style and collection of topics. The publisher had to use market information to set a price for the book, along with information on reliable wholesalers and distribution partners to get the books from the publisher to you, the customer.

In addition to using databases to create this book, the publisher also uses databases to keep track of the book's sales, to determine royalties for the authors, to set salaries and wages for employees, to pay employees, to prospect for new book opportunities, to pay bills, and to perform nearly every other function in the business. For example, to determine authors' royalties on books sold, the publisher must collect information from hundreds of bookstores and consolidate it into a single report. Large publishers, such as Prentice Hall/Pearson Education, rely on computer databases to perform these tasks.

Other organizations also make use of the database processes used to create and sell this book. For example, Adidas uses databases to design and produce its clothing catalog and to market and sell products. Companies such as Adidas also use databases to gather and store information about customers and their purchasing behavior. Companies such as Nordstrom and Victoria's Secret even produce tailor-made catalogs and other mailings for specific individuals, based on the purchasing information stored in corporate databases. Additionally, database technology fuels electronic commerce on the Web, from tracking available products for sale to providing customer service.

As these examples make clear, database management systems have become an integral part of the total information systems solution for many organizations. Database management systems allow organizations to retrieve, store, and analyze information easily. Next we examine some basic concepts, advantages of the database approach, and database management.

The Database Approach: Foundation Concepts

The database approach now dominates nearly all of the computer-based information systems used today. To understand databases, we must familiarize ourselves with some terminology. In Figure TB3.1, we compare database terminology (middle column) with equivalents in a library (left column) and a business office (right column). We use **database management systems (DBMSs)** to interact with the data in databases. A DBMS is a software application with which you create, store, organize, and retrieve data from a single database or several databases. Microsoft Access is an example of a popular DBMS for personal computers. In the DBMS, the individual database is a collection of related attributes about entities. An **entity** is something you collect data about, such as people or classes (see Figure TB3.2). We often think of entities as **tables**, where each row is a **record** and each column is an **attribute** (also referred to as field). A record is a collection of related attributes about a single entity. Each record typically consists of many attributes, which are individual pieces of information. For example, a name and a Social Security number are attributes of a person.

Advantages of the Database Approach

Before there were DBMSs, organizations used the file processing approach to store and manipulate data electronically. Data were usually kept in a long, sequential computer file, which was often stored on tape. Information about entities often appeared in several different places throughout the information system, and the data was often stored along with, and sometimes embedded within, the programming code that used the data. People

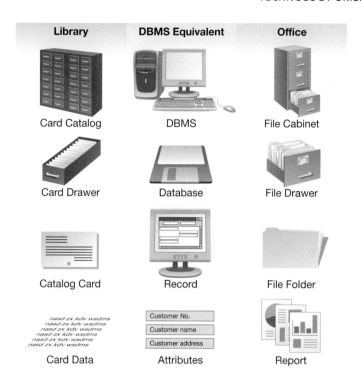

FIGURE TB3.1

Computers make the process of storing and managing data much easier.

had not yet envisioned the concept of separately storing information about entities in nonredundant databases, so files often had repetitive data about a customer, a supplier, or another entity. When someone's address changed, it had to be changed in every file where that information occurred, an often tedious process. Similarly, if programmers changed the code, they typically had to change the corresponding data along with it. This was often no better than the pen-and-paper approach to storing data.

It is possible for a database to consist of only a single file or table. However, most databases managed under a DBMS consist of several files, tables, or entities. A DBMS can manage hundreds or even thousands of tables simultaneously by linking the tables as part of a single system. The DBMS helps us manage the tremendous volume and complexity of

FIGURE TB3.2

This sample data table for the entity Student includes eight attributes and 11 records.

Attribute Types →

ID Number	Last Name	First Name	Street Address	City	State	Zip code	Major
209345	Vance	James	1242 N. Maple	Bloomington	Indiana	47401	Recreation
213009	Haggarty	Joe	3400 E. Longvi	Bloomington	Indiana	47405	Business Management
345987	Borden	Chris	367 Ridge Roa	Bloomington	Indiana	47405	Aeronautical Engineering
457838	Jessup	Mike	12 Long Lake	Bloomington	Indiana	47401	Computer Science
459987	Chan	Virginia	8009 Walnut	Bloomington	Indiana	47405	Sociology
466711	Monroe	Lisa	234 Jamie Lan	Bloomington	Indiana	47401	Pre-Medicine
512678	Austin	John	3837 Wood's E	Bloomington	Indiana	47401	Law
691112	Sherwin	Jordan	988 Woodbridg	Bloomington	Indiana	47404	Political Science
910234	Moore	Larry	1234 S. Grant	Bloomington	Indiana	47403	Civil Engineering
979776	Dunn	Pat	109 Hoosier Av	Bloomington	Indiana	47404	Psychology
983445	Pickett	Steve	989 College	Bloomington	Indiana	47401	Sports Science

→ Attribute

Record (One Row) →

TABLE TB3.1 Advantages of the Database Approach

Advantages	Description
Program–data independence	Much easier to evolve and alter software to changing business needs when data and programs are independent.
Minimal data redundancy	Single copy of data ensures that data storage is minimized.
Improved data consistency	Eliminating redundancy greatly reduces the possibilities of inconsistency.
Improved data sharing	Easier to deploy and control data access using a centralized system.
Increased productivity of application development	Data standards make it easier to build and modify applications.
Enforcement of standards	A centralized system makes it much easier to enforce standards and rules for data creation, modification, naming, and deletion.
Improved data quality	Centralized control, minimized redundancy, and improved data consistency help to enhance the quality of data.
Improved data accessibility	Centralized system makes it easier to provide access for new personnel within or outside organizational boundaries.
Reduced program maintenance	Information changed in the central database is replicated seamlessly throughout all applications.

interrelated data so that we can be sure that a change is automatically made for every instance of that data. For example, if a student or customer address is changed, that change is made through all parts of the system where that data might occur. Using the DBMS prevents unnecessary and problematic redundancies of the data, and the data are kept separate from the programming code in applications. The database need not be changed if a change is made to the code in any of the applications. Consequently, there are numerous advantages to using a database approach to managing organizational data, and these are summarized in Table TB3.1. Of course, moving to the database approach comes with some costs and risks that must be recognized and managed (see Table TB3.2). Nonetheless, most organizations have embraced the database approach because most feel that the advantages far exceed the risks or costs.

Effective Management of Databases

Now that we have outlined why databases are important to organizations, we can talk about how organizational databases can be managed effectively. The **database administrator (DBA)** is responsible for the development and management of the organization's databases. The DBA works with the systems analysts (described in Chapter 9—Developing Information Systems) and programmers to design and implement the database. The DBA must also work with users and managers of the firm to establish policies for managing an organization's databases. The DBA implements security features for the database, such as

TABLE TB3.2 Costs and Risks of the Database Approach

Cost or Risk	Description
New, specialized personnel	Conversion to the database approach may require hiring additional personnel.
Installation and management cost and complexity	Database approach has higher up-front costs and complexity in order to gain long-term benefits.
Conversion costs	Extensive costs are common when converting existing systems, often referred to as *legacy systems*, to the database approach.
Need for explicit backup and recovery	A shared corporate data resource must be accurate and available at all times.
Organizational conflict	Ownership—creation, naming, modification, and deletion—of data can cause organizational conflict.

designating who can look at the database and who is authorized to make changes. The DBA should not make these decisions unilaterally; rather, the DBA merely implements the business decisions made by organizational managers. A good DBA is fundamental to adequately leveraging the investment in database technology.

Key Database Activities

In this section, we describe the key activities involved in the design, creation, use, and management of databases (for more information, see Hoffer, Prescott, and McFadden, 2007). We start by describing how people use databases, beginning with the entry of data.

Entering and Querying Data

DBMS software enables end users to create and manage their own database applications. At some point, data must be entered into the database. A clerk or other data entry professional creates records in the database by entering data. These data may come from telephone conversations, preprinted forms that must be filled out, historical records, or electronic files (see Figure TB3.3a). Most applications enable us to use a graphical user interface (GUI)

FIGURE TB3.3a

A preprinted form used for gathering information that could be stored in a database.

Source: Benjamin-Cummings Publishing.

FIGURE TB3.3b

A computer-based form used for gathering information that could be stored in a database.

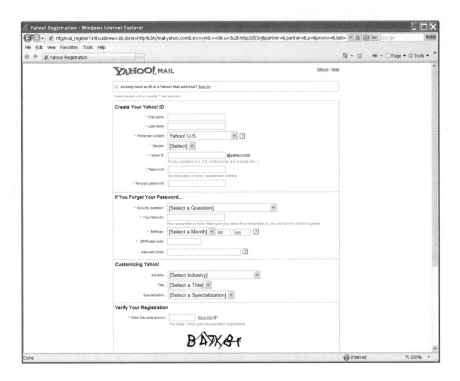

(see Figure TB3.3b) to create a **form**, which typically has blanks where the user can enter the information or make choices, each of which represents an attribute within a database record. This form presents the information to the user in an intuitive way so that the user can easily see and enter the data. The form might be online or printed, and the data could even be entered directly by the customer rather than by a data entry clerk. Forms can be used to add, modify, and delete data from the database.

To retrieve information from a database, we use a **query**. **Structured Query Language (SQL)** is the most common language used to interface with databases. Figure TB3.4 is an example of an SQL statement used to find students who earned an "A" in a particular course. These grades are sorted by student ID number. Writing SQL statements requires time and practice, especially when you are dealing with complex databases with many entities or when you are writing complex queries with multiple integrated criteria—such as adding numbers while sorting on two different attributes. Many DBMS packages have a simpler way of interfacing with the databases—using a concept called **query by example (QBE)**. QBE capabilities in a database enable us to fill out a grid, or template, in order to construct a sample or description of the data we would like to see. Modern DBMS packages, such as Microsoft Access, let us take advantage of the drag-and-drop features of a GUI to create a query quickly and easily. Conducting queries in this manner is much easier than typing the corresponding SQL commands. In Figure TB3.5, we provide an example of the QBE grid from Microsoft Access's desktop DBMS package.

FIGURE TB3.4

This sample SQL statement would be used to find students who earned an "A" in a particular course and to sort that information by student ID number.

```
SELECT DISTINCTROW STUDENT_ID, GRADE
FROM GRADES
WHERE GRADE="A"
ORDER BY STUDENT_ID;
```

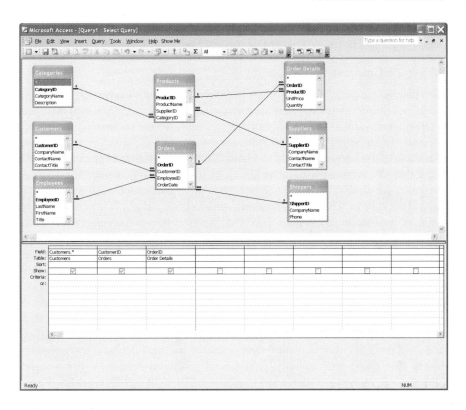

FIGURE TB3.5

Query by example allows you to fill out a form to define what information you want to see.

Creating Database Reports

DBMS packages include a report generation feature. A report is a compilation of data from the database that is organized and produced in printed format. Reports are traditionally produced on paper, but today, many reports are presented to users on-screen, reducing the amount of paper used. **Report generators** are software tools that help users to quickly build reports and describe the data in a useful format.

An example of a report is a quarterly sales report for a restaurant. Adding the daily sales totals, grouping them into quarterly totals, and displaying the results in a table of totals creates a quarterly sales report. Reports are not limited to text and numbers. Report writers enable us to create reports using any data in the databases at whatever level we choose. For example, we could add to the restaurant report breakdowns of the data that show the average daily sales totals by days of the week. We could also show the quarterly sales totals in a bar chart, as shown in Figure TB3.6. Each of these reports could be presented to the user either on paper or online. We could create automatic links between

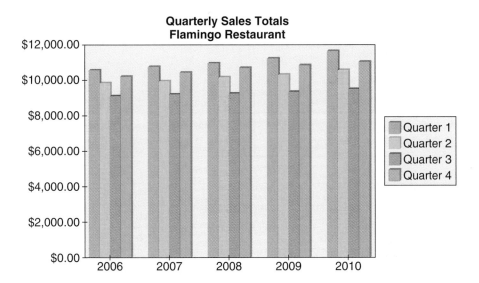

FIGURE TB3.6

The quarterly sales report could show either text and numbers or a bar chart and could include the level of detail captured by the database data.

the underlying sales data located in the database and the attributes on the report in which the underlying data is used so that the reports could be updated automatically.

Database Design

The best database in the world is no better than the data it holds. Conversely, all the data in the world will do you no good if they are not organized in a manner in which there are few or no redundancies and in which you can retrieve, analyze, and understand them. The two key elements of an organizational database are the data and the structure of that data. Let us refer back to the library example in Figure TB3.1 to understand the structure of data. We know that we can find books in the library by using the card catalog. The card catalog is a structure for finding books. Each book has three cards, one each for the title, the author, and the subject. These classifications—title, author, subject—are a model, or representation, of the data in this system. Likewise, we must have a data model for databases. A **data model** is a map or diagram that represents entities and their relationships.

Much of the work of creating an effective organizational database is in the modeling. If the model is not accurate, the database will not be effective. A poor data model will result in data that are inaccurate, redundant, or difficult to search. If the database is relatively small, the effects of a poor design might not be too severe. A corporate database, however, contains many entities, perhaps hundreds or thousands. In this case, the implications of a poor data model can be catastrophic. A poorly organized database is difficult to maintain and process—thus defeating the purpose of having a database management system in the first place. Undoubtedly, your school maintains databases with a variety of entity types—for example, students and grades—with both of these entities having several attributes. Attributes of a Student entity might be Student ID, Name, Campus Address, Major, and Phone. Attributes of a Grades entity might include Student ID, Course ID, Section Number, Term, and Grade (see Figure TB3.7).

For the DBMS to distinguish between records correctly, each instance of an entity must have one unique identifier. For example, each student has a unique Student ID. Note that using the student name (or most other attributes) would not be adequate because students may have the exact same name, live at the same address, or have the same phone number. Consequently, when designing a database, we must always create and use a unique identifier, called a **primary key**, for each type of entity, in order to store and retrieve data accurately. In some instances, the primary key can also be a combination of

FIGURE TB3.7

The attributes for and links between two entities—students and grades.

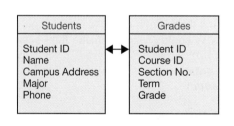

Students

Student ID	Name	Campus Address	Major	Phone
555-39-3232	Joe Jones	123 Any Avenue	Finance	335-2211
289-42-8776	Sally Carter	1200 Wolf Street #12	Marketing	335-8702

Grades

Student ID	Course ID	Section No.	Term	Grade
555-39-3232	MIS 250	2	F'05	D+
555-39-3232	MIS 250	1	F'06	A−
289-42-8776	MIS 250	3	S'07	B+

TABLE TB3.3 Rules for Expressing Associations among Entities and Their Corresponding Data Structures

Relationship	Examples	Instructions
One-to-one	Each team has only one home stadium, and each home stadium has only one team.	Place the primary key from one table into the other as a foreign key.
One-to-many	Each player is on only one team, but each team has many players.	Place the primary key from the table on the one side of the relationship as a foreign key in the table on the many side of the relationship.
Many-to-many	Each player participates in many games and each game has many players.	Create a third table and place the primary keys from each of the original tables together in the third as a combination primary key.

two or more attributes, in which case it is called a **combination primary key**. An example of this is the Grades entity shown in Figure TB3.7, where the combination of Student ID, Course ID, Section Number, and Term uniquely refers to the grade of an individual student, in a particular class (section number), from a particular term. Attributes not used as the primary key can be referred to as **secondary keys** when they are used to identify one or more records within a table that share a common value. For example, a secondary key in the Student entity shown in Figure TB3.7 would be Major when used to find all students who share a particular major.

Associations

To retrieve information from a database, it is necessary to associate or relate information from separate tables. The three types of associations among entities are one-to-one, one-to-many, and many-to-many. Table TB3.3 summarizes each of these three associations and shows how they should be handled in database design for a basketball league.

To understand how associations work, consider Figure TB3.8, which shows four tables—Home Stadium, Team, Player, and Games—for keeping track of the information for a basketball league. The Home Stadium table lists the Stadium ID, Stadium Name, Capacity, and Location, with the primary key underlined. The Team table contains two attributes, Team ID and Team Name, but nothing about the stadium where the team plays. If we wanted to have such information, we could gain it only by making an association between the Home Stadium and Team tables. For example, if each team has only one home stadium and each home stadium has only one team, we have a one-to-one relationship between the team and the home stadium entities. In situations in which we have one-to-one relationships between entities, we place the primary key from one table in the table for the

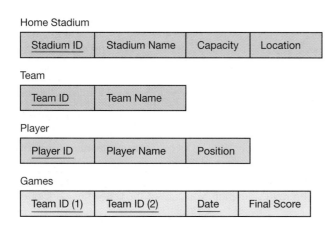

FIGURE TB3.8

Tables used for storing information about several basketball teams, with no foreign key attributes added so that associations cannot be made.

A. One-to-one relationship: Each team has only one home stadium, and each home
   stadium has only one team.

Team

Team ID	Team Name	*Stadium ID*

B. One-to-many relationship: Each player is on only one team, but each team has
   many players.

Player

Player ID	Player Name	Position	*Team ID*

C. Many-to-many relationship: Each player participates in many games, and each game
   has many players.

Player Statistics

Team 1	*Team 2*	*Date*	*Player ID*	Points	Minutes	Fouls

other entity and refer to this attribute as a **foreign key**. In other words, a foreign key refers to an attribute that appears as a nonprimary key attribute in one entity and as a primary key attribute (or part of a primary key) in another entity. By sharing this common—but unique—value, entities can be linked, or associated, together. We can choose in which of these tables to place the foreign key of the other. After adding the primary key of the Home Stadium entity to the Team entity, we can identify which stadium is the home for a particular team and find all the details about that stadium (see section A in Figure TB3.9).

When we find a one-to-many relationship—for example, each player plays for only one team, but each team has many players—we place the primary key from the entity on the one side of the relationship, the Team entity, as a foreign key in the table for the entity on the many side of the relationship, the Player entity (see section B in Figure TB3.9). In essence, we take from the one and give to the many, a Robin Hood strategy.

When we find a many-to-many relationship (e.g., each player plays in many games, and each game has many players), we create a third, new entity—in this case, the Player Statistics entity and corresponding table. We then place the primary keys from each of the original entities together into the third, new table as a new, combination primary key (see section C in Figure TB3.9).

You may have noticed that by placing the primary key from one entity in the table of another entity, we are creating a bit of redundancy. We are repeating the data in different places. We are willing to live with this bit of redundancy, however, because it enables us to keep track of the interrelationships among the many pieces of important organizational data that are stored in different tables. By keeping track of these relationships, we can quickly answer questions such as "Which players on the SuperSonics played in the game on February 16 and scored more than 10 points?" In a business setting, the question might be "Which customers purchased the 2007 forest green Ford Escape from Thom Roberts at the Roberts Ford dealership in Bloomington, Indiana, during the first quarter of 2007, and how much did each pay?" This kind of question would be useful in calculating the bonus money Thom should receive for that quarter or in recalling those specific vehicles in the event of a recall by the manufacturer.

Entity-Relationship Diagramming

A diagramming technique that creates an **entity-relationship diagram (ERD)** is commonly used when designing databases, especially when showing associations between entities. To create an ERD, you draw entities as boxes and draw lines between entities to show relationships. Each relationship can be labeled on the diagram to give additional meaning to the diagram. For example, Figure TB3.10 shows an ERD for the basketball league data previously discussed. From this diagram, you can see the following associations:

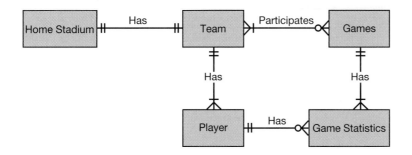

FIGURE TB3.10

An entity-relationship diagram showing the relationships between entities in a basketball league database.

- Each Home Stadium has a Team.
- Each Team has Players.
- Each Team participates in Games.
- For each Player and Game, there are Game Statistics.

When you are designing a complex database, with numerous entities and relationships, ERDs are very useful. They allow the designer to talk with people throughout the organization to make sure that all entities and relationships have been found.

The Relational Model

Now that we have discussed data, data models, and the storage of data, we need a mechanism for joining entities that have natural relationships with one another. For example, there are several relationships among the four entities we described previously—students, instructors, classes, and grades. Students are enrolled in multiple classes. Likewise, instructors teach multiple classes and have many students in their classes in a semester. It is important to keep track of these relationships. We might, for example, want to know which courses a student is enrolled in so that we can notify her instructors that she will miss courses because of an illness. The primary DBMS approach, or model, for keeping track of these relationships among data entities is the relational model. Other models—the hierarchical, network, and object-oriented models—are also used to join entities with commercial DBMSs, but this is beyond the scope of our discussion (see Hoffer et al., 2007).

The most common DBMS approach in use today is the **relational database model**. A DBMS package using this approach is referred to as a relational DBMS, or RDBMS. With this approach, the DBMS views and presents entities as two-dimensional tables, with records as rows and attributes as columns. Tables can be joined when there are common columns in the tables. The uniqueness of the primary key, as mentioned earlier, tells the DBMS which records should be joined with others in the corresponding tables. This structure supports very powerful data manipulation capabilities and linking of interrelated data. Database files in the relational model are three-dimensional: a table has rows (one dimension) and columns (a second dimension) and can contain rows of attributes in common with another table (a third dimension). This three-dimensional database is potentially much more powerful and useful than traditional, two-dimensional, "flat file" databases (see Figure TB3.11).

A good relational database design eliminates unnecessary data duplications and is easy to maintain. To design a database with clear, nonredundant relationships, you perform a process called normalization.

Normalization

To be effective, databases must be efficient. Developed in the 1970s, **normalization** is a technique to make complex databases more efficient and more easily handled by the DBMS (Hoffer et al., 2007). To understand the normalization process, let us return to the scenario in the beginning of this chapter. Think about your report card. It looks like nearly any other form or invoice. Your personal information is usually at the top, and each of your classes is listed, along with an instructor, a class day and time, the number

With the relational model, we represent these two entities, department and instructor, as two separate tables and capture the relationship between them with a common column in each table.

Department Records

Department No	Dept Name	Location	Dean
Dept A			
Dept B			
Dept C			

Instructor Records

Instructor No	Inst Name	Title	Salary	Dept No
Inst 1				
Inst 2				
Inst 3				
Inst 4				

of credit hours, and a location. Now think about how this data is stored in a database. Imagine that this database is organized so that in each row of the database, the student's identification number is listed on the far left. To the right of the student ID are the student's name, local address, major, phone number, course and instructor information, and a final course grade (see Figure TB3.12). Notice that there is redundant data for students, courses, and instructors in each row of this database. This redundancy means that this database is not well organized. If, for example, we want to change the phone number of an instructor who has hundreds of students, we have to change this number hundreds of times.

Elimination of data redundancy is a major goal and benefit of using data normalization techniques. After the normalization process, the student data is organized into five separate tables (see Figure TB3.13). This reorganization helps simplify the ongoing use and maintenance of the database and any associated analysis programs.

Data Dictionary

Each attribute in the database needs to be of a certain type. For example, an attribute may contain text, numbers, or dates. This **data type** helps the DBMS organize and sort the data, complete calculations, and allocate storage space.

Once the data model is created, a format is needed to enter the data in the database. A **data dictionary** is a document that database designers prepare to help individuals enter data. The data dictionary explains several pieces of information for each attribute, such as its name, whether it is a key or part of a key, the type of data expected (dates, alphanumeric, numbers, and so on), and valid values. Data dictionaries can include information such as why the data item is needed, how often it should be updated, and on which forms and reports the data appears.

Database of students, courses, instructors, and grades with redundant data.

ID	Student_ID	Student_Name	Campus_Address	Major	Phone	Course_ID	Course_Title	Instructor_Name	Instructor_Location	Instructor_Phone	Term	Grade
1	A121	Joy Egbert	100 N. State Street	MIS	555-7771	MIS 350	Intro. MIS	Hess	T437C	555-2222	S07	A
2	A121	Joy Egbert	100 N. State Street	MIS	555-7771	MIS 372	Database	Sarker	T437F	555-2224	S07	B
3	A121	Joy Egbert	100 N. State Street	MIS	555-7771	MIS 375	Elec. Comm.	Wells	T437D	555-2228	S07	B+
4	A121	Joy Egbert	100 N. State Street	MIS	555-7771	MIS 448	IS Proj. Mgmt	Schneider	T437E	555-2227	F06	A-
5	A121	Joy Egbert	100 N. State Street	MIS	555-7771	MIS 374	Telecomm	Marrett	T437A	555-2221	S07	C+
6	A123	Larry Mueller	123 S. State Street	MIS	555-1235	MIS 350	Intro. MIS	Hess	T437C	555-2222	S07	A
7	A123	Larry Mueller	123 S. State Street	MIS	555-1235	MIS 372	Database	Sarker	T437F	555-2224	S07	B-
8	A123	Larry Mueller	123 S. State Street	MIS	555-1235	MIS 375	Elec. Comm.	Wells	T437D	555-2228	S07	A-
9	A123	Larry Mueller	123 S. State Street	MIS	555-1235	MIS 448	IS Proj. Mgmt	Schneider	T437E	555-2227	F06	C+
10	A124	Mike Guon	125 S. Elm	MGT	555-2214	MIS 350	Intro. MIS	Hess	T437C	555-2222	S07	A-
11	A124	Mike Guon	125 S. Elm	MGT	555-2214	MIS 372	Database	Sarker	T437F	555-2224	S07	A-
12	A124	Mike Guon	125 S. Elm	MGT	555-2214	MIS 375	Elec. Comm.	Wells	T437D	555-2228	S07	B+
13	A124	Mike Guon	125 S. Elm	MGT	555-2214	MIS 374	Telecomm	Marrett	T437A	555-2221	S07	B
14	A126	Jackie Judson	224 S. Sixth Street	MKT	555-1245	MIS 350	Intro. MIS	Hess	T437C	555-2222	S07	A
15	A126	Jackie Judson	224 S. Sixth Street	MKT	555-1245	MIS 372	Database	Sarker	T437F	555-2224	S07	B+
16	A126	Jackie Judson	224 S. Sixth Street	MKT	555-1245	MIS 375	Elec. Comm.	Wells	T437D	555-2228	S07	B+
17	A126	Jackie Judson	224 S. Sixth Street	MKT	555-1245	MIS 374	Telecomm	Marrett	T437A	555-2221	S07	A-

Record: 1 of 17

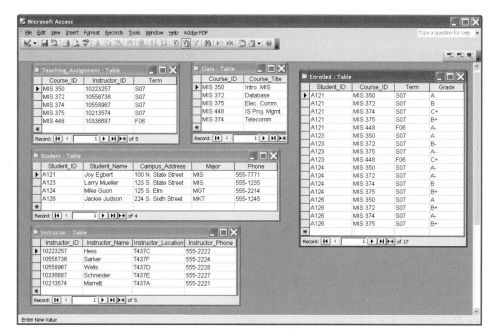

FIGURE TB3.13

Organization of information on students, courses, instructors, and grades after normalization.

Data dictionaries can be used to enforce **business rules**. Business rules, such as who has authority to update a piece of data, are captured by the designers of the database and included in the data dictionary to prevent illegal or illogical entries from entering the database. For example, designers of a warehouse database could capture a rule in the data dictionary to prevent invalid ship dates from being entered into the database.

How Organizations Get the Most from Their Data

Modern organizations are said to be drowning in data but starving for information. Despite being a mixed metaphor, this statement seems to portray quite accurately the situation in many organizations. The advent of Internet-based electronic commerce has resulted in the collection of an enormous amount of customer and transactional data. How this data is collected, stored, and manipulated is a significant factor influencing the success of a commercial Internet Web site. In this section we discuss how organizations are getting the most from their data.

Linking Web Site Applications to Organizational Databases

A recent database development is the creation of links between sites on the Web and organizational databases. For example, many companies are enabling users of their Web site to view product catalogs, check inventory, and place orders—all actions that ultimately read and write to the organizations' databases. Traditionally, databases would have to be located together or have complex software connecting them in order to utilize each other's data. With the wide use of Web services (see Technology Briefing 2—Information Systems Software for more information), data can now easily be integrated into many applications from many sources regardless of where the database physically resides.

Some Internet electronic commerce applications can receive and process millions of transactions per day. To gain the greatest understanding of customer behavior and to ensure adequate system performance for customers, you must manage online data effectively. For example, Amazon.com is the world's largest bookstore, with more than 2.5 million titles, and is open 24 hours a day, 365 days a year, with customers all over the world ordering books and a broad range of other products. Amazon's servers log millions of transactions per day. Amazon is a vast departure from a traditional physical bookstore. In fact, the largest physical bookstore carries "only" about 170,000 titles, and it would not be economically feasible to build a physical bookstore the size of Amazon; a physical bookstore that carried Amazon's 2.5 million titles would need to be the size of nearly 25 football fields. The key to effectively designing an online electronic commerce business is clearly the effective management of online data. In Chapter 4—Managing the Information Systems Infrastructure, you can learn how organizations use databases to gather business intelligence and gain competitive advantage.

Key Points Review

1. *Describe why databases have become so important to modern organizations.* Databases often house mission-critical organizational data, so proper design and management of the databases is critical. If they are designed and managed well, the databases can be used to transform raw data into information that helps people do their jobs faster, better, and more effectively, ultimately helping customers and making the firm more competitive.

2. *Describe what databases and database management systems are and how they work.* A database is a collection of related data organized in a way that facilitates data searches. A database contains entities, attributes, records, and tables. Entities are things about which we collect data, such as people, courses, customers, or products. Attributes are the individual pieces of information about an entity, such as a person's last name or Social Security number, that are stored in a database record.

A record is the collection of related attributes about an entity; usually, a record is displayed as a database row. A table is a collection of related records about an entity type; each row in the table is a record, and each column is an attribute. A database management system is a software application with which you create, store, organize, and retrieve data from a single database or several databases. Data is typically entered into a database through the use of a specially formatted form. Data is retrieved from a database through the use of queries and reports. The data within a database must be adequately organized so that it is possible to store and retrieve information effectively. The main approach for structuring the relationships among data entities is the relational database model. Normalization is a technique to transform complex databases into a more efficient form, allowing them to be more easily maintained and manipulated.

Key Terms

attribute   498
business rules   509
combination primary key   505
data dictionary   508
data model   504
data type   508
databases   497
database administrator
    (DBA)   500

database management systems
    (DBMSs)   498
entity   498
entity-relationship diagram
    (ERD)   506
foreign key   506
form   502
normalization   507
primary key   504

query   502
query by example (QBE)   502
record   498
relational database model   507
report generators   503
secondary keys   505
Structured Query Language
    (SQL)   502
tables   498

Review Questions

1. Describe why databases have become so important to modern organizations.
2. Explain the difference between a database and a database management system.
3. List some reasons that record keeping with physical filing systems is less efficient than using a database on a computer.
4. Describe how the following terms are related: entity, attribute, record, and table.

5. Compare and contrast the primary key, combination key, and foreign key within an entity.
6. How do Structured Query Language and query by example relate to each other?
7. What is the purpose of normalization?
8. Explain how organizations are getting the most from their investment in database technologies.

Self-Study Questions

Visit the Interactive Study Guide on the text Web site for additional Self-Study Questions: **www.prenhall.com/jessup.**

1. A database comprises _____.
   A. attributes
   B. records
   C. organized data for querying
   D. all of the above

2. A database is used to collect, organize, and query information. Which of the following is least likely to use a database as a fundamental part of their job?
   A. airline reservations agent
   B. university registrar
   C. Social Security Administration
   D. security guard

3. A(n) _____ is a unique identifier that can be a combination of two or more attributes.
   A. secondary key
   B. primary key
   C. tertiary key
   D. elementary key

4. Which of the following is not true in regard to the relational database model?
   A. Entities are viewed as tables, with records as rows and attributes as columns.
   B. Databases use keys and redundant data in different tables in order to link interrelated data.
   C. Entities are viewed as children of higher-level attributes.
   D. A properly designed table has a unique identifier that may be one or more attributes.

5. Each team has only one home stadium, and each home stadium has only one team. This is an example of which of the following relationships?
   A. one-to-one
   B. one-to-many
   C. many-to-many
   D. many-to-one

6. A database administrator is _____.
   A. the primary user of a database management system
   B. responsible for the development and management of the organization's database
   C. none of the above
   D. all of the above

7. Which of the following statements about databases is false?
   A. Databases are becoming more popular.
   B. Minimal planning is required since the software is so advanced.
   C. A data warehouse utilizes a database.
   D. A database administrator is responsible for the development and management of a database.

8. A popular diagramming technique for designing databases is called _____.
   A. flowcharting
   B. database diagramming
   C. entity relationship diagramming
   D. none of the above

9. _____ is a technique to make a complex database more efficient by eliminating redundancy.
   A. data repository
   B. associating
   C. normalization
   D. standardization

10. Which of the following is a document, sometimes published as an online interactive application, prepared by the designers of the database to aid individuals in data entry?
    A. data dictionary
    B. database
    C. normalization
    D. data model

Answers are on page 512.

Problems and Exercises

1. Match the following terms with the appropriate definitions:
   i. Database
   ii. Database management system
   iii. Database administrator
   iv. Query by example
   v. Primary key
   vi. Foreign key
   vii. Data dictionary
   viii. Relational model
   ix. Normalization
   x. Business rules

   a. A person responsible for the development and management of the organization's databases
   b. An attribute that appears as a nonprimary key attribute in one entity and as a primary key in another
   c. A field included in a database that assures that each instance of an entity is stored or retrieved accurately
   d. Present in the data dictionary these prevent illegal or illogical entries from entering the database
   e. A collection of related data organized in a way that facilitates data searches

f. A software application with which you can create, store, organize, and retrieve data for one or many databases

g. A technique used to simplify complex databases so that they are more efficient and easier to maintain

h. The capability of a DBMS to enable us to request data by simply providing a sample or a description of the types of data we would like to see

i. A DBMS approach in which entities are presented as two-dimensional tables that can be joined together with common columns

j. A document, sometimes published as an online interactive application, prepared by the designers of the database to aid individuals in data entry

2. You see an announcement for a job as a database administrator for a large corporation but are unclear about what this title means. Research this on the Web and obtain a specific job announcement.

3. How and why are organizations without extensive databases falling behind in competitiveness and growth? Is this simply a database problem that can be fixed easily with some software purchases? Search the Web for stories or news articles that deal with the issue of staying competitive by successfully managing data. How are these stories similar to each other? How are they different? Prepare a 10-minute presentation to the class on your findings.

4. What are six advantages of databases and three costs or risks of a database system? Why are databases becoming more popular?

5. Why would it matter what data type is used for the attributes within a database? How does this relate to programming? How does this relate to queries and calculations? Does the size of the database matter?

6. Discuss the issue of data accuracy based on what you have learned from this briefing. Does a computer database handle accuracy issues better than a filing system? Who (or what) is ultimately responsible for data accuracy?

7. List three different database software applications. Compare and contrast the advantages and disadvantages, including price, program size, and other pertinent factors.

8. Have several classmates interview database administrators within organizations with which they are familiar. To whom do these people report? How many employees report to these people? Is there a big variance in the responsibilities across organizations? Why or why not?

9. Go to www.ecampus.com and search for a couple of textbooks that you either have bought or intend to purchase. What is the selection of books available, and what is the delivery time? Are shipping costs added to the cost of the books? How does this compare with the campus bookstore? Which process is more convenient?

10. Based on your understanding of a primary key and the information in the following sample grades table, determine the best choice of attribute(s) for a primary key.

Student ID	Course	Grade
100013	Visual Programming	A
000117	Telesystems	A
000117	Introduction to MIS	A

11. Search the Web for an organization with a home page that utilizes a link between the home page and the organization's own database. Describe the data that the browser enters and the organization's possible uses for this data. Can you retrieve company information or can you only send information to the company? How are the data displayed on the home page?

12. Select an organization with which you are familiar that utilizes flat file databases for their database management. Determine whether the organization should move to a relational database. Why would you make this recommendation? Is it feasible to do so? Why or why not?

13. What databases are used at your educational institution? Have you filled out a lot of paperwork that was then entered by someone else? Did you actually do some of the data entry for your account? What kind of information were you able to retrieve about your account? From where was the database administered? Were you able to access it online?

Answers to the Self-Study Questions

1. D, p. 498
2. D, p. 498
3. B, p. 504
4. C, p. 507
5. A, p. 505
6. B, p. 500
7. B, p. 498
8. C, p. 506
9. C, p. 507
10. A, p. 508

Technology Briefing

Networking

p r e v i e w > The purpose of this technology briefing is to introduce key networking concepts, technologies, and applications. This discussion provides you with a solid foundation for understanding how computers are connected across a room or across the world. After reading this briefing, you will be able to do the following:

1. Describe the evolution of and types of computer networks.

2. Understand networking fundamentals, including network services and transmission media.

3. Describe network software and hardware, including media access control, network topologies, and protocols, as well as connectivity hardware for both local area and wide area networks.

Telecommunications and networking technologies are taking on more and more importance as organizations rely more on computer-based information systems. Understanding how the underlying networking technologies work and where these technologies are heading will help you better understand the potential of information systems. In this briefing, we describe the enabling technologies underlying computer networks, how they form networks, and how these networks are used. The discussion begins with a description of the fundamental elements of computer networking.

Evolution of Computer Networking

Human communication involves the sharing of information and messages between senders and receivers. The sender of a message formulates the message in her brain and codes the message into a form that can be communicated to the receiver—through voice, for example. The message is then transmitted along a communication pathway to the receiver. The receiver, using his ears and brain, then attempts to decode the message, as shown in Figure TB4.1. This basic model of human communication helps us to understand telecommunications or computer networking.

Messages, Senders, and Receivers

Computer networking is the sharing of information or services. As with human communication, all computer networks require three things:

- Senders and receivers that have something to share
- A pathway or transmission medium, such as a cable, to send the message
- Rules or protocols dictating communication between senders and receivers

The easiest way to understand computer networking is through the human communication model. Suppose you are planning to study abroad in Europe for a semester. You need information about schools that accept exchange students. The first requirement for a network—information to share—has now been met. You start your search by writing a letter (coding your message) and faxing it to several schools. You have met the second requirement: a means of transmitting the coded message. The fax system is the pathway or transmission medium used to contact the receiver. Transmission media refers to the physical pathway—cable(s) and wireless—used to carry network information. At this point, you may run into some difficulties. Not all the receivers of your fax may understand what you have written—decode your message—because they speak other languages. Although you have contacted the receiver, you and the receiver of your message must meet the third requirement for a successful network: you must establish a language of communication—the rules or protocols governing your communication. **Protocols** define the procedures that different computers follow when they transmit and receive data. You both might decide that one communication protocol will be that you communicate in English. This communication session is illustrated in Figure TB4.2.

Computer Networks

A fundamental difference between human and computer communication is that human communication consists of words, whereas computer communication consists of bits, the fundamental information units of computers, as depicted in Figure TB4.3. Virtually all types of information can be transmitted on a computer network—documents, art,

FIGURE TB4.1

Communication requires senders and receivers.

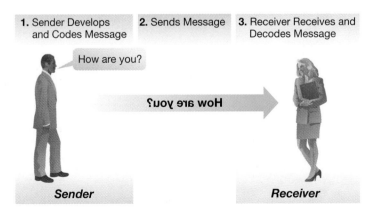

1. Sender Develops and Codes Message 2. Sends Message 3. Receiver Receives and Decodes Message

How are you?

How are you?

Sender *Receiver*

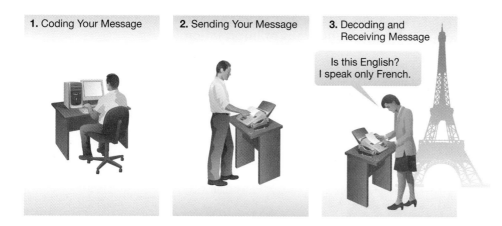

1. Coding Your Message

2. Sending Your Message

3. Decoding and Receiving Message

Is this English?
I speak only French.

FIGURE TB4.2

Coding, sending, and decoding a message.

music, or film—although each type of information has vastly different requirements for effective transmission. For example, a single screen of text is approximately 14 KB of data, whereas a publication-quality photograph could be larger than 200 MB of data (see Table TB4.1). The process of converting a photograph or a song into digital information, or bits, is called **digitizing**. After information is converted into bits, it can travel across a network. To transmit either the screen of text or the picture in a timely manner from one location to another, adequate bandwidth is needed. For example, using an old-fashioned 56-kilobits-per-second (Kbps) modem—a modem that transmits approximately 56,000 bits of data in a second—a single screen of text would be transferred in under one second, while a publication-quality photograph could take more than eight hours. Hence, different types of information have different communication bandwidth requirements (see www.numion.com/Calculators/Time.html for a tool that helps you calculate download times).

Now that you understand the basic elements of networks, we will talk about how they have evolved. Since the beginning of the information age in the 1950s, people and enterprises have used computers to process data and information. Over the years, however, computer networks have gotten better and better.

Human Communication

Words Are Spoken

Computer Communication

Bits

010110111010011010

Art
Film
Music
Business Information

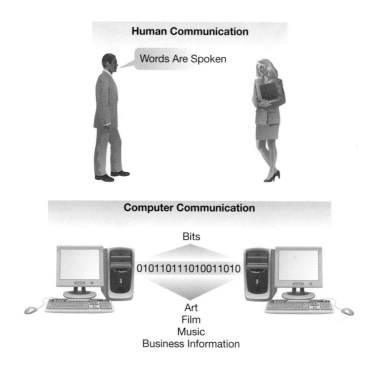

FIGURE TB4.3

In human communication, words are spoken and transmitted in the air. In computer communication, digital data are transmitted over some type of communication medium.

TABLE TB4.1 Communication and Storage/Bandwidth Requirements for Different Types of Information

Type of Information	Raw Size	Compressed Size
Voice		
Telephone	64 KBps	16–32 KBps
Teleconference	96 KBps	32–64 KBps
Compact disc	1.41 MBps	63–128 KBps
Data		
Single screen of text	14.4 KB	4.8–7 KB
Typed page, single-spaced	28.8 KB	9.6–14.4 KB
Faxed page (low to high resolution)	1.68–3.36 MB	130–336 KB
Super VGA screen image	6.3 MB	315–630 KB
Digital X-ray	50.3 MB	16.8–25.1 MB
Publication-quality photograph	230.4 MB	23–46 MB
Video		
Video telephony	9.3 MBps	64–384 KBps
Video teleconferencing	37.3 MBps	384 KBps–1.92 MBps
Studio-quality digital tv	166 MBps	1.7 MBps
High definition television	1.33 GBps	20–50 MBps

Note: KB = kilobytes, MB = megabytes; KBps = kilobytes per second; MBps = megabytes per second; GBps = gigabytes per second.

Source: Adapted from *Business Data Communications*, 2nd ed., by Stallings/VanSlyke © 1997. Reprinted by permission of Prentice Hall, Inc., Upper Saddle River, NJ.

Centralized Computing

Centralized computing, depicted in Figure TB4.4, remained largely unchanged through the 1970s. In this model, large centralized computers, called mainframes, were used to process and store data. During the mainframe era (beginning in the 1940s), people entered data on mainframes through the use of local input devices called **terminals**. These devices were called "dumb" terminals because they did not conduct any processing, or "smart," activities. The centralized computing model is not a true network because there is no sharing of information and capabilities. The mainframe provides all the capabilities, and the terminals are only input/output devices. Computer networks evolved in the 1980s when organizations needed separate, independent computers to communicate with each other.

Distributed Computing

The introduction of personal computers in the late 1970s and early 1980s gave individuals control over their own computing. Organizations also realized that they could use multiple small computers to achieve many of the same processing goals of a single

FIGURE TB4.4

In the centralized computing model, all processing occurs in one central mainframe.

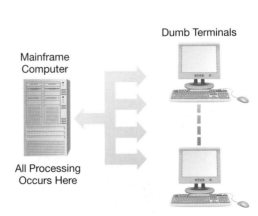

Dumb Terminals

Mainframe Computer

All Processing Occurs Here

large computer. People could work on subsets of tasks on separate computers rather than using one mainframe to perform all the processing. Achieving the goal of separate processing required computer networks so that information and services could be easily shared between these distributed computers. The 1980s were characterized by an evolution to a computing model called **distributed computing**, shown in Figure TB4.5, in which multiple types of computers are networked together to share information and services.

Collaborative Computing

In the 1990s, a new computing model, called **collaborative computing**, emerged. Collaborative computing is a synergistic form of distributed computing in which two or more networked computers are used to accomplish a common processing task. That is, in this model of computing, computers are not simply communicating data but also sharing processing capabilities. For example, one computer may be used to store a large employee database. A second computer may be used to process and update individual employee records selected from this database. The two computers collaborate to keep the company's employee records current, as depicted in Figure TB4.6.

Collaborative computing has also been introduced at the consumer level with innovations in instant messaging (IM). All the major players have integrated collaborative functionality into their IM platforms. Now users can share files to particular folders that will then synchronize to other users' folders (see Figure TB4.7).

Also in use are business-oriented Web collaborative tools. One example of this is Microsoft's SharePoint technology. SharePoint, like other Web-based collaborative tools, allows users to use office automation tools to create documents that are linked to Web sites

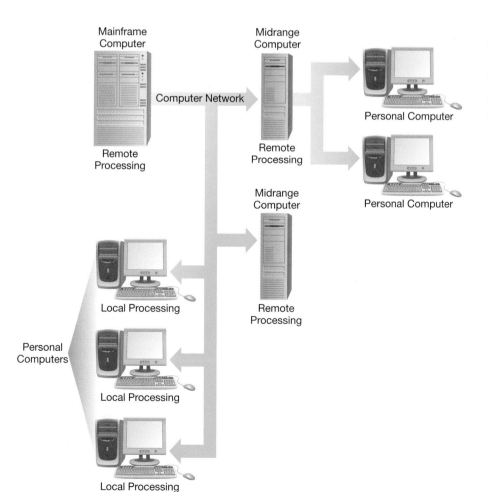

Mainframe Computer

Midrange Computer

Computer Network

Personal Computer

Remote Processing

Remote Processing

Midrange Computer

Personal Computer

Personal Computers

Local Processing

Remote Processing

Local Processing

Local Processing

FIGURE TB4.5

In the distributed computing model, separate computers work on subsets of tasks and then pool their results by communicating over a network.

FIGURE TB4.6

In the collaborative computing model, two or more networked computers are used to accomplish a common processing task.

1. Computer Requests Record to Change

2. Returns Requested Record

4. Returns Changed Record

3. Modifies Record

5. Stores Changed Record in Database

that then can be distributed, checked out, modified, and even published to the public. With the rise in collaborative tools, most office automation applications now integrate some sort of collaborative components.

Types of Networks

Computing networks today include all three computing models: centralized, distributed, and collaborative. The emergence of new computing models did not mean that organizations completely discarded older technologies. Rather, a typical computer network includes mainframes, minicomputers, personal computers, and a variety of other devices. Computer networks are commonly classified by size, distance covered, and structure. The most commonly used classifications are a private branch exchange, local area network, wide area network, metropolitan area network, and personal area network. Each is described in the following sections.

FIGURE TB4.7

Microsoft Live Messenger.

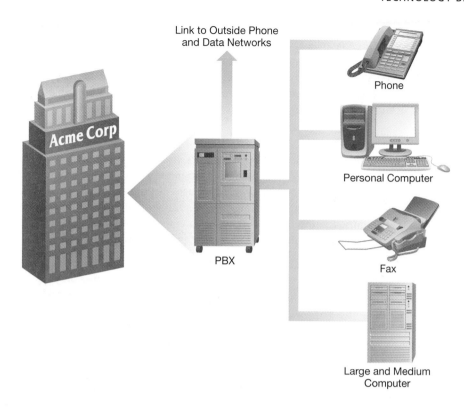

FIGURE TB4.8

A private branch exchange (PBX) supports local phone and data communications as well as links to outside phone and data networks.

Private Branch Exchange

A **private branch exchange (PBX)** is a telephone system that serves a particular location, such as a business (see Figure TB4.8). It connects one telephone extension to another within the system and connects the PBX to the outside telephone network. It can also connect computers within the system to other PBX systems, to an outside network, or to various office devices, such as fax machines or photocopiers. Since they use ordinary telephone lines, PBX systems have limited bandwidth. This prevents them from transmitting such forms of information as interactive video, digital music, or high-resolution photos. Using PBX technology, a business requires few outside phone lines but has to purchase or lease the PBX equipment.

Local Area Network

A **local area network (LAN)**, shown in Figure TB4.9, is a computer network that spans a relatively small area, allowing all computer users to connect with each other to share information and peripheral devices, such as a printer. LAN-based communications may involve the sharing of data, software applications, or other resources between several users. LANs

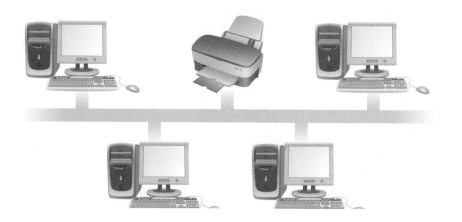

FIGURE TB4.9

A local area network (LAN) allows multiple computers located near each other to communicate directly with each other and to share peripheral devices, such as a printer.

typically do not exceed tens of kilometers in size and are typically contained within a single building or a limited geographical area. They typically use only one kind of transmission medium or cabling, such as twisted-pair wire or coaxial cable. There are also wireless local area network (WLAN) products available. These are very popular because they are relatively easy to set up and enable you to have a network without any network cables strewn around your home or office. WLANs will be discussed more thoroughly later.

Wide Area Network

A **wide area network (WAN)** is a computer network that spans a relatively large geographical area. WANs are typically used to connect two or more LANs. Different hardware and transmission media are often used in WANs because they must cover large distances efficiently. Used by multinational companies, WANs transmit and receive information across cities and countries. A discussion follows of four specific types of WANs—global networks, enterprise networks, value-added networks, and metropolitan area networks.

Global Networks A **global network** spans multiple countries and may include the networks of several organizations. The Internet is an example of a global network. The Internet is the world's largest computer network, consisting of thousands of individual networks supporting millions of computers and users in almost every country of the world. We provide a detailed discussion of the Internet in Technology Briefing 5—The Internet and World Wide Web.

Enterprise Networks An **enterprise network** is a WAN that is the result of connecting disparate networks of a single organization into a single network (see Figure TB4.10).

Value-Added Networks Medium-speed WANs, called **value-added networks (VANs)**, are private, third-party-managed networks that are economical because they are shared by multiple organizations. Customers lease communication lines rather than investing in dedicated network equipment. The "added value" provided by VANs can include network management, e-mail, EDI, security, and other special capabilities. Consequently, VANs can be more expensive than generic communication lines leased from a common telecommunication company like AT&T or Sprint, but they provide valuable services for customers.

Metropolitan Area Networks A **metropolitan area network (MAN)** is a computer network of limited geographic scope, typically a citywide area, that combines both LAN and high-speed fiber-optic technologies. MANs are attractive to organizations that need high-speed data transmission within a limited geographic area.

FIGURE TB4.10

An enterprise network allows an organization to connect distributed locations into a single network.

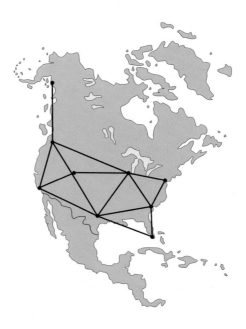

FIGURE TB4.11

The Toyota Prius can be equipped with a Bluetooth network that allows drivers to operate their Bluetooth-enabled cellular phones, using hands-free operation through the car's onboard navigation system.

Source: Photo by Scott Halleran/Getty Images.

Personal Area Networks

A final type of computer network, called a **personal area network (PAN)**, is an emerging technology that uses wireless communication to exchange data between computing devices using short-range radio communication, typically within an area of 10 meters. The enabling technology for PAN is called **Bluetooth**, a specification for personal networking of desktop computers, peripheral devices, mobile phones, pagers, portable stereos, and other handheld devices. Bluetooth's founding members include Ericsson, IBM, Intel, Nokia, and Toshiba. Bluetooth is rapidly being integrated into a variety of personal devices to ease interoperability and information sharing (see Figure TB4.11).

Now that you have an understanding of the general types of networks, the next sections examine some of their fundamental components. This discussion is divided into two areas: networking fundamentals and networking software and hardware. Together, these sections provide a foundation for understanding various types of networks.

Networking Fundamentals

Telecommunications advances have enabled individual computer networks—constructed with a variety of hardware and software—to connect together in what appears to be a single network. Networks are increasingly being used to dynamically exchange relevant, value-adding knowledge and information throughout global organizations and institutions. The following sections take a closer look at the fundamental building blocks of these complex networks and the services they provide.

Servers, Clients, and Peers

A **network** consists of three separate components—servers, clients, and peers—as depicted in Figure TB4.12. A **server** is any computer on the network that makes access to files, printing, communications, and other services available to users of the network. Servers only provide services. A server typically has a more advanced microprocessor, more memory, a larger cache, and more disk storage than a single-user workstation. A **client** is any computer, such as a user's workstation or PC on the network, or any software application, such as a word processing application, that uses the services provided by the server. Clients only request services. A client usually has only one user, whereas many different users share the server. A **peer** is any computer that may both request and provide services. The trend in business is to use **server-centric networks** in which servers and

FIGURE TB4.12

A server is a computer on the network that enables multiple computers (or "clients") to access data. A peer is a computer that may both request and provide services.

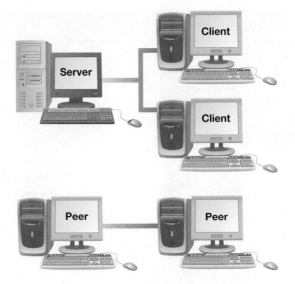

clients have defined roles. However, **peer-to-peer networks** (often abbreviated as P2P) that enable any computer or device on the network to provide and request services can be found in small offices and homes. In P2P networks, all peers have equivalent capabilities and responsibilities; this is the network architecture behind popular file sharing applications such as BitTorrent and KaZaA, where peers are able to connect directly to the hard drives of other peers on the Internet that are utilizing the software.

Although much has been written about how P2P has spawned the illegal trade of music and movies, little has been done on the business advantages technologies such as BitTorrent offers. Only few companies are using these technologies; one example is Warner Brothers, which is using BitTorrent technology to distribute its media. Other companies will soon follow suit and use P2P networks as distribution channels.

Network Services

Network services are the capabilities that networked computers share through the multiple combinations of hardware and software. The most common network services are file services, print services, message services, and application services. **File services** are used to store, retrieve, and move data files in an efficient manner, as shown in Figure TB4.13a. An individual can use the file services of the network to move a customer file electronically to multiple recipients across the network. **Print services** are used to control and manage users' access to network printers and fax equipment, as shown in Figure TB4.13b. Sharing printers on a network reduces the number of printers an organization needs. **Message services** include the storing, accessing, and delivering of text, binary, graphic, digitized video, and audio data across a network. These services are similar to file services, but they also deal with communication interactions between users and applications. Message services include electronic mail or the transfer of messages between two or more networked computers, as shown in Figure TB4.13c. **Application services** run software for network clients and enable computers to share processing power, as shown in Figure TB4.13d. Application services highlight the concept of client/server computing, in which processing is distributed between the client and server. Clients request information or services from the servers. The servers store data and application programs. For example, the physical search of database records may take place on the server, while a much smaller database application that handles the user-interface functions runs on the client.

When an organization decides to network its computers and devices, it must decide what services will be provided and whether these services will be centralized (a server-centric approach), distributed (a peer-to-peer approach), or some combination of both. These decisions ultimately affect the choice of the network operating system. The **network operating system (NOS)** is system software that controls the network and

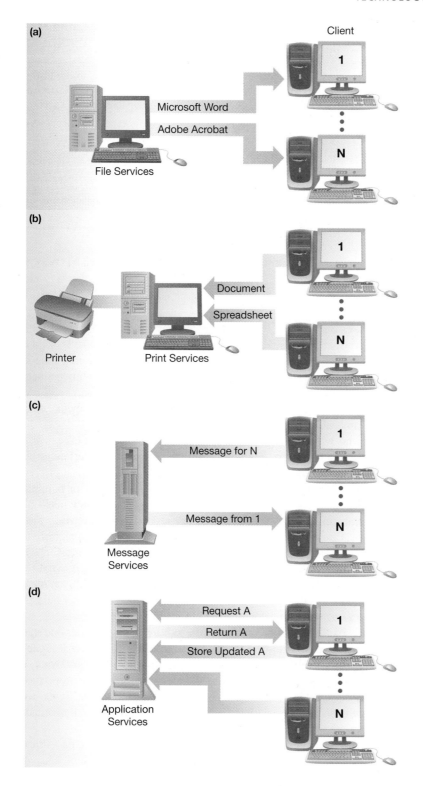

FIGURE TB4.13

Networks can provide (a) file, (b) print, (c) message, and (d) application services.

enables computers to communicate with each other. In other words, the NOS enables network services. In most LAN environments, the NOS consists of two parts. The first and most complex part is the system software that runs on the network server. The system software coordinates many functions, including user accounts, access information, security, and resource sharing. The second and much smaller part of the NOS runs on each workstation connected to the network. In peer-to-peer networks, usually a piece of the NOS is installed on each attached workstation and runs on top of the local operating system. A recent trend is to integrate the NOS into the workstation operating system itself. Recent

TABLE TB4.2 Key Benefits and Drawbacks of Different Cable Media

Medium	Key Benefit(s)	Drawback(s)
Twisted pair	Inexpensive; easy to install and reconfigure	Highly susceptible to EMI, eavesdropping, and attenuation; unsuitable for high speeds
Coaxial	Higher bandwidth than twisted pair; lower susceptibility to EMI, eavesdropping, and attenuation than twisted pair	More expensive than twisted pair; more difficult to install, reconfigure, and manage attenuation than twisted pair; bulky
Fiber optic	Very high bandwidth; low attenuation and immune to EMI and eavesdropping	Expensive cable and hardware; complex installation and maintenance

versions of Windows use this approach. Examples of NOSs are Novell NetWare, Microsoft Windows Server, and Converging Technologies LANtastic.

Transmission Media

Every network uses one or more types of **transmission media**—the physical pathways to send data and information between two or more entities on a network. To send messages, computers send energy-based signals—electric currents using electromagnetic waves—to contact each other. These electromagnetic waves can be altered by semiconductor materials and are represented in two discrete, or binary, states—the 0s and 1s of a computer, known as bits. These bits are transmitted over physical pathways, or media, as computers communicate with each other.

When deciding which type of medium to use in a network, an organization should consider bandwidth, attenuation, immunity from electromagnetic interference and eavesdropping, the cost of the cable, and ease of installation, as summarized in Table TB4.2. Recall that **bandwidth** is the transmission capacity of a computer or communications channel, measured in megabits per second (Mbps), and represents how much binary data can be reliably transmitted over the medium in one second. Some networks have a bandwidth of 10 Mbps; others have 100 Mbps, 1 Gbps, or even more. To appreciate the importance of bandwidth for speed, consider how long it would take to transmit a document the length of this book (about 2 million characters, or 16 million bits). It would take about 1.6 seconds at 10 Mbps and .16 seconds at 100 Mbps. In contrast, using an old-fashioned PC modem that transmits data at a rate of 56K bits per second (bps), it would take nearly five minutes to transmit the same document.

In addition to bandwidth, a second key issue to consider is transmission media's vulnerability to attenuation. **Attenuation** results when the power of an electric signal weakens as it is sent over increasing distance, as shown in Figure TB4.14. In a network, an important concern is how far a signal can travel and still maintain its original properties or meaning. **Electromagnetic interference (EMI)** occurs when fluorescent lights, weather, or other electronic signals interfere with the original signal being sent. All media differ as to how immune they are to EMI, as we will see in the next sections.

Two forms of media are used in networks: cable and wireless media. Although wireless data communication is being used increasingly, it is generally somewhat slower and less stable than wired cable media. Nevertheless, the capabilities of wireless media are rapidly improving, and wireless media have many useful applications. The following sections describe the characteristics of both cable and wireless media.

FIGURE TB4.14

Signals weaken when sent over increasing distances.

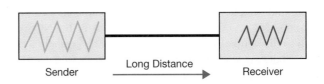

Sender   Long Distance   Receiver

FIGURE TB4.15

A cable spliced open showing several twisted pairs (a); a sample network installation that utilizes many twisted pair cables at once (b).

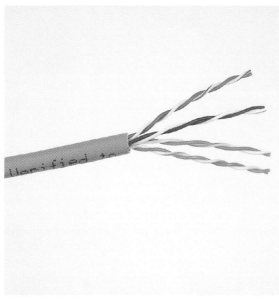

(a)

(b)

Sources: (a) ©Belkin Components; (b) ©Getty Images, Inc.

Cable Media

Cable media physically link computers and other devices in a network. The most common forms of cable media are twisted pair, coaxial, and fiber-optic.

Twisted Pair Cable **Twisted pair (TP) cable** is made of two or more pairs of insulated copper wires twisted together (see Figure TB4.15). The cable may be unshielded (UTP) or shielded (STP). Telephone wire installations use UTP cabling. UTP is rated according to its quality; category 5 (Cat 5) and Cat 6 UTP are often used in network installations. Unshielded cable is cheap, easy to install, and has a capacity up to 1 Gbps at distances up to 100 meters. However, like all copper wiring, it has rapid attenuation and is very sensitive to EMI and eavesdropping—the undetected capturing of network information. Shielded twisted cable is cable wrapped in an insulation that makes it less prone to EMI and eavesdropping. Shielded twisted cable is more expensive than unshielded twisted cable, and it is more difficult to install because it requires special grounding connectors to drain EMI. STP can support bandwidths up to 500 Mbps at distances up to 100 meters. However, it is most commonly used to support networks running at 16 Mbps.

Coaxial Cable **Coaxial (or coax) cable** contains a solid inner copper conductor, surrounded by plastic insulation and an outer braided copper or foil shield (see Figure TB4.16). Coax cable comes in a variety of thicknesses—thinnet coax and thicknet coax—based on resistance to EMI. Though less costly than TP, thinnet coax is not commonly used in networks anymore; thicknet coax is more expensive than TP. The cable is cut, and a connector, called a T-connector, is attached to the cable and each device. Coax cable is most commonly used for cable television installations and for networks operating at 10 to 100 Mbps. Its attenuation is lower than twisted pair cable's, and it is moderately susceptible to EMI and eavesdropping.

Fiber-Optic Cable **Fiber-optic cable** is made of a light-conducting glass or plastic core, surrounded by more glass, called cladding, and a tough outer sheath (see Figure TB4.17). The sheath protects the fiber from changes in temperature as well as from bending or

FIGURE TB4.16

FIGURE TB4.16

These sample coaxial cables are ready to be connected to a computer or other device.

Source: ©Getty Images, Inc.

breaking. This technology uses pulses of light sent along the optical cable to transmit data. Fiber-optic cable transmits clear and secure data because it is immune to EMI and eavesdropping. Transmission signals do not break up because fiber-optic cable has low attenuation. It can support bandwidths from 100 Mbps to greater than 2 Gbps (gigabits per second) and distances from 2 to 25 kilometers. It can transmit video and sound. Fiber-optic cable is more expensive than copper wire because the cost and difficulties of installation and repair are higher for fiber-optic. Fiber-optic cables are used for high-speed **backbones**—the high-speed central networks to which many smaller networks can be connected. A backbone may connect, for example, several different buildings in which other, smaller LANs reside. Table TB4.2 provides a comparison of benefits and drawbacks of the three different cable media that have been discussed.

Wireless Media

With the popularity of cellular phones, **wireless media** are rapidly gaining popularity. Wireless media transmit and receive electromagnetic signals using methods such as infrared line of sight, high-frequency radio, and microwave systems.

Infrared Line of Sight **Infrared line of sight** uses high-frequency light waves to transmit data on an unobstructed path between nodes—computers or some other device such as a printers—on a network at a distance of up to 24.4 meters. The remote controls for most audiovisual equipment, such as your TV, stereo, and other consumer electronics equipment, use infrared light. Infrared systems may be configured as either point-to-point or broadcast. For example, when you use your TV remote control, you have to be in front of the TV to have successful communication. This is an example of point-to-point infrared. Many new printers and notebooks have the capability to transmit data using infrared communication, allowing these devices to be easily connected. With broadcast infrared communication, devices do not

FIGURE TB4.17

Fiber-optic cable consists of a light-conducting glass or plastic core, surrounded by more glass, called cladding, and a tough outer sheath.

Source: ©Getty Images, Inc.

need to be positioned directly in front of each other but simply have to be located within some distance of each other. Infrared equipment is relatively inexpensive, but point-to-point systems require strict line-of-sight positioning. Installation and maintenance focus on ensuring proper optical alignment between nodes on the network. Point-to-point infrared systems can support up to 16 Mbps at one meter, with transmission speeds reducing as distances increase; broadcast systems support less than 1 Mbps. Attenuation and susceptibility to EMI and eavesdropping are problematic, particularly when objects obstruct the light path or when environmental conditions such as smoke or high-intensity light are prevalent.

High-Frequency Radio **High-frequency radio** signals can transmit data at rates of up to several hundred Mbps to network nodes from 12.2 up to approximately 40 kilometers apart, depending on the nature of any obstructions between them. The flexibility of the signal path makes high-frequency radio ideal for mobile transmissions. For example, most police departments use high-frequency radio signals that enable police vehicles to communicate with each other as well as with the dispatch office. This medium is expensive due to the cost of antenna towers and high-output transceivers. Installation is complex and often dangerous because of the high voltages. Although attenuation is fairly low, this medium is very susceptible to EMI and eavesdropping.

Two common applications of high-frequency radio communication are cellular phones and wireless networks. A **cellular phone** gets its name from how the signal is distributed. In a cellular system a coverage area is divided into **cells** with a low-powered radio antenna/receiver in each cell; these cells are monitored and controlled by a central computer (see Figure TB4.18). Any given cellular network has a fixed number of radio frequencies. When a user initiates or receives a call, the mobile telephone switching office assigns the caller a unique frequency for the duration of the call. As a person travels within the network, the central computer at the switching office monitors the quality of the signal and automatically assigns the call to the closest cellular antenna. Cellular phones have gone through rapid changes since their first commercial use in the mid-1980s (see Table TB4.3). Cellular phones are now mostly digital in the United States except for a few rural areas. Digital transmission and reception offers many advantages over analog, some of which include wider reception range, less static, and the capability of data transmission.

High-frequency radio-waves technology is increasingly being used to support **wireless local area networks (WLANs)**. WLANs are also referred to as **Wi-Fi (wireless fidelity)** and are based on a family of standards called **802.11**. The 802.11 family of standards has been universally adopted and has transmission speeds up to 540 Mbps (using the 802.11n standard). The ease of installation has made WLANs popular for business and home use. For example, some homes and many buildings have (or want) multiple

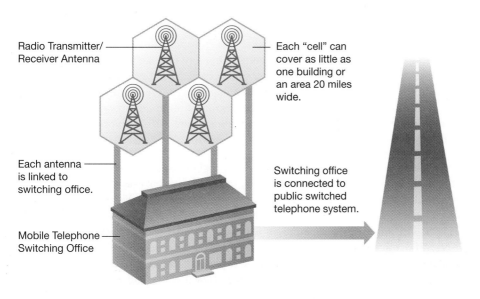

Radio Transmitter/
Receiver Antenna

Each "cell" can
cover as little as
one building or
an area 20 miles
wide.

Each antenna
is linked to
switching office.

Switching office
is connected to
public switched
telephone system.

Mobile Telephone
Switching Office

FIGURE TB4.18

A cellular network divides a geographic region into cells.

TABLE TB4.3 Evolution of Cell Phone Technology

Generation	Description	Data Transfer	Advantages
0G	Preceded modern cellular mobile telephony and was usually mounted in cars or trucks and was a closed circuit so you could call only other radio telephone users.	Analog	Communicate on the go.
1G	This technology, introduced in the 1980s, used circuit switching with poor voice quality, unreliable handoffs between towers, and non-existent security.	Analog	Can communicate with other cell phones and land lines.
2G	The first all-digital signal that was divided into TDMA and CDMA standards. Allowed for SMS (text) messaging and e-mails being sent/received to the phones.	Digital (up to 9.6-Kbps transfer)	Lower-powered radio signals allow longer battery life. Digital format allows for clearer signal and reduced signal noise.
2.5G	Allows for faster data transmission via a packet-switched domain in addition to the circuit-switched domain.	Digital (up to 115-Kbps transfer)	Higher data speeds allow for more complex data to be transmitted (e.g., sports scores, news stories).
3G	Even faster. Requires a new cellular network, different from that already available in 2G systems.	Digital (up to 128 Kbps when moving and 2 MBps when stationary)	Transfer full video and audio.
4G	Appears to be the future standard of wireless devices.	Digital (up to 100 Mbps when moving and 1 GBps when stationary)	Data speeds similar to wired networks.

computers and need to share Internet access, files, and peripheral devices. Unfortunately, many older buildings and homes do not have a wired infrastructure to easily connect computers and devices, making wireless networking particularly attractive. For example, Washington State University wanted to transform a traditional computer classroom—with obtrusive desktop computers sitting atop rows of desks that had wires and cables everywhere—into a flexible and comfortable team-learning environment where technology was present but not overwhelming. With the help of the Boeing Company, Dell Computers, and Intel, students now sit in one of several comfortable learning stations using a variety of mobile wireless technologies (see Figure TB4.19). Through the use of wireless technologies, many organizations are transforming their work environments into better team collaboration environments.

The last example where high-frequency radio is being used is in the operation of PANs. As discussed previously, PANs use low-powered Bluetooth radio-wave technology. Using Bluetooth, PANs are becoming extremely popular to connect cell phones to headsets, MP3 players to music servers, automobiles to cell phones, and countless other applications. Recently, Nokia released a new standard for PANs, called Wibree; with low cost, small size, and ultra-low power consumption, Wibree can bring wireless connectivity into even more devices, such as heart rate monitors, MP3 player remote controls, or even golf clubs.

Microwave **Microwave transmission** is a high-frequency radio signal that is sent through the air using either terrestrial (earth-based) systems or satellite systems. Both terrestrial and satellite microwave transmission require line-of-sight communications between the signal sender and the signal receiver. Terrestrial microwave, shown in Figure TB4.20, uses antennae that require an unobstructed path or line of sight between nodes. **Terrestrial microwave** systems are used to cross inaccessible terrain or to connect buildings where cable installation would be expensive. The cost of a terrestrial microwave system depends on the distance to be covered. Typically, businesses lease access to these

FIGURE TB4.19

The Boeing Wireless Classroom of the Future at Washington State University provides a flexible and comfortable learning environment for students.

Source: Courtesy Boeing.

microwave systems from service providers rather than invest in antenna equipment. Data may be transmitted at up to 274 Mbps. Over short distances, attenuation is not a problem, but signals can be obstructed over longer distances by environmental conditions such as high winds and heavy rain. EMI and eavesdropping are significant problems with microwave communications.

Satellite microwave, shown in Figure TB4.21, uses a relay station that transfers signals between antennae located on earth and satellites orbiting the earth. In other words, a **satellite** is a microwave station located in outer space. Satellite transmissions are delayed because of the distance signals must travel (also known as **propagation delay**). Satellites orbit from 400 to 22,300 miles above the earth and have different uses and characteristics (see Table TB4.4). This technology has become very viable for media such as radio. There are two main players in the U.S. market in the satellite radio marketplace: XM and Sirius. Both have their own satellites that send out scrambled signals to proprietary receivers.

Another of satellite communication's strength is that it can be used to access very remote and undeveloped locations on the earth. Such systems are extremely costly because

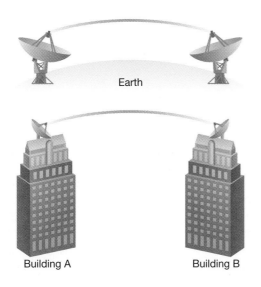

Earth

Building A   Building B

FIGURE TB4.20

Terrestrial microwave requires a line-of-sight path between a sender and a receiver.

FIGURE TB4.21

Communications satellites are relay stations that receive signals from one earth station and rebroadcast them to another.

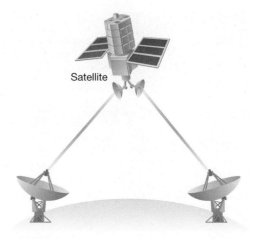

Satellite

their use and installation depends on space technology. Companies such as AT&T sell satellite services with typical transmission rates ranging from less than 1 to 10 Mbps, but the rates can be as high as 90 Mbps. Like terrestrial microwave, satellite systems are prone to attenuation and susceptible to EMI and eavesdropping.

A popular application of satellite communication is the **Global Positioning System (GPS)**. The GPS uses 24 active satellites to allow users to triangulate their position anywhere on the planet. At any point in time, at any place on Earth, signals from at least four GPS satellites can be picked up by a GPS receiver; each of the satellites sends a signal containing a time stamp. Using this time stamp, the GPS receiver can determine the distance from each satellite, and can thus triangulate its own position on earth with very high accuracy. GPS technology includes the first generation systems having location resolution down to 10 square meters (about 107 square feet), and the newer second generation technology having location resolution down to 10 square centimeters (about 1.5 square inches).

As with cable media, there are key differences between the types of wireless media. Table TB4.5 summarizes the key benefits and drawbacks of each wireless medium. Table TB4.6 compares wireless media across several criteria.

TABLE TB4.4 Characteristics of Satellites with Different Orbits

Name	Distance from Earth	Characteristics/Common Application
Low Earth Orbit (LEO) Satellite	400–1,000 miles	• Not fixed in space in relation to the rotation of the earth; circle the earth several times per day. • Photography for mapping and locating mineral deposits; monitoring ice caps, coastlines, volcanoes, and rain forests; research plant and crop changes; monitor wildlife and animal habitat and animal changes; search and rescue for downed aircraft or ships that are in trouble; research projects in astronomy and physics.
Medium Earth Orbit (MEO)	1,000–22,300 miles	• Not fixed in space in relation to the rotation of the earth; circle the earth more than one time per day. • Primarily used in geographical positioning systems (GPS mapping) for navigation of ships at sea, spacecraft, airplanes, automobiles, and military weapons.
Geosynchronous Earth Orbit (GEO)	22,300 miles	• Fixed in space in relation to the rotation of the earth; circle the earth one time per day. • Because it is fixed in space, transmission is simplified. • Transmission of high-speed data for television, weather information, remote Internet connections, satellite digital radio, telecommunications (satellite phones).

TABLE TB4.5 Key Benefits and Drawbacks of Different Wireless Media

Medium	Key Benefit(s)	Drawback(s)
Infrared line of sight	Easy to install and configure; inexpensive	Very limited bandwidth; line of sight required; environmental factors influence signal quality
High-frequency radio	Mobile stations; low attenuation	Frequency licensing; complex installation
Terrestrial microwave	Can access remote locations or congested areas; high bandwidth; low attenuation	Frequency licensing; complex installation; environmental factors influence signal quality
Satellite microwave	Can access remote locations; high bandwidth; earth stations can be fixed or mobile	Frequency licensing; complex installation; environmental factors influence signal quality; propagation delays

Network Software and Hardware

Standards play a key role in creating networks. The physical elements of networks—adapters, cables, and connectors—are defined by a set of standards that have evolved since the early 1970s. Standards ensure the interoperability and compatibility of network devices. The Institute of Electrical and Electronics Engineers has established a number of telecommunications standards. The three major standards for LAN cabling and media access control are Ethernet, token ring, and ARCnet. See Table TB4.7 for a summary of LAN standards. Each standard combines a media access control technique, network topology, and media in different ways. Software is blended with hardware to implement protocols that allow different types of computers and networks to communicate successfully. Protocols are often implemented within a computer's operating system or within the network operating system. Each of these topics is described more thoroughly next.

Media Access Control

Media access control is the set of rules that governs how a given node or workstation gains access to the network to send or receive information. There are two general types of access control: distributed and random access. With distributed control, only a single workstation at a time has authorization to transmit its data. This authorization is transferred sequentially from workstation to workstation. Under random control, any workstation can transmit its data by checking whether the medium is available. No specific permission is required. The following sections describe each type in more detail.

Distributed Access Control The most commonly used method of distributed access control is called **token passing**. Token passing is an access method that uses a constantly circulating electronic token, a small packet of data, to prevent collisions and give all workstations equal access to a ring-shaped network. A collision occurs when two or more

TABLE TB4.6 Relative Comparison of Wireless Media

Medium	Expense	Speed	Attenuation	EMI	Eavesdropping
Infrared line of sight	Low	Up to 16 Mbps	High	High	High
High-frequency radio	Moderate	Up to 54 Mbps	Low	High	High
Terrestrial microwave	Moderate	Up to 274 Mbps	Low	High	High
Satellite microwave	High	Up to 90 Mbps	Moderate	High	High

Note: Mbps = megabits per second.

TABLE TB4.7 Summary of Major LAN Standards

Network Standards	Access Control	Topology	Typical Media	Speed
Ethernet	CSMA/CD	Bus	Coax or twisted pair	10 Mbps–1 Gbps
Token ring	Token passing	Ring	Twisted pair	4–100 Mbps
ARCnet	Token passing	Star or bus	Coax or twisted pair	2.5–20 Mbps

workstations simultaneously transmit messages onto the network. A workstation must possess the token before it can transmit a message onto the network.

A workstation that receives the token and wants to send a message marks the token as busy, appends a message to it, and transmits both. The message and token are passed around the ring, as depicted in Figure TB4.22. Each workstation copies the message and retransmits the token/message combination. When it is received back at the originating workstation, the message is removed, the token is marked as free, and it is transmitted to the next workstation on the network.

Random Access Control The most commonly used method of random access control is called **CSMA/CD (carrier sense multiple access/collision detect)**. In CSMA/CD, each workstation "listens" to the network to determine whether a message is being transmitted. If the network is quiet, the workstation sends its message; otherwise, it waits. When a workstation gains access to the medium and sends information onto the network, messages are sent to all workstations on the network; however, only the destination with the proper address is able to "open" the message. If two or more workstations try to send a message simultaneously, all workstations detect that a collision has occurred, and all sending is ceased. After a short random period of time, the workstations again try to send their messages. When network traffic is light, there are few collisions, and data are quickly transmitted. However, the speed of transmission deteriorates rapidly under heavy traffic conditions.

Network Topologies

Network topology refers to the shape of a network. The four common network topologies are star, ring, bus, and mesh.

FIGURE TB4.22

Station A receives the token and adds a message for station C; station C receives the message and token, then forwards both back to station A; station A removes the message and forwards the empty token on to the next station on the network.

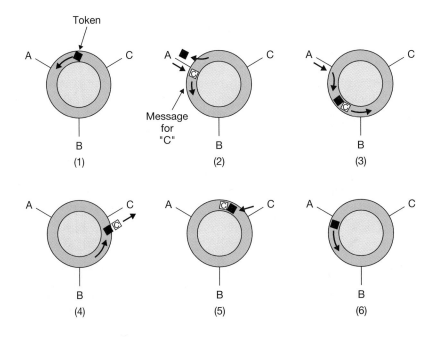

Star Network A **star network** is configured, as you might expect, in the shape of a star, as shown in Figure TB4.23a. That is, all nodes or workstations are connected to a central hub, or concentrator, through which all messages pass. Active hubs amplify transmission signals, so long cable lengths may be used. The workstations represent the points of the star. Star topologies are easy to lay out and modify. However, they are also the most costly because they require the largest amount of cabling. Although it is easy to diagnose problems at individual workstations, star networks are susceptible to a single point of failure at the hub, which would result in all workstations losing network access.

Ring Network A **ring network** is configured in the shape of a closed loop or circle, with each node connecting to the next node, as shown in Figure TB4.23b. In ring networks, messages move in one direction around the circle. As a message moves around the circle,

FIGURE TB4.23

(a) The star network has several workstations connected to a central hub. (b) The ring network is configured in a closed loop, with each workstation connected to another workstation. (c) The bus network is configured in the shape of an open-ended line where each workstation receives the same message simultaneously. (d) The mesh network consists of computers and other devices that are either fully or partially connected to each other.

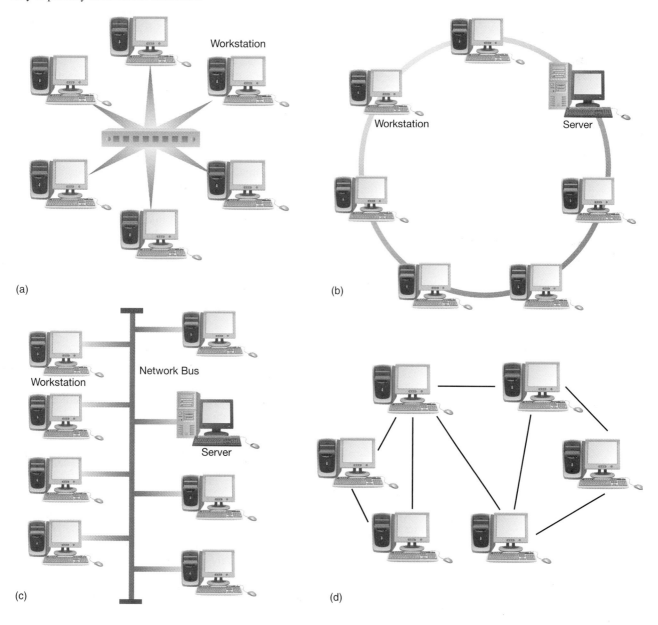

each workstation examines it to see whether the message is for that workstation. If not, the message is regenerated and passed on to the next node. This regeneration process enables ring networks to cover much larger distances than star or bus networks can. Relatively little cabling is required, but a failure of any node on the ring network can cause complete network failure. Self-healing ring networks avoid this by having two rings with data flowing in different directions; thus, the failure of a single node does not cause the network to fail. In either case, it is difficult to modify and reconfigure a ring network. Ring networks normally use some form of token-passing media access control method to regulate network traffic.

Bus Network A **bus network** is in the shape of an open-ended line, as shown in Figure TB4.23c; as a result, it is the easiest network to extend and has the simplest wiring layout. This topology enables all network nodes to receive the same message through the network cable at the same time. However, it is difficult to diagnose and isolate network faults. Bus networks use CSMA/CD for media access control.

Mesh Network A **mesh network** consists of computers and other devices that are either fully or partially connected to each other. In a *full* mesh design, every computer and device is connected to every other computer and device. In a *partial* mesh design, many but not all computers and devices are connected (see Figure 4.13). Like a ring network, mesh networks provide relatively short routes from one node to another. Mesh networks also provide many possible routes through the network—a design that prevents one circuit or computer from becoming overloaded when traffic is heavy. Given these benefits, most WAN networks, including the Internet, use a partial mesh design.

Protocols

In addition to media access control and network topologies, all networks employ protocols to make sure communication between computers is successful. *Protocols* are agreed-on formats for transmitting data between connected computers. They specify how computers should be connected to the network, how errors will be checked, what data compression method will be used, how a sending computer will signal that it has finished sending a message, and how a receiving computer will signal that it has received a message. Protocols allow packets to be correctly routed to and from their destinations. There are literally thousands of protocols for programmers to use, but a few are a lot more important than the others. In this section, we will first review the worldwide standard, called the OSI model, for implementing protocols. Next, we briefly review two of the more important network protocols: Ethernet and TCP/IP.

The OSI Model The need of organizations to interconnect computers and networks that use different protocols has driven the industry to an open system architecture in which different protocols can communicate with each other. The International Organization for Standardization defined a networking model called the Open Systems Interconnection (OSI), which divides computer-to-computer communications into seven connected layers. The **OSI model** is a protocol that represents a group of specific tasks, represented in Figure TB4.24 as successive layers, that enable computers to communicate data. Each successively higher layer builds on the functions of the layers below. For example, suppose you are using a PC running Windows and are connected to the Internet and you want to send a message to a friend who is connected to the Internet through a large workstation computer running Unix—two different computers and two different operating systems. When you transmit your message, it is passed down from layer to layer in the Windows protocol environment of your system. At each layer, special bookkeeping information specific to the layer, called a header, is added to the data. Eventually, the data and headers are transferred from the Windows Layer 1 to Unix's Layer 1 over some physical medium. On receipt, the message is passed up through the layers in the Unix application. At each

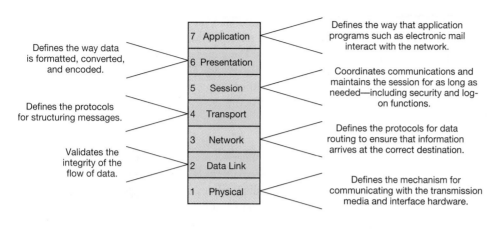

The Open Systems Interconnection (OSI) model has seven layers and provides a framework for connecting different computers with different operating systems to a network.

layer, the corresponding header information is stripped away, the requested task is performed, and the remaining data package is passed on until your message arrives as you sent it, as shown in Figure TB4.25. In other words, protocols represent an agreement between different parts of the network about how data are to be transferred.

Ethernet **Ethernet** is a LAN protocol developed by Xerox Corporation in 1976. It uses a bus network topology and uses random access control to send data. The original Ethernet supports data transfer rates of 10 Mbps. A later version, called 100Base-T or Fast Ethernet, supports transfer rates of 100 Mbps; the latest version, called Gigabit Ethernet, supports transfer rates of 1 gigabit, or 1,000 megabits, per second. Most new computers have some type of Ethernet card installed, allowing you to use this type of network connection.

TCP/IP The Internet was based on the idea that individual networks could be separately designed and developed yet still connect their users to the Internet by using their own unique interfaces. **Transmission Control Protocol/Internet Protocol (TCP/IP)**, the

FIGURE TB4.25

Message passing between two different computers.

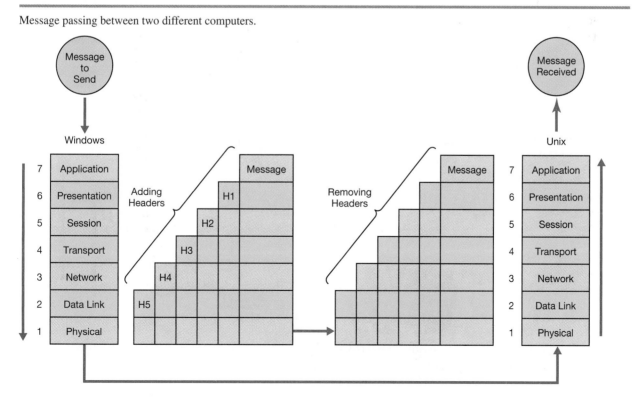

protocol of the Internet, allows different interconnected networks to communicate using the same language. For example, TCP/IP allows IBM, Macintosh, and Unix users to communicate despite any system differences. Computer scientist Vinton Cerf and engineer Robert Kahn defined the Internet Protocol (IP), by which packets are sent from one computer to another on their way to a destination, as part of the DARPA project. TCP/IP is discussed more thoroughly in Technology Briefing 5.

Connectivity Hardware

Stand-alone computers can be physically connected to create different types of networks. Transmission media connectors, network interface cards, and modems are used to connect computers or devices in a network. After individual devices are connected to the network, multiple segments of transmission media can be connected to form one large network. Repeaters, hubs, bridges, and multiplexers are used to extend the range and size of the network. These devices are described next.

Transmission Media Connectors Transmission media connectors, or simply **connectors**, are used to terminate cable in order to be plugged into a network interface card or into other network components. Connectors include T-connectors for coax cable and RJ-45 connectors (similar to a phone jack) for twisted pair cable.

Network Interface Cards A **network interface card (NIC)** is a PC expansion board that plugs into a computer so that it can be connected to a network. Each NIC has a unique identifier (determined by the manufacturer) that is used to identify the address of the computer on the network.

Modems A **modem** (MOdulator/DEModulator) enables computers to transmit data over telephone lines and thereby connect your PC with other PCs in a computer network, or to the Internet. Because the dial-up telephone system was designed to pass the sound of voices in the form of analog signals, it cannot pass the electrical pulses—**digital signals**—that computers use. The only way to pass digital data over conventional voice telephone lines is to convert it to audio tones—**analog signals**—that the telephone lines can carry. Hence, a modem converts digital signals from a computer into analog signals so that telephone lines may be used as a transmission medium to send and receive electronic information, as shown in Figure TB4.26. In Technology Briefing 5—The Internet and World Wide Web, we contrast dial up modems with various other methods for connecting to the Internet including *digital subscriber lines (DSL)* and *cable modems*.

FIGURE TB4.26

Modems convert digital signals into analog and analog signals into digital.

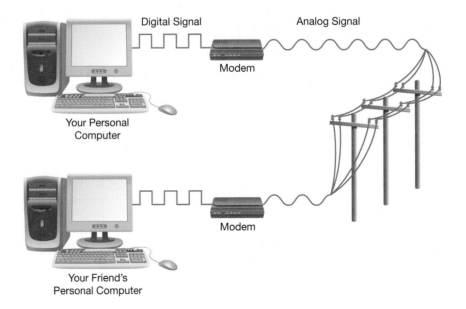

TABLE TB4.8 Networking Hardware

Networking Hardware	Description
Repeaters	A **repeater** is used to regenerate or replicate a signal as it weakens when traveling on a network. A repeater also moves data from one media segment to another and effectively extends the size of the network.
Hub	A **hub** is used as a central point of connection between media segments. Like repeaters, hubs enable the network to be extended to accommodate additional workstations. Hubs are commonly used in 10Base-T networks.
Bridges	A **bridge** is used to connect two different LANs or two segments of the same LAN by forwarding network traffic between network segments. However, unlike repeaters, bridges determine the physical location of the source and destination computers. They are typically used to divide an overloaded network into separate segments, helping to minimize intersegment traffic. Bridges are also used to connect segments that use different wiring or network protocols.
Multiplexers	A **multiplexer (MUX)** is used to share a communications line or medium among a number of users. Sometimes the transmission medium provides more capacity than a single signal can occupy. To use the entire media bandwidth effectively, multiplexers are used to transmit several signals over a single channel.
Router	A **router** is an intelligent device used to connect two or more individual networks. When a router receives a signal, it looks at the network address and passes the signal or message on to the appropriate network.
Brouter	A **brouter**, short for bridge router, provides the capabilities of both a bridge and a router.
Channel service unit	A **channel service unit (CSU)** is a device that acts as a "buffer" between a LAN and a public carrier's WAN. CSUs ensure that all signals placed on the public lines from the LAN are appropriately timed and formed for the public network.
Gateway	A **gateway** performs protocol conversion so that different networks can communicate even though they "speak" different languages. For example, communications between a LAN and a large system, such as a mainframe, whose protocols are different, require a gateway.

Networking Hardware

Because of the complexity of current networks, there are several specialized pieces of equipment needed for computers to connect and transfer data. Not all pieces of equipment are necessary in order to connect computers together. The use of this equipment is dependent on the configuration of the network and the use of the network. As seen in Table TB4.8, each piece of network hardware is designed for a specific function at a specific OSI layer. Most Internet traffic will at some point have to cross both a gateway, which allows the packets to leave the LAN, and a router, which designates the addressing for the packets.

Key Points Review

1. *Describe the evolution of and types of computer networks.* Since the 1950s, three models of computing have been used. First, from the 1950s until the 1970s, the centralized computing model was dominant. In the centralized computing model, all processing occurs at a large central computer, and users interact with the system through the use of terminals. From the late 1970s until the late 1980s, a distributed computing model was dominant. In this model, separate computers work on subsets of tasks and then pool their results by communicating via a network. In the 1990s, the collaborative computing model

emerged. In this model, two or more networked computers work together to accomplish a common processing task. There are several types of computer networks. A private branch exchange (PBX) is a private telephone exchange, located in a single facility, that provides both voice and data communication. A local area network (LAN) is a group of computers at one location that share hardware and software resources; wireless LANs have gained popularity because of their ease of installation. A wide area network (WAN) refers to two or more LANs from different locations that are linked together. There are four general types of WANs: global networks, enterprise networks, value-added networks, and metropolitan area networks. A global network is a WAN that spans multiple countries and may include the networks of several organizations. An enterprise network is a WAN that connects all the LANs of a single location. Value-added networks are private, third-party-managed networks that are shared by multiple organizations. Metropolitan area networks span a limited geographic scope, typically a citywide area with both LAN and high-speed fiber-optic technologies. A final type of computer network, called a personal area network, is an emerging technology that uses wireless communication to exchange data between computing devices using short-range radio communication, typically within an area of 10 meters.

2. *Understand networking fundamentals, including network services and transmission media.* In networking, a distinction is made between servers, clients, and peers. A server is a computer that stores information (programs and data) and provides services to users through a network. A client is any device or software application that makes use of the information or services provided by a server. Peers are two separate computers or devices on a network that request and provide services to each other. Servers and clients are combined to create server-centric networks. Peers are combined to create peer-to-peer networks. Networks provide file, print, message, and application services that extend the capabilities of stand-alone computers. The network operating system (NOS) is the major piece of software that controls the network. In a typical LAN, the NOS consists of two parts. The first and most complex is the system software that runs on the server.

The NOS software coordinates many functions, including user accounts, access information, security, and resource sharing. The second and much smaller part of the NOS runs on each workstation connected to the LAN. Networks exchange information by using cable or wireless transmission media. Cable media include twisted pair, coaxial, and fiber-optic. Wireless media include infrared line of sight, high-frequency radio, and microwave.

3. *Describe network software and hardware, including media access control, network topologies, and protocols, as well as connectivity hardware for both LANs and WANs.* Network access control refers to the rules that govern how a given workstation gains access to the network. There are two general types: distributed and random access. With distributed access, only a single workstation at a time has authorization to transmit its data. Under random access control, any workstation can transmit its data by checking whether the medium is available. The shape of a network can vary; the four most common topologies are star, ring, bus, and mesh configurations. Protocols are agreed-on formats for transmitting data between connected computers. The need of organizations to interconnect devices that use different protocols has driven the industry to an open system architecture in which different protocols can communicate with each other. The International Organization for Standardization defined a networking model called the Open Systems Interconnection (OSI) that divides computer-to-computer communications into seven connected layers. Each successively higher layer builds on the functions of the layers below. Hardware and software vendors can use networking standards such as OSI to build devices that can be more easily interconnected. Ethernet is an important protocol for LANs, whereas the Transmission Control Protocol/Internet Protocol is most widely used for the world's largest WAN, the Internet. In a network, each device or computer must be connected to the medium or cable segment. To accomplish this, transmission media connectors, network interface cards, and modems are used. After individual devices are connected to the network, multiple segments of transmission media can be connected to form one large network. A variety of different devices is used to extend the range and size of the network and to interconnect wide area networks.

Key Terms

Review Questions

1. Compare and contrast centralized, distributed, and collaborative computing.
2. How are local area networks, wide area networks, enterprise networks, and global networks related to each other?
3. Explain the difference between servers, clients, and peers.
4. What are the major types of network services available?
5. What are three common types of transmission media that use cabling?
6. What are four common methods of wireless transmission media for networking, and how do they differ from each other?
7. What is a network topology? Describe the four common topologies that are used today.
8. What is the purpose of the OSI model?
9. What is Ethernet, and why is it so popular?
10. What is TCP/IP, and what roles does it play in the use of the Internet?
11. What are the various types of hardware used to connect computers together into networks?
12. What is a modem used for, and how does it work?

Self-Study Questions

Visit the Interactive Study Guide on the text Web site for additional Self-Study Questions: **www.prenhall.com/jessup**.

1. Which of the following is a type of computer on the network that makes access to files, printing, communications, and other services available to users of the network?
   A. server
   B. client
   C. peer
   D. pager

2. Which of the following is not a type of cable medium?
   A. twisted pair
   B. coaxial
   C. fiber-optic
   D. tertiary groups

3. Which of the following is a type of wireless medium?
   A. fiber-optic
   B. TCP/IP
   C. infrared
   D. microterminal

4. Which of the following are types of networks?
   A. star, ring, bus
   B. star, box, ring
   C. star, ring, triangle
   D. ring, bus, rectangle

5. All of the following are common applications of high-frequency radio communication except _____.
   A. pagers
   B. cellular phones
   C. wireless networks
   D. facsimiles

6. The International Organization for Standardization (ISO) defined a networking model called the _____ that divides computer-to-computer communications into seven connected layers.
   A. Network Allocation System (NAS)
   B. Open Systems Network (OSN)
   C. Open Systems Interconnection (OSI)
   D. Network Transfer System (NTS)

7. Which of the following is a type of local area network protocol developed by Xerox Corporation in 1976 that typically uses a bus or star network topology and uses random access control to send data?
   A. Ethernet
   B. bridge
   C. star
   D. gateway

8. Which of the following is the protocol of the Internet, allowing different interconnected networks to communicate using the same language?
   A. Ethernet
   B. C++
   C. Transmission Control Protocol/Internet Protocol (TCP/IP)
   D. router

9. After individual devices are connected to a network, multiple segments of transmission media can be connected to form one large network. All of the following except _____ are used to extend the range and size of the network.
   A. bridges
   B. repeaters
   C. modems
   D. hubs

10. A _____ performs protocol conversion so that different networks can communicate even though they "speak" different languages.
    A. gateway
    B. channel service unit
    C. modem
    D. brouter

Answers are on page 541.

Problems and Exercises

1. Match the following terms with the appropriate definitions:
   i. Protocols
   ii. Digitizing
   iii. Token passing
   iv. Network operating system
   v. Router
   vi. Bus network
   vii. Mesh network
   viii. Peer-to-peer network
   ix. Attenuation
   x. Wi-Fi
      a. A decrease in the power of an electrical signal as it is sent over a distance
      b. Wireless local area network based on the 802.11 standard
      c. A network access control method in which a token circulates around a ring topology and stations can transmit messages onto the network only when a nonbusy token arrives at a station
      d. A network topology in which all stations are connected to a single open-ended line
      e. A group of software programs that manages and provides network services
      f. An intelligent device used to connect two or more individual networks
      g. A network that enables any computer or device on the network to provide and request services
      h. A network that consists of computers and other devices that are either fully or partially connected to each other
      i. The procedures that different computers follow when they transmit and receive data
      j. The process of converting analog information to digital information

2. Discuss the difference between PBX networks and LANs. What are the advantages of each? What are possible disadvantages of each? When would you recommend one over the other?

3. Personal area networks using Bluetooth are becoming increasingly popular. Visit www.bluetooth.com and investigate the types of products that this wireless technology is being used to enhance. Find three products that you find interesting and prepare a 10-minute presentation on what these products are and how Bluetooth is enhancing their operation and usage.

4. Using terms such as *digital, analog, dial-up telephone lines,* and *modem,* explain how a file is sent from your

computer to your friend's computer through the regular phone system. What happens when and where?

5. Compare and contrast client-server and peer-to-peer networks. How do the computers and devices interact with each other in these networks? How does the term *client* relate to a peer-to-peer network? Under what circumstances is one type of network better than the other? Why?

6. Describe one of your experiences with a computer network. What type of topology was being used? What was the network operating system? Was the network connected to any other networks? How?

7. Scan the popular press and/or the Web for clues concerning emerging technologies for computer networking. This may include new uses for current technologies or new technologies altogether. Discuss as a group the "hot" issues. Do you feel they will become a reality in the near future? Why or why not? Prepare a 10-minute presentation of your findings to be given to the class.

8. Working in a group, have everyone describe what type of network would be most appropriate for a small office with about 10 computers, one printer, and one scanner, all within one floor in one building and relatively close to one another. Be sure to talk about transmission media, network topology, hardware, and software. Did all group members come up with the same option? Why or why not? What else would you need to know to make a good recommendation?

9. Investigate the popular press, Web, or people you know working in companies to see to what extent firms are using twisted pair versus coaxial cable versus fiber-optic cabling. Under which circumstances is each being used, and what appear to be the trends in the use of cabling types?

10. Perform the same analysis as in question 9, but this time check into uses of wireless networking. Which forms of wireless networking appear to be most popular and why?

11. Do some shopping on the Web and/or at a local computer store to determine what you would need and what it would cost to set up a wireless local area network in your home.

12. Ask questions of IS personnel at your workplace or at your school and determine which types of networks are being used in your office or classroom and how these local area networks are connected to the broader backbone network for this organization.

13. Search the Web for background information on the origin and uses of the Ethernet protocol. How did it begin, and how popular is it today?

14. Search the Web for background information on the origin and uses of the TCP/IP protocol. Why has it become so popular and powerful?

15. Investigate Cisco's Web site and determine what types of networking products the company produces and sells. Why are its products so popular, and who are its competitors?

16. Investigate the options for high-speed, broadband Internet access into your home. What options are available to you, and how much do they cost?

Answers to the Self-Study Questions

1. A, p. 521	**2.** D, p. 525	**3.** C, p. 526	**4.** A, p. 532	**5.** D, p. 527
6. C, p. 534	**7.** A, p. 535	**8.** C, p. 535	**9.** C, p. 537	**10.** A, p. 537

Technology Briefing
The Internet and the World Wide Web

p r e v i e w > Organizations need to bring products to a global market quickly and to be closely integrated with their customers and suppliers. These and related demands have driven the rapid development of telecommunications technologies, particularly the Internet. These technologies enable people and enterprises to share information across time and distance, and they can lower boundaries between markets and cultures. The Internet revolution is changing how we live and work and how we communicate with each other. This technology briefing introduces how the Internet works, providing a solid foundation for understanding how organizations use the Internet to connect computers across a city or across the world. After reading this briefing, you will be able to do the following:

1. Describe the Internet and how it works.

2. Describe the basic Internet services and the use of the World Wide Web.

The Internet

The name **Internet** is derived from the concept of *internetworking,* which means connecting host computers and their networks together to form even larger networks. The Internet is a large worldwide collection of networks that use a common protocol to communicate with each other.

How Did the Internet Get Started?

You can trace the roots of the Internet back to the late 1960s, when the U.S. **Defense Advanced Research Projects Agency (DARPA)** began to study ways to interconnect networks of various kinds. This research effort produced the **Advanced Research Projects Agency Network (ARPANET)**, a large wide area network (WAN) that linked many universities and research centers. The first two nodes on the ARPANET were the University of California, Los Angeles, and the Stanford Research Institute, followed by the University of Utah.

ARPANET quickly evolved and was combined with other networks. For example, in 1986, the U.S. **National Science Foundation (NSF)** initiated the development of the **National Science Foundation Network (NSFNET)**, which became a major component of the Internet. Other networks throughout the United States and the rest of the world were interconnected and/or morphed into the growing "Internet." Among these were the BIT-NET, CSNET, NSINET, ESNET, and NORDUNET. Throughout the world, support for the Internet has come from a combination of federal and state governments, universities, national and international research organizations, and industry.

The Internet Uses Packet-Switching Technology

The Internet relies on packet-switching technology to deliver data and information across networks. Packet switching enables millions of users to send large and small chunks of data across the Internet concurrently. **Packet switching** is based on the concept of turn taking. To minimize delays, network technologies limit the amount of data that a computer can transfer on each turn. Consider a conveyor belt as a comparison. Suppose that the conveyor belt connects a warehouse and a retail store. When a customer places an order, it is sent from the store to the warehouse, where a clerk assembles the items in the order. The items are placed on the conveyor belt and delivered to the customer in the store. In most situations, clerks finish sending items from one order before proceeding to send items from another order. This process works well when orders are small, but when a large order with many items comes in, sharing a conveyor belt can introduce delays for others. Consider waiting in the store for your one item while another order with 50 items is being filled.

Local area networks (LANs), WANs, and the Internet all use packet-switching technologies so that users can share the communication channel and minimize delivery delays. Figure TB5.1 illustrates how computers use packet switching. Computer A wants to send a message to computer C; similarly, computer B wants to send a message to computer D. For example, computer A is trying to send an e-mail message to computer C, while computer B is trying to send a word processing file to computer D. The outgoing messages are divided into smaller packets of data, and then each sending computer (A and B) takes turns sending the packets over the *transmission media.* The incoming packets are reassembled at their respective destinations, using previously identified packet sequence numbers.

For packet switching to work, each packet being sent across a network must be labeled with a header. This header contains the network address of the source (sending computer)

FIGURE TB5.1

Using packet switching to send messages from files on computers A and B to computers C and D.

Source: Douglas E. Comer, *The Internet Book,* 2nd ed. (Upper Saddle River, NJ: Prentice Hall, 1997).

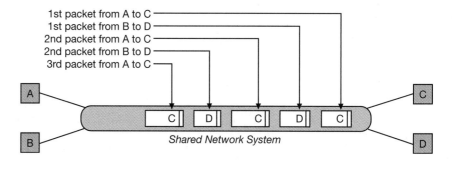

and the network address of the destination (receiving computer). Each computer attached to a network has a unique network address. As packets are sent, network hardware detects whether a particular packet is destined for a local machine. Packet-switching systems adapt instantly to changes in network traffic. If only one computer needs to use the network, it can send data continuously. As soon as another computer needs to send data, packet switching, or turn taking, begins. Now let us see how the Internet handles this packet switching.

Transmission Control Protocol/Internet Protocol

Organizations use diverse network technologies that may or may not be compatible with the technologies of other organizations. Because so many different networks are interconnected today, they must have a common language, or *protocol,* to communicate. As described in Technology Briefing 4—Networking, the protocol of the Internet is called *Transmission Control Protocol/Internet Protocol (TCP/IP).* The first part, TCP, breaks information into small chunks called data packets and manages the transfer of those packets from computer to computer (via packet switching, as described previously). For example, a single document may be broken into several packets, each containing several hundred characters, as well as a destination address, which is the IP part of the protocol. The IP defines how a data packet must be formed and to where a router must forward each packet. Packets travel independently to their destination, sometimes following different paths and arriving out of order. The destination computer reassembles all the packets on the basis of their identification and sequencing information. Together, TCP and IP provide a reliable and efficient way to send data across the Internet.

A data packet that conforms to the IP specification is called an **IP datagram**. Datagram routing and delivery are possible because, as previously mentioned, every computer and router connected to the Internet is assigned a unique address, called its **IP address**. When an organization connects to the Internet, it obtains a set of IP addresses that it can assign to its computers. TCP helps IP guarantee delivery of datagrams by performing three main tasks. First, it automatically checks for datagrams that may have been lost en route from their source to their destination. Second, TCP collects the incoming datagrams and puts them in the correct order to re-create the original message. Finally, TCP discards any duplicate copies of datagrams that may have been created by network hardware.

Connecting Independent Networks

Now that you understand how computers share a transmission path, we can examine how packet-switching networks are interconnected to form the Internet. The Internet uses special purpose computers, called *routers,* to interconnect independent networks. For example, Figure TB5.2 illustrates a router that connects network 1 and network 2. A router, like a conventional computer, has a central processor, memory, and network interfaces. However, routers do not use conventional software, nor are they used to run applications.

FIGURE TB5.2

Routers connect networks.

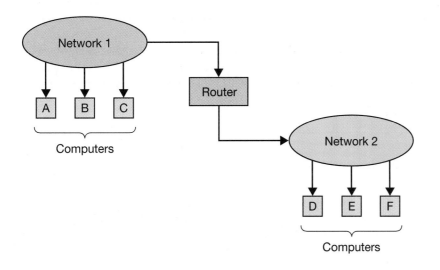

FIGURE TB5.3

LANs connect to wide area backbones.

Source: Douglas E. Comer, *The Internet Book,* 2nd ed. (Upper Saddle River, NJ: Prentice Hall, 1997).

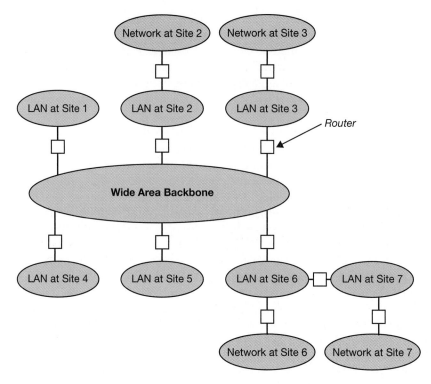

Their only job is to interconnect networks and forward data packets from one network to another. For example, in Figure TB5.2, computers A and F are connected to independent networks. If computer A generates a data packet destined for computer F, the packet is sent to the router that interconnects the two networks. The router forwards the packet onto network 2, where it is delivered to its destination at computer F.

Routers are the fundamental building blocks of the Internet because they connect thousands of LANs and WANs. LANs are connected to backbone WANs, as depicted in Figure TB5.3. A *backbone network* manages the bulk of network traffic and typically uses a higher-speed connection than the individual LAN segments. For example, a backbone network might use fiber-optic cabling, which can transfer data at a rate of 2 Gbps (gigabits per second), whereas a LAN connected to the backbone may use Ethernet with twisted pair cabling, transferring data at a rate of 10 MBps to 1 GBps. To gain access to the Internet, an organization connects a router between one of its own networks and the closest Internet site. Business organizations typically connect to the Internet not only with personal computers but with Web servers (see below) as well.

Web Domain Names and Addresses

A **Uniform Resource Locator (URL)** is used to identify and locate a particular **Web page**. For example, www.google.com is the URL used to find the main Google Web server. The URL has three distinct parts: the domain, the top-level domain, and the host name (see Figure TB5.4).

The **domain name** is a term that helps people recognize the company or person that domain name represents. For example, Google's domain name is google.com. The prefix *google* lets you know that it is very likely that this domain name will lead you to the **Web site** of Google. Domain names also have a suffix that indicates which **top-level domain** they belong to. For example the "com" suffix is reserved for commercial organizations. Some other popular suffixes are listed here:

- edu—educational institutions
- org—organizations (nonprofit)
- mil—military
- net—network organizations
- ca—Canada

FIGURE 5.4

Dissecting a URL.

Domain names ending with .com, .net, or .org can be registered through many different companies (known as registrars) that compete with one another. An alphabetical listing of these registrars is provided in the *ICANN* Registrar Directory on the ICANN site at www.icann.org/registrars/accredited-list.html. Given the proliferation of domain names, more of these top-level domain categories are being added, such as .aero for the air transport industry, .name for individuals, .coop for business industry cooperatives, and .museum for museums.

The host name is the particular Web server or group of Web servers (if it is a larger Web sites) that will respond to the Web request. In most cases, the www host name refers to the default Web site or the home page of the particular domain. Other host names can be used. For example, spreadsheets.google.com will take you to the group of Web servers that are responsible for serving up Google's spreadsheet application. Larger companies have several host names for their different functions. Some examples used in Google are the following:

- mail.google.com (Google's free e-mail service)
- labs.google.com (Google's test applications)
- trends.google.com (see what other people are searching)
- maps.google.com (Google's mapping application)

All of the domain names and the host names are associated with one or more IP addresses. For example, the domain name google.com represents about a dozen underlying IP addresses. IP addresses serve to identify all the computers or devices on the Internet (or on any TCP/IP network). The IP address serves as the destination address of that computer or device and enables the network to route messages to the proper destination. The format of an IP address is a 32-bit numeric address written as four numbers separated by periods. Each of the four numbers can be any number between 0 and 255. For example, 1.160.10.240 could be an IP address. You could set up a private network using the TCP/IP protocol and assign your own domain names and IP addresses for computers and other devices on that network. On the other hand, if you wish to connect to the Internet, you must use registered IP addresses.

IP addresses can also be used as a URL to navigate to particular Web addresses. This practice is not done regularly, as IP addresses are far more difficult to remember than domain names.

Who Manages the Internet?

So, who keeps track of these IP addresses on the Internet? A number of national and international standing committees and task forces have been used to manage the development and use of the Internet. Among these is the Coordinating Committee for Intercontinental Research Networks, which has helped to coordinate government-sponsored research in this area. The Internet Society is a professional membership society with over 150 organizational and 16,000 individual members around the world that helps to shape the future of the Internet and is home for the Internet Engineering Task Force and the Internet Architecture Board (IAB). These groups help manage Internet standards. For example, the IAB has guided the evolution of the TCP/IP Protocol Suite. The Internet Assigned Numbers Authority has provided the recording of system identifiers on the Internet and has helped to manage an **Internet Registry** that acts as a central repository for Internet-related information and that provides central allocation of network system identifiers. The Internet Registry also provides central maintenance of the **Domain Name System (DNS)** root database, which points to distributed DNS servers replicated throughout the Internet. This database is used to associate Internet host names with their Internet IP addresses. As mentioned previously, users can access Web sites using domain name or IP addresses. The functionality of the DNS is to provide users easy to remember domain names to access Web sites. In other words, it is far easier to remember www.apple.com than it is to remember 17.254.0.91, but both will work as a URL in any Web browser, as the DNS servers will translate the domain names into the accompanying IP address.

In 1993, the NSF created **InterNIC**, a government–industry collaboration, to manage directory and database services, domain registration services, and other information services on the Internet. In the late 1990s, this Internet oversight was transitioned more fully out into industry when InterNIC morphed into the **Internet Corporation for Assigned Names and Numbers (ICANN)**, a nonprofit corporation that assumed responsibility for managing IP addresses, domain names, and root server system management. The number of unassigned Internet addresses is running out, so new classes of addresses are being added as we adopt **IPv6**, the latest version of the IP.

How to Connect to the Internet

Now you can see how the Internet works and how it is managed. How do you connect to the Internet? For personal use (i.e., from home), we typically connect to the Internet through **Internet service providers (ISPs)**, also called Internet access providers. ISPs provide several different ways to access the Internet from home (see Table TB5.1).

TABLE TB5.1 Methods for Connecting to the Internet

Service	Outlook	Typical Bandwidth
Dial-up	Although still used heavily in the United States, there are very few new dial-up customers. This market should dry up as broadband is moved to the rural areas of the United States.	52 Kbps
ISDN	This technology has limited market share because of its expense. Typically, ISDN connections are more expensive than broadband connections, although they offer less bandwidth.	128 Kbps
DSL	DSL technology has gained market share over cable. With many companies offering higher speeds at lower cost, DSL should continue to cut into cable's market share.	Upload: 1.5 Mbps Download: 3 Mbps
Cable	Coaxial cable used for cable TV provides much greater bandwidth than telephone lines and therefore is the market leader in broadband use for home users. Overselling of bandwidth that causes slower-than-average speeds tends to be a major problem for home users.	Upload: 768 Kbps Download: 30 Mbps
Satellite	Although satellite connectivity had a promising future, many users are moving away from this expensive technology in order to access faster and cheaper cable or DSL connections.	Upload: 50 Kbps Download: 5 Mbps
Wireless	Wireless offers the most promise of any of the current technologies, as the speeds are increasing while the coverage areas continue to grow.	Up to 54 Mbps
Fiber to the home	FTTH has been adopted by many major players in the ISP industry. Although the technology typically can be placed only in new developments, the demand for fast connections is helping make FTTH a significant technology for ISPs.	Up to 100 Mbps

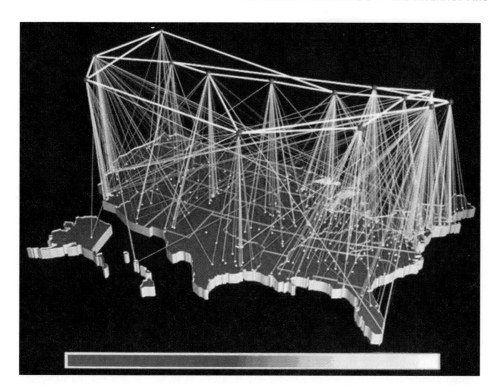

ISPs connect to one another through **network access points (NAPs)**. Much like railway stations, these NAPs serve as access points for ISPs and are an exchange point for Internet traffic. They determine how traffic is routed and are often the points of most Internet congestion. NAPs are a key component of the **Internet backbone**, which is the collection of main network connections and telecommunications lines that make up the Internet (see Figure TB5.5).

The Internet follows a hierarchical structure, similar to the interstate highway system. High-speed central network lines are like interstate highways, enabling traffic from midlevel networks to get on and off. Think of midlevel networks as city streets that, in turn, accept traffic from their neighborhood streets or member networks. However, you cannot get on an interstate or city street whenever you want to. You have to share the highway and follow traffic control signs to arrive safely at your destination. The same holds true for traffic on the Internet.

Home Internet Connectivity

People can connect to the Internet in a number of ways. The following outline how typical home users connect to the Internet.

Dial-Up Traditionally, most people connected to the Internet through a telephone line at home or work. The term we use for standard telephone lines is **plain old telephone service (POTS)**. The speed, or bandwidth, of POTS is generally about 52 Kbps (52,000 bits per second). The POTS system is also called the **public switched telephone network (PSTN)**. Today, most people connect to the Internet using some form of digital, high-speed connection.

Integrated Services Digital Network **Integrated services digital network (ISDN)** is a standard for worldwide digital communications. ISDN was designed in the 1980s to replace all analog systems, such as most telephone connections in the United States, with a completely digital transmission system. ISDN uses existing twisted pair telephone wires to provide high-speed data service. ISDN systems can transmit voice, video, and data. Because ISDN is a purely digital network, you can connect your PC to the Internet without the use of a traditional modem. Removing the analog-to-digital conversion for sending information and the digital-to-analog conversion for receiving information greatly increases the data transfer rate. However, a small electronic box called an "ISDN modem" is typically required so that computers and older, analog-based devices such as telephones and fax machines can utilize and share the ISDN-based service. While ISDN has had moderate success in various parts of the world such as Germany, it has largely been surpassed by DSL and cable modems.

Digital Subscriber Line **Digital subscriber line (DSL)** is one of the more popular ways of connecting to the Internet. DSL is referred to as a "last-mile" solution because it is used only for connections from a telephone switching station to a home or office and generally is not used between telephone switching stations.

The abbreviation DSL is used to refer collectively to **asymmetric digital subscriber line (ADSL)**, **symmetric digital subscriber line (SDSL)**, and other forms of DSL. DSL enables more data to be sent over existing copper telephone lines by sending digital pulses in the high-frequency area of telephone wires. Because these high frequencies are not used by normal voice communications, DSL enables your computer to operate simultaneously with voice connections over the same wires. ADSL speeds range from 1.5 to 9 Mbps downstream and from 16 to 640 Kbps upstream. SDSL is said to be symmetric because it supports the same data rates for upstream and downstream traffic (up to 3 Mbps). Like ISDN, ADSL and SDSL require a special modem-like device. ADSL is most popular in North America, whereas SDSL is being developed primarily in Europe.

Cable Modems In most areas, the company that provides cable television service also provides Internet service. With this type of service, a special **cable modem** is designed to transmit data over cable TV lines. Coaxial cable used for cable TV provides much greater bandwidth than telephone lines, and millions of homes in the United States are already wired for cable TV, so cable modems are a fast, popular method for accessing the Internet. Cable modems offer speeds up to 30 Mbps.

Satellite Connections In many regions of the world, people can now access the Internet via *satellite,* referred to as **Internet over satellite (IoS)**. IoS technologies allow users to access the Internet via satellites that are placed in fixed positions above the earth's surface in what is known as a **geostationary or geosynchronous orbit** (i.e., the satellite moves with the earth's rotation). With these services, your PC is connected to a satellite dish hanging out on the side of your home or placed out on a pole (much like satellite services for your television) and is able to maintain a reliable connection to the satellite in the sky because the satellite orbits the earth at the exact speed of the earth's rotation. Given the vast distance that signals must travel from the earth up to the satellite and back again, IoS is slower than high-speed terrestrial (i.e., land-based) connections to the Internet over copper or fiber-optic cables. In remote regions of the world, IoS is the only option available because installing the cables necessary for Internet connection is not economically feasible or, in many cases, is just not physically possible.

Broadband Wireless **Broadband wireless** is a technology that is becoming more prevalent with home users today. With speeds similar to DSL and cable, broadband wireless is usually found in rural areas where other connectivity options, such as DSL and cable, are not available. A common scenario is that the ISP will install an antenna at a high point, such as a large building or radio tower. The consumer will mount a small dish to the roof and point it at the antenna. Although broadband wireless can bridge a distance of up to 50 kilometers, line of sight between the sender and receiver is necessary for wireless access to work.

Mobile Wireless Access In addition to the fixed wireless approach, there are also many new **mobile wireless** approaches for connecting to the Internet. For example, there are Internet-enabled *cellular phones* that give you Internet access nearly anywhere. Also, special network adapter cards from a cellular service provider allow a notebook computer, tablet PC, or personal digital assistant (PDA) to connect to cellular networks. The advantage of these systems is that as long as you are in the coverage area of that cell provider you have access to the Internet (much like coverage with cellular phones). One other option for wireless access to the Internet is to use a wireless Ethernet network adapter card (typically built into most mobile computers) as long as you are within the range of a *wireless local area network* (WLAN). Using a WLAN, you are free to roam around your office or building; with a cellular-based technology, you are able to connect anywhere within the cellular coverage area.

Fiber to the Home **Fiber to the home (FTTH)**, also known as **fiber to the premises (FTTP)**, refers to connectivity technology that allows for superspeed connection to people's homes. This is usually done by fiber-optic cabling running directly into new homes. With several players entering the FTTH marketplace, including the largest FTTH company, Verizon, there will be a wide use of this technology shortly. The growth in FTTH is dependent on new home building, as it is currently cost prohibitive to distribute the technology to existing structures.

Until now, we have talked about ways that individuals rather than organizations typically access the Internet. In the following section, we talk more about ways that organizations typically access the Internet.

Business Internet Connectivity

Although home users have enjoyed a consistent increase in bandwidth availability, the demand for corporate use has increased at a greater pace; therefore, the need for faster speeds has become of great importance. In addition to the home connectivity options, business customers also have several high-speed options, described next.

T1 Lines To gain adequate access to the Internet, organizations are turning to long-distance carriers to lease a dedicated **T1 line** for digital transmissions. The T1 line was developed by AT&T as a dedicated digital transmission line that can carry 1.544 Mbps of information. In the United States, companies such as MCI that sell long-distance services are called **interexchange carriers (IXC)** because their circuits carry service between the major telephone exchanges. A T1 line usually traverses hundreds or thousands of miles over leased long-distance facilities.

AT&T and other carriers charge as little as $400 per month for a dedicated T1 circuit, and some providers will waive the installation fee if you sign up for some specified length of service. If you need an even faster link, you might choose a **T3 line**. T3 provides about 45 Mbps of service at about 10 times the cost of leasing a T1 line. Alternatively, organizations often choose to use two or more T1 lines simultaneously rather than jump to the more expensive T3 line. Higher speeds than the T3 are also available but are not typically used for normal business activity. For example, fiber-optic networks offer speeds considerably faster than T3 lines. See Table TB5.2 for a summary of telecommunication line capacities, including optical carrier (OC) lines that use the Synchronous Optical Network (SONET) standard.

Asynchronous Transfer Mode **Asynchronous transfer mode (ATM)** is a method of transmitting voice, video, and data over high-speed LANs at speeds of up to 2.2 Gbps. ATM has found wide acceptance in the LAN and WAN arenas as a solution to integrating disparate networks over large geographic distances. ATM uses a form of packet transmission

TABLE TB5.2 Capacity of Telecommunication Lines

Type of Line	Data Rate
T1	1.544 Mbps
T3	44.736 Mbps
OC-1	51.85 Mbps
OC-3	155.52 Mbps
OC-12	622.08 Mbps
OC-24	1.244 Gbps
OC-48	2.488 Gbps

in which data is sent over a packet-switched network in fixed-length, 53-byte cells. Although it is based on packet-switching technology, ATM has the potential to do away with routers, allocated bandwidth, and contention for communications media. Organizations in the movie and entertainment industries that need to deliver synchronized video and sound, for example, are particularly interested in ATM.

The Future of Connectivity

Although there are many options for both business and home user alike, there are still many innovations yet to gain widespread acceptance. One such innovation is broadband over power lines. **Power line communication**, or power line telecoms, is a system that uses the existing power distribution wires for data transmission. Currently, the data rates are 1 Mbps and increasing every year. This technology is promising, as the infrastructure is currently available to virtually all consumers.

WiMax is another promising innovation. WiMAX, or Worldwide Interoperability for Microwave Access, is a standards-based technology that enables the delivery of the "last mile" in wireless form. WiMax is similar to broadband wireless in that it offers high-speed stationary wireless, but is different in that it is not a line-of-sight technology. Further, WiMax can also be used for mobile application. Currently, WiMax is being used primarily by corporate customers and ISPs because of the large investment needed in equipment. However, as equipment becomes less expensive, consumer versions of the technology will become available (see www.clearwire.com).

The Current State of Internet Usage

The Internet is now the most prominent global network. Internet World Stats (www.internetworldstats.com) reports that just over 1 billion people worldwide use the Internet. This means that over 15 percent of the world's population has Internet access at home, an increase of 183 percent since 2000. Most Internet users are found in Asia, but North America has the largest percentage of users (68.6 percent). Africa, on the other hand, has the smallest percentage of its population using the Internet since 2000 (just 2.6 percent) but is experiencing rapid growth (423 percent).

One other way to measure the rapid growth of the Internet, in addition to the number of users, is to examine the growth in the number of **Internet hosts**—that is, computers working as servers on the Internet—as shown in Figure TB5.6.

FIGURE TB5.6

Growth in Internet servers (hosts).

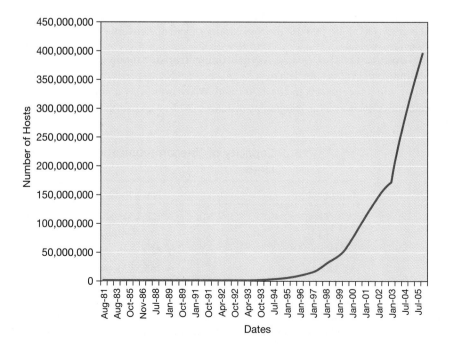

What Are People Doing on the Internet?

The Internet enables people to access a wide range of data, including text, video, audio, graphics, databases, maps, and other data types. The Internet is more, however, than just access to data. The Internet also enables people to connect with each other. Recently, with increases in bandwidth and decreases in prices for computers and Internet access, there have been substantial changes in the ways people are using the Internet. For example, recent advancements in communication technologies and increasingly high transmission speeds have made interactivity—real-time collaboration between people—possible over the Internet.

A number of popular uses of the Internet are summarized in Table TB5.3. Essentially, these involve ways to access information and to communicate with other people. For access to a variety of free software that will enable you to better use the Internet, visit one of the popular software download Web sites, such as www.cnet.com.

While the Internet is an amazing collection of technologies, the real power of the Internet was not realized until the early 1990s, with the invention of the World Wide Web and the Web browser. The Web and the Web browser have essentially given us a graphical user interface with which to use the Internet and, as a result, have made the Internet much more accessible and easy to use and opened the door for some very innovative uses of the Internet.

TABLE TB5.3 Popular Internet Uses and Tools

Internet Use	Description	Popular Free Applications
E-mail	Enables users to send and receive messages	Apple Mail, Mozilla Thunderbird, Outlook Express
File sharing	Making files available for users to download; files can be provided by a server or peer to peer (P2P) based.	Bittorrent, FreeNET, WSFTP
Instant Messaging	Uses a client application to have real-time messaging	AIM, GTalk, Jabber, Windows Live Messenger, Yahoo! Messenger
Search engine	Uses Internet applications to provide a list of documents stored on other computers connected to the Web	Google, Windows Live, Yahoo!, Dogpile
Web browsing	View documents (usually Web pages) on computers connected to the Web	Opera, Internet Explorer, Firefox
Voice communication	Enables users to transmit and receive voice conversations	Skype, GTalk, Windows Live Messenger

World Wide Web

One of the most powerful uses of the Internet is something that you have no doubt heard a great deal about—the World Wide Web. More than likely, you have probably browsed the Web using Netscape Navigator, Microsoft's Internet Explorer, Firefox, or some other popular Web browser, as shown in Figure TB5.6. A **Web browser** is a software application that can be used to locate and display Web pages, including text, graphics, and multimedia content. Browsers have become a standard Internet tool. As previously mentioned, the **World Wide Web (WWW)** is a graphical user interface to the Internet that provides users with a simple, consistent interface to a wide variety of information.

History of the World Wide Web

Prior to the invention of the Web by Tim Berners-Lee in 1991, content posted on the Internet could be accessed through the Internet tool **Gopher**. Gopher provides a menu-driven, hierarchical interface to organize files stored on servers, providing a way to tie together related files from different Internet servers across the world. The Web took Gopher one step further by introducing **hypertext**. A hypertext document, otherwise known as a Web page, contains not only information but also references or links to other documents that contain related information. These links are known as **hyperlinks**. The Web also introduced the *Hypertext Markup Language (HTML)*, which is the standard method of specifying the format of Web pages. Specific content within each Web page is enclosed within codes, or markup tags, that stipulate how the content should appear to the user. Web pages are stored on **Web servers**, which process user requests for pages using the **Hypertext Transfer Protocol (HTTP)**. Web servers typically host a collection of interlinked Web pages, called a Web site, that are owned by the same organization or by an individual. Web sites and specific Web pages within those sites have a unique Internet URL address. A user who wants to access a Web site enters the URL, and the Web server hosting the Web site retrieves the desired page and delivers it to the user.

The introduction of the Web was the first of three events that led to its proliferation. The second event was the Information Infrastructure Act (Berghel, 1996), passed by the U.S. government in 1992, which opened the Web for commercial purposes. Prior to this legislation, universities and government agencies were the Web's main users. The third event was the arrival of a graphical Web browser, Mosaic, which quickly transcended Gopher by adding a graphical front end to the Web. Mosaic's graphical interface allowed Web pages to be constructed to deliver an extended range of content, including images, audio, video, and other multimedia, all of which could be included and displayed within the same Web page. Mosaic was the predecessor to Netscape's Navigator.

World Wide Web Architecture

The Web uses Web browsers, Web servers, and the TCP/IP networking protocol to facilitate the transmission of Web pages over the Internet. Figure TB5.7 depicts the architecture of the Web. To access information on the Web, a Web browser, as well as the TCP/IP protocol, must be installed on a user's computer. Users can access Web pages by entering into their Web browser the URL of the Web page. Once the user enters the URL in the Web

FIGURE TB5.7

World Wide Web architecture.

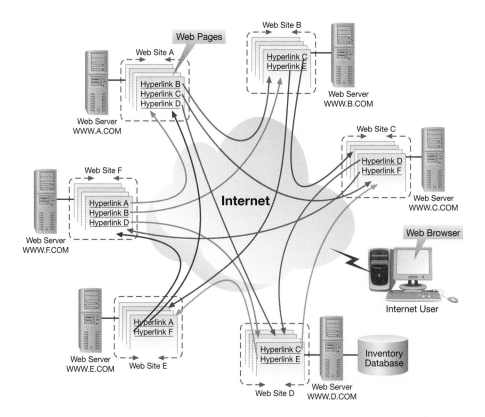

browser, TCP/IP breaks the request into packets and routes them over the Internet to the Web server, where the requested Web page is stored. When the packets reach their destination, TCP/IP reassembles them and passes the request to the Web server. The Web server understands that the user is requesting a Web page (indicated by the http:// prefix in the URL) and retrieves the Web page, which is packetized by TCP/IP and transmitted over the Internet back to the Web browser. TCP/IP reassembles the packets at the destination and delivers the Web page to the Web browser. In turn, the Web browser translates the HTML code contained in the Web page, formats its physical appearance, and displays the results. If the Web page contains a hyperlink, the user can click on it and the process repeats itself.

World Wide Web Applications

Because the powerful and relatively inexpensive Web platform is extremely well suited for disseminating information on a global basis, organizations are constantly trying to devise innovative applications for the Web. Over the years, many organizations have become very sophisticated users of Web technologies. The first wave of Web-based commerce occurred around 1994, when new businesses brought product marketing to the Web, pioneering an explosion of commercial activity that will continue into the foreseeable future (see Chapter 5—Enabling Commerce Using the Internet).

Key Points Review

1. *Describe the Internet and how it works.* The Internet is composed of networks that are developed and maintained by many different entities; it follows a hierarchical structure, similar to the interstate highway system. High-speed central networks called backbones are like interstate highways, enabling traffic from midlevel networks to get on and off. The Internet relies on packet-switching technology to deliver data and information across networks. Routers are used to interconnect independent networks. Because so many different networks are connected to the Internet, they use a common communication protocol (TCP/IP). TCP/IP is divided into two parts. TCP breaks information into small chunks, called data packets, which are transferred from computer to computer. IP defines how a data packet must be formed and how a router must forward each packet. All computers, including routers, are assigned unique IP addresses. Data routing and delivery are possible because of the unique addressing of every computer attached to the Internet. Together, TCP and IP provide a reliable and efficient way to send data across the Internet.

2. *Describe the basic Internet services and the use of the World Wide Web.* A collection of tools enables us to use the Internet in order to exchange messages, share information, or connect to remote computers. The many ways we can do this include e-mail, file sharing, instant messaging, search engines, voice communication, and Web browsing. Perhaps the most powerful application of the Internet is the World Wide Web, which binds together the various tools used on the Internet, providing users with a simple, consistent interface to a wide variety of information through the use of Web browsers.

Key Terms

Advanced Research Projects Agency Network (ARPANET)   544
asymmetric digital subscriber line (ADSL)   550
asynchronous transfer mode (ATM)   551
broadband wireless   550
cable modem   550

Defense Advanced Research Projects Agency (DARPA)   544
digital subscriber line (DSL)   550
domain name   546
Domain Name System (DNS)   548
fiber to the home (FTTH)   551

fiber to the premises (FTTP)   551
geostationary or geosynchronous orbit   550
Gopher   553
hyperlinks   554
hypertext   554
Hypertext Transfer Protocol (HTTP)   554

Review Questions

1. What is the Internet, and why was it created?
2. What are packet switching and TCP/IP?
3. Other than the telephone, what are three alternatives for connecting to the Internet at home?
4. What are the alternatives for corporations to connect to the Internet?
5. What organization manages the registration for domain names?
6. List and describe five popular uses of the Internet.
7. What is the World Wide Web, and what is its relationship to the Internet?
8. Name four top-level domains.
9. Name two future technologies that people will be using to connect to the Internet.
10. What are URLs, and why are they important to the World Wide Web?

Self-Study Questions

Visit the Interactive Study Guide on the text Web site for additional Self-Study Questions: **www.prenhall.com/jessup**.

1. All of the following are correct domain suffix pairs except
   A. edu—educational institutions
   B. mil—military
   C. neo—network organizations
   D. com—commercial businesses
2. Which of the following is faster and becoming more popular than the standard telephone as a way to connect to the Internet?
   A. DSL
   B. satellite
   C. cable
   D. all of the above
3. Web sites and specific Web pages within those sites have a unique Internet address called a URL, or _____.
   A. Universal Resource Login
   B. Universal Router Locator
   C. Uniform Resource Locator
   D. Uniform Resource Language
4. Which is the fastest connection available for home users?

   A. dial-up
   B. DSL
   C. broadband wireless
   D. FTTH
5. Which of the following is a typical way large corporations connect to the Internet?
   A. satellite
   B. cable
   C. T1 Lines
   D. all of the above
6. What specialized piece of hardware allows for packets to be sent to different computers on the Internet?
   A. router
   B. DNS
   C. Web browser
   D. ISP
7. What system relates domain names to IP addresses?
   A. ISP
   B. router
   C. DNS
   D. Web browser

8. What is the newest version of the Internet protocol that allows for far more IP addresses than is currently available?

A. IPX

B. IPv6

C. IPv4

D. SPX

9. Which language allows for documents to be shared and linked on the World Wide Web?

A. FTP

B. SSL

C. HTML

D. HTTP

10. What organization was the first to link computers together to form the predecessor to the Internet?

A. InterNIC

B. Internet Corporation for Assigned Names and Numbers (ICANN)

C. U.S. Defense Department

D. NASA

Answers are on page 558.

Problems and Exercises

1. Match the following terms to the appropriate definitions:

i. Instant messaging

ii. DNS

iii. FTTH

iv. ICANN

v. T1

vi. Internet service provider

vii. Web browser

viii. Domain name

ix. Hypertext

x. DSL

a. To gain adequate access to the Internet, organizations are turning to long-distance carriers to lease this dedicated high-speed line

b. Used in Uniform Resource Locators (URLs) to identify a source or host entity on the Internet

c. This database is used to associate Internet host names with their Internet IP addresses

d. Text in a Web document that is highlighted and, when clicked on by the user, evokes an embedded command that goes to another specified file or location and brings up that file or location on the user's screen

e. Refers to connectivity technology that allows for superspeed connection to home, usually done by fiber-optic cabling running directly into new homes

f. A software application that can be used to locate and display Web pages, including text, graphics, and multimedia content

g. An application that allows typed conversations with others in real time on the Internet

h. An individual or organization that enables other individuals and organizations to connect to the Internet

i. A nonprofit corporation responsible for managing IP addresses, domain names, and the root server system.

j. High-speed Internet connection using digital pulses in the high-frequency area of telephone wires

2. Do you have your own Web site with a specific domain name? How did you decide on the domain name? If you don't have your own domain, research possibilities of obtaining one. Would your preferred name be available? Why might your preferred name not be available?

3. Table TB5.3 lists a variety of different popular Internet tools. Research the Web for different tools from one category. What are the benefits and drawbacks of each? Have you used one of the tools? If so, what are your experiences?

4. You have probably experienced several different types of connection—from the university T1 connections to a home DSL or even dial-up connection. If you had to balance between cost and speed, which connection would you choose?

5. Scan the popular press and search the Web for clues concerning emerging technologies for telecommunications. This may include new uses for current technologies or new technologies altogether. Discuss as a group the "hot" issues. Do you feel they will become a reality in the near future? Why or why not? Prepare a 10 minute presentation to the class of your findings.

6. Explain in simple language how the Internet works. Be sure to talk about backbones, packet switching, networks, routers, TCP/IP, and Internet services. What technologies, hardware, and software do you utilize when using the Internet? What would you like to use that isn't available to you?

7. How long, on average, are you willing to wait for a Web page to load in your browser on your computer? Under what conditions would you be willing to wait longer for a page to come up in your browser? Based on your answers, what are the implications for Web site design? Do you wait longer if you know what you will be seeing, that is, if you are loading a page at a site you have been to in the past?

8. Search through recent articles in your favorite technology publication—whether print or online. What are some of the issues being discussed that relate to the Internet and/or the Web in particular? Have you experienced any of these technologies, applications, and/or issues? What is your opinion about them? How will they affect your life and career? Prepare a 10-minute presentation to the class of your findings.

9. Research projects can now be accomplished by using the Internet as the sole source of information. Conduct such a research project using solely the Internet for source information and answer the following questions: (1) what is the history of the Internet, (2) what are the demographics of the users of the Internet, and (3) what are the historic growth and the projected growth of the Internet? Remember, use only the Internet itself to research and write this short paper and reference all of your sources completely and accurately.

10. Surf the Web to explore three different ways hyperlinks are used. Which ways of using (or naming) hyperlinks seem to be most effective? Why? If you were to design your own Web site, how would you implement hyperlinks in your Web pages?

Answers to the Self-Study Questions

1. C, p. 546	**2.** D, p. 548	**3.** C, p. 546	**4.** D, p. 551	**5.** C, p. 551
6. A, p. 545	**7.** C, p. 548	**8.** B, p. 548	**9.** C, p. 554	**10.** C, p. 544

Glossary

802.11: A family of universally adopted wireless transmission standards having transmission speeds up to 540 Mbps.

Acceptable use policy: Computer and/or Internet usage policy for people within an organization, with clearly spelled-out penalties for noncompliance.

Access control software: Software for securing information systems by only allowing specific users access to specific computers, applications, or data.

Adaptive maintenance: Making changes to an information system to make its functionality meet changing business needs or to migrate it to a different operating environment.

Ad-hoc reports: Reports created due to unplanned information requests in which information is gathered to support a nonroutine decision.

Advanced Research Projects Agency Network (ARPANET): A wide area network that came about as a result of research efforts by the Defense Advanced Research Projects Agency (DARPA) to interconnect networks of various kinds. The ARPANET evolved into the Internet.

Adware: A special type of spyware which collects information about a person in order to customize Web browser banner advertisements.

Affiliate marketing: A type of marketing that allows individual Web site owners to earn revenue by posting other companies' ads on their Web pages.

Alpha testing: Testing performed by the development organization to assess whether the entire system meets the design requirements of the users.

Analog signals: Audio tones used to transmit data over conventional voice telephone lines.

Analytical CRM: Systems for analyzing customer behavior and perceptions in order to provide business intelligence.

Applet: A program designed to be executed within another application such as a Web page.

Application-level control: The prevention of unauthorized access to selected applications by some form of security.

Application Service Provider (ASP): A company offering on-demand software on an as-needed basis to its clients over the Web.

Application services: Processes that run software for network clients and enable computers to share processing power.

Application software: Software used to perform a specific task that the user needs to accomplish.

Arithmetic/Logic Unit (ALU): Part of the central processing unit (CPU) that performs mathematics, including all forms of addition, subtraction, multiplication, and division and logical operations.

Artificial intelligence (AI): The science of enabling information technologies—software, hardware, networks, and so on—to simulate human intelligence, such as reasoning and learning, as well as gaining sensing capabilities, such as seeing, hearing, walking, talking, and feeling.

ASCII (American Standard Code for Information Interchange): Character encoding method that is based on the English alphabet and provides codes to represent symbols (letters and numbers) in binary form.

Asymmetric digital subscriber line (ADSL): A data transfer format that enables large amounts of data to be sent relatively quickly over existing copper telephone lines with speeds ranging from 15 to 9 Mbps downstream and from 16 to 640 Kbps upstream.

Asynchronous transfer mode (ATM): A method of transmitting voice, video, and data over high-speed LANs at speeds of up to 22 Gbps.

Attenuation: The weakening of an electric signal as it is sent over increasing distance.

Attribute: Individual pieces of information about an entity in a database.

Audio: Sound that has been digitized for storage and replay on a computer.

Audit control software: Software used to keep track of computer activity so that auditors can spot suspicious activity and take action if necessary.

Authentication: The process of confirming the identity of a user who is attempting to access a system or Web site.

Automating: Using information systems to do an activity faster, cheaper, and perhaps with more accuracy and/or consistency.

Autonomic computing: Self-managing computing systems needing only minimal human intervention to operate.

Backbone: A network that manages the bulk of network traffic and typically uses a higher-speed connection than the individual LAN segments connected to it.

Back-office system: Systems designed to support activities without direct customer contact. See analytical CRM.

Backup: Copies of critical systems and data, maintained on a regular basis.

Backup site: Facilities that allow businesses to continue functioning in the event a disaster strikes (can be thought of as a company's office in a temporary location).

Bandwidth: The transmission capacity of a computer or communications channel, often measured in megabits per second (Mbps); it represents how much binary data can be reliably transmitted over the medium in one second.

Batch input: Input method where information is entered in "batches," rather than on a continuous or interactive basis.

Batch processing: The processing of transactions after some quantity of transactions are collected and then processed together as a "batch" at some later time.

Best-cost provider strategy: Strategy to offer products or services of reasonably good quality at competitive prices.

Best practices: Procedures and processes from business organizations that are widely accepted as being among the most effective and/or efficient.

Beta testing: Testing performed by actual system users, who test the capabilities of the system with actual data in their work environment.

Bid luring: A type of e-auction fraud where bidders are lured to leave a legitimate auction in order to buy the same item at a lower price.

Bid shielding: A type of e-auction fraud where sellers use another account to bid on their own item to artificially inflate its price.

Binary code: Methods for representing digital data and information using sequences of zeros and ones.

Biometrics: A type of security that grants or denies access to a resource (e.g., facility, computer systems) through the analysis of fingerprints, retinal patterns in the eye, or other bodily characteristics.

Bits: The individual ones and zeros that make up a byte.

Blogging: The creation of online text diaries, usually organized chronologically, that can focus on anything the user desires. Also called weblogging.

Bluetooth: A wireless specification for personal area networking (PAN) of desktop computers, peripheral devices, mobile phones, pagers, portable stereos, and other handheld devices.

Bot: Short for "software robot"; a program that works in the background to provide some service when a specific event occurs.

Break-even analysis: A type of cost-benefit analysis to identify at what point (if ever) tangible benefits equal tangible costs.

Brick-and-mortar business strategy: A business approach where an organization exclusively utilizes physical locations, such as department stores, business offices, and manufacturing plants, without any type of online presence.

Bricks-and-clicks business strategy: A business approach where an organization utilizes both physical locations and virtual locations. Also referred to as click-and-mortar.

Bridge: Device used to connect two different LANs or two segments of the same LAN by forwarding network traffic between network segments; unlike repeaters, bridges determine the physical location of the source and destination computers.

Broadband wireless: Wireless transmission technology with speeds similar to DSL and cable requiring line-of-sight between the sender and receiver.

Brouter: Short for bridge router (pronounced *brow-ter*); provides the capabilities of both a bridge and a router for managing network traffic.

Business intelligence: (1) The processes of gathering information from both external and internal sources to make better decisions. (2) The data derived from these processes.

Business model: Summary of how a company will generate revenue, identifying the product offering, value-added services, revenue sources, and target customers.

Business processes: Activities organizations perform in order to reach their business goals, consisting of core processes and supporting processes.

Business process management (BPM): A systematic, structured improvement approach by all or part of an organization whereby people critically examine, rethink, and redesign business processes in order to achieve dramatic improvements in one or more performance measures such as quality, cycle time, or cost.

Business process reengineering (BPR): Legacy term for business process management (BPM).

Business rules: Rules included in data dictionaries to prevent illegal or illogical entries from entering the database.

Business-to-business (B2B): Electronic commerce between business partners, such as suppliers and intermediaries.

Business-to-consumer (B2C): Electronic commerce between businesses and consumers.

Business-to-employee (B2E): Electronic commerce between businesses and their employees.

Bus network: Network in the shape of an open-ended line; it is the easiest network to extend and has the simplest wiring layout.

Buyer agents: Intelligent agents that search to find the best price for a particular product you wish to purchase. Also known as a shopping bot.

Byte: Typically 8 bits or about one typed character.

Bytes per inch (BPI): The numbers of bytes that can be stored on one inch of magnetic tape.

Cable modem: A specialized piece of equipment that enables a computer to access Internet service via cable TV lines.

Cache: Pronounced "cash." A small block of memory used by processors to store those instructions most recently or most often used.

CAPTCHA: Completely Automated Public Turing Test to tell Computers and Humans Apart. A way to prevent automated mechanisms from repeatedly attempting to submit an online form or gain access to a system by requiring users to interpret and reenter distorted letters or numbers.

Carding: Stealing credit card information for one's own use, or to sell.

CD-R (compact disc–recordable): A type of optical disk that data can be written to.

CD-ROM (compact disc–read-only memory): A type of optical disk that cannot be written to, but can only be read.

CD-RW (compact disc–rewritable): A type of optical disk that be written onto multiple times.

Cell: A geographic area containing a low-powered radio antenna/receiver for transmitting telecommunications signals within that area; monitored and controlled by a central computer.

Cellular phone: Mobile phone, which uses a communications system that divides a geographic region into sections, called cells.

Censorship: Governmental attempts to control Internet traffic, thus preventing some material from being viewed by a country's citizens.

Centralized computing: A computing model where large centralized computers, called mainframes, are used to process and store data.

Central processing unit (CPU): Also called a microprocessor, processor, or chip. Is responsible for performing all the operations of the computer.

Certificate authority: A trusted middleman between computers that verifies that a Web site is a trusted site and is used when implementing public-key encryption on a large scale.

Channel service unit (CSU): A device that acts as a "buffer" between a LAN and a public carrier's WAN. CSUs ensure that all signals placed on the public lines from the LAN are appropriately timed and formed for the public network.

Characters per inch (CPI): The numbers of characters that can be stored on one inch of magnetic tape.

Chief information officer (CIO): Title given to executive-level individuals who are responsible for leading the overall information systems component within their organizations and integrating new technologies into the organization's business strategy.

Child Online Protection Act (COPA): A law to protect minors from accessing inappropriate content on the Internet.

Circuit-level control: Firewall allowing unrestricted traffic for certain communication/circuits.

Click-and-mortar business strategy: A business approach where an organization utilizes both physical locations and virtual locations. Also referred to as bricks-and-clicks.

Click fraud: Abuse of pay-per-click advertising models by repeatedly clicking on a link to inflate revenue to the host or increase the costs for the advertiser.

Click-only business strategy: A business approach that exclusively utilizes an online presence. Companies using this strategy are also referred to as virtual companies.

Client: Any computer, such as a user's workstation or PC on the network; or any software application, such as a word processing application, that requests and uses the services provided by the server.

Clock speed: The speed of the system clock, typically measured in hertz (Hz).

Clock tick: A single pulse of the system clock.

Cloning: Using scanners to steal wireless transmitter codes for cell phones, then duplicating the phones for illegal use.

Coaxial (coax) cable: Network cable containing a solid inner copper conductor, surrounded by plastic insulation and an outer braided copper or foil shield; most commonly used for cable television installations and for networks operating at 10 Mbps.

Cold backup site: A backup facility consisting of an empty warehouse with all necessary connections for power and communication, but nothing else.

Collaboration: Cooperation between different individuals or entities.

Collaborative computing: A synergistic form of distributed computing, in which two or more networked computers are used to accomplish common processing tasks.

Collaborative CRM: Systems for providing effective and efficient communication with the customer from the entire organization.

Collectivism: A cultural characteristic emphasizing the importance of the collective/group over the individual in society.

Collocation facilities: Facilities in which businesses can rent space for servers or other information systems equipment.

Combination primary key: A unique identifier consisting of two or more attributes.

Command-based interface: Computer interface that requires the user to enter text-based commands to instruct the computer to perform specific operations.

Competitive advantage: A firm's ability to do something better, faster, cheaper, or uniquely when compared with rival firms in the market.

Competitive click fraud: A computer crime where a person—competitor, disgruntled employee, and so on—inflates an organization's online advertising costs by repeatedly clicking on an advertiser's link.

Compiler: A software program that translates a programming language into machine language by taking the entire program written in a programming language and converting it into a completely new program in machine language that can be read and executed directly by the computer.

Computer-aided software engineering (CASE): Software tools that provide automated support for some portion of the systems development process.

Computer assisted auditing tools (CAAT): Software used to test information systems controls.

Computer-based information system: A combination of hardware, software, and telecommunication networks that people build and use to collect, create, and distribute data.

Computer crime: The use of a computer to commit an illegal act.

Computer ethics: A broad range of issues and standards of conduct that have emerged through the use and proliferation of information systems.

Computer forensics: The use of formal investigative techniques to evaluate digital information for judicial review.

Computer literacy: The knowledge of how to operate a computer.

Concept of time: A cultural characteristic that reflects the extent to which a culture has a longer- or shorter-term orientation.

Confidentiality: Ensuring that no one can read the message except the intended recipient.

Connectors: Also called transmission media connectors; used to terminate cable in order to be plugged into a network interface card or into other network components.

Consumer-to-consumer (C2C): A form of electronic commerce that does not involve business firms, such as an online textbook exchange service for students at a university or an online trading Web site such as eBay.

Control objectives for information and related technology (COBIT): A set of best practices that help organizations to both maximize the benefits from their information systems infrastructure, while at the same time establishing appropriate controls.

Control unit: Part of the central processing unit (CPU) that works closely with the ALU (arithmetic logic unit) by fetching and decoding instructions as well as retrieving and storing data.

Conversion: The process of transferring information from a legacy system to a new computing platform.

Cookie: A message passed to a Web browser on a user's computer by a Web server, that is then stored in a text file by the browser; that message is sent back to the server each time the user's browser requests a page from that server.

Core processes: Business processes, such as manufacturing goods, selling products, and providing service, that make up the primary activities in a value chain.

Corrective maintenance: Making changes to an information system to repair flaws in its design, coding, or implementation.

Cost-benefit analysis: Techniques that contrast the total expected tangible costs versus the tangible benefits for an investment.

Cracker: An individual who breaks into computer systems with the intention of doing damage or committing a crime.

Critical success factor (CSF): Something that must go well to ensure success for a manager, department, division, or organization.

Crowdsourcing: The use of everyday people as a cheap labor force, enabled by information technology.

CSMA/CD (carrier sense multiple access/collision detect): A format in which each workstation "listens" to the network to determine whether a message is being transmitted. If the network is quiet, the workstation sends its message; otherwise, it waits. When a workstation gains access to the medium and sends information onto the network, messages are sent to all workstations on the network; however, only the destination with the proper address is able to "open" the message.

Culture: The collective programming of the mind that distinguishes the members of one group or category of people from another.

Custom applications: Software programs that are designed and developed by company personnel as opposed to being bought off-the-shelf.

Customer Interaction Center (CIC): A part of operational CRM that provides a central point of contact for an organization's customers, employing multiple communication channels to support the communication preferences of customers.

Customer Relationship Management (CRM): A corporate-level strategy designed to create and maintain lasting relationships with customers by concentrating on the downstream information flows, through the introduction of reliable systems, processes, and procedures.

Customer Service and Support (CSS): A part of operational CRM that automates service requests, complaints, product returns, and information requests.

Customer Verification Value (CVV2): A three-digit code located on the back of a credit card; used in transactions where the physical card is not present.

Customization: Modifying software so that it better suits user needs.

Customized application software: Software that is developed based on specifications provided by a particular organization.

Cybersquatting: The dubious practice of registering a domain name, then trying to sell the name to the person, company, or organization most likely to want it.

Cyberterrorism: The use of computer and networking technologies against persons or property to intimidate or coerce governments, individuals, or any segment of society to attain political, religious, or ideological goals.

Cyberwar: An organized attempt by a country's military to disrupt or destroy information and communications systems of another country.

Data: Recorded, unformatted information, such as words and numbers, that often has no meaning in and of itself.

Database: A collection of related data organized in a way to facilitate data searches.

Database administrator (DBA): A person responsible for the development and management of the organization's databases.

Database management system (DBMS): A software application used to create, store, organize, and retrieve data from a single database or several databases.

Data dictionary: A document prepared by database designers to describe the characteristics of all items in a database.

Data diddling: A type of computer crime where the data going into or out of a computer is altered.

Data flows: Data moving through an organization or within an information system.

Data mart: A data warehouse that is limited in scope and customized for the decision support applications of a particular end-user group.

Data mining: A method used by companies to sort and analyze information to better understand their customers, products, markets, or any other phase of their business for which data has been captured.

Data-mining agents: Intelligent agents that continuously analyze large data warehouses to detect changes deemed important by a user, sending a notification when such changes occur.

Data model: A map or diagram that represents the entities of a database and their relationships.

Data type: The type (e.g., text, number, date) of an attribute in a database.

Data warehouse: An integration of multiple, large databases and other information sources into a single repository or access point that is suitable for direct querying, analysis, or processing.

Decision support system (DSS): A special-purpose information system designed to support organizational decision making.

Dedicated grid: A grid computing architecture consisting of homogeneous computers that are dedicated to performing the grid's computing tasks; a dedicated grid does not use unutilized resources.

Defense Advanced Research Projects Agency (DARPA): A U.S. governmental agency that began to study ways to interconnect networks of various kinds, which lead to the development of the ARPANET (Advanced Research Projects Agency Network).

Denial-of-service (DoS): Attack by unauthorized users—often zombie computers—that makes a network resource (e.g., Web site) unavailable to users or available with only a poor degree of service.

Density: The storage capacity of magnetic type that is typically referred in either characters per inch (CPI) or bytes per inch (BPI).

Desktop videoconferencing: The use of integrated computer, telephone, video recording, and playback technologies—typically by two people—to interact with each other using their desktop computers from remote sites.

Destructive agents: Malicious agents designed by spammers and other Internet attackers to farm e-mail addresses off Web sites or deposit spyware on machines.

Developmental testing: Testing performed by programmers to ensure that each module is error free.

Differentiation strategy: Strategy in which an organization differentiates itself by providing better products or services than its competitors.

Digital dashboard: A display delivering summary information to managers and executives.

Digital divide: The gap between those individuals in our society who are computer literate and have access to information resources like the Internet and those who do not.

Digital rights management (DRM): A technological solution that allows publishers to control their digital media (music, movies, and so on) to discourage, limits or prevent illegal copying and distribution.

Digital signals: The electrical pulses that computers use to send bits of information.

Digital signature: A mechanism to prove that a message did, in fact, originate from the claimed sender.

Digital subscriber line (DSL): A high-speed data transmission method that uses special modulation schemes to fit more data onto traditional copper phone wires.

Digital video disk: A DVD used for storing movies.

Digitizing: The process of converting analog into digital information, or bits, which then can travel across a network.

Disaster recovery plan: Organizational plans that spell out detailed procedures for recovering from systems-related disasters, such as virus infections and other disasters, that might strike critical information systems.

Discount rate: The rate of return used by an organization to compute the present value of future cash flows.

Disintermediation: The phenomenon of cutting out the "middleman" in transactions and reaching customers more directly and efficiently.

Diskette: A removable storage medium with a capacity of 1.44 MB; also called floppy disk.

Disruptive innovation: A new technology, product, or service that eventually surpasses the existing dominant technology, product, or service in a market.

Distributed computing: A model of using separate computers to work on subsets of tasks and then pooling their results by communicating over a network.

Distribution portal: Enterprise portals that automate the business processes involved in selling, or distributing, products from a single supplier to multiple buyers.

Docking station: Hardware that allows a portable computer to be easily connected to desktop peripherals including full-sized monitors, keyboards, and mice.

Domain name: Used in Uniform Resource Locators (URLs) to identify a source or host entity on the Internet.

Domain Name System (DNS): A database used to associate Internet host names with their Internet IP addresses.

Domestic company: A company operating solely in its domestic market.

Dot matrix printer: A printing technology where characters and images are formed using a series of small dots; most commonly found printing voluminous batch information, such as periodic reports and forms.

Downsizing: When companies slash costs, streamline operations, and/or let employees go.

Downstream information flows: Information flows that relate to the information that is produced by a company and sent along to another organization, such as a distributor.

Drill-down report: Reports that provide details behind the summary values on a key-indicator or exception report.

Drive-by hacking: Computer attack in which an attacker accesses a wireless computer network, intercepts data, uses network services, and/or sends attack instructions without entering the office or organization that owns the network.

Dumpster diving: A type of computer crime where individuals go through dumpsters and garbage cans for company documents, credit card receipts, and other papers containing information that might be useful.

DVD-ROM (digital versatile disk–read-only memory): A storage technology similar to a CD-ROM, but with much higher capacity; there are recordable (DVD-R) and rewritable (DVD-RW) versions.

E911: Enhanced 911; a part of a federal mandate to improve the effectiveness and reliability of 911 service.

E-auctions: Electronic auctions.

E-business: Term used to refer to the use of a variety of types of information technologies and systems to support every part of the business.

E-business innovation cycle: The extent to which an organization derives value from a particular information technology over time.

Economic opportunities: Opportunities that a firm finds for making more money and/or making money in new ways.

Edge computing: The location of relatively small servers close to the end users to save resources in terms of network bandwidth and access time.

E-government: The use of information systems to provide citizens, organizations, and other governmental agencies with information about public services.

E-information: The use of the Internet to provide electronic brochures and other types of information for customers.

E-integration: The use of the Internet to provide customers with the ability to gain personalized information by querying corporate databases and other information sources.

Electromagnetic interference (EMI): Occurs when fluorescent lights, weather, or other electronic signals interfere with a signal being sent.

Electronic bill pay: The use of online banking for bill paying.

Electronic commerce (EC): Exchanges of goods and services via the Internet among and between customers, firms, employees, business partners, suppliers, etc.

Electronic Data Interchange (EDI): The digital, or electronic, transmission of business documents and related data between organizations via telecommunications networks that enables the online exchange and sale of goods and services between firms.

Electronic meeting system (EMS): A collection of personal computers networked together with sophisticated software tools to help group members solve problems and make decisions through interactive, electronic idea generation, evaluation, and voting.

Embargo: A type of export regulation concerning the flow of goods and services, typically limiting (or prohibiting) trade with one particular country.

Embedded systems: Systems (such as a digital video recorder [TiVo] or a network router) designed to perform specific, predefined tasks.

Enabling technologies: Information technologies that enable a firm to accomplish a task or goal or to gain or sustain competitive advantage in some way.

Encryption: The process of encoding messages before they enter the network or airwaves, then decoding them at the receiving end of the transfer, so that only the intended recipients can read or hear them.

End-user development: A systems development method whereby users in the organization develop, test, and maintain their own applications.

Enterprise licensing: A type of software licensing that is usually negotiated and covers all users within an organization. Also known as volume licensing.

Enterprise Marketing Automation (EMA): A part of operational CRM that provides a comprehensive view of an organization's competitive environment including: competitors, industry trends, and a broad range of environmental factors.

Enterprise network: A WAN that is the result of connecting disparate networks of a single organization into a single network.

Enterprise portal: Information systems that provide a single point of access to secured, proprietary information, which may be dispersed throughout an organization.

Enterprise Resource Planning (ERP): Information system that supports and integrates all facets of the business, including planning, manufacturing, sales, marketing, and so on.

Enterprise systems: Information systems that allow companies to integrate information across operations on a company-wide basis.

Enterprise-wide information systems: Information systems that allow companies to integrate information across operations on a company-wide basis. Also known as enterprise systems.

Entity: Something we collect data about, such as people or classes.

Entity-relationship diagram (ERD): A diagramming technique that is commonly used when designing databases, especially when showing associations between entities.

Ergonomic keyboard: Keyboard resembling a widened V shape that is designed to reduce the stress placed on the wrists, hands, and arms when typing.

ERP core components: ERP components that support the important internal activities of an organization for producing products and services.

ERP extended components: ERP components that support the primary external activities of an organization for dealing with suppliers and customers.

E-tailing: Electronic retailing; the online sales of goods and services.

Ethernet: A local area network protocol developed by Xerox Corporation in 1976. It uses a bus network topology and uses random access control to send data.

E-transaction: The use of the Internet to allow customers to place orders and make payments.

Exception report: Report that highlights situations that are out of the normal operating range.

Executive information system (EIS): An information system designed to provide information in a highly aggregated form so that managers at the executive level of the organization can quickly scan it for trends and anomalies.

Executive level: The top level of the organization, where executives focus on long-term strategic issues facing the organization.

Expert system (ES): A special-purpose information system designed to mimic human expertise by manipulating knowledge—understanding acquired through experience and extensive learning—rather than simply information.

Explicit knowledge assets: Knowledge assets that can be documented, archived, and codified.

Export regulations: Regulations directed at limiting the export of certain goods to other countries.

Extensible Business Reporting Language (XBRL): An XML-based specification for publishing financial information.

Extensible Markup Language (XML): A data presentation standard that allows designers to create customized features that enable data to be more easily shared between applications and organizations.

External acquisition: The process of purchasing an existing information system from an external organization or vendor.

External (or secondary) cache: Special high-speed cache memory that is usually not built into the CPU, but is located within easy reach of the CPU on the motherboard.

Externally focused systems: Information systems that coordinate business activities with customers, suppliers, business partners, and others who operate outside an organization's boundaries.

Extranet: The use of the Internet by firms and companies for business-to-business interactions.

Eye-tracking device: A pointing device that uses the movement of someone's eyes to move the pointer.

Fiber-optic cable: Transmission medium made of light-conducting glass or plastic core, surrounded by more glass, called cladding, and a tough outer sheath; used for high-speed data transmission.

Fiber to the home (FTTH): High-speed network connectivity to homes and offices that is typically implemented using fiber-optic cabling. Also known as fiber to the premise.

Fiber to the premise (FTTP): High-speed network connectivity to homes and offices that is typically implemented using fiber-optic cabling. Also known as fiber to the home.

Fifth-generation language (5GL): Computer language developed for application within some expert system or artificial intelligence application, using English sentences.

File services: Processes used to store, retrieve, and move data files in an efficient manner across a network.

Financial flow: The movement of financial assets throughout the supply chain.

Firewall: Hardware or software designed to keep unauthorized users out of network systems.

Firewall architecture: The manner in which a firewall is implemented, such as hardware only, software only, or a combination of hardware and software.

Flash: Software used to create and display dynamic content on Web sites.

Flash drive: Portable, removable data storage device using flash memory.

Flash memory: A variation of ROM that can be repeatedly written to and erased that it retains its information after power is turned off.

Foreign key: An attribute that appears as a nonprimary key attribute in one entity and as a primary key attribute (or part of a primary key) in another entity.

Form: (1) A collection of blank entry boxes, each representing a field, that is used to enter information into a database. (2) A business document that contains some predefined data and may include some areas where additional data is to be filled in, typically for a single record.

Forward auction: A form of e-auctions that allows sellers to post goods and services for sale and buyers to bid on these items.

Fourth-generation language (4GL): Outcome-oriented programming language using English-like sentences.

Front-office system: Systems designed for direct interaction with an organization's customers. See operational CRM.

Fully-automated data entry: Data entry into an information system that does not require any human intervention.

Functional area information system: A cross-organizational-level information system designed to support a specific functional area.

Fuzzy logic: Type of logic used in intelligent systems that allows rules to be represented using approximations or subjective values in order to handle situations where information about a problem is incomplete.

Gateway: A networking hardware component used for protocol conversion so that different networks can communicate even though they "speak" different languages.

Geoeconomics: The combination of economic and political factors that influence a region.

Geographic information system (GIS): A system for creating, storing, analyzing, and managing geographically referenced information.

Geostationary or geosynchronous orbit: An orbit in which a satellite moves with the earth's rotation.

Global business strategy: An international business strategy employed to achieve economies of scale by producing identical products in large quantities for a variety of different markets. This strategy is characterized by extensive data flows from the subsidiaries to the home location, and by strong control of the home location on the subsidiaries.

Global information dissemination: The use of the Internet as an inexpensive means for distributing an organization's information.

Global IS strategy: An information systems strategy using a centralized infrastructure and tight controls are utilized to support the centralized nature of the decision making; typically employed by companies pursuing a global business strategy.

Globalization: The integration of economies throughout the world, enabled by innovation and technological progress.

Globalization 1.0: The first stage of globalization (fifteenth century through the 1800s), primarily driven by power from horses, wind, and steam. Countries (mainly European) were globalizing, shrinking the world from size large to size medium. Industries changed slowly and the effects of globalization on individuals was barely noticed.

Globalization 2.0: The second stage of globalization (1800 to 2000), driven by a reduction of transportation and telecommunication costs. Companies (mainly American and European) were globalizing, shrinking the world from size medium to size small. Changes were happening at a fairly slow pace.

Globalization 3.0: The third stage of globalization (starting around 2000), driven by the convergence of the 10 "flatteners." Individuals and small groups from virtually every nation were globalizing, shrinking the world from size small to size tiny. Changes are happening at a faster pace, making people readily feel the effects of industry changes.

Global network: Network spanning multiple countries and may include the networks of several organizations. The Internet is an example of a global network.

Global positioning system: A worldwide navigation system that utilizes 24 middle earth orbiting (MEO) satellites to determine the exact position of a GPS receiver.

Gopher: A text-based, menu-driven interface that enables users to access a large number of varied Internet resources as if they were in folders and menus on their own computers.

Government-to-business (G2B): Electronic commerce that involves a country's government and businesses.

Government-to-citizens (G2C): Online interactions between federal, state, and local governments and their constituents.

Government-to-government (G2G): Electronic interactions that take place between countries, or between different levels of government within a country.

Graphical user interface (GUI): Computer interface that enables the user to select pictures, icons, and menus to send instructions to the computer.

Grid computing: A computing architecture that combines the computing power of a large number of smaller, independent, networked computers (often regular desktop PCs) into a cohesive system in order to solve problems that only supercomputers were previously capable of solving.

Groupware: Software that enables people to work together more effectively.

Hackers: Individuals who gain unauthorized access to computer systems.

Hacktivists: Hackers pursuing political, religious, or ideological goals.

Hard data: Facts and numbers that are typically generated by transaction processing systems and management information systems.

Hard drive or hard disk: A secondary storage device usually located inside the system unit of a computer for storing data.

Hardware: Physical computer equipment, such as the computer monitor, central processing unit, or keyboard.

Head crash: A hard disk failure occurring when the read/write head touches the disk, resulting in the loss of the data and/or the operation of the hard disk.

High-frequency radio: Wireless transmission medium that can transmit data at rates of up to 54 Mbps to network nodes from 12.2 to 39.6 kilometers apart.

Hot backup site: A fully equipped backup facility, having everything from hardware, software, current data, and office equipment.

Hub: Used as a central point of connection between media segments; like repeaters, hubs enable the network to be extended to accommodate additional workstations; commonly used in 10Base-T networks.

Hyperlink: A reference or link on a Web page to other documents that contain related information.

Hypertext: Text in a Web document that is highlighted and, when clicked on by the user, evokes an embedded command that goes to another specified file or location and brings up that file or location on the user's screen.

Hypertext Markup Language (HTML): The standard method of specifying the format of Web pages. Specific content within each Web page is enclosed within codes, or markup tags, which stipulate how the content should appear to the user.

Hypertext Transfer Protocol (HTTP): The process by which servers process user requests for Web pages.

Identity theft: Stealing of another person's social security number, credit card number, and other personal information for the purpose of using the victim's credit rating to borrow money, buy merchandise, and otherwise run up debts that are never repaid.

Individualism: A cultural characteristic emphasizing the importance of the individual over the collective/group in society.

Inferencing: The matching of user questions and answers to information in a knowledge base within an expert system in order to make a recommendation.

Informating: The ability of information technology to provide information about the operation within a firm and/or about the underlying work process that the system supports.

Information: Data that has been formatted and/or organized in some way as to be useful to people.

Information accessibility: An ethical issue that focuses on defining what information a person or organization has the right to obtain about others and how this information can be accessed and used.

Information accuracy: An ethical issue concerned with the authenticity and fidelity of information, as well as identifying who is responsible for informational errors that harm people.

Information Age: A period of time in society where information became a valuable or dominant currency.

Information flow: The movement of information along the supply chain.

Information modification: An information systems security attack by unauthorized users where electronic information is intentionally changed.

Information privacy: An ethical issue that is concerned with what information an individual should have to reveal to others through the course of employment or through other transactions such as online shopping.

Information property: An ethical issue that focuses on who owns information about individuals and how information can be sold and exchanged.

Information systems (IS): Assumed to mean computer-based information systems, which are combinations of hardware, software, and telecommunications networks that people build and use to collect, create, and distribute useful data; this term is also used to represent the field in which people develop, use, manage, and study computer-based information systems in organizations.

Information systems audit: An assessment of the state of an organization's information systems controls to determine necessary changes and to help ensure the information systems' availability, confidentiality, and integrity.

Information systems controls: Controls helping to ensure the reliability of information, consisting of policies and their physical implementation, access restrictions, or recordkeeping of actions and transactions.

Information systems infrastructure: The hardware, software, networks, data, facilities, human resources, and services used by organizations to support their decision making, business processes, and competitive strategy.

Information systems planning: A formal organizational process for identifying and assessing all possible information systems development projects of an organization.

Information systems security: Precautions taken to keep all aspects of information systems safe from unauthorized use or access.

Information systems security plan: An ongoing planning process involving risk assessment, risk-reduction planning, and plan implementation as well as ongoing monitoring.

Information technology (IT): Refers to machine technology that is controlled by or uses information.

Informational systems: The systems designed to support decision making based on stable point-in-time or historical data.

Informing: Individuals' access to a wealth of information, enabled by the Internet.

Infrared line of sight: Uses high-frequency light waves to transmit data on an unobstructed path between nodes—computers or some other device such as printers—on a network, at a distance of up to 24.4 meters.

Infrastructure: The interconnection of various structural elements to support an overall entity, such as an organization, city, or country.

Ink-jet printer: Type of printer that uses a small cartridge to transfer ink onto paper.

Innovator's dilemma: The notion that disruptive innovations can cause established firms or industries to lose market dominance, often leading to failure.

Input devices: Hardware that is used to enter information into a computer.

In-sourcing: The delegation of a company's core operations to a subcontractor that specializes in that operation.

Intangible benefit: A benefit of using a particular system or technology that is difficult to quantify.

Intangible cost: A cost of using a particular system or technology that is difficult to quantify.

Integrated services digital network (ISDN): A standard for worldwide digital communications that is intended to replace analog systems and uses existing twisted-pair telephone wires to provide high-speed data service.

Integration: The use of Web technologies to link Web sites to corporate databases to provide real-time access to personalized information.

Integrity: Assuring the recipient that the received message has not been altered in any way from the original that was sent.

Intelligent agent: A program that works in the background to provide some service when a specific event occurs.

Intelligent system: System comprised of sensors, software, and computers embedded in machines and devices, which emulate and enhance human capabilities.

Interactive communication: Immediate communication and feedback between a company and its customers using Web technologies.

Interexchange carriers (IXC): Companies that sell long-distance services, with circuits carrying service between the major telephone exchanges.

Interface: The way in which the user interacts with the computer.

Internal cache: Special high-speed cache memory that is incorporated into the microprocessor's design.

Internally focused systems: Information systems that support functional areas, business processes, and decision making within an organization.

International business strategy: Set of strategies employed by organizations operating in different global markets.

Internet: A term derived from the concept of Internetworking, which means connecting host computers and their networks together to form even larger networks. The Internet is a large worldwide collection of networks that use a common protocol to communicate with each other.

Internet backbone: The collection of main network connections and telecommunications lines comprising the Internet.

Internet Corporation for Assigned Names and Numbers (ICANN): A nonprofit corporation that assumed responsibility from InterNIC for managing IP addresses, domain names, and the root server system management.

Internet hoax: A false message circulated online about new viruses, funds for alleged victims of crime or the September 11, 2001, terrorist attacks, kids in trouble, cancer causes, or any other topic of public interest.

Internet hosts: Computers working as servers on the Internet.

Internet over Satellite (IoS): Technologies that allow users to access the Internet via satellites that are placed in a geostationary or geosynchronous orbit.

Internet Registry: A central repository for Internet-related information and which provides a central allocation of network system identifiers.

Internet service providers (ISPs): Individuals or organizations that enable other individuals and organizations to connect to the Internet.

Internet tax freedom act: An act mandating a moratorium on electronic commerce taxation in order to stimulate electronic commerce.

Internetworking: Connecting host computers and their networks together to form even larger networks.

InterNIC: A government-industry collaboration created by the NSF in 1993, to manage directory and database services, domain registration services, and other information services on the Internet.

Interorganizational system (IOS): An information system that communicates across organizational boundaries.

Interpreter: A software program that translates a programming language into machine language one statement at a time.

Intranet: An internal, private network using Web technologies to facilitate the secured transmission of proprietary information within an organization, thereby limiting the viewing access to authorized users within the organization.

IP address: An Internet protocol address assigned to every computer and router to connect to the Internet; it serves as the destination address of that computer or device and enables the network to route messages to the proper destination.

IP convergence: The use of the Internet protocol for transporting voice, video, fax, and data traffic.

IP datagram: A data packet that conforms to the Internet protocol specification.

IPv6: The latest version of the Internet protocol, also referred to as IPng, for IP next generation.

Java: An object-oriented programming language developed at Sun Microsystems in the early 1990s that is used in developing applications on the Web and other environments.

JavaScript: A scripting language, created by Netscape, that allows developers to add dynamic content to Web sites.

Joint application design (JAD): A special type of a group meeting in which all (or most) users meet with the analyst to *jointly* define and agree on system requirements or designs.

Keyboard: Input device for entering text and numbers into a computer.

Key-indicator report: Reports that provide a summary of critical information on a recurring schedule.

Knowledge: A body of governing procedures, such as guidelines or rules, which are used to organize or manipulate data to make it suitable for a given task.

Knowledge assets: The set of skills, routines, practices, principles, formulas, methods, heuristics, and intuitions (both explicit and tacit) used by organizations to improve efficiency, effectiveness, and profitability.

Knowledge management: The processes an organization uses to gain the greatest value from its knowledge assets.

Knowledge management system: A collection of technology-based tools that include communications technologies and information storage and retrieval systems to enable the generation, storage, sharing, and management of tacit knowledge assets.

Knowledge portal: Specific portals used to share knowledge collected into a repository with employees (often using an intranet), with customers and suppliers (often with an extranet), or the general public (often using the Internet).

Knowledge society: Term coined by Peter Drucker to refer to a society in which there is a relatively high proportion of knowledge workers, these types of people have risen in importance and leadership, and where education is the cornerstone of the society.

Knowledge worker: Term coined by Peter Drucker to refer to professionals who are relatively well educated and who create, modify, and/or synthesize knowledge as a fundamental part of their jobs.

Laser printer: An electrostatic printing process that forces toner onto the paper, literally "burning" the image onto the paper.

Learning organization: An organization that is skilled at creating, acquiring, and transferring knowledge, and at modifying its behavior to reflect new knowledge and insights.

Legacy systems: Older stand-alone computer systems within an organization with older versions of applications that are either fast approaching or beyond the end of their useful life within the organization.

Life focus: The extent to which a culture focuses on the *quantity* versus the *quality* of life.

Liquid crystal display (LCD): A type of computer monitor that is most commonly used on notebook and desktop computers.

Local area network (LAN): A computer network that spans a relatively small area, allowing all computer users to connect with each other to share information and peripheral devices, such as a printer.

Location-based services: Highly personalized mobile services based on a user's location.

Logic bombs: A type of computer virus that lies in wait for unsuspecting computer users to perform a triggering operation before executing its instructions.

Low-cost leadership strategy: Strategy to offer the best prices in the industry on goods or services.

Machine language: A binary-level computer language that computer hardware understands.

Magnetic tape: A secondary storage method that consists of narrow plastic tape coated with a magnetic substance.

Mainframe computer: A very large computer that is used as the main, central computing system for many major corporations and governmental agencies.

Making the business case: The process of identifying, quantifying, and presenting the value provided by an information system.

Malware: Malicious software such as viruses, worms, or Trojan horses.

Management information system (MIS): (1) A field of study that encompasses the development, use, management, and study of computer-based information systems in organizations. (2) An information system designed to support the management of organizational functions at the managerial level of the organization.

Managerial level: The middle level of the organization, where functional managers focus on monitoring and controlling operational-level activities and providing information to higher levels of the organization.

Manual data entry: Having a person enter information by hand into an information system.

Maquiladoras: Assembly plants located on the Mexican side of the United States-Mexican border; utilized mainly to take advantage of lower wages and less stringent regulations.

Masculinity/Femininity: The degree to which a society is characterized by masculine qualities, such as assertiveness, or by feminine characteristics, such as nurturance.

Mass Customization: Tailoring products and services to meet particular needs of individual customers on a large scale.

M-Commerce: Any electronic transaction or information interaction conducted using a wireless, mobile device and mobile networks that leads to a transfer of real or perceived value in exchange for information, services, or goods.

Media access control: The rules that govern how a given node or workstation gains access to a network to send or receive information.

Memory wall: A term used to describe the disparity between the large increase in clock speed of CPUs and the relatively smaller increase in memory speed and size, limiting performance increases.

Menu-driven pricing: A pricing system in which companies set and present negotiable prices for products to consumers.

Menu interface: List of options from which a user invokes a command or system operation.

Mesh network: A network that consists of computers and other devices that are either fully or partially connected to each other.

Message services: The storing, accessing, and delivering of text, binary, graphic, digitized video, and audio data across a network; similar to file services, but they also deal with communication interactions between users and applications.

Metropolitan area network (MAN): A computer network of limited geographic scope, typically a city-wide area, which combines both LAN and high-speed fiber-optic technologies.

Microcomputer: A category of computer that is generally used for personal computing, for small business computing, and as a workstation attached to large computers or to other small computers on a network.

Microsoft.NET: A programming platform that is used to develop applications that are highly interoperable across a variety of platforms and devices.

Microwave transmission: A high-frequency radio signal sent through the air using either terrestrial (earth-based) systems or satellite systems.

Midrange computer: Often referred to as minicomputers, these are computers whose performance is lower than that of mainframes but higher than microcomputers.

Mirror: The synchronous storage of data on independent systems to achieve redundancy for purposes of reliability and/or performance.

Mobile wireless: Wireless approaches for connecting to the Internet where the computer or handheld device can be moved and will continue to connect.

Models: Conceptual, mathematical, logical, and analytical formulas used to represent or project business events or trends.

Modem: Short for modulator-demodulator; a modem is a device or program that enables a computer to transmit data over telephone lines.

Modules: In a software application, components (classified software functions) that can be selected and implemented as needed.

Monitor: A computer display screen.

Monitoring and sensing agents: Intelligent agents that keep track of key information, such as inventory levels or competitors' prices, notifying the user when conditions change.

Moore's Law: The prediction that computer processing performance would double every 18 months.

Motherboard: A large printed plastic or fiberglass circuit board that holds or connects to all the computer's electronic components.

Multidomestic business strategy: An international business strategy employed to be flexible and responsive to needs and demands of heterogeneous local markets.

Multinational IS strategy: An information systems strategy using decentralized systems are used to support the decentralized nature of the decision making; typically employed by companies pursuing a multidomestic business strategy.

Multiplexer (MUX): Used to share a communications line or medium among a number of users.

National Science Foundation (NSF): The organization in the United States that initiated the development of the NSFNET (National Science Foundation Network), which became a major component of the Internet.

National Science Foundation Network (NSFNET): A network developed by the United States in 1986 that became a major component of the Internet.

Net Neutrality: A concept that data sent over the Internet using Internet protocol should be routed and handled in a neutral matter, regardless of the content of the data.

Net-present-value analysis: A type of cost-benefit analysis that compares discounted benefit and cost cash flow streams associated with an investment.

Network: A group of computers and associated peripheral devices connected by a communication channel capable of sharing information and other resources (e.g., a printer) among users.

Network access points (NAPs): Access points used by ISPs to connect to each other.

Network address translation (NAT): The process of hiding computers' true network addresses by replacing the computers' IP addresses with a firewall's address; thus, potential attackers only "see" the network address of the firewall.

Network click fraud: A form of click fraud where a site hosting an advertisement creates fake clicks in order to get revenue from the advertiser.

Network computer: A microcomputer with minimal memory and storage designed to connect to networks, especially the Internet, to use the resources provided by servers.

Network interface card (NIC): An expansion board that plugs into a computer so that it can be connected to a network.

Network operating system (NOS): System software that controls the network and enables computers to communicate with each other.

Network services: Capabilities of networked computers that enable them to share files, print, send and receive messages, and to use shared software applications.

Network topology: The shape of a network; the three common network topologies are star, ring, bus, and mesh.

Neural network: An information system that attempts to approximate the functioning of a human brain.

New economy: An economy in which information technology plays a significant role and that enables producers of both the tangible (computers, shoes, etc.) and intangible (services, ideas, etc.) to compete efficiently in global markets.

Nonrecurring costs: One-time costs that are not expected to continue after the system is implemented.

Nonrepudiation: A mechanism using a digital signature to prove that a message did, in fact, originate from the claimed sender.

Nonshipment: A type of e-auction fraud where a seller fails to ship an item after payment has been received.

Normalization: A technique for converting complex databases into ones that are simple and clear.

Notebook computer: A mobile microcomputer which can be as light as 2.5 pounds and can be easily carried in a briefcase or backpack.

Object-oriented analysis and design (OOA&D): Systems development methodologies and techniques based on objects rather than on data and processes.

Object-oriented languages: Programming languages that group together data and its corresponding instructions into manipulatable objects.

Office automation system (OAS): A collection of software and hardware for developing documents, scheduling resources, and communicating.

Offshoring: The set up of entire factories in countries such as China in order to mass produce goods at a fraction of the price it would cost to produce these goods in the United States or even in Mexico.

Off-the-shelf application software: Software designed and used to support general business processes that does not require any specific tailoring to meet the organization's needs.

OLAP server: The chief component of an OLAP system that understands how data is organized in the database and has special functions for analyzing the data.

On-demand computing: Allocation of computing resources on the basis of users' needs, often on a pay-per-use basis.

On-demand software: Software provided over the Web on an as-needed basis.

Online analytical processing (OLAP): The process of quickly conducting complex analysis of data stored in a database, typically using graphical software tools.

Online banking: The use of the Internet to conduct financial transactions.

Online investing: The use of the Internet to get information about stock quotes and manage financial portfolios.

Online processing: Processing of source documents as they are created, providing immediate results to the system operator or customer.

Online transaction processing (OLTP): Immediate automated responses to the requests from multiple concurrent transactions from customers.

Open source software: Systems software, applications, and programming languages of which the source code is freely available for use and/or modification.

Operating system: Software that coordinates the interaction between hardware devices, peripherals, application software, and users.

Operational CRM: Systems for automating the fundamental business processes—marketing, sales, and support—for interacting with the customer.

Operational level: The bottom level of an organization, where the routine, day-to-day business processes and interaction with customers occur.

Operational systems: The systems that are used to interact with customers and run a business in real time.

Optical disk: A storage disk coated with a metallic substance that is written to (or read from) when a laser beam passes over the surface of the disk.

Organizational learning: The ability of an organization to learn from past behavior and information, improving as a result.

Organizational strategy: A firm's plan to accomplish its mission and goals as well as to gain or sustain competitive advantage over rivals.

OSI model: Open systems interconnection; a protocol that represents a group of specific, successive tasks that enable computers to communicate with one another.

Output devices: Hardware devices that deliver information in a usable form.

Outsourcing: The moving of routine jobs and/or tasks to people in another firm, in another part of the country, or in another country, at less cost.

Packaged applications: Software programs written by third-party vendors.

Packet filtering: Prevention of unauthorized access to a computer network by a firewall at the data-packet level; data packets are accepted or rejected based on predefined rules.

Packet switching: The process of breaking information into small chunks called data packets and then managing the transfer of those packets from computer to computer via the Internet.

Paid inclusion: Inclusion in a search engine's listing after payment of a fee.

Patch management system: An online system that utilizes Web services to automatically check for software updates, downloading and installing these "patches" as they are made available.

Pay per click: A payment model used in online advertising, where the advertiser pays the Web site owner a fee for visitors visiting a certain link.

Payment failure: A type of e-auction fraud where buyers fail to pay for an item after the conclusion of an auction.

Peer: Any computer that may both request and provide services.

Peer-to-peer networks: Networks that enable any computer or device on the network to provide and request services.

Perfective maintenance: Making enhancements to improve processing performance, to improve interface usability, or to add desired, but not necessarily required, system features.

Personal area network (PAN): An emerging technology that uses wireless communication to exchange data between computing devices using short-range radio communication, typically within an area of 10 meters.

Personal computer (PC): A class of computers that fit on desktops and are used in homes and offices. Also called microcomputer.

Personal digital assistant (PDA): A handheld microcomputer that is approaching the functionality levels of desktop PCs.

Phishing: Attempts to trick financial account and credit card holders into giving away their authorization information, usually by sending spam messages to literally millions of e-mail accounts. Also known as spoofing.

Phreaking: Crimes committed against telephone company computers with the goal of making free long distance calls, impersonating directory assistance or other operator services, diverting calls to numbers of the perpetrator's choice, or otherwise disrupting telephone service for subscribers.

Piggybacking or shoulder-surfing: The act of simply standing in line behind a card user at an automated teller machine (ATM), looking over that person's shoulder, and memorizing the card's personal identification number (PIN).

Plain old telephone service (POTS): Standard telephone lines with a speed, or bandwidth, that is generally about 52 Kbps (52,000 bits per second); also called the public switched telephone network (PSTN).

Plotter: Device used for transferring engineering designs from the computer to drafting paper, which is often as big as 34 by 44 inches.

Pointing devices: Input devices for pointing at items and selecting menu items on a computer.

Port: A hardware interface by which a computer communicates with another device or system.

Power distance: A cultural characteristic related to how different societies view authority and hierarchical structures.

Power line communication (PLC): A connectivity technology that uses existing power distribution wires for data transmission. Also referred to as power line telecoms (PLT).

Power supply: A device that converts electricity from the wall socket to a lower voltage appropriate for computer components and regulates the voltage to eliminate surges common in most electrical systems.

Preventive maintenance: Making changes to a system to reduce the chance of future system failure.

Primary key: A field included in a database that assures that each instance of entity is stored or retrieved accurately.

Primary memory: The computer's main or random access memory (RAM).

Primary storage: Temporary storage for current calculations.

Print-on-Demand: Publishing original works using customized printing that is done in small batches.

Print services: Used to control and manage users' access to network printers and tax equipment.

Privacy: Ensuring that no one can read the message except the intended recipient.

Private branch exchange (PBX): A telephone system that serves a particular location, such as a business, connecting one telephone extension to another within the system and connecting the PBX to the outside telephone network.

Processing devices: Computer hardware that transforms inputs into outputs.

Processing logic: The steps by which data is transformed or moved, as well as a description of the events that trigger these steps.

Procurement portal: Enterprise portals that automate the business processes involved in purchasing, or procuring, products between a single buyer and multiple suppliers.

Product flow: The movement of goods from the supplier to production, from production to distribution, and from distribution to the consumer.

Productivity paradox: The observation that productivity increases at a rate that is lower than expected when new technologies are introduced.

Propagation delay: The delay in the transmission of a satellite signal because of the distance the signal must travel.

Protocols: Procedures that different computers follow when they transmit and receive data.

Prototyping: An iterative systems development process in which requirements are converted into a working system that is continually revised through close work between analysts and users.

Proxy server: A firewall that serves as, or creates the appearance of, an alternative server that intercepts all messages entering and leaving the network, effectively hiding the true network addresses. Proxy servers are also commonly used to locally store (cache) Web sites to provide for faster access of popular sites.

Proxy variables: A measurement of changes as a result of a systems implementation in terms of their perceived value to the organization, particularly where it is difficult to determine and measure direct effects from a system.

Public key: A data encryption technique that uses two keys—a private key and a public key—to encrypt and decode messages.

Public switched telephone network (PSTN): Standard telephone lines with a speed, or bandwidth, that is generally about 52 Kbps (52,000 bits per second); also called plain old telephone service (POTS).

Query: Method used to retrieve information from a database.

Query by example (QBE): A capability of a DBMS that enables data to be requested by providing a sample or a description of the types of data we would like to see.

Quota: Regulations permitting foreign businesses to export only a certain number of products to a specific country.

QWERTY keyboard: The default keyboard layout for entering numbers and letters (QWERTY stands for how the letters are arranged on the keyboard, with *Q-W-E-R-T-Y* being the first six letters going from left to right on the keyboard).

Radio frequency identification (RFID): The use of electromagnetic or electrostatic coupling in the RF portion of the electromagnetic spectrum in order to transmit signals; an RFID system uses a transceiver and antenna to transfer information to a processing device, or RFID tag.

RAID (redundant array of independent [inexpensive] disks): A secondary storage technology that makes redundant copies of data on two or more hard drives.

Random-access memory (RAM): A type of primary storage that is volatile and can be accessed randomly by the CPU.

Rapid application development (RAD): A four-phase systems development methodology that combines prototyping, computer-based development tools, special management practices, and close user involvement.

Read-only memory (ROM): A type of primary storage on which data has been prerecorded and is nonvolatile.

Read/write heads: Components that inscribe data to or retrieve data from hard disks, diskettes, and tapes.

Record: A record is a collection of related attributes about a single entity.

Recovery point objectives: Objectives specifying how timely backup data should be preserved.

Recovery time objectives: Objectives specifying the maximum time allowed to recover from a catastrophic event.

Recurring costs: Ongoing costs that occur throughout the life cycle of systems development, implementation, and maintenance.

Registers: Temporary storage locations inside the CPU where data must reside while being processed or manipulated.

Relational database model: The most common DBMS approach in which entities are presented as two-dimensional tables, with records as rows and attributes as columns.

Repeater: A network device used to regenerate or replicate a signal as it weakens when traveling on a network; also moves data from one media segment to another and effectively extends the size of the network.

Report: A compilation of data from a database that is organized and produced in printed format.

Report generator: Software tools that help users to quickly build reports and describe the data in a useful format.

Reproductions: A type of e-auction fraud where something is sold as an original but is actually a reproduction.

Request for proposal: A communication tool indicating buyer requirements for a given system and requesting information from potential vendors.

Requirements collection: The process of gathering and organizing information from users, managers, business processes, and documents to understand how a proposed information system should function.

Revenue model: Organization model that describes how the organization will earn revenue, generate profits, and produce a return on invested capital.

Reverse auction: A type of auction in which buyers post a request for proposal (RFP) and sellers respond with bids.

Reverse pricing system: A pricing system in which customers specify the product they are looking for and how much they are willing to pay, and this information is routed to appropriate companies who either accept or reject this offer.

RFID tag: The processing device used in an RFID system that uniquely identifies an object.

Ring network: A network that is configured in the shape of a closed loop or circle, with each node connecting to the next node.

Risk acceptance: A computer system security policy in which no countermeasures are adopted, and any damages that occur are simply absorbed.

Risk analysis: The process in which the value of the assets being protected are assessed, the likelihood of their being compromised is determined, and the costs of their being compromised are compared with the costs of the protections to be taken.

Risk assessment: An assessment of the type of risks an organization's information systems infrastructure faces, the criticality of those risks to the infrastructure, and the level of risks the organization is willing to tolerate.

Risk reduction: The process of taking active countermeasures to protect information systems.

Risk transference: A computer system security policy in which someone else absorbs the risk, as with insurance.

Router: An intelligent device used to connect and route data traffic across two or more individual networks.

RSS (really simple syndication): A set of standards for sharing updated Web content, such as news and sports scores, across sites.

Rule: A way of encoding knowledge, typically expressed using an "if-then" format, within an expert system.

Salami slicing: A form of data diddling that occurs when a person shaves small amounts from financial accounts and deposits them in a personal account.

Sales Force Automation (SFA): CRM systems to support the day-to-day sales activities of an organization.

Sarbanes-Oxley Act: Government regulation formed as a reaction to large-scale accounting scandals that led to the downfall of large corporations that includes the use of information systems controls in compliance reviews.

Satellite: A device launched to orbit Earth and enable network communication.

Satellite microwave: The process of using relay stations that transfer high-frequency radio signals between antennas located on Earth and satellites orbiting the Earth.

Scanners: Input devices that convert printed text and images into digital data.

Scheduled reports: Reports produced at predefined intervals—daily, weekly, or monthly—to support the routine informational needs of managerial-level decision making.

Scripting languages: A programming technique for providing interactive components to a Web page.

Search engine advertising: Prominent inclusion in Web search results that provides revenue to the search engine host on a pay-per-click basis. Also called sponsored search.

Search engine marketing: The practice of trying to increase a company's visibility in search engine results.

Search engine optimization: Methods for improving a site's ranking in search engine results.

Secondary key: Attributes not used as the primary that can be used to identify one or more records within a table that share a common value.

Secondary nonvolatile storage: Methods for permanently storing data to a large-capacity storage component, such as a hard disk, diskette, CD-ROM disk, or tape.

Secure Sockets Layer (SSL): A popular public-key encryption method used on the Internet.

Semi-automated data entry: Data entry into an information system using some type of data capture device, such as a grocery store checkout scanner.

Semi-structured decisions: Managerial-level decision making where solutions and problems are not clear-cut and often require judgment and expertise.

Server: Any computer on the network that enables access to files, printing, communications, and other services available to users of the network; it typically has a more advanced microprocessor, more memory, a larger cache, and more disk storage than a single-user workstation.

Server-centric networks: Networks in which servers and clients have defined roles.

Server farm: Massive clusters of computers used to support the information processing needs of large organizations.

Service mentality: The belief among information systems personnel that their chief goal is satisfying their systems customers within the firm while fundamentally believing that the customers, not the systems personnel, own the technology and the information.

Service-oriented architecture: A software architecture that enables the integration of different applications using Web services.

Shipping fraud: E-Auction fraud. Charging irregular shipping and handling fees, far above actual cost.

Shrink-wrap license: A type of software license that is used primarily for consumer products where the contract is activated when the shrink wrap on the packaging has been removed.

Slingbox: A device acting as a personal media server that can "placeshift" television content to any Internet-enabled device.

Smart cards: Special credit card-sized cards, containing a microprocessor chip, memory circuits, and often a magnetic stripe.

Social engineering or masquerading: Misrepresenting oneself in order steal equipment or to trick others into revealing sensitive information.

Social online communities: Web sites enabling social networking.

Soft data: Textual news stories or other nonanalytical information.

Software: A program or set of programs that tell the computer to perform certain processing functions.

Software asset management (SAM): A set of activities performed to better manage an organization's software infrastructure by being able to consolidate and standardize their software titles, decide to retire unused software, or decide when to upgrade or replace software.

Software engineering: A disciplined approach for constructing information systems through the use of common methods, techniques, or tools.

Software piracy: A type of computer crime where individuals make illegal copies of software protected by copyright laws.

Sound card: A specialized circuit board that supports the ability to convert digital information into sounds that can be listened to on speakers or headphones plugged into the card; a microphone can also be plugged into the card for capturing audio for storage or processing.

Source documents: Documents that serve as a stimulus to a transaction processing system from some external source.

Spam: Electronic junk mail.

Speech recognition: The process of converting spoken words into commands and data.

Sponsored search: Prominent inclusion in Web search results that provides revenue to the search engine host on a pay-per-click basis. Also called search engine advertising.

Spoofing: Attempts to trick financial account and credit card holders into giving away their authorization information, usually by posting false Web sites that duplicate legitimate sites. Also known as phishing.

Spyware: Software that covertly gathers information about a user through an Internet connection without the user's knowledge.

Stand-alone applications: Systems that focus on the specific needs of individual departments and are not designed to communicate with other systems in the organization.

Star network: A network with several workstations connected to a central hub.

Strategic: A way of thinking in which plans are made to accomplish specific goals.

Strategic necessity: Something an organization must do in order to survive.

Strategic planning: The process of forming a vision of where the organization needs to head, convert that vision into measurable objectives and performance targets, and craft a plan to achieve the desired results.

Streaming media: Streaming video with sound.

Streaming video: A sequence of compressed moving images that can be sent over the Internet.

Streamlined Sales Tax Project: A project to simplify tax codes and make it mandatory for out-of-state sellers to collect taxes.

Structured decisions: Decisions where the procedures to follow for a given situation can be specified in advance.

Structured Query Language (SQL): The most common language used to interface with databases.

Supercomputer: The most expensive and most powerful category of computers. It is primarily used to assist in solving massive research and scientific problems.

Supply chain: The network of producers of supplies that a company uses.

Supply chain effectiveness: The extent to which a company's supply chain is focusing on maximizing customer service, regardless of procurement, production, and transportation costs.

Supply chain efficiency: The extent to which a company's supply chain is focusing on minimizing procurement, production, and transportation costs, sometimes by reducing customer service.

Supply Chain Execution (SCE): The execution of supply chain planning, involving the management of product flow, information flow, and financial flow.

Supply Chain Management (SCM): Information systems focusing on improving upstream information flows with two main objectives—to accelerate product development and to reduce costs associated with procuring raw materials, components, and services from suppliers.

Supply Chain Planning (SCP): The process of developing various resource plans to support the efficient and effective production of goods and services.

Supply network: The flow of materials from multiple suppliers involved in the process of servicing a single organization.

Supporting processes: Business processes, such as accounting, human resources, and general management, that are needed to support the execution of an organization's value chain.

Symmetric digital subscriber line (SDSL): A data transfer format that enables large amounts of data to be sent relatively quickly over existing copper telephone lines; said to be symmetric because it supports the same data rates (up to 3 Mbps) for upstream and downstream traffic; works by sending digital pulses in the high-frequency area of telephone wires.

Symmetric secret key system: An encryption system where both the sender and recipient use the same key for encoding (scrambling) and decoding the message.

System analysis: The second phase of the systems development life cycle, in which the current ways of doing business are studied and alternative replacement systems are proposed.

System clock: An electronic circuit inside a computer that generates pulses at a rapid rate for setting the pace of processing events.

System conversion: The process of decommissioning the current system and installing a new system into the organization.

System design: The third phase of the systems development life cycle, in which details of the chosen approach are developed.

System effectiveness: The extent to which a system enables people and/or the firm to accomplish goals or tasks well.

System efficiency: The extent to which a system enables people and/or the firm to do things faster, at lower cost, or with relatively little time and effort.

System identification, selection, and planning: The first phase of the systems development life cycle, in which potential projects are identified, selected, and planned.

System implementation: The fourth phase of the systems development life cycle, in which the information system is programmed, tested, installed, and supported.

System maintenance: The fifth (and final) phase of the systems development life cycle, in which an information system is systematically repaired and/or improved.

Systems analysis and design: The process of designing, building, and maintaining information systems.

Systems analyst: The primary person responsible for performing systems analysis and design activities.

Systems benchmarking: A standardized set of performance tests designed to facilitate comparison between systems.

Systems development life cycle (SDLC): Describes the life of an information system from conception to retirement.

Systems integration: Connecting separate information systems and data to improve business processes and decision making

Systems software: The collection of programs that controls the basic operations of computer hardware.

System unit: The physical box that houses all the electronic components that do the work of the computer.

T1 line: Developed by AT&T as a dedicated digital transmission line that can carry 1.544 Mbps of information.

T3 line: A digital transmission line that provides about 45 Mbps of service at about 10 times the cost of leasing a T1 line.

Table: A collection of related records in a database where each row is a record and each column is an attribute.

Tablet PC: Notebook computer accepting input from a stylus or a keyboard.

Tacit knowledge assets: Knowledge assets that reflect the processes and procedures located in employees' minds.

Tag: A command that is inserted into a document to specify how the document is to be formatted or used.

Tangible benefit: A benefit of using a particular system or technology that is quantifiable.

Tangible cost: A cost of using a particular system of technology that is quantifiable

Tariff: Government-imposed fees to regulate the flow of goods and services in and out of a country.

Technology: Any mechanical and/or electrical means to supplement, extend, or replace human, manual operations or devices.

Telecommunications network: A group of two or more computer systems linked together with communications equipment.

Terminals: Local input devices used to enter data onto mainframes in centralized computing systems.

Terrestrial microwave: The process of using Earth-based antennas that require an unobstructed path or line-of-sight between nodes: often used to cross inaccessible terrain or to connect buildings where cable installation would be expensive.

Text mining: Analytical techniques for extracting information from textual documents.

Text recognition software: Software designed to convert handwritten text into computer-based characters.

Time bombs: A type of computer virus that lies in wait for a specific date before executing its instructions.

Token passing: An access method that uses a constantly circulating electronic token, a small packet of data, to prevent collisions and give all workstations equal access to the network.

Top-level domain: Categories of Internet domain names as indicated by their suffix (i.e., .com, .edu, or .org).

Total cost of ownership (TCO): The cost of owning and operating a system, including the total cost of acquisition, as well as all costs associated with its ongoing use and maintenance.

Trading exchange: A Web site where multiple buyers and sellers come together to conduct business; also called an electronic marketplace.

Transaction processing system (TPS): An information system designed to process day-to-day business event data at the operational level of the organization.

Transactions: Repetitive events in organizations that occur as a regular part of conducting day-to-day operations.

Transaction support: Utilizing the Web to provide automatic support to clients and firms for conducting business online without human assistance.

Transborder data flows: Data flowing across national boundaries.

Transmission control protocol/internet protocol (TCP/IP): The protocol of the Internet, which allows different interconnected networks to communicate using the same language.

Transmission media: The physical pathways to send data and information between two or more entities on a network.

Transnational business strategy: An international business strategy that allows companies to leverage the flexibility offered by a decentralized organization (to be more responsive to local conditions), while at the same time reaping economies of scale enjoyed by centralization. Characterized by a balance between centralization and decentralization and interdependent resources.

Transnational IS strategy: Information systems strategy using integrated networks between the home office and the multiple local subsidiaries to enable different degrees of integration; typically employed by companies pursuing a transnational business strategy.

Trojan horse: A destructive computer code whose instructions remain hidden to the user because the computer appears to function normally, but, in fact, it is performing underlying functions dictated by the intrusive code.

Tunneling: A technology used by VPNs to encapsulate, encrypt, and transmit data over the Internet infrastructure, enabling business partners to exchange information in a secured, private manner between organizational networks.

Twisted pair cable: Cable made of two or more pairs of insulated copper wires twisted together.

Unauthorized access: An information systems security breach where an unauthorized individual sees, manipulates, or otherwise handles electronically stored information.

Uncertainty avoidance: A cultural characteristic related to the risk-taking nature of a culture.

Uniform Resource Locator (URL): The unique Internet address for a Web site and specific Web pages within sites.

Unstructured decisions: Decisions where few or no procedures to follow for a given situation can be specified in advance.

Upstream information flow: An information flow consisting of information received from another organization, such as from a supplier.

USA PATRIOT Act: Officially known as *Uniting and Strengthening America by Providing Appropriate Tools to Intercept and Obstruct Terrorism*, is a law giving law enforcement agencies, at both the local and federal levels, broader ranges of power to aid in the protection of Americans.

User agents: Intelligent agents that automatically perform tasks for a user, such as automatically sending a report at the first of the month, assembling customized news, or filling out a Web form with routine information.

Utilities or utility programs: Software designed to manage computer resources and files.

Utility computing: A form of on-demand computing where resources in terms of processing, data storage, or networking are rented on an as-needed basis and the organization receives a bill for the services used from the provider at the end of each month.

Value-added network (VAN): (1) Medium-speed WANs that are private, third-party managed networks and are economical because they are shared by multiple organizations. Value-added services include network management, e-mail, or security. (2) Telephone lines that are leased from telecommunications providers, creating a secure, dedicated circuit between a company and its business partners.

Value chain: The set of primary and support activities in an organization where value is added to a product or service.

Value chain analysis: The process of analyzing an organization's activities to determine where value is added to products and/or services and the costs that are incurred for doing so.

Value system: A collection of interlocking company value chains.

Vanilla version: The features and modules that the ERP comes with out of the box.

Vertical market: A market comprised of firms within a specific industry sector.

Video: Still and moving images that can be recorded, manipulated, and displayed on a computer.

Videoconferencing: The use of integrated telephone, video recording, and playback technologies by two or more people to interact with each other from remote sites.

Videoconferencing over IP: The use of Internet technologies for videoconferences.

Virtual company: A firm that exists either on paper or on the Internet but has little or no physical components or attributes. Also referred to as click-only companies.

Virtual private network (VPN): A network connection that is constructed dynamically within an existing network—often called a secure tunnel—in order to securely connect remote users or nodes to an organization's network.

Virtual teams: Work teams that are composed of members that may be from different organizations and different locations that form and disband as needed.

Virus: Destructive programs that disrupt the normal functioning of computer systems.

Virus prevention: Set of activities designed to detect and prevent computer viruses.

Vishing: Phone scams that attempt to defraud people by asking them to call a bogus telephone number to "confirm" their account information. Also known as voice phishing.

Visualization: The display of complex data relationships using a variety of graphical methods.

Visual programming languages: Programming languages that have a graphical user interface (GUI) for the programmer and are designed for programming applications that will have a GUI.

Vlogging: Video blogging.

Voice over IP (VoIP): The use of Internet technologies for placing telephone calls.

Voice-to-text software: An application that uses a microphone to monitor a person's speech and then converts the speech into text.

Volatile memory: Memory that loses its contents when the power is turned off.

Volume licensing: A type of software licensing that is usually negotiated and covers all users within an organization. Also known as enterprise licensing.

Warez: Slang term for stolen proprietary software that is sold or shared for free over the Internet.

Watermarked: The process of marking products so that they can be traced to the original purchaser.

Web analytics: The analysis of Web surfers' behavior in order to improve a site's performance

Web browser: A software application that can be used to locate and display Web pages including text, graphics, and multimedia content.

Web cam: A small camera that is used to transmit real-time video images within desktop videoconferencing systems.

Web crawlers: Intelligent agents that continuously browse the Web for specific information (e.g., used by search engines). Also known as Web spiders.

Weblogging: The creation of online text diaries, usually organized chronologically, that can focus on anything the user desires. Also called blogging.

Web page: A hypertext document that contains not only information, but also references or links to other documents that contain related information.

Web page builders or HTML editors: Programs for assisting in the creation and maintenance of Web pages.

Web server: A computer used to host Web sites.

Web services: Web-based software systems used to integrate information from different applications and databases as well as allow different applications from different sources to interact over a network.

Web site: A collection of interlinked Web pages created by the same author.

Web spiders: Intelligent agents that continuously browse the Web for specific information (e.g., used by search engines). Also known as Web crawlers.

What-if analysis: An analysis of the effects hypothetical changes to data have on the results.

Wide area network (WAN): A computer network that spans a relatively large geographic area; typically used to connect two or more LANs.

Wi-Fi (wireless fidelity): Wireless LAN, based on 802.11 standard.

Wiki: Web site allowing users to add, remove, or edit content. Often used synonymously with open source dictionaries.

WiMax: Worldwide Interoperability for Microwave Access (IEEE 802.16), is similar to broadband wireless in that it offers high-speed stationary wireless, but does not require line of sight.

Wireless local area network (WLAN): Local area network using a wireless transmission protocol.

Wireless media: The pathways used to transmit and receive electromagnetic signals using methods such as infrared line of sight, high-frequency radio, and microwave systems.

Wisdom: Accumulated knowledge, gained through a combination of academic study and personal experience, that goes beyond knowledge by representing broader, more generalized rules and schemas for understanding a specific domain or domains; wisdom allows you to understand how to apply concepts from one domain to new situations or problems.

Workflow software: One of the 10 flatteners; referring to a variety of software applications that allow people worldwide to communicate.

World Wide Web (WWW): A system of Internet servers that support documents formatted in HTML, which supports links to other documents, as well as graphics, audio, and video files.

Worm: Destructive computer code that is designed to copy and send itself throughout networked computers.

Zombie computer: Virus infected computers that launch attacks on Web sites.

References

CHAPTER 1

Carr, N. 2003. IT doesn't matter. *Harvard Business Review* 81(5).

CIO. 2004. Metrics: Offshore spending swells. http://www2 .cio.com/metrics/2004/metric667.html (accessed February 3, 2007).

Collett, S. 2006. Hot skills, cold skills: The IT worker of 2010 won't be a technology guru but rather a "versatilist." *Computerworld.* http://www.computerworld.com/action/ article.do?command=viewArticleTOC&specialReportId= 9000100&articleId=112360 (accessed February 3, 2007).

Drucker, P. 1959. *Landmarks of tomorrow.* New York: Harper.

Lundberg, A. 2004. Interview with N. Carr. *CIO.* May 1. http://www.cio.com (accessed February 3, 2007).

Porter, M. E. 1985. *Competitive advantage: Creating and sustaining superior performance.* New York: Free Press.

Porter, M. E., and V. Millar. 1985. How information gives you competitive advantage. *Harvard Business Review* 63(4): 149–161.

Rifkin, J. 1987. *Time wars: The primary conflict in human history.* New York: Henry Holt.

Rothfeder, J., and L. Driscoll. 1990. CIO is starting to stand for "career is over": Once deemed indispensable, the chief information officer has become an endangered species. *BusinessWeek.* February 26, 78.

Sims-Taylor, K. The brief reign of the knowledge worker: Information technology and technological unemployment. Paper presented at the International Conference on the Social Impact of Information Technologies, St. Louis, Missouri, October 12–14, 1998.

Songini, M. 2005. GAO: Navy sinks $1B into failed ERP pilot projects. *Computerworld.* http://www.computerworld.com/ industrytopics/defense/story/0,10801,106121,00.html (accessed February 3, 2007).

Stevens, D. 1994. Reinvent IS or Jane will. *Datamation.* December 15, 84.

Tapscott, D. 2004. The engine that drives success: The best companies have the best business models because they have the best IT strategies. *CIO.* May 1.

Todd, P., J. McKeen, and R. Gallupe. 1995. The evolution of IS job skills: A content analysis of IS jobs. *MIS Quarterly* 19(1): 1–27.

CHAPTER 2

Bartlett, C., and S. Ghoshal. 1998. *Managing across borders: The transnational solution.* Boston: Harvard Business School Press.

Engardio, P., M. Arndt, and G. Smith. 2006. Emerging giants. *BusinessWeek,* July 31. http://www.businessweek.com/magazine/ content/06_31/b3995001.htm (accessed February 3, 2007).

Farrell, D., N. Kaka, and S. Stürze. 2005. Ensuring India's offshoring future. *McKinsey Quarterly,* September. http://

www.mckinsey.com/mgi/publications/India_offshoring.asp (accessed February 3, 2007).

Friedman, T. L. 2004. *The world is flat.* New York: Farrar, Straus and Giroux.

Ghoshal, S. 1987. Global strategy: An organizing framework. *Strategic Management Journal* 8(5): 425–440.

Heichler, E. 2000. A head for the business. CIO.com, June 15. http://www.cio.com/archive/061500_head.html (accessed February 3, 2007).

Hitt, M. A., R. D. Ireland, and R. E. Hoskisson. 2005. *Strategic management. Concepts and cases.* 6th ed. Stamford, CT: Thomson.

Hofstede, G. 2001. *Culture's consequences, comparing values, behaviors, institutions, and organizations across nations.* Thousand Oaks, CA: Sage Publications.

Holmes, S. 2006. Boeing's global strategy takes off. *BusinessWeek,* January 30. http://yahoo.businessweek.com/ magazine/content/06_05/b3969417.htm. (accessed February 3, 2007).

IMF. 2002. Globalization: Threat or opportunity? http:// www.imf.org/external/np/exr/ib/2000/041200.htm (accessed February 3, 2007).

Jinging, J. 2004. Wal-Mart's China inventory to hit US$18b this year. *China Daily.* November 11. http://www.chinadaily .com.cn/english/doc/2004-11/29/content_395728.htm (accessed February 3, 2007).

King, J. 2003. IT's global itinerary: Offshore outsourcing is inevitable. Computerworld.com, September 15. http://www. computerworld.com/managementtopics/outsourcing/story/ 0,10801,84861,00.html (accessed February 3, 2007).

Mallaby, S. 2006. In India, engineering success. WashingtonPost.com, January 2. http://www .washingtonpost.com/wp-dyn/content/article/2006/ 01/02/AR2006010200566.html (accessed February 3, 2007).

Netcraft.com. 2006. May 2006 Web server survey. http://news.netcraft.com/archives/2006/09/index.html (accessed February 3, 2007).

Prahalad, C. K., and Y.L. Doz. 1987. *The multinational mission: Balancing local demands and global vision.* New York: Free Press.

Ramarapu, N. K., and A. A. Lado. 1995. Linking information technology to global business strategy to gain competitive advantage: An integrative model. *Journal of Information Technology* 10: 115–124.

Viotti, P. R., and M. V. Kauppi. 2006. *International relations and world politics: Security, economy, identity.* 3rd ed. Upper Saddle River, NJ: Prentice Hall.

CHAPTER 3

Applegate, L. M., R. D. Austin, and F. W. McFarlan. 2007. *Corporate information strategy and management.* 7th ed. Burr Ridge, IL: Richard D. Irwin.

Bakos, J. Y., and M. E. Treacy. 1986. Information technology and corporate strategy: A research perspective. *MIS Quarterly* 10(2): 107–120.

Brynjolfsson, E. 1993. The productivity paradox of information technology. *Communications of the ACM* 36(12): 66–76.

Christensen, C. M. 1997. *The innovator's dilemma*. Boston: Harvard Business School Press.

Christensen, C. M., and Raynor, M. E. 2003. *The innovator's solution: Creating and sustaining successful growth*. Boston: Harvard Business School Press.

Garvin, D. A. 1993. Building a learning organization. *Harvard Business Review* 71(4): 78–91.

Goldratt, E. M., and J. Cox. 1992. *The goal: A process of ongoing improvement*. Great Barrington, MA: North River Press.

Harris, S. E., and J. L. Katz. 1991. Organizational performance and information technology investment intensity in the insurance industry. *Organization Science* 2(3): 263–295.

Maddox, J. 1999. The unexpected science to come. *Scientific American* 281(December): 62–67.

McKeen, J. D., T. Guimaraes, and J. C. Wetherbe. 1994. A comparative analysis of MIS project selection mechanisms. *Database* 25(2): 43–59.

Porter, M. E. 1979. How competitive forces shape strategy. *Harvard Business Review* 57(March–April): 137–145.

Porter, M. E. 1985. *Competitive advantage: Creating and sustaining superior performance*. New York: Free Press.

Porter, M. E. 2001. Strategy and the Internet. *Harvard Business Review* 79(3): 62–78.

Rubin, H. 2004. Practical counsel for capturing IT value: The elusive value of infrastructure. *CIO*. June 1. http://www.cio.com/archive/060104/real.html (accessed February 3, 2007).

Shank, J., and V. Govindarajan. 1993. *Strategic cost management: Three key themes for managing costs effectively*. New York: Free Press.

Wheeler, B. C. 2002a. Making the business case for it investments through facts, faith, and fear. Online teaching case and teaching note. http://www.coba.usf.edu/departments/isds/faculty/abhatt/cases/TN-ITInvestments.doc.

Wheeler, B. C. 2002b. NeBIC: A dynamic capabilities theory for assessing net-enablement. *Information Systems Research* 13(2), 125–146.

Zuboff, S. 1988. *In the age of the smart machine: The future of work and power*. New York: Basic Books.

CHAPTER 4

CSI. 2006. 2006 CSI/FBI computer crime survey. http://i.cmpnet.com/gocsi/db_area/pdfs/fbi/FBI2006.pdf (accessed February 3, 2007).

Friedman, T. L. 2005. *The world is flat*. New York, Farrar, Straus and Giroux.

Gray, J. 2004. Distributed computing economics, in A. Herbert and K. Sparck Jones, eds. *Computer systems theory, technology, and applications, a tribute to Roger Needham*. New York: Springer, 93–101.

Malhotra, Y. 2005. Integrating knowledge management technologies in organizational business processes: Getting real time enterprises to deliver real business performance. *Journal of Knowledge Management* 9(1): 7–28.

Netcraft. 2006. http://news.netcraft.com/archives/2006/02/02/february_2006_web_server_survey.html (accessed February 3, 2007).

Santosus, M., and J. Surmacz. 2001. The ABCs of knowledge management. *CIO*. May 23. http://www.cio.com/research/knowledge/edit/kmabcs.html.

Top 500. (2007). http://www.top500.org/stats (accessed February 3, 2007).

Winter, S. G. (2001). Framing the issues: Knowledge asset strategies. The Conference of Managing Knowledge Assets: Changing Rules and Emerging Strategies. http://emertech.wharton.upenn.edu/ConfRpts_Folder/WhartonKnowledgeAssets_Report.pdf (accessed February 3, 2007).

CHAPTER 5

Anderson, C. 2004. The long tail. *Wired*. http://www.wired.com/wired/archive/12.10/tail.html (accessed February 3, 2007).

Anderson, C. 2006. *The long tail: Why the future of business is selling less of more*. New York: Hyperion.

American Life Project. 2005. Reports: Online activities and pursuits. About 25 million people have used the internet to sell something. http://www.pewinternet.org/PPF/r/169/report_display.asp (accessed February 3, 2007).

Chatterjee, D., and V. Sambamurthy. 1999. Business implications of web technology: An insight into uof the world wide web by U.S. companies. Electronic markets. *International Journal of Electronic Commerce and Business Media* 9(2): 126–131.

Fraud.org. 2005. 2005 Internet fraud report. http://www.fraud.org/2005_Internet_Fraud_Report.pdf (accessed February 3, 2007).

Hitwise. 2006. MySpace is the number one website in the U.S. according to Hitwise. http://www.hitwise.com/press-center/hitwiseHS2004/social-networking-june-2006.php (accessed February 3, 2007).

Kalakota, R., R. A. Oliva, and E. Donath. 1999. Move over, e-commerce. *Marketing Management* 8(3): 23–32.

Laudon, K. and C. Guercio Traver. 2007. *E-commerce: Business, technology, society*. New York: Pearson Addison Wesley.

Looney, C., and D. Chatterjee. 2002. Web enabled transformation of the brokerage industry: An analysis of emerging business models. *Communications of the ACM* 45(8): 75–81.

Looney, C., L. Jessup, and J. Valacich. 2004. Emerging business models for mobile brokerage services. *Communications of the ACM* 47(6): 71–77.

Microsoft Corporation. 2002. Microsoft IT: MS expense: U.S.-based Employees. http://www.microsoft.com/resources/casestudies/CaseStudy.asp?CaseStudyID=13724 (accessed February 3, 2007).

Microsoft Corporation. 2005. Virgin Entertainment Group uses Microsoft SharePoint products and technologies to boost sales and reduce operational costs. https://members.microsoft.com/customerevidence/search/EvidenceDetails.aspx?EvidenceID=2959&LanguageID=1&PFT=developers&TaxID=25396 (accessed February 3, 2007).

MobileInfo. 2006. M-commerce. MobileInfo.com. http://www.mobileinfo.com/Mcommerce/index.htm (accessed February 3, 2007).

Priceline.com. Information from http://www.priceline.com (accessed February 4, 2007).

Princeton Survey Research Associates. 2005. Leap of faith: Using the Internet despite the dangers. http://www.consumerwebwatch.org/pdfs/princeton.pdf (accessed February 3, 2007).

Quelch, J. A., and L. R. Klein. 1996. The Internet and internal marketing. *Sloan Management Review* 63 (Spring): 60–75.

Schonfeld, E. 2006. Cyworld ready to attack MySpace. *Business 2.0*, July 27. http://money.cnn.com/2006/07/27/technology/cyworld0727.biz2/index.htm (accessed February 3, 2007).

Szuprowicz, B. 1998. *Extranet and Intranet: E-commerce business strategies for the future*. Charleston, SC: Computer Technology Research Corporation.

Turban, E., D. King, J. K. Lee, and D. Viehland. 2004. *Electronic commerce 2004. A managerial perspective*. 3rd ed. Upper Saddle River, NJ: Pearson Education.

U.S. Census Bureau News. 2006. Report No. CB06-19. Washington, DC: U.S. Department of Commerce.

Vollmer, K. 2003. IT trends 2003: Electronic data interchange. http://www.forrester.com/findresearch/results?SortType=Date&geo=0&dAg=10000&N=50645+10849 (accessed February 3, 2007).

Zwass, V. 1996. Electronic commerce: Structures and issues. *International Journal of Electronic Commerce* 1(1): 3–23.

CHAPTER 6

CSI. 2006. 2006 CSI/FBI computer crime and security survey. http://i.cmpnet.com/gocsi/db_area/pdfs/fbi/FBI2006.pdf (accessed February 4, 2007).

Panko, R. 2007. *Corporate computer and network security*. Upper Saddle River, NJ: Pearson Prentice Hall.

CHAPTER 7

Awad, E. M., and H. M. Ghaziri. 2004. *Knowledge management*. Upper Saddle River, NJ: Pearson Prentice Hall.

Checkland, P. B. 1981. *Systems thinking, systems practice*. Chichester, UK: John Wiley.

Leonard, D. 2005. How to salvage your company's deep smarts. *CIO*. May 1. http://www.cio.com/archive/050105/keynote.html (accessed February 3, 2007).

Santosus, M., and J. Surmacz. 2001. The ABCs of knowledge management. *CIO*. May 23. http://www.cio.com/research/knowledge/edit/kmabcs.html (accessed February 3, 2007).

Sprague, R. H., Jr. 1980. A framework for the development of decision support systems. *MIS Quarterly* 4(4): 1–26.

Turban, E., J. E. Aronson, and T. P. Liang. 2005. *Decision support systems and intelligent systems*. 7th ed. Upper Saddle River, NJ: Prentice Hall.

Winter, S. G. 2001. Framing the issues: Knowledge asset strategies. The Conference of Managing Knowledge Assets: Changing Rules and Emerging Strategies. http://emertech.wharton.upenn.edu/ConfRpts_Folder/WhartonKnowledgeAssets_Report.pdf (accessed February 3, 2007).

CHAPTER 8

Edwards, J. 2003. Tag, you're it: RFID technology provides fast, reliable asset identification and management. *CIO*. February 15. http://www.cio.com/archive/021503/et_article.html (accessed February 4, 2007).

Hammer, M., and J. Champy. 1993. *Reengineering the corporation: A manifesto for business revolution*. New York: Harper Business Essentials.

Hewlett-Packard. Information from http://www.hp.com (accessed February 3, 2007).

Koch, C., D. Slater, and E. Baatz. 2000. The ABCs of ERP. *CIO*. http://www.cio.com (accessed August 6, 2001).

Kumar, R. L., and C. W. Crook. 1999. A multi-disciplinary framework for the management of interorganizational systems. *The DATABASE for Advances in Information Systems* 30(1): 22–36.

Langenwalter, G. A. 2000. *Enterprise resources planning and beyond*. Boca Raton, FL: St. Lucie Press.

Larson, P. D., and D. S. Rogers. 1998. Supply chain management: Definition, growth, and approaches. *Journal of Marketing Theory and Practice* 6(4): 1–5.

Porter, M. E., and V. E. Millar. 1985. How information gives you competitive advantage. *Harvard Business Review* (July–August): 149–160.

CHAPTER 9

Applegate, L. M., R. D. Austin, and F. W. McFarlan. 2007. *Corporate information strategy and management*. 6th ed. Chicago: Irwin.

Boynton, A. C., and R. W. Zmud. 1994. An assessment of critical success factors. In *Management information systems*. eds. Gray, King, McLean, and Watson. 2nd ed. Fort Worth, TX: Dryden Press.

Court, R. 1998. Disney buys out Starwave. *Wired*. April 30. www.wired.com/news/business/0,1367,12031,00.html (accessed February 3, 2007).

Fryer, B. 1994. Outsourcing support: Kudos and caveats. *Computerworld*. April 11. http://www.computerworld.com.

George, J. F., D. Batra, J. S. Valacich, and J. A. Hoffer. 2007. *Object-oriented systems analysis and design*. 2nd ed. Upper Saddle River, NJ: Prentice Hall.

Hoffer, J. A., J. F. George, and J. S. Valacich. 2008. *Modern systems analysis and design*. 5th ed. Upper Saddle River, NJ: Prentice Hall.

Martin, J. 1991. *Rapid application development*. New York: Macmillan Publishing.

McConnell, S. 1996. *Rapid development*. Redmond, WA: Microsoft Press.

McFarlan, F. W., and R. L. Nolan. 1995. How to manage an IT outsourcing alliance. *Sloan Management Review* 36(2): 9–24.

McKeen, J. D., T. Guimaraes, and J. C. Wetherbe. 1994. A comparative analysis of MIS project selection mechanisms. *Database* 25(2): 43–59.

Nunamaker, J. F., Jr. 1992. Build and learn, evaluate and learn. *Informatica* 1(1): 1–6.

CHAPTER 10

Business Software Alliance. 2006. Third annual BSA and IDC global software piracy study. May 2006. http://www.bsa.org/ globalstudy/upload/2005%20Piracy%20Study%20- %20Official%20Version.pdf (accessed February 4, 2007).

CSI. 2006. 2006 CSI/FBI computer crime and security survey. Computer Security Institute. http://i.cmpnet.com/gocsi/ db_area/pdfs/fbi/FBI2006.pdf (accessed February 5, 2007).

Mason, R. O. 1986. Four ethical issues for the information age. *MIS Quarterly* (16): 423–433.

Panko, R. 2007. *Corporate computer and network security*. Upper Saddle River, NJ: Prentice Hall.

Sipior, J. C., and B. T. Ward. 1995. The ethical and legal quandary of e-mail privacy. *Communications of the ACM* 38(12): 48–54.

Volonino, L., and S. R. Robinson. 2004. *Principles and practice of information security*. Upper Saddle River, NJ: Prentice Hall.

Weimann, G. 2006. *Terror on the Internet: The new arena, the new challenges*. Washington, DC: USIP Press Books.

Weisband, S. P., and B. A. Reinig. 1995. Managing user perceptions of e-mail privacy. *Communications of the ACM* (December): 40–47.

TECHNOLOGY BRIEFING 1

Evans, A., K. Martin, and M. A. Poatsy. 2007. *Technology in action, complete*. 3rd ed. Upper Saddle River, NJ: Prentice Hall.

Te'eni, D., J. M. Carey, and P. Zhang. 2007. *Human-computer interaction: Developing effective organizational information systems*. Chichester, UK: John Wiley.

TECHNOLOGY BRIEFING 2

Hoffer, J. A., J. F. George, and J. S. Valacich. 2008. *Modern systems analysis and design*. 5th ed. Upper Saddle River, NJ: Prentice Hall.

TECHNOLOGY BRIEFING 3

Hoffer, J. A., M. B. Prescott, and F. R. McFadden. 2007. *Modern database management*. 8th ed. Upper Saddle River, NJ: Prentice Hall.

TECHNOLOGY BRIEFING 4

Panko, R. R. 2007. *Business data networks and telecommunications*. 6th ed. Upper Saddle River, NJ: Prentice Hall.

TECHNOLOGY BRIEFING 5

Berghel, H. 1996. U.S. technology policy in the information age. *Communications of the ACM* 39(6): 15–18.

Laudon, K. and C. Guercio Traver. 2007. *E-commerce: Business, technology, society*. New York: Pearson Addison Wesley.

Name Index

Organization Index

A

Adidas, 498
Adobe, 491
Aeroflot, 81
Airbus, 80, 81, 227–228, 262, 358
Akamai, 140
Alaska Airlines, 179
Albertsons, 331
AllBookstores, 197
Amazon.com, 197, 198, 210, 218, 265–266, 300, 316
American Airlines, 124
American Gaming Association (AGA), 42
American Management Association (AMA), 182
Apple Computer, 3–4, 113, 215, 467, 470
auctionrp.com, 217
Augusta, Maine, Police Department, 243

B

Best Buy, 180
BitTorrent, 407
BizRate, 197
Blockbuster, 123
Blue Security, 365
Boeing Company, 39, 45, 80, 81, 124–125, 172–173, 186, 190, 191–192, 195, 227–229, 262, 308–309, 358, 404, 445
BookSurge, 210
Business Software Alliance, 175

C

Canon, 117
Census Bureau of the Department of Commerce, 177
Charles Schwab, 184
ChoicePoint, 29
Cisco, 9
Columbia University, 219
Comcast Cable Company, 84
Comedy Central, 219
Compaq Computers, 114
Computer Emergency Response Team, Coordination Center (CERT/CC), 254
Computer Ethics Institute, 422
Computer Security Division (CSD), 255
Computer Security Institute (CSI), 256
Computer Technology Industry Foundation, 356
Connexion by Boeing, 39
Cray, 468
Cyworld, 209

D

DaimlerChrysler, 344
Dell, Inc., 87, 95, 98, 183, 316, 344
Digital Equipment Company (DEC), 113–114
Dodgeball.com, 214
Dreamworks SKG, 62

E

eBay, 175–176, 208
eEye Digital Security, 428
Eli Lilly, 215
eLSG.SkyChefs, 348
EnfoTrust Networks, 307–308
Expedia, 220

F

Federal Trade Commission (FTC), 29
FedEx, 16, 17, 28, 29, 356–357
Florists Transworld Delivery (FTD), 208
Ford Motor Company, 74–75, 344, 345
Forrester Research, 199

G

Geek Squad, 180
General Motors, 70, 137, 344
GlobalSpec, 368
Goodwill Industries International Inc., 69
Google, 9, 47, 127–130, 135, 142, 155, 202–203, 205, 397

H

Hewlett-Packard, 62, 114, 317, 343, 469
Home Depot, 307–308

I

IBM, 13, 14, 88, 140, 226–227, 462, 467, 469
In2Movies, 407–408
Internal Revenue Service, 20, 216
Internet Architecture Board (IAB), 547
InterNIC, 548
iStockphoto.com, 214–215

J

Jeppesen, 172

K

Kodak, 111, 117, 118

L

Lands' End, 198
Lawrence Livermore National Laboratory, 137
Livedoor Co., 272
Lotus Development, 293
Ludicorp, 79–80
Lufthansa, 39, 405

M

Macromedia, 491
Major League Baseball Advanced Media (MLBAM), 311–312
Major League Baseball (MLB), 311
Marvel Comics, 351
McDonald's, 318
McKinsey and Company, 59
Meta Group, 105
MGM Grand, 41
Microsoft, 9, 47, 62, 143, 193, 200, 235, 327, 357, 365, 381, 429–430, 490
Ministry of Sound, 275
Misuho Securities Co., 272
MIT, 248–249, 427
Morgan Stanley, 165
Motion Picture Association of America (MPAA), 407–408
MTV, 30
MTV Networks, 412
MySpace.com, 209

N

Napster, 407
National Association of Colleges and Employers, 14
National Security Agency (NSA), 239
Nestlé, 73
Netegrity, 193
Netflix, 123, 198
Netscape, 47, 491
Nielsen Norman Group, 226
Nike, 51, 273
Nordstrom, 88
NTP, Incorporated, 162

O

Open Source Initiative (OSI), 403
Oracle Corporation, 319
Orbitz, 220

P

Pan Am, 80
PayPal, 175, 205
Pearson Prentice Hall, 214
Pew Internet and American Life Project, 102–103
PharmaMaster, 365
Pixar Animation Studios, 21
Polaroid, 118
Porsche, 88
Prairie Wave Telecommunications, 421
Prentice Hall/Pearson Education, 498
Priceline.com, 196
PriceWaterhouseCoopers, 109
Procter & Gamble, 97
Project Entropia, 65

Q

QFC grocery chain, 331

R

RealNetworks, 276
Reporters Without Borders, 9, 61
Research in Motion (RIM), 162, 472
RJR Nabisco, 188
Robert Half International, 14

S

Salami.com, 200
Samsung, 462
Sandia National Laboratories, 45
Sanyo, 111
SBS International, 309
Sears, 112
Shop.org, 199
SideStep, 197
Sirius, 166
Skype, 54
Sony, 117
Sony BMG, 91
Stride Rite, 208
Sundance Film Festival, 171
Sun Microsystems, 182, 489

T

Target, 88
Tele2, 55

Subject Index

Credits

Cover: Dave Cutler/Stock Illustration Source Inc.

Chapter 1: Page 16, © Dave Cutler/Images.com; 17 (left bottom), Erik Dreyer, Getty Images Inc.–Stone Allstock; 17 (top), Mark Richards, PhotoEdit Inc.; 17 (right bottom), Jon Feingersh, Getty Images; 21, Alan Levenson, Corbis/Outline; 24, IBM Corporate Archives; 27, www.internet worldstatscom. Copyright © 2006, Miniwatts Marketing Group. All rights reserved worldwide; 30, Steve Finn, Getty Images, Inc.–Liaison; 39, Jeff Christensen, Reuters Limited.

Chapter 2: Page 41, Tony Freeman, PhotoEdit, Inc.; 46, R. Bossu, Corbis/Sygma; 47 (lower top) eBay, Inc.; 47 (page bottom), Reprinted by permission of Incisive Media. © 2006 Incisive Interactive Marketing LLC. www.clickz.com; 48 (left), Reprinted with permission from Adobe Systems Incorporated; 48 (middle), Don Bishop, Getty Images Inc.–Artville LLC; 48 (right), David Young-Wolff, PhotoEdit Inc.; 49, AP Wide World Photos; 50 (left), © Mozilla.org; 50 (right), Courtesy of Wikipedia; 50 (bottom) Red Hat Inc.; 51, STR/AFP, Getty Images, Inc.–Agence France Presse; 52 (right middle), Allen Birnbach, Masterfile Corporation; 52 (left middle), © Ellen B. Senisi; 52 (bottom), Mike Clarke, Getty Images, 53 (right), David Young-Wolff, PhotoEdit Inc.; 53 (left), © 2006 Yahoo! Inc. YAHOO and the YAHOO! Logo are trademarks of Yahoo! Inc.; 54 (left top), Ralph Krubner/The Stock Connection; 54 (left bottom), Bonnie Kamin, PhotoEdit, Inc.; 54 (right), Blackberry Research in Motion Ltd, 55, Daniel Acker, Landov LLC; 58, Courtesy of Wikipedia; 63, Courtesy of Wikipedia; 68, Sean Young, Landov LLC; 81, Pawel Kopczynski, Landov LLC.

Chapter 3: Page 83, TiVo, Inc.; 95, Dell/Getty Images, Inc.–Liaison; 103, www.pewinternet.org/PPF/r/153/report_display.asp 3/23/05.

Chapter 4: Page 127, AFP, Getty Images, Inc.–Agence France Presse; 130, Craig Mitchelldyer, Getty Images; 132, Lucidio Studio, Inc., The Stock Connection; 133, Reprinted with permission from Microsoft Corporation; 134, Erik Von Weber, Getty Images, Inc.–PhotoDisc; 137, Jamstec/Earth Simulator Center; 141 (left-TiVo logo), © 2006 Tivo Inc.; 142, © Mozilla.org; 143, Courtesy of Google Inc.; 148, HP Imaging and Printing Group; 149, Wireless Garden, Inc.; 153, Copyright © 1988, NCR Corporation. Used with permission; 155, AP Wide World Photos; 157 (right middle), Recognition Systems, Inc.; 157 (top left), Laurance B. Aiuppy, The Stock Connection; 157 (far left middle), AFC Cable Systems, Inc.; 157 (far right); Steve Mitchell, AP Wide World Photos; 157 (bottom), SGM, The Stock Connection; 157 (middle left), Jerry Mason, Photo Researchers, Inc.; 157 (page bottom) Sungard Availability Services; 172, AP Wide World Photos.

Chapter 5: Page 175; eBay Inc.; 180, Butler Photography; 181 (top) Joshua Lutz, Redux Pictures; 181 (bottom), I. Uimonen, Magnum Photos, Inc.; 183, © 2006 Dell Inc. All rights reserved; 185, Charles Schwab & Company, Inc.; 192, Boeing Commerical Airplane Group; 203, Google Inc.; 204 (top), © Microsoft; 204 (bottom), Visa U.S.A. Brand Management; 206, Reprinted by permission of e-gold.com; 208, AP Wide World Photos; 209, David Young-Wolff, PhotoEdit Inc.; 211, Gawker Media LLC; 215, Sling Media, Inc.

Chapter 6: Page 234, Reprinted with permission from Microsoft Corporation; 237 Barracuda Networks, Inc; 240, DALLAL, SIPA Press; 250, Symantec Corporation; 263, Alamy Images.

Chapter 7: Page 265, David Young-Wolff/PhotoEdit Inc.; 276, Reprinted by permission of RealNetworks; 278, Burke, Inc.; 283, Reprinted with permission from Microsoft Corporation; 284 (left), Spencer Platt, Getty Images, Inc.–Liasion; 284 (right), Everett Collection; 285, Reprinted by permission of Mathmedics, Inc./Easydiagnosis www.easydiagnosis.com; 288, NCSA Media Techology Resources; 300, AP Wide World Photos; 301, Ag-Chem Equipment Company, Inc.

Chapter 8: Page 311, David Madison, Getty Images Inc.–Stone Allstock; 318, AP Wide World Photos; 319, Jochen Siegle, Landov LLC; 329, August Stein, Getty Images, Inc.–Artville LLC; 345 (bottom), Courtesy of Ford Motor Company and Covisint.com; 348, Reprinted by permission of Reed Business; 349, Kruell/laif, Redux Pictures; 351, R. Maiman, Corbis/Sygma.

Chapter 9: Page 375, Reprinted with permission from Microsoft Corporation; 378, Chris Farina, Corbis/Bettmann; 395, © The 5th Wave, www.the5thwave.com; 397, Copyright © 2005 O'Reilly Media, Inc. All rights reserved. Used with permission.

Chapter 10: Page 407, Jeff Christensen/Reuters CORBIS–NY; 410 (left), Omni-Photo Communications, Inc.; 410 (second from left), Michael Newman, PhotoEdit, Inc.; 410 (third from left), John Stuart, Creative Eye/MIRA.com; 410 (right), MicroTouch Systems, Inc.; 412, MTV Networks/via Bloomberg News/Landov, Landov LLC; 413, David Young-Wolff, PhotoEdit, Inc.; 417, Frank LaBua, Pearson Education/PH College; 418, Reprinted with permission from Microsoft Corporation; 423 (bottom), Reprinted with permission of Computer Economics.

Techology Briefing 1: Page 448, Dell Inc.; 449, Martin Meissner, AP Wide World Photos; 453, David Young-Wolff,

PhotoEdit, Inc.; 454, Logitech Inc.; 456, Dell Inc.; 458, Landov LLC; 461 (top left), Paul Wilkinson, Dorling Kindersley Media Library; 461 (right), Swissbit; 461 (left bottom), Sony Electronics, Inc.; 464, Yoshikazu Tsuno, Getty Images; 466 (page top), David Young-Wolff, PhotoEdit Inc.; 466 (middle left), Summagraphics Corporation; 466 (middle right), Panasonic Communications Systems Division; 466 (bottom right), Dell Inc.; 472 (left), NextGen; 472 (top right), Patrick Olear, PhotoEdit Inc.

Technology Briefing 2: Page 489, Used with permission. All rights reserved; 490, Reprinted with permission from Microsoft Corporation.

Techology Briefing 3: Page 508, Reprinted with permission from Microsoft Corporation; 509, Reprinted with permission from Microsoft Corporation.

Technology Briefing 4: Page 518, Reprinted with permission from Microsoft Corporation.